www.wadsworth.com

www.wadsworth.com is the World Wide Web site for
Wadsworth and is your direct source to dozens of
online resources.

At *www.wadsworth.com* you can find out about
supplements, demonstration software, and
student resources. You can also send email to many of
our authors and preview new publications and exciting
new technologies.

www.wadsworth.com
Changing the way the world learns®

The Criminal Justice System

Politics and Policies

Ninth Edition

GEORGE F. COLE
University of Connecticut

MARC G. GERTZ
Florida State University

AMY BUNGER
Florida State University

THOMSON
™
WADSWORTH

Australia • Canada • Mexico • Singapore • Spain
United Kingdom • United States

THOMSON

WADSWORTH

Senior Executive Editor: *Sabra Horne*
Technology Project Manager: *Susan DeVanna*
Marketing Manager: *Dory Schaeffer*
Marketing Assistant: *Alanna Kelly*
Advertising Project Manager: *Stacy Purviance*
Project Manager, Editorial Production:
   Jane Brundage
Art Director: *Vernon Boes*

Print/Media Buyer: *Rebecca Cross*
Permissions Editor: *Sommy Ko*
Production Service: *Scott Rohr, Buuji, Inc.*
Copy Editor: *Alan DeNiro, Buuji, Inc.*
Cover Designer: *Yvo Riezebos*
Cover Image: © *Getty Images*
Compositor: *Buuji, Inc.*
Cover and Text Printer: *Webcom*

Printed in Canada
2   3   4   5   6   7   07   06   05   04   03

For more information about our products,
contact us at:
Thomson Learning Academic Resource Center
1-800-423-0563

For permission to use material from this text,
contact us by:
Phone: 1-800-730-2214   Fax: 1-800-730-2215
Web: http://www.thomsonrights.com

Library of Congress Control Number:
2003112637

ISBN 0-534-62874-5

Wadsworth/Thomson Learning
10 Davis Drive
Belmont, CA 94002-3098
USA

Asia
Thomson Learning
5 Shenton Way #01-01
UIC Building
Singapore 068808

Australia/New Zealand
Thomson Learning
102 Dodds Street
Southbank, Victoria 3006
Australia

Canada
Nelson
1120 Birchmount Road
Toronto, Ontario M1K 5G4
Canada

Europe/Middle East/Africa
Thomson Learning
High Holborn House
50/51 Bedford Row
London WC1R 4LR
United Kingdom

Latin America
Thomson Learning
Seneca, 53
Colonia Polanco
11560 Mexico D.F.
Mexico

Spain/Portugal
Paraninfo
Calle Magallanes, 25
28015 Madrid, Spain

Contents

✪

Preface

Entering into the fourth decade of publication with this Ninth Edition, we see scholarship further supporting this book's fundamental premise: the link between law, politics, and public policy must be understood to accurately grasp the workings of the criminal justice system. Since our last edition, world events in the aftermath of the bombing of the World Trade Center and Pentagon have affirmed and deepened our belief in this premise. Media attention on everything from duct tape to airport security to schoolyards has yet again refocused our citizens on crime. The public continues to express high levels of fear and worry about crime. Citizens react strongly to events like child abductions, school shootings, and terrorism, despite data that our crime rate is declining. Crime continues to be listed as an important public problem relative to other social problems. Therefore, politicians respond with "tough on crime" campaigns and legislation. We also see increased funds for homeland security—which is criminal justice by a different name. Culture, public opinion, and public interest campaigns and interest groups are becoming more educated and more vocal. We see more public participation in crime legislation in the wake of 9/11, as evidenced by Amber Alerts, sex offender registration, trying juveniles as adults, and the impact of race and science on the imposition of the death penalty.

Our goal remains to bring you the classics that help illustrate the nexus between policy and politics, and reconcile some of these works with a sampling of the latest research. Survey and foundational courses remain our target audience, and we feel a deep responsibility to a collection of classics. Many of you will take issue with our definition of a classic, but our aim is to provide works that have had staying power, or works whose impact on politics or society was so influential that the works framed scholarly debate for years to come. We walk the reader through the seminal works that established the links between criminal justice and law, politics, and culture. That path reveals times when the empirical tools of social science debunk or demystify many of our publicly held assumptions. In exhibiting some of today's most contemporary criminal justice debates, like gun control, three strikes laws, mandatory arrests, and drug legalization, our journey shows how popular opinion, or possibly legislative reaction to popular opinion, can lead to laws and choices that are at odds with the experts. Expert opinion has also changed over time, and our selection of readings demonstrates this as well. No longer is expert opinion limited to academia, but it is increasingly conducted also by members of government agencies, nonprofit organizations, and private research companies.

We are pleased by the widespread attention that this collection has received, and encourage its continued use in criminal justice, political science, public administration, and sociology courses. We limit jargon and extensive discussions of methodologies, to make this accessible and user friendly for undergraduates, as well as to provide an efficient introduction to graduate students who have the skills to go to those original works if need be. Our duty is to stay abreast of present day work, but we would be remiss to not provide the undergirdings of current research—those scholars who blazed trails on works of race and sentencing or culture, for example, and an array of works whom scholars may still argue against.

In this Ninth Edition, our introductory sections now address the influence or impact of a culturally defining moment like 9/11, and how it shapes our institutions and laws. This book is more than a collection of works, and we continue to integrate the individual articles. There are eight readings new to this edition, including Maxwell, Ganer, and Fagan's "The Preventative Effects of Arrest on Intimate Partner Violence"; Tonry's "Racial Disproportion in U.S. Prisons"; Johnson's "Mature Coping: The Challenge of Adjustment in Contemporary Prisons"; Travis and Petersilia's "Reentry Reconsidered: A New Look at an Old Question"; Olgetree's "Black Man's Burden: Race and the Death Penalty in America"; Kovandzic, Sloan, and Vieraitis's "Unintended Consequences of Politically Popular Sentencing Policy: The Homicide Promoting Effects of 'Three Strikes' in U.S. Cities (1980-1999)"; Kleck's "An Overview of Gun Control Policy in the United States"; and Goode's "Drugs and Crime." Although we keep many classics, our new selections maintain our tradition of understanding and viewing the criminal justice system as exactly that, a system which can best be understood as a relationship between politics and policy, as well as between citizen and state. We provide discussion questions at the end of each section which serve this synthetic goal, and provide useful tools for class discussions stressing critical thinking, essay exam preparations, and comprehensive exam overviews.

Special thanks are extended to our colleagues, both at our respective universities, and from our professional time in criminal justice agencies, and to the many faculty currently using this text, who took the time and energy to give us feedback. Sabra Horne, executive editor of criminal justice at Wadsworth, continues to be an important source of encouragement.

George F. Cole
Marc G. Gertz
Amy Bunger

PART I

✪

Politics and the Administration of Justice

The close relationship between law, policy, and politics has been recognized since ancient times. Yet the social conflicts of the second half of the twentieth century helped us to see that the way criminal justice is allocated reflects the values of the individuals and groups that hold the power in the political system. Consider the changes over the past decade, and at the dawn of a new century. Policies toward crime and justice, formulated in a more liberal political era, have changed along with the attitudes of the American public. Consequently, governments and legislators are reacting to what they think the public wants, and in effect have increased the power that the state has over individuals.

In a democracy such as the United States, a purposeful tension was created between the need to: (1) maintain public order, (2) ensure public safety, and (3) protect such precious values as individual liberties, the rule of law, and democratic government. Ideally, citizens in the "land of the free" could live without spending time, angst, energy and resources on personal protection, but for many Americans the possibility of being victimized by criminals is ever present, and the fear of victimization omnipresent. In 1973 the National Advisory Commission on Criminal Justice Standards and Goals set as a target the reduction of crime over the ensuing ten years, stating that a time would come in the immediate future when:

- A couple could walk in the evening in their neighborhood without fear of assault and robbery.

- A family could go away for the weekend without fear of returning to a house ransacked by burglars.

- A woman could take a night job without fear of being raped on her way to or from work.

- Every citizen could live without fear of being brutalized by unknown assailants.

Although crime levels have been cut dramatically in recent years, these goals are still elusive. Indeed, the number of crimes committed by strangers has grown. The symbols of personal threat are also highly visible in a post-9/11 world, in which literal barricades, screening machines, and uniformed officers have become common place.

Public opinion polls indicate that Americans remain steadfast in identifying crime as one of the top five public problems to be addressed by government. Criminality and fear of crime are not new phenomena; they have always been part of the American experience. Yet the Founders structured a society juxtaposing crime control with primacy for due process protections for the individual, later asserting that if the "constable blundered" the criminal should go free. Worry about crime in all its forms—violence as well as robberies, thefts, and assaults—has always been present in the United States, but is balanced by fear of an intrusive government. Incidents of extreme, large-scale violence threatened the social order. For example, farmers and others openly rebelled in the earliest years of the country. Military policies produced significant draft riots during the Civil War. In the early twentieth century, mobs of whites set upon and murdered African Americans in cities throughout the United States, including St. Louis, Kansas City, and Chicago. In other decades, police officers battled labor union organizers, veterans seeking payment of benefits, war protesters, and civil rights advocates. Thus, when riots erupted in Los Angeles in 1992 in the aftermath of the acquittal of police officers who were videotaped beating African-American motorist Rodney King, the country was not witnessing a new kind of event. Americans tolerate crime as the unacceptable end of the continuum of freedom. Until triggering events—real or media driven—force the issue into public consciousness, most citizens are either desensitized or immune to its effects.

Experts agree that, contrary to public opinion and the claims of politicians, crime rates have not been steadily rising. Rates for most crimes have dropped since the early 1980s. The National Crime Victimization Surveys show that the victimization rate peaked in 1981 and has declined since then. The greatest declines are in property crimes, but crimes of violence have also dropped, especially since 1993. The *Uniform Crime Reports* show similar results. They reveal a rapid rise in crime rates beginning in 1964 and continuing until 1980, when the rates began to level off or decline. The overall crime rate has declined each year since 1991.

CRIME AND JUSTICE
AS PUBLIC POLICY ISSUES

Crime and justice are crucial public policy issues. In a democracy, striking a balance between maintaining public order and protecting individual freedom is a struggle. Policies could be imposed that make citizens feel safe from crime, such as placing a police officer on every street corner and executing suspected criminals. Such severe practices have been used elsewhere in the world. Although they may reduce crime, they also betray our democratic values. If law enforcement officers were given a free hand to work their will on the public, citizens in a democracy would be giving up individual freedom, due process, and their conception of justice. Even in this post–"terror on our soil" era, we see strong pockets of resistance against too much crime control.

Dealing with the crime problem concerns not only the arrest, conviction, and punishment of offenders. Policies must also be developed to deal with a host of issues such as gun control, stalking, domestic violence, cybertheft, drugs, child abductions, and global criminal organizations. Many of these issues are controversial. Policies must be hammered out in the political arenas of state legislatures and Congress.

Crime Control and American Ideals

How we choose to curb crime is a testimonial to our democratic ideals. The administration of justice in a democracy can be distinguished from that in an authoritarian state by the extent and form of protections provided for the accused as guilt is determined and punishment is imposed.

In our nation all people have rights, the guilty as well as the innocent. We balance this by placing the burden of proof for a defendant's guilt on the state. Unlike many nations in the news of late, our laws reflect our concern to avoid unnecessarily depriving people of liberty, either by permitting police to search people at will or by mistakenly punishing an innocent person for a crime that he or she did not commit. Our greatest challenge may be to find ways to remain true to these principles of fair treatment and justice while also operating a system that can effectively protect, investigate, and punish. Significant divisions exist within our populace, especially between liberals and conservatives, in respect to policies about how to deal with crime within our democratic framework. Indeed, a single individual can hold seemingly contradictory views regarding crime. People often support their commitment to democratic ideals until it conflicts with protection of their own family.

On one side, there are people who believe that the answer lies in stricter enforcement of the law through the expansion of police forces and the enactment of punitive measures that will result in the swift and certain punishment of criminals. The holders of this view have remained politically dominant since the early 1980s. They argue that we must strengthen the agents of crime control, who they assert have been hurt by decisions of the U.S. Supreme Court and by liberal programs that have weakened traditional values of responsibility and family.

In contrast, there are those who argue that the strengthening of crime control has endangered our cherished values of due process and justice. They claim that strict approaches are ineffective in reducing crime because the answer lies in reshaping the lives of individual offenders and changing the social and economic conditions from which they believe criminal behavior springs. These opponents also disagree on what crimes should actually be punished under the law.

As you encounter these arguments, think about how they relate to actual crime trends. Crime increased in the 1960s when we were trying the approach of rehabilitating offenders. Does this mean that the approach does not work? Perhaps the liberal approach was merely overwhelmed by the number of people in their crime-prone years at that time. Perhaps there would have been even more crime if not for the efforts to rehabilitate. On the other hand, crime rates diminished when tough policies were implemented in the 1980s. But was that because of the policies or because of the shrinking size of the crime-prone age group? If the policies were effective, then why did certain violent crime rates move upward in the early 1990s when tough policies were still in force? Why has there been such a decrease in crime during the past decade? Obviously, there are no easy answers, yet we cannot avoid making choices about how to use our police, courts, and corrections system most effectively.

The Politics of Crime and Justice

As we examine alternative criminal justice policies, we need to remember that such policies are developed in national, state, and local political arenas. Because the public is so deeply concerned about crime, there is always a risk that politicians will simply say what they believe the voters want to hear, rather than think seriously about whether the policies will achieve their goals.

The crime bill passed by Congress in 1994 expanded the death penalty to sixty additional crimes, including murder of members of Congress, the Supreme Court, and the president's staff. These are tough provisions, but do they actually accomplish anything relevant to crime in America or to people's fear of crime? Politicians may claim that they "got tough on crime," but the public has little knowledge of the specific provisions of most legislation.

The most visible connection between politics and criminal justice is in the arguments and posturing by Republicans and Democrats who attempt to outdo each other in showing the voters how tough they can be. Equally important are the more "routine" linkages between politics and the justice system. Penal codes and the budgets of criminal justice agencies are passed by legislators who are responsive to the voters. Congress appropriates millions of dollars to assist states and cities in waging the War on Drugs but prohibits any expenditures for legal counsel for poor defendants, and the same can be said for our newly created War on Terror. At the state and local level, many criminal justice authorities, including sheriffs, prosecutors, and judges, are also elected officials. Thus, their decisions will be influenced by the community's concerns and values.

As you learn about each part of the criminal justice system, keep in mind the ways in which decision makers and institutions are connected to politics and government. Criminal justice is intimately connected to society and its institutions, and to fully understand it we must recognize those connections.

CRIMINAL JUSTICE AS A SYSTEM

To achieve the goals of criminal justice, many organizational subunits—police, courts, corrections—have been developed. Each of these organizations has its own personnel, functions, and responsibilities. If we were to construct an organizational chart, we might assume that criminal justice is an orderly process in which a variety of professionals act on the accused's case in the interests of society. To understand how the system really works, however, we must look beyond the formal organizational chart. To assist in this task, we can use the social science concept of system: a complex whole consisting of interdependent parts whose operations are directed toward goals and are influenced by the environment within which they function. This system operates in a market model context, where economic assumptions about free will and efficiency fashion an assembly line response to be carried out by seemingly autonomous rational individuals.

Criminal Justice from a System Perspective

Criminal justice is a system made up of a number of parts or subsystems—police, courts, and corrections. The subsystems have their own goals and needs—and sometimes goals that can be at odds with another piece of the system—but are also interdependent. When one unit changes its policies, practices, or resources, other units will be affected. An increase in the number of people arrested by the police on felony charges, for example, will affect the work not only of the judicial subsystem but also of the probation and correctional subsystems. For criminal justice to achieve its goals, each part must make its own distinctive contribution; each part must also have at least minimal contact with at least one other component of the system.

Although it is important to understand the characteristics and operations of the entire criminal justice system and its individual subsystems, we must also see how individual actors play their roles. The criminal justice system is made up of a great many persons performing specific tasks. Some, such as police officers and judges, are well known to the public. Other important actors, such as bail bond agents and probation officers, are less visible and less well known.

A key concept for analysis of the relationships among individual decision makers is *exchange*. In this context, exchange refers to a mutual transfer of resources among individual decision makers, each of whom has interests and goals that he or she cannot readily accomplish alone. Therefore, each needs to gain cooperation and assistance from other actors by contributing to their interests and goals. The concept of exchange allows us to see interpersonal behavior as the result of individual decisions about the values and costs of alternative courses of action.

A variety of exchange relationships characterize the criminal justice system, some of which are more visible than others. Probably the most obvious example of an exchange relationship is plea bargaining. In this situation, a defendant's fate is determined not through a trial but rather through an agreement between the defense attorney and the prosecutor whereby the defendant agrees to plead guilty in exchange for surety of sentence, which may include a reduction of charges. As a result of the exchange, the defendant achieves a shorter sentence, or no risk as to what the sentence could be; the prosecutor secures a quick, sure conviction; and the defense attorney can move on to the next case. Thus, the cooperation underlying the exchange promotes the goals of each participant.

The concept of exchange reminds us that decisions are the products of interactions among individuals and that the major subsystems—police, courts, and corrections—are tied together by the actions of individual decision makers.

The concepts of system and exchange are closely linked, and their value as tools for the analysis of criminal justice cannot be overemphasized. These concepts can be used as the basis for an organizing framework to describe individual subsystems and actors and to help us understand how the justice process really works. However, several additional characteristics of the criminal justice system help to shape its composition and functioning.

Characteristics of the Criminal Justice System

Four important attributes characterize the workings of the criminal justice system: (1) discretion, (2) resource dependence, (3) sequential tasks, and (4) filtering.

Discretion   At all levels of the justice process, officials exercise a high degree of discretion—the ability to act according to one's own judgment and conscience. For example, police officers decide how to handle a crime situation, prosecutors decide what charges to file against the accused, judges decide how long a sentence will be, and parole boards decide when an offender should be released from prison.

The fact that discretion exists throughout the criminal justice system may seem odd given that our country is ruled by law and has created procedures to ensure that decisions are made in accordance with that law. However, instead of a mechanical system in which law preempts human decision making, criminal justice is a system in which the participants may consider a wide variety of circumstances and exercise many options as they dispose of a case.

Two primary arguments are frequently used to justify discretion in the criminal justice system. First, discretion is needed because the system lacks the resources to treat every case in the same fashion. If every violation of the law were pursued through trial, the costs would be staggering. Second, many officials in the system believe that their discretionary authority permits them to achieve greater justice than rigid rules would produce.

Resource Dependence   Criminal justice agencies generally do not generate their own resources—operating funds, staff, and equipment—but depend on others for them. Therefore, criminal justice actors (police chiefs, prosecutors, and judges) frequently must cultivate and maintain good relationships with people responsible for the allocation of resources—that is, the political decision makers (legislators, mayors, city council members, and so on).

Because the budgetary decision makers are elected officials who seek to please the public, criminal justice officials must also maintain a positive image and good relations with the voters. If the police enjoy strong public support, for example, then the mayor will be reluctant to reduce the law enforcement budget. In maintaining positive public relations, criminal justice officials inevitably seek favorable coverage from local news media. Because the media often provide a crucial link between government agencies and the public, criminal justice officials may publicize notable achievements while simultaneously seeking to limit or control publicity about controversial cases and decisions.

Sequential Tasks Decisions in the criminal justice system are made in a particular sequence. The police must make an arrest before defendants are passed to the prosecutor, whose decisions ultimately determine the nature of the workload for courts and corrections. Officials cannot achieve their objectives by acting out of sequence. For example, prosecutors and judges cannot bypass the police by making arrests on their own, and corrections officials cannot punish anyone who has not already passed through the decision-making stages administered by the police, prosecution, and courts. Obviously, the sequential nature of the system is a key element in the exchange relationships that characterize the interactions of decision makers who depend on each other to achieve their respective goals. Thus, the system is highly interdependent.

Filtering The criminal justice system may be viewed as a filtering process through which cases are screened. At each stage, some defendants are sent on to the next stage of decision making while others are either released or processed under changed conditions. It should be noted that very few suspects arrested by the police are prosecuted, tried, and convicted. Some go free because the police decide that a crime has not been committed or that the evidence is not sound. The prosecutor may drop charges by deciding that justice would be better served by diverting the suspect to a substance abuse clinic. Large numbers of defendants will plead guilty, the judge may dismiss charges against others, and the jury may acquit a few defendants. Most of the offenders who are actually tried, however, will be convicted. Thus, the criminal justice system is often described as a "funnel" into which many cases enter but only a few result in conviction and punishment.

The administration of criminal justice may be viewed as having goals that run counter to the ideals of due process, but we must remember that this reflects the design of our nation's Founders—the creation of a constant tension between government and liberty, the state and the individual. Our government wasn't established to have no conflict; it was designed to prescribe how to handle conflict. Decisions concerning the disposition of cases are influenced by the selective nature of the filtering process in which administrative discretion and interpersonal exchange relationships are extremely important. At each decision-making level, actors in the judicial system are able to determine which types of crime will come to official notice, which kinds of offenders will be processed, and how enthusiastically a conviction will be sought. It is in these day-to-day practices and policies of criminal justice agencies that the law is put into effect, and it is out of this activity that organizations and individuals shape the law.

QUESTIONS FOR FURTHER EXPLORATION

1. What ideology (or ideologies) do you see reflected in the American system of punishment?

2. What are the neccessary elements of an adversarial system in the United States? Describe and explain them. What are the consequences of these protections?

3. Does the media coverage of crime in America tell Americans what to think, or what to think about?

4. There is a dynamic and constant tension between due process, equal protection, the use of discretion, and the preservation of public order in the criminal justice system. What are some examples of these competing values?

SUGGESTIONS FOR FURTHER READING

Cole, David, *No Equal Justice.* New York: New Press, 1999. Argues that a double standard compromises the legitimacy of criminal justice and exacerbates racial divisions.

Friedman, Lawrence M. *Crime and Punishment in American History.* New York: Basic Books, 1993. A historical overview of criminal justice from colonial times. Argues that the evolution of criminal justice reflects transformations in American character.

Hall, Jerome. *General Principles of Criminal Law,* 2d ed. Indianapolis: Bobbs-Merrill, 1947. One of the clearest texts outlining the foundations of criminal law and the defenses that may be used.

Reiman, Jeffrey. *The Rich Get Richer and the Poor Get Prision: Economic Bias in American Criminal Justice.* Boston: Allyn & Bacon, 1996. A stinging critique of the system. Argues that the criminal justice system serves the powerful by its failure to reduce crime.

Roberts, J.V., and A. N. Doob. *Public Opinion, Crime and Criminal Justice.* Boulder,

Colo.: Westview Press, 1997. Details areas in criminal justice policy that are influenced by public opinion or politicians' response to it, such as "three strikes you're out" laws, drugs, and gun control.

Scheingold, Stuart A. *The Politics of Law and Order: Street Crime and Public Policy.* New York: Longman, 1984. Broad overview of the political context of the criminal justice system arguing the importance of considering the symbolic nature of crime policy, and the simultaneous complexity of the phenomenon of crime.

Tonry, Michael, ed. *The Handbook of Crime and Punishment.* New York: Oxford University Press, 1998. This encyclopedia volume provides current literature reviews in criminal justice and its context.

Walker, Samuel. *Sense and Nonsense About Crime and Drug Policy,* 5th ed. Belmont, Calif.: Wadsworth, 2001. A provocative look at crime policies.

1

✪

Two Models of the Criminal Process

Herbert L. Packer

In one of the most important contributions to systematic thought about the administration of criminal justice, Herbert Packer articulates the values supporting two models of the justice process. He notes the gulf existing between the "Due Process Model" of criminal administration, with its emphasis on the rights of the individual, and the "Crime Control Model," which sees the regulation of criminal conduct as the most important function of the judicial system.

Two models of the criminal process will let us perceive the normative antinomy at the heart of the criminal law. These models are not labeled Is and Ought, nor are they to be taken in that sense. Rather, they represent an attempt to abstract two separate value systems that compete for priority in the operation of the criminal process. Neither is presented as either corresponding to reality or representing the ideal to the exclusion of the other. The two models merely afford a convenient way to talk about the operation of a process whose day-to-day functioning involves a constant series of minute adjustments between the competing demands of two value systems and whose normative future likewise involves a series of resolutions of the tensions between competing claims.

I call these two models the Due Process Model and the Crime Control Model. . . . As we examine the way the models operate in each successive

Source: Reprinted from *The Limits of the Criminal Sanction* by Herbert L. Packer, with the permission of the publisher, Stanford University Press.

stage, we will raise two further inquiries: first, where on a spectrum between the extremes represented by the two models do our present practices seem approximately to fall; second, what appears to be the direction and thrust of current and foreseeable trends along each such spectrum?

There is a risk in an enterprise of this sort that is latent in any attempt to polarize. It is, simply, that values are too various to be pinned down to yes-or-no answers. The models are distortions of reality. And, since they are normative in character, there is a danger of seeing one or the other as Good or Bad. The reader will have his preferences, as I do, but we should not be so rigid as to demand consistently polarized answers to the range of questions posed in the criminal process. The weighty questions of public policy that inhere in any attempt to discern where on the spectrum of normative choice the "right" answer lies are beyond the scope of the present inquiry. The attempt here is primarily to clarify the terms of discussion by isolating the assumptions that underlie competing policy claims, and examining the conclusions that those claims, if fully accepted, would lead to.

VALUES UNDERLYING THE MODELS

Each of the two models we are about to examine is an attempt to give operational content to a complex of values underlying the criminal law. As I have suggested earlier, it is possible to identify two competing systems of values, the tension between which accounts for the intense activity now observable in the development of the criminal process. The actors in this development—lawmakers, judges, police, prosecutors, defense lawyers—do not often pause to articulate the values that underlie the positions that they take on any given issue. Indeed, it would be a gross oversimplification to ascribe a coherent and consistent set of values to any of these actors. Each of the two competing schemes of values we will be developing in this section contains components that are demonstrably present some of the time in some of the actors' preferences regarding the criminal process. No one person has ever identified himself as holding all of the values that underlie these two models. The models are polarities, and so are the schemes of values that underlie them. A person who subscribed to all of the values underlying the other would be rightly viewed as a fanatic. The values are presented here as an aid to analysis, not as a program for action.

Some Common Ground

However, the polarity of the two models is not absolute. Although it would be possible to construct models that exist in an institutional vacuum, it would not serve our purposes to do so. We are postulating, not a criminal process that operates in any kind of society at all, but rather one that operates within the framework of contemporary American society. This leaves plenty of room for polarization, but it does require the observance of some limits. A model of the criminal process that left out of account relatively stable and enduring features of the American legal system would not have much relevance to our central inquiry. For convenience, these elements of stability and continuity can be roughly equated with minimal agreed limits expressed in the Constitution of the United States and, more importantly, with unarticulated assumptions that can be perceived to underlie those limits. Of course, it is true that the Constitution is constantly appealed to by proponents and opponents of many measures that affect the criminal process. And only the naive would deny that there are few conclusive positions that can be reached by appeal to the Constitution. Yet there are assumptions about the criminal process that are widely shared and that may be viewed as common ground for the operation of any model of the criminal process. Our first task is to clarify these assumptions.

First, there is the assumption, implicit in the ex post facto clause of the Constitution, that the function of defining conduct that may be treated as criminal is separate from and prior to the process of identifying and dealing with persons as criminals. How wide or narrow the definition of criminal conduct must be is an important question of policy that yields highly variable results depending on the values held by those making the relevant decisions. But that there must be a means of definition that is in some sense separate from and prior to the operation of the process is clear. If this were not so, our efforts to deal with the phenomenon of organized crime would appear ludicrous indeed (which is not to say that we have by any means exhausted the possibilities for dealing with that problem within the limits of this basic assumption).

A related assumption that limits the area of controversy is that the criminal process ordinarily ought to be invoked by those charged with the responsibility for doing so when it appears that a crime has been committed and that there is a reasonable prospect of apprehending and convicting its perpetrator. Although police and prosecutors are allowed broad discretion for deciding not to invoke the criminal process, it is commonly agreed that these officials have no general dispensing power. If the legislature has decided that certain conduct is to be treated as criminal, the decision makers at every level of the criminal process are expected to accept that basic decision as a premise for action. The controversial nature of the occasional case in which the relevant decision makers appear not to have played their appointed role only serves to highlight the strength with which the premise holds. This assumption may be viewed as the other side of the ex post facto coin. Just as conduct that is not proscribed as criminal may not be dealt with in the criminal process, so conduct that has been denominated as criminal must be treated as such by the participants in the criminal process acting within their respective competences.

Next, there is the assumption that there are limits to the powers of government to investigate and apprehend persons suspected of committing crimes. I do not refer to the controversy (settled recently, at least in broad outline) as to whether the Fourth Amendment's prohibition against unreasonable searches and seizures applies to the states with the same force with which it applies to the federal government. Rather, I am talking about the general assumption that a degree of scrutiny and control must be exercised with respect to the activities of law-enforcement officers, that the security and privacy of the individual may not be invaded at will. It is possible to imagine a society in which even lip service is not paid to this assumption. Nazi Germany approached but never quite reached this position. But no one in our society would maintain that any individual may be taken into custody at any time and held without any limitation of time during the process of investigating his possible commission of crimes, or would argue that there should be no form of redress for violation of at least some standards for official investigative conduct. Although this assumption may not appear to have much in the way of positive content, its absence would render moot some of our most hotly controverted problems. If there were not general agreement that there must be some limits on police power to detain and investigate, the highly controversial provisions of the Uniform Arrest Act, permitting the police to detain a person for questioning for a short period even though they do not have grounds for making an arrest, would be a magnanimous concession by the all-powerful state rather than, as it is now perceived, a substantial expansion of police power.

Finally, there is a complex of assumptions embraced by terms such as "the adversary system," "procedural due process," "notice and an opportunity to be heard," and "day in court." Common to them all is the notion that the alleged criminal is not merely an object to be acted upon but an independent entity in the process who may, if he so desires, force the operators of the process to demonstrate to an independent authority (judge and jury) that he is guilty of the charges against him. It is a minimal assumption. It speaks in terms of "may" rather than "must." It permits but does not require the accused, acting by himself or through his own agent, to play an active role in the process. By virtue of that fact the process becomes or has the capacity to become a contest between, if not equals, at least independent actors. As we shall see, much of the space between the two models is occupied by stronger or weaker notions of how this contest is to be arranged, in what cases it is to be played, and by what rules. The Crime Control Model tends to de-emphasize this adversary aspect of the process; the Due Process Model tends to make it central. The common ground, and it is important, is the agreement that the process has, for everyone subjected to it, at least the potentiality of becoming to some extent an adversary struggle.

So much for common ground. There is a good deal of it, even in the narrowest view. Its existence should not be overlooked, because it is, by definition, what permits partial resolutions of the tension between the two models to take place. The rhetoric of the criminal process consists largely of claims that disputed territory is "really" common ground: that, for example, the premise of an adversary system "necessarily" embraces the appointment of counsel for everyone accused of crime, or conversely, that the obligation to pursue persons suspected of committing crimes "necessarily" embraces interrogation of suspects without the intervention of counsel. We may smile indulgently at such claims; they are rhetoric, and no more. But the form in which they are made suggests an important truth: that there *is* a common ground of value assumption about the criminal process that makes continued discourse about its problems possible.

Crime Control Values

The value system that underlies the Crime Control Model is based on the proposition that the repression of criminal conduct is by far the most important function to be performed by the criminal process. The failure of law enforcement to bring criminal conduct under tight control is viewed as leading to the breakdown of public order and thence to the disappearance of an important condition of human freedom. If the laws go unenforced—which is to say, if it is perceived that there is a high percentage of failure to apprehend and convict in the criminal process—a general disregard for legal controls tends to develop. The law-abiding citizen then becomes the victim of all sorts of unjustifiable invasions of his interests. His security of person and property is sharply diminished, and, therefore, so is his liberty to function as a member of society. The claim ultimately is that the criminal process is a positive guarantor of social freedom. In order to achieve this high purpose, the Crime Control Model requires that primary attention be paid to the efficiency with which the criminal process operates to screen suspects, determine guilt, and secure appropriate dispositions of persons convicted of crime.

Efficiency of operation is not, of course, a criterion that can be applied in a vacuum. By "efficiency" we mean the system's capacity to apprehend, try, convict, and dispose of a high proportion of criminal offenders whose offenses become known. In a society in which only the grossest forms of antisocial behavior were made criminal and in which the crime rate was exceedingly low, the criminal process might require the devotion of many more man-hours of police, prosecutorial, and judicial time per case than ours does, and still operate with tolerable efficiency. A society that was prepared to increase even further the resources devoted to the suppression of crime might cope with a rising crime rate without sacrifice of efficiency while continuing to maintain an elaborate and time-consuming set of criminal processes. However, neither of these possible characteristics corresponds with social reality in this country. We use the criminal sanction to cover an increasingly wide spectrum of behavior thought to be antisocial, and the amount of crime is very high indeed, although both level and trend are hard to assess. At the same time, although precise measures are not available, it does not appear that we are disposed in the public sector of the economy to increase very drastically the quantity, much less the quality, of the resources devoted to the suppression of criminal activity through the operation of the criminal process. These factors have an important bearing on the criterion of efficiency, and therefore on the nature of the Crime Control Model.

The model, in order to operate successfully, must produce a high rate of apprehension and conviction, and must do so in a context where the magnitudes being dealt with are very large and the resources for dealing with them are very limited. There must then be a premium on speed and finality. Speed, in turn, depends on informality and on uniformity; finality depends on minimizing the occasions for challenge. The process must not be cluttered up with ceremonious rituals that do not advance the progress of a case. Facts can be established more quickly through interrogation in a police station than through the formal process of examination and cross-examination in a court. It follows that extrajudicial processes should be preferred to judicial processes, informal operations to formal ones. But informality is not enough; there must also be uniformity. Routine, stereotyped procedures are essential if large numbers are being handled. The model that will operate successfully on these presuppositions must be an administrative, almost a managerial, model. The image that comes to mind is an assembly-line conveyor belt down which moves an endless stream of cases, never stopping, carrying the cases to workers who stand at fixed stations and who perform on each case as it comes by the same small but essential operation that brings it one step closer to being a finished product, or, to exchange the metaphor for the reality, a closed file. The criminal process, in this model, is seen as a screening process in which each successive state—prearrest investigation, arrest, postarrest investigation, preparation for trial, trial or entry of plea, conviction, disposition—involves a series of routinized operations whose success is gauged primarily by their tendency to pass the case along to a successful conclusion.

What is a successful conclusion? One that throws off at an early stage those cases in which it appears unlikely that the person apprehended is an offender and then secures, as expeditiously as possible, the conviction of the rest, with a minimum of occasions for challenge, let alone post-audit. By the application of administrative expertness, primarily that of the police and prosecutors, an early determination of the probability of innocence or guilt emerges. Those who are probably innocent are screened out. Those who are probably guilty are passed quickly through the remaining stages of the process. The key to the operation of the model regarding those who are not screened out is what I shall call a presumption of guilt. The concept requires some explanation, since it may appear startling to assert that what appears to be the precise converse of our generally accepted ideology of a presumption of innocence can be an essential element of a model that does correspond in some respects to the actual operation of the criminal process.

The presumption of guilt is what makes it possible for the system to deal efficiently with large numbers, as the Crime Control Model demands. The supposition is that the screening processes operated by police and prosecutors are reliable indicators of probable guilt. Once a man has been arrested and investigated without being found to be probably innocent, or, to put it differently, once a determination has been made that there is enough evidence of guilt to permit holding him for further action, then all subsequent activity directed toward him is based on the view that he is probably guilty. The precise point at which this occurs will vary from case to case; in many cases it will occur as soon as the suspect is arrested, or even before, if the evidence of probable guilt that has come to the attention of the authorities is sufficiently strong. But in any case the presumption of guilt will begin to operate well before the "suspect" becomes a "defendant."

The presumption of guilt is not, of course, a thing. Nor is it even a rule of law in the usual sense. It simply is the consequence of a complex of attitudes, a mood. If there is confidence in the reliability of informal administrative fact-finding activities that take place in the early stages of the criminal process, the remaining stages of the process can be relatively perfunctory without any loss in operating efficiency. The presumption of guilt, as it operates in the Crime Control Model, is the operational expression of that confidence.

It would be a mistake to think of the presumption of guilt as the opposite of the presumption of innocence that we are so used to thinking of as the polestar of the criminal process and that, as we shall see, occupies an important position in the Due Process Model. The presumption of innocence is not its opposite; it is irrelevant to the presumption of guilt; the two concepts are different rather than opposite ideas. The difference can perhaps be epitomized by an example. A murderer, for reasons best known to himself, chooses to shoot his victim in plain view of a large number of people. When the police arrive, he hands them his gun and says, "I did it and I'm glad." His account of what happened is corroborated by several eyewitnesses. He is placed under arrest and led off to jail. Under these circumstances, which may seem extreme but which in fact characterize with rough accuracy the evidentiary situation in a large proportion of criminal cases, it would be plainly absurd to maintain that more probably than not the suspect did not commit the killing. But that is not what the presumption of innocence means. It means that until there has been an adjudication of guilt by an authority legally competent to make such an adjudication, the suspect is to be treated, for reasons that have nothing whatever to do with the probable outcome of the case, as if his guilt is an open question.

The presumption of innocence is a direction to officials about how they are to proceed, not a prediction of outcome. The presumption of guilt, however, is purely and simply a prediction of outcome. The presumption of innocence is, then, a direction to the authorities to ignore the presumption of guilt in their treatment of the suspect. It tells them, in effect, to close their eyes to what will frequently seem to be factual probabilities. The reasons why it tells them this are among the animating presuppositions of the Due Process Model, and we will come to them shortly. It is enough to note at this point that the presumption of guilt is descriptive and factual; the presumption of innocence is normative and legal. The pure Crime Control Model has no truck with the presumption of innocence, although its real-life emanations are, as we shall see, brought into uneasy compromise with the dictates of this dominant ideological position. In the presumption of guilt this model finds a factual predicate for the position that the dominant goal of repressing crime can be achieved through highly summary processes without any great loss of efficiency (as previously defined), because of the probability that, in the run of cases, the preliminary screening process operated by the police and the prosecuting officials contains adequate guarantees of reliable fact-finding. Indeed, the model takes an even stronger position. It is that subsequent processes, particularly those of a formal adjudicatory nature, are unlikely to produce as reliable fact-finding as the expert administrative process that precedes them is capable of. The criminal process thus must put special weight on the quality of administrative fact-finding. It becomes important, then, to place as few restrictions as possible on the character of the administrative fact-finding processes and to limit restrictions to such as enhance reliability, excluding those designed for other purposes. As we shall see, this view of restrictions on administrative fact-finding is a consistent theme in the development of the Crime Control Model.

In this model, as I have suggested, the center of gravity of the process lies in the early, administrative fact-finding stages. The complementary proposition is that the subsequent stages are relatively unimportant and should be truncated as much as possible. This, too, produces tensions with presently dominant ideology. The pure Crime Control Model has very little use for many conspicuous features of the adjudicative process, and in real life works out a number of ingenious compromises with them. Even in the pure model, however, there have to be devices for dealing with the suspect after the preliminary screening process has resulted in a determination of probable guilt. The focal device, as we shall see, is the plea of guilty; through its use, adjudicative fact-finding is reduced to its barest essentials and operating at its most successful pitch, it offers two possibilities: an administrative fact-finding process leading (1) to exoneration of the suspect, or (2) to the entry of a plea of guilty.

Due Process Values

If the Crime Control Model resembles an assembly line, the Due Process Model looks very much like an obstacle course. Each of its successive stages is designed to present formidable impediments to carrying the accused any further along in the process. Its ideology is not the converse of that underlying the Crime Control Model. It does not rest on the idea that it is not socially desirable to repress crime, although critics of its application have been known to claim so. Its ideology is composed of a complex of ideas, some of them based on judgments about the efficacy of crime control devices, others having to do with quite different considerations. The ideology of due process is far more deeply impressed on the formal structure of the law than is the ideology of crime control; yet an accurate tracing of the strands that make it up is strangely difficult. What follows is only an attempt at an approximation.

The Due Process Model encounters its rival on the Crime Control Model's own ground in respect to the reliability of fact-finding processes. The Crime Control Model, as we have suggested, places heavy reliance on the ability of investigative and prosecutorial officers, acting in an informal setting in which their distinctive skills are given full sway, to elicit and reconstruct a tolerably accurate account of what actually took place in an alleged criminal event. The Due Process Model rejects this premise and substitutes for it a view of informal, nonadjudicative fact-finding that stresses the possibility of error. People are notoriously poor observers of disturbing events—the more emotion-arousing the context, the greater the possibility that recollection will be incorrect; confessions and admissions by persons in police custody may be induced by physical or psychological coercion so that the police end up hearing what the suspect thinks they want to hear rather than the truth; witnesses may be animated by bias or interest that no one would trouble to discover except one specially charged with protecting the interests of the accused (as the police are not). Considerations of this kind all lead to a rejection of informal fact-finding processes as definitive of factual guilt and to an insistence on formal, adjudicative, adversary fact-finding processes in which the factual case against the accused is publicly heard by an impartial tribunal and is evaluated only after the accused has had a full opportunity to discredit the case against him. Even then, the distrust of fact-finding processes that animates the Due Process Model is not dissipated. The possibilities of human error being what they are, further scrutiny is necessary, or at least must be available, in case facts have been overlooked or suppressed in the heat of battle. How far this subsequent scrutiny must be available is a hotly controverted issue today. In the pure Due Process Model the answer would be: at least as long as there is an allegation of factual error that has not received an adjudicative hearing in a fact-finding context. The demand for finality is thus very low in the Due Process Model.

This strand of due process ideology is not enough to sustain the model. If all that were at issue between the two models was a series of questions about the reliability of fact-finding processes, we would have but one model of the criminal process, the nature of whose constituent elements would pose questions of fact not of value. Even if the discussion is confined, for the moment, to the question of reliability, it is apparent that more is at stake than simply an evaluation of what kinds of fact-finding processes, alone or in combination, are likely to produce the most nearly reliable results. The stumbling block is this: How much reliability is compatible with efficiency? Granted that informal fact-finding will make some mistakes that can be remedied if backed up by adjudicative fact-finding, the desirability of providing this backup is not affirmed or negated by factual demonstrations or predictions that the increase in reliability will be x percent or x plus n percent. It still remains to ask how much weight is to be given to the competing demands of reliability (a high degree of probability in each case that factual guilt has been accurately determined) and efficiency (expeditious handling of the large numbers of cases that the process ingests). The Crime Control Model is more optimistic about the improbability of error in a significant number of cases: but it is also, though only in part therefore, more tolerant about the amount of error that it will put up with. The Due Process Model insists on the prevention and elimination of mistakes to the extent possible; the Crime Control Model accepts the probability of mistakes up to the level at which they interfere with the goal of repressing crime, either because too many guilty people are escaping or, more subtly, because general awareness of the unreliability of the process leads to a decrease in the deterrent efficacy of the criminal law. In this view, reliability and efficiency are not polar opposites but rather complementary characteristics. The system is reliable *because* efficient; reliability becomes a matter of independent concern only when it becomes so attenuated as to impair efficiency. All of this the Due Process Model rejects. If efficiency demands shortcuts around reliability, then absolute efficiency must be rejected. The aim of the process is at least as much to protect the factually innocent as it is to convict the factually guilty. It is a little like quality control in industrial technology;

tolerable deviation from standard varies with the importance of conformity to standard in the destined uses of the product. The Due Process Model resembles a factory that has to devote a substantial part of its input to quality control. This necessarily cuts down on quantitative output.

All of this is only the beginning of the ideological difference between the two models. The Due Process Model could disclaim any attempt to provide enhanced reliability for the fact-finding process and still produce a set of institutions and processes that would differ sharply from those demanded by the Crime Control Model. Indeed, it may not be too great an oversimplification to assert that in point of historical development the doctrinal pressures emanating from the demands of the Due Process Model have tended to evolve from an original matrix of concern for the maximization of reliability into values quite different and more far-reaching. These values can be expressed in, although not adequately described by, the concept of the primacy of the individual and the complementary concept of limitation on official power.

The combination of stigma and loss of liberty that is embodied in the end result of the criminal process is viewed as being the heaviest deprivation that government can inflict on the individual. Furthermore, the processes that culminate in these highly afflictive sanctions are seen as in themselves coercive, restricting, and demeaning. Power is always subject to abuse—sometimes subtle, other times, as in the criminal process, open and ugly. Precisely because of its potency in subjecting the individual to the coercive power of the state, the criminal process must, in this model, be subjected to controls that prevent it from operating with maximal efficiency. According to this ideology, maximal efficiency means maximal tyranny. And, although no one would assert that minimal efficiency means minimal tyranny, the proponents of the Due Process Model would accept with considerable equanimity a substantial diminution in the efficiency with which the criminal process operates in the interest of preventing official oppression of the individual.

The most modest-seeming but potentially far-reaching mechanism by which the Due Process Model implements these antiauthoritarian values is the doctrine of legal guilt. According to this doctrine, a person is not to be held guilty of a crime merely on a showing that in all probability, based upon reliable evidence, he did factually what he is said to have done. Instead, he is to be held guilty if and only if these factual determinations are made in procedurally regular fashion and by authorities acting within competences duly allocated to them. Furthermore, he is not to be held guilty, even though the factual determination is or might be adverse to him, if various rules designed to protect him and to safeguard the integrity of the process are not given effect: the tribunal that convicts him must have the power to deal with his kind of case ("jurisdiction") and must be geographically appropriate ("venue"); too long a time must not have elapsed since the offense was committed ("statute of limitations"); he must not have been previously convicted or acquitted of the same or a substantially similar offense ("double jeopardy"); he must not fall within a category of persons, such as children or the insane, who are legally immune to conviction ("criminal responsibility"); and so on. None of these requirements has anything to do with the factual question of whether the person did or did not engage in the conduct that is charged as the offense against him; yet favorable answers to any of them will mean that he is legally innocent. Wherever the competence to make adequate factual determination lies, it is apparent that only a tribunal that is aware of these guilt-defeating doctrines and is willing to apply them can be viewed as competent to make determinations of legal guilt. The police and the prosecutors are ruled out by lack of competence, in the first instance, and by lack of assurance of willingness, in the second. Only an impartial tribunal can be trusted to make determinations of legal as opposed to factual guilt.

In this concept of legal guilt lies the explanation for the apparently quixotic presumption of innocence of which we spoke earlier. A man who, after police investigation, is charged with having committed a crime can hardly be said to be presumptively innocent, if what we mean is factual innocence. But if what we mean is that it has yet to be determined if any of the myriad legal doctrines that serve in one way or another the end of limiting official power through the observance of certain substantive and procedural regularities may be appropriately invoked to exculpate the accused man, it is apparent that as a matter of prediction it cannot be said with confidence that more probably than not he will be found guilty.

Beyond the question of predictability this model posits a functional reason for observing the presumption of innocence: by forcing the state to prove its case against the accused in an adjudicative context, the presumption of innocence serves to force into play all the qualifying and disabling doctrines that limit the use of the criminal sanction against the individual, thereby enhancing his opportunity to secure a favorable outcome. In this sense, the presumption of innocence may be seen to operate as a kind of self-fulfilling prophecy. By opening up a procedural situation that permits the successful assertion of defenses having nothing to do with factual guilt, it vindicates the proposition that the factually guilty may nonetheless be legally innocent and should therefore be given a chance to qualify for that kind of treatment.

The possibility of legal innocence is expanded enormously when the criminal process is viewed as the appropriate forum for correcting its own abuses. This notion may well account for a greater amount of the distance between the two models than any other. In theory the Crime Control Model can tolerate rules that forbid illegal arrests, unreasonable searches, coercive interrogations, and the like. What it cannot tolerate is the vindication of those rules in the criminal process itself through the exclusion of evidence illegally obtained or through the reversal of convictions in cases where the criminal process has breached the rules laid down for its observance. And the Due Process Model, although it may in the first instance be addressed to the maintenance of reliable fact-finding techniques, comes eventually to incorporate prophylactic and deterrent rules that result in the release of the factually guilty even in cases in which blotting out the illegality would still leave an adjudicative fact-finder convinced of the accused person's guilt. Only by penalizing errant police and prosecutors within the criminal process itself can adequate pressure be maintained, so the argument runs, to induce conformity with the Due Process Model.

Another strand in the complex of attitudes underlying the Due Process Model is the idea—itself a shorthand statement for a complex of attitudes—of equality. This notion has only recently emerged as an explicit basis for pressing the demands of the Due Process Model, but it appears to represent, at least in its potential, a most powerful norm for influencing official conduct. Stated most starkly, the ideal of equality holds that "there can be no equal justice where the kind of trial a man gets depends on the amount of money he has." The factual predicate underlying this assertion is that there are gross inequalities in the financial means of criminal defendants as a class, that in an adversary system of criminal justice an effective defense is largely a function of the resources that can be mustered on behalf of the accused, and that the very large proportion of criminal defendants who are, operationally speaking, "indigent" will thus be denied an effective defense. This factual premise has been strongly reinforced by recent studies that in turn have been both a cause and an effect of an increasing emphasis upon norms for the criminal process based on the premise.

The norms derived from the premise do not take the form of an insistence upon governmental responsibility to provide literally equal opportunities for all criminal defendants to challenge the process. Rather, they take as their point of departure the notion that the criminal process, initiated as it is by the government and containing as it does the likelihood of severe deprivations at the hands of government, imposes some kind of public obligation to ensure that financial inability does not destroy the capacity of an accused to assert what may be meritorious challenges to the processes being invoked against him. At its most gross, the norm of equality would act to prevent situations in which financial inability forms an absolute barrier to the assertion of a right that is in theory generally available, as where there is a right to appeal that is, however, effectively conditional upon the filing of a trial transcript obtained at the defendant's expense. Beyond this, it may provide the basis for a claim whenever the system theoretically makes some kind of challenge available to an accused who has the means to press it. If, for example, a defendant who is adequately represented has the opportunity to prevent the case against him from coming to the trial stage by forcing the state to its proof in a preliminary hearing, the norm of equality may be invoked to assert that the same kind of opportunity must be available to others as well. In a sense the system, as it functions for the small minority whose resources permit them to exploit all its defensive possibilities, provides a benchmark by which its functioning in all other cases is to be tested: not, perhaps, to guarantee literal identity but rather to provide a measure of whether the process as a whole is recognizably of the same general order. The demands made by a norm of this kind are likely by their very nature to be quite sweeping. Although the norm's imperatives may be initially limited to determining whether in a particular case the accused was injured or prejudiced by his relative inability to make an appropriate challenge, the norm of equality very quickly moves to another level on which the demand is that the process in general be adapted to minimize discriminations rather than that a mere series of post hoc determinations of discriminations be made or makeable.

It should be observed that the impact of the equality norm will vary greatly depending upon the point in time at which it is introduced into a model of the criminal process. If one were starting from scratch to decide how the process ought to work, the norm of equality would have nothing very important to say on such questions as, for example, whether an accused should have the effective assistance of counsel in deciding whether to enter a plea of guilty. One could decide, on quite independent considerations, that it is or is not a good thing to afford that facility to the generality of persons accused of crime. But the impact of the equality norm becomes far greater when it is brought to bear on a process whose contours have already been shaped. If our model of the criminal process affords defendants who are in a financial position to do so the right to consult a lawyer before entering a plea, then the equality norm exerts powerful pressure to provide such an opportunity to all defendants and to regard the failure to do so as a malfunctioning of the process of whose consequences the accused is entitled to be relieved. In a sense, this has been the role of the equality norm in affecting the real-world criminal process. It has made its appearance on the scene comparatively late and has therefore encountered a system in which the relative financial inability of most persons accused of crime results in treatment very different from that accorded the small minority of the financially capable. For this reason, its impact has already been substantial and may be expected to be even more so in the future.

There is a final strand of thought in the Due Process Model that is often ignored but that needs to be candidly faced if thought on the subject is not to be obscured. This is a mood of skepticism about the morality and utility of the criminal sanction, taken either as a whole or in some of its applications. The subject is a large and complicated one, comprehending as it does much of the intellectual history of our times. It is properly the subject of another essay altogether. To put the matter briefly, one cannot improve upon the statement by Professor Paul Bator:

> In summary we are told that the criminal law's notion of just condemnation and punishment is a cruel hypocrisy visited by a smug society on the psychologically and economically crippled; that its premise of a morally autonomous will with at least some measure of choice whether to comply with the values expressed in a penal code is unscientific and outmoded; that its reliance on punishment as an educational and deterrent agent is misplaced, particularly in the case of the very members of society most likely to engage in criminal conduct; and that its failure to provide for individualized and humane rehabilitation of offenders is inhuman and wasteful.[1]

This skepticism, which may be fairly said to be widespread among the most influential and articulate contemporary leaders of informed opinion, leads to an attitude toward the processes of the criminal law that, to quote Mr. Bator again, engenders "a peculiar receptivity toward claims of injustice which arise within the traditional structure of the system itself; fundamental disagreement and unease about the very bases of the criminal law has, inevitably, created acute pressure at least to expand and liberalize those of its processes and doctrines which serve to make more tentative its judgments or limit its power." In short, doubts about the ends for which power is being exercised create pressure to limit the discretion with which that power is exercised.

The point need not be pressed to the extreme of doubts about or rejection of the premises upon which the criminal sanction in general rests. Unease may be stirred simply by reflection on the variety of uses to which the criminal sanction is put and by a judgment that an increasingly large proportion of those uses may represent an unwise invocation of so extreme a sanction. It would be an interesting irony if doubts about the propriety of certain uses of the criminal sanction prove to contribute to a restrictive trend in the criminal process that in the end requires a choice among uses and finally an abandonment of some of the very uses that stirred the original doubts, but for a reason quite unrelated to those doubts.

There are two kinds of problems that need to be dealt with in any model of the criminal process. One is what the rules shall be. The other is how the rules shall be implemented. The second is at least as important as the first, as we shall see time and again in our detailed development of the models. The distinctive difference between the two models is not only in the rules of conduct that they lay down but also in the sanctions that are to be invoked when a claim is presented that the rules have been breached and, no less importantly, in the timing that is permitted or required for the invocation of those sanctions.

As I have already suggested, the Due Process Model locates at least some of the sanctions for breach of the operative rules in the criminal process itself. The relation between these two aspects of the process—the rules and the sanctions for their breach—is a purely formal one unless there is some mechanism for bringing them into play with each other. The hinge between them in the Due Process Model is the availability of legal counsel. This has a double aspect. Many of the rules that the model requires are couched in terms of the availability of counsel to do various things at various stages of the process—this is the conventionally recognized aspect; beyond it, there is a pervasive assumption that counsel is necessary in order to invoke sanctions for breach of any of the rules. The more freely available these sanctions are, the more important is the role of counsel in seeing to it that the sanctions are appropriately invoked. If the process is seen as a series of occasions for checking its own operation, the role of counsel is a much more nearly central one than is the case in a process that is seen as primarily concerned with expeditious determination of factual guilt. And if equality of operation is a governing norm, the availability of counsel is seen as requiring it for all. Of all the controverted aspects of the criminal process, the right to counsel, including the role of government in its provision, is the most dependent on what one's model of the process looks like, and the least susceptible of resolution unless one has confronted the antinomies of the two models.

I do not mean to suggest that questions about the right to counsel disappear if one adopts a model of the process that conforms more or less closely to the Crime Control Model, but only that such questions become absolutely central if one's model moves very far down the spectrum of possibilities toward the pure Due Process Model. The reason for this centrality is to be found in the assumption underlying both models that the process is an adversary one in which the initiative in invoking relevant rules rests primarily on the parties concerned, the state, and the accused. One could construct models that placed central responsibility on adjudicative agents such as committing magistrates and trial judges. And there are, as we shall see, marginal but nonetheless important adjustments in the role of the adjudicative agents that enter into the models with which we are concerned. For present purposes it is enough to say that these adjustments are marginal, that the animating presuppositions that underlie both models in the context of the American criminal system relegate the adjudicative agents to a relatively passive role, and therefore place central importance on the role of counsel.

One last introductory note: . . . What assumptions do we make about the sources of authority to shape the real-world operations of the criminal process? Recognizing that our models are only models, what agencies of government have the power to pick and choose between their competing demands? Once again, the limiting features of the American context come into play. Ours is not a system of legislative supremacy. The distinctively American institution of judicial review exercises a limiting and ultimately a shaping influence on the criminal process. Because the Crime Control Model is basically an affirmative model, emphasizing at every turn the existence and exercise of official power, its validating authority is ultimately legislative (although proximately administrative). Because the Due Process Model is basically a negative model, asserting limits on the nature of official power and on the modes of its exercise, its validating authority is judicial and requires an appeal to supralegislative law, to the law of the Constitution. To the extent that tensions between the two models are resolved by deference to the Due Process Model, the authoritative force at work is the judicial power, working in the distinctively judicial mode of invoking the sanction of nullity. That is at once the strength and the weakness of the Due Process Model: its strength because in our system the appeal to the Constitution provides the last and overriding word; its weakness because saying no in specific cases is an exercise in futility unless there is a general willingness on the part of the officials who operate the process to apply negative prescriptions across the board. It is no accident that statements reinforcing the Due Process Model come from the courts, while at the same time facts denying it are established by the police and prosecutors.

NOTE

1. Paul Bator, "Finality in Criminal Law and federal Habeas Corpus for State Prisoners," *Harvard Law Review* 76 (1963): 441–442.

2

❖

Racial Politics, Racial Disparities, and the War on Crime

Michael Tonry

African Americans make up more than 50 percent of the prison population but only 12 percent of all U.S. residents. When all punishments—probation, intermediate sanctions, incarceration—are taken into account, one in three African-American men in their twenties are currently under correctional supervision. Michael Tonry believes that racial disparities are a reflection of racial politics, especially the War on Drugs.

Racial disparities in arrests, jailing, and imprisonment steadily worsened after 1980 for reasons that have little to do with changes in crime patterns and almost everything to do with two political developments. First, conservative Republicans in national elections "played the race card" by using anticrime slogans (remember Willie Horton?) as a way to appeal to anti-Black sentiments of White voters. Second, conservative politicians of both parties promoted and voted for harsh crime control and drug policies that exacerbated existing racial disparities.

The worsened disparities might have been ethically defensible if they had been based on good faith beliefs that some greater policy good would thereby have been achieved. Sometimes unwanted side effects of social policy are inevitable. Traffic accidents and fatalities are a price we pay for the convenience of automobiles. Occupational injuries are a price we pay for engaging in the industries in which they occur.

Source: Michael Tonry, "Racial Politics, Racial Disparities, and the War on Crime," *Crime and Delinquency* 40 (1994): 475–497.

The principal causes of worse racial disparities have been the War on Drugs launched by the Bush and Reagan administrations, characterized by vast increases in arrests and imprisonment of street-level drug dealers, and the continuing movement toward harsher penalties. Policies toward drug offenders are a primary cause of recent increases in jail and prison admissions and populations. Racial disparities among drug offenders are worse than among other offenders.

It should go without saying in the late 20th century that governments detest racial injustice and desire racial justice, and that racial disparities are tolerable only if they are unavoidable or are outweighed by even more important social gains. There are no offsetting gains that can justify the harms done to Black Americans by recent drug and crime control policies.

This article presents data on racial trends in arrests, jailing, and imprisonment; examines the rationales for the policies that have produced those trends; and considers whether the adoption of policies known to have disparate adverse effects on Blacks can be ethically justified. First, the evidence concerning the effectiveness of recent drug and crime control policies that have exacerbated racial disparities is examined. Next, data on arrests, jail, and imprisonment trends are presented and demonstrate that racial disparities have worsened, but not because Blacks are committing larger proportions of the serious offenses (homicide, rape, robbery, aggravated assault) for which offenders were traditionally sent to prison. Finally, the reasons why recent policies were adopted and whether they can be ethically justified are considered.

CRIME REDUCTION EFFECTS
OF CRIME CONTROL POLICY

There is no basis for a claim that recent harsh crime control policies or the enforcement strategies of the War on Drugs were based on good faith beliefs that they would achieve their ostensible purposes. In this and other countries, practitioners and scholars have long known that manipulation of penalties has few, if any, effects on crime rates.

Commissions and expert advisory bodies have been commissioned by the federal government repeatedly over the last 30 years to survey knowledge of the effects of crime control policies, and consistently they have concluded that there is little reason to believe that harsher penalties significantly enhance public safety. In 1967, the President's Commission on Law Enforcement and Administration of Justice observed that crime control efforts can have little effect on crime rates without much larger efforts being directed at crime's underlying social and economic causes. "The Commission . . . has no doubt whatever that the most significant action that can be taken against crime is action designed to eliminate slums and ghettos, to improve education, to provide jobs. . . . We shall not have dealt effectively with crime until we have alleviated the conditions that stimulate it."

In 1978, the National Academy of Sciences Panel on Research on Deterrent and Incapacitative Effects, funded by President Ford's department of justice and asked to examine the available evidence on the crime-reductive effects of sanctions, concluded: "In summary, we cannot assert that the evidence warrants an affirmative conclusion regarding deterrence" (Blumstein, Cohen, and Nagin 1978). Fifteen years later, the National Academy of Sciences Panel on the Understanding and Control of Violent Behavior, created and paid for with funds from the Reagan and Bush administration departments of justice, surveyed knowledge of the effects of harsher penalties on violent crime (Reiss and Roth 1993). A rhetorical question and answer in the panel's final report says it all: "What effect has increasing the prison population had on violent crime? Apparently very little. . . . If tripling the average length of sentence of incarceration per crime [between 1976 and 1989] had a strong preventive effect," reasoned the panel, "then violent crime rates should have declined" (p. 7). They had not.

I mention that the two National Academy of Sciences panels were created and supported by national Republican administrations to demonstrate that skepticism about the crime-preventive effects of harsher punishments is not a fantasy of liberal Democrats. Anyone who has spent much time talking with judges or corrections officials knows that most, whatever their political affiliations, do not believe that harsher penalties significantly enhance public safety.

Likewise, outside the United States, conservative governments in other English-speaking countries have repudiated claims that harsher penalties significantly improve public safety. In Margaret Thatcher's England, for example, a 1990 White Paper (an official policy statement of the government), based on a 3-year study, expressed its skepticism about the preventive effects of sanctions:

> Deterrence is a principle with much immediate appeal. . . . But much crime is committed on impulse, given the opportunity presented by an open window or an unlocked door, and it is committed by offenders who live from moment to moment: their crimes are as impulsive as the rest of their feckless, sad, or pathetic lives. It is unrealistic to construct sentencing arrangements on the assumption that most offenders will weigh up the possibilities in advance and base their conduct on rational calculation. (Home Office 1990)

Canada is the other English-speaking country that has recently had a conservative government. In Brian Mulroney's Canada, the Committee on Justice and the Solicitor General (in American terms, the judiciary committee) proposed in 1993 that Canada shift from an American-style crime control system to a European-style preventive approach. In arguing for the shift in emphasis, the committee observed that "the United States affords a glaring example of the limited effect that criminal justice responses may have on crime. . . . If locking up those who violate the law contributed to safer societies then the United States should be the safest country in the world" (Standing Committee on Justice and the Solicitor General 1993). Six years earlier, the Canadian Sentencing

Commission (1987) had reached similar conclusions: "Deterrence cannot be used, with empirical justification, to guide the imposition of sanctions."

There is no better evidentiary base to justify recent drug control policies. Because no other western country has adopted drug policies as harsh as those of the United States, a bit of background may be useful before I show why there was no reasonable basis for believing recent policies would achieve their ostensible goals. In drug policy jargon, the United States has adopted a prohibitionistic rather than a harm-reduction strategy and has emphasized supply-side over demand-side tactics (Wilson 1990). This strategic choice implies a preference for legal threats and moral denunciation of drug use and users instead of a preference for minimizing net costs and social harms to the general public, the law enforcement system, and drug users. The tactical choice is between a law enforcement emphasis on arrest and punishment of dealers, distributors, and importers, interdiction, and source-country programs or a prevention emphasis on drug treatment, drug-abuse education in schools, and mass media programs aimed at public education. The supply-side bias in recent American policies was exemplified throughout the Bush administration by its insistence that 70% of federal antidrug funds be devoted to law enforcement and only 30% to treatment and education (Office of National Drug Control Policy 1990).

It has been a long time since most researchers and practitioners believed that current knowledge justifies recent American drug control policies. Because the potential income from drug dealing means that willing aspirants are nearly always available to replace arrested street-level dealers, large-scale arrests have repeatedly been shown to have little or no effect on the volume of drug trafficking or on the retail prices of drugs (e.g., Chaiken 1988; Sviridoff, Sadd, Curtis, and Grinc 1992). Because the United States has long and porous borders, and because an unachievably large proportion of attempted smuggling would have to be stopped to affect drug prices significantly, interdiction has repeatedly been shown to have little or no effect on volume or prices (Reuter 1988). Because cocaine, heroin, and marijuana can be grown in many parts of the world in which government controls are weak and peasant farmers' incentives are strong, source-country programs have seldom been shown to have significant influence on drug availability or price in the United States (Moore 1990).

The evidence in support of demand-side strategies is far stronger. In December 1993, the President's Commission on Model State Drug Laws, appointed by President Bush, categorically concluded, "Treatment works." That conclusion is echoed by more authoritative surveys of drug treatment evaluations by the U.S. General Accounting Office (1990), the National Institute of Medicine (Gerstein and Jarwood 1990), and in *Crime and Justice* by Anglin and Hser (1990). Because drug use and offending tend to coincide in the lives of drug-using offenders, the most effective and cost-effective way to deal with such offenders is to get and keep them in well-run treatment programs.

A sizable literature now also documents the effectiveness of school-based drug education in reducing drug experimentation and use among young people (e.g., Botvin 1990; Ellickson and Bell 1990). Although there is no credible literature that documents the effects of mass media campaigns on drug use, a judge could take judicial notice of their ubiquity. It is not unreasonable to believe that such campaigns have influenced across-the-board declines in drug use in the United States since 1980 (a date, incidentally, that precedes the launch of the War on Drugs by nearly 8 years).

That the preceding summary of our knowledge of the effectiveness of drug control methods is balanced and accurate is shown by the support it receives from leading conservative scholars. Senator-scholar Daniel Patrick Moynihan (1993) has written, "Interdiction and 'drug busts' are probably necessary symbolic acts, but nothing more." James Q. Wilson (1990), for two decades America's leading conservative crime control scholar, observed that "significant reductions in drug abuse will come only from reducing demand for those drugs. . . . The marginal product of further investment in supply reduction is likely to be small" (p. 534). He reports that "I know of no serious law-enforcement official who disagrees with this conclusion. Typically, police officials tell interviewers that they are fighting either a losing war or, at best, a holding action" (p. 534).

Thus a fair-minded survey of existing knowledge provides no grounds for believing that the War on Drugs or the harsh policies exemplified by "three strikes and you're out" laws and evidenced by a tripling in America's prison population since 1980 could achieve their ostensible purposes. If such policies cannot be explained in instrumental terms, how can they be explained? The last section answers that question, but first a summary of recent data on racial trends in arrests, jailing, and incarceration.

RACIAL DISPARITIES
IN ARRESTS, JAIL, AND PRISON

Racial disparities, especially affecting Blacks, have long bedeviled the criminal justice system. Many hundreds of studies of disparities have been conducted and there is now widespread agreement among researchers about causes. Racial bias and stereotyping no doubt play some role, but they are not the major cause. In the longer term, disparities in jail and prison are mainly the result of racial differences in offending patterns. In the shorter term, the worsening disparities since 1980 are not primarily the result of racial differences in offending but were foreseeable effects of the War on Drugs and the movement toward increased use of incarceration. These patterns can best be seen by approaching the recent increases in racial disparities in imprisonment as a mystery to be solved. (Because of space limitations, jail data are not discussed here at length, but the trends parallel those for prisons. Between 1980 and 1991, e.g., the percentage of jail inmates who were Black increased from 40% to 48%.)

Figure 1, showing the percentages of prison inmates who were Black or White from 1960 to 1991, reveals two trends. First, for as long as prison population data have been compiled, the percentage of inmates who are Black has

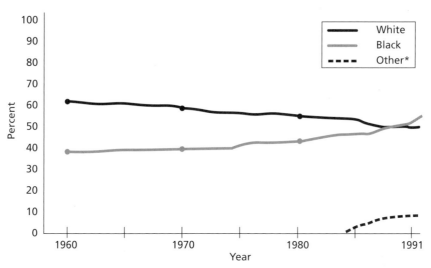

* Hispanics in many states, Asians, Native Americans.

FIGURE 1 Prisoners in State and Federal Prisons on Census Data by Race, 1960–1991

Sources: For 1960, 1970, 1980: Cahalan 1986, table 3.31; for 1985–1991: Bureau of Justice Statistics 1993, 1991a, 1991b, 1989a, 1989b, 1987.

by several times exceeded the percentage of Americans who are Black (10% to 13% during the relevant period). Second, since 1980 the Black percentage among prisoners has increased sharply.

Racial disproportions among prison inmates are inherently undesirable, and considerable energy has been expended on efforts to understand them. In 1982, Blumstein showed that around 80% of the disproportion could be explained on the basis of racial differences in arrest patterns. Of the unexplained 20%, Blumstein argued, some might represent bias and some might reflect racial differences in criminal history or arguably valid case-processing differences. Some years earlier, Hindelang (1976, 1978) had demonstrated that racial patterns in victims' identifications of their assailants closely resembled racial differences in arrests. Some years later, Langan (1985) skipped over the arrest stage altogether and showed that racial patterns in victims' identifications of their assailants explained about 80% of disparities in prison admissions. In 1990, Klein, Petersilia, and Turner showed that, after criminal history and other legitimate differences between cases were taken into account, the offender's race had no independent predictive effect in California on whether he was sent to prison or for how long. There the matter rests. Blumstein (1993a) updated his analysis and reached similar conclusions (with one important exception that is discussed below).

Although racial crime patterns explain a large part of racial imprisonment patterns, they do not explain why the Black percentage rose so rapidly after 1980. Table 1 shows Black and White percentages among people arrested for the eight

Table 1 Percentage Black and White Arrests for Index 1 Offenses, 1976–1991 (3-year intervals)*

	1976		1979		1982		1985		1988		1991		1992	
	White	Black	White	Black	White	Black	White	Black	White	Black	White	Black	White	Black
Murder and nonnegligent manslaughter	45.0	53.5	49.4	47.7	48.8	49.7	50.1	48.4	45.0	53.5	43.4	54.8	43.5	55.1
Forcible rape	51.2	46.6	50.2	47.7	48.7	49.7	52.2	46.5	52.7	45.8	54.8	43.5	55.5	42.8
Robbery	38.9	59.2	41.0	56.9	38.2	60.7	37.4	61.7	36.3	62.6	37.6	61.1	37.7	60.9
Aggravated assault	56.8	41.0	60.9	37.0	59.8	38.8	58.0	40.4	57.6	40.7	60.0	38.3	59.5	38.8
Burglary	69.0	29.2	69.5	28.7	67.0	31.7	69.7	28.9	67.0	31.3	68.8	29.3	67.8	30.4
Larceny-theft	65.7	32.1	67.2	30.2	64.7	33.4	67.2	30.6	65.6	32.2	66.6	30.9	66.2	31.4
Motor vehicle theft	71.1	26.2	70.0	27.2	66.9	31.4	65.8	32.4	58.7	39.5	58.5	39.3	58.4	39.4
Arson	—	—	78.9	19.2	74.0	24.7	75.7	22.8	73.5	25.0	76.7	21.5	76.4	21.9
Violent crime†	50.4	47.5	53.7	44.1	51.9	46.7	51.5	47.1	51.7	46.8	53.6	44.8	53.6	44.8
Property crime‡	67.0	30.9	68.2	29.4	65.5	32.7	67.7	30.3	65.3	32.6	66.4	31.3	65.8	31.8
Total crime index	64.1	33.8	65.3	32.4	62.7	35.6	64.5	33.7	62.4	35.7	63.2	34.6	62.7	35.2

*Because of rounding, the percentages may not add to total.

†Violent crimes are offenses of murder, forcible rape, robbery, and aggravated assault.

‡Property crimes are offenses of burglary, larceny-theft, motor vehicle theft, and arson.

SOURCES: *Sourcebook of Criminal Justice Statistics.* Various years. Washington, DC: U.S. Department of Justice, Bureau of Justice Statistics; FBI 1993, Table 43.

serious FBI Index Crimes at 3-year intervals from 1976 to 1991 and for 1992. Within narrow bands of fluctuation, racial arrest percentages have been stable since 1976. Comparing 1976 with 1992, for example, Black percentages among people arrested for murder, robbery, and burglary were slightly up and Black percentages among those arrested for rape, aggravated assault, and theft were slightly down. Overall, the percentage among those arrested for violent crimes who were Black fell from 47.5% to 44.8%. Because prison sentences have traditionally been imposed on people convicted of violent crimes, Blumstein's and the other analyses suggest that the Black percentage among inmates should be flat or declining. That, however, is not what Figure 1 shows. Why not?

Part of the answer can be found in prison admissions. Figure 2 shows racial percentages among prison admissions from 1960 to 1992. Arrests of Blacks for violent crimes may not have increased since 1980, but the percentage of Blacks among those sent to prison has increased starkly, reaching 54% in 1991 and 1992. Why? The main explanation concerns the War on Drugs.

Table 2 shows racial percentages among persons arrested for drug crimes between 1976 and 1992. Blacks today make up about 13% of the U.S. population and, according to National Institute on Drug Abuse (1991) surveys of Americans' drug use, are no more likely than Whites ever to have used most drugs of abuse. Nonetheless, the percentages of Blacks among drug arrestees were in the low 20% range in the late 1970s, climbing to around 30% in the early 1980s and peaking at 42% in 1989. The number of drug arrests of Blacks more than doubled between 1985 and 1989, whereas White drug arrests increased only by 27%. Figure 3 shows the stark differences in drug arrest trends by race from 1976 to 1991.

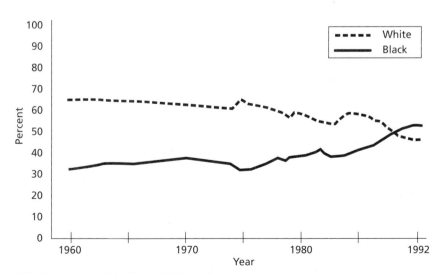

NOTE: Hispanics are included in Black and White populations.

FIGURE 2 Admissions to Federal and State Prisons by Race, 1960–1992

Source: Langan 1991; Gilliard 1992; Perkins 1992, Perkins and Gilliard 1992.

Table 2 U.S. Drug Arrests by Race, 1976–1992

Year	Total Violations	White	White %	Black	Black %
1976	475,209	366,081	77	103,615	22
1977	565,371	434,471	77	122,594	22
1978	592,168	462,728	78	127,277	21
1979	516,142	396,065	77	112,748	22
1980	531,953	401,979	76	125,607	24
1981	584,776	432,556	74	146,858	25
1982	562,390	400,683	71	156,369	28
1983	615,081	423,151	69	185,601	30
1984	560,729	392,904	70	162,979	29
1985	700,009	482,486	69	210,298	30
1986	688,815	463,457	67	219,159	32
1987	809,157	511,278	63	291,177	36
1988	844,300	503,125	60	334,015	40
1989	1,074,345	613,800	57	452,574	42
1990	860,016	503,315	59	349,965	41
1991	763,340	443,596	58	312,997	41
1992	919,561	546,430	59	364,546	40

SOURCES: FBI 1993, Table 43; *Sourcebook of Criminal Justice Statistics*—1978–1992. Various tables. Washington, DC: U.S. Department of Justice, Bureau of Justice Statistics.

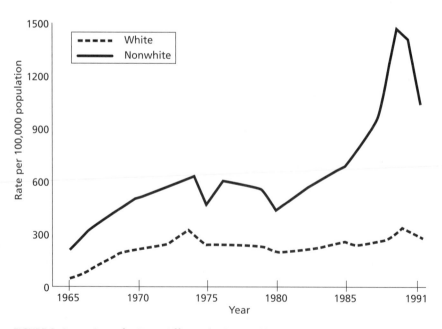

FIGURE 3 Arrest Rates for Drug Offenses by Race, 1965–1991

Source: Blumstein 1993b.

Drug control policies are a major cause of worsening racial disparities in prison. In the federal prisons, for example, 22% of new admissions and 25% of the resident population were drug offenders in 1980. By 1990, 42% of new admissions were drug offenders and in 1992 were 58% of the resident population. In state prisons, 5.7% of inmates in 1979 were drug offenders, a figure that by 1991 had climbed to 21.3% to become the single largest category of prisoners (robbers, burglars, and murderers were next at 14.8%, 12.4%, and 10.6%, respectively) (Beck et al. 1993).

The effect of drug policies can be seen in prison data from a number of states. Figure 4 shows Black and White prison admissions in North Carolina from 1970 to 1990. White rates held steady; Black rates doubled between 1980 and 1990, rising most rapidly after 1987. Figure 5 shows prison admissions for drug crimes in Virginia from 1983 to 1989; the racial balance flipped from two-thirds White, one-third non-White in 1983 to the reverse in 1989. Similarly, in Pennsylvania, Clark (1992) reports, Black male prison admissions for drug crimes grew four times faster (up 1,613%) between 1980 and 1990 than did White male admissions (up 477%). In California, according to Zimring and Hawkins (1994), the number of males in prison for drug crimes grew 15 fold between 1980 and 1990 and "there were more people in prison in California for drug offences in 1991 than there were for *all* offences in California at the end of 1979" (p. 89; emphasis in original).

Why, if Blacks in their lives are no more likely than Whites to use illicit drugs, are Blacks so much more likely to be arrested and imprisoned? One possible answer, which is almost certainly wrong, is that Blacks are proportionately

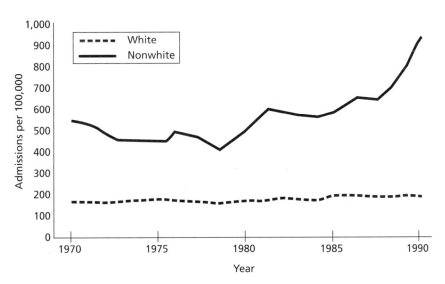

FIGURE 4 Prison Admissions per 100,000 General Population, North Carolina, by Race, 1970–1990

Source: Clarke 1992.

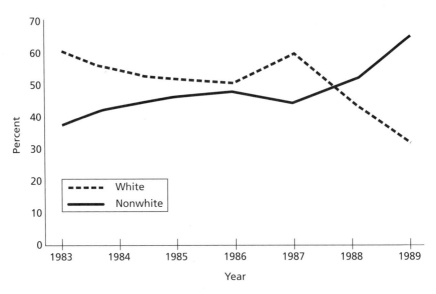

FIGURE 5 Percentage of New Drug Commitments by Race, Virginia, Fiscal Years 1983–1989

Source: Austin and McVey 1989.

more likely to sell drugs. We have no representative surveys of drug dealers and so cannot with confidence paint demographic pictures. However, there is little reason to suspect that drug crimes are more interracial than are most other crimes. In addition, the considerations that make arrests of Black dealers relatively easy make arrests of White dealers relatively hard.

Drug arrests are easier to make in socially disorganized inner-city minority areas than in working- or middle-class urban or suburban areas for a number of reasons. First, although drug sales in working- or middle-class areas are likely to take place indoors and in private spaces where they are difficult to observe, drug sales in poor minority areas are likely to take place outdoors in streets, alleys, or abandoned buildings, or indoors in public places like bars. Second, although working- or middle-class drug dealers in stable areas are unlikely to sell drugs to undercover strangers, dealers in disorganized areas have little choice but to sell to strangers and new acquaintances. These differences mean that it is easier for police to make arrests and undercover purchases in urban minority areas than elsewhere. Because arrests are fungible for purposes of both the individual officer's personnel file and the department's year-to-year statistical comparisons, more easy arrests look better than fewer hard ones. And because, as ethnographic studies of drug trafficking make clear (Fagan 1993; Padilla 1992), arrested drug dealers in disadvantaged urban minority communities are generally replaced within days, there is a nearly inexhaustible potential supply of young minority Americans to be arrested.

There is another reason why the War on Drugs worsened racial disparities in the justice system. Penalties for drug crimes were steadily made harsher since the mid-1980s. In particular, purveyors of crack cocaine, a drug used primarily by poor urban Blacks and Hispanics, are punished far more severely than are purveyors of powder cocaine, a pharmacologically indistinguishable drug used primarily by middle-class Whites. The most notorious disparity occurs under federal law, which equates 1 gram of crack with 100 grams of powder. As a result, the average prison sentence served by Black federal prisoners is 40% longer than the average sentence for Whites (McDonald and Carlson 1993). Although the Minnesota Supreme Court and two federal district courts have struck down the 100-to-1 rule as a denial of constitutional equal protection to Blacks, at the time of writing, every federal court of appeals that had considered the question had upheld the provision.

The people who launched the drug wars knew all these things—that the enemy troops would mostly be young minority males, that an emphasis on supply-side antidrug strategies, particularly use of mass arrests, would disproportionately ensnare young minority males, that the 100-to-1 rule would disproportionately affect Blacks, and that there was no valid basis for believing that any of these things would reduce drug availability or prices.

Likewise, as the first section showed, there was no basis for a good faith belief that the harsher crime control policies of recent years—more and longer mandatory minimum sentences, tougher and more rigid sentencing guidelines, and three-strikes-and-you're-out laws—would reduce crime rates, and there was a good basis for predicting that they would disproportionately damage Blacks. If Blacks are more likely than Whites to be arrested, especially for drug crimes, the greater harshness of toughened penalties will disproportionately be borne by Blacks. Because much crime is intraracial, concern for Black victims might justify harsher treatment of Black offenders if there were any reason to believe that harsher penalties would reduce crime rates. Unfortunately, as the conservative national governments of Margaret Thatcher and Brian Mulroney and reports of National Academy of Sciences Panels funded by the administrations of Republican Presidents Ford, Reagan, and Bush all agree, there is no reason to believe that harsher penalties significantly reduce crime rates.

JUSTIFYING THE UNJUSTIFIABLE

There is no valid policy justification for the harsh drug and crime control policies of the Reagan and Bush administrations, and for their adverse differential effect on Blacks. The justification, such as it is, is entirely political. Crime is an emotional subject and visceral appeals by politicians to people's fears and resentments are difficult to counter.

It is easy to seize the low ground in political debates about crime policy. When one candidate campaigns with pictures of clanging prison gates and grief-stricken relatives of a rape or murder victim, and with disingenuous promises that newer, tougher policies will work, it is difficult for an opponent to explain that crime is a complicated problem, that real solutions must be long term, and that simplistic toughness does not reduce crime rates. This is why, as a result, candidates often compete to establish which is tougher in his views about crime. It is also why less conservative candidates often try to preempt their more conservative opponents by adopting a tough stance early in the campaign. Finally, it is why political pundits congratulate President Clinton on his acumen in proposing federal crime legislation as or more harsh than his opponents. He has, it is commonly said, "taken the crime issue away from the Republicans."

Conservative Republican politicians have, since the late 1960s, used welfare, especially Aid to Families with Dependent Children, and crime as symbolic issues to appeal to anti-Black sentiments and resentments of White voters, as Thomas and Mary Edsall's *Chain Reaction: The Impact of Race, Rights, and Taxes on American Politics* (1991) makes clear. The Edsalls provide a history, since the mid-1960s, of "a conservative politics that had the effect of polarizing the electorate along racial lines." Anyone who observed Ronald Reagan's portrayal in several campaigns of Linda Evans, a Black Chicago woman, as the "welfare queen" or George Bush's use of Black murderer Willie Horton to caricature Michael Dukakis's criminal justice policies knows of what the Edsalls write.

The story of Willie Horton is the better known and makes the Edsalls' point. Horton, who in 1975 had been convicted of the murder of a 17-year-old boy, failed to return from a June 12, 1986, furlough. The following April, he broke into a home in Oxon Hill, Maryland, where he raped a woman and stabbed her companion.

Lee Atwater, Bush's campaign strategist, after testing the visceral effects of Willie Horton's picture and story on participants in focus groups, decided a year later to make Horton a wedge issue for Republicans. Atwater reportedly told a group of Republican activists that Bush would win the presidency "if I can make Willie Horton a household name." He later told a Republican gathering in Atlanta, "there's a story about a fellow named Willie Horton who, for all I know, may end up being Dukakis's running mate." Atwater for a time denied making both remarks but in 1991, dying of cancer, recanted: "In 1988, fighting Dukakis, I said that I would . . . make Willie Horton his running mate. I am sorry."

The sad reality is that tragedies like the crimes of Willie Horton are inevitable. So are airplane crashes, 40,000 to 50,000 traffic fatalities per year, and defense department cost overruns. Every person convicted of a violent crime cannot be held forever. Furloughs are used in most corrections systems as a way to ease offenders back into the community and to test their suitability for eventual release on parole or commutation. Horton had successfully completed nine previous furloughs, from each of which he had returned without incident, under a program established in 1972 not by Michael Dukakis but by Governor Francis Sargent, a Republican.

Public discourse about criminal justice issues has been debased by the cynicism that made Willie Horton a major participant in the 1988 presidential election. That cynicism has made it difficult to discuss or develop sensible public policies, and that cynicism explains why conservative politicians have been able year after year successfully to propose ever harsher penalties and crime control and drug policies that no informed person believes can achieve their ostensible goals.

Three final points, arguments that apologists for current policies sometimes make, warrant mention. First, it is sometimes said to be unfair to blame national Republican administrations for the failures and disparate impacts of recent crime control policies. This ignores the efforts of the Reagan and Bush administrations to encourage and, through federal mandates and funding restrictions, to coerce states to follow the federal lead. Attorney General William Barr (e.g., 1992) made the most aggressive efforts to compel state adoption of tougher criminal justice policies, and the Bush administration's final proposed crime bills restricted eligibility for federal funds to states that, like the federal government, abolished parole release and adopted sentencing standards no less severe than those in the federal sentencing guidelines. In any case, as the Edsalls' book makes clear, the use of crime control issues (among others including welfare reform and affirmative action) to elicit anti-Black sentiments from White voters has long been a stratagem of both state and federal Republican politicians.

Second, sometimes it is argued that political leaders have merely followed the public will; voters are outraged by crime and want tougher policies (DiIulio 1991). This is a half-truth that gets the causal order backwards. Various measures of public sentiment, including both representative surveys like Gallup and Harris polls and work with focus groups, have for many years consistently shown that the public is of two minds about crime (Roberts 1992). First, people are frustrated and want offenders to be punished. Second, people believe that social adversity, poverty, and a troubled home life are the principal causes of crime, and they believe government should work to rehabilitate offenders. A number of surveys have found that respondents who would oppose a tax increase to pay for more prisons would support a tax increase to pay for rehabilitative programs. These findings of voter ambivalence about crime should not be surprising. Most people have complicated views about complicated problems. For example, most judges and corrections officials have the same ambivalent feelings about offenders that the general public has. Conservative politicians have seized upon public support of punishment and ignored public support of rehabilitation and public recognition that crime presents complex, not easy, challenges. By presenting crime control issues only in emotional, stereotyped ways, conservative politicians have raised [crime's] salience as a political issue but made it impossible for their opponents to respond other than in the same stereotyped ways.

Third, sometimes it is argued that disparate impacts on Black offenders are no problem and that, because much crime is intraracial, failure to adopt tough policies would disserve the interests of Black victims. As former Attorney General Barr (1992) put it, perhaps in ill-chosen words, "the benefits of increased incarceration would be enjoyed disproportionately by Black Americans" (p. 17). This argument also is based on a half-truth. No one wants to live in unsafe neighborhoods or to be victimized by crime, and in a crisis, people who need help will seek it from the police, the public agency of last resort. Requesting help in a crisis and supporting harsh policies with racially disparate effects are not the same thing. The relevant distinction is between acute and chronic problems. A substantial body of public opinion research (e.g., National Opinion Research Center surveys conducted throughout the 1980s summarized in Wood 1990) shows that Blacks far more than Whites support establishment of more generous social welfare policies, full employment programs, and increased social spending. The congressional Black and Hispanic caucuses have consistently opposed bills calling for tougher sanctions and supported bills calling for increased spending on social programs aimed at improving conditions that cause crime. Thus, in claiming to be concerned about Black victims, conservative politicians are responding to natural human calls for help in a crisis while ignoring evidence that Black citizens would rather have government support efforts to ameliorate the chronic social conditions that cause crime and thereby make calls for help in a crisis less necessary.

The evidence on the effectiveness of recent crime control and drug abuse policies, as the first section demonstrated, cannot justify their racially disparate effects on Blacks, nor, as this section demonstrates, can the claims that such policies merely manifest the peoples' will or respect the interests of Black victims. All that is left is politics of the ugliest kind. The War on Drugs and the set of harsh crime control policies in which it was enmeshed were adopted to achieve political, not policy, objectives, and it is the adoption for political purposes of policies with foreseeable disparate impacts, the use of disadvantaged Black Americans as means to the achievement of White politicians' electoral ends, that must in the end be justified. It cannot.

REFERENCES

Anglin, M. Douglas, and Yih-Ing Hser (1990). "Treatment of Drug Abuse." In M. Tonry and J. Q. Wilson (eds.), *Drugs and Crime.* Chicago: University of Chicago Press.

Austin, James, and Aaron David McVey (1989). *The Impact of the War on Drugs.* San Francisco: National Council on Crime and Delinquency.

Barr, William P. (1992). "The Case for More Incarceration." Washington, D.C.: U.S. Department of Justice, Office of Policy Development.

Blumstein, Alfred (1982). "On the Racial Disproportionality of United States' Prison Populations." *Journal of Criminal Law and Criminology* 73:1259–81.

———— (1993a). "Racial Disproportionality of U.S. Prison Populations Revisited."

University of Colorado Law Review 64:743–60.

———— (1993b). "Making Rationality Relevant—The American Society of Criminology 1992 Presidential Address." *Criminology* 31:1–16.

Blumstein, Alfred, Jacqueline Cohen, and Daniel Nagin (1978). *Deterrence and Incapacitation.* Report of the National Academy of Sciences Panel on Research on Deterrent and Incapacitative Effects. Washington, D.C.: National Academy Press.

Botvin, Gilbert J. (1990). "Substance Abuse Prevention: Theory, Practice, and Effectiveness." In M. Tonry and J. Q. Wilson (eds.), *Drugs and Crime.* Chicago: University of Chicago Press.

Bureau of Justice Statistics (1987). *Correctional Populations in the United States, 1985*. Washington, D.C.: U.S. Department of Justice, Bureau of Justice Statistics.

———— (1989a). *Correctional Populations in the United States, 1987*. Washington, D.C.: U.S. Department of Justice, Bureau of Justice Statistics.

———— (1989b). *Correctional Populations in the United States, 1986*. Washington, D.C.: U.S. Department of Justice, Bureau of Justice Statistics.

———— (1991a). *Correctional Populations in the United States, 1989*. Washington, D.C.: U.S. Department of Justice, Bureau of Justice Statistics.

———— (1991b). *Correctional Populations in the United States, 1988*. Washington, D.C.: U.S. Department of Justice, Bureau of Justice Statistics.

———— (1993). *Correctional Populations in the United States, 1991*. Washington, D.C.: U.S. Department of Justice, Bureau of Justice Statistics.

Cahalan, Margaret Werner (1986). *Historical Corrections Statistics in the United States, 1850–1984*. Washington, D.C.: U.S. Department of Justice, Bureau of Justice Statistics.

Canadian Sentencing Commission (1987). *Sentencing Reform: A Canadian Approach*. Ottawa: Canadian Government Publishing Centre.

Chaiken, Marcia, ed. (1988). *Street Level Enforcement: Examining the Issues*. Washington, D.C.: U.S. Government Printing Office.

Clark, Stover (1992). "Pennsylvania Corrections in Context." *Overcrowded Times* 3:4–5.

Clarke, Stevens H. (1992). "North Carolina Prisons Growing." *Overcrowded Times* 3:1, 11–13.

DiIulio, John J. (1991). *No Escape: The Future of American Corrections*. New York: Basic Books.

Edsall, Thomas, and Mary Edsall (1991). *Chain Reaction: The Impact of Race, Rights, and Taxes on American Politics*. New York: Norton.

Ellickson, Phyllis L., and Robert M. Bell (1990). *Prospects for Preventing Drug Use Among Young Adolescents*. Santa Monica, Calif.: RAND.

Fagan, Jeffrey (1993). "The Political Economy of Drug Dealing Among Urban Gangs." In R. C. Davis, A. J. Lurigio, and D. P. Rosenbaum (eds.), *Drugs and the Community*. Springfield, Ill.: Charles C. Thomas.

Federal Bureau of Investigation (1993). *Uniform Crime Reports for the United States—1992*. Washington, D.C.: U.S. Government Printing Office.

Gerstein, Dean R., and Henrik J. Jarwood, eds. (1990). *Treating Drug Problems*. Report of the Committee for Substance Abuse Coverage Study, Division of Health Care Services, National Institute of Medicine. Washington, D.C.: National Academy Press.

Gilliard, Darrell K. (1992). *National Corrections Reporting Program, 1987*. Washington, D.C.: U.S. Department of Justice, Bureau of Justice Statistics.

Hindelang, Michael. (1976). *Criminal Victimization in Eight American Cities: A Descriptive Analysis of Common Theft and Assault*. Washington, D.C.: Law Enforcement Assistance Administration.

———— (1978). "Race and Involvement in Common Law Personal Crimes." *American Sociological Review* 43:93–108.

Home Office (1990). *Protecting the Public*. London: H. M. Stationery Office.

Klein, Stephen, Joan Petersilia, and Susan Turner (1990). "Race and Imprisonment Decisions in California." *Science* 247: 812–16.

Langan, Patrick A. (1985). "Racism on Trial: New Evidence to Explain the Racial Composition of Prisons in the United States." *Journal of Criminal Law and Criminology* 76:666–83.

———— (1991). *Race of Persons Admitted to State and Federal Institutions, 1926–86*. Washington, D.C.: U.S. Department of Justice, Bureau of Justice Statistics.

McDonald, Douglas, and Ken Carlson (1993). *Sentencing in the Federal Courts: Does Race Matter?* Washington, D.C.: U.S. Department of Justice, Bureau of Justice Statistics.

Moore, Mark H. (1990). "Supply Reduction and Drug Law Enforcement." In

M. Tonry and J. Q. Wilson (eds.), *Drugs and Crime*. Chicago: University of Chicago Press.

Moynihan, Daniel Patrick (1993). "Iatrogenic Government—Social Policy and Drug Research." *American Scholar* 62:351–62.

National Institute on Drug Abuse (1991). *National Household Survey on Drug Abuse: Population Estimates 1990*. Washington, D.C.: U.S. Government Printing Office.

Office of National Drug Control Policy (1990). *National Drug Control Strategy—January 1990*. Washington, D.C.: Author.

Padilla, Felix (1992). *The Gang as an American Enterprise*. New Brunswick, N.J.: Rutgers University Press.

Perkins, Craig (1992). *National Corrections Reporting Program, 1989*. Washington, D.C.: U.S. Department of Justice, Bureau of Justice Statistics.

Perkins, Craig, and Darrell K. Gilliard (1992). *National Corrections Reporting Program, 1988*. Washington, D.C.: U.S. Department of Justice, Bureau of Justice Statistics.

Reiss, Albert J., Jr., and Jeffrey Roth (1993). *Understanding and Controlling Violence, Report of the National Academy of Sciences Panel on the Understanding and Control of Violence*. Washington, D.C.: National Academy Press.

Reuter, Peter (1988). "Can the Borders Be Sealed?" *Public Interest* 92:51–65.

Roberts, Julian V. (1992). "Public Opinion, Crime, and Criminal Justice." In M. Tonry (ed.), *Crime and Justice: A Review of Research*, vol. 16. Chicago: University of Chicago Press.

Sourcebook of Criminal Justice Statistics (1978–1992). Washington, D.C.: Department of Justice, Bureau of Justice Statistics.

Standing Committee on Justice and the Solicitor General (1993). *Crime Prevention in Canada: Toward a National Strategy*. Ottawa: Canada Communication Group.

Sviridoff, Michele, Susan Sadd, Richard Curtis, and Randolph Grinc (1992). *The Neighborhood Effects of Street-Level Drug Enforcement*. New York: Vera Institute of Justice.

U.S. General Accounting Office (1990). *Drug Abuse: Research on Treatment May Not Address Current Needs*. Washington, D.C.: U.S. General Accounting Office.

Wilson, James Q. (1990). "Drugs and Crime." In M. Tonry and J. Q. Wilson (eds)., *Drugs and Crime*. Chicago: University of Chicago Press.

Wood, Floris W. (1990). *An American Profile: Opinions and Behavior, 1972–1989*. New York: Gale Research.

Zimring, Franklin E., and Gordon Hawkins (1994). "The Growth of Imprisonment in California." *British Journal of Criminology* 34:83–95.

3

✸

The Media, Moral Panics, and the Politics of Crime Control

Ted Chiricos

Criminologists use the concept of the "moral panic" to try to understand why the public becomes almost hysterical over some perceived threat to societal values and interests. In recent years moral panics about serial killers, drug dealers, and child sexual abuse have dominated the headlines. Public pressures have been directed at political leaders to "do something!" Ted Chiricos argues that moral panics are used by political leaders to justify expansion of the power of the state.

In the summer and fall of 1993, violent crime captured popular consciousness in the United States with a speed and intensity seldom seen. Searing images of "random" violence—tourists in Florida, a truck driver in Los Angeles, passengers on a train—competed with natural disasters to hold a nation in awe.

By January 1994, television networks had run week-long series on *Kids and Crime* (CNN) and *America the Violent* (NBC) or had featured specials on *Florida, the State of Fear* (ABC) and *"Monster" Kody Scott* (CBS), the notorious gangbanger from Los Angeles. Newsmagazines ran cover stories on "Growing Up Scared" (*Newsweek*), "Lock 'Em Up and Throw Away the Key" (*Time*) and "Florida: The State of Rage" (*U.S. News and World Report*).

In the wake of the media feeding frenzy, Americans ranking crime/violence as the nation's foremost problem jumped from 9 percent to 49 percent between January 1993 and January 1994 (Gallup 1994:6). Not surprising was

Source: Written specifically for this book.

the response of politicians and moral entrepreneurs who swam furiously to stay atop the wave of public anxiety. Proposals to deal with the "epidemic" of violence escalated demands for "getting tough"—more police, more prison beds, longer mandatory sentences, "hard time" for kids, more and faster executions, "three strikes, you're out."

In April of 1999, the tragedy of Columbine High School captured the nation's attention, becoming the focal point of public, media and congressional attention. The importance of Columbine was elevated, in part, by several prior school shootings, especially since 1996, none of which reached the level of devastation witnessed in Littleton, Colorado. Columbine served as a focusing event for youth violence. Indeed, the massacre of Columbine became the most covered news story of 1999 (Pew Research Center 2000). Coverage of juvenile crime included school shootings, club drugs, and "raves."

When asked about watching the continuing coverage of the aftermath of the violence at Columbine, 50 percent of respondents indicated they followed it "very closely," while 32 percent watched "fairly closely" (Henry J. Kaiser Family Foundation 1999). Events in Littleton, Colorado, had significant influence on the public's perception of safety in schools. When asked, "How much, if at all, did the Columbine shooting last year change your views about how safe your child is at school?" 44 percent of those surveyed reported, "a lot," while 27 percent indicated "some" (Pew Research Center 2000). News and polling organizations began surveying the public on the sources of this seeming rise in youth violence, asking questions about parenting, Internet access and monitoring for weapons and bomb making information, the availability of guns to youth, the Goth culture and the influence of the entertainment industry.

In response to this widespread attention, the White House convened a summit within a few weeks of events at Columbine. The violence in Colorado seemingly prompted the most intense period of legislative activity on school violence in the 106th Congress. During this time, 35 percent of all bills addressing school violence were introduced in April and May of 1999 whereas no other month of the year for the legislative session contained more than 9 percent of bills on juvenile crime (Lawrence and Birkland 2000).

THE CONCEPT OF MORAL PANIC

Hysteria over violent crime is a classic example of "moral panic." This concept was developed by Cohen, who noted that at certain times a "condition, episode, person or group of persons emerges to become defined as a threat to societal values and interests" (Cohen 1972:9). He notes that typically the threat is presented in the media in a simplistic fashion; spokespersons such as editors, the clergy, and politicians man the moral barricades; and experts pronounce their diagnoses of the problem and present solutions. As he emphasizes, the point of moral panic is "not that there's nothing there" but that societal responses are fundamentally inappropriate (Cohen 1972:204).

Cohen studied a moral panic involving British teenagers—"Mods" and "Rockers"—in the 1960s. Though substantially peaceful, large gatherings of these youths at several beaches provoked massive popular concern. A flood of media reports were used to justify an emergent "control culture" that included everything from local "action groups" to a largely symbolic "malicious damage" bill passed by Parliament. "Mods" and "Rockers" were typified as "folk devils" whose "premature affluent and aggressive" ways were the consequence of "permissiveness" and—at a time of rapid social change—a threat to established values of "sobriety and hard work." The beaches involved had already lost prosperous and even working-class clientele. Desperate to shore up declining status, they adopted what Cohen described as "the rhetoric of moral panics—'We won't allow our seafront/area/town/country to be taken over by hooligans/hippies/blacks/Pakistanis'" (1972:177–198).

Stuart Hall (1978:140–147) and his colleagues studied a British "mugging" panic during which the media helped mobilize popular support for commands to get tougher on crime. That the typical "mugger" was portrayed as a young black man simplified the process of defining the problem of crime as a reflection of the "erosion of 'traditional' working-class neighborhoods and communities." In a number of English cities, black youth were increasingly unemployed, militant, and at odds with the police. Concerns were expressed about the apparent decline of "core values" such as respectability, work, discipline, family—England. As the authors note, a consequence of changes in society is the "emergence of a predisposition to the use of 'scapegoats' into which *all* the disturbing experiences are condensed and then symbolically rejected or 'cast out'" (1978:157).

Moral panics can be understood as having an ideological dimension in that they initiate *partisan* calls to "do something" and there is a *distortion of reality* in pursuit of that objective. Gouldner (1976:23–66) argues that ideology is discourse that "seeks to gather, assemble, husband, defer and control the *discharge* of political energies." Popular support for "public projects" is mobilized without reference to tradition, authority, or faith. Instead, *reports* are made about the world that justify *commands* to do something of a public nature. Moreover, the core of ideology—a relationship between reports and commands—is rooted in partisanship, yet mobilization of broad public support generally requires the misrepresentation of partisan interests. Thus, the function of ideology is not merely to report and to reveal but also to blur and conceal.

Specifically, the moral panic over violence is used to justify expanding the punitive apparatus of the state—even as crime rates are falling. In addition, the panic diverts attention from contradictions of the nation's political economy that have promoted an extraordinary growth of economic inequality and expansion of the urban underclass. It is precisely this underclass that has become an increasingly "privileged target group" for incarceration.

In short, these moral panics not only provide the "vocabularies of punitive motive" to justify an explosive growth of prison populations, but they obscure the declining condition of those most victimized by a changing political economy and by crime—even as they are incarcerated in unprecedented numbers.

Over the past fifteen years, the United States has had an *expanding* under-class, a *declining* crime rate and an *exploding* prison population. An expanding underclass has not led to an increase in crime, but members of that underclass are being incarcerated in unprecedented numbers. Something is missing in the chain linking political economy and punishment. Melossi (1985) has suggested that an important link in this chain may be provided by *discourse* that justifies repression.

The central point of this paper is that moral panics provide one part of that discursive link. They provide a "vocabulary of punitive motive" (Melossi 1985) that justifies a massive increase in prison population—even in the face of declining crime rates. At the same time, they divert attention from the conse-quences of investment decisions that include a rapid expansion in the number of people who either have nothing to lose from crime or who may actually derive value from the use of drugs or involvement in violence.

THE RECENT MORAL PANICS:
DRUGS AND VIOLENCE

The United States has experienced two major moral panics in the past decade. The first, involving crack cocaine, began in the summer and peaked in the fall of 1986; the second, involving violent crime, began in the summer of 1993 and peaked early in 1994.

The two panics share several key features that underscore their common ideological substance and significance. The first was an explosion in the *volume* of media *reports*—increasing in each case more than 400 percent during a six-month period. Moreover, these panics had several common *thematic emphases.* Both reported (1) that behaviors thought characteristic of urban ghettos were spreading to previously "safe" places and (2) that "carriers" of the spreading menace were increasingly children. In both instances the panics promoted a critical *misunderstanding* of the underlying behaviors which helped to justify *commands* for a radical expansion of *punitive controls.* At the same time, these panics *displaced* attention from the coercive consequences of investment deci-sions that diminished the value of work for so many and devastated the cir-cumstances of America's urban ghettos.

Volume of Media Reports:
Crack Cocaine and Violent Crime

Figure 1 shows media coverage of drug issues from January 1985 through March 1987. In the early 1980s, drugs accounted for about 1 percent of total news coverage tracked by the Conference on Issues and Media (CIM). At the beginning of 1986 the CIM index was still below 1 percent after a brief surge in 1985 (Merriam 1989:22–24).

Spurred by the death of basketball star Len Bias (June 19) media coverage of drugs shot up to 6 percent of all news in the two weeks ending August 10.

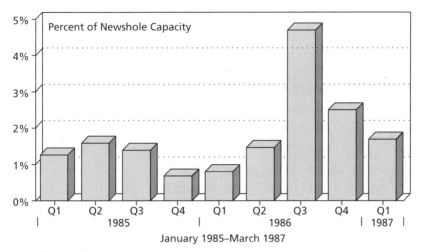

*Adapted from: Merriam, 1989:23.

FIGURE 1 Media Coverage of Drug Issues*

Ironically, the White House declared a renewed "war" on drugs in August and coverage began to fall. By the first quarter of 1987 the CIM index was back down to 1.1 percent (Merriam 1989:24–25).

The explosion of media coverage was punctuated by key reports in both print and television media. The *New York Times* assigned a full-time reporter to cover illegal drugs in November 1985 and ran its first front-page story on crack during that month. On March 17, 1986, a *Newsweek* cover story reported on the "Coke Plague" and the "almost instant addiction" of "crack" that moved a Los Angeles detective to conclude "we have lost the cocaine battle." By May 23, NBC News anchor Tom Brokaw declared that "crack" was "flooding America" and had become the nation's "drug of choice." In June, *Newsweek* proclaimed crack the biggest story since Vietnam and Watergate. On September 2, Dan Rather of CBS News hosted *48 Hours on Crack Street*—the most widely watched documentary in five years. NBC followed three days later with a prime-time special: *Cocaine Country*. This was just one of four hundred crack or cocaine stories—fifteen hours of air time—that NBC ran between April and November of 1986 (Reinarman and Levine 1989:118). By September, *Time* had recognized crack as "the issue of the year." Between March 30 and December 31, 1986, the *New York Times* carried 139 cocaine stories and the *Washington Post* carried 60 more (Danielian and Reese 1989:49).

The pattern of media coverage during the panic over violent crime was remarkably similar. Figure 2 shows the combined frequency of television and newspaper stories involving violent crime and juvenile violence between January 1992 and March 1994. By these measures, media attention varied within narrow parameters until the middle of 1993. Monthly newspaper citations rose from a low of eighteen in June to a high of ninety-five in November,

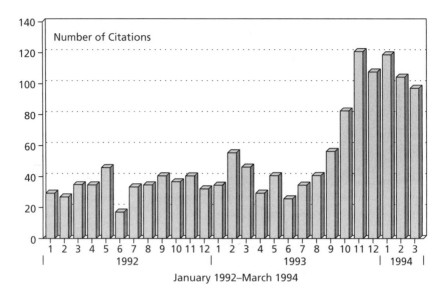

FIGURE 2 Media Coverage of Violent Crime and Juvenile Violence

dropping only slightly thereafter. Network television stories rose from a low of four in April to a high of thirty-four in January 1994.

Noting that Los Angeles "has the equivalent of a St. Valentine's Day massacre every day," a May 31 editorial in *U.S. News & World Report* ascribed a mood of "panic" to the citizens of that city. That mood seemed to escalate nationally after the July rape and murder of two teenage girls by six Houston gang members to whom "life means nothing" (*Newsweek* 1993a:16). Two weeks later (August 2) each of the national newsmagazines ran cover stories on violent crime and the panic was on.

The images of violence escalated further with the murder of a German tourist in Miami (September 11) and a British tourist at a highway rest stop in North Florida. *Newsweek* headlined its coverage a "State of Terror" and noted that the incident "sends shock waves overseas and reminds Americans of the epidemic violence in our streets." Two weeks later, *U.S. News* headlined Florida as "The State of Rage" where "nine foreign visitors [had] been murdered since last October," and *Time's* report on "Taming the Killers" asked if young murderers can be reformed or if "they are fated to repeat their crimes." On October 1, twelve-year-old Polly Klaas was kidnapped from her California home—a story that galvanized all media outlets until her body was found two months later.

The media blitz continued through the end of the year with a major *U.S. News* report (November 8) on "Violence in Schools" followed the next week with "The Voters Cry for Help" in dealing with "the wave of crime fear gripping Americans." *Newsweek* headlined "Death at an Early Age" on November 8 (1993) and three weeks later ran an eight-page cover story on "Gangsta Rap and the Culture of Violence." On December 8, CBS aired a one-hour special on Florida—"State of Fear."

The mid-December "Massacre on the Long Island Railroad," which left five dead and nineteen wounded, pushed the panic to its greatest heights. Most major media outlets gave the story front-page and lead coverage. *U.S. News* carried the headline "Violence and Its Terrifying Randomness" and asked, "Is no place in America safe from violence?" Shortly thereafter NBC News and CNN ran week-long series on *America the Violent* and *Kids and Crime*, respectively.

Reports: Qualitatively Different Dangers

In addition to the escalating volume of media attention, the moral panics over crack, violence, and youth crime were characterized by reports emphasizing new and greater dangers. Both drugs and violence were common to the American experience, and the warrant for panic included, in both cases, reports of a menace that was qualitatively different and more terrifying.

Out of the Ghetto—Out of Control A key element in both panics was a presumption that dangerous behaviors thought common to inner-city neighborhoods were suddenly spreading out of the ghetto into middle America. By the early 1980s, freebasing—the precursor to "crack" as a form of cocaine use—was common to inner-city after-hours clubs (base houses) in Los Angeles and New York. Cocaine freebase, packaged in retail form as "crack" or "rock," appeared in 1984. Its low price encouraged widespread use in the poor neighborhoods of many cities by 1986.

The March 17 *Newsweek*—which some consider pivotal for the emerging "panic"—sounded the alarm on its cover: "An Epidemic Strikes Middle America." The seven-page story included these descriptions of crack's expanding menace:

> Crack . . . is already creating social havoc in the ghettos of Los Angeles, New York and other large cities, and it is rapidly spreading into the suburbs on both coasts.

> And in Camden County NJ . . . prosecutor Samuel Asbell is convinced that the city's contagion has already spread to suburbia.

> There is simply no question that cocaine in all its forms is seeping into the nation's schools.

Subsequent issues of Newsweek in the summer of 1986 repeated the message of a spreading contagion:

> Crack has captured the ghetto and is inching its way into the suburbs. (1986b:16)

> There are ominous signs that crack and rock dealers are expanding well beyond the inner city. (1986b:20)

> In part, the change in the public mood has a racist tinge: drugs simply have moved from the black and Hispanic underclass to the middle-class mainstream and are being felt as a problem there. (1986c:15)

One analysis of television reporting on the "crack epidemic" compared it with coverage given to "Black Tar"—an especially potent form of heroin—that NBC News (March 28, 1986) identified as responsible "for a growing number of addicts and corpses." Why did crack become a major story in 1986 when Black Tar did not? Writing in *TV Guide*, Diamond, Acosta, and Thornton suggest:

> One reason has to do with those who are being affected and where those victims live. Black Tar stays in the ghetto, while crack is depicted as moving into "our"—that is the comfortable TV viewers—neighborhoods. (1987:7)

Extraordinary violence has been a fact of life in many inner-city neighborhoods for more than twenty years, drive-by shootings, gang-banging and narco-warfare have plagued many inner-city neighborhoods—terrifying their residents, and shortening their lives. Yet through all of this, from July 1980 to January 1993 no more than 9 percent of Americans considered crime to be the nation's most important problem (U.S. Justice Department 1993a:162). Suddenly in January of 1994 this measure jumped to 49 percent (Gallup 1994:6).

A central issue in the moral panic of 1993 was the presumption that violence was spreading from the inner city into places once considered safe. *Time* (1993b:45) was especially active in developing this theme. First, a carjacking feature—"Hell on Wheels"—noted that "the generation that fled the cities to escape violent crime finds that crime commutes too." A week later *Time* (1993c:29) featured "Danger in the Safety Zone," which chronicled violence "in virtually all public places once regarded as safe havens," such as schools, hospitals, libraries, and homes.

Reports about the spread of violence to places like Omaha, Nebraska, and Kenosha, Wisconsin, or Tomball, Texas—"the sort of safe town where many residents leave their front doors unlocked at night" (*Time*, 1993c:31)—established the premise that no place is safe. Quoting a Texas sociologist, *Newsweek* (1993b:40) observed that "We can be followed home from the supermarket, followed when we rent a car"—possibilities that "reinforce the sense that there is no protection, there is nothing you can do."

Littleton, Colorado, was a "safe" upper-middle-class suburb of Denver, Colorado, where massacres like this "didn't happen." In the case of Columbine and other school shootings the previous year, these random acts of violence occurred in small-town America, or the prototypical bedroom community, suburbs of larger cities.

The vehicle by which youth violence "spread" is a different one from crack cocaine, and represents a different avenue for threat to enter. What is more frightening here is the failure of geography to limit this dissemination of information—all roads lead to home, when the destination is a personal computer. The Internet has proven to be a steady source of information for school shooters. There are now Web sites on "how to build a bomb." E-mail has proven to be a source of communication to coordinate attacks. Computers are now regularly confiscated in the wake of school shootings. Schools across the country are now requiring consent forms from parents for their children to be allowed to access the Internet. Other protection-oriented techniques include blocking access to certain sites, and restricting particular search engines.

The presumed *randomness* of violence elevates its threat to people who had learned to avoid "dangerous" places. After the Long Island Railroad murders, *U.S. News* (1993e:6) decried "Violence and its Terrifying Randomness" and *Newsweek* (1993g:27) reported that Americans are "sick at heart about the recurrent episodes of random violence which mock our pretensions to order and civility." *U.S. News* (1993f:49) concluded that "it's the randomness and viciousness of crime in the 1990s, not just its extent, that elevates it as an issue," and *Time* (1993c:29) noted "the fear is getting worse because there is no pattern . . . it is random, spontaneous and episodic."

Reports: It's Spreading to Our Children   The panics over crack cocaine and violent crime both drew heavily from reports emphasizing the escalating involvement of young people in drugs and violence. Menace, both to and from youth, is a common theme in the anxiety of moral panics. Among the reasons may be that youngsters are presumably (1) more vulnerable, (2) less predictable, (3) less remorseful, and (4) physically closer to the rest of us, because they still live in our homes. Moreover, as Hall et al. observed, fears and panics about youth center on the "indiscipline" of the young (1978:145)—an episodic if not perennial threat to social order. Spread of the "ghetto pathologies" of crack and violence to and through children clearly escalated the moral purchase for urgent punitive *commands* to deal with the behavior.

As noted previously, the crack "epidemic" was touched off by a *Newsweek* cover story—"Kids and Cocaine"—that emphasized the availability of crack to young people due to its low cost. The story offered the following observations:

> An epidemic of cheap, deadly "crack" exposes a generation of American children to the nightmare of cocaine addiction. (1986a:58)

> In New York, eager buyers queue up outside crack houses . . . and the lines according to one drug agent "are loaded with kids." There are white kids, black kids, Hispanic kids—kids from the ghetto and kids from the suburbs. (1986a:59–60)

> "There are two trends in cocaine use" says Frank LaVecchia, a former high-school guidance counselor who runs a drug-treatment center in suburban Miami: "*Younger and younger and more and more.*" (1986a:58)

Television, too, reported that cocaine was claiming younger and younger victims as it spread from college campuses to maternity wards. Tom Brokaw, on NBC *Nightly News* (July 7), reported that cocaine "is becoming the college drug of the eighties" and ABC's *World News Tonight* (July 11) reported on babies born with a cocaine addiction ". . . the newest victims of the American cocaine epidemic" (Diamond, Acosta, and Thornton 1987:8).

At the height of the panic, President and Nancy Reagan appeared on television from the White House. He emphasized that "Drugs . . . [are] killing our children," and she warned that drug use was so pervasive that "no one is safe from it—not you, not me and certainly not our children because this epidemic has *their* name on it" (*Time* 1986:25).

The involvement of youth in violence—as both assailant and victim—is a major theme of the recent panic. In April of 1993, the New York Times ran a ten-part series entitled "Children of the Shadows" that chronicled the violence-filled world of ten kids from New York, Memphis, and Oakland. On November 1, the *Washington Post* presented a front-page story titled: "Getting Ready to Die Young: Children in Violent D.C. Neighborhoods Plan Their Own Funerals" (Brown, 1993). On November 7, "Monster" Kody Scott—who began gangbanging at age 11—was featured on *60 Minutes.*

In the six months between July 19, 1993, and January 10, 1994, the three major weekly newsmagazines ran the following headlines either on stories or covers:

> "Life Means Nothing: In Houston six teenagers are accused of mindlessly killing two young girls and seem not to care. Is adolescent brutality on the rise?" (*Newsweek* 1993a:16)
>
> "Teen Violence: Wild in the Streets" (*Newsweek* 1993f: Cover)
>
> "A Boy and His Gun: Even in a town like Omaha, Nebraska, the young are packing weapons in a deadly battle against fear and boredom." (*Time* 1993e:20–21)
>
> "Taming the Killers: Can young murderers be reformed?" (*Time* 1993a:58)
>
> "Death at an Early Age" (Newsweek 1993c:69)
>
> "Violence in the Schools: When Killers Come to Class" (*U.S. News* 1993c: Cover)
>
> "When is Rap 2 Violent?" (*Newsweek* 1993d: Cover)
>
> "Growing Up Scared" (*Newsweek* 1994a: Cover)

U.S. News called attention to a "chilling shift in adolescent attitudes: a sharp drop in respect for life" (1993c:31), and *Time* led a story with this:

> The names of the teenagers in this story aren't real, but the kids are—and they are all killers. They have murdered, some more than once, and are serving time. And they will still be young when they come up for parole. (1993a:58)

A sixteen-year-old was quoted as saying: "If you have a gun you have power. . . . Guns are just a part of growing up these days" (*Time* 1993b:21). In the same article Attorney General Janet Reno noted that violence is devastating this generation as surely as polio cut down young people forty years ago, and concluded that youth violence is "the single greatest crime problem in America today" (*Time* 1993b:43).

THE RECENT PANICS:
MISUNDERSTANDING DRUGS
AND VIOLENCE

Like other moral panics, those concerning crack cocaine and violence involved key ideological distortions—"misunderstandings"—with important conse- quence for the commands developed to deal with them. In particular, while drug abuse and violence have been *substantial* and *enduring* problems in many inner-city neighborhoods for decades, moral panic created the impression of a *sudden* and *escalating* firestorm spreading through society. The result is a political response that is—in Cohen's (1972) terms—*fundamentally inappropriate*.

In fact, in the United States, cocaine use *declined* during 1986 and violent crime rates *declined* during 1993—the years of spreading moral panic. What did *not* decline in those years of panic were the dissolution, despair, and nihilism (West 1994) increasingly characteristic of inner-city neighborhoods, where the choice of drugs or violence has become, for many, as reasonable and available as the choice of work. The consequence of treating the substan- tial and enduring problems of drugs and violence as if they are a sudden and escalating firestorm is that commands to deal with them seek *sudden* solutions that are *fundamentally inappropriate*. In an atmosphere of panic, building walls and stacking people behind them is faster and easier than doing the difficult work of restoring work and community to neighborhoods devastated by dis- investment and de-skilling.

In showing how moral panic has misunderstood drug abuse and violence, I am *not* suggesting that these are somehow inconsequential problems. Rather, I argue that panic disguises the fact that drugs and violence have been *extraordi- nary* problems for several decades—problems borne disproportionately by the residents of inner-city neighborhoods. Indeed, these inner-city residents have been doubly victimized—first, by the profound changes in the political econ- omy of cities and then by the drugs and violence that long ago began taking the place of work and community in many of those neighborhoods.

The principal misunderstanding helping to fuel the panic about cocaine in 1986 was that its use was increasing and spreading—especially among youth outside of the urban underclass. The spread was presumably a function of the low unit cost of the "rock" or crack form of the drug.

Most important, whatever was happening to the *forms* of cocaine, there is little evidence that cocaine use *per se* was increasing—particularly in the gen- eral population. In fact, the annual survey of high school seniors conducted by the University of Michigan showed that reported use of cocaine *dropped* during 1986—and has continued to drop—after reaching a ten-year high in 1985 (U.S. Justice Department 1993a:329). Among college students, reported use of cocaine "in the last year" was also *lower* in 1986 than in 1985 (U.S. Justice Department 1993a:330-331). And with regard to the general population, the Justice Department reports that

Trend data from the national Household Survey on Drug Abuse indicates that current use of most drugs [including cocaine] rose from the early to late 1970s, peaked between 1979 and 1982 and has since declined. The increase in cocaine use was especially sharp in the late 1970s. (U.S. Justice Department 1992:30)

The limits of survey data as a measure of behavior are well known, but there is little reason to conclude that reports of declining drug use after 1985 (or increasing drug use before 1985) reflect variation in the validity of self-reports more than variation in drug-using behavior. And while there *is* evidence from hospital data that "emergency room mentions" of cocaine and "drug-related deaths" increased between 1985 and 1986, the Drug Enforcement Administration issued a report at the height of the "crack" panic that concluded that crack was a "secondary, not a primary drug problem in most cities" and that "its prevalence has been exaggerated by heavy news media attention" (*Washington Post* 1986:A18).

Even within the underclass, the *spread* of cocaine use during the crack "epidemic" was likely exaggerated. In a major review essay on "Drug Abuse in the Inner City," Bruce Johnson and his colleagues concluded that "the number of cocaine users has not increased substantially because of crack. Rather, the relatively few regular cocaine users appear to have increased the frequency of their consumption"—presumably due to the addictiveness of crack (Johnson, Williams, Dei, and Sanabria 1990:16–17).

While it is clear and widely acknowledged that the panic over crack cocaine greatly exaggerated its spreading menace, it is not as clear *why* the panic assumed the proportions it did *when* it did. Several hypotheses have been suggested. These include (1) competition among the various news media to stay on top of an issue that had so captured the attention of the agenda-setting *New York Times* and *Washington Post* and (2) preelection competition between congressional Democrats and Republicans to—in the words of presidential spokesman Marlin Fitzwater—"outdrug each other in terms of political rhetoric" (Reinarman and Levine 1989:129). Whatever the reason, the ideological consequence of the cocaine panic was realized in repressive measures of uncommon proportions.

The recent moral panic over violence has involved a similar pattern of exaggeration, distortion, or "misunderstanding." Specifically, during 1993, when media coverage of violent crime increased by more than 400 percent and Americans ranking crime/violence as the nation's foremost problem also increased by more than 400 percent, the rate of violent crime, as measured by the *Uniform Crime Reports*, showed a *decrease* of 1.5 percent from the previous year (see Fig. 3). The National Crime Victimization Survey showed similar though not identical patterns for 1993. Overall, the rate of violent victimizations—including attempts—increased slightly (5.6 percent) from the previous year. However, rates of *completed* violence actually *decreased* (3.2 percent) (U.S. Justice Department 1995a:2).

So if crime and violence were declining in 1993, what accounts for the 400 percent increase in media coverage for these issues in the last six months of

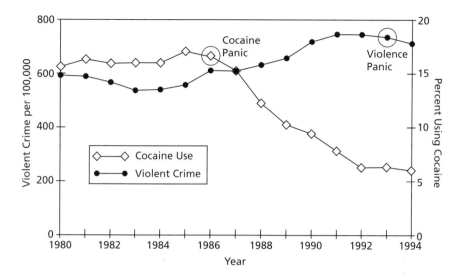

FIGURE 3 Violent Crime and Cocaine Trends: 1980–1994

Sources: U.S. Justice Dept. 1994a; U.S. Justice Dept. 1995b; and Johnston , 1994; High School Survey.

1993 and the more than 400 percent increase in concern about crime and violence in the twelve months ending in January 1994? One possibility is that there was little competing news, and as Sabato has noted, media "feeding frenzies are more likely to develop in slow news periods such as the doldrums of summer" (1991:79).

It is also possible that in the summer of 1993, several highly publicized violent attacks so captured public consciousness that they came to define for many the essence of the crime problem. Because of saturation news coverage, there are few Americans who could not recount at least some details of the Reginald Denny beating in South Central Los Angeles, or the Monticello, Florida, rest area murder, or the Fort Lauderdale tourist murders, or the Long Island Railroad killings, in which a gunman walked the aisles of a speeding train and emptied his gun several times. And as noted above, all three national news magazines did lengthy features on violence two weeks after the gang-rape and murder of two teenage girls who took a short-cut through the woods to their homes in Houston.

One common theme to these crimes is that each involved *white* victims and allegedly *black male* assailants who were unknown to the victims. Except for the Houston murders, each involved *adult* victims and except for the Long Island Railroad "massacre" each of the assailants was *young*. Yet far from typical criminal violence these are tragic exceptions to the norm of victimization that occurs overwhelmingly *within* age and race bounds. Departures from the norm are often considered newsworthy. They may become more so when they resonate criminal stereotypes and tap into deeply held racial anxieties.

It is almost as if the recent panic emerged precisely when the violence that has devastated inner-city neighborhoods for decades threatened—even if by stunning exception—to leap the boundaries and defy the norms of violent victimization. And as we have noted previously, this is precisely what the reports of the moral panic tried to convey.

RECENT PANICS: COMMANDS

The bottom line of all ideological discourse is the use of reports—whether they distort reality or not—to mobilize popular support to *do* something in the public arena. Because moral panics have such relentless energy and because they employ rhetoric like "epidemic," "firestorm," "rising tide," and "plague," the *urgency* of swift and serious action is explicitly justified. The character of decision making in the context of frenzied media attention is well captured by presidential adviser George Stephanopolous (1993), appearing on the ABC *Nightline* special concerning the media's coverage of violence:

> What happens when a picture that powerful, even if incomplete, is presented on television? The only governing virtue is decisiveness. The question is: "What are you going to do?" It doesn't really matter what the answer is. It's just "Do something!" [The media] starts the drumbeat . . . "What are you going to do?" "What are you going to do?" "What are you going to do?"

Indeed, the command implications of moral panic over drugs and violence have been decisive, if nothing else. The response to the crack cocaine panic has been well documented elsewhere (Belenko et al. 1991) and is briefly summarized here. In Washington, drug politics were rapidly transformed in the summer of 1986 by several factors, none more significant than the explosion of media reports. According to members of Congress and their aides "when the media started talking about it, it lit a fire" (Kerr 1986:B6).

Commands—Drugs

On July 23, House Speaker Tip O'Neill announced plans for comprehensive drug legislation to be voted on by September. The extraordinary pace of action was justified by House Democratic leader Jim Wright, who commented that "his most pressing concern was that Congress act before television lost interest in the drug story." And Republican leader Robert Michel expressed fears that "unless House Republicans joined in quickly, the Democrats could grab the issue as their own in time for the [November] election" (Kerr 1986:B6). In September, President and Nancy Reagan went on television to call for a new "crusade" against drugs and on October 17, 1986, Congress passed the Anti-Drug Abuse Act of 1986—called by some "the most far-reaching drug law ever passed" (Kerr 1986:B6).

Even as the panic quickly subsided in Washington (Kerr 1986), enthusiasm for getting tough on drugs—particularly crack cocaine offenders—mushroomed in the states. The "no lose" proposition of moving swiftly and severely against marginalized segments of the urban underclass, who were seen as responsible for the spreading menace of crack—among other things—became a centerpiece of state and local social policy in the last half of the 1980s.

Nationwide, drug arrests increased more than 65 percent between 1986 and 1989 (U.S. Justice Department, 1993b:9), and state prison admissions for drug crimes mushroomed 214 percent (33,100 to 103,800) between 1986 and 1990 (U.S. Justice Department, 1994b:10). As a proportion of all state prison admissions in the United States, those for drug offenses increased 372 percent during the 1980s—rising from 6.8 percent in 1980 to 32.1 percent in 1990 (U.S. Justice Department, 1994b:10).

The most celebrated feature of this newest war on drugs was the extraordinary set of penalties applied to the possession, sale, or trafficking of *crack* as opposed to powder cocaine. Under federal law, 1 gram of crack counts as much as 100 grams of powder. Possession of 50 grams of crack brings a ten-year sentence; to get ten years for powder cocaine one would need 5,000 grams. Though patterns vary among the states, at least eight have adopted sentences for crack cocaine that are much more severe than for other drugs. Moreover, in federal law, only crack has mandatory minimum sentences for simple possession. All other drugs require possession with intent to sell.

A direct consequence of this panic-inspired legislation has been a substantial increase in the flow of African Americans into prison. Specifically, because almost 92 percent of federal crack defendants are black (as opposed to 27 percent for powder cocaine) harsher penalties for crack weigh most heavily against African-American drug users. As a result, the rate of incarceration (per 100,000) increased 48 percent for blacks between 1986 and 1991 as compared to 34 percent for whites (U.S. Justice Department 1994b:9). Looked at another way, African Americans accounted for 38.2 percent of those in state prisons for drugs in 1986 and 53.2 percent by 1991. More remarkably, blacks incarcerated for drugs made up 3.3 percent of all state prisoners in 1986 and 11.3 percent—a 242 percent increase—in 1991 (U.S. Justice Department 1993b:623). By 1992, the rate of incarceration for African-American males (2,678 per 100,000) was almost eight times as great as for the total population (344) (U.S. Justice Department 1994b:9). If those in jail, on probation, or on parole are included, almost *one of every ten* adult black males in America was in the punitive custody of the state by 1991 (U.S. Justice Department 1993b, 1994c).

Commands—Violent Crime

Commands "justified" by the panic over violent crime in late 1993 are still being realized, and their full consequence can only be known in years to come. However, the variety of measures proposed, if not always implemented, has given freer rein to repressive imaginations than even the drug panic did. Proposals in one state—"Florida, the State of Fear"—have included fingerprinting and uniforms for all school children, curfews, caning, and castration. While these have yet to gain legislative approval, more traditional measures, such as boot camps and easier transfer to adult court for juveniles, as well as a massive increase in prison capacity, certainly have. In fact, Florida, which doubled its prison population (19,700 to 39,991) between 1980 and 1990, will see it doubled again to more than 80,000 by June, 1996. Early in 1994, at the peak of the panic over violence, Florida legislators appropriated almost as many *new* prison beds—17,000—as existed in 1980.

At the federal level, the "Violent Crime Control and Law Enforcement Act of 1994" was passed in August of that year. Touted by the Justice Department as "the largest crime bill in the history of the country," it "will provide for 100,000 new police officers, $9.7 billion in funding for prisons and $6.1 billion in funding for prevention programs" (U.S. Justice Department, 1994c:1). Beyond that, it expands the death penalty to cover sixty additional federal offenses; authorizes adult prosecution for thirteen year olds charged with serious violent crimes; provides "stiffer penalties for violent and drug trafficking crimes committed by gang members"; has its own version of a "three strikes" provision; doubles the maximum term for repeat Federal sex offenders, creates new crimes and enhances penalties for others.

Several states, including California, have implemented "three strikes" provisions mandating sentences between twenty-five years and life for persons convicted of a third felony. Many states have extended the reach of mandatory minimum sentencing, and many are greatly expanding their prison capacities. In state after state, during the 1994 political campaigns, candidates fired competing "get tough" salvos in efforts to cash in on the wave of crime fear sweeping the nation.

Almost immediately following the shooting in Littleton, Colorado, the White House called a meeting of politically odd bedfellows—Hollywood and media executives, gun industry officials, religious leaders and crime and mental health experts.

Coverage of Columbine was omnipresent, but the type of coverage varied between print and broadcast media (Lawrence and Birkland 2000). Common themes included: school violence and shootings; school safety and design; guns (safety, lobbying, and gun control); media, pop culture, the Internet and movie violence; American sociocultural context, including Goth; mental health; the culture of teenage life, including alienation and peer pressure; and parenting and parental liability (Lawrence and Birkland 2000). In ways previously described by Iyengar (1991), television coverage was mostly detailing the chaos in Littleton, while stories in the *Los Angeles Times* and the *New York Times* were more thematic and explored the range of themes. The amount of media attention is less important than the lack of congruence between the media's definition of school shootings and the congressional definition of the problem.

While the media fueled attention to the problem, it did not define how the problem was addressed. Press coverage did elevate youth violence above other competing social problems, but it did not influence competing definitions within the problem (Lawrence and Birkland 2000). The media and public opinion polls helped "tell" Congress that school shootings were a problem, but the debates in Congress did not track the debates in the press. What was notably absent from print and broadcast coverage, with respect to Columbine, but was front and center in congressional debate, was illicit drug use. An analysis of 675 news stories about Columbine reveal only two stories about illicit drug use, while nine of the fifty-six bills in Congress were about drugs, particularly as related to the Safe and Drug-Free Schools acts (Lawrence and Birkland 2000). It is also important what *wasn't* focused on in Congress. A Gallup report shows that 62 percent of Americans supported more mental health counseling for teenagers, the same number of respondents who supported stricter gun control laws (Newport 1999).

Congress is motivated to create avenues to their ideological or parochial initiatives. Indeed, contrary to the idea that the media is defining the problem for Congress, it may alternatively be possible that media attention simply serves as a resource—a moral panic as resource—for partisan initiative. While Gusfield (1981) developed the idea of public problems in his discussion of drunk driving in the United States—whereby the problem is constructed as one of individual responsibility—Lawrence and Birkland conceptualize "institutions like the media and Congress as public arenas for the social construction of public problems" (2000:3). Congress, in recognizing certain problems officially, tells us how the federal government is defining problems. The case of school shootings illustrates more than competition among social problems; it tells about "alternative ways of framing the problem" (Hilgartner and Bosk 1988:70).

The tragedy in Littleton, Colorado, combines things with symbolic relevance—violence, children, and suburban America. Hilgartner and Bosk argue that the more innately dramatic certain events are, the more likely they are to tap "broad cultural preoccupations" (1988:71). These are likely to be the types of problems that are championed by commanding political and economic coalitions (Lawrence and Birkland 2000). The grand-scale public reaction builds on the collective fear begun with crack and cocaine and violent crime: "It's spreading to our children."

Columbine was a "free pass" for Congress and Washington officialdom. It demonstrates responsiveness by convening White House summits, and showing live C-SPAN coverage on the House and Senate floors. Ultimately, however, the amount of attention criminal justice receives is disproportionate to the ability to truly do something about crime. Most real change in criminal justice stems from local authorities and how they mold or implement federal monies or guidelines (Scheingold 1991). This allows Congress to demonstrate action without ultimate accountability.

CONCLUSION: MORAL PANIC
AS IDEOLOGICAL DISPLACEMENT

And so it's off to war again—if not the metaphorical war on drugs, then the literal war in the streets. And prisoners *will* be taken. The "success" of moral panic as an ideological phenomenon could be no more aptly demonstrated. It not only mobilizes a massive expansion of the state's repressive apparatus—even as drug use and crime *decline*—but it diverts attention from the consequences of a one-sided class war that has involved not only disinvestment and de-skilling, but regressive taxation, the pillaging of pension funds and the social safety net, and assaults on the well-being of both the workplace and the environment (Barlett and Steele 1992; Lind 1995).

These actions, which have made American capital more competitive in the "global marketplace," have also assisted in the dismantling of the middle class, the growth of an isolated underclass, and a more unequal distribution of wealth and opportunity than at any time since the onset of the last Great Depression (Batra 1987; Lind 1995). The same conditions that have made enormous fortunes for a handful of investors have made most Americans work harder for less and have consigned so many others—particularly in the urban underclass—to a superfluous present and a hopeless future.

But instead of waging war on the inhuman conditions fostered by policies of disinvestment and de-skilling that have hollowed our inner-city neighborhoods, we wage war on those individuals dehumanized by the lack of reasonable choices. Instead of waging war on unemployment, inadequate schools, and the loss of hope we wage war on individuals destroyed by those very conditions. Instead of waging war on the factors contributing to an increasingly isolated underclass—for whom life has less and less meaning—we wage war against individuals who seek meaning in drugs and violence.

Instead of seeing the world as it is—one in which investment decisions by the owners of capital have caused the devastation of inner-city neighborhoods, communities, and families and the economic stagnation of almost all others— these moral panics force us to see as "in all ideology, men and their circumstances . . . upside-down as in a *camera obscura*" (Marx and Engels 1846/1970:47). The greatest victims of private and public policies that have literally determined that people will count less than profits are demonized by moral panics and herded behind ever-widening walls of exclusion.

As noted previously, the real danger of the recent moral panics is that they treat problems that have been *substantial* and *enduring* for several decades in many inner-city neighborhoods as if they are a *sudden* firestorm. An atmosphere of panic mobilizes demands for immediate repression and causes us to ignore the root problems of urban America, which have grown and festered for decades. The same media frenzy that raises *decisiveness* to the cardinal virtue of public policy lowers the chance that meaningful response to enduring problems will be undertaken.

Put behind walls another hundred thousand or five hundred thousand or a million young men for whom drugs and violence have become meaningful choices—and what will happen? If nothing is done to restore work, family, and community to our central city neighborhoods, then successive waves of children will have made and will make those same choices.

The triumph of moral panic as ideology is realized in the promotion of "solutions" to the contradictions of capitalism that literally misrepresent and conceal their existence while mobilizing support to repress their most disadvantaged and visible victims. At the same time, and perhaps most important, moral panic keeps the vast majority of Americans—who are "doing with less so that big business can have more"—focused on ostensible dangers from the underclass instead of the policies and profits of the investors of capital, who are responsible not only for the growth of that underclass but the frustrations and anxieties plaguing so many Americans.

REFERENCES

Barlett, Donald L., and James B. Steele (1992). *America: What Went Wrong?* Kansas City: Andrews & McMeel.

Batra, Ravi (1987). *The Great Depression of 1990.* New York: Simon & Schuster.

Belenko, Steven, Jeffrey Fagan, and Ko-Lin Chin (1991). "Criminal justice responses to crack." *Journal of Research in Crime & Delinquency* 28:55–74.

Brown, DeNeen L. (1993). Getting ready to die young: Children in violent D.C. neighborhoods plan their own funerals. *Washington Post 1* November: A1.

Cohen, Stan (1972). *Folk Devils and Moral Panics: The Creation of the Mods and Rockers.* Oxford: Blackwell.

Danielian, Lucig H., and Stephen D. Reese (1989). "A closer look at intermedia influences on agenda setting: The cocaine issue of 1986." In *Communication Campaigns About Drugs,* ed. Pamela J. Shoemaker, 47–66. Hillsdale, N.J.: Lawrence Erlbaum Associates.

Diamond, Edwin, Frank Acosta, and Leslie-Jean Thornton (1987). "Is TV news hyping America's cocaine problem?" *TV Guide* (7 February): 4–10.

Gallup, George Jr. (1994). *The Gallup Poll, No. 341* (February). Wilmington, Del.: Scholarly Resources, Inc.

Gouldner, Alvin (1976). *The Dialectic of Ideology and Technology.* New York: Oxford University Press.

Gusfield, Joseph (1981). *The Culture of Public Problems.* Chicago: University of Chicago Press.

Hall, Stuart, Chas Critcher, Tony Jefferson, John Clarke, and Brian Roberts (1978). *Policing the Crisis: Mugging, the State and Law and Order.* London: MacMillan.

Henry J. Kaiser Family Foundation, Harvard School of Public Health, Health News Interest Index Poll (June 18, 1999).

Hilgartner, S., and James Bosk (1988). "The rise and fall of social problems: A public arena's model." *American Journal of Sociology* 94(1):53–78.

Iyengar, Shanto (1991). *Is Anyone Responsible?* Chicago: University of Chicago Press.

Johnson, Bruce D., Terry Willliams, Kojo A. Dei, and Harry Sanabria (1990). "Drug Abuse in the Inner City: Impact on Hard-Drug Users and the Community." In Michael Tonry and James Q. Wilson (eds.), *Drugs and Crime.* Chicago: University of Chicago Press, pp. 9–67.

Johnston, Lloyd D. (1994). "Drug use continues to climb among American teenagers." Press Release by the University of Michigan News and Information Services (8 December).

Kerr, Peter (1986). "Anatomy of the Drug Issue: How, After Years, It Erupted." *New York Times* November 17: A1, B6.

Lawrence, Regina G., and Thomas A. Birkland (2000). "Guns, Hollywood and Criminal Justice: Defining the School Shootings Problem Across Public Arenas." American Political Science Association Meeting (August).

Lind, Michael (1995). "To Have and to Have Not: Notes on the Progress of the American Class War." *Harpers Magazine* (June) pp. 35–47.

Marx, Karl, and Frederick Engels (1846/1970). *The German Ideology.* New York: International Publishers.

Melossi, Dario (1985). "Punishment and Social Action: Changing Vocabularies of Punitive Motive within a Political Business Cycle." *Current Perspectives in Social Theory* 6:169–197.

Merriam, John E. (1989). "National Media Coverage of Drug Issues, 1983–1987." In Pamela J. Shoemaker (ed.), *Communication Campaigns About Drugs: Government, Media and the Public.* Hillsdale, N.J.: Lawrence Erlbaum, pp. 21–28.

Newport, Frank (1999). Media Portrayals of Violence Seen by Many as Causes of Real-Life Violence. Gallup News Services. http://www.gallup.com/poll/release/pr990510.asp.

Pew Research Center, News Interest Index Poll (April 19, 2000).

Newsweek (1986a). "Kids and Cocaine." March 17: 58–65.

——— (1986b). "Crack and Crime." June 16: 15–22.

——— (1986c). "Trying to Say No." August 11: 14–19.

——— (1993a). "Life Means Nothing." July 19: 16–17.

——— (1993b). "In a State of Terror." September 27: 40–41.

——— (1993c). "Death at an Early Age." November 8: 69.

——— (1993d). "Criminal Records: Gangsta Rap and the Culture of Violence." November 29: 60–64.

——— (1993e). "Death Ride: Massacre on the LIRR." December 20: 26–31.

——— (1993f). "Wild in the Streets." August 2: 40–47.

——— (1993g). "Brutality as a Teen Fashion Statement." August 23: 61.

——— (1993h). "Growing Up Fast and Frightened." November 22: 52.

——— (1994a). "Kids Growing Up Scared." January 10: 43–50.

Reinarman, Craig, and Harry G. Levine (1989). "The Crack Attack: Politics and Media in America's Latest Drug Scare." In Joel Best (ed.), *Images of Issues: Typifying Contemporary Social Problems.* New York: Aldine de Gruyter, pp. 115–137.

Sabato, Larry J. (1991). *Feeding Frenzy: How Attack Journalism Has Transformed American Politics.* New York: Free Press.

Scheingold, Stuart (1991). *The Politics of Street Crime.* Philadelphia: Temple University Press.

Stephanopolous, George (1993). Comments recorded in appearance on "Crime, violence and T.V. news," an ABC News *Nightline* special (December 10).

Time (1986). "Bringing Out the Big Guns: The First Couple and Congress Press the Attack on Drugs." September 22: 25–26.

——— (1993a). "Taming the Killers." October 11: 58–59.

——— (1993b). "Hell on Wheels." August 16: 44–48.

——— (1993c). "Danger in the Safety Zone." August 23: 29–32.

——— (1993d). "Up in Arms." December 20: 18–26.

——— (1993e). "A Boy and His Gun." August 2: 20–27.

U.S. Justice Department (1992). Drugs, Crime, and the Justice System. Washington, D.C.: U.S. Government Printing Office.

——— (1993a). Sourcebook of Criminal Justice Statistics—1992. Washington, D.C.: U.S. Government Printing Office.

——— (1993b). Drugs and Crime Facts, 1992. Washington, D.C.: Bureau of Justice Statistics.

——— (1994a). Crime in the United States—1993. Washington, D.C.: U.S. Government Printing Office.

——— (1994b). Prisoners in 1993. Washington, D.C.: Bureau of Justice Statistics.

——— (1994c). Fact Sheet: Violent Crime Control and Law Enforcement Act of 1994. Washington, D.C. (24, October).

——— (1995a). Criminal Victimization 1993. Washington, D.C.: Bureau of Justice Statistics.

———— (1995b). Uniform Crime Reports: 1994 Preliminary Annual Release. Washington, D.C. (21, May).

U.S. News & World Report (1993a). "Los Angeles under the Gun." May 31: 82.

———— (1993b). "Florida: The State of Rage." October 11: 40–44.

———— (1993c). "Violence in the Schools." November 8: 31–36.

———— (1993d). "The Voters Cry for Help." November 15: 26–30.

———— (1993e). "Violence and Its Terrifying Randomness." December 20: 6.

———— (1993f). "A New Attack on Crime." October 18: 49.

Washington Post (1986). New York leads in "crack" use: DEA says prevalence elsewhere overstated. 25 September: A18.

West, Cornel (1994). *Race Matters.* New York: Vintage Books.

4

☸

Criminal Justice, Legal Values, and the Rehabilitative Ideal

Francis A. Allen

In this classic article written in 1959 Francis A. Allen notes the rise during the twentieth century of the rehabilitative ideal. He asserts that the rhetorical influence of the "rehabilitative ideal" compromised its real meaning. He describes the ways that this more scientific approach to an understanding of criminality and its correction had a number of unintended consequences for the criminal justice system, allowing it to effectively be used as a justification for net widening.

Although one is sometimes inclined to despair of any constructive changes in the administration of criminal justice, a glance at the history of the past half-century reveals a succession of the most significant developments. Thus, the last fifty years have seen the widespread acceptance of three legal inventions of great importance: the juvenile court, systems of probation, and systems of parole. During the same period, under the inspiration of Continental research and writing, scientific criminology has become an established field of instruction and inquiry in American universities and in other research agencies. At the same time, psychiatry has made its remarkable contributions to the theory of human behavior and, more specifically, to that form of human behavior described as criminal. These developments have been accompanied by nothing less than a revolution in public conceptions of the nature of

Source: Francis A. Allen, *The Borderland of Criminal Justice* (Chicago: University of Chicago Press, 1964), pp. 25–41. First delivered as a lecture at the Institute for Juvenile Research, Chicago, Illinois, on March 17, 1959. Some footnotes deleted, one renumbered.

crime and the criminal and in public attitudes toward the proper treatment of the convicted offender.

This history with its complex developments of thought, institutional behavior, and public attitudes must be approached gingerly; for in dealing with it we are in peril of committing the sin of oversimplification. Nevertheless, despite the presence of contradictions and paradox, it seems possible to detect one common element or theme I shall describe, for want of a better phrase, as the rise of the rehabilitative ideal.

The rehabilitative ideal is itself a complex of ideas which, perhaps, defies an exact definition. The essential points, however, can be identified. It is assumed, first, that human behavior is the product of antecedent causes. These causes can be identified as part of the physical universe, and it is the obligation of the scientist to discover and to describe them with all possible exactitude. Knowledge of the antecedents of human behavior makes possible an approach to the scientific control of human behavior. Finally, and of primary significance for the purposes at hand, it is assumed that measures employed to treat the convicted offender should serve a therapeutic function; that such measures should be designed to effect changes in the behavior of the convicted person in the interests of his own happiness, health, and satisfactions and in the interest of social defense.

Although these ideas are capable of quite simple statement, they have provoked some of the modern world's most acrimonious controversies. And the disagreements among those who adhere in general to these propositions have been hardly less intense than those prompted by the dissenters. This is true, in part, because these ideas possess a delusive simplicity. No idea is more pervaded with ambiguity than the notion of reform or rehabilitation. Assuming, for example, that we have the techniques to accomplish our ends of rehabilitation, are we striving to produce in the convicted offender something called "adjustment" to his social environment or is our objective something different from or more than this? By what scale of values do we determine the ends of therapy?

These are intriguing questions, well worth extended consideration. But it is not my purpose to pursue them here. Rather, I am concerned with describing some of the dilemmas and conflicts of values that have resulted from efforts to impose the rehabilitative ideal on the system of criminal justice. There is no area in which a more effective demonstration can be made of the necessity for greater mutual understanding between the law and the behavioral disciplines.

There is, of course, nothing new in the notion of reform or rehabilitation of the offender as being one objective of the penal process. This idea is given important emphasis, for example, in the thought of the medieval churchmen. The church's position, as described by Sir Francis Palgrave, was that punishment was not to be "thundered in vengeance for the satisfaction of the state, but imposed for the good of the offender: in order to afford the means of amendment and to lead the transgressor to repentance, and to mercy." Even Jeremy Bentham, whose views modern criminologists have often scorned and more often ignored, is found saying: "It is a great merit in a punishment to contribute to the *reformation of the offender*, not only through fear of being punished again, but by a change in his character and habits." But this is far from saying that the modern expression of the rehabilitative ideal is not to be sharply distinguished form earlier expressions. The most important differences, I believe, are two. First, the modern statement of the rehabilitative ideal is accompanied by, and largely stems from, the development of scientific disciplines concerned with human behavior, a development not remotely approximated in earlier periods when notions of reform of the offender were advanced. Second, and of equal importance for the purposes at hand, in no other period has the rehabilitative ideal so completely dominated theoretical and scholarly inquiry, to such an extent that in some quarters it is almost assumed that matters of treatment and reform of the offender are the only questions worthy of serious attention in the whole field of criminal justice and correction.

THE NARROWING
OF SCIENTIFIC INTERESTS

This narrowing of interests prompted by the rise of the rehabilitative ideal during the past half-century should put us on our guard. No social institutions as complex as those involved in the administration of criminal justice serve a single function or purpose. Social institutions are multivalued and multipurposed. Values and purposes are likely on occasion to prove inconsistent and to produce internal conflict and tension. A theoretical orientation that evinces concern for only one or a limited number of the purposes served by the institution must inevitably prove partial and unsatisfactory. In certain situations it may prove positively dangerous. This stress on the unfortunate consequences of the rise of the rehabilitative ideal need not involve failure to recognize the substantial benefits that have also accompanied its emergence. Its emphasis on the fundamental problems of human behavior, its numerous contributions to the decency of the criminal-law processes are of vital importance. But the limitations and dangers of modern trends of thought need to be clearly identified in the interest, among others, of the rehabilitative ideal itself.

My first proposition is that the rise of the rehabilitative ideal has dictated what questions are to be investigated, with the result that many matters of equal or even greater importance have been ignored or insufficiently examined. This tendency can be abundantly illustrated. Thus, the concentration of interest on the nature and needs of the criminal has resulted in a remarkable absence of interest in the nature of crime. This is, indeed, surprising, for on reflection it must be apparent that the question of what is a crime is logically the prior issue: how crime is defined determines in large measure who the criminal is who becomes eligible for treatment and therapy. A related observation was made some years ago by the late Karl Llewellyn: "When I was younger I used to hear smuggish assertions among my sociological friends, such as: 'I take the sociological, *not* the legal, approach to crime'; and I suspect an inquiring reporter could still hear much the same (perhaps with 'psychiatric' often substituted for 'sociological')—though it is surely somewhat obvious that when you take 'the legal' out, you also take out 'crime'." This disinterest in the definition of criminal behavior has afflicted the lawyers quite as much as the behavioral scientists. Even the criminal law scholar has tended, until recently, to assume that problems of procedure and treatment are the things that "really matter." Only the issue of criminal responsibility as affected by mental disorder has attracted the consistent attention of the non-lawyer, and the literature reflecting this interest is not remarkable for its cogency or its wisdom. In general, the behavioral sciences have left other issues relevant to crime definition largely in default. There are a few exceptions. Dr. Hermann Mannheim, of the London School of Economics has manifested intelligent interest in these matters. The late Professor Edwin Sutherland's studies of "white-collar crime" may also be mentioned, although, in my judgment, Professor Sutherland's efforts in this field are among the least perceptive and satisfactory of his many valuable contributions.

The absence of widespread interest in these areas is not to be explained by any lack of challenging questions. Thus, what may be said of the relationships between legislative efforts to subject certain sorts of human behavior to penal regulation and the persistence of police corruption and abuse of power? Studies of public attitudes toward other sorts of criminal legislation might provide valuable clues as to whether given regulatory objectives are more likely to be attained by the provision of criminal penalties or by other kinds of legal sanctions. It ought to be re-emphasized that the question, What sorts of behavior should be declared criminal? is one to which the behavioral sciences might contribute vital insights. This they have largely failed to do, and we are the poorer for it.

Another example of the narrowing of interests that has accompanied the rise of the rehabilitative ideal is the lack of concern with the idea of deterrence—indeed, many modern criminologists are hostile toward it. This, again, is a most surprising development. It must surely be apparent that the criminal law has a general preventive function to perform in the interests of public order and of security of life, limb, and possessions. Indeed, there is reason to assert that the influence of criminal sanctions on the millions who never engage in serious criminality is of greater social importance than their impact on the hundreds of thousands who do. Certainly, the assumptions of those who make our laws is that the denouncing of certain kinds of conduct as criminal and providing the means for the enforcement of legislative prohibitions will generally prevent or minimize such behavior. Just what the precise mechanisms of deterrence are is not well understood. Perhaps it results, on occasion, from the naked threat of punishment. Perhaps, more frequently, it derives from a more subtle process wherein the mores and moral sense of the community are recruited to advance the attainment of the criminal law's objectives. The point is that we know very little about these vital matters, and the resources of the behavioral sciences have rarely been employed to contribute knowledge and insight in their investigation. Not only have the criminologists displayed little interest in these matters, some have suggested that the whole idea of general prevention is invalid or worse. Thus, speaking of the deterrent theory of punishment, the authors of a leading textbook in criminology assert: "This is simply a derived rationalization of revenge. Though social revenge is the actual psychological basis of punishment today, the apologists for the punitive regime are likely to bring forward in their defense the more sophisticated, but equally futile, contention that punishment deters from [*sic*] crime." We are thus confronted by a situation in which the dominance of the rehabilitative ideal not only diverts attention from many serious issues but leads to a denial that these issues even exist.

DEBASEMENT OF THE
REHABILITATIVE IDEAL

I now turn to another kind of difficulty that has accompanied the rise of the rehabilitative ideal in the areas of corrections and criminal justice. It is a familiar observation that an idea once propagated and introduced into the active affairs of life undergoes change. The real significance of an idea as it evolves in actual practice may be quite different from that intended by those who conceived it and gave it initial support. An idea tends to lead a life of its own; and modern history is full of the unintended consequences of seminal ideas. The application of the rehabilitative ideal to the institutions of criminal justice presents a striking example of such a development. My second proposition, then, is that the rehabilitative ideal has been debased in practice and that the consequences resulting from this debasement are serious and, at times, dangerous.

This proposition may be supported, first, by the observation that, under the dominance of the rehabilitative ideal, the language of therapy is frequently employed, wittingly or unwittingly, to disguise the true state of affairs that prevails in our custodial institutions and at other points in the correctional process. Certain measures, like the sexual psychopath laws, have been advanced and supported as therapeutic in nature when, in fact, such a characterization seems highly dubious. Too often the vocabulary of therapy has been exploited to serve a public-relations function. Recently, I visited an institution devoted to the diagnosis and treatment of disturbed children. The institution had been established with high hopes and, for once, with the enthusiastic support of the state legislature. Nevertheless, fifty minutes of an hour's lecture, delivered by a supervising psychiatrist before we toured the building, were devoted to custodial problems. This fixation on problems of custody was reflected in the institutional arrangements which included, under a properly euphemistic label, a cell for solitary confinement.[1] Even more disturbing was the tendency of the staff to justify these custodial measures in therapeutic terms. Perhaps on occasion the requirements of institutional security and treatment coincide. But the inducements to self-deception in such situations are strong and all too apparent. In short, the language of therapy has frequently provided a formidable obstacle to a realistic analysis of the conditions that confront us. And realism in considering these problems is the one quality that we require above all others.

There is a second kind of unintended consequence that results from the application of the rehabilitative ideal to the practical administration of criminal justice. Surprisingly enough, the rehabilitative ideal has often led to increased severity of penal measures. This tendency may be seen in the operation of the juvenile court. Although frequently condemned by the popular press as a device for leniency, the juvenile court is authorized to intervene punitively in many situations in which the conduct, were it committed by an adult, would be wholly ignored by the law or would subject the adult to the mildest of sanctions. The tendency of proposals for wholly indeterminate sentences, a clearly identifiable fruit of the rehabilitative ideal, is unmistakably in the direction of lengthened periods of imprisonment. A large variety of statutes authorizing what is called "evil" commitment of persons, but which, except for the reduced protections afforded the parties proceeded against, are essentially criminal in nature, provide for absolutely indeterminate periods of confinement. Experience has demonstrated that, in practice, there is a strong tendency for the rehabilitative ideal to serve purposes that are essentially incapacitative rather than therapeutic in character.

THE REHABILITATIVE IDEAL
AND INDIVIDUAL LIBERTY

This reference to the tendency of the rehabilitative ideal to encourage increasingly long periods of incarceration brings me to my final proposition. It is that the rise of the rehabilitative ideal has often been accompanied by attitudes and measures that conflict, sometimes seriously, with the values of individual liberty and volition. As I have already observed, the role of the behavioral sciences in the administration of criminal justice and in the area of public policy lying on the borderland of the criminal law is one of obvious importance. But I suggest that, if the function of criminal justice is considered in its proper dimensions, it will be discovered that the most fundamental problems in these areas are not those of psychiatry, sociology, social case work, or social psychology. On the contrary, the most fundamental problems are those of political philosophy and political science. The administration of the criminal law presents to any community the most extreme issues of the proper relations of the individual citizen to state power. We are concerned here with the perennial issue of political authority: Under what circumstances is the state justified in bringing its force to bear on the individual human being? These issues, of course, are not confined to the criminal law, but it is in the area of penal regulation that they are most dramatically manifested. The criminal law, then, is located somewhere near the center of the political problem, as the history of the twentieth century abundantly reveals. It is no accident, after all, that the agencies of criminal justice and law enforcement are those first seized by an emerging totalitarian regime. In short, a study of criminal justice is fundamentally a study in the exercise of political power. No such study can properly avoid the problem of the abuse of power.

The obligation of containing power within the limits suggested by a community's political values has been considerably complicated by the rise of the rehabilitative ideal. For the problem today is one of regulating the exercise of power by men of good will, whose motivations are to help not to injure, and whose ambitions are quite different from those of the political adventurer so familiar to history. There is a tendency for such persons to claim immunity from the usual forms of restraint and to insist that professionalism and a devotion to science provide sufficient protection against unwarranted invasion of individual rights.

• • •

There is one proposition which, if generally understood, would contribute more to clear thinking on these matters than any other. It is not a new insight. Garofalo asserted: "The mere deprivation of liberty, however benign the administration of the place of confinement, is undeniably punishment." This proposition may be rephrased as follows: Measures which subject individuals to the substantial and involuntary deprivation of their liberty contain an inescapable punitive element, and this reality is not altered by the facts that the motivations that prompt incarceration are to provide therapy or otherwise contribute to the person's well-being or reform. As such, these measures must be closely scrutinized to insure that power is being applied consistently with those values of the community that justify interference with liberty for only the most clear and compelling reasons.

But the point I am making requires more specific and concrete application to be entirely meaningful. It should be pointed out, first, that the values of individual liberty may be imperiled by claims to knowledge and therapeutic technique that we, in fact, do not possess and by our failure to concede candidly what we do not know. At times, practitioners of the behavioral sciences have been guilty of these faults. At other times, such errors have supplied the assumptions on which legislators, lawyers, and lay people generally have proceeded. An illustration of these dangers is provided by the sexual psychopath laws, to which I return, for they epitomize admirably some of the worst tendencies of modern practice. Doubts almost as serious can be raised as to a whole range of other measures. The laws providing for the commitment of persons displaying the classic symptoms of psychosis and advanced mental disorder have proved a seductive analogy for other proposals. But does our knowledge of human behavior really justify the extension of these measures to provide for the indefinite commitment of persons otherwise afflicted?

There are other ways in which the modern tendencies of thought accompanying the rise of the rehabilitative ideal have imperiled basic political values. The most important of these is the encouragement of procedural laxness and irregularity. It is my impression that there is a greater awareness of these dangers today than at some other times in the past. Nevertheless, in our courts of so-called socialized justice one may still observe, on occasion, a tendency to assume that, since the purpose of the proceeding is to "help" rather than to "punish," some lack of concern in establishing the charges against the person before the court may be justified. Thus, in some courts the judge is supplied with a report on the offender by the psychiatric clinic before the judgment of guilt or acquittal is announced. Such reports, while they may be relevant to the defendant's need for therapy or confinement, are ordinarily wholly irrelevant to the issue of his guilt of the particular offense charged. Yet it asks too much of human nature to assume that the judge is never influenced on the issue of guilt or innocence by a strongly adverse psychiatric report.

Let me give one final illustration of the problems that have accompanied the rise of the rehabilitative ideal. Some time ago we encountered a man in his eighties incarcerated in a state institution. He had been confined for some thirty years under a statute calling for the automatic commitment of defendants acquitted on grounds of insanity in criminal trials. It was generally agreed by the institution's personnel that he was not then psychotic and probably had never been psychotic. The fact seemed to be that he had killed his wife while drunk. An elderly sister of the old man was able and willing to provide him with a home, and he was understandably eager to leave the institution. When we asked the director of the institution why the old man was not released, he gave two significant answers. In the first place, he said, the statute requires me to find that this inmate is no longer a danger to the community; this I cannot do, for he may kill again. And of course the director was right. However unlikely commission of homicide by such a man in his eighties might appear, the director could not be certain. But, as far as that goes, he could not be certain also about himself or about you or me. The second answer was equally interesting. The old man, he said, is better off here. To understand the full significance of this reply it is necessary to know something about the place of confinement. Although called a hospital, it was in fact a prison, and not at all a progressive prison. Nothing worthy of the name of therapy was provided and very little even by way of recreational facilities.

This case points several morals. It illustrates, first, a failure of the law to deal adequately with the new requirements which are being placed upon it. The statute, as a condition of the release of the inmate, required the director of the institution virtually to warrant the future good behavior of the inmate, and, in so doing, made unrealistic and impossible demands on expert judgment. This might be remedied by the formulation of release criteria more consonant with actuality. Provisions for conditional release to test the inmate's reaction to the free community would considerably reduce the strain on administrative decision-making. But there is more here. Perhaps the case reflects that arrogance and insensitivity to human values to which men who have no reason to doubt their own motives appear peculiarly susceptible.

I have attempted to describe some of the continuing problems and difficulties associated with, what I have called, the rise of the rehabilitative ideal. In so doing, I have not sought to cast doubt on the substantial benefits associated with that movement. It has exposed some of the most intractable problems of our time to the solvent properties of human intelligence. Moreover, the devotion to the ideal of empirical investigation provides the movement with a self-correcting mechanism of great importance and justifies hopes for constructive future development.

Nevertheless, no intellectual movement produces only unmixed blessings. I have suggested that the ascendancy of the rehabilitative ideal has, as one of its unfortunate consequences, diverted attention from other questions of great criminological importance. This has operated unfavorably to the full development of criminological science. Not only is this true, but the failure of many students and practitioners in the relevant areas to concern themselves with the full context of criminal justice has produced measures dangerous to basic political values and has, on occasion, encouraged the debasement of the rehabilitative ideal to produce results which are unsupportable whether measured by the objectives of therapy or of correction. The worst manifestations of these tendencies are undoubtedly deplored as sincerely by competent therapists as by others. But the occurrences are neither so infrequent nor so trivial that they can be safely ignored.

NOTE

1. As I recall, it was referred to as the "quiet room." In another institution the boy was required to stand before a wall while a seventy pound fire hose was played on his back. This procedure went under the name of "hydrotherapy."

PART II

Police

Contemporary democratic societies debate whether police exist for protection or prevention. History doesn't resolve this debate, because police agencies have played many different and contradictory roles. Are the police to be concerned primarily with crime fighting or peace keeping? Should they be social workers with guns or gun-toters in social work? Should they be instruments of social change or defenders of the faith?

THREE ERAS OF AMERICAN POLICING

American policing is often described in terms of three historical periods: the Political Era (1840–1920), the Professional Era (1920–1970), and the Community Era (1970–present). This division of history has been criticized as describing policing only in the urban areas of the Northeast without taking into account the very different development of the police in rural areas of the South and West. Even so, it is useful as a framework through which we can note differences in the organization of the police, the primary tasks they are charged with, and the specific policies and strategies that they are instructed to follow.

The Political Era: 1840–1920

Early policing in the United States is referred to as the Political Era because of the close ties that existed between the police and urban political leaders. Urban police often appeared to work for the mayor or the political party in power rather than for the citizens in general. Some jurisdictions issued guns and badges to white males who supported the mayor or those in political power. These police officers would then help their political patrons stay in power by working to get out the vote on election day. Ranks in the force were often for sale to the highest bidder, and many police officers were "on the take."

During this era the police focused on crime prevention and order maintenance by foot patrol. The officer on the beat dealt with crime, disorder, and other problems as they arose. In addition, the police in urban areas carried out service functions such as caring for derelicts, operating soup kitchens, regulating public health, and handling medical and social emergencies. Through their closeness to the communities they served, the police became both city servants and crime control officers. Because of this, the police often enjoyed citizen support.

Urbanization increased during the twentieth century, and so did criticism of the influence of politics on the police in these urban enclaves. Efforts to reform the nature and organization of the police began, and reformers sought to make police into law enforcement professionals, reducing their connection to local politics.

The Professional Era: 1920–1970

The Progressive reform movement of the early twentieth century had a significant influence on policing. These typically educated, upper-middle-class Progressives were interested in two primary goals: efficient government and the provision of government services to improve the conditions of the less fortunate. Belief in the importance of expertise was high, and the growth in an expert-driven administrative state provided impetus for professionalization and bureaucratization at all levels of government. A related goal was the removal of political influences, such as party politics and patronage, on government. When the Progressives applied these goals to the police, they envisioned professional law enforcement officials who would use modern technology to benefit the entire society, not just the local politicians.

August Vollmer, chief of police of Berkeley, California, from 1909 to 1932, was one of the leading advocates of professional policing. He and other reformers argued that the police should be a professional force, a nonpartisan agency of government committed to the highest ideals of public service. Six essential elements comprise this model of professional policing:

1. The force should stay out of politics.
2. Members should be well trained, disciplined, and tightly organized.
3. Laws should be equally enforced.
4. The force should take advantage of technological developments.
5. Personnel procedures should be based on merit.
6. The crime-fighting role should be prominent.

Reemphasizing crime control instead of maintaining order probably did more than anything else to change the nature of American policing. This narrow focus on crime fighting severed many of the ties that the police had developed with the communities they served. Cops became crime fighters. By the

1930s, with their new orientation toward fighting crime, the police were adopting modern technologies and methods in order to combat serious crimes. Citizen support became important, and effectiveness in fighting serious crimes like murder, rape, and robbery received the most attention. Alternatively, victimless crimes, and efforts to strictly maintain order, often aroused citizen opposition. The clean, professionalized model of policing advocated by the reform movement would only be tolerated if police responsibility was narrowed to crime fighting.

The 1960s were a time of social awakenings, with the civil rights and antiwar movements, urban riots, and rising crime rates. These cultural markers challenged many assumptions of the professional model. With American cities increasingly populated by low-income members of racial minorities, the professional style alienated officers from the communities they served. In the eyes of many inner-city residents, the police were an occupying army keeping them at the bottom of society rather than public servants providing help to all citizens.

The police continued to portray their public identity as that of a crime fighting force, but citizens recognized that the police were often ineffective in this role. Crime rates rose for many offenses, and the police were unable to change the perception that the quality of urban life was diminishing.

Community Policing Era: 1970–Present

The 1970s revealed calls for a movement away from the overriding crime-fighting focus and toward greater emphasis on maintaining order and providing services to the community. The complexities of police work were increasingly illlustrated in academic and policy research, fueled by the extent to which day-to-day practices deviated from the ideals of the professional model. The research also questioned the effectiveness of the police in catching and deterring criminals.

Three findings of the research are especially noteworthy:

1. Increasing the number of patrol officers in a neighborhood has little effect on the crime rate.
2. Rapid response to calls for service does not greatly increase the arrest rate.
3. Improving the percentage of crimes solved is difficult. These findings undermined the principles of the professional crime-fighter model.

Critics argued that the professional style isolated the police from the community and reduced their knowledge about and accountability to the neighborhoods they served. Motorized patrols sealed officers inside their patrol cars so that they had few personal contacts with citizens. Alternatively, it was argued that officers should get out of their cars and spend more time directly meeting and assisting citizens.

Advocates of the community policing approach urged greater use of foot patrols so that officers would become known to citizens, which has the potential to maximize cooperation with the police. They believe that through attention to little problems, the police may not only reduce disorder and fear but also improve public attitudes toward policing. Through a problem-oriented approach to policing, officers should identify the underlying causes of problems such as rowdy teenagers, spouse batterers, and abandoned buildings used as drug houses. By addressing various problems, small or large, within neighborhoods, the police can reduce disorder and the fear of crime.

Questions still remain about community policing and whether it can or should be implemented throughout the nation. The populations of some cities, especially in the West, are too dispersed to permit a switch from motorized to foot patrols. In addition, some critics of community policing question whether the professional model really disconnected police from community residents and whether Americans actually want their police to be something other than crime fighters.

POLICE CULTURE

The position of "police officer" is more than a cluster of formally prescribed duties and role expectations held jointly by criminal justice officials and members of the political community. There is a formal administrative language that specifies duties and responsibilities. There is also a cultural dimension to the position that has a profound influence on the operational code of the police, both as a unit and as individuals behaving within a bureaucratic framework. What remains is an inherent tension between an officer's role conception and the mandate required by the law.

Social scientists have demonstrated that there is a definite relationship between one's occupational environment and the way one interprets events; an occupation may be seen as a major badge of identity that an individual acts to protect as a facet of his or her self-esteem and person. Thus, entry requirements, training, and professional socialization produce a homogeneity of attitudes that guides the police in their daily work.

National studies of occupational status have shown that the public ascribes more prestige to the police now than in prior decades, even though police officers do not believe the public regards their calling as honorable. Publications of police organizations repeatedly take up the theme that the public does not appreciate law enforcement agents, particularly relative to other Western industrialized democracies where the police are often quite revered. In a Denver survey, 98 percent of police officers reported that they had experienced verbal or physical abuse and that these incidents tended to occur in neighborhoods of minority and underprivileged groups. Part of the burden of the police is that they have doubts about their professional status. Yet opinion polls consistently indicate that the overwhelming majority of citizens, even those in the ghetto, see the police as protectors of persons and property.

Discretion is a characteristic of bureaucracy. Unlike most organizations, the discretion the police have increases as one moves down the hierarchy. This means that the patrol officer, the most common and lowest ranking person in law enforcment, has the greatest amount of discretion. He or she deals with clients alone and is almost solely in charge of enforcing the most ambiguous laws—conflicts among citizens in which the definition of offensive behavior is most often open to dispute. The police officer's perception of the situation, as shaped by his or her personal values and norms, is crucial in determining what action the officer will take and what charges will be filed.

The police officer's world is circumscribed by the all-encompassing demands of the job. The police are socialized to a culture of loyalty known as the "thin blue line," a professional esprit de corps, and the symbolism of authority, but the situational context of their position limits their freedom to isolate their vocational role from other aspects of their lives. From the time they are first given their badges and guns, they must always carry these reminders of their position—the tools of the trade—and be prepared to use them. Thus, the requirements that the police maintain vigilance against crime even when off duty and that they work at "odd hours," along with the limited opportunities for social contact with persons other than fellow officers, reinforce the values of the police subculture.

THE "IMPOSSIBLE" MANDATE

In a thoughtful essay Peter Manning wrote that the police agree with their audiences, their professional interpreters—the American family, criminals, and politicians—in at least one respect: they have an "impossible" mandate. In society, various occupational groups are given license to carry out certain activities that others are not. Indeed, groups achieving professional status have formal rules and codes of ethics that not only set their own standards but also define their occupational mandate. Medical doctors, for example, have the right to prescribe drugs and perform operations, but they are also able to set the boundaries of their mandate. Because over time the practice of medicine has become a secure profession, there is little disagreement in society about the tasks, attitudes, and values that set its practitioners apart.

The police in contemporary society remain susceptible to criticism largely because they have been unable to define their mandate; it has been defined for them by those they serve. As a result, citizens have a distorted notion of police work. People are aware of the excitement of a small portion of police work, but then mistakenly broaden this notion to include all police activities. For much of the public, the police are viewed as always ready to respond to citizen demands—as highly organized crime fighters able to keep society from falling apart.

Sociopolitical changes in the United States have added to the tensions between the mandate of the police and their ability to fulfill it. In the past hundred years there have been massive shifts of population from rural areas to the cities. Criminal law has been called upon to serve a variety of purposes that are only tangentially related to law enforcement and order maintenance. Affluence has brought the criminal justice system new problems—such as the ease of communication and the abundance of property. Police have been assigned the tasks of crime prevention, crime detection, and the apprehension of criminals. They have a mandate that claims to include efficient, apolitical, and professional enforcement of the law. All this is to be accomplished within the bounds dictated by a democratic society that values due process of law. The mandate given the police is indeed "impossible." This will be true so long as there are misunderstandings, on the part of the police and the public, about the nature of law enforcement, the potential for success in controlling crime, and the role of law in a democratic society.

QUESTIONS FOR FURTHER EXPLORATION

1. What is the role conception of a police officer? What effect does this have on their exercise of discretion?

2. A sense of danger and isolation are often cited as daily feelings for police officers. How would these feelings influence their job performance?

3. What is most effective in eliciting a desired behavior from the police?

4. What does each era of policing imply about the relationship between police and citizens?

5. How is the productivity of police measured?

6. What role does the police play in an individualistic society versus a communitarian society?

7. When the government changes laws that control citizens, how are patrol strategies impacted?

8. Is the decision making behavior of police officers shaped by their individual backgrounds, occupational attitudes, influences across the criminal justice system, or societal conditions?

SUGGESTIONS FOR FURTHER READING

Bayley, David H. *Police for the Future.* New York: Oxford University Press, 1994. A thoughtful examination of police work with a blueprint for the future.

Goldstein, Herman. *Problem-Oriented Policing.* New York: McGraw-Hill, 1990. Basic examination of the move toward problem-oriented, or community, policing.

Lawrence, Regina. *The Politics of Force: Media and the Construction of Police Brutality.* Berkeley: University of California Press, 2000. Emphasizes the interplay between the criminal justice system and the media, using coverage of use of force incidents. Shows how coverage influences public perception of crime, and may shape political reaction.

Skolnick, Jerome H., and James J. Fyfe. *Above the Law: Police and the Excessive Use of Force.* New York: Free Press, 1993. Written in light of the Rodney King beating and the riots that followed. The authors believe that only by recruiting and supporting police chiefs who will uphold a policy of strict accountability can brutality be eliminated.

Tonry, Michael, and Norval Morris, eds. *Modern Policing.* Chicago: University of Chicago Press, 1992. An outstanding collection of essays by leading scholars examining the history, organization, and operational tactics of the police.

Wilson, James Q. *Varieties of Police Behavior.* Cambridge, Mass.: Harvard University Press, 1968. A classic study of the styles of policing in different types of communities. Shows the impact of politics on the operations of the force.

5

Police Discretion
Not to Invoke
the Criminal Process

Low-Visibility Decisions in the
Administration of Justice

Joseph Goldstein

Legislatures write the criminal laws as if they were commands to be enforced by the police, but officers have wide latitude in determining how the laws will be enforced. Professor Joseph Goldstein of the Yale Law School notes that decisions not to invoke the law are shielded from the public's view. Of particular interest is his development of the concepts of "total," "full," and "actual" enforcement. The extent to which the police pursue a policy approaching "full" enforcement for all offenses depends upon the values of the community.

Police decisions not to invoke the criminal process largely determine the outer limit of law enforcement. By such decisions, the police define the ambit of discretion throughout the process of other decision makers— prosecutor, grand and petit jury judge, probation officer, correction authority, and parole and pardon boards. These police decisions, unlike their decisions to invoke the law, are generally of extremely low visibility and consequently are seldom the subject of review. Yet an opportunity for review and appraisal of nonenforcement decisions is essential to the functioning of the rule of law in our system of criminal justice. This article will therefore be an attempt to

Source: Yale Law Journal Company and Fred B. Rothman & Company from *The Yale Law Journal,* Vol. 69, pp. 543–594. Footnotes omitted.

determine how the visibility of such police decisions may be increased and what procedures should be established to evaluate them on a continuing basis in the light of the complex of objectives of the criminal law and of the paradoxes toward which the administration of criminal justice inclines.

I. The criminal law is one of many intertwined mechanisms for the social control of human behavior. It defines behavior which is deemed intolerably disturbing to or destructive of community values and prescribes sanctions which the state is authorized to impose upon persons convicted or suspected of engaging in prohibited conduct. Following a plea or verdict of guilty, the state deprives offenders of life, liberty, dignity, or property through convictions, fines, imprisonments, killings, and supervised releases, and thus seeks to punish, restrain, and rehabilitate them, as well as to deter others from engaging in proscribed activity. Before a verdict, and despite the presumption of innocence which halos every person, the state deprives the suspect of life, liberty, dignity, or property through the imposition of deadly force, search and seizure of persons and possessions, accusation, imprisonment, and bail, and thus seeks to facilitate the enforcement of the criminal law.

These authorized sanctions reflect the multiple and often conflicting purposes which now surround and confuse criminal law administration at and between key decision points in the process. The stigma which accompanies conviction, for example, while serving a deterrent, and possibly retributive, function, becomes operative upon the offender's release and thus impedes the rehabilitation objective of probation and parole. Similarly, the restraint function of imprisonment involves the application of rules and procedures which, while minimizing escape opportunities, contributes to the deterioration of offenders confined for reformation. Since police decisions not to invoke the criminal process may likewise further some objectives while hindering others, or, indeed, run counter to all, any meaningful appraisal of these decisions should include an evaluation of their impact throughout the process on the various objectives reflected in authorized sanctions and in the decisions of other administrators of criminal justice.

Under the rule of law, the criminal law has both a fair-warning function for the public and a power-restricting function for officials. Both post- and preverdict sanctions, therefore, may be imposed only in accord with authorized procedures. No sanctions are to be inflicted other than those which have been prospectively prescribed by the Constitution, legislation, or judicial decision for a particular crime or a particular kind of offender. These concepts, of course, do not preclude differential disposition, within the authorized limits, of persons suspected or convicted of the same or similar offenses. In an ideal system differential handling, individualized justice, would result, but only from an equal application of officially approved criteria designed to implement officially approved objectives. And finally a system which presumes innocence requires that preconviction sanctions be kept at a minimum consistent with assuring an opportunity for the process to run its course.

A regularized system of review is a requisite for ensuring substantial compliance by the administrators of criminal justice with these rule-of-law principles. Implicit in the word "review" and obviously essential to the operation of any review procedure is the visibility of the decisions and conduct to be scrutinized. Pretrial hearings on motions, the trial, appeal, and the writ of habeas corpus constitute a formal system for evaluating the actions of officials invoking the criminal process. The public hearing, the record of proceedings, and the publication of court opinions—all features of the formal system—preserve and increase the visibility of official enforcement activity and facilitate and encourage the development of an informal system of appraisal. These proceedings and documents are widely reported and subjected to analysis and comment by legislative, professional, and other interested groups and individuals.

But police decisions not to invoke the criminal process, except when reflected in gross failures of service, are not visible to the community. Nor are they likely to be visible to official state reviewing agencies, even those within the police department. Failure to tag illegally parked cars is an example of gross failure of service, open to public view and recognized for what it is. An officer's decision, however, not to investigate or report adequately a disturbing event which he has reason to believe constitutes a violation of the criminal law does not ordinarily carry with it consequences sufficiently visible to make the community, the legislature, the prosecutor, or the courts aware of a possible failure of service. The police officer, the suspect, the police department, and frequently even the victim, when directly concerned with a decision not to invoke, unlike the same parties when responsible for or subject to a decision to invoke, generally have neither the incentive nor the opportunity to obtain review of that decision or the police conduct associated with it. Furthermore, official police records are usually too incomplete to permit evaluations of nonenforcement decisions in the light of the purposes of the criminal law. Consequently, such decisions, unlike decisions to enforce, are generally not subject to the control which would follow from administrative, judicial, legislative, or community review and appraisal.

Confidential reports detailing the day-to-day decisions and activities of a large municipal police force have been made available to the author by the American Bar Foundation. These reports give limited visibility to a wide variety of police decisions not to invoke the criminal process. Three groups of such decisions will be described and analyzed. Each constitutes a police "program" of nonenforcement either based on affirmative departmental policy or condoned by default. All of the decisions, to the extent that the officers concerned thought about them at all, represent well-intentioned, honest judgments, which seem to reflect the police officer's conception of his job. None of the decisions involve bribery or corruption, nor do they concern "obsolete," though unrepealed, criminal laws. Specifically, these programs involve police decisions (1) not to enforce the narcotics laws against certain violators, who inform against other "more serious" violators; (2) not to enforce the felonious assault laws against an assailant whose victim does not sign a complaint; and (3) not to enforce gambling laws against persons engaged in the numbers racket, but instead to harass them. Each of these decisions is made even though the police "know" a crime has been committed and even though they may "know" who the offender is and may, in fact, have apprehended him. But before describing and evaluating these nonenforcement programs, as an agency of review might do, it is necessary to determine what discretion, if any, the police, as invoking agents, have, and conceptually to locate the police in relation to other principal decision makers in the criminal law process.

II. The police have a duty not to enforce the substantive law of crimes unless invocation of the process can be achieved within bounds set by constitution, statute, court decision, and possibly official pronouncements of the prosecutor. *Total enforcement*, were it possible, is thus precluded, by generally applicable due process restrictions on such police procedures as arrest, search, seizure, and interrogation. *Total enforcement* is further precluded by such specific procedural restrictions as prohibitions on invoking an adultery statute unless the spouse of one of the parties complains, or an unlawful-possession-of-firearms statute if the offender surrenders his dangerous weapons during a statutory period of amnesty. Such restrictions of general and specific application mark the bounds, often ambiguously, of an area of *full enforcement* in which the police are not only authorized but expected to enforce fully the law of crimes. An area of *no enforcement* lies, therefore, between the perimeter of *total enforcement* and the outer limits of *full enforcement*. In this *no-enforcement* area, the police have no authority to invoke the criminal process.

Within the area of *full enforcement*, the police have not been delegated discretion not to invoke the criminal process. On the contrary, those state statutes providing for municipal police departments which define the responsibility of police provide:

> It shall be the duty of the police . . . under the direction of the mayor and chief of police and in conformity with the ordinances of the city, and the laws of the state, . . . to pursue and arrest any persons fleeing from justice . . . to apprehend any and all persons in the act of committing any offense against the laws of the state . . . and to take the offender forthwith before the proper court or magistrate, to be dealt with for the offense; to make complaints to the proper officers and magistrates of any person known or believed by them to be guilty of the violation of the ordinances of the city or the penal laws of the state; and at all times diligently and faithfully to enforce all such laws. . . .

Even in jurisdictions without such a specific statutory definition, declarations of the *full enforcement* mandate generally appear in municipal charters, ordinances, or police manuals. Police manuals, for example, commonly provide, in sections detailing the duties at each level of the police hierarchy, that the captain, superintendent, lieutenant, or patrolman shall be responsible, so far as is in his power, for the prevention and detection of crime and the enforcement of all criminal laws and ordinances. Illustrative of the spirit and policy of *full enforcement* is this protestation from the introduction to the Rules and Regulations of the Atlanta, Georgia, Police Department:

> Enforcement of all Criminal Laws and City Ordinances, is my obligation. There are no specialties under the Law. My eyes must be open to traffic

problems and disorders, though I move on other assignments, to slinking vice in back streets and dives though I have been directed elsewhere, to the suspicious appearance of evil wherever it is encountered. . . . I must be impartial because the Law surrounds, protects, and applies to all alike, rich and poor, low and high, black and white. . . .

Minimally, then, *full enforcement,* so far as the police are concerned, means (1) the investigation of every disturbing event which is reported to or observed by them and which they have reason to suspect may be a violation of the criminal law; (2) following a determination that some crime has been committed, an effort to discover its perpetrators; and (3) the presentation of all information collected by them to the prosecutor for his determination of the appropriateness of further invoking the criminal process.

Full enforcement, however, is not a realistic expectation. In addition to ambiguities in the definitions of both substantive offenses and due process boundaries, countless limitations and pressures preclude the possibility of the police seeking or achieving *full enforcement.* Limitations of time, personnel, and investigative devices—all in part but not entirely functions of budget—force the development, by plan or default, of priorities of enforcement. Even if there were "enough police" adequately equipped and trained, pressures from within and without the department, which is after all a human institution, may force the police to invoke the criminal process selectively. By decisions not to invoke within the area of *full enforcement,* the police largely determine the outer limits of *actual enforcement* throughout the criminal process. This relationship of the police to the total administration of criminal justice can be seen in the diagram [Figure 1]. They may reinforce, or they may undermine, the legislature's objectives in designating certain conduct "criminal" and in authorizing the imposition of certain sanctions following conviction. A police decision to ignore a felonious assault "because the victim will not sign a complaint" usually precludes the prosecutor or grand jury from deciding whether to accuse, judge or jury from determining guilt or innocence, judge from imposing the most "appropriate" sentence, probation or correctional authorities from instituting the most "appropriate" restraint and rehabilitation programs, and finally parole or pardon authorities from determining the offender's readiness for release to the community. This example is drawn from one of the three programs of nonenforcement about to be discussed.

III. Trading enforcement against a narcotics suspect for information about another narcotics offense or offender may involve two types of police decisions not to invoke fully the criminal process. First, there may be a decision to ask for the dismissal or reduction of the charge for which the informant is held; second, there may be a decision to overlook future violations while the suspect serves as an informer. The second type is an example of a relatively pure police decision not to invoke the criminal process while the first requires, at a minimum, tacit approval by prosecutor or judge. But examination of only the pure types of decisions would oversimplify the problem. They fail to illustrate the extent to which police nonenforcement decisions may permeate the process as well as influence, and be influenced by, prosecutor and court action in settings

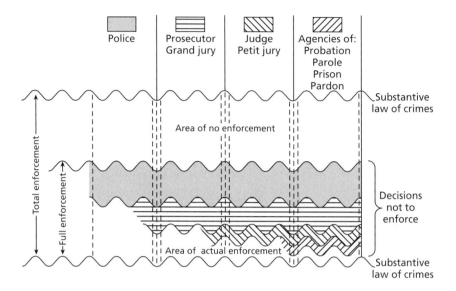

FIGURE 1 The Police in Relation to Other Decision Makers in the Criminal Process

which fail to prompt appraisal of such decisions in light of the purposes of the criminal law. Both types of decision, pure and conglomerate, are nonetheless primarily police decisions. They are distinguishable from a prosecutor's or court's decision to trade information for enforcement under an immunity statute, and from such parliamentary decisions as the now-repealed seventeenth- and eighteenth-century English statutes which gave a convicted offender who secured the conviction of his accomplice an absolute right to pardon. Such prosecutor and parliamentary decisions to trade information for enforcement, unlike the police decisions to be described, have not only been authorized by a legislative body but have also been made sufficiently visible to permit review.

In the municipality studied, regular uniformed officers, with general law enforcement duties on precinct assignments, and a special narcotics squad of detectives, with citywide jurisdiction, are responsible for enforcement of the state narcotics laws. The existence of the special squad acts as a pressure on the uniformed officer to be the first to discover any sale, possession, or use of narcotics in his precinct. Careful preparation of a case for prosecution may thus become secondary to this objective. Indeed, approximately 80 percent of those apprehended for narcotics violations during one year were discharged. In the opinion of the special squad, which processes each arrested narcotics suspect, either the search was illegal or the evidence obtained inadequate. The precinct officer's lack of interest in carefully developing a narcotics case for prosecution often amounts in effect to a police decision not to enforce but rather to harass.

But we are concerned here primarily with the decisions of the narcotics squad, which, like the Federal Narcotics Bureau, has established a policy of concentrating enforcement efforts against the "big supplier." The chief of the squad claimed that informers must be utilized to implement that policy, and that in order to get informants it is necessary to trade "little ones for big ones." Informers are used to arrange and make purchases of narcotics, to elicit information from suspects, including persons in custody, and to recruit additional informants.

Following arrest, a suspect will generally offer to serve as an informer to "do himself some good." If an arrestee fails to initiate such negotiations, the interrogating officer will suggest that something may be gained by disclosing sources of supply and by serving as an informer. A high mandatory minimum sentence for selling, a high maximum sentence for possession, and, where users are involved, a strong desire on their part to avoid the agonies of withdrawal, combine to place the police in an excellent bargaining position to recruit informers. To assure performance, each informer is charged with a narcotics violation, and final disposition is postponed until the defendant has fulfilled his part of the bargain. To protect the informer, the special squad seeks to camouflage him in the large body of releasees by not disclosing his identity even to the arresting precinct officer, who is given no explanation for release. Thus persons encountered on the street by a uniformed patrolman the day after their arrest may have been discharged, or they may have been officially charged and then released on bail or personal recognizance to await trial or to serve as informers.

While serving as informers, suspects are allowed to engage in illegal activity. Continued use of narcotics is condoned; the narcotics detective generally is not concerned with the problem of informants who make buys and use some of the evidence themselves. Though informers are usually warned that their status does not give them a "license to peddle," possession of a substantial amount of narcotics may be excused. In one case, a defendant found guilty of possession of marijuana argued that she was entitled to be placed on probation since she had cooperated with the police by testifying against three persons charged with the sale of narcotics. The sentencing judge denied her request because he discovered that her cooperation was related to the possession of a substantial amount of heroin, an offense for which she was arrested (but never charged) while on bail for the marijuana violation. A narcotics squad inspector, in response to an inquiry from the judge, revealed that the defendant had not been charged with possession of heroin because she had been cooperative with the police on that offense.

In addition to granting such outright immunity for some violations, the police will recommend to the prosecutor either that an informer's case be *nolle prossed* or, more frequently, that the charge be reduced to a lesser offense. And, if the latter course is followed, the police usually recommend to the judge, either in response to his request for information or in the presentence report, that informers be placed on probation or given relatively light sentences. Both the prosecutor and judge willingly respond to police requests for reducing a charge of sale to a lesser offense because they consider the mandatory minimum too severe. As a result, during a four-year period in this jurisdiction, less than 2.5

percent of all persons charged with the sale of narcotics were convicted of that offense.

The narcotics squad's policy of trading *full enforcement* for information is justified on the grounds that apprehension and prosecution of the "big supplier" is facilitated. The absence of any such individual is attributed to this policy. As one member of the squad said, "[The city] is too hot. There are too many informants." A basic, though untested, assumption of the policy is that ridding the city of the "big supplier" is the key to solving its narcotics problem. Even if this assumption were empirically validated, the desirability of continuing such a policy cannot be established without taking into account its total impact on the administration of criminal justice in the city, the state, and the nation. Yet no procedure has been designed to enable the police and other key administrators of criminal justice to obtain such an appraisal. The extent and nature of the need for such a procedure can be illustrated, despite the limitations of available data, by presenting in the form of a mock report some of the questions, some of the answers, and some of the proposals a policy appraisal and review board might consider.

Following a description of the informer program, a report might ask: *To what extent, if at all, has the legislature delegated to the police the authority to grant, or obtain a grant of, complete or partial immunity from prosecution, in exchange for information about narcotics suppliers?* No provisions of the general immunity or narcotics statutes authorize the police to exercise such discretion. The general immunity statute requires a high degree of visibility by providing that immunity be allowed only on a written motion by the prosecuting attorney to the court and that the information given be reduced to writing under the direction of the judge to preclude future prosecution for the traded offense or offenses. The narcotics statutes, unlike comparable legislation concerning other specific crimes, make no provision for obtaining information by awarding immunity from prosecution. Nor is there any indication, other than possibly in the maximum sentences authorized, that the legislature intended that certain narcotics offenses be given high priority or be enforced at the expense of other offenses. What evidence there is of legislative intent suggests the contrary; this fact is recognized by the local police manual. And nothing in the statute providing for the establishment of local police departments can be construed to authorize the policy of trading enforcement for information. That statute makes *full enforcement* a duty of the police. The narcotics squad has ignored this mandate and adopted an informer policy which appears to constitute a usurpation of legislative function. It does not follow that the police must discontinue employing informers, but they ought to discontinue trading enforcement for information until the legislature, the court, or the prosecutor explicitly initiates such a program. Whether the police policy of trading enforcement for information should be proposed for legislative consideration would depend upon the answers to some of the questions which follow.

Does trading enforcement for information fulfill the retributive, restraining, and reformative functions of the state's narcotics laws? By in effect licensing the user–informer to satisfy his addiction and assuring the peddler–informer, who may also be a user, that he will obtain dismissal or reduction of the pending charge to a lesser offense, the police undermine, if not negate, the retributive and restraining functions of the narcotics laws. In addition, the community is deprived of an opportunity to subject these offenders, particularly the addicts, to treatment aimed at reformation. In fact, the police ironically acknowledge the inconsistency of their program with the goal of treatment: "cured" addicts are not used as informers for fear that exposure to narcotics might cause their relapse. A comparison of the addict-release policies of the police, sentencing judge, and probation and parole authorities demonstrates the extent to which the administration of criminal justice can be set awry by a police nonenforcement program. At one point on the continuum, the police release the addict to informer status so that he can maintain his association with peddlers and users. The addict accepts such status on the tacit condition that continued use will be condoned. At other points on the continuum, the judge and probation and parole authorities make treatment a condition of an addict's release and continued use or even association with narcotics users the basis for revoking probation or parole. Thus the inherent conflict between basic purposes of the criminal law is compounded by conflicts among key decision points in the process.

Does trading enforcement for information implement the deterrent function of criminal law administration? If deterrence depends—and little if anything is really known about the deterrent impact of the criminal law—in part at least, upon the potential offender's perception of law enforcement, the informer policy can have only a negative effect. In addition to the chance of nondetection which accompanies the commission of all crimes in varying degrees, the narcotics suspect has four-to-one odds that he will not be charged following detection and arrest. And he has a high expectation, even if charged, of obtaining a reduction or dismissal of an accurate charge. These figures reflect and reinforce the offender's view of the administration of criminal justice as a bargaining process initiated either by offering information "to do himself some good" or by a member of the narcotics squad advising the uninformed suspect, the "new offender," of the advantages of disclosing his narcotics "connections." Such law enforcement can have little, if any, deterrent impact.

That the "big supplier," an undefined entity, has been discouraged from using the city as a headquarters was confirmed by a local federal agent and a U.S. attorney in testimony before a Senate committee investigating illicit narcotics traffic. They attributed the result, however, to the state's high mandatory minimum sentence for selling, not to the informer policy. In fact, that municipal police policy was not made visible at the hearings. It was mentioned neither in their testimony nor in the testimony of the chief of police and the head of the narcotics squad. These local authorities may have reasoned that since the mandatory sentence facilitates the recruitment of informers who, in turn, are essential to keeping the "big supplier" outside city limits, the legislature's sentencing policy could be credited with the "achievement."

Whether the police informer program, the legislature's sentencing policy, both, or neither, caused the "big supplier" to locate elsewhere is not too significant; the traffic and use of narcotics in the city remain major problems. Since user demand is maintained, if not increased, by trading enforcement for information, potential and actual peddlers are encouraged to supply the city's addicts. Testimony before the Senate committee indicates that although the "big suppliers" have moved their headquarters to other cities, there are now in the city a large number of small peddlers serving a minimum of 1,500 and in all probability a total of 2,500 users, and that the annual expenditure for illicit narcotics in the city is estimated at not lower than $10 million and probably as high as $18 million. Evaluated in terms of deterrent effect, the program of trading enforcement for information to reach the "big supplier" has failed to implement locally the ultimate objective of the narcotics laws—reducing addiction. Furthermore, the business of the "big supplier" has not been effectively deterred. At best suppliers have been discouraged from basing their operations in the city, which continues to be a lucrative market. Thus by maintaining the market, local policy, although a copy of national policy, may very well hinder the efforts of the Federal Narcotics Bureau.

A report of a policy appraisal and review board might find: "Trading little ones for big ones" is outside the ambit of municipal police discretion and should continue to remain so because it conflicts with the basic objectives of the criminal law. Retribution, restraint, and reformation are subverted by a policy which condones the use and possession of narcotics. And deterrence cannot be enhanced by a police program which provides potential and actual suppliers and users with more illustrations of nonenforcement than enforcement.

A report might conclude by exploring and suggesting alternative programs for coping with the narcotics problem. No attempt will be made here to exhaust or detail all possible alternatives. An obvious one would be a rigorous program of *full enforcement* designed to dry up, or at least drastically reduce, local consumer and peddler demand for illicit narcotics. If information currently obtained from suspects is essential and worth a price, compensation might be given to informers, with payments deferred until a suspect's final release. Such a program would neither undermine the retributive and restraining objectives of the criminal law nor deprive the community of an opportunity to impose rehabilitation regimes on the offender. Funds provided by deferred payments might enhance an offender's chances of getting off to a good start upon release. Moreover, changing the picture presently perceived by potential violators from nonenforcement to enforcement would at least not preclude the possibility of deterrence. Such a program might even facilitate the apprehension of "big suppliers" who, faced with decreasing demand, might either be forced to discontinue serving the city because sales would no longer be profitable or to adopt bolder sales methods which would expose them to easier detection.

Full enforcement will place the legislature in a position to evaluate its narcotics laws by providing a basis for answering such questions as: Will *full enforcement* increase the price of narcotics to the user? Will such inflation increase the frequency of crimes committed to finance narcotics purchases? Or will *full enforcement* reduce the number of users and the frequency of connected crimes? Will too great or too costly an administrative burden be placed on the prosecutor's office and the courts by *full enforcement*? Will correctional institutions be filled beyond "effective" capacity? The answers to these questions are now buried or obscured by decisions not to invoke the criminal process.

Failure of a *full enforcement* program might prompt a board recommendation to increase treatment or correctional personnel and facilities. Or a board, recognizing that *full enforcement* would be either too costly or inherently ineffective, might propose the repeal of statutes prohibiting the use and sale of narcotics and/or the enactment, as part of a treatment program, of legislation authorizing sales to users at a low price. Such legislative action would be designed to reduce use and connected offenses to a minimum. By taking profits out of sales it would lessen peddler incentive to create new addicts and eliminate the need to support the habit by the commission of crimes.

These then are the kinds of questions, answers, and proposals a policy appraisal and review board might explore in its report examining this particular type of police decision not to invoke the criminal process.

IV. Another low-visibility situation which an appraisal and review board might uncover in this municipality stems from police decisions not to invoke the felonious assault laws unless the victim signs a complaint. Like the addict–informer, the potential complainant in an assault case is both the victim of an offense and a key source of information. But unlike him, the complainant, who is not a suspect, and whose initial contact with the police is generally self-imposed, is not placed under pressure to bargain. And in contrast with the informer program, the police assault program was clearly not designed, if designed at all, to effectuate an identifiable policy.

During one month under the nonenforcement program of a single precinct, thirty-eight out of forty-three felonious assault cases, the great majority involving stabbings and cuttings, were cleared "because the victim refused to prosecute." This program, which is coupled with a practice of not encouraging victims to sign complaints, reduces the pressure of work by eliminating such tasks as apprehending and detaining suspects, writing detailed reports, applying for warrants to prefer charges, and appearing in court at inconvenient times for long periods without adequate compensation. As one officer explained, "run-of-the-mill" felonious assaults are so common in his precinct that prosecution of each case would force patrolmen to spend too much time in court and leave too little time for investigating other offenses. This rationalization exposes the private value system of individual officers as another policy-shaping factor. Some policemen feel, for example, that assault is an acceptable means of settling disputes among Negroes, and that when both assailant and victim are Negro, there is no immediate discernible harm to the public which justifies a decision to invoke the criminal process. Anticipation of dismissal by judge and district attorney of cases in which the victim is an uncooperative witness, the police claim, has been another operative factor in the development of the assault policy. A policy appraisal and review board, whose investigators had been specifically directed to examine the assault policy, should be able to identify these or other policy-shaping factors more precisely. Yet on the basis of the data available, a board could tentatively conclude that court and prosecutor responses do not explain why the police have failed to adopt a policy of encouraging assault victims to sign complaints, and, therefore, that the private value system of department members, as reflected in their attitude toward work load and in a stereotypical view of the Negro, is of primary significance.

Once some of the major policy-shaping factors have been identified, an appraisal and review board might formulate and attempt to answer the following or similar questions: Would it be consistent with any of the purposes of the criminal law to authorize police discretion in cases of felonious assaults as well as other specified offenses? Assuming that it would be consistent or at least more realistic to authorize police discretion in some cases, what limitations and guides, if any, should the legislature provide? Should legislation provide that factors such as work load, willingness of victims or certain victims to sign a complaint, the degree of violence, and attitude of prosecutor and judge be taken into account in the exercise of police discretion? If work load is to be recognized, should the legislature establish priorities of enforcement designed to assist the police in deciding which offenses among equally pressing ones are to be ignored or enforced? If assaults are made criminal in order to reduce threats to community peace and individual security, should a victim's willingness to prosecute, if he happens to live, be relevant to the exercise of police discretion? Does resting prosecution in the hands of the victim encourage him to "get even" with the assailant through retaliatory lawlessness? Or does such a policy place the decision in the hands of the assailant whose use of force has already demonstrated an ability and willingness to fulfill a threat?

Can the individual police officer, despite his own value system, sufficiently respond to officially articulated community values to be delegated broad powers of discretion? If not, can or should procedures be designed to enable the police department to translate these values into rules and regulations for individual policemen? Can police officers or the department be trained to evaluate the extent to which current practice undermines a major criminal law objective of imposing upon all persons officially recognized minimum standards of human behavior? For example, can the individual officer of the department be trained to evaluate the effect of decisions in cases of felonious assault among Negroes on local programs for implementing national or state policies of integration in school, employment, and housing, and to determine the extent to which current policy weakens or reinforces stereotypes which are used to justify not only police policy but, more importantly, opposition to desegregation programs? Or should legislation provide that the police invoke the process in all felonious assault cases unless the prosecutor or court publicly provides them in recorded documents with authority and guides for exercising discretion, and thus make visible both the policy of nonenforcement and the agency or agencies responsible for it?

Some of these issues were considered and resolved by the Oakland, California, Police Department in 1957 when, after consultation with prosecutors and judges, it decided to abandon a similar assault policy and seek *full enforcement.* Chief of Police W. W. Vernon, describing Oakland's new program, wrote:

> In our assault cases for years we had followed this policy of releasing the defendant if the complainant did not feel aggrieved to the point of being willing to testify. . . . [Since] World War II . . . our assault cases increased tremendously to the point where we decided to do something about the increase.

Training materials prepared by the Oakland Police Academy disclose that between 1952 and 1956, while the decision to prosecute was vested in the victim, the rate of reported felonious assaults rose from 93 to 161 per 100,000 population and the annual number of misdemeanor assaults rose from 618 to 2,630. The materials emphasize that these statistics mean a work load of "nearly ten assault reports a day every day of the year." But they stress:

> The important point about these figures is not so much that they represent a substantial police workload, which they do, but more important, that they indicate an increasing lack of respect for the laws of society by a measurable segment of our population, and a corresponding threat to the rest of the citizens of our city. The police have a clear responsibility to develop respect for the law among those who disregard it in order to ensure the physical safety and well-being of those who do. . . .
>
> We recognize that the problem exists mainly because the injured person has refused to sign a complaint against the perpetrator. The injured person has usually refused to sign for two reasons: first, because of threats of future bodily harm or other action by the perpetrator and, secondly, because it has been a way of life among some people to adjust grievances by physical assaults and not by the recognized laws of society which are available to them.
>
> We, the police, have condoned these practices to some extent by not taking advantage of the means at our disposal: that is, by not gathering sufficient evidence and signing complaints on information and belief in those cases where the complainant refuses to prosecute. The policy and procedure of gathering sufficient evidence and signing complaints on information and belief should instill in these groups the realization that the laws of society must be resorted to in settling disputes. When it is realized by many of these people that we will sign complaints ourselves and will not condone fighting and cuttings, many of them will stop such practices.

Following conferences with the police, the local prosecutors and judges pledged their support for the new assault program. The district attorney's office will deny a complainant's request that a case be dropped and suggest that it be addressed to the judge in open court. The judge, in turn, will advise the complainant that the case cannot be dismissed, and that a perjury, contempt, or false-report complaint will be issued in "appropriate cases" against the victim who denies facts originally alleged. The police have been advised that the court and prosecutor will actively cooperate in the implementation of the new program, but that every case will not result in a complaint since it is the "job [of the police] to turn in the evidence and it's the prosecuting attorney's job to determine when a complaint will be issued." Thus the role of each of the key decision-making agencies with preconviction invoking authority is clearly delineated and integrated.

With the inauguration of a new assault policy, an appraisal and review board might establish procedures for determining how effectively the objectives of the policy are fulfilled in practice. A board might design intelligence-retrieving devices which would provide more complete data than the following termed by Chief Vernon "the best evidence that our program is accomplishing the purpose for which it was developed." Prior to the adoption of the new policy, 80 percent of the felonious assault cases "cleared" were cleared because "complainant refuses to prosecute," while only 32.2 percent of the clearances made during the first three months in 1958 were for that reason, even though the overall clearance rate rose during that period. And "during the first quarter of this year Felony Assaults dropped 11.1 percent below the same period last year, and in March they were 35.6 percent below March of last year. Battery cases were down 19.0 percent for the first three months of 1958." An appraisal and review board might attempt to determine the extent to which the police in cases formerly dropped because "complainant refused to testify" have consciously or otherwise substituted another reason for "case cleared." And it might estimate the extent to which the decrease in assaults *reported* reflects, if it does, a decrease in the *actual* number of assaults or only a decrease in the number of victims willing to report assaults. Such follow-up investigations and what actually took place in Oakland on an informal basis between police, prosecutor, and judge illustrate some of the functions an appraisal and review board might regularly perform.

V. Police decisions to harass, though generally perceived as overzealous enforcement, constitute another body of nonenforcement activities meriting investigation by an appraisal and review board. Harassment is the imposition by the police, acting under color of law, of sanctions prior to conviction as a means of ultimate punishment, rather than as a device for the invocation of criminal proceedings. Characteristic of harassment are efforts to annoy certain "offenders" both by temporarily detaining or arresting them without intention to seek prosecution and by destroying or illegally seizing their property without any intention to use it as evidence. Like other police decisions not to invoke the criminal process, harassment is generally of extremely low visibility, probably because the police ordinarily restrict such activity to persons who are unable to afford the costs of litigation, who would, or think they would, command little respect even if they were to complain, or who wish to keep themselves out of public view in order to continue their illicit activities. Like the informer program, harassment is conducted by the police in an atmosphere of cooperation with other administrators of criminal justice. Since harassment, by definition, is outside the rule of law, any benefits attributed to such police activity cannot justify its continuation. An appraisal and review board, however, would not limit its investigations to making such a finding. It would be expected to identify and analyze factors underlying harassment and to formulate proposals for replacing harassment—lawless nonenforcement—with enforcement of the criminal law.

Investigators for an appraisal and review board in this jurisdiction would discover, for example, a mixture of enforcement and harassment in a police program designed to regulate the gambling operations of mutual-numbers syndicates. The enforcement phase is conducted by a highly trained unit of less than a dozen men who diligently gather evidence in order to prosecute and convict syndicate operators of conspiracy to violate the gambling laws. This specialized unit, which operates independently of and without the knowledge of other officers, conducts all its work within the due process boundaries of *full enforcement*. Consequently, the conviction rate is high for charges based upon its investigations. The harassment phase is conducted by approximately sixty officers who tour the city and search on sight, because of prior information, or such telltale actions as carrying a paper bag, a symbol of the trade, persons who they suspect are collecting bets. They question the "suspect" and proceed to search him, his car, or home without first making a valid arrest to legalize the search. If gambling paraphernalia are found, the police, fully aware that the exclusionary rule prohibits its use as evidence in this jurisdiction, confiscate the "contraband" and arrest the individual without any intention of seeking application of the criminal law.

Gambling operators treat the harassment program as a cost of doing business, "a risk of the trade." Each syndicate retains a bonding firm and an attorney to service members who are arrested. When a "runner" or "bagman" is absent from his scheduled rounds, routine release procedures are initiated. The bondsman, sometimes prematurely, checks with the police to determine if a syndicate man has been detained. If the missing man is in custody, the syndicate's attorney files an application for a writ of habeas corpus and appears before a magistrate who usually sets bail at a nominal amount and adjourns hearing the writ, at the request of the police, until the following day. Prior to the scheduled hearing, the police usually advise the court that they have no intention of proceeding, and the case is closed. Despite the harassee's release, the police retain the money and gambling paraphernalia. If the items seized are found in a car, the car is confiscated, with the cooperation of the prosecutor, under a nuisance abatement statute. Cars are returned, however, after the harassee signs a "consent decree" and pursuant to it, pays "court costs"—a fee which is based on the car's value and which the prosecutor calls "the real meat of the harassment program." The "decree," entered under a procedure devised by the court and prosecutor's office, enjoins the defendant from engaging in illegal activity and, on paper, frees the police from any tort liability by an acknowledgment that seizure of the vehicle was lawful and justified—even though one prosecutor has estimated that approximately 80 percent of the searches and seizures were illegal. A prosecuting attorney responsible for car confiscation initially felt that such procedures "in the ordinary practice of law would be unethical, revolting, and shameful," but explained that he now understands why he acted as he did:

To begin with . . . laws in . . . [this state] with respect to gambling are most inadequate. This is equally true of the punishment feature of the law. To illustrate . . . a well-organized and productive gambling house or numbers racket would take in one-quarter of a million dollars each week. If, after a long and vigorous period of investigation and observation, the defendant was charged with violating the gambling laws and convicted therefor, the resulting punishment is so obviously weak and unprohibitive that the defendants are willing to shell out a relatively small fine or serve a relatively short time in prison. The . . . [city's] gamblers and numbers men confidently feel that the odds are in their favor. If they operate for six months or a year, and accumulate untold thousands of dollars from the illegal activity, then the meager punishment imposed upon them if they are caught is well worth it. Then, too, because of the search and seizure laws in . . . [this state], especially in regard to gambling and the numbers rackets, the hands of the police are tied. Unless a search can be made prior to an arrest so that the defendant can be caught in the act of violating the gambling laws, or a search warrant issued, there is no other earthly way of apprehending such people along with evidence sufficient to convict them that is admissible in court.

Because of these two inadequacies of the law (slight punishment and conservative search and seizure laws with regard to gambling) the prosecutor's office and the police department are forced to find other means of punishing, harassing, and generally making life uneasy for gamblers.

This position, fantastic as it is to be that of a law-trained official, a guardian of the rule of law, illustrates how extensively only one of many police harassment programs in this jurisdiction can permeate the process and be tolerated by other decision makers in a system of criminal administration where decisions not to enforce are of extremely low visibility.

Having uncovered such a gambling-control program, an appraisal and review board should recommend that the police abandon such harassment activities because they are antagonistic to the rule of law. In addition, the board might advance secondary reasons for eliminating harassment by exposing the inconsistencies between this program and departmental justifications for its narcotics and assault policies. While unnecessary to the condemnation of what is fundamentally lawless nonenforcement, such exposure might cause the police to question the wisdom of actions based on a personal or departmental belief that the legislature has authorized excessively lenient sanctions and restrictive enforcement procedures. The comparison might emphasize the inconsistencies of police policy toward organized crime by exposing the clash between an informer program designed to rid the city of the "big supplier" and a harassment program which tends to consolidate control of the numbers racket in a few syndicates "big" enough to sustain the legal, bonding, and other "business" costs of continued interruptions and the confiscation of property. More importantly, it should cause a reexamination and redefinition of "work load" which was so significant in the rationalization of the assault policy. A cost accounting would no doubt reveal that a significant part of "work load," as presently defined by the police, includes expenditures of public funds for personnel and equipment employed in unlawful activities. Once harassment is perceived by municipal officials concerned with budgets as an unauthorized expenditure of public funds, consideration for increased awards to the police department might be conditioned upon a showing that existing resources are now deployed for authorized purposes. Such action should stimulate police cooperation in implementing the board's proposal for curtailing harassment.

Further, to effectuate its recommendation, the board might attempt to clarify and redefine the duties of the police by a reclassification of crimes which would emphasize the mandate that no more than *full enforcement* of the existing criminal law as defined by the legislature is expected. For many crimes, this may mean little or no *actual enforcement* because the values protected by procedural limitations are more important than the values which may be infringed by a particular offense. A board might propose, for example, that crimes be classified not only as felonies and misdemeanors, but in terms of active and passive police enforcement. An *active enforcement* designation for an offense would mean that individual police officers or specialized squads are to be assigned the task of ferreting out and even triggering violations. *Passive enforcement* would mean that the police are to assume a sit-back-and-wait posture, that is, that they invoke the criminal process only when the disturbing event is brought to their attention by personal observation during a routine tour of duty or by someone outside the police force registering a complaint. Designation of gambling, for example, as a *passive enforcement* offense would officially apprise the police that substantial expenditures of personnel and equipment for enforcement are not contemplated unless the local community expresses a low tolerance for such disturbing events by constantly bringing them to police attention. The adoption of this or a similar classification scheme might not only aid in training the police to understand that harassment is unlawful, but it may also provide the legislature with a device for officially allowing local differences in attitude toward certain offenses to be reflected in police practice and for testing the desirability of removing criminal sanctions from certain kinds of currently proscribed behavior.

VI. The mandate of *full enforcement,* under circumstances which compel selective enforcement, has placed the municipal police in an intolerable position. As a result, nonenforcement programs have developed undercover, in a hit-or-miss fashion, and without regard to impact on the overall administration of justice or the basic objectives of the criminal law. Legislatures, therefore, ought to reconsider what discretion, if any, the police must or should have in invoking the criminal process, and what devices, if any, should be designed to increase visibility and hence reviewability of these police decisions.

The ultimate answer is that the police should not be delegated discretion not to invoke the criminal law. It is recognized, of course, that the exercise of discretion cannot be completely eliminated where human beings are involved. The frailties of human language and human perception will always admit of borderline cases (although none of the situations analyzed in this article are "borderline"). But nonetheless, outside this margin of ambiguity, the police should operate in an atmosphere which exhorts and commands them to invoke impartially all criminal laws within the bounds of *full enforcement*. If a criminal law is ill advised, poorly defined, or too costly to enforce, efforts by the police to achieve *full enforcement* should generate pressures for legislative action. Responsibility for the enactment, amendment, and repeal of the criminal laws will not, then, be abandoned to the whim of each police officer or department, but retained where it belongs in a democracy—with elected representatives.

Equating *actual enforcement* with *full enforcement*, however, would be neither workable nor humane nor humanly possible under present conditions in most, if not all, jurisdictions. Even if there were "enough police" (and there are not) to enforce all of the criminal laws, too many people have come to rely on the nonenforcement of too many "obsolete" laws to justify the embarrassment, discomfort, and misery which would follow implementation of *full enforcement* programs for every crime. *Full enforcement* is a program for the future, a program which could be initiated with the least hardship when the states, perhaps stimulated by the work of the American Law Institute, enact new criminal codes clearing the books of obsolete offenses.

In the interim, legislatures should establish policy appraisal and review boards not only to facilitate coordination of municipal police policies with those of other key criminal law administrators, but also to assist commissions drafting new codes in reappraising basic objectives of the criminal law and in identifying laws which have become obsolete. To ensure that board appraisals and recommendations facilitate the integration of police policies with overall state policies and to ensure the cooperation of local authorities, board membership might include the state's attorney general, the chief justice of the supreme court, the chairman of the department of correction, the chairman of the board of parole and the chief of parole supervision, the chairman of the department of probation, the chairman of the judiciary committees of the legislature, the chief of the state police, the local chief of police, the local prosecutor, and the chief judge of each of the local trial courts. In order regularly and systematically to cull and retrieve information, the board should be assisted by a full-time director who has a staff of investigators well trained in social science research techniques. It should be given power to subpoena persons and records and to assign investigators to observe all phases of police activity including routine patrols, bookings, raids, and contacts with both the courts and the prosecutor's office. To clarify its functions, develop procedures, determine personnel requirements, and test the idea itself, the board's jurisdiction should initially be restricted to one or two major municipalities in the state. The board would review, appraise, and make recommendations concerning municipal police nonenforcement policies as well as follow up and review the consequences of implemented proposals. In order to make its job both manageable and less subject to attack by those who cherish local autonomy and who may see the establishment of a board as a step toward centralization, it would have solely an advisory function and limit its investigations to the enforcement of state laws, not municipal ordinances. And to ensure that board activity will not compromise current enforcement campaigns or place offenders on notice of new techniques of detection or sources of information, boards should be authorized, with court approval, to withhold specified reports from general publication for a limited and fixed time.

Like other administrative agencies, a policy appraisal and review board will in time no doubt suffer from marasmus and outlive its usefulness. But while viable, such a board has an enormous potential for uncovering in a very dramatic fashion basic inadequacies in the administration of criminal justice and for prompting a thorough community reexamination of the why of a law of crimes.

6

✵

Broken Windows

The Police
and Neighborhood Safety

James Q. Wilson
George L. Kelling

The role of the police in the United States today is being reexamined. After almost a half-century of emphasis on professionalism, crime control, and efficiency, James Q. Wilson and George L. Kelling argue that there should be a shift in patrol strategy toward a focus on order maintenance and community accountability.

In the mid-1970s, the state of New Jersey announced a "Safe and Clean Neighborhoods Program," designed to improve the quality of community life in twenty-eight cities. As part of that program, the state provided money to help cities take police officers out of their patrol cars and assign them to walking beats. The governor and other state officials were enthusiastic about using foot patrol as a way of cutting crime, but many police chiefs were skeptical. Foot patrol, in their eyes, had been pretty much discredited. It reduced the mobility of the police, who thus had difficulty responding to citizen calls for service, and it weakened headquarters control over patrol officers.

Many police officers also disliked foot patrol, but for different reasons: it was hard work, it kept them outside on cold, rainy nights, and it reduced their chances for making a "good pinch." In some departments, assigning officers to foot patrol had been used as a form of punishment. And academic experts on policing doubted that foot patrol would have any impact on crime rates; it was,

Source: Atlantic Monthly 249 (March 1982): 29–38.

in the opinion of most, little more than a sop to public opinion. But since the state was paying for it, the local authorities were willing to go along.

Five years after the program started, the Police Foundation, in Washington, D.C., published an evaluation of the foot-patrol project. Based on its analysis of a carefully controlled experiment carried out chiefly in Newark, the foundation concluded, to the surprise of hardly anyone, that foot patrol had not reduced crime rates. But residents of the foot-patrolled neighborhoods seemed to feel more secure than persons in other areas, tended to believe that crime had been reduced, and seemed to take fewer steps to protect themselves from crime (staying at home with the doors locked, for example). Moreover, citizens in the foot-patrol areas had a more favorable opinion of the police than did those living elsewhere. And officers walking beats had higher morale, greater job satisfaction, and a more favorable attitude toward citizens in their neighborhoods than did officers assigned to patrol cars.

These findings may be taken as evidence that the skeptics were right—foot patrol has no effect on crime; it merely fools the citizens into thinking that they are safer. But in our view, and in the view of the authors of the Police Foundation study (of whom Kelling was one), the citizens of Newark were not fooled at all. They knew what the foot-patrol officers were doing, they knew it was different from what motorized officers do, and they knew that having officers walk beats did in fact make their neighborhoods safer.

But how can a neighborhood be "safer" when the crime rate has not gone down—in fact, may have gone up? Finding the answer requires first that we understand what most often frightens people in public places. Many citizens, of course, are primarily frightened by crime, especially crime involving a sudden, violent attack by a stranger. This risk is very real, in Newark as in many large cities. But we tend to overlook or forget another source of fear: the fear of being bothered by disorderly people—not violent people, nor, necessarily, criminals, but disreputable or obstreperous or unpredictable people: panhandlers, drunks, addicts, rowdy teenagers, prostitutes, loiterers, the mentally disturbed.

What foot-patrol officers did was to elevate, to the extent they could, the level of public order in these neighborhoods. Though the neighborhoods were predominantly black and the foot patrolmen were mostly white, this "order-maintenance" function of the police was performed to the general satisfaction of both parties.

One of us (Kelling) spent many hours walking with Newark foot-patrol officers to see how they defined "order" and what they did to maintain it. One beat was typical: a busy but dilapidated area in the heart of Newark, with many abandoned buildings, marginal shops (several of which prominently displayed knives and straight-edged razors in their windows), one large department store, and, most important, a train station and several major bus stops. Though the area was run-down, its streets were filled with people, because it was a major transportation center. The good order of this area was important not only to those who lived and worked there but also to many others who had to move through it on their way home, to supermarkets, or to factories.

The people on the street were primarily black; the officers who walked the street were white. The people made up of "regulars" and "strangers." Regulars included both "decent folk" and some drunks and derelicts who were always there but who "knew their place." Strangers were, well, strangers, and viewed suspiciously, sometimes apprehensively. The officer—call him Kelly—knew who the regulars were, and they knew him. As he saw his job, he was to keep an eye on strangers, and make certain that the disreputable regulars observed some informal but widely understood rules. Drunks and addicts could sit on the stoops, but could not lie down. People could drink on the side streets, but not on the main intersection. Bottles had to be in paper bags. Talking to, bothering, or begging from people waiting at the bus stop was strictly forbidden. If a dispute erupted between a businessman and a customer, the businessman was assumed to be right, especially if the customer was a stranger. If a stranger loitered, Kelly would ask him if he had any means of support and what his business was; if he gave unsatisfactory answers, he was sent on his way. Persons who broke the informal rules, especially those who bothered people waiting at bus stops, were arrested for vagrancy. Noisy teenagers were told to keep quiet.

These rules were defined and enforced in collaboration with the "regulars" on the street. Another neighborhood might have different rules, but these, everybody understood, were the rules for *this* neighborhood. If someone violated them, the regulars not only turned to Kelly for help but also ridiculed the violator. Sometimes what Kelly did could be described as "enforcing the law," but just as often it involved taking informal or extralegal steps to help protect what the neighborhood had decided was the appropriate level of public order. Some of the things he did probably would not withstand a legal challenge.

A determined skeptic might acknowledge that a skilled foot-patrol officer can maintain order but still insist that this sort of "order" has little to do with the real sources of community fear—that is, with violent crime. To a degree, that is true. But two things must be borne in mind. First, outside observers should not assume that they know how much of the anxiety now endemic in many big-city neighborhoods stems from a fear of "real" crime and how much from a sense that the street is disorderly, a source of distasteful, worrisome encounters. The people of Newark, to judge from their behavior and their remarks to interviewers, apparently assign a high value to public order, and feel relieved and reassured when the police help them maintain that order.

Second, at the community level, disorder and crime are usually inextricably linked, in a kind of developmental sequence. Social psychologists and police officers tend to agree that if a window in a building is broken *and is left unrepaired*, all the rest of the windows will soon be broken. This is as true in nice neighborhoods as in run-down ones. Window breaking does not necessarily occur on a large scale because some areas are inhabited by determined window breakers whereas others are populated by window lovers; rather, one unrepaired broken window is a signal that no one cares, and so breaking more windows costs nothing. (It has always been fun.)

Philip Zimbardo, a Stanford psychologist, reported in 1969 on some experiments testing the broken-window theory. He arranged to have an automobile without license plates parked with its hood up on a street in the Bronx and a comparable automobile on a street in Palo Alto, California. The car in the Bronx was attacked by "vandals" within ten minutes of its "abandonment." The first to arrive were a family—father, mother, and young son—who removed the radiator and battery. Within twenty-four hours, virtually everything of value had been removed. Then random destruction began—windows were smashed, parts torn off, upholstery ripped. Children began to use the car as a playground. Most of the adult "vandals" were well-dressed, apparently clean-cut whites. The car in Palo Alto sat untouched for more than a week. Then Zimbardo smashed part of it with a sledgehammer. Soon, passersby were joining in. Within a few hours, the car had been turned upside down and utterly destroyed. Again, the "vandals" appeared to be primarily respectable whites.

Untended property becomes fair game for people out for fun or plunder, and even for people who ordinarily would not dream of doing such things and who probably consider themselves law-abiding. Because of the nature of community life in the Bronx—its anonymity, the frequency with which cars are abandoned and things are stolen or broken, the past experience of "no one caring"—vandalism begins much more quickly than it does in staid Palo Alto, where people have come to believe that private possessions are cared for, and that mischievous behavior is costly. But vandalism can occur anywhere once communal barriers—the sense of mutual regard and the obligations of civility—are lowered by actions that seem to signal that "no one cares."

We suggest that "untended" behavior also leads to the breakdown of community controls. A stable neighborhood of families who care for their homes, mind each other's children, and confidently frown on unwanted intruders can change, in a few years or even a few months, to an inhospitable and frightening jungle. A piece of property is abandoned, weeds grow up, a window is smashed. Adults stop scolding rowdy children; the children, emboldened, become more rowdy. Families move out, unattached adults move in. Teenagers gather in front of the corner store. The merchant asks them to move; they refuse. Fights occur. Litter accumulates. People start drinking in front of the grocery; in time, an inebriate slumps to the sidewalk and is allowed to sleep it off. Pedestrians are approached by panhandlers.

At this point it is not inevitable that serious crime will flourish or violent attacks on strangers will occur. But many residents will think that crime, especially violent crime is on the rise, and they will modify their behavior accordingly. They will use the streets less often, and when on the streets will stay apart from their fellows, moving with averted eyes, silent lips, and hurried steps. "Don't get involved." For some residents, this growing atomization will matter little, because the neighborhood is not their "home" but "the place where they live." Their interests are elsewhere; they are cosmopolitans. But it will matter greatly to other people, whose lives derive meaning and satisfaction from local attachments rather than worldly involvement; for them, the neighborhood will cease to exist except for a few reliable friends whom they arrange to meet.

Such an area is vulnerable to criminal invasion. Though it is not inevitable, it is more likely that here, rather than in places where people are confident they can regulate public behavior by informal controls, drugs will change hands, prostitutes will solicit, and cars will be stripped. That the drunks will be robbed by boys who do it as a lark, and the prostitutes' customers will be robbed by men who do it purposefully and perhaps violently. That muggings will occur.

Among those who often find it difficult to move away from this are the elderly. Surveys of citizens suggest that the elderly are much less likely to be the victims of crime than younger persons, and some have inferred from this that the well-known fear of crime voiced by the elderly is an exaggeration: perhaps we ought not to design special programs to protect older persons; perhaps we should even try to talk them out of their mistaken fears. This argument misses the point. The prospect of a confrontation with an obstreperous teenager or a drunken panhandler can be as fear-inducing for defenseless persons as the prospect of meeting an actual robber; indeed, to a defenseless person, the two kinds of confrontation are often indistinguishable. Moreover, the lower rate at which the elderly are victimized is a measure of the steps they have already taken—chiefly, staying behind locked doors—to minimize the risks they face. Young men are more frequently attacked than older women, not because they are easier or more lucrative targets but because they are on the streets more.

Nor is the connection between disorderliness and fear made only by the elderly. Susan Estrich of the Harvard Law School, has recently gathered together a number of surveys on the sources of public fear. One, done in Portland, Oregon, indicates that three-fourths of the adults interviewed cross to the other side of a street when they see a gang of teenagers; another survey, in Baltimore, discovered that nearly half would cross the street to avoid even a single strange youth. When an interviewer asked people in a housing project where the most dangerous spot was, they mentioned a place where young persons gathered to drink and play music, despite the fact that not a single crime had occurred there. In Boston public housing projects, the greatest fear was expressed by persons living in the buildings where disorderliness and incivility, not crime, were the greatest. Knowing this helps one understand the significance of such otherwise harmless displays as subway graffiti. As Nathan Glazer has written, the proliferation of graffiti, even when not obscene, confronts the subway rider with the "inescapable knowledge that the environment he must endure for an hour or more a day is uncontrolled and uncontrollable, and that anyone can invade it to do whatever damage and mischief the mind suggests."

In response to fear, people avoid one another, weakening controls. Sometimes they call the police. Patrol cars arrive, an occasional arrest occurs, but crime continues and disorder is not abated. Citizens complain to the police chief, but he explains that his department is low on personnel and that the courts do not punish petty or first-time offenders. To the residents, the police who arrive in squad cars are either ineffective or uncaring; to the police, the residents are animals who deserve each other. The citizens may soon stop calling the police, because "they can't do anything."

The process we call urban decay has occurred for centuries in every city. But what is happening today is different in at least two important respects. First, in the period before, say, World War II, city dwellers—because of money costs, transportation difficulties, familial and church connections—could rarely move away from neighborhood problems. When movement did occur, it tended to be along public-transit routes. Now mobility has become exceptionally easy for all but the poorest or those who are blocked by racial prejudice. Earlier crime waves had a kind of built-in self-correcting mechanism: the determination of a neighborhood or community to reassert control over its turf. Areas in Chicago, New York, and Boston would experience crime and gang wars, and then normalcy would return, as the families for whom no alternative residences were possible reclaimed their authority over the streets.

Second, the police in this earlier period assisted in that reassertion of authority by acting, sometimes violently, on behalf of the community. Young toughs were roughed up, people were arrested "on suspicion" or for vagrancy, and prostitutes and petty thieves were routed. "Rights" were something enjoyed by decent folk, and perhaps also by the serious professional criminal, who avoided violence and could afford a lawyer.

This pattern of policing was not an aberration or the result of occasional excess. From the earliest days of the nation, the police function was seen primarily as that of a night watchman: to maintain order against the chief threats to order—fire, wild animals, and disreputable behavior. Solving crimes was viewed not as a police responsibility but as a private one. In the March 1969 *Atlantic*, one of us (Wilson) wrote a brief account of how the police role had slowly changed from maintaining order to fighting crimes. The change began with the creation of private detectives (often ex-criminals), who worked on a contingency-fee basis for individuals who had suffered losses. In time, the detectives were absorbed into municipal police agencies and paid a regular salary; simultaneously, the responsibility for prosecuting thieves was shifted from the aggrieved private citizen to the professional prosecutor. The process was not complete in most places until the twentieth century.

In the 1960s, when urban riots were a major problem, social scientists began to explore carefully the order-maintenance function of the police, and to suggest ways of improving it—not to make streets safer (its original function) but to reduce the incidence of mass violence. Order maintenance became, to a degree, co-terminous with "community relations." But, as the crime wave that began in the early 1960s continued without abatement throughout the decade and into the 1970s, attention shifted to the role of the police as crime fighters. Studies of police behavior ceased, by and large, to be accounts of the order-maintenance function and became, instead, efforts to propose and test ways whereby the police could solve more crimes, make more arrests, and gather better evidence. If these things could be done, social scientists assumed, citizens would be less fearful.

A great deal was accomplished during this transition, as both police chiefs and outside experts emphasized the crime-fighting function in their plans, in the allocation of resources, and in deployment of personnel. The police may well have become better crime fighters as a result. And doubtless they remained aware of their responsibility for order. But the link between order maintenance and crime prevention, so obvious to earlier generations, was forgotten.

That link is similar to the process whereby one broken window becomes many. The citizen who fears the ill-smelling drunk, the rowdy teenager, or the importuning beggar is not merely expressing his distaste for unseemly behavior, he is also giving voice to a bit of folk wisdom that happens to be a correct generalization—namely, that serious street crime flourishes in areas in which disorderly behavior goes unchecked. The unchecked panhandler is, in effect, the first broken window. Muggers and robbers, whether opportunistic or professional, believe they reduce their chances of being caught or even identified if they operate on streets where potential victims are already intimidated by prevailing conditions. If the neighborhood cannot keep a bothersome panhandler from annoying passersby, the thief may reason, it is even less likely to call the police to identify a potential mugger or to interfere if the mugging actually takes place.

Some police administrators concede that this process occurs, but argue that motorized patrol officers can deal with it as effectively as foot patrol officers. We are not so sure. In theory, an officer in a squad car can observe as much as an officer on foot; in theory, the former can talk to as many people as the latter. But the reality of police–citizen encounters is powerfully altered by the automobile. An officer on foot cannot separate himself from the street people; if he is approached, only his uniform and his personality can help him manage whatever is about to happen. And he can never be certain what that will be—a request for directions, a plea for help, an angry denunciation, a teasing remark, a confused babble, a threatening gesture.

In a car, an officer is more likely to deal with street people by rolling down the window and looking at them. The door and the window exclude the approaching citizen; they are a barrier. Some officers take advantage of this barrier, perhaps unconsciously, by acting differently if in the car than they would on foot. We have seen this countless times. The police car pulls up to a corner where teenagers are gathered. The window is rolled down. The officer stares at the youths. They stare back. The officer says to one, "C'mere." He saunters over, conveying to his friends by his elaborate casual style the idea that he is not intimidated by authority. "What's your name?" "Chuck." "Chuck who?" "Chuck Jones." "What'ya doing, Chuck?" "Nothin'." "Got a P.O. [parole officer]?" "Nah." "Sure?" "Yeah." "Stay out of trouble, Chuckie." Meanwhile, the other boys laugh and exchange comments among themselves, probably at the officer's expense. The officer stares harder. He cannot be certain what is being said, nor can he join in and, by displaying his own skill at street banter, prove that he cannot be "put down." In the process, the officer has learned almost nothing, and the boys have decided the officer is an alien force who can safely be disregarded, even mocked.

Our experience is that most citizens like to talk to a police officer. Such exchanges give them a sense of importance, provide them with the basis for gossip, and allow them to explain to the authorities what is worrying them (whereby they gain a modest but significant sense of having "done something" about the problem). You approach a person on foot more easily, and talk to him more readily, than you do a person in a car. Moreover, you can more easily retain some anonymity if you draw an officer aside for a private chat. Suppose you want to pass on a tip about who is stealing handbags, or who offered to sell you a stolen TV. In the inner city, the culprit, in all likelihood, lives nearby. To walk up to a marked patrol car and lean in the window is to convey a visible signal that you are a "fink."

The essence of the police role in maintaining order is to reinforce the informal control mechanisms of the community itself. The police cannot, without committing extraordinary resources, provide a substitute for that informal control. On the other hand, to reinforce those natural forces the police must accommodate them. And therein lies the problem.

Should police activity on the street be shaped, in important ways, by the standards of the neighborhood rather than by the rules of the state? Over the past two decades, the shift of police from order maintenance to law enforcement has brought them increasingly under the influence of legal restrictions, provoked by media complaints and enforced by court decisions and departmental orders. As a consequence, the order-maintenance functions of the police are now governed by rules developed to control police relations with suspected criminals. This is, we think, an entirely new development. For centuries, the role of the police as watchmen was judged primarily not in terms of its compliance with appropriate procedures but rather in terms of its attaining a desired objective. The objective was order, an inherently ambiguous term but a condition that people in a given community recognized when they saw it. The means were the same as those the community itself would employ, if its members were sufficiently determined, courageous, and authoritative. Detecting and apprehending criminals, by contrast, was a means to an end, not an end in itself; a judicial determination of guilt or innocence was the hoped-for result of the law-enforcement mode. From the first, the police were expected to follow rules defining that process, though states differed in how stringent the rules should be. The criminal-apprehension process was always understood to involve individual rights, the violation of which was unacceptable because it meant that the violating officer would be acting as a judge and jury—and that was not his job. Guilt or innocence was to be determined by universal standards under special procedures.

Ordinarily, no judge or jury ever sees the persons caught up in a dispute over the appropriate level of neighborhood order. That is true not only because most cases are handled informally on the street but also because no universal standards are available to settle arguments over disorder, and thus a judge may not be any wiser or more effective than a police officer. Until quite recently in many states, and even today in some places, the police make arrests on such charges as "suspicious person" or "vagrancy" or "public drunkenness"—charges with scarcely any legal meaning. These charges exist not because society wants judges to punish vagrants or drunks but because it wants an officer to have the legal tools to remove undesirable persons from a neighborhood when informal efforts to preserve order in the streets have failed.

Once we begin to think of all aspects of police work as involving the application of universal rules under special procedures, we inevitably ask what constitutes an "undesirable person" and why we should "criminalize" vagrancy or drunkenness. A strong and commendable desire to see that people are treated fairly makes us worry about allowing the police to rout persons who are undesirable by some vague or parochial standard. A growing and not-so-commendable utilitarianism leads us to doubt that any behavior that does not "hurt" another person should be made illegal. And thus many of us who watch over the police are reluctant to allow them to perform, in the only way they can, a function that every neighborhood desperately wants them to perform.

This wish to "decriminalize" disreputable behavior that "harms no one"— and thus remove the ultimate sanction the police can employ to maintain neighborhood order—is, we think, a mistake. Arresting a single drunk or a single vagrant who has harmed no identifiable person seems unjust, and in a sense it is. But failing to do anything about a score of drunks or a hundred vagrants may destroy an entire community. A particular rule that seems to make sense in the individual case makes no sense when it is made a universal rule and applied to all cases. It makes no sense because it fails to take into account the connection between one broken window left untended and a thousand broken windows. Of course, agencies other than the police could attend to the problems posed by drunks or the mentally ill, but in most communities—especially where the "deinstitutionalization" movement has been strong—they do not.

The concern about equity is more serious. We might agree that certain behavior makes one person more undesirable than another, but how do we ensure that age or skin color or natural origin or harmless mannerisms will not also become the basis for distinguishing the undesirable from the desirable? How do we ensure, in short, that the police do not become the agents of neighborhood bigotry?

We can offer no wholly satisfactory answer to this important question. We are not confident that there *is* a satisfactory answer, except to hope that by their selection, training, and supervision the police will be inculcated with a clear sense of the outer limit of their discretionary authority. That limit, roughly, is this—the police exist to help regulate behavior, not to maintain the racial or ethnic purity of a neighborhood.

Consider the case of the Robert Taylor Homes in Chicago, one of the largest public housing projects in the country. It is home for nearly 20,000 people, all black, and extends over ninety-two acres along South State Street. It was named after a distinguished black who had been, during the 1940s, chairman of the Chicago Housing Authority. Not long after it opened, in 1962, relations between project residents and the police deteriorated badly. The citizens felt that the police were insensitive or brutal; the police, in turn, complained of unprovoked attacks on them. Some Chicago officers tell of times when they were afraid to enter the Homes. Crime rates soared.

Today, the atmosphere has changed. Police—citizen relations have improved—apparently, both sides learned something from the earlier experience. Recently, a boy stole a purse and ran off. Several young persons who saw the theft voluntarily passed along to the police information on the identity and residence of the thief, and they did this publicly, with friends and neighbors looking on. But problems persist, chief among them the presence of youth gangs that terrorize residents and recruit members in the project. The people expect the police to "do something" about this, and the police are determined to do just that.

But do what? Though the police can obviously make arrests whenever a gang member breaks the law, a gang can form, recruit, and congregate without breaking the law. And only a tiny fraction of gang-related crimes can be solved by an arrest; thus, if an arrest is the only recourse for the police, the residents' fears will go unassuaged. The police will soon feel helpless, and the residents will again believe that the police "do nothing." What the police in fact do is to chase known gang members out of the project. In the words of one officer, "We kick ass." Project residents both know and approve of this. The tacit police—citizen alliance in the project is reinforced by the police view that the cops and the gangs are the two rival sources of power in the area, and that the gangs are not going to win.

None of this is easily reconciled with any conception of due process or fair treatment. Since both residents and gang members are black, race is not a factor. But it could be. Suppose a white project gang confronted a black gang, or vice versa. We would be apprehensive about the police taking sides. But the substantive problem remains the same: How can the police strengthen the informal social-control mechanisms of natural communities in order to minimize fear in public places? Law enforcement, per se, is no answer. A gang can weaken or destroy a community by standing about in a menacing fashion and speaking rudely to passersby without breaking the law.

We have difficulty thinking about such matters, not simply because the ethical and legal issues are so complex but because we have become accustomed to thinking of the law in essentially individualistic terms. The law defines *my* rights, punishes *his* behavior, and is applied by *that* officer because of *this* harm. We assume, in thinking this way, that what is good for the individual will be good for the community, and what doesn't matter when it happens to one person won't matter when it happens to many. Ordinarily, those are plausible assumptions. But in cases where behavior that is tolerable to one person is intolerable to many others, the reactions of the others—fear, withdrawal, flight—may ultimately make matters worse for everyone, including the individual who first professed his indifference.

It may be their greater sensitivity to communal as opposed to individual needs that helps explain why the residents of small communities are more satisfied with their police than are the residents of similar neighborhoods in big cities. Elinor Ostrom and her co-workers at Indiana University compared the perception of police services in two poor, all-black Illinois towns—Phoenix and East Chicago Heights—with those of three comparable all-black neighborhoods in Chicago. The level of criminal victimization and the quality of police-community relations appeared to be about the same in the towns and the Chicago neighborhoods. But the citizens living in their own villages were much more likely than those living in the Chicago neighborhoods to say that they do not stay at home for fear of crime, to agree that the local police have "the right to take any action necessary" to deal with problems, and to agree that the police "look out for the needs of the average citizen." It is possible that the residents and the police of the small towns saw themselves as engaged in a collaborative effort to maintain a certain standard of communal life, whereas those of the big city felt themselves to be simply requesting and supplying particular services on an individual basis.

If this is true, how should a wise police chief deploy his meager forces? The first answer is that nobody knows for certain, and the most prudent course of action would be to try further variations on the Newark experiment, to see more precisely what works in what kinds of neighborhoods. The second answer is also a hedge—many aspects of order maintenance in neighborhoods can probably best be handled in ways that involve the police minimally, if at all. A busy, bustling shopping center and a quiet, well-tended suburb may need almost no visible police presence. In both cases, the ratio of respectable to disreputable people is ordinarily so high as to make informal social control effective.

Even in areas that are in jeopardy from disorderly elements, citizen action without substantial police involvement may be sufficient. Meetings between teenagers who like to hang out on a particular corner and adults who want to use that corner might well lead to an amicable agreement on a set of rules about how many people can be allowed to congregate, where, and when. Where no understanding is possible—or, if possible, not observed—citizen patrols may be a sufficient response. There are two traditions of communal involvement in maintaining order. One, that of the "community watchmen," as old as the first settlement of the New World. Until well into the nineteenth century, volunteer watchmen, not policemen, patrolled their communities to keep order. They did so, by and large, without taking the law into their own hands—without, that is, punishing persons or using force. Their presence deterred disorder or alerted the community to disorder that could not be deterred. There are hundreds of such efforts today in communities all across the nation. Perhaps the best known is that of the Guardian Angels, a group of unarmed young persons in distinctive berets and T-shirts, who first came to public attention when they began patrolling the New York City subways but who claim now to have chapters in more than thirty American cities. Unfortunately, we have little information about the effect of these groups on crime. It is possible, however, that whatever their effect on crime, citizens find their presence reassuring, and that they thus contribute to maintaining a sense of order and civility.

The second tradition is that of the "vigilante." Rarely a feature of the settled communities of the East, it was primarily to be found in those frontier towns that grew up in advance of the reach of government. More than 350 vigilante groups are known to have existed; their distinctive feature was that their members did take the law into their own hands, by acting as judge, jury, and often executioner as well as policeman. Today, the vigilante movement is conspicuous by its rarity, despite the great fear expressed by citizens that the older cities are becoming "urban frontiers." But some community watchmen groups have skirted the line, and others may cross it in the future. An ambiguous case,

Communal involvement

reported in the *Wall Street Journal*, involved a citizens' patrol in the Silver Lake area of Belleville, New Jersey. A leader told the reporter, "We look for outsiders." If a few teenagers from outside the neighborhood enter it, "we ask them their business," he said. "If they say they're going down the street to see Mrs. Jones, fine, we let them pass. But then we follow them down the block to make sure they're really going to see Mrs. Jones."

Though citizens can do a great deal, the police are plainly the key to order maintenance. For one thing, many communities, such as the Robert Taylor Homes, cannot do the job by themselves. For another, no citizen in a neighborhood, even an organized one, is likely to feel the sense of responsibility that wearing a badge confers. Psychologists have done many studies on why people fail to go to the aid of persons being attacked or seeking help, and they have learned that the cause is not "apathy" or "selfishness" but the absence of some plausible grounds for feeling that one must personally accept responsibility. Ironically, avoiding responsibility is easier when a lot of people are standing about. On streets and in public places, where order is so important, many people are likely to be "around," a fact that reduces the chance of any one person acting as the agent of the community. The police officer's uniform singles him out as a person who must accept responsibility if asked. In addition, officers, more easily than their fellow citizens, can be expected to distinguish between what is necessary to protect the safety of the street and what merely protects its ethnic purity.

But the police forces of America are losing, not gaining, members. Some cities have suffered substantial cuts in the number of officers available for duty. These cuts are not likely to be reversed in the near future. Therefore, each department must assign its existing officers with great care. Some neighborhoods are so demoralized and crime-ridden as to make foot patrol useless; the best the police can do with limited resources is respond to the enormous number of calls for service. Other neighborhoods are so stable and serene as to make foot patrol unnecessary. The key is to identify neighborhoods at the tipping point—where the public order is deteriorating but not unreclaimable, where the streets are used frequently but by apprehensive people, where a window is likely to be broken at any time, and must quickly be fixed if all are not to be shattered.

Most police departments do not have ways of systematically identifying such areas and assigning officers to them. Officers are assigned on the basis of crime rates (meaning that marginally threatened areas are often stripped so that police can investigate crimes in areas where the situation is hopeless) or on the basis of calls for service (despite the fact that most citizens do not call the police when they are merely frightened or annoyed). To allocate patrol wisely, the department must look at the neighborhoods and decide, from firsthand evidence, where an additional officer will make the greatest difference in promoting a sense of safety.

One way to stretch limited police resources is being tried in some public housing projects. Tenant organizations hire off-duty police officers for patrol work in their buildings. The costs are not high (at least not per resident), the officer likes the additional income, and the residents feel safer. Such arrangements are probably more successful than hiring private watchmen, and the Newark experiment helps us understand why. A private security guard may deter crime or misconduct by his presence, and he may go to the aid of persons needing help, but he may well not intervene—that is, control or drive away—someone challenging community standards. Being a sworn officer—a "real cop"—seems to give one the confidence, the sense of duty, and the aura of authority necessary to perform this difficult task.

Patrol officers might be encouraged to go to and from duty stations on public transportation and, while on the bus or subway car, enforce rules about smoking, drinking, disorderly conduct, and the like. The enforcement need involve nothing more than ejecting the offender (the offense, after all, is not one with which a booking officer or a judge wishes to be bothered). Perhaps the random but relentless maintenance of standards on buses would lead to conditions on buses that approximate the level of civility we now take for granted on airplanes.

But the most important requirement is to think that to maintain order in precarious situations is a vital job. The police know this is one of their functions, and they also believe, correctly, that it cannot be done to the exclusion of criminal investigation and responding to calls. We may have encouraged them to suppose, however, on the basis of our oft-repeated concerns about serious, violent crime, that they will be judged exclusively on their capacity as crime fighters. To the extent that this is the case, police administrators will continue to concentrate police personnel in the highest-crime areas (though not necessarily in the areas most vulnerable to criminal invasion), emphasize their training in the law and criminal apprehension (and not their training in managing street life), and join too quickly in campaigns to decriminalize "harmless" behavior (though public drunkenness, street prostitution, and pornographic displays can destroy a community more quickly than any team of professional burglars).

Above all, we must return to our long-abandoned view that the police ought to protect communities as well as individuals. Our crime statistics and victimization surveys measure individual losses, but they do not measure communal losses. Just as physicians now recognize the importance of fostering health rather than simply treating illness, so the police—and the rest of us—ought to recognize the importance of maintaining, intact, communities without broken windows.

7

❂

A Sketch of
the Policeman's
"Working Personality"

Jerome H. Skolnick

Each of us views the real world through cognitive lenses that influence our perception and interpretation of events. Because their role contains the two important variables of danger and authority, police officers develop a distinctive view of the world. Sociologist Jerome Skolnick explores this view and shows how the "working personality" affects the actions of the police.

A recurrent theme of the sociology of occupations is the effect of a man's work on his outlook on the world.[1] Doctors, janitors, lawyers, and industrial workers develop distinctive ways of perceiving and responding to their environment. Here we shall concentrate on analyzing certain outstanding elements in the police milieu, danger, authority, and efficiency, as they combine to generate distinctive cognitive and behavioral responses in police: a "working personality." Such an analysis does not suggest that all police are alike in "working personality," but that there are distinctive cognitive tendencies in police as an occupational grouping. Some of these may be found in other occupations sharing similar problems. So far as exposure to danger is concerned, the policeman may be likened to the soldier. His problems as an authority bear a certain similarity to those of the school-teacher, and the pressures he feels to prove himself efficient are not unlike

Source: From *Justice without Trial: Law Enforcement in a Democratic Society* by Jerome H. Skolnick (New York: John Wiley & Sons, 1966), pp. 42–62. Reprinted by permission of the author and publisher.

those felt by the industrial worker. The combination of these elements, however, is unique to the policeman. Thus, the police, as a result of combined features of their social situation, tend to develop ways of looking at the world distinctive to themselves, cognitive lenses through which to see situations and events. The strength of the lenses may be weaker or stronger depending on certain conditions, but they are ground on a similar axis.

Analysis of the policeman's cognitive propensities is necessary to understand the practical dilemma faced by police required to maintain order under a democratic rule of law. . . . A conception of order is [essential] to the resolution of this dilemma. [We suggest] that the paramilitary character of police organization naturally leads to a high evaluation of similarity, routine, and predictability. Our intention is to emphasize features of the policeman's environment interacting with the paramilitary police organization to generate a "working personality." Such an intervening concept should aid in explaining how the social environment of police affects their capacity to respond to the rule of law.

[Emphasis] will be placed on the division of labor in the police department . . . ; "operational law enforcement" [cannot] be understood outside these special work assignments. It is therefore important to explain how the hypothesis emphasizing the generalizability of the policeman's "working personality" is compatible with the idea that police division of labor is an important analytic dimension for understanding "operational law enforcement." Compatibility is evident when one considers the different levels of analysis at which the hypotheses are being developed. Janowitz states, for example, that the military profession is more than an occupation; it is a "style of life" because the occupational claims over one's daily existence extend well beyond official duties. He is quick to point out that any profession performing a crucial "life and death" task, such as medicine, the ministry, or the police, develops such claims.[2] A conception like "working personality" of police should be understood to suggest an analytic breadth similar to that of "style of life." That is, just as the professional behavior of military officers with similar "styles of life" may differ drastically depending upon whether they command an infantry battalion or participate in the work of an intelligence unit, so too does the professional behavior of police officers with similar "working personalities" vary with their assignments.

The policeman's "working personality" is most highly developed in his constabulary role of the man on the beat. For analytical purposes that role is sometimes regarded as an enforcement specialty, but in this general discussion of policemen as they comport themselves while working, the uniformed "cop" is seen as the foundation for the policeman's "working personality." There is a sound organizational basis for making this assumption. The police, unlike the military, draw no caste distinction in socialization, even though their order of ranked titles approximates the military's. Thus, one cannot join a local police department as, for instance, a lieutenant, as a West Point graduate joins the army. Every officer of rank must serve an apprenticeship as a patrolman. This feature of police organization means that the constabulary role is the primary one for all police officers, and that whatever the special requirements of roles in enforcement specialties, they are carried out with a common background of constabulary experience.

The process by which this "personality" is developed may be summarized: the policeman's role contains two principal variables, danger and authority, which should be interpreted in the light of a "constant" pressure to appear efficient.[3] The element of danger seems to make the policeman especially attentive to signs indicating a potential for violence and lawbreaking. As a result, the policeman is generally a "suspicious" person. Furthermore, the character of the policeman's work makes him less desirable as a friend, since norms of friendship implicate others in his work. Accordingly, the element of danger isolates the policeman socially from that segment of the citizenry which he regards as symbolically dangerous and also from the conventional citizenry with whom he identifies.

The element of authority reinforces the element of danger in isolating the policeman. Typically, the policeman is required to enforce laws representing puritanical morality, such as those prohibiting drunkenness, and also laws regulating the flow of public activity, such as traffic laws. In these situations the policeman directs the citizenry, whose typical response denies recognition of his authority and stresses his obligation to respond to danger. The kind of man who responds well to danger, however, does not normally subscribe to codes of puritanical morality. As a result, the policeman is unusually liable to the charge of hypocrisy. That the whole civilian world is an audience for the policeman further promotes police isolation and, in consequence, solidarity. Finally, danger undermines the judicious use of authority. Where danger, as in Britain, is relatively less, the judicious application of authority is facilitated. Hence, British police may appear to be somewhat more attached to the rule of law, when, in fact, they may appear so because they face less danger, and they are as a rule better skilled than American police in creating the appearance of conformity to procedural regulations.

THE SYMBOLIC ASSAILANT
AND POLICE CULTURE

In attempting to understand the policeman's view of the world, it is useful to raise a more general question: What are the conditions under which police, as authorities, may be threatened?[4] To answer this, we must look to the situation of the policeman in the community. One attribute of many characterizing the policeman's role stands out: the policeman is required to respond to assaults against persons and property. When a radio call reports an armed robbery and gives a description of the man involved, every policeman, regardless of assignment, is responsible for the criminal's apprehension. The raison d'être of the policeman and the criminal law, the underlying collectively held moral sentiments which justify penal sanctions, arises ultimately and most clearly from the threat of violence and the possibility of danger to the community. Police who "lobby" for severe narcotics laws, for instance, justify their position on grounds that the addict is a harbinger of danger since, it is maintained, he requires $100 a day to support his habit, and he must steal to get it. Even though the addict is not typically a violent criminal, criminal penalties for addiction are supported on grounds that he may become one.

The policeman, because his work requires him to be occupied continually with potential violence, develops a perceptual shorthand to identify certain kinds of people as symbolic assailants, that is, as persons who use gesture, language, and attire that the policeman has come to recognize as a prelude to violence. This does not mean that violence by the symbolic assailant is necessarily predictable. On the contrary, the policeman responds to the vague indication of danger suggested by appearance.[5] Like the animals of the experimental psychologist, the policeman finds the threat of random damage more compelling than a predetermined and inevitable punishment.

Nor, to qualify for the status of symbolic assailant, need an individual ever have used violence. A man backing out of a jewelry store with a gun in one hand and jewelry in the other would qualify even if the gun were a toy and he had never in his life fired a real pistol. To the policeman in the situation, the man's personal history is momentarily immaterial. There is only one relevant sign: a gun signifying danger. Similarly, a young man may suggest the threat of violence to the policeman by his manner of walking or "strutting," the insolence in the demeanor being registered by the policeman as a possible preamble to later attack.[6] Signs vary from area to area, but a youth dressed in a black leather jacket and motorcycle boots is sure to draw at least a suspicious glance from a policeman.

Policemen themselves do not necessarily emphasize the peril associated with their work when questioned directly, and may even have well-developed strategies of denial. The element of danger is so integral to the policeman's work that explicit recognition might induce emotional barriers to work performance. Thus, one patrol officer observed that more police have been killed and injured in automobile accidents in the past ten years than from gunfire. Although his assertion is true, he neglected to mention that police are the only peacetime occupational group with a systematic record of death and injury from gunfire and other weaponry. Along these lines, it is interesting that of the 224 working Westville policemen (not including the sixteen juvenile policemen) responding to a question about which assignment they would like most to have in the police department,[7] 50 percent selected the job of detective, an assignment combining elements of apparent danger and initiative. The next category was adult street work, that is, patrol and traffic (37 percent). Eight percent selected the juvenile squad,[8] and only 4 percent selected administrative work. Not a single policeman chose the job of jail guard. Although these findings do not control for such factors as prestige, they suggest that confining and routine jobs are rated low on the hierarchy of police preferences, even though such jobs are least dangerous. Thus, the policeman may well, as a personality, enjoy the possibility of danger, especially its associated excitement, even though he may at the same time be fearful of it. Such "inconsistency" is easily understood. Freud has by now made it an axiom of personality theory that logical and emotional consistency are by no means the same phenomenon.

However complex the motives aroused by the element of danger, its consequences for sustaining police culture are unambiguous. This element requires him, like the combat soldier, the European Jew, the South African (white or black), to live in a world straining toward duality, and suggesting danger when "they" are perceived. Consequently, it is in the nature of the policeman's situation that his conception of order emphasizes regularity and predictability. It is, therefore, a conception shaped by persistent *suspicion*. The English "copper," often portrayed as a courteous, easygoing, rather jolly sort of chap, on the one hand, or as a devil-may-care adventurer, on the other, is differently described by Colin MacInnes:

> The true copper's dominant characteristic, if the truth be known, is neither those daring nor vicious qualities that are sometimes attributed to him by friend or enemy, but an ingrained conservatism, and almost desperate love of the conventional. It is untidiness, disorder, the unusual, that a copper disapproves of most of all: far more, even than of crime which is merely a professional matter. Hence his profound dislike of people loitering in streets, dressing extravagantly, speaking with exotic accents, being strange, weak, eccentric, or simply any rare minority—of their doing, in fact, anything that cannot be safely predicted.[9]

Policemen are indeed specifically *trained* to be suspicious, to perceive events or changes in the physical surroundings that indicate the occurrence or probability of disorder. A former student who worked as a patrolman in a suburban New York police department describes this aspect of the policeman's assessment of the unusual:

> The time spent cruising one's sector or walking one's beat is not wasted time, though it can become quite routine. During this time, the most important thing for the officer to do is notice the *normal*. He must come to know the people in his area, their habits, their automobiles and their friends. He must learn what time the various shops close, how much money is kept on hand on different nights, what lights are usually left on, which houses are vacant . . . only then can he decide what persons or cars under what circumstances warrant the appellation "suspicious."[10]

The individual policeman's "suspiciousness" does not hang on whether he has personally undergone an experience that could objectively be described as hazardous. Personal experience of this sort is not the key to the psychological importance of exceptionality. Each, as he routinely carries out his work, will experience situations that threaten to become dangerous. Like the American Jew who contributes to the "defense" organizations such as the Anti-Defamation League in response to Nazi brutalities he has never experienced personally, the policeman identifies with his fellow cop who has been beaten, perhaps fatally, by a gang of young thugs.

SOCIAL ISOLATION

The patrolman in Westville, and probably in most communities, has come to identify the black man with danger. James Baldwin vividly expresses the isolation of the ghetto policeman:

> The only way to police a ghetto is to be oppressive. None of the police commissioner's men, even with the best will in the world, have any way of understanding the lives led by the people they swagger about in twos and threes controlling. Their very presence is an insult, and it would be, even if they spent their entire day feeding gumdrops to children. They represent the force of the white world, and that world's criminal profit and ease, to keep the black man corralled up here, in his place. The badge, the gun in the holster, and the swinging club make vivid what will happen should his rebellion become overt. . . .
>
> It is hard, on the other hand, to blame the policeman, blank, good-natured, thoughtless, and insuperably innocent, for being such a perfect representative of the people he serves. He, too, believes in good intentions and is astounded and offended when they are not taken for the deed. He has never, himself, done anything for which to be hated—which of us has?—and yet he is facing, daily and nightly, people who would gladly see him dead, and he knows it. There is no way for him not to know it; there are few things under heaven more unnerving than the silent, accumulating contempt and hatred of a people. He moves through Harlem, therefore, like an occupying soldier in a bitterly hostile country; which is precisely what, and where he is, and is the reason he walks in twos and threes.[11]

While Baldwin's observations on police—black relations cannot be disputed seriously, there is greater social distance between police and "civilians" in general regardless of their color than Baldwin considers. Thus, Colin MacInnes has his English hero, Mr. Justice, explaining:

> The story is all coppers are just civilians like anyone else, living among them not in barracks like on the Continent, but you and I know that's just a legend for mugs. We *are* cut off: we're *not* like everyone else. Some civilians fear us and play up to us, some dislike us and keep out of our way but no one—well, very few indeed—accepts us as just ordinary like them. In one sense, dear, we're just like hostile troops occupying an enemy country. And say what you like, at times that makes us lonely.[12]

MacInnes' observation suggests that by not introducing a white control group, Baldwin has failed to see that the policeman may not get on well with anybody regardless (to use the hackneyed phrase) of race, creed, or national origin. Policemen whom one knows well often express their sense of isolation from the public as a whole, not just from those who fail to share their color. Westville police were asked, for example, to rank the most serious problems police have. The category most frequently selected was not racial problems, but some form of public relations: lack of respect for the police, lack of cooperation in enforcement of law, lack of understanding of the requirements of police work.[13] One respondent answered:

> As a policeman my most serious problem is impressing on the general public just how difficult and necessary police service is to all. There seems to be an attitude of "law is important, but it applies to my neighbor— not to me."

Of the 282 Westville policemen who rated the prestige police work receives from others, 70 percent ranked it as only fair or poor, while less than 2 percent ranked it as "excellent" and another 29 percent as "good." Similarly, in Britain, two-thirds of a sample of policemen interviewed by a royal commission stated difficulties in making friends outside the force; of those interviewed 58 percent thought members of the public to be reserved, suspicious, and constrained in conversation; and 12 percent attributed such difficulties to the requirements that policemen be selective in associations and behave circumspectly.[14]

A Westville policeman related the following incident:

> Several months after I joined the force, my wife and I used to be socially active with a crowd of young people, mostly married, who gave a lot of parties where there was drinking and dancing, and we enjoyed it. I've never forgotten, though, an incident that happened on one Fourth of July party. Everybody had been drinking, there was a lot of talking, people were feeling boisterous, and some kid there—he must have been twenty or twenty-two—threw a firecracker that hit my wife in the leg and burned her. I didn't know exactly what to do—punch the guy in the nose, bawl him out, just forget it. Anyway, I couldn't let it pass, so I walked over to him and told him he ought to be careful. He began to rise up at me, and when he did, somebody yelled, "Better watch out, he's a cop." I saw everybody standing there, and I could feel they were all against me and for the kid, even though he had thrown the firecracker at my wife. I went over to the host and said it was probably better if my wife and I left because a fight would put a damper on the party. Actually, I'd hoped he would ask the kid to leave, since the kid had thrown the firecracker. But he didn't, so we left. After that incident, my wife and I stopped going around with that crowd, and decided that if we were going to parties where there was to be drinking and boisterousness, we weren't going to be the only police people there.

Another reported that he seeks to overcome his feelings of isolation by concealing his police identity:

> I try not to bring my work home with me, and that includes my social life. I like the men I work with, but I think it's better that my family doesn't become a police family. I try to put my police work into the background, and try not to let people know I'm a policeman. Once you do, you can't have normal relations with them.[15]

Although the policeman serves a people who are, as Baldwin says, the established society, the white society, these people do not make him feel accepted. As a result, he develops resources within his own world to combat social rejection.

POLICE SOLIDARITY

All occupational groups share a measure of inclusiveness and identification. People are brought together simply by doing the same work and having similar career and salary problems. As several writers have noted, however, police show an unusually high degree of occupational solidarity.[16] It is true that the police have a common employer and wear a uniform at work, but so do doctors, milkmen, and bus drivers. Yet it is doubtful that these workers have so close knit an occupation or so similar an outlook on the world as do police. Set apart from the conventional world, the policeman experiences an exceptionally strong tendency to find his social identity within his occupational milieu.

Compare the police with another skilled craft. In a study of the International Typographical Union, the authors asked printers the first names and jobs of their three closest friends. Of the 1,236 friends named by the 412 men in their sample, 35 percent were printers.[17] Similarly, among the Westville police, of 700 friends listed by 250 respondents, 35 percent were policemen. The policemen, however, were far more active than printers in occupational social activities. Of the printers, more than half (54 percent) had never participated in any union clubs, benefit societies, teams, or organizations composed mostly of printers, or attended any printers' social affairs in the past five years. Of the Westville police, only 16 percent had failed to attend a single police banquet or dinner in the *past year* (as contrasted with the printers' *five years*); and of the 234 men answering this question, 54 percent had attended three or more such affairs *during the past year*.

These findings are striking in light of the interpretation made of the data on printers. Lipset, Trow, and Coleman do not, as a result of their findings, see printers as an unintegrated occupational group. On the contrary, they ascribe the democratic character of the union in good part to the active social and political participation of the membership. The point is not to question their interpretation, since it is doubtless correct when printers are held up against other manual workers. However, when seen in comparison to police, printers appear a minimally participating group; put positively, police emerge as an exceptionally socially active occupational group.

POLICE SOLIDARITY AND DANGER

There is still a question, however, as to the process through which danger and authority influence police solidarity. The effect of danger on police solidarity is revealed when we examine a chief complaint of police: lack of public support and public apathy. The complaint may have several referents including police pay, police prestige, and support from the legislature. But the repeatedly voiced broader meaning of the complaint is resentment at being taken for granted. The policeman does not believe that his status as civil servant should relieve the public of responsibility for law enforcement. He feels, however, that payment out of public coffers somehow obscures his humanity and, therefore, his need for help.[18] As one put it:

> Jerry, a cop, can get into a fight with three or four tough kids, and there will be citizens passing by, and maybe they'll look, but they'll never lend a hand. It's their country too, but you'd never know it the way some of them act. They forget that we're made of flesh and blood too. They don't care what happens to the cop so long as they don't get a little dirty.

Although the policeman sees himself as a specialist in dealing with violence, he does not want to fight alone. He does not believe that his specialization relieves the general public of citizenship duties. Indeed, if possible, he would prefer to be the foreman rather than the workingman in the battle against criminals.

The general public, of course, does withdraw from the workday world of the policeman. The policeman's responsibility for controlling dangerous and sometimes violent persons alienates the average citizen perhaps as much as does his authority over the average citizen. If the policeman's job is to ensure that public order is maintained, the citizen's inclination is to shrink from the dangers of maintaining it. The citizen prefers to see the policeman as an automaton, because once the policeman's humanity is recognized, the citizen necessarily becomes implicated in the policeman's work, which is, after all, sometimes dirty and dangerous. What the policeman typically fails to realize is the extent he becomes tainted by the character of the work he performs. The dangers of their work not only draw policemen together as a group but separate them from the rest of the population. Banton, for instance, comments:

> Patrolmen may support their fellows over what they regard as minor infractions in order to demonstrate to them that they will be loyal in situations that make the greatest demands upon their fidelity. . . .
>
> In the American departments I visited it seemed as if the supervisors shared many of the patrolmen's sentiments about solidarity. They too wanted their colleagues to back them up in an emergency, and they shared similar frustrations with the public.[19]

Thus, the element of danger contains seeds of isolation which may grow in two directions. In one, a stereotyping perceptual shorthand is formed through which the police come to see certain signs as symbols of potential violence. The police probably differ in this respect from the general middle-class white population only in degree. This difference, however, may take on enormous significance in practice. Thus, the policeman works at identifying and possibly apprehending the symbolic assailant; the ordinary citizen does not. As a result, the ordinary citizen does not assume the responsibility to implicate himself in the policeman's required response to danger. The element of danger in the policeman's role alienates him not only from populations with a potential for crime but also from the conventionally respectable (white) citizenry, in short, from that segment of the population from which friends would ordinarily be drawn. As Janowitz has noted in a paragraph suggesting similarities between the police and the military, ". . . any profession which is continually preoccupied with the threat of danger requires a strong sense of solidarity if it is to operate effectively. Detailed regulation of the military style of life is expected to enhance group cohesion, professional loyalty, and maintain the martial spirit."[20]

SOCIAL ISOLATION AND AUTHORITY

The element of authority also helps to account for the policeman's social isolation. Policemen themselves are aware of their isolation from the community, and are apt to weight authority heavily as a causal factor. When considering how authority influences rejection, the policeman typically singles out his responsibility for enforcement of traffic violations.[21] Resentment, even hostility, is generated in those receiving citations, in part because such contact is often the only one citizens have with police, and in part because municipal administrations and courts have been known to utilize police authority primarily to meet budgetary requirements, rather than those of public order. Thus, when a municipality engages in "speed trapping" by changing limits so quickly that drivers cannot realistically slow down to the prescribed speed or, while keeping the limits reasonable, charging high fines primarily to generate revenue, the policeman carries the brunt of public resentment.

That the policeman dislikes writing traffic tickets is suggested by the quota system police departments typically employ. In Westville, each traffic policeman has what is euphemistically described as a working "norm." A motorcyclist is supposed to write two tickets an hour for moving violations. It is doubtful that "norms" are needed because policemen are lazy. Rather, employment of quotas most likely springs from the reluctance of policemen to expose themselves to what they know to be public hostility. As a result, as one traffic policeman said:

> You learn to sniff out the places where you can catch violators when
> you're running behind. Of course, the department gets to know that you
> hang around one place, and they sometimes try to repair the situation
> there. But a lot of the time it would be too expensive to fix up the
> engineering fault, so we keep making our norm.

When meeting "production" pressures, the policeman inadvertently gives a false impression of patrolling ability to the average citizen. The traffic cyclist waits in hiding for moving violators near a tricky intersection, and is reasonably sure that such violations will occur with regularity. The violator believes he has observed a policeman displaying exceptional detection capacities and may have two thoughts, each apt to generate hostility toward the policeman: "I have been trapped," or "They can catch me; why can't they catch crooks as easily?" The answer, of course, lies in the different behavior patterns of motorists and "crooks." The latter do not act with either the frequency or predictability of motorists at poorly engineered intersections.

While traffic patrol plays a major role in separating the policeman from the respectable community, other of his tasks also have this consequence. Traffic patrol is only the most obvious illustration of the policeman's general responsibility for maintaining public order, which also includes keeping order at public accidents, sporting events, and political rallies. These activities share one feature: the policeman is called upon to *direct* ordinary citizens and therefore to restrain their freedom of action. Resenting the restraint, the average citizen in such a situation typically thinks something along the lines of "He is supposed to catch crooks; why is he bothering me?" Thus, the citizen stresses the "dangerous" portion of the policeman's role while belittling his authority.

Closely related to the policeman's authority-based problems as *director* of the citizenry are difficulties associated with his injunction to *regulate public morality*. For instance, the policeman is obliged to investigate "lovers' lanes" and to enforce laws pertaining to gambling, prostitution, and drunkenness. His responsibility in these matters allows him much administrative discretion since he may not actually enforce the law by making an arrest, but instead merely interfere with continuation of the objectionable activity.[22] Thus, he may put the drunk in a taxi, tell the lovers to remove themselves from the backseat, and advise a man soliciting a prostitute to leave the area.

Such admonitions are in the interest of maintaining the proprieties of public order. At the same time, the policeman invites the hostility of the citizen so directed in two respects: he is likely to encourage the sort of response mentioned earlier (that is, an antagonistic reformulation of the policeman's role) and the policeman is apt to cause resentment because of the suspicion that policemen do not themselves strictly conform to the moral norms they are enforcing. Thus, the policeman, faced with enforcing a law against fornication, drunkenness, or gambling, is easily liable to a charge of hypocrisy. Even when the policeman is called on to enforce the laws relating to overt homosexuality, a form of sexual activity for which police are not especially noted, he may encounter the charge of hypocrisy on grounds that he does not adhere strictly to prescribed heterosexual codes. The policeman's difficulty in this respect is shared by all authorities responsible for maintenance of disciplined activity, including industrial foremen, political leaders, elementary schoolteachers, and college professors. All are expected to conform rigidly to the entire range of norms they espouse.[23] The policeman, however, as a result of the unique combination of the elements of danger and authority, experiences a special predicament. It is difficult to develop qualities enabling him to stand up to danger and to conform to standards of puritanical morality. The element of danger demands that the policeman be able to carry out efforts that are in their nature overtly masculine. Police work, like soldiering, requires an exceptional caliber of physical fitness, agility, toughness, and the like. The man who ranks high on these masculine characteristics is, again like the soldier, not usually disposed to be puritanical about sex, drinking, and gambling.

On the basis of observations, policemen do not subscribe to moralistic standards for conduct. For example, the morals squad of the police department, when questioned, was unanimously against the statutory rape age limit, on grounds that as late teenagers they themselves might not have refused an attractive offer from a seventeen-year-old girl.[24] Neither, from observations, are policemen by any means total abstainers from the use of alcoholic beverages. The policeman who is arresting a drunk has probably been drunk himself; he knows it and the drunk knows it.

More than that, a portion of the social isolation of the policeman can be attributed to the discrepancy between moral regulation and the norms and behavior of policemen in these areas. We have presented data indicating that police engage in a comparatively active occupational social life. One interpretation might attribute this attendance to a basic interest in such affairs; another might explain the policeman's occupational social activity as a measure of restraint in publicly violating norms he enforces. The interest in attending police affairs may grow as much out of security in "letting oneself go" in the presence of police, and a corresponding feeling of insecurity with civilians, as an authentic preference for police social affairs. Much alcohol is usually consumed at police banquets with all the melancholy and boisterousness accompanying such occasions. As Horace Cayton reports on his experience as a policeman:

> Deputy sheriffs and policemen don't know much about organized recreation: all they usually do when celebrating is get drunk and pound each other on the back, exchanging loud insults which under ordinary circumstances would result in a fight.[25]

To some degree the reason for the behavior exhibited on these occasions is the company, since the policeman would feel uncomfortable exhibiting insobriety before civilians. The policeman may be likened to other authorities who prefer to violate moralistic norms away from onlookers for whom they are routinely supposed to appear as normative models. College professors, for instance, also get drunk on occasion, but prefer to do so where students are not present. Unfortunately for the policeman, such settings are harder for him to come by than they are for the college professor. The whole civilian world watches the policeman. As a result, he tends to be limited to the company of other policemen for whom his police identity is not a stimulus to carping normative criticism.

CORRELATES OF SOCIAL ISOLATION

The element of authority, like the element of danger, is thus seen to contribute to the solidarity of policemen. To the extent that policemen share the experience of receiving hostility from the public, they are also drawn together and become dependent upon one another. Trends in the degree to which police may exercise authority are also important considerations in understanding the dynamics of the relation between authority and solidarity. It is not simply a question of how much absolute authority police are given, but how much authority they have relative to what they had, or think they had, before. If, as Westley concludes, police violence is frequently a response to a challenge to the policeman's authority, so too may a perceived reduction in authority result in greater solidarity. Whitaker comments on the British police as follows:

As they feel their authority decline, internal solidarity has become increasingly important to the police. Despite the individual responsibility of each police officer to pursue justice, there is sometimes a tendency to close ranks and to form a square when they themselves are concerned.[26]

These inclinations may have positive consequences for the effectiveness of police work, since notions of professional courtesy or colleagueship seem unusually high among police.[27] When the nature of the policing enterprise requires much joint activity, as in robbery and narcotics enforcement, the impression is received that cooperation is high and genuine. Policemen do not appear to cooperate with one another merely because such is the policy of the chief, but because they sincerely attach a high value to teamwork. For instance, there is a norm among detectives that two who work together will protect each other when a dangerous situation arises. During one investigation, a detective stepped out of a car to question a suspect who became belligerent. The second detective, who had remained overly long in the backseat of the police car, apologized indirectly to his partner by explaining how wrong it had been of him to permit his partner to encounter a suspect alone on the street. He later repeated this explanation privately, in genuine consternation at having committed the breach (and possibly at having been culpable in the presence of an observer). Strong feelings of empathy and cooperation, indeed almost of "clannishness," a term several policemen themselves used to describe the attitude of police toward one another, may be seen in the daily activities of police. Analytically, these feelings can be traced to the elements of danger and shared experiences of hostility in the policeman's role.

Finally, to round out the sketch, policemen are notably conservative, emotionally and politically. If the element of danger in the policeman's role tends to make the policeman suspicious, and therefore emotionally attached to the status quo, a similar consequence may be attributed to the element of authority. The fact that a man is engaged in enforcing a set of rules implies that he also becomes implicated in *affirming* them. Labor disputes provide the commonest example of conditions inclining the policeman to support the status quo. In these situations, the police are necessarily pushed on the side of the defense of property. Their responsibilities thus lead them to see the striking and sometimes angry workers as their enemy and, therefore, to be cool, if not antagonistic, toward the whole conception of labor militancy.[28] If a policeman did not believe in the system of laws he was responsible for enforcing, he would have to go on living in a state of conflicting cognitions, a condition which a number of social psychologists agree is painful.[29]

This hypothetical issue of not believing in the laws they are enforcing simply does not arise for most policemen. In the course of the research, however, there was one example. A Negro civil rights advocate (member of CORE) became a policeman with the conviction that by so doing he would be aiding the cause of impartial administration of laws for Negroes. For him, however, this outside rationale was not enough to sustain him in administering a system of laws that depends for its impartiality upon a reasonable measure of social and economic equality among the citizenry. Because this recruit identified so much with the Negro community as to be unable to meet the enforcement requirements of the Westville Police Department, his efficiency was impaired, and he resigned in his rookie year.

Police are understandably reluctant to appear to be anything but impartial politically. The police are forbidden from publicly campaigning for political candidates. The London police are similarly prohibited, and before 1887 were not allowed to vote in parliamentary elections or in local ones until 1893.[30] It was not surprising that the Westville chief of police forbade questions on the questionnaire that would have measured political attitudes.[31] One policeman, however, explained the chief's refusal on grounds that "A couple of jerks here would probably cut up, and come out looking like Commies."

During the course of administering the questionnaire over a three-day period, I talked with approximately fifteen officers and sergeants in the Westville department, discussing political attitudes of police. In addition, during the course of the research itself, approximately fifty were interviewed for varying periods of time. Of these, at least twenty were interviewed more than once, some over time periods of several weeks. Furthermore, twenty police were interviewed in Eastville, several for periods ranging from several hours to several days. Most of the time was *not* spent on investigating political attitudes, but I made a point of raising the question, if possible, making it part of a discussion centered around the contents of a right-wing newsletter to which one of the detectives subscribed. One discussion included a group of eight detectives. From these observations, interviews, and discussions, it was clear that a Goldwater type of conservatism was the dominant political and emotional persuasion of police. I encountered only three policemen who claimed to be politically "liberal," at the same time asserting that they were decidedly exceptional.

Whether or not the policeman is an "authoritarian personality" is a related issue, beyond the scope of this discussion partly because of the many questions raised about this concept. Thus, in the course of discussing the concept of "normality" in mental health, two psychologists make the point that many conventional people were high scorers on the California F scale and similar tests. The great mass of the people, according to these authors, is not much further along the scale of ego development than the typical adolescent who, as they describe him, is "rigid, prone to think in stereotypes, intolerant of deviations, punitive and anti-psychological—in short, what has been called an authoritarian personality."[32] Therefore it is preferable to call the policeman's a conventional personality.

Writing about the New York police force, Thomas R. Brooks suggests a similar interpretation. He writes:

> Cops are conventional people. . . . All a cop can swing in a milieu of marijuana smokers, interracial dates, and homosexuals is the night stick. A policeman who passed a Lower East Side art gallery filled with paintings of what appeared to be female genitalia could think of doing only one thing—step in and make an arrest.[33]

Despite his fundamental identification with conservative conventionality, however, the policeman may be familiar, unlike most conventional people, with the argot of the hipster and the underworld. (The policeman tends to resent the quietly respectable liberal who comes to the defense of such people on principle but who has rarely met them in practice.) Indeed, the policeman will use his knowledge of the argot to advantage in talking to a suspect. In this manner, the policeman *puts on* the suspect by pretending to share his moral conception of the world through the use of "hip" expressions. The suspect may put on a parallel show for the policeman by using only conventional language to indicate his respectability. (In my opinion, neither fools the other.)

NOTES

1. For previous contributions in this area, see the following: Ely Chinoy, *Automobile Workers and the American Dream* (Garden City: Doubleday and Company, Inc., 1955); Charles R. Walker and Robert H. Guest, *The Man on the Assembly Line* (Cambridge: Harvard University Press, 1952); Everett C. Hughes, "Work and the Self," in his *Men and Their Work* (Glencoe, Ill.: The Free Press, 1958), pp. 42–55; Harold L. Wilensky, *Intellectuals in Labor Unions: Organizational Pressures on Professional Roles* (Glencoe, Ill.: The Free Press, 1956); Wilensky, "Varieties of Work Experience," in Henry Borow, ed., *Man in a World at Work* (Boston: Houghton Mifflin Company, 1964), pp. 125–154; Louis Kriesberg, "The Retail Furrier: Concepts of Security and Success," *American Journal of Sociology* 57 (March 1952): 478–485; Waldo Burchard, "Role Conflicts of Military Chaplains," *American Sociological Review* 19 (October 1954): 528–535; Howard S. Becker and Blanche Geer, "The Fate of Idealism in Medical School," *American Sociological Review* 23 (1958): 50–56; and Howard S. Becker and Anselm L. Strauss, "Careers, Personality, and Adult Socialization," *American Journal of Sociology* 62 (November 1956): 253–363.

2. Morris Janowitz, *The Professional Soldier: A Social and Political Portrait* (New York: The Free Press of Glencoe, 1964), p. 175.

3. By no means does such an analysis suggest there are no individual or group differences among police. On the contrary, most of this study emphasizes differences, endeavoring to relate these to occupational specialties in police departments. This [section], however, explores similarities rather than differences, attempting to account for the policeman's general disposition to perceive and to behave in certain ways.

4. William Westley was the first to raise such questions about the police, when he inquired into the conditions under which police are violent. Whatever merit this analysis has, it owes much to his prior insights, as all subsequent sociological studies of the police must. See his "Violence and the Police," *American Journal of Sociology* 59 (July 1953): 34–41; also his unpublished Ph.D. dissertation "The Police: A Sociological Study of Law, Custom, and Morality," University of Chicago, Department of Sociology, 1951.

5. Something of the flavor of the policeman's attitude toward the symbolic assailant comes across in a recent article by a police expert. In discussing the problem of selecting subjects for field interrogation, the author writes:

A. Be suspicious. This is a healthy police attitude, but it should be controlled and not too obvious.

B. Look for the unusual.

   1. Persons who do not "belong" where they are observed.

   2. Automobiles which do not "look right."

   3. Businesses opened at odd hours, or not according to routine or custom.

C. Subjects who should be subjected to field interrogations.

   1. Suspicious persons known to the officer from previous arrests, field interrogations, and observations.

   2. Emaciated appearing alcoholics and narcotics users who invariably turn to crime to pay for cost of habit.

3. Person who fits description of wanted suspect as described by radio, teletype, daily bulletins.

4. Any person observed in the immediate vicinity of a crime very recently committed or reported as "in progress."

5. Known troublemakers near large gatherings.

6. Persons who attempt to avoid or evade the officer.

7. Exaggerated unconcern over contact with the officer.

8. Visibly "rattled" when near the policeman.

9. Unescorted women or young girls in public places, particularly at night in such places as cafés, bars, bus and train depots, or streetcorners.

10. "Lovers" in an industrial area (make good lookouts).

11. Persons who loiter about places where children play.

12. Solicitors or peddlers in a residential neighborhood.

13. Loiterers around public rest rooms.

14. Lone male sitting in car adjacent to schoolground with newspaper or book in his lap.

15. Lone male sitting in car near shopping center who pays unusual amount of attention to women, sometimes continuously manipulating rearview mirror to avoid direct eye contact.

16. Hitchhikers.

17. Person wearing coat on hot days.

18. Car with mismatched hub caps, or dirty car with clean license plate (or vice versa).

19. Uniformed "deliverymen" with no merchandise or truck.

20. Many others. How about your own personal experiences?
From Thomas F. Adams, "Field Interrogation," *Police* (March–April 1963): 28.

6. See Irving Piliavin and Scott Briar, "Police Encounters with Juveniles," *American Journal of Sociology* 70 (September 1964): 206–214.

7. A questionnaire was given to all policemen in operating divisions of the police force: patrol, traffic, vice control, and all detectives. The questionnaire was administered at police lineups over a period of three days, mainly by the author but also by some of the police personnel themselves. Before the questionnaire was administered, it was circulated to and approved by the policemen's welfare association.

8. Indeed, the journalist Paul Jacobs, who has ridden with the Westville juvenile police as part of his own work in poverty, observed in a personal communication that juvenile police appear curiously drawn to seek out dangerous situations, as if juvenile work without danger is degrading.

9. Colin MacInnes, *Mister Love and Justice* (London: New English Library, 1962), p. 74.

10. Peter J. Connell, "Handling of Complaints by Police," unpublished paper for course in criminal procedure, Yale Law School, Fall 1961.

11. James Baldwin, *Nobody Knows My Name* (New York: Dell Publishing Company, 1962), pp. 65–67.

12. MacInnes, op. cit., p. 20.

13. Respondents were asked, "Anybody who knows anything about police work knows that police face a number of problems. Would you please state—in order—what you consider to be the most serious problems police have." On the basis of a number of answers, the writer and J. Richard Woodworth devised a set of categories. Then Woodworth classified each response into one of the categories (see table, p. 129). When a response did not seem clear, he consulted with the writer. No attempt was made to independently check Woodworth's classifications because the results are used impressionistically, and do not test a hypothesis. It may be, for instance, that "relations with public" is sometimes used to indicate racial problems, and vice versa. "Racial problems" include only those answers having specific reference to race.

14. Royal Commission on the Police, 1962. Appendix IV to *Minutes of Evidence*, cited in Michael Banton, *The Policeman in the Community* (London: Tavistock Publications, 1964), p. 198.

15. Similarly, Banton found Scottish police officers attempting to conceal their occupation when on holiday. He quotes one as

Westville Police Ranking of Number-One Problem Faced by Police

	Number	Percent
Relations with public	74	26
Racial problems and demonstrations	66	23
Juvenile delinquents and delinquency	23	8
Unpleasant police tasks	23	8
Lack of cooperation from authorities (DA, legislature, courts)	20	7
Internal departmental problems	17	6
Irregular life of policeman	5	2
No answer or other answer	56	20
	284	100

saying: "If someone asks my wife 'What does your husband do?', I've told her to say, 'He's a clerk,' and that's the way it went because she found that being a policeman's wife—well, it wasn't quite a stigma, she didn't feel cut off, but that sort of invisible wall was up for conversation purposes when a policeman was there" (p. 198).

16. In addition to Banton, William Westley and James Q. Wilson have noted this characteristic of police. See Westley, op. cit., p. 294; Wilson, "The Police and Their Problems: A Theory," *Public Policy* 12 (1963): 189–216.

17. S. M. Lipset, Martin H. Trow, and James S. Coleman, *Union Democracy* (New York: Anchor Books, 1962), p. 123.

18. On this issue there was no variation. The statement "the policeman feels" means that there was no instance of a negative opinion expressed by the police studies.

19. Banton, op. cit., p. 114.

20. Janowitz, op. cit.

21. O. W. Wilson, for example, mentions this factor as a primary source of antagonism toward police. See his "Police Authority in a Free Society," *Journal of Criminal Law, Criminology, and Police Science* 54 (June 1964): 175–177. In the current study, in addition to the police themselves, other people interviewed, such as attorneys in the system, also attribute the isolation of police to their authority. Similarly, Arthur L. Stinchcorabe, in "The Control of Citizen

Resentment in Police Work," provides a stimulating analysis, to which I am indebted, of the ways police authority generates resentment.

22. See Wayne R. La Fave, "The Police and Nonenforcement of the Law," *Wisconsin Law Review* (1962): 104–137, 179–239.

23. For a theoretical discussion of the problems of leadership, see George Homans, *The Human Group* (New York: Harcourt, Brace and Company, 1950), especially the chapter on "The Job of the Leader," pp. 415–440.

24. The work of the Westville morals squad is analyzed in detail in an unpublished master's thesis by J. Richard Woodworth, "The Administration of Statutory Rape Complaints: A Sociological Study" (University of California, 1964).

25. Horace R. Cayton, *Long Old Road* (New York: Trident Press, 1965), p. 154.

26. Ben Whitaker, *The Police* (Middlesex, England: Penguin Books, 1964), p. 137.

27. It would be difficult to compare this factor across occupations, since the indicators could hardly be controlled. Nevertheless, I felt that the sense of responsibility to policemen in other departments was on the whole quite strong.

28. In light of this, the most carefully drawn lesson plan in the "professionalized" Westville police department, according to the officer in charge of training, is the one dealing with the policeman's demeanor in

Closest Friends of Printers and Police, by Occupation

	Printers N = 1.236 (%)	Police N = 700 (%)
Same occupation	35	35
Professionals, business executives, and independent business owners	21	30
White-collar or sales employees	20	12
Manual workers	25	22

labor disputes. A comparable concern is now being evidenced in teaching policemen appropriate demeanor in civil rights demonstrations. See, e.g., Juby E. Towler, *The Police Role in Racial Conflicts* (Springfield, Ill.: Charles C Thomas, 1964).

29. Indeed, one school of social psychology asserts that there is a basic "drive," a fundamental tendency of human nature, to reduce the degree of discrepancy between conflicting cognitions. For the policeman, this tenet implies that he would have to do something to reduce the discrepancy between his beliefs and his behavior. He would have to modify his behavior, his beliefs, or introduce some outside factor to justify the discrepancy. If he were to modify his behavior, so as not to enforce the law in which he disbelieves, he would not hold his position for long. Practically, then, his alternatives are to introduce some outside factor, or to modify his beliefs. However, the outside factor would have to be compelling in order to reduce the pain resulting from the dissonance between his cognitions. For example, he would have to be able to convince himself that the only way he could possibly make a living was by being a policeman. Or he would have to modify his beliefs. See Leon Festinger, *A Theory of Cognitive Dissonance* (Evanston, Ill.: Row-Peterson, 1957). A brief explanation of Festinger's theory is reprinted in Edward E. Sampson, ed., *Approaches, Contexts, and Problems of Social Psychology* (Englewood Cliffs, N.J.: Prentice-Hall, 1964), pp. 9–15.

30. Whitaker, op. cit., p. 26.

31. The questions submitted to the chief of police were directly analogous to those asked of printers in the study of the I.T.U. See Lipset et al., op. cit., "Appendix II–Interview Schedule," pp. 493–503.

32. Jane Loevinger and Abel Ossorio, "Evaluations of Therapy by Self-Report: A Paradox," *Journal of Abnormal and Social Psychology* 58 (May 1959): 392; see also Edward A. Shils, "Authoritarianism: 'Right' and 'Left'," in R. Christie and M. Jahoda, eds., *Studies in Scope and Method of "The Authoritarian Personality"* (Glencoe, Ill.: The Free Press, 1954), pp. 24–49.

33. Thomas R. Brooks, "New York's Finest," *Commentary* 40 (August 1965): 29–30.

8

The Preventive Effects of Arrest on Intimate Partner Violence

Research, Policy, and Theory

Christopher D. Maxwell
Joel H. Garner
Jeffrey A. Fagan

There is a large literature measuring varied police responses to calls for assistance. In incidents of domestic violence, jurisdictions have experimented with whether police tactical response—in this case, an arrest—may deter future acts of domestic violence. Mandatory removal or arrest does not increase the future risk for violence against women. Maxwell, Garner, and Fagan argue that arresting the offending partner for intimate violence does produce a reduction in subsequent violent offenses.

In the past quarter-century, many alternatives for the appropriate law enforcement response to intimate partner violence have been proposed, studied, recommended, adopted as policy, and enacted in federal and state laws. These alternatives have varied from doing nothing to on-scene counseling, temporary separation, and more formal criminal justice sanctions such as arrest, restraining orders, and coerced treatment (Fagan, 1996). The rationales for these policies were based on theories about deterrence rehabilitation, incapacitation, victim empowerment, officer safety, and a general concern for the efficacy of criminal law regarding intimate private relationships (Pagan and Browne, 1994:3; Zimring, 1989:11). Until the 1980s, the empirical base for

Source: Christopher D. Maxwell, Joel H. Garner, and Jeffrey A. Fagan. "The Preventive Effects of Arrest on Intimate Partner Violence," in *Criminology and Public Policy*, vol 2, no. 1 (2002), pp. 51–80.

assessing the extent to which the alternative policies fulfilled the promises of their theoretical rationales was thin. In the foreword to a domestic violence research report that showed domestic violence was repetitive and highly visible to police, James Q. Wilson asserted that the criminal justice field lacks "reliable information as to the consequences of following different approaches" when responding to intimate partner violence. He argued that "gathering such information in a systematic and objective manner ought to be a high-priority concern for local police and prosecutors" (Wilson, 1977:v).

For the past 25 years, the law enforcement and research community has addressed Wilson's challenge by gathering systematic and objective information about alternative police responses to intimate partner violence. However, gathering information alone has not led to a clear understanding of the consequences of alternative policies or to the strength of the theories underlying those policies (Davis and Smith, 1995; Fagan, 1996). To alleviate this shortcoming, we use common data and consistent measures from 4,032 incidents of misdemeanor assault compiled in five jurisdictions to test the preventive effects of arrest on intimate partner violence. We begin by reviewing the published results from six field experiments that tested for the deterrent effects of arrest on intimate partner violence. Then we describe our methods for pooling data and conducting our analyses of the five coordinated field experiments known collectively as the Spouse Abuse Replication Program (SARP). Next, we present the results of analyses using multiple data sources, methods, and measures. We conclude with a discussion of the policy implications of our re-analysis.

BACKGROUND

In 1980, the Minneapolis Police Department and the Police Foundation accepted Wilson's challenge and proposed to compare three alternative police responses to partner violence: arrest, on-scene counseling, and separation (Sherman, 1980). This proposal was innovative in using arrest as the tested sanction rather than conviction or prison time. However, it took a more traditional approach to confirm specific deterrence theory by testing for a negative relationship between the use of a formal sanction against an individual and that person's subsequent illegal behavior. In this study, volunteer Minneapolis officers carried out one of the three alternative responses based on an experimental design. Sherman and Berk (1984b) reported that when police did not arrest the suspect during a misdemeanor spouse assault incident, 21% re-offended within six months according to official records, a rate 50% higher than the 14% re-offending rate of arrested suspects. Results were similar when re-offending was measured by victim interviews. Thus, the experiment designed to test a specific deterrence theory found consistent, statistically significant, and supportive findings for what was by 1984 becoming the preferred policy option among domestic violence reform advocates—arresting the suspect.

Policy Impact of the Minneapolis Experiment

Although the results of this experiment received extensive coverage on national television and in newspapers, the actual impact of this research is difficult to gauge. The policy debate about police response to domestic violence shifted quickly during the 1980s from one in which many jurisdictions did not authorize police officers to make arrests in misdemeanor assault unless they occurred in the officer's presence, to laws and policies that encouraged the use of arrest, to laws and policies that mandated arrest in at least some circumstances (Hirschel and Hutchison, 1991:3). Sherman and Berk (1984a) interpreted the Minneapolis findings as support for using arrest but not necessarily for the mandated use of arrest. Nevertheless, several indications show that the Minneapolis experiment influenced the policy debate about the appropriate police response to domestic violence (Boffey, 1983; Lempert, 1984; Sherman and Cohn, 1989; U.S. Attorney General's Task Force on Family Violence, 1984). What is less clear is whether this experiment's impact stems from its grounding in theory, experimental design, consistent findings, visibility of the research results, or compatibility of its pro-arrest findings with growing public support for more formal sanctions for domestic violence.

The Spouse Assault Replication Program

Support for replication of the Minneapolis experiment was widespread among researchers and policy makers. Sherman and Berk (1984b) urged replication, and some academics' early praise for the study also was tempered by others preference for replication (Boffey, 1983; Lempert, 1984). The U.S. Attorney General's Task Force on Family Violence also encouraged replicating the Minneapolis experiment (1984). By 1986, six new experiments were initiated in Atlanta, Charlotte, Colorado Springs, Dade County, Milwaukee, and Omaha. Each new study involved experimental comparisons of arrest with alternative police responses to misdemeanor spouse assault incidents and measured victim safety using official police records and victim interviews (Gamer and Maxwell, 2000).

> These new experiments became known as the Spouse Assault Replication Program (SARP), but that name is a misnomer because the designers of the new experiments changed several crucial aspects of the Minneapolis design. For instance, in each new experiment, police officers determined case eligibility before the researchers assigned an alternative treatment to carry out. This method of determining eligibility without knowing the randomized treatment is preferred for experimental studies. The Minneapolis experiment, however, permitted officers to know the treatment before they decided case eligibility (Sherman and Berk, 1984b). In addition, the Minneapolis experiment attempted to interview victims by phone every two weeks. In the design of the SARP experiments, victim interviews were to occur twice, once within a month of the experimental incident and once at six months after the experimental incident.[1] The SARP experiments also developed a series of common

measures about suspects, victims, treatments, and outcomes. Overall, the SARP experiments built on the Minneapolis design, increasing the number of sites and experimental incidents, enhancing the rigor of the random assignment, archiving the research data, and promoting commonality among the new experiments at the expense of commonality with the original Minneapolis experiment (Garner and Maxwell, 2000; National Institute of Justice, 1985).

Synthesizing SARP Findings

The published findings from the SARP experiments generated a complex mixture of deterrence, null, and escalation effects. Where there once had been one experiment with two statistically significant and consistent results, there now were six experiments with their own set of internally and externally inconsistent findings. Seven prior efforts have tried synthesizing the substantive findings from these experiments. These efforts found deterrent effects where the original authors did not (Zorza and Woods, 1994), identified the inconsistent and incomplete nature of the published findings (Garner et al., 1995), produced deterrent effects from a meta-analysis of prevalence findings (Sugarman and Boney-McCoy, 2000), reported mixed effects by site in a review of each experiment including Minneapolis (Sherman, 1992b), asserted that the effects of arrest vary by the marital and employment status of suspects (Berk et al., 1992; Schmidt and Sherman, 1992), and made an expert assessment that "arrest in all misdemeanor cases will not, on average, produce a discernable effect on recidivism" (Chalk and King, 1998:176). Thus, prior efforts at synthesis vary almost as much as do the published reports from the individual sites.

Although alternative approaches to synthesizing a large body of research, such as qualitative literature reviews and meta-analysis of published findings, have contributed to our understanding of this and other bodies of research, the secondary analysis of case-level data provide the most rigorous method for combining information across a variety of studies (Cooper and Hedges, 1994). Although efforts at secondary analysis of the archived data from the SARP experiments (see Berk et al., 1992; Sherman et al., 1992) have provided insights into the conditions under which arrest may or may not improve women's safety, they still are incomplete for several reasons. First, they use only the official records as a measure of repeat offending and do not consider information generated by thousands of victim interviews. Second, Sherman et al. (1992a) considered only the frequency of re-offending and Berk et al. (1992) considered only the prevalence of re-offending. Finally, Sherman et al. (1992a) reported two single site analyses (Milwaukee and Omaha) and Berk et al. (1992) did not use information from the Charlotte experiment. For these and other reasons, the published syntheses of the SARP experiments cannot be the definitive assessments of the average effect of arrest on subsequent offending.

SARP's Policy Impact

The inconsistencies in the site-specific and the multisite analyses reported in the various SARP reviews generated some ambivalence among researchers (Berk, 1993; Fagan, 1996; Sherman, 1992b) and policy makers (Clark, 1993; Frisch, 1992; Lerman, 1992; Mitchell, 1992) about the efficacy of arrest as the primary mechanism to control intimate partner violence. However, this ambivalence does not appear to have influenced police practices. We know of no jurisdiction that revised its policy to reflect the concerns these scholars raised. Furthermore, under the authority of the 1994 Violence Against Women Act, the U.S. Department of Justice initiated the Grants to Encourage Arrest Policies Program. To support this program, Congress appropriated nearly $120 million between 1994 and 1996 for the Violence Against Women Office to help local jurisdictions "implement mandatory arrest or proarrest programs and policies in police departments, including mandatory arrest programs and policies for protection order violations" (Violence Against Women Grants Office, 1996:5). Thus, presently, the findings (and the interpretation of findings) from the SARP experiments are not as closely connected to current policies and practices as the findings from the Minneapolis experiment were in the 1980s and 1990s.

METHODS

This study builds on a body of research that addresses the specific deterrent effect of arrest on the subsequent aggressive behavior by intimate partners. We synthesize the original data generated by the SARP experiments and conduct analyses that differ from the site-specific analyses in several ways. First, in contrast to prior secondary analyses (see Berk et al., 1992; Sherman et al., 1992a), our design conforms to the program's original plans for a multisite analysis of the case-level data.[2] Second, we use information about subsequent offenses from all victim interviews and from all official police records. Third, we use common measures about suspects, victims, incidents, and treatments to apply consistent case eligibility standards across the five experiments in which arrest was one possible treatment. Finally, we address (1) the complexities of combining data from five independent studies with systematic design differences; (2) the variability in the existence, number, and timing of victim interviews; and (3) the differences in the collection of the official data. The SARP experiments, by design, drew cases from different populations. They varied in size from 330 to 1,600 cases. They randomly assigned arrest to two-thirds (Milwaukee), one-half (Dade), one-third (Omaha and Charlotte), and one-fourth (Colorado Springs) of the eligible cases. In Dade County, the experiment was initially limited to married couples; in Milwaukee, the experiment included assaults between siblings and gathered cases only from selected neighborhoods. Although there were other differences in incident eligibility rules between sites, this is the first effort to synthesize the SARP experiments that addresses these issues (see Maxwell, 1998 for a detailed listing of differences among sites).

Selection of Cases from the Pooled Data

We used common measures about suspects and experimental incidents (e.g., the incident at which the treatment was assigned and delivered) to select a research sample that best represents the archetypical male-on-female assaults that drive much of the policy debate about controlling intimate partner violence. The five sites collected data about 4,792 experimental incidents; we use information from the 4,032 incidents involving adult male suspects who assaulted their female intimate partner. To arrive at 4,032 cases, we excluded 306 incidents that involved a female suspect and 314 incidents that involved a male victim. Other experimental incidents excluded in our study involved victims and offenders whose relationships were not spouse-like, such as brothers and sisters ($n = 85$), and experimental incidents that did not involve an assault or victim injury ($n = 34$) (see Maxwell et al., 2001 for additional details about sample selection).

Treatments Assigned and Compared

One of the SARP requirements was that arrest be one of the alternative police treatments tested. The nature of the alternatives to arrest and the proportion of cases assigned to arrest and nonarrest treatments were left to the implementing teams of researchers and police agencies. Of the 4,032 suspects in the research sample, 43.4% were assigned to the arrest treatment and the remaining 56.6% were assigned to a variety of nonarrest treatments (see Table 1). In our analyses, we compare the arrest treatment with all of the nonarrest treatments. Binder and Meeker (1988) suggested this comparison of the formal sanction of arrest with the informal alternatives in their critique of the original Minneapolis analysis. This method also was used in subsequent analysis of the Minneapolis experiment (see Berk and Sherman, 1988), and in some original SARP analyses (see Pate and Hamilton, 1992; Sherman et al., 1992a).

The designs in each of the SARP sites allowed officers to avoid using the randomly assigned treatment and apply an alternative treatment under certain conditions, such as an assault on the victim in the officers' presence or an assault on the officers. Consequently, the treatments delivered differed from the treatment assigned in 6.7% of the incidents.[3] We chose to compare suspects based on the treatment randomly assigned. This is the only comparison for which we have a statistical basis for assuming uncorrelated error terms for both measured and unmeasured characteristics of suspects (Armitage, 1996:13; Heckman and Robb, 1986). This choice also was consistent with the method used in the original Minneapolis experiment, the SARP design, each of the original SARP analyses, and clinical trials in medical research.[4]

Sample characteristics vary by site and by treatment assigned. For instance, Colorado Springs contributes 30.7% of the research sample and Milwaukee provides 23.7% (see Table 1). The Omaha experiment contributed only 7.3% of the total sample. Thus, the larger sites contributed three or four times as many experimental incidents as did the smallest site. Approximately 19% of subjects in the research sample were less than 24 years of age, and almost 45% were older than 31. At the time of the experimental incident, either the police determined or the victim reported that the suspect was using an intoxicant—either alcohol or illegal drugs-—in 45% of the incidents. In 37.5% of the research sample, the suspect's race was white. At the time of the experimental incident, most suspects were married to the victim (58.8%), most were employed (71.5%). and 40% had at least one prior arrest. As displayed in Table 2, the proportion of cases assigned to the arrest treatment varied significantly by site as well as by suspect's race, marital status, arrest record, employment condition, and use of intoxicants at the time of the experimental incident. All of these differences are statistically significant ($p < 0.05$). Suspect age was the only characteristic with similar distributions between the arrest and the nonarrest cases.

Characteristics of the Pooled Sample

Thus, Table 2 established that the research sample has unequal proportions in the characteristics of suspects assigned to arrest and nonarrest treatments. Unequal proportions in the treatment and control groups are unlikely in a single site experiment, but when we merged the data from the five experiments, three differences emerged: (1) Both criminal histories and social characteristics of suspects vary by site, (2) the sites have different numbers and types of incidents, and (3) the sites assigned different proportions of suspects to the arrest treatment. Accordingly, the unequal proportions of cases, the uneven distribution of victim and suspect characteristics, and the uneven allocation of cases to treatment groups are factors we must address in our multisite analyses that test for the effects of arrest on subsequent criminal behavior.

Victim Interviews

The SARP design called for initial victim interviews within a month of the experimental incident and a second interview six months after the experimental incident. However, the SARP researchers were not able to interview all of the victims; those victims interviewed were rarely interviewed according to the plan, and several sites added additional interviews or deviated from the basic design for some of their cases.[5] Initial victim interviews were completed in more than 70% of the research sample (see Table 1), but the rate varied from 60% in Milwaukee (where, by design, initial interviews were not attempted in 25% of the cases) to almost 80% in Omaha. In just less than 63% of the research sample, a final interview was obtained. Milwaukee had the highest proportion of final interviews, with more than 79%, and Charlotte, at 50%, had the lowest. In more than 78% of the research sample ($n = 3,147$), at least one interview took place with the victim. Besides site differences in the proportion interviewed, the timing of the initial interviews varied from 1 to 776 days after the experimental incident; the mean number of days was 39.2. The actual time

Table 1 Sample Characteristics, Treatments Assigned, Victim Interview Rates by Site

	CHARLOTTE				COLORADO SPRINGS				DADE COUNTY				MILWAUKEE				OMAHA				ALL SITES			
Research Sample	Row %	N	Col. %	N	Row %	N	Col. %	N	Row %	N	Col. %	N	Row %	N	Col. %	N	Row %	N	Col. %	N	Row %	N	Col. %	N
	15.8	638	100.0	638	30.7	1,238	100.0	1,238	22.5	906	100.0	906	23.7	954	100.0	954	7.3	296	100.0	296	100.0	4,032	100.0	4,032
Treatment assigned																								
Arrest			33.2	212			26.3	325			51.1	463			67.9	648			33.8	100			43.4	1,748
Non-arrest			66.8	426			73.7	913			48.9	443			32.1	306			66.2	196			56.6	2,284
Suspect characteristics																								
Mean age			32.8				30.8				35.1				31.0				31.4				32.2	
Use of intoxicant			54.2	346			59.3	734			30.6	277			29.4	280			59.1	175			44.9	1,812
Race/Ethnicity																								
African-American			69.9	446			30.2	374			41.8	379			75.4	719			41.9	124			50.6	2,042
White			27.7	177			54.2	671			36.1	327			19.9	190			50.3	149			37.5	1,514
Hispanic			0.3	2			14.5	180			22.1	200			4.2	40			4.7	14			10.8	436
Asian/Other			2.0	13			1.1	13			0.0	0			0.5	5			3.0	9			1.0	40
Relationship with victim																								
Married			48.4	309			66.7	826			78.7	713			30.9	295			46.3	137			56.5	2,280
Separated			1.6	10			4.3	53			2.9	26			0.3	3			0.0	0			2.3	92
Divorced			0.3	2			0.6	8			2.0	18			0.7	7			1.4	4			1.0	39
Current/Past intimate			49.7	317			28.4	351			16.4	149			68.0	649			52.4	155			40.2	1,621
Prior arrest			30.7	196			42.8	530			12.1	110			61.8	590			64.9	192			40.1	1,618
Employed			77.1	492			86.7	1,073			70.5	639			47.2	450			78.0	231			71.6	2,885
Extent of victim interviews completion																								
Initial			64.4	411			82.9	1,026			65.5	593			60.2	574			79.4	235			70.4	2,839
Final			50.2	320			70.4	872			42.4	384			77.9	743			73.0	216			62.9	2,535
Any victim interview			64.4	411			87.9	1,088			65.7	595			85.7	818			79.4	235			78.1	3,147

Table 2 Site, Suspect and Incident Characteristics by Treatment Assigned (N = 4.032)

	TREATMENT ASSIGNMENT					
	NON-ARREST		ARREST		TOTAL	
	Row %	N	Row %	N	Row %	N
Selected incidents	56.6	2,284	43.3	1,748	100	4,032
	Col. %	N	Col. %	N	Col. %	N
Selected incidents	100	2,284	100	1,748	100	4,032
Site						
Charlotte	18.7	426	12.1	212	15.8	638
Colorado Springs	40.0	913	18.6	325	30.7	1,238
Dade Co.	19.4	443	26.5	463	22.5	906
Milwaukee	13.4	306	37.1	648	23.7	954
Omaha	8.6	196	5.7	100	7.3	296
Age						
18 to 24	19.7	449	17.3	303	18.7	752
25 to 28	21.1	481	20.7	361	20.9	842
29 to 31	15.6	356	16.1	281	15.8	637
32 to 37	22.3	510	22.9	400	22.6	910
38 to 82	21.4	488	23.1	403	22.1	891
Use of intoxicant	49.5	1,130	39.0	682	44.9	1,812
Race						
Non-White	59.1	1350	66.8	1168	62.5	2,518
White	40.9	934	33.2	580	37.5	1514
Marital status						
Non-married	38.4	877	44.9	784	41.2	1,661
Married	61.6	1,407	55.1	964	58.8	2,371
Prior arrest	36.9	843	44.3	774	40.1	1,617
Employed	74.3	1,697	67.9	1,187	71.5	2,884

to the final interviews varied from 12 to 674 days, and the mean number of days was 280. Thus, the actual exposure time covered by the final interviews was, on average, 97 days longer than the planned 183 days.

We addressed the methodological issues created by the difference in victim interview rates and length of follow-up in several ways. First, we extended the basic Heckman selection model (Heckman, 1979) and produced a time-dependent latent-hazard selection measure. This approach used as its dependent measure the maximum length of time that the researchers tracked each victim during the study, rather than the traditional dichotomized measure of interview completion or noncompletion. For the 22% of victims who never were interviewed, their interview exposure time was set to one day. For the remaining victims with one or more interviews, their follow-up time was set to equal the number of days between the experimental incident and the date of their last interview. We then modeled the length of all 4,032 victim interview times as a function of the site and victim characteristics using a semiparametric maximum-likelihood Cox regression model. Using this process, we then produced a latent interview exposure rate for every victim. In our analyses of repeat offending, we used this measure as one means of addressing measured differences between the interviewed and noninterviewed victims, as well as to control for the different lengths of victim follow-up. This measure also permitted us to take advantage of the information about new victimizations gathered from all interviews regardless of the number or timing of interviews, rather than just those victimizations reported in the final interviews.

In the model predicting the length of victim interview follow-up, two of the seven measures tested, the site and the victim's age, predicted variation in the time covered by a victim's interviews. Dade County, Milwaukee, and Omaha had longer follow-up periods on average compared with Charlotte. In all sites, older victims also were observed over a longer follow-up period. The suspect's assigned treatment, the victim's relationship with the suspect, the victim's employment status, race, and the timing of any subsequent criminal offenses filed with the police involving the suspect did not significantly predict differences in whether the victim was interviewed or the average length of the follow-up period.

Outcome Measures

The SARP design called for collecting data that would permit the computation of the prevalence, frequency, and time-to-failure dimensions of the criminal career paradigm (Blumstein et al., 1986). In addition, the design called for computing each of these dimensions separately for violent offenses, property damage, and other types of offenses against the same victim, other victims, and any victim. This approach resulted in potentially hundreds of outcome measures derived from the official records and victim interviews. However, after review of the raw data and each site's data collection instruments and protocols, we found that not all of the data needed to calculate all of these measures were available for each of the five SARP experiments (see Maxwell, 1998 for details on the diversity and commonality of available measures in the archived data).

Using the available information in the victim interviews, we constructed composite outcome measures that capture incidents of subsequent assaults, verbal threats of assault, or property damage by the suspect against the original victim. From local law enforcement criminal history records, we constructed a measure that captured any reported offense against the same victim after the experimental incident. Using this measure, we then calculated a six-month prevalence rate, an annual incident rate, and a time-to-first-failure rate. From the victim interview data, we also calculated prevalence and six-month incident rates. Because sufficient information to determine the date of subsequent incidents reported in victim interviews was not always present in the victim interviews, we were unable to calculate a time-to-first-failure rate for all five sites. Both measures also are limited to incidents involving the offender and the victim identified in the original experimental incident. The interview measure captures threats, but police records typically do not include threats. Of course, many victims do not report offenses to the police (Bachman and Coker, 1995), and police do not always document all citizen complaints (Klinger and Bridges, 1997). Thus, we expected that victim interviews would identify more frequent victimization than would the official records. Therefore, we preferred the victim interview information over the official records for a measure of repeat offending and victim safety.

Multivariate Analytical Models

We estimated the effects of arrest on the recurrence of intimate partner violence in a series of models using (1) the treatment and site measures; (2) treatment, site, and the interview exposure measures; (3) treatment, site, interview exposure, and site by treatment interaction measures; and (4) treatment, site, interview exposure, and six suspect characteristics measurements thought to be associated with increased risk of re-offending. The choice of the appropriate estimation routine for the five outcome measures reflected the three measurement dimensions: The prevalence of any new victimization is a dichotomy, the rate of aggressive incidents is a count, and the time-to-first-offense is a right-hand censored interval measure of days between the experimental incident and the first officially recorded offense. For dichotomous dependent measures of prevalence, models were estimated using logistic regression methods. To estimate the number of incidents, models were tested using Negative Binomial Regression.[6] We estimated the time-to-first-failure rates using the Cox semi-parametric regression.[7] For each regression procedure, we report the unstandardized coefficients, the coefficient's standard errors, and the odds ratios. We use the odds ratio as a rough measure of the relative size of the effect of arrest.

RESULTS

Offenses and Victimizations Base Rates

Table 3 reports prevalence and mean incident rates of new incidents reported in the victim interviews and found in the official police records. In the official police records, 23.1% of the suspects in the research sample had one or more reported offenses after the experimental incident. The annual incident rate averaged 0.39 offenses per suspect. Among 3.149 victims interviewed at least once, 42.5% reported at least one new victimization by the suspect through the final victim interview. These same victims reported 9,009 incidents (an average of 2.86 incidents per suspect) during this period after the experimental treatment. Thus, similar to what was found in other domestic violence research (see Feld and Straus, 1989; Langan and Innes, 1986; Quigley and Leonard, 1996), analysis of the official criminal history records indicated no new offenses against three-quarters of all suspects, and almost three-fifths of the interviewed victims reported no new victimizations. However, when victims report at least

Table 3　Base Rates of Failure by Treatment Assigned

	NON-ARREST		ARREST		TOTAL	
Official Record Sample	(N = 2,284)		(N = 1,748)		(N = 4,032)	
	%	N	%	N	%	N
Six-month prevalence of recidivism	21.1	481	25.7	450	23.1	931
		Chi-sqr. = 0.725				
Mean annual frequency of recidivism	0.32		0.48		0.39	
		F-value = 25.397 ***				
Mean survival time (days)	865		816		850	
		Log-rank = 15.8 ***				

	NON-ARREST		ARREST		TOTAL	
Victim Interview Sample	(N = 1,789)		(N = 1,358)		(N = 3,147)	
	%	N	%	N	%	N
Prevalence of victimization	42.3	756	42.9	583	42.5	1,339
		Chi-sqr. = 0.14				
Mean 6-month frequency of victimization	2.74		3.03		2.86	
		F-value = 1.075				

one new incident, the average number of victimizations was 6.7, or greater than one victimization per month.

Effects of Arrest

With multiple outcome measures and sources, our criteria for judging across the five models for the existence of an effect for arrest are a combination of the consistency of direction, its relative size compared with other measures in the models, and its statistical significance. Among these three criteria, we place greater stock in the consistency of direction effects and in the size of effects, and we de-emphasize statistical significance tests. As other criminologists have noted, the use of statistical significance tests is technically not appropriate for nonprobability samples (Sampson and Laub, 1993), such as those used in the Minneapolis and SARP experiments. Nagin and Farrington (1992:519) similarly argue that "empirical regularities" such as the consistent direction of effects are the "grist for useful theory," rather than one or two tests for statistical significance. Yet, like Sampson and Laub (1993), we also report statistical significance tests to help avoid type I errors.

As reported in Table 4, arrest reduced the prevalence of new victimization by 25% and the incidents of victimizations by 30%. In the official criminal history data, arrest also was associated with reductions of 4% in the prevalence and 8% in the incidence of recidivism, as well as a 12% reduction in the hazard rate. In other words, based on five outcome measures from two sources, there were consistently smaller rates of subsequent victimization and recidivism among the suspects assigned to the arrest treatment versus the nonarrest interventions.

Table 4 Multivariate Tests of the Effects of Arrest on Intimate Partner Violence

Independent Variable:	VICTIM REPORTS (N = 3,147)						OFFICIAL REPORTS (N = 4,032)								
	PREVALENCE[a]			6-MONTH RATE[b]			6-MONTH PREVALENCE[a]			ANNUAL RATE[b]			TIME-TO-FAILURE[c]		
	B	S.E.	Exp(B)	B	S.E.	Exp(B)	B	S.E.	Exp(B)	B	S.E.	Exp(B)	B	S.E.	Exp(B)
Arrest	-0.28	0.08	0.75 ***	-0.35	0.08	0.70 ***	-0.04	0.08	0.96	-0.08	0.07	0.92	-0.03	0.06	0.88
Site (Charlotte)															
Colorado Springs	-0.97	0.13	0.38 ***	-0.49	0.15	0.61 ***	0.28	0.12	1.33 *	-0.02	0.13	0.98	-0.02	0.10	0.76 **
Dade Co.	-0.49	0.14	0.61 ***	-0.01	0.16	0.99	0.64	0.13	1.89 ***	0.64	0.12	1.89 ***	0.35	0.11	1.61 ***
Milwaukee	0.48	0.13	1.61 ***	0.96	0.16	2.62 ***	0.23	0.13	1.26	0.67	0.12	1.96 ***	0.16	0.11	1.10
Omaha	0.42	0.17	1.52 *	-1.01	0.20	0.36 ***	-0.54	0.19	0.58 **	-0.60	0.19	0.55 ***	-0.80	0.16	0.39 ***
Interview exposure	0.86	0.11	2.36 ***	-0.55	0.09	0.58 ***	0.54	0.09	1.71 ***	0.08	0.10	1.09	0.26	0.07	1.28 ***
Suspect's															
Age	-0.39	0.15	0.68 **	-0.83	0.14	0.44 ***	-0.50	0.15	0.61 ***	-0.32	0.13	0.72 *	-0.41	0.13	0.71 **
Use of intoxicant	-0.01	0.08	0.99	0.36	0.07	1.43 ***	0.21	0.08	1.23 **	0.10	0.08	1.10	0.14	0.06	1.12
White	0.23	0.08	1.26 **	0.30	0.07	1.35 ***	-0.39	0.08	0.68 ***	-0.36	0.07	0.70 ***	-0.33	0.07	0.74 ***
Married	0.04	0.09	1.05	0.11	0.07	1.11	-0.01	0.08	0.99	0.10	0.08	1.10	-0.03	0.07	0.74 ***
Prior arrest	0.45	0.08	1.56 ***	0.11	0.09	1.12	0.92	0.08	2.50 ***	0.86	0.08	2.36 ***	0.78	0.07	3.34 ***
Employed	0.02	0.09	1.02	-0.23	0.08	0.79 ***	-0.06	0.09	0.94	-0.16	0.07	0.85 *	-0.07	0.07	0.94
Constant	0.20	0.53		3.98	0.47		-0.07	0.52		-0.11	0.46				
Negative binomial scalar				5.02	0.17					2.12	0.13				
Initial likelihood	4292.51			-20158.7			4735.61			-4224.08			17656.49		
Final likelihood	3949.93		***	-5537.95		***	4476.31		***	-3618.03		***	17384.65		***

a = Logistic Regression; b = Negative Binomial Regression; c = Cox Regression.
* = $p < 0.05$; ** = $p < 0.02$; *** = $p < 0.001$.

For the two outcome measures based on victim interview data, these negative effects were statistically significant at the traditional $p < 0.05$ level.[8] Using the three outcome measures derived from the criminal history information, the arrest treatment also was associated with a reduction in the recidivism rates, but none of the differences between the two treatment groups were statistically significant.

The results reported in Table 4 also show that there were statistically significant differences in the base rates of failures across the five sites for all five outcome measures. We therefore tested to determine whether the effects of arrest were related to the site for any of the five measures, but did not find any evidence that was the case (see Maxwell, 1998 for detailed results of these tests). Thus, because the effects for arrest were in the same direction across all five measures and in the same direction in each of the five sites, as well as statistically significant in two of the five models, the results support the notion that, compared with nonarrest interventions, arrest provides additional safety to female victims of intimate partner assault. This finding is consistent with the specific deterrence hypothesis that these studies originally were testing.[9]

Effect of the Victim Interview Process

As mentioned above, we had to address the issue of missing victim interviews. We did so by including in the outcome models our interview exposure measure to assess the impact of the interview process on the outcome measures and on the effect of arrest. As reported in Table 4, we found higher victimization rates among those whose last interview occurred later in time after the initial experimental incident in four of the five comparisons. The one effect that was not significant was the relationship between exposure and failure measured by the victim's six-month victimization rate. This measure showed a negative association between the length of follow-up and the frequency of offenses reported by the victims.

Because our approach to controlling for missing victim interviews and time covered by the interviews was innovative, we also tested for relationships between arrest and our five outcomes without specifying the victim interview exposure measure. For the five models reported in Table 4, the exclusion of the exposure measure did not change the direction or statistical significance of either the treatment or site measures and the size of the arrest coefficients increased by an average of 3%. As an additional test of the interview selection process, we then modeled the criminal history data using only the suspects that had at least one victim interview ($n = 3,147$). The substantive results were similar to those reported in Table 4 for the full sample. Among this subsample, arrest led to a 7% reduction in the odds of any subsequent recidivism, but again this reduction was not significant ($p = 0.44$). The timing of the first subsequent incident ($b = 0.001; p = 0.988$) and the difference in the incident rates between the arrest and nonarrest groups were also not significant ($b = -0.01; p = 0.839$). Lastly, we compared the prevalence and incident rates of re-offending among those with and without a victim interview and found that suspects with non-interviewed victims have significantly smaller rates of recidivism across all three measures. This finding is contrary to our concern that noninterviewed victims in the SARP experiments might have had higher rates of repeat victimizations. From these results, we conclude that discrepancies in the size and statistical significance of the arrest coefficients from the victim interviews and from the official records were due less to differences in the interviewed and noninterviewed samples, and more to the ability of the victim interviews to capture subsequent victimizations not included in official police reports.

Effects of Suspect Characteristics

In Table 4, we also included statistical tests for the suspect's age, use of intoxicants at the experimental incident, race, marital status, prior arrest record, and employment status. Older suspects were less likely to aggress against their female intimate partners (cf., Farrington, 1986:7). Intimate partner aggression is perhaps also resistant to low-cost legal sanctions: Having one or more prior arrests for any offense against any victim was consistently associated with greater quantity of incidents, and this relationship was statistically significant in four of our five regression models (cf., Moffitt et al., 2000). The size of the relationship between prior arrest and new incidents ranged from about a 12% increase in the odds of a new victimization to a 234% increase in the odds for the time-to-first-failure in the official criminal history records. Alcohol use increased the risk of intimate partner aggression: The use of intoxicants at the time of the experimental incident was similarly associated with increased failures in four out of five outcome measures, and two of these positive relationships were statistically significant (the prevalence of victimization and the prevalence of recidivism) (cf., Fagan and Browne, 1994:3; Kantor and Straus, 1987).[10]

The suspect's race had a substantial and statistically significant relationship to subsequent failures, but the direction of the association depended on whether the data came from the victim interviews or official records. Based on victim interview data, victims were more likely to report new offenses if the suspect was white. Based on the criminal history information, white suspects were less likely to recidivate compared with all other suspects. The sizes of these relationships was substantial, from a 35% increase in the odds of victimization to a 30% decrease in the odds of recidivism. The role of the suspect's marital relationship with the victim also varied in size and direction by outcome measure. By three outcome measures, married suspects were more likely to fail, and by two measures, they were less likely to fail. However, only for the prevalence of new victimization was the increase statistically associated with married suspects. This one relationship was nearly a 5% increase. Finally, in four out of five models, employed suspects were less likely to commit additional incidents (cf., Sherman et al., 1992a). Two of the four negative relationships were statistically significant and ranged from 15% to 21% decreases in the odds of new incidents.

The results regarding the additional covariates suggest that the preventive effect of arrest was modest relative to the size of the relationships between suspect and victim characteristics and failure rates. We base this assessment primarily on comparing the sizes of Menard's (1995) standardized logistic regression coefficients, which corresponds to a one standard deviation increase in the independent measure for every b standard deviation change in logit (Y). The standardized coefficients based on the official criminal history data were arrest = −0.01; interview exposure = 0.09; prior arrest = 0.19; white = −0.08; age = −0.05; intoxication = 0.04; employed = 0.01; and married = 0.00. The standardized coefficients for the victim interview data were arrest = −0.06; interview exposure = 0.15; prior record = 0.10; arrest = −0.06; age = −0.05; white = 0.05; married = 0.01; intoxication = 0.00; and employment = 0.00.

DISCUSSION AND CONCLUSION

The design and implementation of the Spouse Assault Replication Program approaches the standards for criminological research put forth by the National Academy of Sciences (Blumstein et al., 1978; Sechrest et al., 1979). The five experiments used a common protocol that included random assignment of treatment after selecting incidents, documentation of suspect and victim characteristics, collection of outcome data from multiple sources, and data elements that allowed for the construction of multiple dimensions of subsequent offending. Earlier efforts to synthesize the SARP results have failed to capitalize on these important characteristics. Instead, these earlier syntheses relied on qualitative methods (Schmidt and Sherman, 1993), tested models using data from only a few sites (Sherman et al., 1992a), modeled just one outcome from one data source (Berk et al., 1992), or relied on published results (Sugarman and Boney-McCoy, 2000). To address these shortcomings, our research integrated original data from all five experiments, standardized cases according to the nature of incidents, employed three dimensions of outcomes, controlled for natural variation between suspects and incidents, used multiple sources of information about outcomes, and controlled for variability in victim interview rates and timing.

Policy Implications

Our findings of a consistent reduction in the incidents of victimization due to arrest, independent of other criminal justice sanctions and individual processes, support the continued use of arrests as a preferred law enforcement response for reducing subsequent victimization of women by their intimate partners.[11] Although the size and statistical significance of the effect of arrest varied depending on whether victim interviews or law enforcement records measured the suspect's subsequent aggression, in all five measures, arrest is associated with fewer incidents of subsequent intimate partner aggression. This finding exists during the first several days after the experimental incident as well as beyond one year. Thus, our research does not find that arrest will eventually increase the risk for violence against women.

In several ways, the results we generated from the Spouse Assault Replication Program provide stronger support for pro-arrest policies than do the results from the Minneapolis Domestic Violence experiment. First, our findings stem from five jurisdictions with a total sample of more than 4,000 male suspects, whereas the Minneapolis findings were based on 314 incidents collected in one jurisdiction. Second, the random assignment procedures used in SARP were more rigorous than the one used in Minneapolis. Third, SARP researchers interviewed almost 80% of the female victims, whereas only about 60% were interviewed in Minneapolis. Finally, our analyses control for missing victim interviews, the variability in timing of victim interviews, and suspect characteristics. Sherman and Berk's (1984b) published findings consider only the assigned treatment effects.

In addition, our data and methods may underestimate the current empirical support for arrest for a number of reasons. First, although Sherman and Berk's (1984b) Minneapolis results provide strong support for the deterrent effect for arrest, we could not incorporate cases from Minneapolis into our analyses. If the archived Minneapolis data were sufficiently complete and similar to SARP's common data, their use would likely enhance the evidence for the effectiveness of arrest. Second, our analyses compared cases assigned to arrest with those cases not assigned to arrest. However, the police arrested about 10% of the cases assigned to an informal treatment. Thus, the comparison between the arrest and the nonarrest treatments is diluted. Had the treatment assignment been implemented perfectly, the size of our reported deterrent effect might have been even larger.

On the other hand, because the size of the deterrent effects found in our analyses is smaller than those reported in the Minneapolis experiment, and because the results from our analyses of the official criminal history data do not reach statistical significance, our findings provide weaker support for pro-arrest policies than the Minneapolis findings provided. Nevertheless, on balance, we believe that the predominate weight of the empirical regularities favors a conclusion that arrest has a modest preventive effect on intimate partner violence.

Unlike most criminological research, the Minneapolis Domestic Violence Experiment and SARP were part of a continuing program of research that focused on a theory-driven policy addressing an important social problem. The results of these efforts have identified some benefits of arrest, specifically, the reduction of victimization of female intimate partners. However, as extensive as this program was, it does not provide a complete basis for a systematic examination of the costs and the benefits of the use of arrest to address violence against women. For instance, some academics (e.g., Stark, 1993) have argued for arresting batterers no matter its deterrent benefits because the forced separation provides immediate, presumably incapacitative, protection for the victims. Others have pondered whether arrest may create negative outcomes when other effects on the victims, the suspects, and their families are considered. Binder and Meeker (1992) suggest that arrest may have both positive and negative collateral consequences on children in the household, the likelihood that a spouse will call the police in the future, the stability of the marriage, and the suspect's employment status (see also Berk and Sherman, 1985; McCord, 1992). In addition, both fiscal and resource expenditures are attached to arresting suspects as well as possible reductions in expenditures due to law enforcement agencies responding to fewer subsequent encounters with suspects. However, neither SARP nor other systematic research has generated evidence about other possible costs or benefits of arrests. Although this type of assessment is routine in the development of environmental, health, and safety regulations (Cohen, 2000), we are unaware of any attempt to address the question of whether the benefits we find outweigh the cost of arrest to society. Therefore, a more thorough assessment of a policy promoting or mandating arrest needs to capture both the major costs and benefits of arrest.

The findings from the SARP experiment also suggest real limitations in the effectiveness of arrest in reducing violence against women. The evidence from this study shows that regardless of the treatment assigned and irrespective of the data source, most victims reported no subsequent victimization by their male partner during follow-up periods that ranged from six months to more than two years. The mere physical presence of a police officer may redefine the parameters of the violence from an interpersonal struggle for power to one that now involves, formally or informally, outsiders. Although the presence of an outsider may last from a few minutes to an hour, it may be enough to convince many suspects that the victim and the police mean business. In other words, the threat of arrest may suffice as the best specific deterrent for most suspects.[12]

However, victimizations also persisted for about 40% of victims. We estimate that the average suspect with at least one subsequent incident had committed about an average of seven new incidents of aggression against the same victim within just the first six months of follow-up. Apparently, some women continue to be victimized multiple times by their intimate partners, even after the police have responded to a request for help. For these reasons, the SARP experiments show that arresting suspects, although effective on average, is not a panacea for all victims of intimate partner violence. This suggests that other policies, either replacing or enhancing the use of arrest, that focus on identifying potential repeat offenders and either treating, sanctioning, or incapacitating them might produce larger reductions in intimate partner violence. The challenge is twofold: developing plausible policies and carrying out a long-term, systematic research program that rigorously tests the underlying theories of those policies.

Testing Theory

Sherman (1980) designed the Minneapolis Domestic Violence Experiment as a test of specific deterrence theory. Its apparent impact on public policy might be a coincidence or a single example that illustrates a point—successful efforts at policy relevance need not be atheoretical. We believe that the use of theory in the Minneapolis and SARP experiments should enhance their policy relevance because the theoretical framework provides a basis for generalizing the results beyond a few jurisdictions at one point in time. However, the theoretical formulation used in the Minneapolis and SARP experiments was not fully devel-oped. It merely asserted that there would be some reduction in criminal behav-ior with use of a formal sanction. This simple formulation makes specific deterrence theory infallible; because with any contrary finding, researchers can assert that the sanction was not swift, certain, or severe enough.

With our research, the field now has systematic evidence about how much reduction in subsequent violence is associated with arresting suspects for inti-mate partner violence. However, we agree with Lempert (1989) that additional sanctions need to be tested in ways that experimentally compare variations in the certainty, celerity, and severity across a variety of offenses, offenders, and victims. SARP contributes to this kind of theory-testing effort by examining one sanction for one offense in a variety of contexts. One of our concerns is that others might instead overgeneralize our results to support the use of more severe sanctions, particularly to control intimate partner violence, despite other research reporting no gains for domestic violence victims from more punitive practices such as prosecution (Davis et al., 1998; Ford, 1991; Steinman, 1990; Thistlethwaite et al., 1998). For these reasons, we advise against simple extrap-olations of the preventive effects of arrest to other criminal justice sanctions, such as the restraining orders or incarceration of batterers without further sys-tematic research and evaluation.

In addition, we suggest that future research obtain measurements of the offender's immediate and long-term cognitive reactions to sanctions and treat-ments. Subsequent research also would be stronger if it measured secondary outcomes like changes in offenders' employment status and familial relation-ships, or the victims' and children's welfare.[13] These measurements could fur-ther our understanding of the "black box" of specific deterrence (Manning, 1993:641) and permit an assessment of whether there are unintended conse-quences of sanctions on those not directly punished. As McCord (1992:233) argued, further research on domestic violence needs to go beyond the concept of deterrence by also assessing whether sanctions lead to outcomes like "loss of support for children or loss of shelter." Except for interviewing some arrestees in Milwaukee (Sherman et al., 1990), the SARP experiments did not measure the suspects' attitudes and perceptions and therefore cannot address the variety of underlying mechanisms suggested by Gibbs (1975) that might account for the association between increased sanctions and reduced offending found here. At this time, the available research can only estimate the amount of subsequent aggression reduced because of arrest. We need further research to understand more completely why and when sanctions deter and whether secondary con-sequences of arrest exist.

Suspect Characteristics

Several suspect characteristics are significantly related to the prevalence, fre-quency, and timing of the first new incident of victimization and recidivism. For instance, the odds of new victimization were 30% to 60% less for each additional year of age. Also, according to the official data, suspects with prior arrests for any offense are from 250% to 330% more likely to commit new acts of intimate partner violence. Unlike the consistent effects for suspect's age and prior record, the contradictory findings regarding their race in victim interviews and official records present a conundrum for this and subsequent research. From official records, white suspects are less likely to re-offend after the experimental incident. The effect size is large, with a 30% reduction in the odds for both the frequency and timing of an officially recorded failure. However, the victim interview data yielded the opposite result: White suspects are 30% more likely than are nonwhite suspects to continue victimization. There are several plausible explanations for this contradiction, including race interactions with the severity of violence, the different treatments, or the willingness of victims to report incidents to the police.[14] Future research will need to address these possibilities to unravel the complex role of race and should also incorporate the suspect's age and arrest record.

NOTES

1. In Omaha, victims were to be interviewed three times over a year. In Colorado Springs, three-quarters of the victims were to be interviewed every two weeks for the first three months, and all were interviewed at six months. In Milwaukee, 25% of victims were not interviewed until six months after the experimental incident. For more details about the SARP designs, see Maxwell (1998) and Garner and Maxwell (2000).

2. The idea for this design was originally proposed by Albert J. Reiss, Jr. and Robert F. Boruch.

3. The majority of decisions to avoid the random assignment (78% of misdelivered treatments) involved suspects who were randomly assigned to nonarrest treatments but were arrested. Officers chose not to arrest when arrest was assigned in 59 (22%) of all misdelivered treatments.

4. A logistic regression model found that the only suspect characteristics that predicted misdelivery of treatment are intoxication ($b = 0.57; p < 0.001$) and unemployment ($b = 0.30; p < 0.05$).

5. The Colorado Springs design called for interviews in the first and sixth month for 25% of the cases and for monthly interviews for 75% of the sample. The archived data from this site did not identify the actual date of any interview. To avoid losing the Colorado Springs data, we used the dates the interview was scheduled to occur.

6. We compared a poisson regression with a negative binomial regression, but in every instance, there was too much overdispersion to justify using the results based on the Poisson Regression model. This result is consistent with what has been found with other criminal justice data of similar format (Land et al., 1996).

7. We tested the Cox regression assumption of equal or proportional hazards by introducing a time-dependent covariate that indicates whether the effect of arrest is dependent on the passage of time. While controlling for site effects, we found that the time-dependent covariate is not significantly associated ($b = 0.00; p = 0.08$) with the hazard rate.

8. We report findings from the models that include controls for suspect characteristics because we believe these provide the most precise estimate of the effect of arrest.

9. In addition to arrest, some suspects received additional criminal justice sanctions or controls, such as restraining orders, conviction, probation, fines, or incarceration. In the Milwaukee experiment, the researcher found that 60% of the suspects appeared at the prosecutor's office for charging, 3.2% were charged, and 2.7% were required to attend counseling. The researchers also asked the victims about the presence of restraining orders and found that 12% reported having one against the suspect (Bousa et al., 1990). In the Charlotte site,

about 25% of the suspects either pled guilty or were found guilty regardless of their assigned treatment. The Omaha and Colorado sites also collected data on court disposition, but no disposition information was collected in Dade. Although it may have been valuable to include measures of additional sanctions, there were several reasons we could not do so in our multisite analysis. First, these subsequent treatments were not randomly assigned. Thus, any analysis would be confounded with selection biases. Second, we do not know the timing of subsequent sanctions so we would not know whether re-offending started before or after the sanction. Third, although some of the experiments collected and archived data about some of these issues, these items were not common data elements in the SARP design.

10. The high correlation between victim and suspect demographics precluded us from including both in the same model.

11. One alternative explanation for our findings is that arrest does not change suspect offending as much as it changes the victim's willingness to report offenses to the police and to interviewers. Two recent empirical studies do not support this speculation. Using data from SARP's Metro-Dade County Experiment, Hickman (2000) found that the use of arrest in the experimental incident was not related to reporting subsequent incidents to the police. Felson and Ackerman (2001), using NCVS data,

found that the existence of prior domestic assaults increased the respondent's willingness to sign a police complaint.

12. The argument that there is desistance from calling the police is consistent with Bowker (1984) and Dutton et al.'s (1991) claim that social disclosure alone deters further domestic violence. Although these scholars were speaking about disclosure originating out of an arrest, the same effect seems likely to occur from just calling the police.

13. See, for instance, Paternoster and Brame's (1997) test of the effect of police procedural justice on recidivism using information from interviews of arrested offenders from the Milwaukee Domestic Violence Experiment.

14. Similar to our finding concerning the relationship between aggression and race, Bachman and Coker (1995) found evidence using the National Crime Victimization Survey that victimized African-American women were more likely to call the police compared with victimized white women. They also found that if the police were called to the scene, the officers were more likely to arrest the suspect if the victim and suspect were both African-American. Together, these two findings suggest an explanation for the relationship between the suspect's race and the likelihood of officially recorded failure found in SARP.

REFERENCES

Armitage, Peter (1996). The design and analysis for clinical trials. In Subir Ghosh and Caly-ampudi Radhakrishna Rao (eds.), *Design and Analysis of Experiments, Vol. 13, Handbook of Statistics.* Amsterdam: Elsevier.

Bachman, Ronet and Ann L. Coker (1995). Police involvement in domestic violence: The interactive effects of victim injury, offender's history of violence, and race. *Violence and Victims* 10:91–106.

Berk, Richard A. (1993). What the scientific evidence shows: On the average, we can do no better than arrest. In Richard J. Gelles and Donileen R. Loseke (eds.), *Current Controversies on Family Violence.* Newbury Park, Calif.: Sage.

Berk, Richard A. and Lawrence W. Sherman (1985). Data collection strategies in the Minneapolis domestic violence experiment. In Leigh Burstein, Howard E. Freeman, and Peter H. Rossi (eds.), *Collecting Evaluation Data:*

Problems and Solutions. Beverly Hills, Calif.: Sage.

Berk, Richard A., Alec Campbell, Ruth Klap, and Bruce Western (1988). Police responses to family violence incidences: An analysis of an experimental design with incomplete randomization. *Journal of the American Statistical Association* 83:70–76.

Berk, Richard A., Alec Campbell, Ruth Klap, and Bruce Western (1992). The deterrent effect of arrest in incidents of domestic violence: A Bayesian analysis of four field experiments. *American Journal of Sociology* 57:698–708.

Binder, Arnold and James Meeker (1988). Experiments as reforms. *Journal of Criminal Justice* 16:347–358.

Binder, Arnold and James Meeker (1992). Arrest as a method to control spouse abuse. In Eve S. Buzawa and Carl G. Buzawa (eds.), *Domestic Violence: The Changing Criminal Justice Response.* Westport, Colo.: Greenwood.

Blumstein, Alfred, Jacqueline Cohen, and Daniel Nagin (eds.) (1978). *Estimating the Effects of Criminal Sanctions on Crime Rates.* Washington, D.C.: National Academy Press.

Blumstein, Alfred, Jacqueline Cohen, Jeffrey A. Roth, and Christy A. Visher (eds.) (1986). *Criminal Careers and "Career Criminals."* Washington, D.C.: National Academy Press.

Boffey, Philip M. (1983). Domestic violence: Study favors arrest. *New York Times* (5 April):Cl.

Bousa, Dominick, Sherman, Janell D. Schmidt, Dennis Rogan, and Patrick Gartin (1990). *Codebook and Frequencies for the Milwaukee Domestic Violence Experiment: The Criminal Justice Processing File.* Washington, D.C.: Crime Control Institute.

Bowker, Lee N. (1984). Coping with wife abuse: Personal and social networks. In Albert R. Roberts (ed.), *Battered Women and Their Families.* New York: Springer.

Chalk, Rosemary A. and Patricia A. King (eds.) (1998). *Violence in Families: Assessing Prevention and Treatment Programs.* Committee on the Assessment of Family Violence Intervention, Board on Children, Youth, and Families, National Research Council and Institute of Medicine. Washington, D.C: National Academy of Science.

Clark. Jacob R. (1993). Where to now on domestic-violence? Studies offer mixed policy guidance. *Law Enforcement News* (30 April):1,17.

Cohen, Mark A. (2000). Measuring the Costs and Benefits of Crime and Justice. David Duffee (ed.). *Criminal Justice* 2000,4, no. NCJ 182411. Washington, D.C.: U.S. Department of Justice, Office of Justice Programs, National Institute of Justice.

Cooper, Harris and Larry V. Hedges (1994). Research synthesis as a scientific enterprise. In Harris Cooper and Larry V. Hedges (eds.), *The Handbook of Research Synthesis.* New York: Russell Sage.

Davis, Robert C., and Barbara Smith (1995). Domestic violence reforms: Empty promises or fulfilled expectations? *Crime & Delinquency* 41:541–552.

Davis, Robert C., Barbara E. Smith, and Laura B. Nickles (1998). The deterrent effect of prosecuting domestic violence misdemeanors. *Crime & Delinquency* 3:434–442.

Dutton, Donald G., Stephen G. Hart, Leslie W. Kennedy, and Kirk R. Williams (1991). Arrest and the reduction of repeat wife assault. In Eve Buzawa and Carl Buzawa (eds.), *Domestic Violence: The Changing Criminal Justice Response.* Westport, Conn.: Greenwood.

Fagan, Jeffrey A. (1996). The Criminalization of Domestic Violence: Promises and limits. Presented at the Conference on Criminal Justice Research and Evaluation. Washington, D.C., National Institute of Justice.

Fagan, Jeffery A. and Angela Browne (1994). Violence against spouses and intimates. Panel on the Understanding and Control of Violent Behavior, Committee on Law and Justice, Commission on Behavioral and Social Science and Education, National Research Council. In Albert J. Reiss, Jr. and

Jeffrey A. Roth (eds.), *Understanding and Controlling Violence,* Vol. 3. Washington, D.C.: National Academy Press.

Farrington, David P. (1986). Age and crime. In Michael Tonry and Noval Morris (eds.), *Crime and Justice: An Annual Review of Research, Vol. 7, Crime and Justice.* Chicago, Ill.: University of Chicago Press.

Feld, Scott L. and Murray Straus (1989). Escalation and desistance of wife assault in marriage. *Criminology* 27:141–161.

Felson, Richard B. and Jeff Ackerman (2001). Arrest for domestic violence and other assaults. *Criminology* 39:655–675.

Ford, David (1991). Prosecution as a victim power source: A note on empowering women in violent conjugal relationships. *Law & Society Review* 25:313–334.

Frisch, Lisa A. (1992). Research that succeeds, policies that fail. *Journal of Criminal Law & Criminology* 83:209–216.

Garner, Joel H. and Christopher D. Maxwell (2000). What are the lessons of the police arrest studies? *Journal of Aggression. Maltreatment & Trauma* 4(1):83–114.

Garner, Joel H., Jeffrey A. Fagan, and Christopher D. Maxwell (1995). Published findings from the Spouse Assault Replication Program: A critical review. *Journal of Quantitative Criminology* 11:3–28.

Gibbs, Jack P. (1975). *Crime, Punishment and Deterrence.* New York: Elsevier.

Heckman, James J. (1979). Sample selection bias as a specification error. *Econometrica* 47:153–161.

Heckman, James J. and Richard Robb (1986). Alternative methods for solving the problem of selection bias in evaluating the impact of treatment outcomes. In Howard Wainer (ed.), *Drawing Inferences from Self-Selected Samples.* Papers from a conference sponsored by Education Testing Services. New York: Springer-Verlag.

Hickman, Laura Jean (2000). Exploring the impact of police behavior on the subsequent reporting of domestic violence

victims. Ph.D. dissertation, University of Maryland at College Park.

Hirschel, J. David and Ira W. Hutchison III (1991). Police-preferred arrest policies. In Michael Steinman (ed.), *Women Battering: Policy Responses,* Vol. 3. Highland Heights, KY and Cincinnati, Ohio: Anderson Publishing Co. and Academy of Criminal Justice Science.

Kantor, Glenda K. and Murray A. Straus (1987). The "drunken bum" theory of wife beating. *Social Problems* 34:213–321

Klinger, David A. and George S. Bridges (1997). Measurement error in calls-for-service as an indicator of crime. *Criminology* 35:705–726.

Land, Kenneth C., Patricia L. McCall, and Daniel S. Nagin (1996). A comparison of Poisson, negative binomial, and semiparametric mixed regression models with empirical applications to criminal careers data. *Sociological Methods and Research* 24:387–442.

Langan, Patrick A. and Christopher A. Innes (1986). *Preventing Domestic Violence Against Women, Special Report.* Washington, D.C.: U.S. Government Printing Office.

Lempert, Richard (1984). From the editor. *Law & Society Review* 18:505–513. (1989). Humility is a virtue: On the publication of policy relevant research. *Law & Society Review* 23:145–161.

Lerman, Lisa G. (1992). The decontextualization of domestic violence. *Journal of Criminal Law & Criminology* 83:217–240.

Manning, Peter K. (1993). The preventive conceit: The black box in market context. *American Behavioral Scientist* 36:639–650.

Maxwell, Christopher D. (1998). The specific deterrent effect of arrest on aggression between intimates and spouses. Ph.D. dissertation, Newark, N.J.: Rutgers, the State University of New Jersey.

Maxwell, Christopher D., Joel H. Garner. and Jeffrey A. Fagan (2001). *The Effects of Arrest on Intimate Partner Violence: New Evidence from the Spouse Assault*

Replication Program. Research in Brief. Washington, D.C.: U.S. Department of Justice, Office of Justice Programs, National Institute of Justice.

McCord, Joan (1992). Deterrence of domestic violence: A critical view of research. *Journal of Research in Crime and Delinquency* 29(2):229–239.

Menard, Scott (1995). *Applied Logistic Regression Analysis, Quantitative Applications in the Social Sciences.* 07–106. Michael S. Lewis-Beck (ed.). Thousand Oaks, Calif.: Sage.

Mitchell, David B. (1992). Contemporary police practices in domestic violence cases: Arresting the abuser: Is it enough? *Journal of Criminal Law & Criminology* 83:241–249.

Moffitt, Terrie E., Robert F. Krueger, Avshalom Caspi, and Jeffrey Fagan (2000). Partner abuse and general crime: How are they the same? How are they different? *Criminology* 38:199–232.

Nagin, Daniel S. and David P. Farrington (1992). The onset and persistence of offending. *Criminology* 30:501–523.

National Institute of Justice (1985). *Replicating an Experiment in Specific Deterrence: Alternative Police Responses to Spouse Assault.* Washington, D.C.: National Institute of Justice.

Pate, Anthony and Edwin E. Hamilton (1992). Formal and informal deterrents to domestic violence. *American Sociological Review* 57:691–697.

Paternoster, Raymond and Robert Brame (1997). Multiple routes to delinquency? A test of developmental and general theories of crime. *Criminology* 35:49–84.

Quigley, Brian M. and Kenneth E. Leonard (1996). Desistance of husband aggression in the early years of marriage. *Violence and Victims* 11:355–370.

Sampson, Robert J. and John H. Laub (1993). Structural variations in juvenile court processing: Inequality, the underclass, and social control. *Law and Society Review* 27:285–311.

Schmidt, Janell D. and Lawrence W. Sherman (1993). Does arrest deter domestic violence? *American Behavioral Scientist* 36:601–610.

Sechrest, Lee, Susan O. White, and Elizabeth Brown (eds.) (1979). *The Rehabilitation of Criminal Offenders: Problems and Prospects.* Washington, D.C.: National Academy of Sciences.

Sherman, Lawrence W. (1980). Specific deterrent effect of spouse assault. Proposal submitted to the National Institute of Justice Crime Control Theory Program. U.S. Department of Justice, Washington, D.C.

Sherman, Lawrence W. (1992). *Policing Domestic Violence: Experiments and Dilemmas.* New York: Free Press.

Sherman, Lawrence W. and R. A. Berk (1984a). The Minneapolis Domestic Violence Experiment. Police Foundation Reports, No. 1. Washington, D.C.

Sherman, Lawrence W. and R. A. Berk (1984b). The specific deterrent effects of arrest for domestic assault. *American Sociological Review* 49:261–272.

Sherman, Lawerence W. and Ellen G. Cohn (1989). The impact of research on legal policy: The Minneapolis Domestic Violence Experiment. *Law and Society Review* 23:117–144

Sherman, Lawrence W., Douglas A. Smith, Janell D. Schmidt, and Dennis P. Rogan (1992a). Crime, punishment, and stake in conformity: Legal and informal control of domestic violence. *American Sociological Review* 57:680–690.

Sherman, Lawerence W., Janell D. Schmidt, Dennis P. Rogan, Douglas A. Smith, Patrick Gartin, Ellen G. Cohen, Dean J. Collins, and Anthony R. Bacich (1992b). The variable effects of arrest on crime control: The Milwaukee Domestic Violence Experiment. *Journal of Criminal Law & Criminology* 83:137–169.

Sherman, Lawrence W., Janell D Schmidt, Dennis P. Rogan, Patrick R. Gartin, Dean J. Collins, Anthony Bacich, and Ellen G. Cohn (1990). *The Milwaukee*

Domestic Violence Experiment. Final Report. Washington, D.C.: Crime Control Institute.

Stark, Evan (1993). Mandatory arrest of batterers: A reply to its critics. *American Behavioral Scientist* 36:651–680.

Steinman, Michael (1990). Lowering recidivism among men who batter women. *Journal of Police Science and Administration* 17:124–132.

Sugarman, David B. and Sue Boney-McCoy (2000). Research synthesis in family violence: The art of reviewing the research. *Journal of Aggression, Maltreatment & Trauma* 4:55–82.

Thistlethwaite, Amy, John Wooldredge, and David Gibbs (1998). Severity of disposition and domestic violence recidivism. *Crime & Delinquency* 3:388–398.

U.S. Attorney General's Task Force on Family Violence (1984). *Attorney General's Task Force on Family Violence. Final Report*. Washington, D.C.: U.S. Government Printing Office.

Violence Against Women Grants Office (1996). Grants to Encourage Arrest Policies Programs. Proposed Regulations No. 28 CFR Part 90 [OJP No. 1019] RIN 1121–AA35. Washington, D.C.: Office for Justice Programs, U.S. Department of Justice, 13.

Wilson, James O. (1977). Forward. In Police Foundation (ed.), *Domestic Violence and the Police*. Washington, D.C.: Police Foundation.

Zimring, Franklin E. (1989). Toward a jurisprudence of family violence. In Lloyd Oblin and Michael Tonry (eds.), *Family Violence, Vol. 11, Crime and Justice: A Review of Research*. Chicago, Ill.: University of Chicago Press.

Zorza, Joan and Laurie Woods (1994). *Analysis and Policy Implications of the New Police Domestic Violence Studies*. New York: National Center on Women and Family Law.

9

❂

Police Use of Deadly Force

Research and Reform

James J. Fyfe

Police use of deadly force first became a major public issue in the 1960s when many urban riots were precipitated by police killings of citizens. Since then, departments have made significant reforms in their policies regarding the use of deadly force, and the U.S. Supreme Court in Tennessee v. Garner *(1985) voided the rule existing in about half the states that allowed the use of deadly force to apprehend unarmed, nonviolent, fleeing felony suspects. James Fyfe examines the factors that seem to distinguish the extensive use of deadly force in some departments.*

W hen police officers fire their guns, the immediate consequences of their decisions are realized at the rate of 750 feet per second and are beyond reversal by any level of official review. As most police recruits learn in the academy, the cop on the street . . . carries in his holster more power than has been granted the Chief Justice of the Supreme Court. When used injudiciously, this power has led to riot and additional death, civil and criminal litigation against police and their employers, and the ousters of police chiefs, elected officials, and entire city administrations. Even when used with great restraint, police deadly force has created polarization, suspicion, and distrust on the part of those who need the police most.

• • •

Source: From James J. Fyfe, "Police Use of Deadly Force: Research and Reform," *Justice Quarterly* 5 (June 1988), pp. 165–166, 168–170, 171–174, 180–189, 199–205. Some footnotes and references deleted.

LEGAL AND ADMINISTRATIVE
CONTROLS ON DEADLY FORCE

. . . The President's Commission on Law Enforcement and Administration of Justice looked carefully at police-community relations. In the report of its Task Force on the Police—which, in my view, remains the single most significant and most influential contribution to American police policy and practice to date—the commission made clear its dismay at the virtual absence of administrative policies to guide police officers' decisions to use deadly force (President's Commission 1967:189-190). In a report to the commission, Police Task Force chair Samuel Chapman cited the full text of one unnamed police department's policy on use of firearms as an illustration of the need for direction in this most critical matter of police discretion:

> Never take me out in anger; never put me back in disgrace (Chapman 1967).

Chapman also saw to it that the final report of the task force included a model administration policy on use of firearms (President's Commission 1967:188-189). This was not the first time he had championed this cause; in 1963 he and Thompson Crockett reported on a 1961 survey of seventy-one Michigan police departments serving populations of 10,000 or more. They found that

> 54 percent (27 of 50) of the agencies furnishing information had no written policies in effect to govern the use of firearms. These twenty-seven departments, which relied upon "oral policy," were asked to indicate the main points of oral instructions given to their officers regarding when to use firearms. Of the twenty-seven, only five departments mentioned such basic situations as self-defense and fleeing felons where firearms may be used. Thus, based on the reported practice in these Michigan cities, it would appear reasonable to regard with grave reservation that suitability of relying singularly upon "oral policy" (Chapman and Crockett 1963:42).

Further:

> "[W]hen to fire" is frequently trusted to the "judgment" or "discretion" of officers as individuals . . . (1963:41).

• • •

The Breadth of Law

In the absence of such policies, police shooting discretion generally was limited only by state criminal statutes or by case law defining justifiable homicide. These laws have several inadequacies. First, even the most restrictive state laws permit police to use their weapons in an extremely broad range of situations. Every state historically has permitted police officers to use deadly force to defend themselves or others against imminent death or serious physical harm, a provision that cannot be debated seriously. Indeed, except that generally they are obliged to attempt to retreat to safety before resorting to deadly force, American citizens enjoy the same justification for homicide. Because we ask the police to put their lives on the line in our behalf, it follows that they should enjoy this slight advantage over the rest of us.

Yet many states also have codified some variant of the common-law "flee-ing felon" rule, which authorizes use of deadly force as a means of apprehend-ing persons fleeing from suspected felonies. The Tennessee statute that eventually became the focus of *Tennessee v. Garner* (1985) illustrates the broadest category of such laws:

> *Resistance to Officer*—If after notice of the intention to arrest the [felony] defendant, he either flees or forcibly resists, the officer may use all the necessary means to effect the arrest (Tennessee Code Annotated sec. 40-7-108:55).

• • •

The manner in which felony suspects are pursued and apprehended has changed in important ways over the centuries. When the fleeing felon rule originated, those who typically pursued felons were ordinary male citizens who were obliged by law to respond to the *hue and cry* and to join in pursuit. Because they were usually armed only with clubs or knives, discharging their duty to arrest compelled them to overpower physically people who knew that arrest was likely to result in execution. These circumstances also are a far cry from more modern applications of the fleeing felon rule. The officer involved in *Garner*, for example, fired his fatal shot from the relative safety of 30 feet at the back of an unarmed, 5'4", 100-pound juvenile burglary suspect who, if apprehended alive, would likely have been sentenced to probation.

Debates about the merits of the *any* fleeing felon laws came to an abrupt end in 1985, when the Supreme Court ruled in *Garner* that the Tennessee statute, when applied against unarmed, nondangerous fleeing suspects, violated the Fourth Amendment's guarantees against unreasonable seizure. In his opin-ion for the majority, Justice White wrote that deadly force was a constitutional means of effecting arrest only when a felony "suspect threatens the officer with a weapon or there is probable cause to believe that he has committed a crime involving the infliction or threatened infliction of serious physical harm" (*Tennessee v. Garner*, 471 U.S. at 4). This decision affects the laws not only of the twenty-three states that followed the broad *any* fleeing felon rule; because Garner was a suspect in a nighttime residential burglary, it also affects the laws of several other states that included this offense under the limited category of offenses justifying deadly force for purposes of apprehension.

The Law as a Control on Professional Discretion

Although *Garner* moots some of the arguments about the great breadth of deadly force statutes, it does little to ameliorate a second and more general lim-itation of law in describing police shooting discretion: in no field of human endeavor does the criminal law alone define adequately the parameters of acceptable occupational behavior. In the course of their work, doctors, lawyers, psychologists, professors, soldiers, nursing home operators, truck drivers, government officials, and journalists can do many outrageous, unacceptable, and hurtful things without violating criminal law. In exchange for the monopolies on the activities performed by those in their crafts, the most highly developed of these professions keep their members' behavior in check by developing and enforcing codes of conduct that are both more specific and more restrictive than are criminal definitions. Who would submit to treatment by a surgeon whose choices in deciding how to deal with patients were limited only by the laws of homicide and assault?

Apply that logic to use of police firearms. Even post-*Garner*, no state law tells officers whether it is advisable to fire warning shots into the air on streets lined by high-rise buildings. The law provides no direction to officers who must decide quickly whether to shoot at people in moving vehicles and thereby risk turning them into speeding unguided missiles. The law related to police use of force, in short, is simply too vague to be regarded as a comprehensive set of operational guidelines.

RESISTANCE TO RULE MAKING REGARDING DEADLY FORCE

Even so, many police administrators did not act on policy recommendations like Chapman's until their officers had become involved in shootings that (although noncriminal) generated community outcries and crises (Sherman 1983). Their sometimes vigorous resistance to change was rooted in many considerations. First, police authority to restrict shooting discretion more tightly than state law was uncertain. In 1971, for example, the Florida Attorney General issued a written opinion that administrative policies overriding the state's any fleeing felon law were legally impermissible (Florida Attorney General 1971:68–75); this narrow view of the separation of powers has been cast aside since in favor of more realistic interpretations of police chiefs' administrative prerogatives. In addition, apparently on the theory that jurors were unlikely to find police behavior unreasonable unless officers had violated their own departments' formal rules and policies, some police officials refrained from committing deadly force policies to paper. Time also has shown that this rather self-serving attempt to avoid accountability and liability was counterproductive: jurors don't need a piece of paper to tell them whether an individual officer acted reasonably, but typically they do find that a police department's failure to provide officers with such paper is inexcusable. Finally, many police officers feared that restrictive deadly force policies would endanger the public and the police; by removing whatever deterrent value inhered in the fleeing felon rule, such policies would result in an increase in crime and a decrease in police ability to apprehend fleeing criminals. Indeed, even when research suggested that this was not the case (Fyfe 1979), many police chiefs continued to regard restrictive deadly force policies as invitations to public accusations that they were "weak on crime" or had "handcuffed the police."

By now, however, the question of whether police should promulgate restrictive deadly force policies has been answered in the affirmative; at least among larger agencies, it is the rare department whose manual does not include such a policy. Social science research has played some part in easing police resistance to formulation of deadly force policy, and in the Supreme Court's *Garner* decision as well.

• • •

EXPLANATIONS OF VARIATIONS IN POLICE HOMICIDE RATES

In attempts to explain why officers in some police departments are more likely than those in others to use deadly force and to kill, researchers generally have identified two sets of variables as salient. One is environmental and lies beyond the direct control of police administrators; the other is internal and is subject to control by police chiefs. The former category includes such variables as the level of violence among the constituencies of the police and the extent of lawful police authority to use deadly force. Included in the second category are such variables as general police operating philosophies and specific policies, both formal and unstated.

Environmental Explanations

Because police exposure to situations likely to precipitate shooting is presumably greatest where levels of general community violence are high, we would expect to find strong relationships between police homicide rates and measures of community violence and police contact with offenders. Perhaps the first researchers to explore such a hypothesis were Kania and Mackey (1977), who reported strong associations between the National Center for Health Statistics police homicide rates (however inaccurate) and rates of public homicide and violent crime across the states. In their intercity study, Sherman and Langworthy (1979) found the same kinds of associations between police homicide rates and such measures of potential police—citizen violence as gun density and rates of arrest for all offenses and for violent offenses. Finally, I (Fyfe 1980b) found strong associations between rates of shooting by onduty officers and rates of public homicide and arrests for violent crime across twenty police subjurisdictions within New York City.

There is a statistically significant association ($p = .002$) between the police homicide rates shown in Table 1 and the most easily derivable measure of public violence, the corresponding public homicide rates. As even a cursory examination of the table would suggest, however (is New Orleans really four times as violent as Washington, D.C., for example?), this measure accounts for only 13 percent of the variation in police homicide rates ($r = .37$; $r^2 = .13$).

The table also suggests that the second environmental factor, the law of police deadly force, is of little help in explaining variation in police homicide rates. If the law were operative here, one would not expect to find (for example) that officers in Long Beach (rate = 6.10) killed citizens twice as often as their colleagues across the city line in Los Angeles (rate = 3.05), or that the police homicide rate in Jacksonville (7.17) was twice as high as in the more notorious Miami (3.50).

Internal Organizational Explanations

Certainly the police reflect the violence of the environments in which they work, and the police are duty-bound to operate within the law. Yet the limits of the law have been discussed already, and it is apparent that other things also are at work here. More specifically, as Uelman (1973) suggested in his research on variations in shooting rates among fifty police departments in Los Angeles County, it is clear that such internal organizational variables as the philosophies, policies, and practices of individual police chiefs and supervisors account for a considerable amount of variation in police homicide rates. Uelman's conclusion has been buttressed by studies (Fyfe 1979; Gain 1971; Meyer 1980; Milton, Halleck, Lardner, and Abrecht 1977; Scharf and Binder 1983) that report, with varying degrees of rigor and certainty, that reductions in police shooting frequency and changes in police shooting patterns have followed implementation of restrictive administrative policies on deadly force and weapons use.

A Case in Point

Without detailed analysis of the context and content of police officials' utterances and policy statements, it is impossible in an essay of this type to sort out their effects in a manner that would satisfy methodological purists. Even so, the effect of police operating philosophy and policy on police deadly force has been most striking in Philadelphia. There the police commissioner in 1970 and 1971 was Frank Rizzo, the flamboyant hard-liner[1] who went on to serve as mayor from 1972 through 1979. In 1973, when the Pennsylvania legislature modified its deadly force statute to prohibit shooting at fleeing persons who were not suspected of "forcible felonies" (Pennsylvania Statutes Annotated 1973), the Philadelphia Police Department (PPD) abolished its former restrictive policy on deadly force on the grounds that the legislature had not defined "forcible felonies" adequately. From that point until Rizzo left office, PPD adopted an operating style in which police were effectively free to do anything with their guns, as long as they did not use them to resolve their own personal disputes.[2]

Figure 1 suggests that some PPD officers took great advantage of this freedom. During 1972, the last full year in which PPD operated under a restrictive deadly force policy, the PPD homicide rate per 1,000 officers was 1.47 (with twelve deaths resulting); the rate jumped to 2.87 (twenty-three deaths) in 1973 and peaked at 3.52 (twenty-nine deaths) in 1974. In 1976, when the city was cooperating in a federal court request to develop means of ending abuse of citizens, the police homicide rate dipped briefly to 1.35. In 1977, after the

Table 1 Mean Annual Rate of Police Homicide per 1,000 Officers by Geographic Region and City, 1975–1983

	Rate per 1,000	Number		Rate per 1,000	Number
Northeast	1.39	480	Memphis	3.75	42
Boston	1.19	22	Miami	3.50	25
Buffalo	0.50	5	Nashville	3.28	28
Newark	1.90	22	New Orleans	6.80	91
New York	1.36	295	Norfolk	1.68	9
Philadelphia	1.66	116	Tampa	3.14	17
Pittsburgh	0.81	10	Washington	1.55	56
Rochester	1.78	10	West	2.85	751
North Central	2.24	628	Albuquerque	1.94	9
Akron	0.97	4	Austin	0.87	4
Chicago	1.71	197	Dallas	4.32	78
Cincinnati	1.88	17	Denver	2.26	28
Cleveland	2.59	44	El Paso	1.88	11
Columbus	2.94	28	Fort Worth	1.91	12
Detroit	3.33	143	Honolulu	0.37	5
Indianapolis	3.75	34	Houston	4.73	130
Kansas City	2.71	29	Long Beach	6.10	34
Milwaukee	0.86	16	Los Angeles	3.05	192
Minneapolis	1.62	11	Oakland	5.22	30
Omaha	2.42	12	Oklahoma City	4.79	30
St. Louis	3.61	64	Phoenix	1.84	27
St. Paul	0.42	2	Portland, OR	0.81	5
Toledo	1.86	11	Sacramento	0.44	2
Wichita	4.33	16	San Antonio	2.74	28
South	3.10	447	San Diego	2.87	32
Atlanta	3.28	37	San Francisco	1.40	22
Baltimore	1.82	53	San Jose	2.62	19
Birmingham	5.19	31	Seattle	1.86	17
Charlotte	1.31	7	Tucson	3.08	15
Jacksonville	7.17	61	Tulsa	3.54	21
Louisville	3.11	20	Totals	2.24	2,236

SOURCE: Derived from Kenneth Matulia, *A Balance of Forces,* 2d ed. (Gaithersburg, Md.: International Association of Chiefs of Police, 1985), pp. A–4, A–5.

Supreme Court dismissed the case that had resulted in this agreement, the rate doubled (deaths rose from eleven to twenty-one). In 1981, the first full year of a new restrictive deadly force policy,[3] the rate decreased to 0.80 and remained relatively low during the next two years. Overall, the PPD police homicide rates were 2.09 while Rizzo was police commissioner, 2.29 while he was mayor, and 1.05 after he was out of office (as compared to the annual PPD homicide rate of 0.61 over 1950–1960; see Robin 1963).

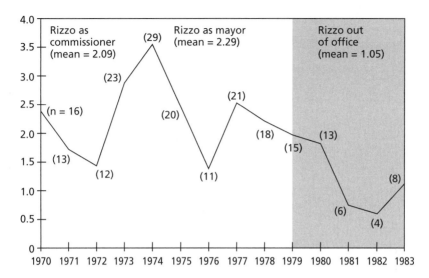

Figure 1 Fatal Shootings per 1,000 Police Officers, Philadelphia,
1970–1983

Source: Data for 1970–1978 from Philadelphia Police Department, Homicide Division, *Shooting Files*; 1979–1983 from Matulia (1985), p. A.5.

These are powerful numbers. Indeed, when I attempted to quantify Rizzo's influence (R) over PPD operations . . . I found that the extent of his authority was a strong predictor of the annual PPD police homicide rate ($r = .72$; $p = .002$), and that adding the public homicide rate to this equation added only marginally to predictive ability ($r = .26$; $R = .78$). In short—and except for the bizarre MOVE incident—knowing what Frank Rizzo was doing was far more valuable for estimating the PPD police homicide rate than were data on public homicides.

ELECTIVE AND NONELECTIVE SHOOTINGS

This analysis obviously suffers from the body count flaw; it includes only fatal shootings rather than all incidents of deadly force by PPD officers. Further, although I am convinced otherwise, many researchers will argue that my analysis of PPD homicides may have omitted some critical variable or set of variables. In addition, and if we assume for the moment that I am correct in asserting that Frank Rizzo *was* the critical variable in all Philadelphia police issues during the years in question, analysis of trends in police use of deadly force typically involves far more sophistication than when police or government administrators are as straightforward as Rizzo in espousing and executing their views.

In less extreme cases, examining in detail the circumstances of shootings is perhaps the most direct way to measure the relative effects of organizational and environmental variables on officers' use of deadly force. For these purposes it is useful to conceive of police shootings as incidents on a continuum that runs from *elective* situations, in which officers may decide to shoot or to refrain from shooting at no risk to themselves or to others, to *nonelective* situations, in which officers have no choice but to shoot or die (see Fyfe 1981c).

By these standards, Edward Garner's death—the shot at the back of the flee-ing, unarmed, nonthreatening, property crime suspect who presents no apparent danger to anybody—was the prototypical elective shooting. Shootings such as this are influenced by internal police organizational variables; Garner and others in Memphis were shot in such circumstances because the police department encouraged or tolerated such action. Yet, as in the case of the Memphis Police Department in 1979, the police also can put an end to such shootings by simple administrative fiat (Memphis Police Department 1979). Shootings at the other end of the continuum are a different manner; no police department can direct officers to refrain from shooting when failure to do so may mean imminent death. Formal discretionary guidelines are of little relevance in such situations because, by any reasonable standard, the officers involved have only one choice.

Between these two extremes are more ambiguous police shootings that may be influenced to varying degrees by such variables as general organizational culture and the presence or absence of training in tactics. It is my experience, for example, that officers in some departments sometimes find themselves in harm's way because they respond to encouragement, both formal and from peers, to take charge of threatening situations quickly with as little assistance (and as little inconvenience to colleagues) as possible. In other departments, the operative norm encourages officers to use caution, to take cover, and to search for nonlethal means of resolving potential violence. These midrange shootings typically involve officers who, for whatever reasons, find themselves danger-ously close to individuals who are armed with knives or other weapons, who attempt to run them down with vehicles, or who are determined to overpower them through mere physical force. Thus, in decreasing order of potential lethal-ity, we can derive the following typology of police shootings, which will be useful in reexamining data already published elsewhere:

> *Gun assault:* Citizen(s) armed with gun uses or attempts to use it against police.
>
> *Knife or other assault:* Citizens(s) armed with cutting instrument or other weapon (for example, bat, chain, club, hammer, vehicle) uses or attempts to use it against police.
>
> *Physical assault:* Citizen(s) attacks or attempts to attack police with fists, feet, or other purely physical means.
>
> *Unarmed, no assault:* Unarmed citizen(s) makes no threat and attempts no attack on police or on any other person.

As inexact as this typology may be, it does allow for some assessment of the relative extent to which police shootings are influenced by environmental and internal organizational forces. One would expect, for example, that shootings by officers whose discretion is limited carefully would tend toward the nonelective end of this continuum, and that a great percentage of shootings by officers in less stringently regulated departments would be elective.

This said, we move to Table 2, which demonstrates great variation in the nature of reported shootings across Chicago, New York, and Philadelphia ($p < .0001$). Even though the data included in the table are not absolutely compatible (my coding scheme for New York and Philadelphia includes accidental shootings and others that Geller and Karales [1981] treated separately, and that are described in note b of the table), it is clear that shootings occurred in significantly different circumstances in the places and times included in the table. About eight in ten of the shootings in Chicago and New York involved citizens who reportedly attacked officers with guns (Chicago = 62.1%; New York = 53.0%) or other weapons (Chicago = 15.3%; New York = 34.0%), but fewer than six in ten Philadelphia shootings (39% guns; 19.6% knives and other) fell into either of these two categories. At the other end of the continuum, the percentage of "unarmed, no-assault" incidents in New York City, which operated under an essentially "defense of life only" deadly force policy during much of the period studied (see Fyfe 1979), was considerably smaller than in either Chicago or Philadelphia (8.5% versus 20.9% and 24.9%, respectively), where police were given relatively more freedom to use their guns in elective situations. Therefore, not surprisingly, the rates presented on the table also indicate that the greatest discrepancies among these three police agencies' shooting experiences are found at the elective end of our continuum ("unarmed, no-assault" rates from New York, Philadelphia, and Chicago = 0.52, 2.94, and 1.36, respectively).

The rates in this table also illustrate the dangers of attempting to describe deadly force in terms of body counts. The three departments included in Table 2 do not appear to differ much in regard to deadly force resulting in fatalities (1971–1975 police homicide rates per 1,000 officers = 2.39 and 2.42 for New York and Philadelphia; 1974–1978 Chicago rate = 1.97). When incidents resulting in nonfatal wounds are added to these figures, however, the differences among these cities grow and change direction (rates = 6.09, 7.57, and 11.82 for New York, Chicago, and Philadelphia). In other words, Philadelphia police officers were only slightly more likely than New York or Chicago officers to shoot and kill citizens during the periods included in Table 2, but they were nearly twice as likely to shoot and kill *or wound* citizens. Further, because Chicago police apparently maintained records of missed shots only from 1975 through 1977 (Geller and Karales 1981:162) and because PPD did not do so at all during the period studied, there is no way to determine with any precision how great these discrepancies might have been if we had been able to include incidents in which officers' bullets failed to hit their targets.

Even so, there is reason to believe that the differences among these cities would be even more striking if such data were available. First, police departments that permit shooting in elective situations are likely to experience high percentages of missed shots. Just as nonelective shootings are extremely dangerous for the officers involved, they are also very dangerous for their opponents. It is far easier to hit someone who is standing 8 or 10 feet away with a shotgun in his hands than someone who is running away in the dark (see, e.g., Horvath

Table 2 Shooting Incident Types in New York City, Philadelphia, and Chicago

Shooting Type	New York 1971–1975[a]	Philadelphia 1971–1975[a]	Chicago 1974–1978[b]
Gun assault	53.0%	39.0%	62.1%
	(n = 481)	(n = 185)	(n = 264)
Rate[c]	3.20	4.60	4.02
Knife/other assault	34.0%	19.6%	15.3%
	(n = 308)	(n = 93)	(n = 65)
Rate	2.07	2.32	0.99
Physical assault	4.5%	16.5%	1.7%
	(n = 41)	(n = 78)	(n = 7)
Rate	0.28	1.95	0.11
Unarmed, no assault	8.5%	24.9%	20.9%
	(n = 77)	(n = 118)	(n = 89)
Rate	0.52	2.94	1.36
Totals	100.0%	100.0%	100.0%
	(n = 907)	(n = 474)	(n = 497)[d]
Rate	6.09	11.82	7.57

Chi-square = 216.45

$p < .0001$

[a]SOURCE: Fyfe (1988). Includes all reported incidents in which police officers shot and wounded or killed others.

[b]Derived from Geller and Karales (1981:103). Includes the number of persons shot rather than the number of incidents in which persons were shot. Excludes persons shot and wounded or killed for the following reasons:

Reason for shooting	n	Rate[c]
Not ascertained	6	0.09
Stray bullet	17	0.26
Mistaken identity	4	0.06
Accidental	52	0.79
Other intentional	7	0.11
Civilian appeared to display an unknown object without pointing it.	5	0.08
Civilian appeared to possess an unknown concealed object without pointing it.	7	0.11
Total	98	1.49

[c]Mean annual rate per 1,000 officers.

[d]Total number of incidents in which citizens were shot.

and Donahue 1982:87). Second, such departments also tend to experience high percentages of woundings in relation to fatalities. The four-to-one ratio of nonfatal to fatal wounds for Philadelphia did not result from any extraordinary humaneness on the part of PPD officers. It came about because an extraordinary percentage of the people shot at by the Philadelphia police were running targets; the officers fired at ranges so great that they were unable to hit the center body mass at which they were trained to shoot.

The data in my own work and in Geller and Karales's (1981) study support these assertions. The differences among police homicide rates for these cities are relatively small, but become more marked when nonfatal woundings are added to the equation. Finally, when the 1975–1977 data on all Chicago police shootings at citizens (n = 1,145; Geller and Karales 1981:162) are compared to the corresponding 1971–1975 data ($n = 2,234$; Fyfe 1978:390), the derived shooting rates per 1,000 officers differ greatly (Chicago = 29.07; New York = 14.09). It is difficult to imagine that inclusion of data from Philadelphia—where officers had by far the most liberal shooting license among these three cities—would not skew this contrast even further.

• • •

CONCLUSIONS

On balance, and even though the available data are skimpier than we would like, it appears that the frequency of police use of deadly force is influenced heavily by organizational philosophies, expectations, and policies; that levels of community violence are marginal predictors, useful chiefly when organizational variables may be held constant (as in studying a single police jurisdiction); and that variations in law play a role in determining frequency of deadly force only when administrators abdicate their responsibility to see that propriety is not limited only by statutory definitions of criminal assault and homicide.

For this last reason, *Tennessee* v. *Garner* probably is not as sweeping as many suspect. By the time this case was decided, virtually all major police departments had adopted their own administrative policies that were at least as restrictive as the *violent* felon rule propounded by the Supreme Court. In his decision for the majority, in fact, Justice White made repeated suggestions that the Court's holding was not a major intervention into police administrative prerogatives because most large police departments already were in compliance. Indeed, the fact that Memphis itself had abolished administratively the *any* fleeing felon rule five years before the case came to the Court weakened seriously the city attorney's oral argument that the *any* fleeing felon rule was a valuable adjunct to the effectiveness of law enforcement. Thus it is likely that the major effects of *Garner* will be (and have been) felt in smaller police jurisdictions where, as Neilsen (1983) suggests, administrative rule making related to deadly force has been less frequent.

Still, although *Garner* itself will not revolutionize American law enforcement, the process leading up to it has altered dramatically the police community's view of the whole deadly force issue. As recently as 1980, for example, attendees at the annual International Association of Chiefs of Police (IACP) meeting voted "by a 4-to-1 margin reaffirming [the association's] support of laws and policies permitting police to shoot fleeing felony suspects" (*St. Louis Post-Dispatch* 1980). In the same year, the International Union of Police Associations passed a resolution seeking to remove Patrick Murphy "as President of a private corporation known as the Police Foundation and to boycott any organization or foundation that supports the Police Foundation" because Murphy had criticized "police officers' use of weapons," "notoriously accused our nation's police officers as the immediate cause of the riots that took place in the 60's," indicated that four police officers who had been acquitted in a Miami beating death (a verdict that sparked Miami's Liberty City riot) had committed the beating of which they were accused, and had "further stated that a restrictive shooting policy not only reduces police shootings of civilians but does not result in any increased danger to police officers or a rise in crime" (International Union of Police Associations 1980).

By 1982, however, IACP had promulgated a model policy on police use of force that would permit shooting at fleeing felony suspects only when "freedom is reasonably believed to represent an *imminent* threat of grave bodily harm or death to the officer or other person(s)" (Matulia 1982:164; emphasis in original). In 1983 IACP joined in recommending that the Commission on Accreditation for Law Enforcement Agencies adopt its present strict *defense of life only* standard for deadly force policies (1983:1–2). In 1984 the Police Foundation's *amici curiae* brief against Tennessee and the Memphis Police Department in *Garner* was joined by "nine national and international associations of police and criminal justice professionals, the chiefs of police associations of two states, and thirty-one law enforcement chief executives" (Police Foundation 1984). Equally significant, and contrary to past practice in cases of substantial constitutional issues involving the police, no *amicus* briefs were filed on the other side of the case. In 1985, when *Garner* was decided, IACP's executive director hailed it as a great step forward. This remarkable turnaround and disavowal of tradition and professional dogma was stimulated in large measure by research findings that suggested that the value of broad police shooting authority was overrated; rarely have researchers had such an effect on criminal justice policies and practices.[4]

Research regarding the people involved in incidents of deadly force by police generally shows that blacks and other minorities are overrepresented at both ends of police guns. Explanations for these disparities vary, but at least by my interpretation they typically involve embarrassing realities over which police have little control. Black citizens are overrepresented in the most violent and most criminogenic neighborhoods; individual black officers, who are still underrepresented in American policing generally, are far more likely than individual white officers to draw the most hazardous police duties in those same neighborhoods. Until these realities are altered, we can expect continuing minority disproportion in deadly force statistics no matter how stringently police officers' discretion is controlled.

This probability, I think, illustrates the central theme that may be drawn from all the research on deadly force reviewed in this essay. Police officers and the people at whom they shoot are simply actors in a much larger play. When police officers' roles in this play are defined carefully by their administrators and when the officers have been trained well to perform those roles, their individual characteristics mean little; the young cop, the old cop, the male cop, the female cop, the white cop, and the black cop all know what is expected of them, and they do it. When such clear expectations are not provided, officers improvise, and often we give their performances bad reviews. Yet because we put them on the stage in the first place, we also should criticize ourselves for failing to ensure that they have been directed adequately. When black children's roles are defined so clearly by the conditions in which so many are raised, we should expect that some will end their lives at the wrong end of police guns.

We should not blame the police for that; we should blame ourselves for creating the stages on which so many black lives are played out.

EDITOR'S POSTSCRIPT

What has been the impact of the Supreme Court's ruling in *Tennessee* v. *Garner* that the police may not use deadly force against a suspected fleeing, unarmed felon? In a 1990 study Fyfe and Walker found that only four of the thirty-one states affected by the *Garner* decision had made statutory changes to bring their laws in line with the Court's interpretation of the Fourth Amendment, yet the authors argue that police officers now know the rules and that *Garner* types of shootings are a thing of the past. From their research the authors draw the following conclusions (Fyfe 1991):

1. Statutes relating to deadly force are irrelevant to officers on the street. Like other professionals or craftsmen, police behavior is most directly affected by organizational and professional guidelines that place limits on their discretion.

2. Most likely changes have not been made in state laws because legislators are reluctant to build political records indicating that they have voted for restrictions that would appear to "handcuff" the police.

3. The decline in fleeing felon shootings is apparently the result of modifications to guidelines made by police administrators.

4. The post-*Garner* impact thus reinforces the belief that control of police street-level decisions is in the chief's office rather than in the legislature's, prosecutor's, or attorney general's chambers.

NOTES

1. Former Mayor Rizzo perhaps is best known for his advice that officers should "break their heads before they break yours." My favorite Rizzoism, however, dates from late 1979, when, in response to a question about a United States Justice Department suit against his administration and the Philadelphia Police Department, Rizzo commented on ABC-TV's *Nightline* that "when I became mayor, the Philadelphia Police Department had only one shotgun. Now we've got enough guns to invade Cuba and win."

2. Despite extensive review of PPD reports of all firearm discharges resulting in injury or death from 1970 through 1978, for example, I can find only two cases that re-

sulted in departmental discipline against officers who had fired their guns while on duty. In one case an officer shot and killed his wife in a police station during an apparent argument over the disposition of his paycheck; the other resulted in the two-day suspension of an officer who had fired unnecessary shots into the air.

3. The policy (Philadelphia Police Department 1980) was promulgated on April 2, 1980. It authorizes officers to shoot in defense of life and, when no alternative exists, to apprehend fleeing suspects who officers know are in possession of deadly weapons that they have used or threatened to use, or who have committed forcible felonies. Of these last, PPD's position was as follows:

Until forcible felony is defined by statute, the Police Department adopts the position that forcible felony includes the crimes of Murder, Voluntary Manslaughter, Rape, Robbery, Kidnapping, Involuntary Deviate Sexual Intercourse, Arson, Burglary of a Private Residence, Aggravated Assault Causing Serious Bodily Injury (Davis 1980).

4. This observation is tempered by the knowledge that increased governmental exposure to civil liability for failure to supervise police officers adequately has served also as a major stimulant to reform of deadly force policies and practices. Almost certainly, *Monell v. New York City Department of Social Services* (1978), in which the Supreme Court holds government entities liable when unreasonable policies and practices are proved to be the causes of constitutional violations suffered at the hands of individual agents, has had more effect on police operations than have any of the Court's more celebrated rulings related to criminal procedure.

REFERENCES

Chapman, S. G. (1967). *Police Firearms Use Policy.* Report to the President's Commission on Law Enforcement and Administration of Justice. Washington, D.C.: United States Government Printing Office.

Chapman, S. G., and T. S. Crockett (1963). "Gunsight Dilemma: Police Firearms Policy." *Police* 6:40–45.

Davis, A. J. (1980). Letter to Burton A. Rose of Peruto, Ryan, and Vitullo, counsel for the Philadelphia chapter of the Fraternal Order of Police, October 15.

Florida Attorney General (1971). *Annual Report.* In Herman Goldstein (ed.), *Policing a Free Society.* Cambridge, Mass.: Ballinger, p. 127.

Fyfe, J. J. (1978). "Shots Fired: An Analysis of New York City Police Firearms Discharge." Ph.D. dissertation, State University of New York at Albany. Ann Arbor: University Microfilms.

——— (1979). "Administrative Interventions on Police Shooting Discretion: An Empirical Examination." *Journal of Criminal Justice* 7:309–324.

——— (1980a). "Always Prepared: Police Off-Duty Guns." *Annals of the American Academy of Political and Social Science* 452:72–81.

——— (1980b). "Geographic Correlates of Police Shooting: A Microanalysis." *Journal of Research in Crime and Delinquency* 17:101–113

——— (1981a). "Observation on Police Deadly Force." *Crime and Delinquency* 27:376–389.

——— (1981b). "Race and Extreme Police-Citizen Violence." In R. L. McNeely and C. E. Pope (eds.), *Race, Crime, and Criminal Justice.* Beverly Hills: Sage, pp. 89–108.

——— (1981c). "Toward a Typology of Police Shootings." In J. J. Fyfe (ed.), *Contemporary Issues in Law Enforcement.* Beverly Hills: Sage, pp. 136–151.

——— (1981d). "Who Shoots? A Look at Officer Race and Police Shooting." *Journal of Police Science and Administration* 9:367–382.

——— (1982). "Blind Justice: Police Shootings in Memphis." *Journal of Criminal Law and Criminology* 73:707–722.

——— (1986). "Enforcement Workshop: The Supreme Court's New Rules for Police Use of Deadly Force." *Criminal Law Bulletin* 22:62–68.

——— (1988). "Police Shooting Environment and License." In J. E. Scott and T. Hirschi (eds.), *Controversial Issues in Crime and Justice.* Beverly Hills: Sage, pp. 79–94.

——— (1991). Communication to the editor.

Fyfe, J. J., and Jeffery T. Walker (1990). "*Garner* Plus Five Years: An Examination of Supreme Court Intervention into Police Discretion and Legislative

Prerogatives." *American Journal of Criminal Justice* 14:167–188.

Gain, C. (1971). "Discharge of Firearms Policy: Effecting Justice through Administrative Regulation." Unpublished statement, Oakland, Calif., December 23.

Geller, W. A., and K. J. Karales (1981). *Split-Second Decisions: Shootings of and by Chicago Police.* Chicago: Chicago Law Enforcement Study Group.

Horvath, F., and M. Donahue (1982). *Deadly Force: An Analysis of Shootings by Police in Michigan, 1976–1981.* East Lansing: Michigan State University.

Illinois Revised Statutes (1975). Chapter 38, Para. 2–8.

International Union of Police Associations (1980). *Resolution of July 15, 1980.* Washington, D.C.: mimeo.

Kania, R. R. E., and W. C. Mackey (1977). "Police Violence as a Function of Community Characteristics." *Criminology* 15:27–48.

Matulia, K. R. (1982). *A Balance of Forces.* Gaithersburg, Md.: International Association of Chiefs of Police.

——— (1985). *A Balance of Forces,* 2d ed. Gaithersburg, Md.: International Association of Chiefs of Police.

Memphis Police Department (1979). *General Order 95–79, Deadly Force Policy,* July 16.

Meyer, M. W. (1980). *Report to the Los Angeles Board of Police Commissioners on Police Use of Deadly Force in Los Angeles: Officer-Involved Shootings, Part IV.* Los Angeles: Los Angeles Board of Police Commissioners.

Milton, C., J. W. Halleck, J. Lardner, and G. L. Abrecht (1977). *Police Use of Deadly Force.* Washington, D.C.: Police Foundation.

Monell v. New York City Department of Social Services. (1978), 436 U.S. 658.

Nielsen, E. (1983). "Policy on the Police Use of Deadly Force: A Cross-National Analysis." *Journal of Police Science and Administration* 11:104–108.

Pennsylvania Statutes Annotated (1973).

Philadelphia Police Department (1980). *Directive* 10, April 2.

Police Foundation, Joined by Nine National and International Associations of Police and Criminal Justice Professionals, the Chiefs of Police Associations of Two States, and Thirty-One Law Enforcement Chief Executives (1984). *Amici Curiae Brief in Tennessee v. Garner.* United States Supreme Court 83–1035, 83–1070. Washington, D.C.: August 6.

President's Commission on Law Enforcement and Administration of Justice (1967). *Task Force Report: The Police.* Washington, D.C.: United States Government Printing Office.

Robin, G. (1963). "Justifiable Homicide by Police." *Journal of Criminal Law, Criminology and Police Science* (May/June): 225–231.

Scharf, P., and A. Binder (1983). *The Badge and the Bullet.* New York: Praeger.

Sherman, L. W. (1980). "Execution without Trial: Police Homicide and the Constitution." *Vanderbilt Law Review* 33:71–110.

——— (1983). "Reducing Police Gun Use: Critical Events, Administrative Policy and Organizational Change." In Maurice Punch (ed.), *The Management and Control of Police Organizations.* Cambridge, Mass.: MIT Press, pp. 98–125.

Sherman, L. W., and R. Langworthy (1979). "Measuring Homicide by Police Officers." *Journal of Criminal Law and Criminology* 70:546–560.

St. Louis Post-Dispatch (1980). "The Police Chiefs on Deadly Force." Editorial, September 21:16.

Tennessee Code Annotated (1977).

Tennessee v. Garner (1985). 471 U.S. 1, 105 S. Ct. 1694, 85 L. Ed. 1.

Uelman, G. (1973). "Varieties of Public Policy: A Study of Police Policy Regarding the Use of Deadly Force in Los Angeles County." *Loyola of Los Angeles Law Review* 6:1–65.

PART III

The Adversarial Process

T ime magazine's 2001 Man of the Year, former New York Mayor Rudy Guiliani, gained his first public fame as a crime-fighting prosecutor. Over the years a number of political leaders at the national and state levels have come to prominence as law-and-order prosecutors. Like Guiliani who convicted members of legendary organized crime families, many aspiring politicians have based their campaigns for higher political office on reputations gained from widely publicized investigations or trials. The prosecutors' influence flows directly from their legal duties, but this must be understood within the context of the administrative and political environment of the system.

Power of the Prosecutor

Prosecutors are powerful because they are concerned with, and have some input in, many parts in the machine of criminal justice. By contrast, other decision makers are involved in only certain segments of the process. From the time of arrest to the final disposition of a case, prosecutors can make a variety of decisions that will largely determine a defendant's fate. The prosecutor chooses the cases to be prosecuted, selects the charges that are to be brought into the courtroom, recommends the bail amount required for pretrial release, approves any negotiated agreements made with the defendant, and urges judges to impose particular sentences.

Throughout the justice process, prosecutors have links with the other actors in the system—police, defense attorneys, judges—and these relationships shape the prosecutor's decisions. Prosecutors may, for example, recommend bail amounts and sentences that demonstrate their understanding of and support for particular judges' preferences. In front of "tough" judges, prosecutors may make "tough" recommendations. However, they are likely to modify their arguments presented to judges who favor leniency or rehabilitation. Likewise, the other actors in the system may adjust their decisions and actions to solidify their relationships with the prosecutor. Police officers' investigation and arrest practices are likely to reflect their understanding of the prosecutor's priorities. Thus, prosecutors influence the decisions of others in the criminal justice process while also shaping their own actions to preserve and reinforce their relationships with police, defense attorneys, and judges.

Prosecutors gain additional power from the fact that their decisions and actions are confidential and hidden from public view. For example, a prosecutor and a defense attorney may strike a bargain outside the courtroom whereby the prosecutor reduces a charge in exchange for a guilty plea or drops a charge altogether if the defendant agrees to seek psychiatric help. In such instances, the justice system reaches a decision about a case in a way that is nearly invisible to the public.

State laws do little to limit or guide prosecutors' decisions. Most laws describe the prosecutor's responsibility in such vague terms as "prosecuting all crimes and civil actions to which state or county may be party." Such laws do not instruct the prosecutor about which cases must be prosecuted and which cases can be dismissed. The prosecutor possesses significant discretion to make such decisions without direct interference from either the law or other actors in the justice system. When people attempt to challenge prosecutors' decisions as improper, judges generally reject such claims by demonstrating their acceptance of broad prosecutorial discretion as a legitimate, important component of the criminal justice process. Because most local prosecutors are elected officials, their decisions may be responsive to changes in public opinion. For some office holders, it is a matter of reelection, while others feel they are obliged to follow the will of the people in holding an office of public trust. When prosecutors feel that the community no longer considers an act proscribed by law as criminal behavior, they will probably refuse to prosecute or will expend every effort to convince the complainant that prosecution should be avoided. Thus, in some communities prostitution may be vigorously prosecuted while in others it is ignored while police and prosecutors focus on other crimes. The fact that about three-fourths of American prosecutors serve counties with populations of fewer than 100,000 accentuates the potential influence of public opinion. Local pressures may bear heavily on the single prosecution official in a community. Without the backing of public opinion, law enforcement and prosecution officers are powerless. Prosecutors develop policies that reflect community attitudes, especially with regard to victimless crimes such as marijuana smoking, petty gambling, and prostitution. A New York prosecutor has remarked, "We are pledged to the enforcement of the law, but we have to use our heads in the process."

Plea Bargaining

For the overwhelming majority of cases, plea bargaining is the most important step in the criminal justice process. Very few cases go to trial; instead, a negotiated guilty plea developed through the interactions of prosecutors, defense lawyers, and judges determines what will finally happen to most criminal defendants. It is generally accepted that up to 90 percent of felony defendants in the United States plead guilty.

Thirty-five years ago, plea bargaining was not publicly acknowledged or discussed; it was the criminal justice system's "little secret." There were doubts about its constitutionality, and it clashed with the idealized image of the courtroom as a place where prosecutors and defense attorneys engaged in legal battles as the jury witnessed the emergence of "truth" amid the "smoke and noise" of courtroom "combat." Yet the quick and quiet resolution of cases through negotiated guilty pleas historically has been common. Indeed, scholars have documented that guilty pleas have been a primary means of finalizing criminal cases at least since the late 1800s. Scholars began to shed light on plea bargaining in the 1960s, and the U.S. Supreme Court openly acknowledged and endorsed the process in the 1970s.

Defendants have great incentives to plea bargain because they can have their cases completed more quickly and they can participate in establishing a definite punishment rather than facing the uncertainty of a judge's discretionary sentencing decision after a trial. Moreover, in exchange for pleading guilty, the defendant is more likely to receive less than the maximum punishment that might have been imposed after a trial. Prosecutors are not being "soft on crime" when they plea-bargain. Instead, they are gaining a relatively easy conviction, even in cases in which there may not have been enough evidence to convince a jury to convict the defendant. They also save time and resources by disposing of cases and recommending a punishment without the need for time-consuming trial preparations. Private defense attorneys also benefit from plea bargaining by saving the time involved in trial preparation, earning their fees quickly, and moving on to the next income-producing case. Likewise, plea bargaining helps public defenders cope with large and often-growing caseloads. Judges, too, avoid time-consuming trials and are spared the difficult prospect of determining what sentence to impose on the defendant. Instead, they frequently adopt the sentence recommended by the prosecutor in consultation with the defense attorney, provided the sentence fits within the range of sentences that the judge believes appropriate for a given crime and offender.

Neither the prosecutor nor the defense attorney is a free agent. Each must count on the cooperation of both defendants and judges. Attorneys often cite the difficulty they have convincing defendants that they should uphold their end of the bargain. Judges must cooperate in the agreement by sentencing the accused according to the prosecutor's recommendation. Although their role requires that they uphold the public interest, judges may be reluctant to interfere with a plea agreement in order to maintain future exchange relationships.

Thus both the prosecutor and the defense attorney usually confer with the judge regarding the sentence to be imposed before agreeing on a plea. At the same time, the judicial role requires that judges hold in reserve their power to reject the agreement. Because uncertainty is one of the hazards of the organizational system, prosecutors and defense attorneys will evaluate each judicial decision as an indication of the judge's future behavior. If particular judges prove to be unpredictable in supporting a plea agreement, defense attorneys may be reluctant to readily reach agreements in subsequent cases.

Legal Issues in Plea Bargaining

The constitutionality of plea bargaining has evolved over the last several decades. Questions concerning the voluntariness of the plea and the parties' obligation to uphold the agreement have forced the U.S. Supreme Court to confront these issues. In deciding these questions the justices have upheld the general constitutionality of the practice and have sought to ensure that due process rights have been upheld in developing and carrying out plea agreements.

The voluntariness of the defendant to plead guilty is a central concern. In *Boykin v. Alabama* (1969) the Court ruled that defendants must make an affirmative statement that the plea was made voluntarily before a judge may accept the plea. Trial judges are required to learn whether the defendant understands the consequences of an agreement to plead guilty, ensuring that pressures were not brought by either the prosecutor or the defense attorney to coerce the plea.

Can a trial court accept a guilty plea if the defendant's innocence is maintained? In *North Carolina v. Alford* (1970) the Court approved, in principle, a pleading of guilty by an innocent defendant for the purpose of obtaining a lesser sentence. Henry C. Alford was charged with first-degree murder, a capital offense. Although maintaining his innocence, Alford plea-bargained to second-degree murder, a charge for which the death penalty was not authorized. After receiving a thirty-year sentence, he complained to the Supreme Court that the plea had been coerced by the death penalty threat. He argued that he had never admitted his guilt throughout the proceedings. The Court disagreed, ruling that it was Alford's privilege to plead guilty to avoid a possible death penalty even though he continued to maintain his innocence. One result of this ruling is that courts in many parts of the country now routinely accept pleas based on the "Alford Doctrine," by which defendants plead guilty but say they are not guilty.

A second issue concerns fulfillment of the plea agreement. If the prosecutor has given a promise of leniency, it must be kept. In *Santobello v. New York* (1971), the Supreme Court ruled that "when a [guilty] plea rests in any significant degree on a promise or agreement of the prosecutor, so that it can be said to be part of the inducement or consideration, such promise must be fulfilled." That defendants must also keep their side of the bargain was decided by the Court in *Ricketts v. Adamson* (1987). Ricketts agreed to plead guilty and testify against a codefendant in exchange for a reduction of the charges from first- to second-degree murder. He carried out the bargain but refused to testify a second time when the codefendant appealed conviction (which was reversed). The prosecutor then withdrew the offer to reduce the charge. The Supreme Court upheld the recharging and said that Ricketts had to suffer the consequences of his voluntary choice not to testify at the codefendant's second trial.

May prosecutors threaten to penalize defendants who insist upon their right to a jury trial? Paul Hayes was indicted in Kentucky for forging an $88.50 check. The prosecutor offered to recommend a sentence of five years imprisonment if a guilty plea were entered, but said that if Hayes pleaded not guilty, he would be indicted under the state's habitual criminal act. If Hayes were then found guilty, a mandatory life sentence would result because he had two prior convictions. Hayes rejected the guilty plea, went to trial, and was sentenced to life imprisonment. On appeal, the U.S. Supreme Court ruled in *Bordenkircher v. Hayes* (1978) that in the "give and take" of plea bargaining, the prosecutor's conduct did not violate constitutional protections.

Plea bargaining, then, is no longer a secret of the courthouse. The Supreme Court has accepted the constitutionality of the practice and has emphasized the importance of protecting defendants' rights as cases are processed. Judges increasingly discuss plea bargaining openly in their courts and admit on the record that they are aware of plea negotiations. In many cases, judges have entered into plea discussions with respect to sentences in cases before them.

DEFENSE ATTORNEYS

Defense attorneys elicit strong public impressions, both positive and negative. On the one hand, they are viewed as defenders of liberty, with a duty to keep the burden of proof on the state. As such, they are involved in a constant searching and creative questioning of official decisions at all stages of the justice process. On the other hand, they are seen as somehow "soiled" by their clients, engaged in shady practices to free clients from the rightful demands of the law. Although the television image of the defense attorney as seen on *The Practice* remains a hero, the public retains the more tarnished image, and the Johnny Cochrans and Mark Gerragoses of the world are respected, but often reviled.

The Environment of Criminal Practice

Defense attorneys face unique difficulties in their work. Their duty typically involves preparing clients and their relatives for the likelihood of conviction and punishment. Although defense attorneys may have actual knowledge that their clients are guilty of a crime, they may become emotionally entangled as the only judicial actors who know the defendants as human beings and see them in the context of social environment and family ties.

Most defense lawyers interact continually with lower-class clients whose lives and problems are depressing. These lawyers may visit the jail at all hours of the day and night. The work setting of the criminal lawyer is far removed from the fancy offices and expensive restaurants that comprise the world of corporate attorneys.

Defense lawyers must also struggle with the fact that criminal practice does not pay well. Public defenders have relatively low salaries, and attorneys appointed to represent poor defendants are paid small sums. If privately retained attorneys do not demand payment from their clients at the start of the case, they may later find themselves trying to persuade the defendants' relatives to pay—since many convicted offenders have no incentive to pay for unsuc-cessful legal ser-vices while sitting in prison. In order to perform their jobs enthusiastically and derive satisfaction from their careers, defense attorneys must focus on goals other than money, such as their important role in protect-ing people's constitutional rights. That these attorneys are usually on the losing side of cases can make it especially difficult for them to feel like successful pro-fessionals. The vast majority of these attorneys are not featured on the six o'clock news.

Defense attorneys face additional pressures. If they mount a vigorous defense and gain an acquittal for their client, the community may blame them for using "technicalities" to keep a criminal on the streets. In addition, if they embarrass the prosecution in court, defense attorneys may harm their prospects for reaching cooperative plea agreements on behalf of future clients. Thus, criminal practice can impose significant financial, social, and psychological bur-dens. As a result, many attorneys get "burned out" after a few years and few criminal law specialists stay in the field past the age of fifty.

Counsel for Indigents

Since the 1960s, the Supreme Court has interpreted the "right to counsel" in the Sixth Amendment of the Constitution as requiring that attorneys be provided for indigent defendants facing imprisonment—namely, those who are too poor to afford their own attorneys. The high court has also required that attorneys be provided early in the criminal justice process to protect suspects' rights during questioning and pretrial proceedings, such as preliminary hearings.

In the United States there are three basic methods of providing counsel to indigent defendants: (1) the *assigned counsel* system, by which a court appoints a private attorney to represent a particular accused; (2) the *contract counsel* system, by which an individual attorney, a nonprofit organization, or a private law firm contracts with a local government to provide legal services to indigent defen-dants for a specified dollar amount; and (3) *public defender* programs, established as public or private nonprofit organizations with full-time or part-time salaried staff. Let us look at these methods in turn.

Assigned Counsel

In the assigned counsel system, the court appoints a lawyer in private practice to represent an indigent defendant. This system is widely used in small cities and in rural areas, but even some urban areas with public defender systems follow the practice of assigning counsel in special circumstances, as when a case has multiple defendants and a conflict of interest might result if one were to be represented by a public lawyer.

Assigned counsel systems are organized on two bases: the ad hoc system and the coordinated system. In ad hoc assignment systems, private attorneys indicate to the judge that they are willing to take the cases of indigent defendants. When an indigent requires counsel the judge then either assigns lawyers in rotation from a prepared list or selects among attorneys who are known and present in the courtroom. In coordinated assignment systems a court administrator oversees the appointment of counsel.

Contract System

The contract system is used in a few rural counties, primarily in Western states. In this system, the government contracts with an individual attorney, nonprofit association, or private law firm to handle all indigent cases. Some jurisdictions use public defenders for most cases but contract for services in multiple-defendant situations that might present conflicts of interest, in extraordinarily complex cases, or in cases that require more time than the government's salaried lawyers can provide.

Public Defender

The public defender is the contemporary response to the legal needs of the indigent. The concept started in Los Angeles County in 1914 when attorneys were first hired by government to work full-time in criminal defense. The most recent survey shows that public defender systems exist in 1,144 counties that cover more than 70 percent of the U.S. population. The public defender system is growing rapidly and is already the dominant form in most large cities, in populous counties, and in about twenty statewide, state-funded jurisdictions. Only two states, North Dakota and Maine, do not have public defenders.

The public defender system is often viewed as superior to the assigned counsel system because the attorneys are full-time specialists in criminal law. Because they are salaried government employees, public defenders, unlike appointed counsel and contract attorneys, do not sacrifice their clients' cases to protect their own financial interests.

Public defenders may have difficulty in gaining the trust and cooperation of their clients. Criminal defendants may assume that attorneys on the state payroll, even with the title "public defender," cannot possibly be devoted to protecting the defendants' rights and interests. A lack of cooperation may make it more difficult for the attorney to prepare the strongest possible arguments for use during hearings, plea negotiations, and trials.

Public defenders may also face burdensome caseloads. In New York City's public defender program, for example, Legal Aid lawyers may be responsible for as many as one hundred felony cases at any time. A public defender in Atlanta may be assigned as many as forty-five new cases *at a single arraignment*. Such heavy caseloads make it difficult for attorneys to be thoroughly familiar with each case.

Overburdened public defenders find it difficult to avoid processing cases by anything other than routine decisions. Decisions are made quickly and with minimal resources. One case may come to be viewed as very much like the next, and the process can become routine and repetitive. When the routine goes too far, no attorney looks closely at individual cases to see if there are special facts or other circumstances that would justify a more vigorous defense or other options.

DEFENSE COUNSEL IN THE SYSTEM

Most criminal lawyers in urban courts work in a difficult professional environment. They work very hard for small fees in unpleasant surroundings and are frequently not given respect by other lawyers or the public. Because plea bargaining is the primary method of deciding cases, defense attorneys believe they must maintain close personal ties with the police, prosecutor, judges, and other court officials. Critics point out that the defenders' independence is reduced by daily interactions with the same prosecutors and judges. When supposed adversaries become close friends from daily contact, there is a risk that the defense attorneys might not fight vigorously on behalf of their clients.

At every step of the criminal justice process, from the first contact with the accused until final disposition of the case, defense attorneys depend upon decisions made by other judicial actors. Even seemingly minor activities, such as visiting the defendant in jail, learning about the case against the defendant from the prosecutor, and setting bail, can be difficult unless defense attorneys have the cooperation of others in the system. Thus, defense attorneys may limit their activities in order to preserve their relationships with other courthouse actors.

For the criminal lawyer who depends on a large volume of petty cases from poor clients and assumes they are probably guilty of some offense, the incentives to bargain are strong. If the attorney is to gain appointments to handle additional cases, he or she must help to make sure that cases flow smoothly through the courthouse. This requires a cooperative relationship with judges, prosecutors, and others in the justice system.

In many cases, there is evidence indicating the defendant's guilt that simply cannot be overcome by skilled lawyering. Thus, good relationships can benefit the defendant by gaining plea agreements for a less-than-maximum sentence. At the same time, these relationships pose risks; if the defense attorney and prosecutor are too friendly, the defendant's case will not be presented in the best possible fashion in plea negotiations or trials.

Defense attorneys have been called "agent-mediators" because they frequently work to prepare the defendant for the likely outcome of the case—usually conviction. By mediating between the defendant and system through, for example, the encouragement of a guilty plea, the attorney helps to save time for the prosecutor and judge in obtaining a conviction and getting the case completed. In addition, appointed counsel and contract attorneys, in particular, may have a financial self-interest in getting the defendant to plead guilty quickly so that they can receive payment and move forward with their next case. A more sympathetic view of defense attorneys labels them as "beleaguered dealers" who cut deals for defendants in a pressurized environment. Although many of their actions assist in pushing cases through the courts, defense attorneys are under tremendous pressure to manage significant caseloads in a difficult court environment. From this perspective, their actions in encouraging clients to plead guilty result from the difficult aspects of their jobs rather than from self-interest.

QUESTIONS FOR FURTHER EXPLORATION

1. As an adversarial system predicated on the due process of law, what are the shared norms and values manifested in the system?

2. Describe the interrelationship between bureaucracy and advocacy and race, class, and ethnicity.

3. Should prosecutors serve as extensions of the police, legal advisors to police work, servants of due process and an American system of law, or as responsive to the concerns of the public they serve?

4. In predicting the outcome of a proceeding, what trumps the question of guilt or innocence and why?

5. There is a dynamic and constant tension among due process, equal protection, the use of discretion and the preservation of public order in the criminal justice system. Provide examples of the ways in which the competition among these valuse may explain shifts and tensions in contemporary criminal justice practices.

SUGGESTIONS FOR FURTHER READING

Heumann, Milton. *Plea Bargaining.* Chicago: University of Chicago Press, 1978. One of the first studies of how prosecutors, judges, and defense attorneys adapt to plea bargaining.

Lewis, Anthony. *Gideon's Trumpet.* New York: Vintage, 1964. The classic case study of the case of *Gideon v. Wainwright.*

McCoy, Candace. *Politics and Plea Bargaining.* Philadelphia: University of Pennsylvania Press, 1993. A study of California victims' rights legislation and its impact on plea bargaining.

McIntyre, Lisa J. *The Public Defender: The Practice of Law in the Shadows of Repute.*

Chicago: University of Chicago Press, 1987. A case study of the public defender's office in Cook County, Illinois.

Toobin, Jeffrey. *The Run of His Life: The People v. O. J. Simpson.* New York: Random House, 1996. A view of the "trial of the century" from the perspective of the defense and prosecution.

Turow, Scott. *Presumed Innocent.* New York: Farrar, Straus, and Giroux, 1987. Fictional account of the indictment and trial of an urban prosecutor for the murder of a colleague. Excellent description of an urban court system.

10

❂

The Decision
to Prosecute

George F. Cole

The prosecuting attorney works within the context of an exchange system of clientele relationships that influence decision making. In this case study I explore the nature of these relationships and link politics to the allocation of justice.

This paper is based on an exploratory study of the Office of Prosecuting Attorney, King County (Seattle), Washington. The lack of social–scientific knowledge about the prosecutor dictated the choice of this approach. An open-ended interview was administered to one-third of the former deputy prosecutors who had worked in the office during the ten-year period 1955–1965. In addition, interviews were conducted with court employees, members of the bench, law-enforcement officials, and others having reputations for participation in legal decision making. Over fifty respondents were contacted during this phase. A final portion of the research placed the author in the role of observer in the prosecutor's office. This experience allowed for direct observation of all phases of the decision to prosecute so that the informal processes of the office could be noted. Discussions with the prosecutor's staff, judges, defendants' attorneys, and the police were held so that the interview data could be placed within an organizational context.

Source: From *Law and Society Review 4* (February 1970): 313–343.

The primary goal of this investigation was to examine the role of the prosecuting attorney as an officer of the legal process within the context of the local political system. The analysis is therefore based on two assumptions. First, that the legal process is best understood as a subsystem of the larger political system. Because of this choice, emphasis is placed upon the interaction and goals of the individuals involved in decision making. Second, and closely related to the first point, it is assumed that broadly conceived political considerations explained to a large extent "who gets or does not get—in what amount—and how, the good (justice) that is hopefully produced by the legal system."[1] By focusing upon the political and social linkages between these systems, it is expected that decision making in the prosecutor's office will be viewed as a principal ingredient in the authoritative allocation of values.

THE PROSECUTOR'S OFFICE
IN AN EXCHANGE SYSTEM

While observing the interrelated activities of the organizations in the legal process, one might ask, "Why do these agencies cooperate?" If the police refuse to transfer information to the prosecutor concerning the commission of a crime, what are the rewards or sanctions that might be brought against them? Is it possible that organizations maintain a form of "bureaucratic accounting" that, in a sense, keeps track of the resources allocated to an agency and the support returned? How are cues transmitted from one agency to another to influence decision making? These are some of the questions that must be asked when decisions are viewed as an output of an exchange system.

The major findings of this study are placed within the context of an exchange system.[2] This serves the heuristic purpose of focusing attention upon the linkages found between actors in the decision-making process. In place of the traditional assumptions that the agency is supported solely by statutory authority, this view recognizes that an organization has many clients with which it interacts and upon whom it is dependent for certain resources. As interdependent subunits of a system, then, the organization and its clients are engaged in a set of exchanges across their boundaries. These will involve a transfer of resources between the organizations that will affect the mutual achievement of goals.

The legal system may be viewed as a set of interorganizational exchange relationships analogous to what Long has called a community game.[3] The participants in the legal system (game) share a common territorial field and collaborate for different and particular ends. They interact on a continuing basis as their responsibilities demand contact with other participants in the process. Thus, the need for cooperation of other participants can have a bearing on the decision to prosecute. A decision not to prosecute a narcotics offender may be a move to pressure the U.S. Attorney's Office to cooperate on another case. It is obvious that bargaining occurs not only between the major actors in a case—the prosecutor and the defense attorney—but also between the clientele groups that are influential in structuring the actions of the prosecuting attorney.

Exchanges do not simply "sail" from one system to another but take place in an institutionalized setting that may be compared to a market. In the market, decisions are made between individuals who occupy boundary-spanning roles and who set the conditions under which the exchange will occur. In the legal system, this may merely mean that a representative of the parole board agrees to forward a recommendation to the prosecutor, or it could mean that there is extended bargaining between a deputy prosecutor and a defense attorney. In the study of the King County prosecutor's office, it was found that most decisions resulted from some type of exchange relationship. The deputies interacted almost constantly with the police and criminal lawyers; the prosecutor was more closely linked to exchange relations with the courts, community leaders, and the county commissioners.

THE PROSECUTOR'S CLIENTELE

In an exchange system, power is largely dependent upon the ability of an organization to create clientele relationships that will support and enhance the needs of the agency. For, although interdependence is characteristic of the legal system, competition with other public agencies for support also exists. Because organizations operate in an economy of scarcity, the organization must exist in a favorable power position in relation to its clientele. Reciprocal and unique claims are made by the organization and its clients. Thus, rather than being oriented toward only one public, an organization is beholden to several publics, some visible and others seen clearly only from the pinnacle of leadership. As Gore notes when these claims are "firmly anchored inside the organization and the lines drawn taut, the tensions between conflicting claims form a net serving as the institutional base for the organization."[4]

An indication of the stresses within the judicial system may be obtained by analyzing its outputs. It has been suggested that the administration of justice is a selective process in which only those cases that do not create strains in the organization will ultimately reach the courtroom.[5] As noted in Figure 1, the system operates so that only a small number of cases arrive for trial, the rest being disposed of through reduced charges, *nolle prosequi*, and guilty pleas.[6] Not indicated are those cases removed by the police and prosecutor prior to the filing of charges. As the focal organization in an exchange system, the office of the prosecuting attorney makes decisions that reflect the influence of its clientele. Because of the scarcity of resources, marketlike relationships, and the organizational needs of the system, prosecutorial decision making emphasizes the accommodations made to the needs of participants in the process.

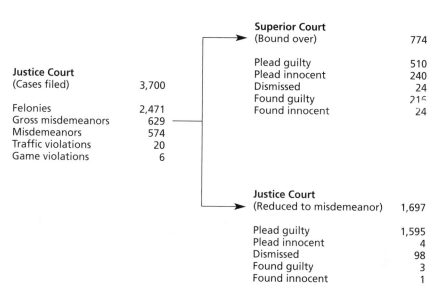

FIGURE 1 Disposition of Felony Cases, King County, 1964

Police

Although the prosecuting attorney has discretionary power to determine the disposition of cases, this power is limited by the fact that usually he is dependent upon the police for inputs to the system of cases and evidence. The prosecutor does not have the investigative resources necessary to exercise the kind of affirmative control over the types of cases that are brought to him. In this relationship, the prosecutor is not without countervailing power. His main check on the police is his ability to return cases to them for further investigation and to refuse to approve arrest warrants. By maintaining cordial relations with the press, a prosecutor is often able to focus attention on the police when the public becomes aroused by incidents of crime. As the King County prosecutor emphasized, "That [investigation] is the job for the sheriff and police. It's their job to bring me the charges." As noted by many respondents, the police, in turn, are dependent upon the prosecutor to accept the output of their system; rejection of too many cases can have serious repercussions affecting the morale, discipline, and work load of the force.

A request for prosecution may be rejected for a number of reasons relating to questions of evidence. Not only must the prosecutor believe that the evidence will secure a conviction, but he must also be aware of community norms relating to the type of acts that should be prosecuted. King County deputy prosecutors noted that charges were never filed when a case involved attempted suicide or fornication. In other actions, the heinous nature of the crime, together with the expected public reaction, may force both the police and prosecutor to press for conviction when evidence is less than satisfactory. As one deputy noted, "In that case [murder and molestation of a six-year-old girl] there was nothing that we could do. As you know the press was on our back and every parent was concerned. Politically, the prosecutor had to seek information."

Factors other than those relating to evidence may require that the prosecutor refuse to accept a case from the police. First, the prosecuting attorney serves as a regulator of caseloads not only for his own office, but for the rest of the legal system. Constitutional and statutory time limits prevent him and the courts from building a backlog of untried cases. In King County, when the system reached the "overload point," there was a tendency to be more selective in choosing the cases to be accepted. A second reason for rejecting prosecution requests may stem from the fact that the prosecutor is thinking of his public exposure in the courtroom. He does not want to take forward cases that will place him in an embarrassing position. Finally, the prosecutor may return cases to check the quality of police work. As a former chief criminal deputy said, "You have to keep them on their toes, otherwise they get lazy. If they aren't doing their job, send the case back and then leak the situation to the newspapers." Rather than spend the resources necessary to find additional evidence, the police may dispose of a case by sending it back to the prosecutor on a lesser charge, implement the "copping out" machinery leading to a guilty plea, drop the case, or in some instances send it to the city prosecutor for action in municipal court.

In most instances, a deputy prosecutor and the police officer assigned to the case occupy the boundary-spanning roles in this exchange relationship. Prosecutors reported that after repeated contacts they got to know the policemen whom they could trust. As one female deputy commented, "There are some you can trust, others you have to watch because they are trying to get rid of cases on you." Deputies may be influenced by the police officer's attitude on a case. One officer noted to a prosecutor that he knew he had a weak case, but mumbled, "I didn't want to bring it up here, but that's what they [his superiors] wanted." As might be expected, the deputy turned down prosecution.

Sometimes the police perform the ritual of "shopping around," seeking to find a deputy prosecutor who, on the basis of past experience, is liable to be sympathetic to their view on a case. At one time, deputies were given complete authority to make the crucial decisions without coordinating their activities with other staff members. In this way the arresting officer would search the prosecutor's office to find a deputy he thought would be sympathetic to the police attitude. As a former deputy noted, "This meant that there were no departmental policies concerning the treatment to be accorded various types of cases. It pretty much depended upon the police and their luck in finding the deputy they wanted." Prosecutors are now instructed to ascertain from the police officer if he has seen another deputy on the case. Even under this more centralized system, it is still possible for the police to request a specific deputy or delay presentation of the case until the "correct" prosecutor is available. Often a prosecutor will gain a reputation for specializing in one type of case. This may mean that the police will assume he will get the case anyway, so they skirt the formal procedure and bring it to him directly.

An exchange relationship between a deputy prosecutor and a police officer may be influenced by the type of crime committed by the defendant. The prototype of a criminal is one who violates person and property. However, a large number of cases involve "crimes without victims." This term refers to those crimes generally involving violations of moral codes, where the general public is theoretically the complainant. In violations of laws against bookmaking, prostitution, and narcotics, neither actor in the transaction is interested in having an arrest made. Hence, vice control men must drum up their own business. Without a civilian complainant, victimless crimes give the police and prosecutor greater leeway in determining the charges to be filed.

One area of exchange involving a victimless crime is that of narcotics control. As Skolnick notes, "The major organizational requirement of narcotics policing is the presence of an informational system."[7] Without a network of informers, it is impossible to capture addicts and peddlers with evidence that can bring about convictions. One source of informers is among those arrested for narcotics violations. Through promises to reduce charges or even to *nolle pros.*, arrangements can be made so that the accused will return to the narcotics community and gather information for the police. Bargaining observed between the head of the narcotics squad of the Seattle police and the deputy prosecutor who specialized in drug cases involved the question of charges, promises, and the release of an arrested narcotics pusher.

In the course of postarrest questioning by the police, a well-known drug peddler intimated that he could provide evidence against a pharmacist suspected by the police of illegally selling narcotics. Not only did the police representative want to transfer the case to the friendlier hands of this deputy, but he also wanted to arrange for a reduction of charges and bail. The police officer believed that it was important that the accused be let out in such a way that the narcotics community would not realize that he had become an informer. He also wanted to be sure that the reduced charges would be processed so that the informer could be kept on the string, thus allowing the narcotics squad to maintain control over him. The deputy prosecutor, on the other hand, said that he wanted to make sure that procedures were followed so that the action would not bring discredit on his office. He also suggested that the narcotics squad "work a little harder" on a pending case as a means of returning the favor.

Courts

The ways used by the court to dispose of cases is a vital influence in the system. The court's actions affect pressures upon the prison, the conviction rate of the prosecutor, and the work of probation agencies. The judge's decisions act as clues to other parts of the system, indicating the type of action likely to be taken in future cases. As noted by a King County judge, "When the number of prisoners gets to the 'riot point,' the warden puts pressure on us to slow down the flow. This often means that men are let out on parole and the number of people given probation and suspended sentences increases." Under such conditions, it would be expected that the prosecutor would respond to the judge's actions by reducing the inputs to the court either by not preferring charges or by increasing the pressure for guilty pleas through bargaining. The adjustments of other parts of the system could be expected to follow. For instance, the police might sense the lack of interest of the prosecutor in accepting charges; hence they will send only airtight cases to him for indictment.

The influence of the court on the decision to prosecute is very real. The sentencing history of each judge gives the prosecutor, as well as other law-enforcement officials, an indication of the treatment a case may receive in a courtroom. The prosecutor's expectation as to whether the court will convict may limit his discretion over the decisions on whether to prosecute. "There is great concern as to whose court a case will be assigned. After Judge ———— threw out three cases in a row in which entrapment was involved, the police did not want us to take any cases to him." Since the prosecutor depends upon the plea-bargaining machinery to maintain the flow of cases from his office, the sentencing actions of judges must be predictable. If the defendant and his lawyer are to be influenced to accept a lesser charge or the promise of a lighter sentence in exchange for a plea of guilty, there must be some basis for belief that the judge will fulfill his part of the arrangement. Because judges are unable formally to announce their agreement with the details of the bargain, their past performance acts as a guide.

Within the limits imposed by law and the demands of the system, the prosecutor is able to regulate the flow of cases to the court. He may control the length of time between accusation and trial; hence he may hold cases until he has the evidence that will convict. Alternatively, he may seek repeated adjournment and continuances until the public's interest dies; problems such as witnesses becoming unavailable and similar difficulties make his request for dismissal of prosecution more justifiable. Further, he may determine the type of court to receive the case and the judge who will hear it. Many misdemeanors covered by state law are also violations of a city ordinance. It is a common practice for the prosecutor to send a misdemeanor case to the city prosecutor for processing in the municipal court when it is believed that a conviction may not be secured in justice court. As a deputy said, "If there is no case—send it over to the city court. Things are speedier, less formal, over there."

In the state of Washington, a person arrested on a felony charge must be given a preliminary hearing in a justice court within ten days. For the prosecutor, the preliminary hearing is an opportunity to evaluate the testimony of witnesses, assess the strength of the evidence, and try to predict the outcome of the case if it is sent to trial. On the basis of this evaluation, the prosecutor has several options: he may bind over the case for trial in superior court; he may reduce the charges to those of a misdemeanor for trial in justice court; or he may conclude that he has no case and drop the charges. The presiding judge of the Justice Courts of King County estimated that about 70 percent of the felonies are reduced to misdemeanors after the preliminary hearing.

Besides having some leeway in determining the type of court in which to file a case, the prosecutor also has some flexibility in selecting the judge to receive the case. Until recently the prosecutor could file a case with a specific judge. "The trouble was that Judge ———— was erratic and independent, [so] no one would file with him. The other judges objected that they were handling the entire work load, so a central filing system was devised." Under this procedure cases are assigned to the judges in rotation. However, as the chief criminal deputy noted, "The prosecutor can hold a case until the 'correct' judge comes up."

Defense Attorneys

With the increased specialization and institutionalization of the bar, it would seem that those individuals engaged in the practice of criminal law have been relegated, both by their profession and by the community, to a low status. The urban bar appears to be divided into three parts. First there is an inner circle, which handles the work of banks, utilities, and commercial concerns; second, another circle includes plaintiffs' lawyers representing interests opposed to those of the inner circle; and finally, an outer group scrapes out an existence by "haunting the courts in hope of picking up crumbs from the judicial table."[8] With the exception of a few highly proficient lawyers who have made a reputation by winning acquittal for their clients in difficult, highly publicized cases, most of the lawyers dealing with the King County prosecutor's office belong to this outer ring.

In this study, respondents were asked to identify those attorneys considered to be specialists in criminal law. Of the nearly 1,600 lawyers practicing in King County, only 8 can be placed in this category. Of this group, 6 were reported to enjoy the respect of the legal community, while the others were accused by many respondents of being involved in shady deals. A larger group of King County attorneys will accept criminal cases, but these lawyers do not consider themselves specialists. Several respondents noted that many lawyers, because of inexperience or age, were required to hang around the courthouse searching for clients. One Seattle attorney described the quality of legal talent available for criminal cases as "a few good criminal lawyers and a lot of young kids and old men. The good lawyers I can count on my fingers."

In a legal system where bargaining is a primary method of decision making, it is not surprising that criminal lawyers find it essential to maintain close personal ties with the prosecutor and his staff. Respondents were quite open in revealing their dependence upon this close relationship to pursue their careers successfully. The nature of criminal lawyer's work is such that his saleable product or service appears to be influence rather than technical proficiency in the law. Respondents hold the belief that clients are attracted partially on the basis of the attorney's reputation as a fixer, or as a shrewd bargainer.

There is a tendency for ex-deputy prosecutors in King County to enter the practice of criminal law. Because of his inside knowledge of the prosecutor's office and friendships made with court officials, the former deputy feels that he has an advantage over other criminal law practitioners. All of the former deputies interviewed said that they took criminal cases. Of the eight criminal law specialists, seven previously served as deputy prosecutors in King County and the other was once prosecuting attorney in a rural county.

Because of the financial problems of the criminal lawyer's practice, it is necessary that he handle cases on an assembly-line basis, hoping to make a living from a large number of small fees. Referring to a fellow lawyer, one attorney said, "You should see ————. He goes up there to Carroll's office with a whole fistful of cases. He trades on some, bargains on others, and never goes to court. It's amazing but it's the way he makes his living." There are incentives, therefore, to bargaining with the prosecutor and other decision makers. The primary aim of the attorney in such circumstances is to reach an accommodation so that the time-consuming formal proceedings need not be implemented. As a Seattle attorney noted, "I can't make money if I spend my time in a courtroom. I make mine on the telephone or in the prosecutor's office." One of the disturbing results of this arrangement is that instances were reported in which a bargain was reached between the attorney and deputy prosecutor on a "package deal." In this situation, an attorney's clients are treated as a group; the outcome of the bargaining is often an agreement whereby reduced charges will be achieved for some, in exchange for the unspoken assent by the lawyer that the prosecutor may proceed as he desires with the other cases. One member of the King County bar had developed this practice to such a fine art that a deputy prosecutor said, "When you saw him coming into the office, you knew that he would be pleading guilty." At one time this situation was so widespread that the "prisoners up in the jail had a rating list which graded the attorneys as either 'good guys' or 'sellouts.'"

The exchange relationship between the defense attorney and the prosecutor is based on their need for cooperation in the discharge of their responsibilities. Most criminal lawyers are interested primarily in the speedy solution of cases because of their precarious financial situation. Because they must protect their professional reputations with their colleagues, judicial personnel, and potential clientele, however, they are not completely free to bargain solely with this objective. As one attorney noted, "You can't afford to let it get out that you are selling out your cases."

The prosecutor is also interested in the speedy processing of cases. This can only be achieved if the formal processes are not implemented. Not only does the pressure of his caseload influence bargaining, but also the legal process, with its potential for delay and appeal, creates a degree of uncertainty that is not present in an exchange relationship with an attorney with whom you have dealt for a number of years. As the presiding judge of the Seattle District Court said, "Lawyers are helpful to the system. They are able to pull things together, work out a deal, keep the system moving."

Community Influentials

As part of the political system, the judicial process responds to the community environment. The King County study indicated that there are different levels of influence within the community and that some people had a greater interest in the politics of prosecution than others. First, the general public is able to have its values translated into policies followed by law-enforcement officers. The public's influence is particularly acute in those gray areas of the law where full enforcement is not expected. Statutes may be enacted by legislatures defining the outer limits of criminal conduct, but they do not necessarily mean that laws are to be fully enforced to these limits. There are some laws defining behavior that the community no longer considers criminal. It can be expected that a prosecutor's charging policies will reflect this attitude. He may not prosecute violations of laws regulating some forms of gambling, certain sexual practices, or violations of Sunday Blue Laws.

Because the general public is a potential threat to the prosecutor, staff members take measures to protect him from criticism. Respondents agreed that decision making occurs with the public in mind—"Will a course of action arouse antipathy toward the prosecutor rather than the accused?" Several deputies mentioned what they called the "aggravation level" of a crime. This is a recognition that the commission of certain crimes, within a specific context, will bring about a vocal public reaction. "If a little girl, walking home from the grocery store, is pulled into the bushes and indecent liberties taken, this is more disturbing to the public's conscience than a case where the father of the girl takes indecent liberties with her at home." The office of the King County prosecuting attorney has a policy requiring that deputies file all cases involving sexual molestation in which the police believe the girl's story is credible. The office also prefers charges in all negligent homicide cases where there is the least possibility of guilt. In such types of cases the public may respond to the emotional context of the case and demand prosecution. To cover the prosecutor from criticism, it is believed that the safest measure is to prosecute.

The bail system is also used to protect the prosecutor from criticism. Thus it is the policy to set bail at a high level with the expectation that the court will reduce the amount. "This looks good for Prosecutor Carroll. Takes the heat off of him, especially in morals cases. If the accused doesn't appear in court the prosecutor can't be blamed. The public gets upset when they know these types are out free." This is an example of exchange where one actor is shifting the responsibility and potential onus onto another. In turn, the court is under pressure from county jail officials to keep the prison population down.

A second community group having contact with the prosecutor is composed of those leaders who have a continuing or potential interest in the politics of prosecution. This group, analogous to the players in one of Long's community games, is linked to the prosecutor because his actions affect their success in playing another game. Hence community boosters want either a crackdown or a hands-off policy toward gambling, political leaders want the prosecutor to remember the interests of the party, and business leaders want policies that will not interfere with their own game.

Community leaders may receive special treatment by the prosecutor if they run afoul of the law. A policy of the King County office requires that cases involving prominent members of the community be referred immediately to the chief criminal deputy and the prosecutor for their disposition. As one deputy noted, "These cases can be pretty touchy. It's important that the boss knows immediately about this type of case so that he is not caught 'flat-footed' when asked about it by the press."

Pressure by an interest group was evidenced during a strike by drugstore employees in 1964. The striking unions urged Prosecutor Carroll to invoke a state law that requires the presence of a licensed pharmacist if the drugstore is open. Not only did union representatives meet with Carroll, but picket lines were set up outside the courthouse protesting his refusal to act. The prosecutor resisted the union's pressure tactics.

In recent years, the prosecutor's tolerance policy toward minor forms of gambling led to a number of conflicts with Seattle's mayor, the sheriff, and church organizations. After a decision was made to prohibit all forms of public gaming, the prosecutor was criticized by groups representing the tourist industry and such affected groups as the bartenders' union, which thought the decision would have an adverse economic effect. As Prosecutor Carroll said, "I am always getting pressures from different interests—business, the Chamber of Commerce, and labor. I have to try and maintain a balance between them." In exchange for these considerations, the prosecutor may gain prestige, political support, and admission into the leadership groups of the community.

SUMMARY

By viewing the King County Office of Prosecuting Attorney as the focal organization in an exchange system, data from this exploratory study suggests the marketlike relationships that exist between actors in the system. Because prosecution operates in an environment of scarce resources and because the decisions have potential political ramifications, a variety of officials influence the allocation of justice. The decision to prosecute is not made at one point, but rather the prosecuting attorney has a number of options he may employ during various stages of the proceedings. But the prosecutor is able to exercise his discretionary powers only within the network of exchange relationships. The police, court congestion, organizational strains, and community pressures are among the factors that influence prosecutorial behavior.

NOTES

1. James R. Klonoski and Robert I. Medelsohn, "The Allocation of Justice: A Political Analysis," *Journal of Public Law* 14 (May 1965): 323–342.

2. William M. Evan, "Toward a Theory of Inter-Organizational Relations," *Management Science* 11 (August 1965): 218–230.

3. Norton Long, *The Polity* (Chicago: Rand McNally, 1962), p. 142.

4. William J. Gore, *Administrative Decision-Making* (New York: John Wiley, 1964), p. 23.

5. William J. Chambliss, *Crime and the Legal Process* (New York: McGraw-Hill, 1969), p. 84.

6. The lack of reliable criminal statistics is well known. These data were gathered from a number of sources, including King County, "Annual Report of the Prosecuting Attorney," State of Washington, 1964.

7. Jerome L. Skolnick, *Justice Without Trial* (New York: John Wiley, 1966), p. 120.

8. Jack Ladinsky, "The Impact of Social Backgrounds of Lawyers on Law Practice and the Law," *Journal of Legal Education* 16 (1963): 128.

11

Adapting to Plea Bargaining

Prosecutors

Milton Heimann

Plea bargaining has been openly discussed only since the late 1960s. Before then, it was a widespread practice that was one of the secrets of criminal justice officials. In this analysis of the way new prosecutors adapt to plea bargaining, Milton Heumann shows how negotiated justice serves the needs of all participants in the process.

The new prosecutor shares many of the general expectations that his counterpart for the defense brings to the court. He expects factually and legally disputable issues, and the preliminary hearings and trials associated with these. If his expectations differ at all from the naive "Perry Mason" orientation, it is only to the extent that he anticipates greater success than the hapless Hamilton Burger of Perry Mason fame.

The new prosecutor's views about plea bargaining parallel those of the defense attorney. He views plea bargaining as an expedient employed in crowded urban courts by harried and/or poorly motivated prosecutors. He views the trial as "what the system is really about" and plea bargaining as a

Source: Reprinted from *Plea Bargaining* by Milton Heumann by permission of the University of Chicago Press and the author.

Editor's note: This study is based on date from Connecticut, where, until a reorganization of the court system in July 1978, prosecution was conducted by state's attorneys in the supreme court and by prosecutors in the circuit court. Readers should understand that the powers of each office are essentially the same; only the workplace is different.

necessary evil dictated by case volume. The following exchange with a newly appointed prosecutor is illustrative.

Q: Let's say they removed the effects of case pressure, provided you with more manpower. You wouldn't have that many cases. . . .

A: Then everybody should go to trial.

Q: Everybody should go to trial?

A: Yeah.

Q: Why?

A: Because supposedly if they're guilty they'll be found guilty. If they're not guilty they'll be found not guilty. That's the fairest way . . . judged by a group of your peers, supposedly.

Q: So you think that plea bargaining is a necessary evil?

A: Yeah.

Q: Would justice be better served if all cases went to trial?

A: That's the way it's supposed to be set up. Sure. Why wouldn't it?

Q: Would prosecutors be more satisfied?

A: Probably.

Q: If cases went to trial?

A: Sure.

Q: Why?

A: Because they could talk in front of twelve people and act like a lawyer. Right. Play the role.

It should be emphasized that these expectations and preferences of the new prosecutor are founded on the minimal law school preparation. . . . The new-comers simply do not know very much about the criminal justice system.

Unlike defense attorneys, however, the new prosecutor is likely to receive some form of structured assistance when he begins his job. The chief prosecutor or chief state's attorney may provide this aid, if the prosecutor's office is staffed by a number of prosecutors or state's attorneys—that is, if the newcomer is not the only assistant prosecutor—it is more common for the chief prosecutor to assign to one or more of his experienced assistants the responsibility for helping the newcomer adjust. Since the newcomer's actions reflect on the office as a whole, it is not surprising that this effort is made.

The assistance the newcomer receives can be described as a form of structured observation. For roughly two weeks, he accompanies an experienced prosecutor to court and to plea-bargaining sessions and observes him in action. The proximity of the veteran prosecutor—and his designation as the newcomer's mentor—facilitates communication between the two. The experienced prosecutor can readily explain or justify his actions, and the newcomer can ask any and all relevant questions. Certainly, this is a more structured form of assistance than defense attorneys receive.

However, new prosecutors still feel confused and overwhelmed during this initial period. Notwithstanding the assistance they receive, they are disoriented by the multitude of tasks performed by the prosecutor and by the environment in which he operates. This is particularly true in the circuit court, where the seemingly endless shuffling of files, the parade of defendants before the court and around the courtroom, the hurried, early-morning plea-bargaining sessions all come as a surprise to the new prosecutor.

Q: What were your initial impressions of the court during this "orientation period"?

A: The first time I came down here was a Monday morning at the arraignments. Let's face it, the majority of people here, you don't expect courts to be as crowded as they are. You don't expect thirty to thirty-five people to come out of the cell block who have been arrested over the weekend. It was . . . you sit in court the first few days, you didn't realize the court was run like this. All you see, you see Perry Mason on TV, or pictures of the Supreme Court, or you see six judges up there in a spotless courtroom, everyone well dressed, well manicured, and you come to court and find people coming in their everyday clothes, coming up drunk, some are high on drugs, it's . . . it's an experience to say the least.

Q: Could you describe your first days when you came down here? What are your recollections? Anything strike you as strange?

A: Just the volume of business and all the stuff the prosecutor had to do. For the first week or two, I went to court with guys who had been here. Just sat there and watched. What struck me was the amount of things he [the prosecutor] has to do in the courtroom. The prosecutor runs the courtroom. Although the judge is theoretically in charge, we're standing there plea bargaining and calling the cases at the same time and chewing gum and telling people to quiet down and setting bonds, and that's what amazed me. I never thought I would learn all the terms. What bothered me also was the paperwork. Not the Supreme Court decisions, not the *mens rea* or any of this other stuff, but the amount of junk that's in those files that you have to know. We never heard about this crap in law school.

As suggested in the second excerpt, the new prosecutor is also surprised by the relative insignificance of the judge. He observes that the prosecutor assumes—through plea bargaining—responsibility for the disposition of many cases. Contrary to his expectations of being an adversary in a dispute moderated by the judge, he finds that often the prosecutor performs the judge's function.

It is precisely this responsibility for resolving disputes that is most vexing to the new superior court state's attorney. Unlike his circuit court counterpart, he does not generally find hurried conferences, crowded courts, and so on. But he observes that, as in the circuit court, the state's attorney negotiates cases, and in the superior court far more serious issues and periods of incarceration are involved in these negotiations. For the novice state's attorney, the notion that he will in short order be responsible for resolving these disputes is particularly disturbing.

Q: What were your initial impressions of your job here [as a state's attorney]?

A: Well, I was frightened of the increased responsibility. I knew the stakes were high here. . . . I didn't really know what to expect, and I would say it took me a good deal of time to adapt here.

Q: Adapt in which way?

A: To the higher responsibilities. Here you're dealing with felonies, serious felonies all the way up to homicides, and I had never been involved in that particular type of situation. . . . I didn't believe that I was prepared to handle the type of job that I'd been hired to do. I looked around me and I saw the serious charges, the types of cases, and the experienced defense counsel on the one hand and the inexperience on my part on the other, and I was, well. . . .

Q: Did you study up on your own?

A: No more than. . . . Before I came over here I had done some research and made a few notes, et cetera, about the procedures. I think I was prepared from the book end of things to take the job, but, again, it was the practical aspects that you're not taught in law school and that you can only learn from experience that I didn't have, and that's what I was apprehensive about.

These first weeks in the court, then, serve to familiarize the newcomer with the general patterns of case resolution. He is not immediately thrust into the court but is able to spend some time simply observing the way matters are handled. The result, though, is to increase his anxiety. The confusion of the circuit court and the responsibilities of a state's attorney in the superior court were not anticipated. The newcomer expects to be able to prepare cases leisurely and to rely on the skills learned in law school. Yet he finds that his colleagues seem to have neither the time nor the inclination to operate in this fashion. As the informal period of orientation draws to a close, the newcomer has a better perspective on the way the system operates, but still is on very uneasy footing about how to proceed when the responsibility for the case is his alone. In short, he is somewhat disoriented by his orientation.

THE PROSECUTOR ON HIS OWN:
INITIAL FIRMNESS AND RESISTANCE
TO PLEA BARGAINING

Within a few weeks after starting his job, the prosecutor and the state's attorney are expected to handle cases on their own. Experienced personnel are still available for advice, and the newcomer is told that he can turn to them with his problems. But the cases are now the newcomer's, and, with one exception, he is under no obligation to ask anyone for anything.

The new prosecutor is confronted by a stream of defense attorneys asking for a particular plea bargain in a case. If the prosecutor agrees, his decision is irreversible. It would be a violation of all the unwritten folkways of the criminal court for either a defense attorney or a prosecutor to break his word. On the other hand, if the prosecutor does not plea bargain, offers nothing in exchange for a plea, he at least does not commit himself to an outcome that may eventually prove to be a poor decision on his part. However, a refusal to plea bargain also places him "out of step" with his colleagues and with the general expectation of experienced defense attorneys.

Like the new attorney, the new prosecutor is in no hurry to dispose of the case. He is (1) inclined toward an adversary resolution of the case through formal hearings and trial, (2) disinclined to plea bargain in general, and (3) unsure about what constitutes an appropriate plea bargain for a particular case. Yet he is faced with demands by defense attorneys to resolve the case through plea bargaining. The new defense attorney has the luxury of postponing his decision for any given case. He can seek the advice of others before committing himself to a particular plea bargain in a particular case. For the new prosecutor, this is more difficult, since he is immediately faced with the demands of a number of attorneys in a number of different cases.

When the new prosecutor begins to handle his own cases, then, he lacks confidence about how to proceed in his dealings with defense attorneys. He often masks his insecurity in this period with an outward air of firmness. He is convinced that he must appear confident and tough, lest experienced attorneys think they can take advantage of him.

Q: What happened during your first few days of handling cases on your own?

A: Well, as a prosecutor, first of all, people try to cater to you because they want you to do favors for them. If you let a lawyer run all over you, you are dead. I had criminal the first day, on a Monday, and I'm in there [in the room where cases are negotiated], and a guy comes in, and I was talking to some lawyer on his file, and he's just standing there. Then I was talking to a second guy, and he was about fourth or fifth. So he looked at me and says: "When the hell you going to get to me?" So I says: "You wait your fucking turn, I'll get to you when I'm ready. If you don't like it, get out." It's sad that you have to swear at people, but it's the only language they understand—especially lawyers. Lawyers are the most obstinate, arrogant, belligerent bastards you will ever meet. Believe me. They come into this court—first of all—and we are really the asshole of the judicial system [circuit court], and they come in here and don't really have any respect for you. They'll come in here and be nice to you, because they feel you'll give them a *nolle*. That's all. Lawyers do not respect this court. I don't know if I can blame them or not blame them. You can come in here and see the facilities here; you see how things are handled; you see how it's like a zoo pushing people in and out. . . . When they do come here, lawyers have two approaches. One, they try to soft-soap and kiss your ass if you give them a *nolle*. Two, they'll come in here and try to ride roughshod over you and try to push you to a corner. Like that lawyer that first day. I had to swear at him and show him I wasn't going to take shit, and that's that. The problem of dealing with lawyers is that you can't let them bullshit you. So, when I first started out I tried to be. . . . It's like the new kid on the block. He comes to a new neighborhood, and you've got to prove yourself. If you're a patsy, you're going to live with that as long as you're in court. If you let a couple of lawyers run over you, word will get around to go to ————, he's a pushover. Before you know it, they're running all over you. So you have to draw a line so they will respect you.

At first I was very tough because I didn't know what I was doing. In other words, you have to be very wary. These guys, some of them, have been practicing in this court for forty years. And they'll take you to the cleaners. You have to be pretty damn careful.

The new prosecutor couples this outward show of firmness toward attorneys with a fairly rigid plea-bargaining posture. His reluctance to offer incentives to the defendant for a plea or to reward the defendant who chooses to plead is, at this point in the prosecutor's career, as much a function of his lack of confidence as it is a reflection of his antipathy toward plea bargaining. During this very early stage he is simply afraid to make concessions. Experienced court personnel are well aware that new prosecutors adopt this rigid stance.

Q: Have you noticed any differences between new prosecutors and prosecutors that have been around a while?

A: Oh, yes. First of all, a new prosecutor is more likely to be less flexible in changing charges. He's afraid. He's cautious. He doesn't know his business. He doesn't know the liars. He can't tell when he's lying or exaggerating. He doesn't know all the ramifications. He doesn't know how tough it is sometimes to prove the case to juries. He hasn't got the experience, so that more likely than not he will be less flexible. He is also more easily fooled. [Circuit court judge]

   I can only answer that question in a general way. It does seem to me that the old workhorses [experienced prosecutors] are more flexible than the young stallions. [Superior court judge]

Q: You were saying about the kids, the new prosecutors, the new state's attorneys. Are they kind of more hard-assed?

A: They tend to be more nervous. They tend to have a less well-defined idea of what they can do and what they can't do without being criticized. So, to the extent that they are more nervous, they tend to be more hard-assed. [Private criminal attorney]

Q: What about new prosecutors? Do they differ significantly from prosecutors who have been around a while?

A: Initially a new prosecutor is going to be reluctant to *nolle,* reluctant to give too good a deal because he is scared. He is afraid of being taken advantage of. And if you are talking about the circuit court, they've got the problem that they can't even talk it over with anybody. They've got a hundred fifty cases or whatever, and they make an offer or don't make an offer, that's it. Maybe at the end of the day they may get a chance to talk it over and say: "Gee, did I do the right thing?" The defense attorney, when the offer is made, has the opportunity to talk to somebody plus his client before making a decision. So I think it takes the prosecutor a longer time to come around and work under the system. [Legal aid attorney]

It is not difficult to understand why the new prosecutor is reluctant to plea bargain and why he appears rigid to court veterans. Set aside for the moment the prosecutor's personal preference for an adversary resolution and consider only the nature of the demands being made on him. Experienced attorneys want charges dropped, sentence recommendations, and *nolles.* They approach him with the standard argument about the wonderful personal traits of the defendant, the minor nature of the crime, the futility of incarceration, and so on. When the new prosecutor picks up the file, he finds that the defendant probably has an extensive prior criminal record and, often, that he has committed a crime that does not sound minor at all. Under the statute for the crime involved, it is likely that the defendant faces a substantial period of incarceration, yet in almost all circuit court cases and in many superior court cases, the attorneys are talking about a no-time disposition. What to the new prosecutor frequently seems like a serious matter is treated as a relatively inconsequential offense by defense attorneys. And, because the newcomer views the matter as serious, his resolve to remain firm—or, conversely, his insecurity about reducing charges—is reinforced.

Illustrations of this propensity for the new prosecutor or state's attorney to be "outraged" by the facts of the case, and to be disinclined to offer "sweet" deals, are plentiful. The following comments by two circuit court prosecutors and a superior court state's attorney, respectively, illustrate the extent to which the newcomer's appraisal of a case differed from that of the defense attorney and from that of his own colleagues.

Q: You used to go to ——— [chief prosecutor] for help on early cases. Were his recommendations out of line with what you thought should be done with the case?

A: Let's say a guy came in with a serious crime . . . a crime that I thought was serious at one time, anyway. Take fighting on ——— Avenue [a depressed area of Arborville]. He got twenty-five stitches in the head and is charged with aggravated assault. One guy got twenty-five stitches, the other fifteen. And the attorneys would want me to reduce it. I'd go and talk to ——— [chief prosecutor]. He'd say: "They both are drunk, they both got head wounds. Let them plead to breach of peace, and the judge will give them a money fine." Things like that

I didn't feel right about doing, since, to me, right out of law school, middle class, you figure twenty-five stitches in the head, Jesus Christ.

Q: How did you learn what a case was worth?

A: What do you mean, what it's worth?

Q: In terms of plea bargaining. What the going rate. . . .

A: From the prosecutors and defense attorneys who would look at me dumbfounded when I would tell them that I would not reduce this charge. And then they would go running to my boss and he'd say, "Well, it's up to him." Some would even go running to the judge, screaming. One guy claimed surprise when I intended to go to trial for assault in second, which is a Class D felony. Two counts of that and two misdemeanor counts. It was set for jury trial. His witnesses were there. His experience in this court, he said, having handled two or three hundred cases, was that none has ever gone to trial. So he claimed surprise the day of trial. He just couldn't believe it.

Q: Were you in any way out of step with the way things were done here when you first began handling cases on your own?

A: In one respect I was. I evaluated a case by what I felt a proper recommendation should be, and my recommendations were almost always in terms of longer time. I found that the other guys in the office were breaking things down more than I expected. As a citizen, I couldn't be too complacent about an old lady getting knocked down, stuff like that. I thought more time should be recommended. I might think five to ten, six to twelve, while the other guys felt that three to seven was enough.

Implicit in these remarks are the seeds of an explanation for a prosecutor's gradually becoming more willing to plea bargain. One can hypothesize that as his experience with handling cases increases, he will feel less outraged by the crime, and thus will be more willing to work out a negotiated settlement. One assistant state's attorney likened his change in attitude to that of a nurse in an emergency room.

It's like nurses in emergency rooms. You get so used to armed robbery that you treat it as routine, not as morally upsetting. In the emergency room, the biggest emergency is treated as routine. And it's happening to me. The nature of the offense doesn't cause the reaction in me that it would cause in the average citizen. Maybe this is a good thing; maybe it isn't.

Though there is merit in this argument—prosecutors do become accustomed to crime—it is hardly a sufficient explanation of prosecutorial adaptation to plea bargaining. Other factors, often far more subtle, must be considered if we are to understand how and why the novice prosecutor becomes a seasoned plea bargainer.

LEARNING ABOUT PLEA BARGAINING

In the preceding sections I have portrayed the new prosecutor as being predisposed toward an adversary resolution of a case, uncertain about his responsibilities, rigid in his relations with defense attorneys, reluctant to drop charges and to plea bargain in cases that he considers serious, and anxious to try out the skills he learned in law school. This characterization of the newcomer contrasts sharply with that of the veteran prosecutor. [The veteran prosecutor takes] an active role in plea bargaining—urging, cajoling, and threatening the defense attorney to share in the benefits of a negotiated disposition. How is the veteran prosecutor to be reconciled with the new prosecutor . . . ?

The answer lies in what the prosecutor learns and is taught about plea bargaining. His education, like the defense attorney's, is not structured and systematic. Instead, he works his way through cases, testing the adversary and plea-bargaining approaches. He learns piecemeal the costs and benefits of these approaches, and only over a period of time does he develop an appreciation for the relative benefits of a negotiated disposition.

Rather than proceed with a sequential discussion of the newcomer's experience, I think it more profitable at this point to distill from his experiences those central concerns that best explain his adaptation to the plea-bargaining system. Some of the "flavor" of the adaptation process is sacrificed by the proceeding in this fashion, but in terms of clarity of presentation, I think it is a justifiable. Thus, I will discuss separately the considerations that move the prosecutor in the plea-bargaining direction, and later tie these together into an overall perspective on prosecutorial adaptation.

THE DEFENDANT'S FACTUAL
AND LEGAL GUILT

Prosecutors and state's attorneys learn that their roles primarily entail the processing of factually guilty defendants. Contrary to their expectations that problems of establishing factual guilt would be central to their job, they find that in most cases the evidence in the file is sufficient to conclude (and prove) that the defendant is factually guilty. For those cases where there is a substantial question as to factual guilt, the prosecutor has the power—and is inclined to exercise it—to nolle or dismiss the case. If he himself does not believe the defendant to be factually guilty, it is part of his formal responsibilities to filter the case out. But of the cases that remain after the initial screening, the prosecutor believes the majority of defendants to be factually guilty.

Furthermore, he finds that defense attorneys only infrequently contest the prosecutor's own conclusion that the defendant is guilty. In their initial approach to the prosecutor they may raise the possibility that the defendant is factually innocent, but in most subsequent discussions their advances focus on disposition and not on the problem of factual guilt. Thus, from the prosecutor's own reading of the file (after screening) and from the comments of his "adversary," he learns that he begins with the upper hand; more often than not, the factual guilt of the defendant is not really disputable.

Q: Are most of the defendants who come to this court guilty?

A: Yeah, or else we wouldn't have charged them. You know, that's something that people don't understand. Basically the people that are brought here are believed very definitely to be guilty or we wouldn't go on with the prosecution. We would *nolle* the case, and, you know, that is something, when people say, "Well, do you really believe. . . ." Yeah. I do. I really do, and if I didn't and we can clear them, then we *nolle* it, there's no question about it.

But most cases are good, solid cases, and in most of them the defendant is guilty. We have them cold-cocked. And they plead guilty because they are guilty . . . a guy might have been caught in a package store with bottles. Now, he wasn't there to warm his hands. The defendant may try some excuse, but they are guilty and they know they are guilty. And we'll give them a break when they plead guilty. I don't think we should throw away the key on the guy just because we got him cold-cocked. We've got good cases, we give them what we think the case is worth from our point of view, allowing the defendant's mitigating circumstances to enter.

Q: The fact that you're willing to offer a pretty good bargain in negotiations might lead a person to plead guilty even if he had a chance to beat it at trial. But if he was found guilty at the trial he might not get the same result?

A: That's possible, I mean, only the accused person knows whether or not he's committed the crime, and. . . . It's an amazing thing, where, on any number of occasions, you will sit down to negotiate with an accused's attorney . . . and you know [he will say]: "No, no, he's not guilty, he wants his trial." But then if he develops a weakness in the case, or points out a weakness to you, and then you come back and say: "Well, we'll take a suspended sentence and probation," suddenly he says, "Yes, I'm guilty." So it leads you to conclude that, well, all these people who are proclaiming innocence are really not innocent. They're just looking for the right disposition. Now, from my point of view, the ideal situation might be if the person is not guilty, that he pleads not guilty, and we'll give him his trial and let the jury decide. But most people who are in court don't want a trial. I'm not the person who seeks them out and says, "I will drop this charge" or "I will reduce this charge. I will reduce the amount of time you have to do." They come to us, so, you know, the conclusion I think is there that any reasonable person could draw, that these people are guilty, that they are just looking for the best disposition possible. Very few people ask for a speedy trial.

In addition to learning of the factual culpability of most defendants, the prosecutor also learns that defendants would be hard-pressed to raise legal challenges to the state's case. As was discussed earlier, most cases are simply barren of any contestable legal issue, and nothing in the prosecutor's file or the defense attorney's arguments leads the prosecutor to conclude otherwise.

The new prosecutor or state's attorney, then, learns that in most cases the problem of establishing the defendant's factual and legal guilt is nonexistent. Typically, he begins with a very solid case, and, contrary to his expectations, he finds that few issues are in need of resolution at an adversary hearing or trial. The defendant's guilt is not generally problematic; it is conceded by the defense attorney. What remains problematic is the sentence the defendant will receive.

DISTINGUISHING AMONG
THE GUILTY DEFENDANTS

Formally, the prosecutor has some powers that bear directly on sentence. He has the option to reduce or eliminate charges leveled against the defendant; the responsibility for the indictment is his, and his alone. Thus, if he *nolles* some of the charges against the defendant, he can reduce the maximum exposure the defendant faces or ensure that the defendant is sentenced only on a misdemeanor (if he *nolles* a felony), and so forth. Beyond these actions on charges, the formal powers of the prosecutor cease. The judge is responsible for sentencing. He is supposed to decide the conditions of probation, the length of incarceration, and so on. Notwithstanding this formal dichotomy of responsibility, prosecutors find that defense attorneys approach them about both charge and sentence reduction.

Since charge reduction bears on sentence reduction, it is only a small step for defense attorneys to inquire specifically about sentence; and, because there is often an interdependence between charge and sentence, prosecutors are compelled at least to listen to the attorney's arguments. Thus, the prosecutor finds attorneys parading before him asking for charge and sentence reduction, and, in a sense, he is obligated to hear them out.

It is one thing to say that prosecutors and state's attorneys must listen to defense attorneys' requests about disposition and another to say that they must cooperate with these attorneys. As already indicated, new prosecutors feel acutely uneasy about charge and sentence reduction. They have neither the confidence nor the inclination to usurp what they view as primarily the judge's responsibility. Furthermore, one would think that their resolve not to become involved in this area would be strengthened by their learning that most defendants are factually and legally guilty. Why should they discuss dispositions in cases in which they "hold all the cards"?

This query presupposes that prosecutors continue to conceive of themselves as adversaries, whose exclusive task is to establish the defendant's guilt or innocence. But what happens is that as prosecutors gain greater experience handling cases, they gradually develop certain standards for evaluating cases, standards that bear not just on the defendant's guilt or innocence but, more importantly, on the disposition of the defendant's case. These standards better explain prosecutorial behavior in negotiating dispositions than does the simple notion of establishing guilt or innocence.

Specifically prosecutors come to distinguish between serious and nonserious cases, and between cases in which they are looking for time and cases in which they are not looking for time. These standards or distinctions evolve after the prosecutor has processed a substantial number of factually and legally guilty defendants. They provide a means of sorting the raw material—the guilty defendants. Indeed, one can argue that the adversary component of the prosecutor's job is shifted from establishing guilt or innocence to determining the seriousness of the defendant's guilt and whether he should receive time. The guilt of the defendant is assumed, but the problem of disposition remains to be informally argued.

Prosecutors and state's attorneys draw sharp distinctions between serious and nonserious cases. In both instances, they assume the defendant guilty, but they are looking for different types of dispositions, dependent upon their classification of the case. If it is a nonserious matter, they are amenable to defense requests for a small fine in the circuit court, some short, suspended sentence, or some brief period of probation; similarly, in a nonserious superior court matter the state's attorney is willing to work out a combination suspended sentence and probation. The central concern with these nonserious cases is to dispose of them quickly. If the defense attorney requests some sort of no-time disposition that is dependent upon either a prosecutorial reduction of charges or a sentence recommendation, the prosecutor and state's attorney are likely to agree. They have no incentive to refuse the attorney's request, since the attorney's desire comports with what they are "looking for." The case is simply not worth the effort to press for greater penalty.

On the other hand, if the case is serious, the prosecutor and state's attorney are likely to be looking for time. The serious case cannot be quickly disposed of by a no-time alternative. These are cases in which we would expect more involved and lengthy plea-bargaining negotiations.

Whether the case is viewed as serious or nonserious depends on factors other than the formal charges the defendant faces. For example, these nonformal considerations might include the degree of harm done the victim, the amount of violence employed by the defendant, the defendant's prior record, the characteristics of the victim and defendant, the defendant's motive; all are somewhat independent of formal charge, and yet all weigh heavily in the prosecutor's judgment of the seriousness of the case. Defendants facing the same formal charges, then, may find that prosecutors sort their cases into different categories. Two defendants charged with robbery with violence may find that in one instance the state's attorney is willing to reduce the charge and recommend probation, while in the second case he is looking for a substantial period of incarceration. In the former case, the defendant may have simply brushed against the victim (still technically robbery with violence), whereas in the second, he may have dealt the victim a severe blow. Or possibly, the first defendant was a junkie supporting his habit, whereas the second was operating on the profit motive. These are, of course, imperfect illustrations, but the point is that the determination as to whether a case is serious or not serious only partially reflects the charges against the defendant. Often the determination is based on a standard that develops with experience in the court and operates, for the most part, independently of formal statutory penalties.

The following excerpts convey a sense of the serious/nonserious dichotomy and also support the argument that charge does not necessarily indicate seriousness.

Q: How did you learn what cases were worth?

A: You mean sentences.

Q: Yeah.

A: Well, that's a hit-or-miss kind of an experience. You take a first offender; any first offender in a nonviolent crime certainly is not going to jail for a nonviolent crime. And a second offender, well, it depends again on the type of crime, and maybe there should be some supervision, some probation. And a third time, you say, well now this is a guy who maybe you should treat a little more strictly. Now, a violent crime, I would treat differently. How did I learn to? I learned because there were a few other guys around with experience, and I got experience, and they had good judgments, workable approaches, and you pick it up like that. In other words, you watch others, you talk to others, you handle a lot of cases yourself.

Q: Does anybody, the public, put pressure on you to be tougher?

A: Not really.

Q: Wouldn't these sentences be pretty difficult for the public to understand?

A: Yeah, somewhat. . . . Sure, we are pretty easy on a lot of these cases except that. . . . We are tough on mugging and crimes by violence. Say an old lady is grabbed by a kid and knocked to the ground and her pocketbook taken as she is waiting for the bus. We'd be as tough as anybody on that one, whether you call it a breach of peace or a robbery. We'd be very tough. And in this case there would be a good likelihood of the first offender going to jail, whatever the charge we give him. The name of the charge isn't important. We'd have the facts regardless.

Q: So you think you have changed? You give away more than you used to?

A: I don't give away more. I think that I have reached the point where. . . . When I started I was trying to be too fair, if you want to say that, you know, to see that justice was done, and I was severe. But, you know, like ———— [head prosecutor] says, you need to look for justice tempered with mercy, you know, substantial justice, and that's what I do now. When I was new, a guy cut [knifed] someone he had to go to jail. But now I look for substantial justice—if two guys have been drinking and one guy got cut, I'm not giving anything away, but a fine, that's enough there.

Q: But you are easier now? I mean, you could look for time?

A: Look, if I get a guy that I feel belongs in jail, I try to sentence bargain and get him in jail. We had this one guy, ———. He was charged with breach of peace. We knew he had been selling drugs but we couldn't prove anything. He hits this girl in ———'s parking lot [large department store], and tried to take her purse. She screams and he runs. This was a real son-of-a-bitch, been pimping for his own wife. On breach of peace I wanted the full year, and eventually got nine months. Cases like that I won't give an inch on. And the lawyer first wanted him to plead to suspended sentence and a money fine. I said this guy is a god-damned animal. Anybody who lets his wife screw and then gets proceeds from it, and deals in drugs . . . well, if you can catch the bastard on it, he belongs behind bars.

· · ·

The second standard used by prosecutors and state's attorneys in processing factually and legally guilty defendants is the time/no-time distinction. There is an obvious relationship between the serious/nonserious standard and this one: in the serious case time is generally the goal; whereas in the nonserious case, a no-time disposition is satisfactory to the prosecutor. But this simple relationship does not always hold, and it is important for us to consider the exceptions.

In some serious cases, the prosecutor or state's attorney may not be looking for time. Generally, these are cases in which the prosecutor has a problem establishing either the factual or legal guilt of the defendant, and thus is willing to settle for a plea to the charge and offer a recommendation of a suspended sentence. The logic is simple: the prosecutor feels the defendant is guilty of the offense but fears that if he insists on time, the defense attorney will go to trial and uncover the factual or legal defects of the state's case. Thus, the prosecutor "sweetens the deal" to extract a guilty plea and to decrease the likelihood that the attorney will gamble on complete vindication.

Of the prosecutors I interviewed, a handful expressed disenchantment with plea bargaining. They felt that their associates were being too lenient, giving away too much in return for the defendant's plea. They argued that the prosecutor's office should stay firm and go to trial if necessary in order to obtain higher sentences. They were personally inclined to act this way: they "didn't like plea bargaining." But when pushed a bit, it became clear that their antipathy to plea bargaining was not without its exceptions. In the serious case with factual or legal defects they felt very strongly that plea bargaining was appropriate. The sentiments of such an "opponent" to plea bargaining are presented below.

Q: So you are saying that you only like some kinds of plea bargaining?

A: I like to negotiate cases where I have a problem with the case. I know the guy is guilty, but I have some legal problem, or unavailability of a witness that the defendant doesn't know about that will make it difficult for us to put the case on. I would have trouble with the case. Then it is in my interest to bargain; even in serious cases with these problems, it is in the best interests of the state to get the guy to plead, even if it's to a felony with suspended sentence.

Q: If there was no plea bargaining, then the state would lose out?

A: Yes, in cases like these. These would be cases that without plea bargaining we would have trouble convicting the defendant. But this has nothing to do with the defendant's guilt or innocence. Yet we might have to let him go. It is just to plea bargain in cases like this. It is fair to get the plea from the defendant, since he is guilty. Now, there is another situation; whereas in the first situation, I have no philosophical problems with plea bargaining. We may have a weak case factually. Maybe the case depends on one witness, and I have talked to the witness and realized how the witness would appear in court. Maybe the witness would be a flop when he testifies. If I feel the defendant is guilty, but the witness is really bad, then I know that we won't win the case at trial, that we won't win a big concession in plea bargaining. So I will evaluate the case, and I will be predisposed to talking about a more lenient disposition.

• • •

The other unexpected cross between the standards—nonserious case/looking for time—occurs in several types of situations. First, there is the case in which the defendant has a long history of nonserious offenses, and it is felt that a short period of incarceration will "teach him a lesson," or at least indicate that there are limits beyond which prosecutors cannot be pushed. Second, there is the situation where the prosecutor holds the defense attorney in disdain and is determined to teach the attorney a lesson. Thus, though the defendant's offense is nonserious, the prosecutor would generally be amenable to a no-time disposition, the prosecutor chooses to hold firm. It is precisely in those borderline cases that the prosecutor can be most successful in exercising sanctions against the uncooperative defense attorney. The formal penalties associated with the charges against the defendant give him ample sentencing range, and by refusing to agree to a no-time disposition, the costs to the defense attorney become great. The attorney is not able to meet his client's demands for no time, and yet he must be leery about trial, given the even greater exposure the defendant faces. These borderline decisions by prosecutors, then, are fertile grounds for exploring sanctions against defense attorneys. It is here that we can expect the cooperative defense attorney to benefit most, and the recalcitrant defense attorney to suffer the most. Relatedly, one can also expect prosecutors to be looking for time in nonserious offenses in which the defendant or his counsel insists on raising motions and going to trial. These adversary activities may be just enough to tip the prosecutor into looking for time.

In addition to its relationship to the serious/nonserious standard, the time/no-time standard bears on prosecutorial plea-bargaining behavior in another way. As prosecutors gain experience in the plea-bargaining system, they tend to stress "certainty of time" rather than "amount of time." This is to say that they become less concerned about extracting maximum penalties from defendants and more concerned with ensuring that in cases in which they are looking for time, the defendant actually receives some time. Obviously, there are limits to the prosecutor's largesse—in a serious case thirty days will not be considered sufficient time. But prosecutors are willing to consider periods of incarceration substantially shorter than the maximum sentence allowable for a particular crime. In return, though, prosecutors want a guarantee of sorts that the defendant will receive time. They want to decrease the likelihood that the defendant, by some means or other, will obtain a suspended sentence. Thus, they will "take" a fixed amount of time if the defendant agrees not to try to "pitch" for a lower sentence, or if the defendant pleads to a charge in which all participants know some time will be meted out by the judge. In the latter instance, the attorney may be free to "pitch," but court personnel know his effort is more a charade for the defendant than a realistic effort to obtain a no-time disposition. The following excerpts illustrate prosecutorial willingness to trade off years of time for certainty of time.

> I don't believe in giving away things. In fact ——— [a public defender] approached me; there's this kid ———, he has two robberies, one first degree, one second, and three minor cases. Now, this kid, I made out an affidavit myself for tampering with a witness. This kid is just n.g. ——— came to me and said, "We'll plead out, two to five." He'll go to state's prison. I agree to that—both these offenses are bindovers. These kids belong in jail. I'd rather take two to five here than bind them over to superior court and take a chance on what will happen there. At least my two to five will be a year and three-quarters in state's prison. The thing is, if I want to get a guy in jail for a year, I'll plea bargain with him, and I'll take six months if I can get it, because the guy belongs in jail, and if I can get him to jail for six months why should I fool around with that case, and maybe get a year if I am lucky? If I can put a guy away for six months I might be cheated out of six months, but at least the guy is doing six months in jail.
>
> What is a proper time? It never bothers me if we could have gotten seven years and instead we got five. In this case, there was no violence; minor stuff was stolen. We got time out of him. That is the important thing.
>
> **A:** It makes no difference to me really if a man does five to ten or four to eight. The important thing is he's off the street, not a menace to society for a period of time, and the year or two less is not going to make that great a difference. If you do get time, I think it's . . . you know, many prosecutors I know feel this way. They have achieved confinement, that's what they're here for.

Q: Let's take another example. Yesterday an attorney walked in here when I was present on that gambling case. He asked you if it could be settled without time?

A: And I said no. That ended the discussion.

Q: What will he do now?

A: He'll file certain motions that he really doesn't have to file. All the facts of our case were spelled out; he knows as much about our cases as he'll ever know. So his motions will just delay things. There'll come a point, though, when he'll have to face trial; and he'll come in to speak with us, and ask if we still have the same position. We'll have the same position. We'll still be looking for one to three. His record goes back to 1923, he's served two or three terms for narcotics, and he's been fined five times for gambling. So we'd be looking for one to three and a fine. Even though he's in his sixties, he's been a criminal all his life, since 1923. . . .

Q: But if the attorney pushes and says, "Now look. He's an old guy. He's sixty-two years old, how about six months?"

A: I might be inclined to accept it because, again, confinement would be involved. I think our ends would be met. It would show his compadres that there's no longer any immunity for gambling, that there is confinement involved. So the end result would be achieved.

Justice Holmes, who is supposed to be the big sage in American jurisprudence, said it isn't the extent of the punishment but the certainty of it. This is my basic philosophy. If the guy faces twelve years in state's prison, I'm satisfied if on a plea of guilty he'll go to state's prison for two or three years.

The experienced prosecutor, then, looks beyond the defendant's guilt when evaluating a case. He learns—from a reading of the file and from the defense attorney's entreaties—that most defendants are factually and legally guilty and that he generally holds the upper hand. As he gains experience in processing these cases, he gradually begins to draw distinctions within this pool of guilty defendants. Some of the cases appear not to be serious, and the prosecutor becomes willing to go along with the defense attorney's request for no-time dispositions. The cases simply do not warrant a firmer prosecutorial posture. In serious cases, when he feels time is in order, he often finds defense attorneys in agreement on the need for some incarceration.

In a sense, the prosecutor redefines his professional goals. He learns that the statutes fail to distinguish adequately among guilty defendants, that they "sweep too broadly," and give short shrift to the specific facts of the offense, to the defendant's prior record, to the degree of contributory culpability of the victim, and so on. Possessing more information about the defendant than the judge does, the prosecutor—probably unconsciously—comes to believe that it is his professional responsibility to develop standards that distinguish among defendants and lead to "equitable" dispositions. Over time, the prosecutor comes to feel that if he does not develop these standards, if he does not make these professional judgments, no one else will.

The prosecutor seems almost to drift into plea bargaining. When he begins his job he observes that his colleagues plea bargain routinely and quickly finds that defense attorneys expect him to do the same. Independent of any rewards, sanctions, or pressures, he learns the strengths of his cases, and learns to distinguish the serious from the nonserious ones. After an initial period of reluctance to plea bargain at all (he is fearful of being taken advantage of by defense attorneys), the prosecutor finds that he is engaged almost unwittingly in daily decisions concerning the disposition of cases. His obligation to consider alternative charges paves the way for the defense attorney's advances; it is only a small jump to move to sentence discussions. And as he plea bargains more and more cases, the serious/nonserious and time/no-time standards begin to hold sway in his judgments. He feels confident about the disposition he is looking for, and if a satisfactory plea bargain in line with his goals can be negotiated, he comes to feel that there is little point to following a more formal adversary process....

CASE PRESSURE
AND POTENTIAL BACKLOG

Though they may do so during the first few weeks, the newcomer's peers and superiors do not generally pressure him to move cases because of volume. Instead, he is thrust in the fray largely on his own and is allowed to work out his own style of case disposition. Contrary to the "conspiratorial perspective" of the adaptation process, he is not coerced to cooperate in processing "onerously large caseloads."

The newcomer's plea-bargaining behavior is conditioned by his reactions to particular cases he handles or learns about and not by caseload problems of the office. The chief prosecutor within the jurisdiction may worry about his court's volume and the speed with which cases are disposed, but he does not generally interfere with his assistant's decision about how to proceed in a case. The newcomer is left to learn about plea bargaining on his own, and for the reason already discussed, he learns and is taught the value of negotiating many of his cases. The absence of a direct relationship between prosecutor plea bargaining and case pressure is suggested in the following remarks.

Q: Is it case pressure that leads you to negotiate?

A: I don't believe it's the case pressure at all. In every court, whether there are five cases or one hundred cases, we should try to settle it. It's good for both sides. If I were a public defender, I'd try to settle all the cases for my guilty clients. By negotiating you are bound to do better. Now take this case. [He reviewed the facts of a case in which an elderly man was charged with raping a seven-year-old girl. The defendant claimed he could not remember what happened, that he was drunk, and that, though the girl might have been in the bed with him, he did not think he raped her.] I think I gave the defense attorney a fair deal. The relatives say she was raped, but the doctor couldn't conclusively establish that. I offered him a plea to a lesser charge, one dealing with advances toward minors, but excluding the sex act. If he takes it, he'll be able to walk away with time served [the defendant had not posted bail and had spent several months in jail]. It's the defendant's option though. He can go through trial if he wants, but if he makes that choice, the kid and her relatives will have to be dragged through the agonies of trial also. Then I would be disposed to look for a higher sentence for the defendant. So I think my offer is fair, and the offer has nothing to do with the volume of this court. It's the way I think the case—all things considered—should be resolved.

Q: You say the docket wasn't as crowded in 1966, and yet there was plea bargaining. If I had begun this interview by saying why is there plea bargaining here. . . .

A: I couldn't use the reason there's plea bargaining because there are a lot of cases. That's not so; that's not so at all. If we had only ten cases down for tomorrow and an attorney walked in and wanted to discuss a case with me, I'd sit down and discuss it with him. In effect, that's plea bargaining. Whether it's for the charge or for an agreed recommendation or reduction of the charge or what have you, it's still plea bargaining. It's part of the process that has been going on for quite a long time.

Q: And you say it's not because of the crowded docket, but if I gave you a list of reasons for why there was plea bargaining and asked you to pick the most important. . . .

A: I never really thought about the. . . . You talk about the necessity for plea bargaining, and you say, well, it's necessary, and one of the reasons is because we have a crowded docket, but even if we didn't we still would plea bargain.

Q: Why?

A: Well, it has been working throughout the years, and the way I look at it, it's beneficial to the defendant, it's beneficial to the court, and not just in saving time but in avoiding police officers coming to court, witnesses being subpoenaed in, and usually things can be discussed between prosecutors and defense counsel which won't be said in the open court and on the record. There are many times that the defense counsel will speak confidentially with the prosecutor about his client or about the facts or about the complainant or a number of things. So I don't know if I can justify plea bargaining other than by speaking of the necessity of plea bargaining. If there were only ten cases down for one day, it still would be something that would be done.

Maybe in places like New York they plea bargain because of case pressure. I don't know. But here it is different. We dispose of cases on the basis of what is fair to both sides. You can get a fair settlement by plea bargaining. If you don't try to settle a case quickly, it gets stale. In New York the volume probably is so bad that it becomes a matter of "getting rid of cases." In Connecticut, we have some pretty big dockets in some cities, but in other areas—here, for example—we don't have that kind of pressure. Sure, I feel some pressure, but you can't say that we negotiate our cases out to clear the docket. And you probably can't say that even about the big cities in Connecticut either.

Prosecutors, then, do not view their propensity to plea bargain as a direct outcome of case pressure. Instead, they speak of "mutually satisfactory outcomes," "fair dispositions," "reducing police overcharging," and so on. We need not here evaluate their claims in detail; what is important is that collectively their arguments militate against according case pressure the "top billing" it so often receives in the literature.

Another way to conceptualize the relationship between case pressure and plea bargaining is to introduce the notion of a "potential backlog." Some prosecutors maintain that if fewer cases were plea bargained, or if plea bargaining were eliminated, a backlog of cases to be disposed of would quickly clog their calendars. A potential backlog, then, lurks as a possibility in every jurisdiction. Even in a low-volume jurisdiction, one complex trial could back up cases for weeks, or even months. If all those delayed cases also had to be tried, the prosecutor feels he would face two not-so-enviable options. He could become further backlogged by trying as many of them as was feasible, or he could reduce his backlog by outright dismissal of cases. The following comments are typical of the potential backlog argument.

Q: Some people have suggested that plea bargaining not be allowed in the court. All cases would go to trial before a judge or jury and. . . .

A: Something like that would double, triple, and quadruple the backlog. Reduce that 90 percent of people pleading guilty, and even if you were to try a bare minimum of those cases, you quadruple your backlog. It's feasible.

Well, right now we don't have a backlog. But if we were to try even 10 percent of our cases, take them to a jury, we'd be so backed up that we couldn't even move. We'd be very much in the position of. . . . Some traffic director in New York once said that there will come a time that there will be one car too many coming into New York and nobody will be able to move. Well, we can get ourselves into that kind of situation if we are going to go ahead and refuse to plea bargain even in the serious cases.

Though a potential backlog is an ever-present possibility, it should be stressed that most prosecutors develop this argument more as a prediction as to the outcome of a rule decreasing or eliminating plea bargaining than as an explanation for why they engage in plea bargaining. If plea bargaining were eliminated, a backlog would develop; but awareness of this outcome does not explain why they plea bargain.

Furthermore, prosecutors tend to view the very notion of eliminating plea bargaining as a fake issue, a straw-man proposition. It is simply inconceivable to them that plea bargaining could or would be eliminated. They maintain that no court system could try all of its cases, even if huge increases in personnel levels were made; trials consume more time than any realistic increase in personnel levels could manage. They were willing to speculate on the outcome of a rule proscribing plea bargaining, but the argument based on court backlog that they evoked was not a salient consideration in understanding their day-in, day-out plea-bargaining behavior.

It is, of course, impossible to refute with complete certainty an argument that prosecutors plea bargain because failure to do so would cause a backlog of unmanageable proportions to develop. However, the interviews indicate other more compelling ways to conceptualize prosecutorial adaptation to plea bargaining, and these do not depend on a potential backlog that always can be conjured up. Though the backlog may loom as a consequence of a failure to plea bargain, it—like its case pressure cousin—is neither a necessary nor sufficient explanatory vehicle for understanding the core aspects of prosecutorial plea-bargaining behavior.

A PERSPECTIVE
ON PROSECUTORIAL ADAPTATION

Perhaps the most important outcome of the prosecutor's adaptation is that he evidences a major shift in his own presumption about how to proceed with a case. As a newcomer, he feels it to be his responsibility to establish the defendant's guilt at trial, and he sees no need to justify a decision to go to trial. However, as he processes more and more cases, as he drifts into plea bargaining, and as he is taught the risks associated with trials, his own assumption about how to proceed with a case changes. He approaches every case with plea bargaining in mind, that is, he presumes that the case will be plea bargained. If it is a "nonserious" matter, he expects it to be quickly resolved; if it is "serious" he generally expects to negotiate time as part of the disposition. In both instances, he anticipates that the case will eventually be resolved by a negotiated disposition and not by a trial. When a plea bargain does not materialize, and the case goes to trial, the prosecutor feels compelled to justify his failure to reach an accord. He no longer is content to simply assert that it is the role of the prosecutor to establish the defendant's guilt at trial. This adversary component of the prosecutor's role has been replaced by a self-imposed burden to justify why he chose to go to trial, particularly if a certain conviction—and, for serious cases, a period of incarceration—could have been obtained by means of a negotiated disposition.

Relatedly, the prosecutor grows accustomed to the power he exercises in these plea-bargaining negotiations. As a newcomer, he argued that his job was to be an advocate for the state and that it was the judge's responsibility to sentence defendants. But, having in fact "sentenced" most of the defendants whose files he plea bargained, the distinction between prosecutor and judge becomes blurred in his own mind. Though he did not set out to usurp judicial prerogatives—indeed, he resisted efforts to engage him in the plea-bargaining process—he gradually comes to expect that he will exercise sentencing powers. There is no fixed point in time when he makes a calculated choice to become adjudicator as well as adversary. In a sense, it simply "happens"; the more cases he resolves (either by charge reduction or sentence recommendations), the greater the likelihood that he will lose sight of the distinction between the roles of judge and prosecutor.

12

✦

The Practice of Law
as Confidence Game

Organization Co-Optation
of a Profession

Abraham S. Blumberg

Central to the adversary system is the defense attorney, who will engage the prosecution in a "fight" to ensure that the defendant's rights are protected and that the case is presented to the judge and jury in the best possible light. What happens when the professional environment of the criminal lawyer moderates the adversarial stance? Bargain justice occurs when it is believed to be in the best interests of both the prosecutor and the defense to avoid the courtroom confrontation. Abraham Blumberg argues that the defense attorney acts as a double agent, to get the defendant to plead guilty.

A recurring theme in the growing dialogue between sociology and law has been the great need for a joint effort of the two disciplines to illuminate urgent social and legal issues. Having uttered fervent public pronouncements in this vein, however, the respective practitioners often go their separate ways. Academic spokesmen for the legal profession are somewhat critical of sociologists of law because of what they perceive as the sociologist's preoccupation with the application of theory and methodology to the examination of legal phenomena, without regard to the solution of legal problems. Further, it is felt that "contemporary writing in the sociology of law . . . betrays the existence of painfully unsophisticated notions about the day-to-day operations of courts, legislatures, and law offices." Regardless of the merit of such criticism, scant attention—apart from explorations of the legal profession

Source: From *Law and Society Review 1* (June 1967): 15–39.

itself—has been given to the sociological examination of legal institutions, or their supporting ideological assumptions. Thus, for example, very little socio- logical effort is expended to ascertain the validity and viability of important court decisions, which may rest on wholly erroneous assumptions about the contextual realities of social structure. A particular decision may rest upon a legally impeccable rationale; at the same time it may be rendered nugatory or self-defeating by contingencies imposed by aspects of social reality of which the lawmakers are themselves unaware.

Within this context, I wish to question the impact of three recent land- mark decisions of the United States Supreme Court, each hailed as destined to effect profound changes in the future of criminal law administration and enforcement in America. The first of these, *Gideon v. Wainwright*, 372 U.S. 335 (1963), required states and localities henceforth to furnish counsel in the case of indigent persons charged with a felony. The Gideon ruling left several major issues unsettled, among them the vital question: What is the precise point in time at which a suspect is entitled to counsel? The answer came rela- tively quickly in *Escobedo v. Illinois*, 378 U.S. 478 (1964), which has aroused a storm of controversy. Danny Escobedo confessed to the murder of his brother- in-law after the police had refused to permit retained counsel to see him, although his lawyer was present in the station house and asked to confer with his client. In a 5 to 4 decision, the court asserted that counsel must be permit- ted when the process of police investigative efforts shifts from merely investiga- tory to that of accusatory: "when its focus is on the accused and its purpose is to elicit a confession—our adversary system begins to operate, and, under the circumstances here, the accused must be permitted to consult with his lawyer."

As a consequence, Escobedo's confession was rendered inadmissible. The decision triggered a national debate among police, district attorneys, judges, lawyers, and other law-enforcement officials, which continues unabated, as to the value and propriety of confessions in criminal cases. On June 13, 1966, the Supreme Court in a 5 to 4 decision underscored the principle enunciated in *Escobedo* in the case of *Miranda v. Arizona*. Police interrogation of any suspect in custody, without his consent, unless a defense attorney is present, is prohibited by the self-incrimination provision of the Fifth Amendment. Regardless of the rel- ative merit of the various shades of opinion about the role of counsel in criminal cases, the issues generated thereby will be in part resolved as additional cases move toward decision in the Supreme Court in the near future. They are of peripheral interest and not of immediate concern in this paper. However, the *Gideon, Escobedo*, and *Miranda* cases pose interesting general questions. In all three decisions, the Supreme Court reiterates the traditional legal conception of a defense lawyer based on the ideological perception of a criminal case as an *adver- sary, combative* proceeding, in which counsel for the defense assiduously musters all the admittedly limited resources at his command to *defend* the accused. The fundamental question remains to be answered: Does the Supreme Court's con- ception of the role of counsel in a criminal case square with social reality?

The task of this paper is to furnish some preliminary evidence toward the illumination of that question. Little empirical understanding of the function of defense counsel exists; only some ideologically oriented generalizations and commitments. This paper is based upon observations made by the writer during many years of legal practice in the criminal courts of a large metropolitan area. No claim is made as to its methodological rigor, although it does reflect a conscious and sustained effort for participant observation.

· · ·

COURT STRUCTURE DEFINES
ROLE OF DEFENSE LAWYER

The overwhelming majority of convictions in criminal cases (usually over 90 percent) are not the product of a combative, trial-by-jury process at all, but instead merely involve the sentencing of the individual after a negotiated, bargained-for plea of guilty has been entered. Although more recently the overzealous role of police and prosecutors in producing pretrial confessions and admissions has achieved a good deal of notoriety, scant attention has been paid to the organizational structure and personnel of the criminal court itself. Indeed, the extremely high conviction rate produced without the features of an adversary trial in our courts would tend to suggest that the "trial" becomes a perfunctory reiteration and validation of the pretrial interrogation and investigation.

The institutional setting of the court defines a role for the defense counsel in a criminal case radically different from the one traditionally depicted. Sociologists and others have focused their attention on the deprivations and social disabilities of such variables as race, ethnicity, and social class as being the source of an accused person's defeat in a criminal court. Largely overlooked is the variable of the court organization itself, which possesses a thrust, purpose, and direction of its own. It is grounded in pragmatic values, bureaucratic priorities, and administrative instruments. These exalt maximum production and the particularistic career designs of organizational incumbents, whose occupational and career commitments tend to generate a set of priorities. These priorities exert a higher claim than the stated ideological goals of "due process of law," and are often inconsistent with them.

Organizational goals and discipline impose a set of demands and conditions of practice on the respective professions in the criminal court to which they respond by abandoning their ideological and professional commitments to the accused client, in the service of these higher claims of the court organization. All court personnel, including the accused's own lawyer, tend to be co-opted to become agent-mediators who help the accused redefine his situation and restructure his perceptions concomitant with a plea of guilty.

Of all the occupational roles in the court, the only private individual who is officially recognized as having a special status and concomitant obligations is the lawyer. His legal status is that of "an officer of the court" and he is held to a standard of ethical performance and duty to his client as well as to the court. This obligation is thought to be far higher than expected of ordinary individuals occupying the various occupational statuses in the court community. However, lawyers, whether privately retained or of the legal-aid, public defender variety, have close and continuing relations with the prosecuting office and the court itself through discreet relations with the judges via their law secretaries or "confidential" assistants. Indeed, lines of communication, influence, and contact with those offices, as well as with the Office of the Clerk of the Court, the Probation Division, and the press, are essential to present and prospective requirements of criminal law practice. Similarly, the subtle involvement of the press and other mass media in the court's organizational network is not readily discernible to the casual observer. Accused persons come and go in the court system schema, but the structure and its occupational incumbents remain to carry on their respective career, occupational, and organizational enterprises. The individual stridencies, tensions, and conflicts a given accused person's case may present to all the participants are overcome, because the formal and informal relations of all the groups in the court setting require it. The probability of continued future relations and interaction must be preserved at all costs.

This is particularly true of the "lawyer regulars"—that is, those defense lawyers, who by virtue of their continuous appearances in behalf of defendants, tend to represent the bulk of a criminal court's nonindigent case work load, and those lawyers who are not "regulars," who appear almost casually in behalf of an occasional client. Some of the lawyer "regulars" are highly visible as one moves about the major urban centers of the nation; their offices line the back streets of the courthouses, at times sharing space with bondsmen. Their political "visibility" in terms of local clubhouse ties, reaching into the judge's chambers and the prosecutor's office, is also deemed essential to successful practitioners. Previous research has indicated that the "lawyer regulars" make no effort to conceal their dependence upon police, bondsmen, and jail personnel. Nor do they conceal the necessity for maintaining intimate relations with all levels of personnel in the court setting as a means of obtaining, maintaining, and building their practice. These informal relations are the *sine qua non* not only of retaining a practice but also in the negotiation of pleas and sentences.

The client, then, is a secondary figure in the court system as in certain other bureaucratic settings. He becomes a means to other ends of the organization's incumbents. He may present doubts, contingencies, and pressures which challenge existing informal arrangements or disrupt them; but these tend to be resolved in favor of the continuance of the organization and its relations as before. There is a greater community of interest among all the principal organizational structures and their incumbents than exists elsewhere in other settings. The accused's lawyer has far greater professional, economic, intellectual, and other ties to the various elements of the court system than he does to his own client. In short, the court is a closed community.

This is more than just the case of the usual "secrets" of bureaucracy which are fanatically defended from an outside view. Even all elements of the press are zealously determined to report on that which will not offend the board of judges, the prosecutor, and probation, legal-aid, or other officials, in return for privileges and courtesies granted in the past and to be granted in the future. Rather than any view of the matter in terms of some variation of a "conspiracy" hypothesis, the simple explanation is one of an ongoing system handling delicate tensions, managing the trauma produced by law enforcement and administration, and requiring almost pathological distrust of "outsiders" bordering on group paranoia.

The hostile attitude toward "outsiders" is in large measure engendered by a defensiveness itself produced by the inherent deficiencies of assembly-line justice, so characteristic of our major criminal courts. Intolerably large caseloads of defendants, which must be disposed of in an organizational context of limited resources and personnel, potentially subject the participants in the court community to harsh scrutiny from appellate courts and other public and private sources of condemnation. As a consequence, an almost irreconcilable conflict is posed in terms of intense pressures to process large numbers of cases, on the one hand, and the stringent ideological and legal requirements of "due process of law," on the other hand. A rather tenuous resolution of the dilemma has emerged in the shape of a large variety of bureaucratically ordained and controlled "work crimes," shortcuts, deviations, and outright rule violations adopted as court practice in order to meet production norms. Fearfully anticipating criticism on ethical as well as legal grounds, all the significant participants in the court's social structure are bound into an organized system of complicity. This consists of a work arrangement in which the patterned, covert, informal breaches and evasions of "due process" are institutionalized but are, nevertheless, denied to exist.

These institutionalized evasions will be found to occur to some degree in all criminal courts. Their nature, scope, and complexity are largely determined by the size of the court and the character of the community in which it is located—for example, whether it is a large, urban institution or a relatively small rural county court. In addition, idiosyncratic, local conditions may contribute to a unique flavor in the character and quality of the criminal law's administration in a particular community. However, in most instances a variety of stratagems are employed—some subtle, some crude, ineffectively disposing of what are often too-large caseloads. A wide variety of coercive devices are employed against an accused client, couched in a depersonalized, instrumental, bureaucratic version of due process of law, and which are in reality a perfunctory obeisance to the ideology of due process. These include some very explicit pressures which are exerted in some measure by all court personnel, including judges, to plead guilty and avoid trial. In many instances the sanction of a potentially harsh sentence is utilized as the visible alternative to pleading guilty, in the case of recalcitrants. Probation and psychiatric reports are "tailored" to organizational needs, or are at least responsive to the court organization's requirements for the refurbishment of a defendant's social biography, consonant with his new status. A resourceful judge can, through his subtle domination of the proceedings, impose his will on the final outcome of a trial. Stenographers and clerks, in their function as record keepers, are on occasion pressed into service in support of a judicial need to "rewrite" the record of a courtroom event. Bail practices are usually employed for purposes other than simply assuring a defendant's presence on the date of a hearing in connection with his case. Too often, the discretionary power as to bail is part of the arsenal of weapons available to collapse the resistance of an accused person. The foregoing is a most cursory examination of some of the more prominent "shortcuts" available to any court organization. There are numerous other procedural strategies constituting due process deviations, which tend to become the work-style artifacts of a court's personnel. Thus, only court "regulars" who are "bound in" are really accepted; others are treated routinely and in almost a coldly correct manner.

The defense attorneys, therefore, whether of the legal-aid, public defender variety or privately retained, although operating in terms of pressures specific to their respective role and organizational obligations, ultimately are concerned with strategies which tend to lead to a plea. It is the rational, impersonal elements involving economies of time, labor, expense, and a superior commitment of the defense counsel to these rationalistic values of maximum production of court organization that prevail in his relationship with a client. The lawyer "regulars" are frequently former staff members of the prosecutor's office and utilize the prestige, know-how, and contacts of their former affiliation as part of their stock-in-trade. Close and continuing relations between the lawyer "regular" and his former colleagues in the prosecutor's office generally overshadow the relationship between the regular and his client. The continuing colleagueship of supposedly adversary counsel rests on real professional and organizational needs of a *quid pro quo*, which goes beyond the limits of an accommodation or *modus vivendi* one might ordinarily expect under the circumstances of an otherwise seemingly adversary relationship. Indeed, the adversary features which are manifest are for the most part muted and exist even in their attenuated form largely for external consumption. The principals, lawyer and assistant district attorney, rely upon one another's cooperation for their continued professional existence, and so the bargaining between them tends usually to be "reasonable" rather than fierce.

FEE COLLECTION AND FIXING

The real key to understanding the role of defense counsel in a criminal case is to be found in the area of the fixing of the fee to be charged and its collection. The problem of fixing and collecting the fee tends to influence to a significant degree the criminal court process itself, and not just the relationship of the lawyer and his client. In essence, a lawyer–client "confidence game" is played. A true confidence game is unlike the case of the emperor's new clothes wherein that monarch's nakedness was a result of inordinate gullibility and credulity. In a genuine confidence game, the perpetrator manipulates the basic dishonesty of his partner, the victim or mark, toward his own (the confidence operator's) ends. Thus, "the victim of a con scheme must have some larceny in his heart."

Legal service lends itself particularly well to confidence games. Usually, a plumber will be able to demonstrate empirically that he has performed a service by clearing up the stuffed drain, repairing the leaky faucet or pipe—and therefore merits his fee. He has rendered, when summoned, a visible, tangible boon for his client in return for the requested fee. A physician, who has not performed some visible surgery or otherwise engaged in some readily discernible procedure in connection with a patient, may be deemed by the patient to have "done nothing" for him. As a consequence, medical practitioners may simply prescribe or administer by injection a placebo to overcome a patient's potential reluctance or dissatisfaction in paying a requested fee, "for nothing."

In the practice of law there is a special problem in this regard, no matter what the level of the practitioner or his place in the hierarchy of prestige. Much legal work is intangible either because it is simply a few words of advice, some preventive action, a telephone call, negotiation of some kind, a form filled out and filed, a hurried conference with another attorney or an official of a government agency, a letter or opinion written, or a countless variety of seemingly innocuous and even prosaic procedures and actions. These are the basic activities, apart from any possible court appearance, of almost all lawyers, at all levels of practice. Much of the activity is not in the nature of the exercise of the traditional, precise professional skills of the attorney such as library research and oral argument in connection with appellate briefs, court motions, trial work, drafting of opinions, memoranda, contracts, and other complex documents and agreements. Instead, much legal activity, whether it is at the lowest or highest "white shoe" law firm levels, is of the brokerage, agent, sales representative, lobbyist type of activity, in which the lawyer acts for someone else in pursuing the latter's interests and designs. The service is intangible.

The large-scale law firm may not speak as openly of their "contacts," their "fixing" abilities, as does the lower-level lawyer. They trade instead upon a facade of thick carpeting, walnut paneling, genteel low pressure, and superficialities of traditional legal professionalism. There are occasions when even the large firm is on the defensive in connection with the fees they charge because the services rendered or results obtained do not appear to merit the fee asked. Therefore, there is a recurrent problem in the legal profession in fixing the amount of fee and in justifying the basis for the requested fee.

Although the fee at times amounts to what the traffic and the conscience of the lawyer will bear, one further observation must be made with regard to the size of the fee and its collection. The defendant in a criminal case and the material gain he may have acquired during the course of his illicit activities are soon parted. Not infrequently the ill-gotten fruits of the various modes of larceny are sequestered by a defense lawyer in payment of his fee. Inexorably, the amount of the fee is a function of the dollar value of the crime committed and is frequently set with meticulous precision at a sum which bears an uncanny relationship to that of the net proceeds of the particular offense involved. On occasion, defendants have been known to commit additional offenses while at liberty on bail, in order to secure the requisite funds with which to meet their obligations for payment of legal fees. Defense lawyers condition even the most obtuse clients to recognize that there is a firm interconnection between fee payment and the zealous exercise of professional expertise, secret knowledge, and organizational "connections" in their behalf. Lawyers, therefore, seek to keep their clients in a proper state of tension, and to arouse in time the precise edge of anxiety which is calculated to encourage prompt fee payment. Consequently, the client attitude in the relationship between defense counsel and an accused is in many instances a precarious admixture of hostility, mistrust, dependence, and sycophancy. By keeping his client's anxieties aroused to the proper pitch, and establishing a seemingly causal relationship between a requested fee and the accused's ultimate extrication from his onerous difficulties, the lawyer will have established the necessary preliminary groundwork to assure a minimum of haggling over the fee and its eventual payment.

In varying degrees, as a consequence, all law practice involves a manipulation of the client and a stage management of the lawyer–client relationship so that at least an *appearance* of help and service will be forthcoming. This is accomplished in a variety of ways, often exercised in combination with each other. At the outset, the lawyer-professional employs with suitable variation a measure of sales puff which may range from an air of unbounding self-confidence, adequacy, and dominion over events, to that of complete arrogance. This will be supplemented by the affectation of a studied, faultless mode of personal attire. In the larger firms, the furnishings and office trappings will serve as the backdrop to help in impression management and client intimidation. In all firms, solo or large-scale, an access to secret knowledge and to the seats of power and influences is inferred, or presumed to a varying degree as the basic vendable commodity of the practitioners.

The lack of visible end product offers a special complication in the course of the professional life of the criminal court lawyer with respect to his fee and in his relations with his client. The plain fact is that an accused in a criminal case always "loses" even when he has been exonerated by an acquittal, discharge, or dismissal of his case. The hostility of an accused which follows as a consequence of his arrest, incarceration, possible loss of job, expense, and other traumas connected with his case is directed, by means of displacement, toward his lawyer. It is in this sense that it may be said that a criminal lawyer never really "wins" a case. The really satisfied client is rare, since in the very nature of the situation even an accused's vindication leaves him with some degree of dissatisfaction and hostility. It is this state of affairs that makes for a lawyer–client relationship in the criminal court which tends to be a somewhat exaggerated version of the usual lawyer–client confidence game.

At the outset, because there are great risks of nonpayment of the fee, due to the impecuniousness of his clients, and the fact that a man who is sentenced to jail may be a singularly unappreciative client, the criminal lawyer collects his fee *in advance*. Often, because the lawyer and the accused both have questionable designs of their own upon each other, the confidence game can be played. The criminal lawyer must serve three major functions, or stated another way, he must solve three problems. First, he must arrange for his fee; second, he must prepare and then, if necessary, "cool out" his client in case of defeat (a highly likely contingency); third, he must satisfy the court organization that he has performed adequately in the process of negotiating the plea, so as to preclude the possibility of any sort of embarrassing incident which may serve to invite "outside" scrutiny.

In assuring the attainment of one of his primary objectives, his fee, the criminal lawyer will very often enter into negotiations with the accused's kin, including collateral relatives. In many instances, the accused himself is unable to pay any sort of fee or anything more than a token fee. It then becomes important to involve as many of the accused's kin as possible in the situation. This is especially so if the attorney hopes to collect a significant part of a proposed substantial fee. It is not uncommon for several relatives to contribute toward the fee. The larger the group, the greater the possibility that the lawyer will collect a sizeable fee by getting contributions from each.

A fee for a felony case which ultimately results in a plea, rather than a trial, may ordinarily range anywhere from $550 to $1,500. Should the case go to trial, the fee will be proportionately larger, depending upon the length of the trial. But the larger the fee the lawyer wishes to exact, the more impressive his performance must be, in terms of his stage-managed image as personage of great influence and power in the court organization. Court personnel are keenly aware of the extent to which a lawyer's stock-in-trade involves the precarious stage management of an image which goes beyond the usual professional flamboyance, and for this reason alone the lawyer is "bound in" to the authority system of the court's organizational discipline. Therefore, to some extent, court personnel will aid the lawyer in the creation and maintenance of that impression. There is a tacit commitment to the lawyer by the court organization, apart from formal etiquette, to aid him in this. Such augmentation of the lawyer's stage-managed image as this affords is the partial basis for the *quid pro quo* which exists between the lawyer and the court organization. It tends to serve as the continuing basis for the higher loyalty of the lawyer to the organization; his relationship with his client, in contrast, is transient, ephemeral, and often superficial.

DEFENSE LAWYER AS DOUBLE AGENT

The lawyer has often been accused of stirring up unnecessary litigation, especially in the field of negligence. He is said to acquire a vested interest in a cause of action or claim which was initially his client's. The strong incentive of possible fee motivates the lawyer to promote litigation which would otherwise never have developed. However, the criminal lawyer develops a vested interest of an entirely different nature in his client's case: to limit its scope and duration rather than do battle. Only in this way can a case be "profitable." Thus, he enlists the aid of relatives not only to assure payment of his fee, but he will also rely on these persons to help him in his agent-mediator role of convincing the accused to plead guilty, and ultimately to help in "cooling out" the accused if necessary.

It is at this point that an accused-defendant may experience his first sense of "betrayal." While he had perhaps perceived the police and prosecutor to be adversaries, or possibly even the judge, the accused is wholly unprepared for his counsel's role performance as an agent-mediator. In the same vein, it is even less likely to occur to an accused that members of his own family or other kin may become agents, albeit at the behest and urging of other agents or mediators, acting on the principle that they are in reality helping an accused negotiate the best possible plea arrangement under the circumstances. Usually, it will be the lawyer who will activate next of kin in this role, his ostensible motive being to arrange for his fee. But soon latent and unstated motives will assert themselves with entreaties by counsel to the accused's next of kin to appeal to the accused to "help himself" by pleading. *Gemeinschaft* sentiments are to this extent exploited by a defense lawyer (or even at times by a district attorney) to achieve specific secular ends, that is, of concluding a particular matter with all possible dispatch.

The fee is often collected in stages, each installment usually payable prior to a necessary court appearance required during the course of an accused's career journey. At each stage, in his interviews and communications with the accused, or in addition, with members of his family, if they are helping with the fee payment, the lawyer employs an air of professional confidence and "inside-dopesterism" in order to assuage anxieties on all sides. He makes the necessary bland assurances, and in effect manipulates his client, who is usually willing to do and say the things, true or not, which will help his attorney extricate him. Since the dimensions of what he is essentially selling, organizational influence and expertise, are not technically and precisely measurable, the lawyer can make extravagant claims of influence and secret knowledge with impunity. Thus, lawyers frequently claim to have inside knowledge in connection with information in the hands of the district attorney, police, or probation officials or to have access to these functionaries. Factually, they often do, and need only to exaggerate the nature of their relationships with them to obtain the desired effective impression upon the client. But, as in the genuine confidence game, the victim who has participated is loath to do anything which will upset the lesser plea which his lawyer has "conned" him into accepting.

In effect, in his role as double agent, the criminal lawyer performs an extremely vital and delicate mission for the court organization and the accused. Both principals are anxious to terminate the litigation with a minimum of expense and damage to each other. There is no other personage or role incumbent in the total court structure more strategically located, who by training and in terms of his own requirements, is more ideally suited to do so than the lawyer. In recognition of this, judges will cooperate with attorneys in many important ways. For example, they will adjourn the case of an accused in jail awaiting plea or sentence if the attorney requests such action. While explicitly this may be done for some innocuous and seemingly valid reason, the tacit purpose is that pressure is being applied by the attorney for the collection of his fee, which he knows will probably not be forthcoming if the case is concluded. Judges are aware of this tactic on the part of lawyers, who, by requesting an adjournment, keep an accused incarcerated a while longer as a not too subtle method of dunning a client for payment. However, the judges will go along with this, on the ground that important ends are being served. Often, the only end served is to protect a lawyer's fee.

The judge will help an accused's lawyer in still another way. He will lend the official aura of his office and courtroom so that a lawyer can stage-manage an impression of an "all-out" performance for the accused in justification of his fee. The judge and other court personnel will serve as a backdrop for a scene charged with dramatic fire, in which the accused's lawyer makes a stirring appeal in his behalf; with a show of restrained passion, the lawyer will intone the virtues of the accused and recite the social deprivations which have reduced him to his present stage. The speech varies somewhat, depending on whether the accused has been convicted after trial or has pleaded guilty. In the main, however, the incongruity, superficiality, and ritualistic character of the total performance is underscored by a visibly impassive, almost bored reaction on the part of the judge and other members of the court retinue.

Afterward, there is a hearty exchange of pleasantries between the lawyer and district attorney, wholly out of context in terms of the supposed adversary nature of the preceding events. The fiery passion in defense of his client is gone, and the lawyers for both sides resume their offstage relations, chatting amiably and perhaps including the judge in their restrained banter. No other aspect of their visible conduct so effectively serves to put even a casual observer on notice that these individuals have claims upon each other. These seemingly innocuous actions are indicative of continuing organizational and informal relations, which, in their intricacy and depth, range far beyond any priorities or claims a particular defendant may have.

Criminal law practice is a unique form of private law practice since it really only appears to be private practice. Actually it is bureaucratic practice, because of the legal practitioner's enmeshment in the authority, discipline, and perspectives of the court organization. Private practice, supposedly, in a professional sense, involves the maintenance of an organized, disciplined body of knowledge and learning; the individual practitioners are imbued with a spirit of autonomy and service, the earning of a livelihood being incidental. In the sense that the lawyer in the criminal court serves as a double agent, serving higher organizational rather than professional ends, he may be deemed to be engaged in bureaucratic rather than private practice. To some extent the lawyer-client "confidence game," in addition to its other functions, serves to conceal this fact.

THE CLIENT'S PERCEPTION

The "cop-out" ceremony, in which the court process culminates, is not only invaluable for redefining the accused's perspectives of himself, but also in reiterating publicly in a formally structured ritual the accused person's guilt for the benefit of significant "others" who are observing. The accused not only is made to assert publicly his guilt of a specific crime, but also a complete recital of its details. He is further made to indicate that he is entering his plea of guilt freely, willingly, and voluntarily, and that he is not doing so because of any promises or in consideration of any commitments that may have been made to him by anyone. This last is intended as a blanket statement to shield the participants from any possible charges of "coercion" or undue influence that may have been exerted in violation of due process requirements. Its function is to preclude any later review by an appellate court on these grounds, and also to obviate any second thoughts an accused may develop in connection with his plea.

However, for the accused, the conception of self as a guilty person is in large measure a temporary role adaptation. His career socialization as an accused, if it is successful, eventuates in his acceptance and redefinition of himself as a guilty person. However, the transformation is ephemeral, in that he will, in private, quickly reassert his innocence. Of importance is that he accept his defeat, publicly proclaim it, and find some measure of pacification in it. Almost immediately after his plea, a defendant will generally be interviewed by a representative of the probation division in connection with a presentence report which is to be prepared. The very first question to be asked of him by the probation officer is: "Are you guilty of the crime to which you pleaded?" This is by way of double affirmation of the defendant's guilt. Should the defendant now begin to make bold assertions of his innocence, despite his plea of guilty, he will be asked to withdraw his plea and stand trial on the original charges. Such a threatened possibility is, in most instances, sufficient to cause an accused to let the plea stand and to request the probation officer to overlook his exclamations of innocence. Table 1 is a breakdown of the categorized responses of a random sample of male defendants in Metropolitan Court during 1962, 1963, and 1964 in connection with their statements during presentence probation interviews following their plea of guilty.

It would be well to observe at the outset that of the 724 defendants who pleaded guilty before trial, only 43 (5.94 percent) of the total group had confessed prior to their indictment. Thus, the ultimate judicial process was predicated upon evidence independent of any confession of the accused.

As the data indicate, only a relatively small number (95) out of the total number of defendants actually will even admit their guilt following the cop-out ceremony. However, even though they have affirmed their guilt, many of these defendants felt that they should have been able to negotiate a more favorable plea. The largest aggregate of defendants (373) were those who reasserted their "innocence" following their public profession of guilt during the cop-out ceremony. These defendants employed differential degrees of fervor, solemnity, and credibility, ranging from really mild, wavering assertions of innocence which were embroidered with a variety of stock explanations and rationalizations, to those of an adamant, "framed" nature. Thus, the "innocent" group, for the most part, were largely concerned with underscoring for their probation interviewer their essential "goodness" and "worthiness," despite their formal plea of guilty. Assertion of innocence at the postplea stage resurrects a more respectable and acceptable self-concept for the accused defendant who has pleaded guilty. A recital of the structural exigencies which precipitated his plea

**Table 1 Defendant Responses as to Guilt or Innocence
After Pleading Guilty (Years: 1962, 1963, 1964; *N* = 724)**

Nature of Response		Number of Defendants
Innocent (manipulated)	"The lawyer, judge, police, or D.A. 'conned me' "	86
Innocent (pragmatic)	"Wanted to get it over with" "You can't beat the system" "They have you over a barrel when you have a record"	147
Innocent (advice of counsel)	"Followed my lawyer's advice"	92
Innocent (defiant)	"Framed"—Betrayed by "complainant," "police," "squealers," "lawyer," "friends," "wife," "girlfriend"	33
Innocent (adverse social data)	Blames probation officer or psychiatrist for "bad report," in cases where there was prepleading investigation	15
Guilty	"But I should have gotten a better deal" Blames lawyer, D.A., police, judge	74
Guilty	Won't say anything further	21
Fatalistic (doesn't press his "innocence," won't admit "guilt")	"I did it for convenience" "My lawyer told me it was only thing I could do" "I did it because it was the best way out"	248
No response		8
Total		724

of guilt serves to embellish a newly proferred claim of innocence, which many defendants mistakenly feel will stand them in good stead at the time of sentence, or ultimately with probation or parole authorities.

Relatively few (33) maintained their innocence in terms of having been "framed" by some person or agent-mediator, although a larger number (86) indicated that they had been manipulated or conned by an agent-mediator to plead guilty, but as indicated, their assertions of innocence were relatively mild.

A rather substantial group (147) preferred to stress the pragmatic aspects of their plea of guilty. They would only perfunctorily assert their innocence and would in general refer to some adverse aspect of their situation which they believed tended to negatively affect their bargaining leverage, including in some instances a prior criminal record.

One group of defendants (92), while maintaining their innocence, simply employed some variation of a theme of following "the advice of counsel" as a covering response to explain their guilty plea in the light of their new affirmation of innocence.

The largest single group of defendants (248) were basically fatalistic. They often verbalized weak suggestions of their innocence in rather halting terms, wholly without conviction. By the same token, they would not admit guilt readily and were generally evasive as to guilt or innocence, preferring to stress aspects of their stoic submission in their decision to plead. This sizeable group of defendants appeared to perceive the total court process as being caught up in a monstrous organizational apparatus, in which the defendant's role expectancies were not clearly defined. Reluctant to offend anyone in authority, fearful that clear-cut statements on their part as to their guilt or innocence would be negatively construed, they adopted a stance of passivity, resignation, and acceptance. Interestingly, they would in most instances invoke their lawyer as being the one who crystallized the available alternatives for them and who was therefore the critical element in their decision-making process.

In order to determine which agent-mediator was most influential in altering the accused's perspectives as to his decision to plead or go to trial (regardless of the proposed basis of the plea), the same sample of defendants were asked to indicate the person who first suggested to them that they plead guilty. They were also asked to indicate which of the persons or officials who made such a suggestion was most influential in affecting their final decision to plead.

Table 2 indicates the breakdown of the responses to the two questions.

It is popularly assumed that the police, through forced confessions, and the district attorney, employing still other pressures, are most instrumental in the inducement of an accused to plead guilty. As Table 2 indicates, it is actually the defendant's own counsel who is most effective in this role. Further, this phenomenon tends to reinforce the extremely rational nature of criminal law administration, for an organization could not rely upon the sort of idiosyncratic measures employed by the police to induce confessions and maintain its efficiency, high production, and overall rational-legal character. The defense counsel becomes the ideal agent-mediator since, as "officer of the court" and confidant of the accused and his kin, he lives astride both worlds and can serve the ends of the two as well as his own.

While an accused's wife, for example, may be influential in making him more amenable to a plea, her agent-mediator role has, nevertheless, usually been sparked and initiated by defense counsel. Further, although a number of first suggestions of a plea came from an accused's fellow jail inmates, he tended to rely largely on his counsel as an ultimate source of influence in his final decision. The defense counsel being a crucial figure in the total organizational scheme for constituting a new set of perspectives for the accused, the same sample of defendants was asked to indicate at which stage of their contact with counsel the suggestion of a plea was made. There are three basic kinds of defense counsel available in Metropolitan Court: legal-aid, privately retained counsel, and counsel assigned by the court (but may eventually be privately retained by the accused).

The overwhelming majority of accused persons, regardless of type of counsel, related a specific incident which indicated an urging or suggestion, either during the course of the first or second contact, that they plead guilty to a lesser charge if this could be arranged. Of all the agent-mediators, it is the lawyer who is most effective in manipulating an accused's perspectives, notwithstanding pressures that may have been previously applied by police, district attorney, judge, or any of the agent-mediators that may have been activated by them.

Table 2 Role of Agent-Mediators in Defendant's Guilty Plea

Person or Official	First Suggested Plea of Guilty	Influenced the Accused Most in His Final Decision to Plead
Judge	4	26
District attorney	67	116
Defense counsel	407	411
Probation officer	14	3
Psychiatrist	8	1
Wife	34	120
Friends and kin	21	14
Police	14	4
Fellow inmates	119	14
Others	28	5
No response	8	10
Total	724	724

Legal-aid and assigned counsel would apparently be more likely to suggest a possible plea at the point of initial interview as response to pressures of time. In the case of the assigned counsel, the strong possibility that there is no fee involved may be an added impetus to such a suggestion at the first contact.

In addition, there is some further evidence in Table 3 of the perfunctory, ministerial character of the system in Metropolitan Court and similar criminal courts. There is little real effort to individualize, and the lawyer's role as agent-mediator may be seen as unique in that he is in effect a double agent. Although, as "officer of the court" he mediates between the court organization and the defendant, his roles with respect to each are rent by conflicts of interest. Too often these must be resolved in favor of the organization which provides him with the means for his professional existence. Consequently, in order to reduce the strains and conflicts imposed in what is ultimately an overdemanding role obligation for him, the lawyer engages in the lawyer–client "confidence game" so as to structure more favorably an otherwise onerous role system.

CONCLUSION

Recent decisions of the Supreme Court, in the area of criminal law administration and defendants' rights, fail to take into account three crucial aspects of social structure which may tend to render the more libertarian rules as nugatory. The decisions overlook (1) the nature of courts as formal organization, (2) the relationship that the lawyer "regular" *actually* has with the court organization, and (3) the character of the lawyer–client relationship in the criminal court (the routine relationships, not those unusual ones that are described in "heroic" terms in novels, movies, and television).

**Table 3 Stage (Contact) at Which Each Type
of Counsel Suggests that Defendant Plead Guilty (N = 724)**

Contact	Privately Retained		Legal-Aid		Assigned		Total	
	N	%	N	%	N	%	N	%
First	66	35	237	49	28	60	331	46
Second	83	44	142	29	8	17	233	32
Third	29	15	63	13	4	9	96	13
Fourth or more	12	6	31	7	5	11	48	7
No response	0	0	14	3	2	4	16	2
Total	190	100	487	100[a]	47	101[a]	724	100

[a]Rounded percentage.

Courts, like many other modern large-scale organizations, possess a monstrous appetite for the co-optation of entire professional groups as well as individuals. Almost all those who come within the ambit of organization authority find that their definitions, perceptions, and values have been refurbished, largely in terms favorable to the particular organization and its goals. As a result, recent Supreme Court decisions may have a long-range effect which is radically different from that intended or anticipated. The more libertarian rules will tend to produce the rather ironic end result of augmenting the *existing* organizational arrangements, enriching court organizations with more personnel and elaborate structure, which in turn will maximize organizational goals of "efficiency" and production. Thus, many defendants will find that courts will possess an even more sophisticated apparatus for processing them toward a guilty plea!

13

Indigent Defenders
Get the Job Done
and Done Well

Roger A. Hanson
Brian J. Ostrom

Data from a nine-state trial court study show that the methods of providing counsel to indigents do not conform to the usual division of public defender, assigned counsel, and contract systems. The article also challenges the common assumption that attorneys for indigents are less successful in representing their clients than privately retained defense attorneys.

INTRODUCTION

It has been nearly thirty years [article originally published in 1989] since the U.S. Supreme Court in the case of *Gideon v. Wainwright* required that the states provide counsel for indigent defendants in criminal cases. Since that time the debate over whether indigent defenders are effective advocates or merely functionaries has continued unabated. Do attorneys paid by the state have the same skill, autonomy, and freedom to represent their clients as privately retained attorneys? Serious doubts were expressed shortly after *Gideon*

Source: "Indigent Defenders Get the Job Done and Done Well" by Roger A. Hanson and Brian J. Ostrom. This article was developed under a grant from the State Justice Institute (SJI-89-05X-B-045) to the National Center for State Courts. Points of view are those of the authors and do not necessarily represent the official position of the State Justice Institute.

and continue to be echoed today. Moreover, current skeptics do not limit their judgments to backwater areas, as evidenced by the following view of McConville and Mirsky concerning New York City's appointed counsel arrangement:

> Against this background, the creation of an indigent defense system whose object is the mass disposal of criminal cases through guilty pleas, lesser pleas, and other non-trial dispositions should not be viewed as a heroic response to the needs of poor people by public-spirited individuals. Nor should it be viewed as a rational response to modern case pressure, as a product of the individual, or collective behavior of courtroom actors, or as the logical result of procedural and evidential complexity attendant upon a trial. Instead, the routine processing of defendants is exactly what the indigent defense system was designed to accomplish.[1]

The assertions that indigent defenders are inferior in training, limited advocates for their clients, and without sufficient resources accentuate the importance of understanding this area of legal policy. Are the critics correct or incorrect in their generalizations? Unfortunately, the answer is not obvious. There are several reasons for taking another look at this topic due to the inherent limitations in past research.

Prior studies have three deficiencies. First, many of the studies fail to go beyond the boundaries of a single court and thereby lack comparative perspective.[2] Second, cross-court studies tend not to incorporate large-, medium-, and small-sized communities.[3] This omission fails to control for the effects of population size, which generally are regarded as influential in shaping the delivery of public policy services. Third, none of the prior studies compare all of the basic types of defenders (for example, public defender, assigned counsel, and contract attorneys) to privately retained counsel.[4] As a result, available evaluations of indigent defense performance are incomplete.

The objective of this article is to describe the knowledge gained from an examination of felony case processing in nine state general jurisdiction trial courts and the role that indigent defenders play in their respective systems. The research was aimed at addressing a series of interrelated issues that are central to understanding the positive and negative effects that indigent defenders have both on court operations and on defendants. Do indigent defenders frustrate or promote the court's desire to dispose of cases expeditiously? How well do indigent defenders serve their clients? Do indigent defenders rush their clients to guilty pleas? When they go to trial, how frequently do they win?

The answers to these questions are drawn from the examination of felony case processing in the following nine diverse courts: (1) Wayne County (Detroit, Michigan) Circuit Court; (2) King County (Seattle, Washington) Superior Court; (3) Denver County (Colorado) District Court; (4) Norfolk (Virginia) Circuit Court; (5) Monterey County (Salinas, California) Superior Court; (6) Oxford County (South Paris, Maine) Superior Court; (7) Gila County (Globe, Arizona) Superior Court; (8) Island County (Coupeville, Washington) Superior Court; and (9) San Juan County (Friday Harbor,

Washington) Superior Court.[5] These courts were selected in order to gain a mixture of the basic categories of indigent defenders (public defender, assigned counsel, contract attorney) in large- and small-sized communities located in different parts of the country. They are not necessarily representative of all courts, but they do represent a broad spectrum along which many courts in the country are found.

Information was obtained from an examination of random samples of felony cases disposed of in 1987. As a result, this article provides a description of the courts in 1987 except where explicit references are made to other years. The analysis of case-level data was augmented with interviews with over 125 defense attorneys, prosecutors, judges, and court staff.

WHAT DO THE INDIGENT DEFENSE SYSTEMS LOOK LIKE?

Legal representation of indigent defendants is viewed commonly as fitting into one of three basic categories: (1) public defender, (2) assigned counsel, and (3) contract attorneys. Each category is assumed to have a particular organizational structure and a particular method of financing, and each is oriented toward achieving one or more of several different goals, such as efficiency, accountability, or effectiveness. Moreover, systems in each category are presumed to be alike (for example, all public defender offices are similar).

One or more of these three basic categories is represented in each of the nine courts. If the courts are classified according to the major provider of services, as shown in Table 1, then Seattle, Denver, and Monterey are public defender systems; Detroit, Norfolk, Oxford, and Island are assigned counsel systems; and Globe and San Juan are contract systems.

This configuration corresponds to the expected pattern of public defender offices existing primarily in large-sized communities and rarely, if at all, in small communities. The occurrence of assigned counsel systems in four of the nine courts is consistent with the national pattern of assigned counsel systems being the most frequent type of system. And the two contract systems in Globe and in San Juan fit the national estimate that this type of system exists in a minority of, usually small-sized, courts.[6]

Table 2 indicates the percent of felony dispositions in 1987 drawn from random samples of case files involving indigent defendants (represented by public defenders, assigned counsel, contract attorneys) and nonindigent defendants (represented by privately retained counsel) in each of the nine courts. Privately retained counsel represent 20 percent or more in five of the courts (Denver, Norfolk, Oxford, Island, and San Juan), and nearly that many in Globe (18 percent) and in Detroit (17.1 percent). Despite assertions to the contrary by some observers,[7] the evidence from the nine courts indicates that the private bar is not an endangered species, unless privately retained counsel are expected to handle a majority of the cases in order to be deemed viable.[8]

Table 1 Defense Representation—Structure and Institutional Issues

	Detroit	Seattle	Denver	Norfolk	Monterey	Globe	Oxford	San Juan and Island
Percent of all felony dispositions handled by indigent defenders	83%	88%	80%	71%	90%	82%	53%	SJ: 61% I: 66%
Type(s) of indigent defense structures	Assigned counsel, public defender	Three public defender firms on contract, assigned counsel	Public defender, assigned counsel, contract attorneys	Assigned counsel	Public defenders, contract attorneys, assigned counsel	Contract attorneys, assigned counsel	Assigned counsel	Contract attorneys, assigned counsel
Level of funding	County	County	State	State	County	County	State	County
Eligibility of attorneys for appointment	Certification by court; judge appoints to case at first appearance	Private assignment rare and handled informally	Pre-1990, no formal requirements and handled informally by judge at first appearance	Attorney requests to be added to list; no formal requirements	No formal requirements on rare occasions when individual attorney assigned	Not applicable	Informal by judge or clerk	SJ: N/A I: Must be approved by defender association
Average attorney tenure	3–6 years (LADA)	3–5 years	6–7 years	Not available	5–8 years	15–18 years	10–12 years	SJ: 3 years (1989) I: 3–8 years

Table 2 Percent of Felony Dispositions Handled
by the Different Types of Defense Attorneys in the Courts

Types of Defense Attorneys	Detroit	Seattle	Denver	Norfolk	Monterey	Globe	Oxford	Island	San Juan
Public defender	18.4% (84)	86.8% (526)	74.6% (276)	0.0 (0)	72.8% (297)	0.0 (0)	0.0 (0)	0.0 (0)	0.0 (0)
Assigned counsel	64.6% (295)	1.2% (7)	5.4% (20)	71.1% (329)	3.7% (15)	0.0 (0)	52.9% (118)	65.6% (82)	0.0 (0)
Contract attorneys	0.0 (0)	0.0 (0)	0.0 (0)	0.0 (0)	13.5% (55)	82.4% (140)	0.0 (0)	0.0 (0)	61.3% (19)
Private counsel	17.1% (78)	12.0% (73)	20.0% (74)	28.9% (134)	10.0% (41)	17.6% (30)	47.1% (105)	34.4% (43)	38.7% (12)
Totals	100.1% (457)	100% (606)	100% (370)	100% (463)	100% (408)	100% (170)	100% (223)	100% (125)	100% (31)

These data also provide a background against which to reconsider the conventional wisdom that indigent defenders fall into three mutually exclusive categories (public defender, assigned counsel, and contract attorney). The experiences of the nine courts suggest that there is considerable flexibility in constructing indigent defense systems. For example, it is neither necessary nor true that the public defender's office must be the major provider of legal services, if it is to be used. Detroit's Legal Aid and Defender Association, which handles 25 percent of the appointments, is a counterexample to that proposition. Additionally, the types of indigent defense structures may be complementary rather than competitive, as commonly supposed. Monterey's use of all three types of indigent defenders illustrates this situation. Finally, the data from the nine courts do not support the inexorable law that says that a particular type of structure must exist in a particular size of community (for example, public defenders in a large-sized community). Again, Detroit, where the dominant category is assigned counsel, is a strong counterexample to that notion. The only linkage between the categories of indigent defenders and size is the absence of public defenders in the four small-sized communities. But even this remnant of the conventional wisdom unravels on closer examination. As noted below, Island County's system of assigned counsel exhibits several characteristics of a public defender office. A closer examination of the nine systems reveals interesting similarities and differences in the defense structures in greater detail.

Detroit's Indigent Defense System[9]

Detroit uses primarily assigned counsel for indigent defense. The assignments, however, are distributed between two major groups. Approximately 75 percent of the caseload is assigned by judges to individual private attorneys, with the remaining 25 percent going to the Legal Aid and Defender Association (LADA). LADA is essentially a public defender's office but without the usual publicly provided budget and management. It is a private, nonprofit defender organization that was established in 1968. The caseload division is the result of a 1972 Michigan Supreme Court ruling that mandated 25 percent of all criminal cases go to LADA. The director of LADA monitors this allocation very closely and ensures that it is met.

All indigent defenders, both assigned counsel and LADA attorneys, operate under the voucher system. The Wayne County payment system for assigned counsel underwent substantial change in 1988. Prior to July 1, 1988, attorneys were paid on an event-based schedule. They were paid separately for every court event (for example, each hearing, motion, trial day, and so forth) based upon the seriousness of the offense. Now attorneys are paid a fixed fee based on the statutory maximum penalty for the offense (ranging from a low of $475 for a twenty-four month maximum case to $1,400 for first-degree murder).

There are currently about 653 individual private attorneys on the assigned counsel list, with about ten new attorneys being added each month and an indeterminate number (less than ten) dropping off the roll or moving to a more occasional status. This total is composed of approximately 200 hard-core "regulars," who depend on the assigned counsel system for a substantial share of their clients and income, and about 450 "irregulars," who use the assigned counsel system to supplement their private (criminal and/or civil) practice.

There are nineteen defense attorneys (in addition to the director and deputy director) who work for the Legal Aid and Defender Association. Although LADA is often referred to as a public defender organization, its structure is closer to an assigned counsel/public defender hybrid. As with a public defender, the operation of LADA is overseen by an independent board, with no formal government connection, that chooses the office head and sets general policy. However, LADA attorneys generate fees in the same way as private assigned counsel (vouchers are submitted to the administrative office of the court and payments are calculated on the same scale), and this accounts for the vast majority of office funding. Finally, LADA attorneys have no overhead to pay and have access to good secretarial support and experienced in-house investigators. The average tenure of attorneys at LADA is three to six years.

Seattle's Indigent Defense System[10]

The provision of indigent defense services is overseen by the King County Office of Public Defense (OPD). The OPD contracts with three nonprofit public defender firms to provide the majority of defense representation for persons charged with felony offenses.[11] Each of the defender firms has its own board of directors and internal management structure. The oldest and largest of the three firms is The Defender Association (TDA). In 1990-1991, TDA was scheduled to handle approximately 41 percent of the felonies, 25 percent of the misdemeanors, 33 percent of the juvenile offender cases, 40 percent of the juvenile dependency cases, 100 percent of the involuntary commitments, and 43 percent of the cases in the Seattle municipal court.[12] The second largest firm is the Associated Counsel for the Accused (ACA), which was assigned 37 percent of the felonies, 50 percent of the misdemeanors, 22 percent of the juvenile offender cases, and 34 percent of the cases in the Seattle municipal court.[13] The third firm, the Society of Counsel Representing Accused Persons (SCRAP), was allocated 22 percent of the felonies, 25 percent of the misdemeanors, 33 percent of the juvenile offender cases, and 60 percent of the juvenile dependency cases.[14]

OPD is a division within the County Department of Human Services that provides management oversight of the indigent defense budget and services, and it assigns all indigent clients to the contracting public defender firms. OPD staff complete a two-page form during a defendant interview. It covers various aspects of the charged offense, whether an interpreter is needed, and the defendant's financial situation. Individuals are determined to be indigent if their total resources are less than 125 percent of the poverty line or if they are on public assistance.

OPD assigns each case to a particular defender firm the same day as indigency is determined. Notice of the case (defendant name, charge, and bail status) is delivered to the defender firm the following day. All payments to each defender firm are specified in the contract, except payments for aggravated homicide and complex fraud cases and conflicts appointments. The payment in these cases is based upon negotiation between OPD and the defender firm. The defense firms are paid monthly through OPD.[15]

Denver's Indigent Defense System[16]

A statewide public defender system has been in place in Colorado since the early 1970s. Organizationally, it is part of the judicial branch. It is responsible for all indigent representation except in conflict cases (in every court, an attorney may decline to accept appointment because it would conflict with the representation of defendants that were already being represented). There are eighteen regional trial offices with attorneys, two regional offices staffed only with support staff (paralegals and investigators), and an appellate division. The system is administered by a state public defender, a chief trial deputy, a chief deputy, and an administrative unit of five (three professionals). The public defender is appointed by an independent public defender commission established by the supreme court.

The Colorado public defender in Denver handles representation for the city and county of Denver. In 1987, the office had twenty-seven staff attorneys and eight contract attorneys. There were twenty-six staff attorneys in 1990. The appointment of counsel in felony cases generally takes place in the Denver County Court. Colorado uses federal guidelines for determining indigency, but the information that defendants give is not verified. Eligibility determination is done by the public defender.

The Denver office is unique in several ways. First, many public defenders begin their employment doing misdemeanor and juvenile casework there and then move to other locations in the state. Denver proper (as opposed to the surrounding counties) is decreasing in caseload, so the office is not expanding. Because it is easy to find private attorneys to do contract work, contract attorneys are used in Denver for county court work on misdemeanors at the rate of $2,025 per month. A similar use of contract attorneys elsewhere in the state is not typical.

The average tenure of public defenders in Denver was six to seven years, with the statewide average estimated at five years. Salaries of public defenders statewide are higher than those of prosecuting attorneys, but in Denver, the salaries start off even, with the public defenders losing ground as they go up. Attorneys who leave tend to go into solo practice, although some have gone to private firms, judgeships, and so forth.

Counsel are appointed by the court when the public defender must decline the representation of an indigent defendant. The assigned counsel attorneys indicate their areas of interest and expertise (for example, misdemeanors, lesser felonies, more serious felonies), and appointments are taken from the appropri-ate lists. The amount of reimbursement is determined by the judge, but since 1985, the state public defender administers the funds appropriated. Control over the conflict budget by the state public defender has created an incentive to minimize conflicts and to scrutinize requests by assigned counsel for payments. The state public defender is said to earn credit with the state legislature by returning unspent funds at the end of the year.

Norfolk's Indigent Defense System[17]

Representation of indigent defendants in the upper (circuit) court is provided by private attorneys who are appointed to individual cases. Appointments gen-erally are made in lower (district) court; however, the circuit court appoints counsel for indigent defendants when the cases do not originate in the lower court.

Appointment of counsel is made from a list of attorneys that is maintained by the circuit court but is also used by the general district court. The list con-tains seventy-eight names. There is apparently no formal process for getting on the list: an individual writes to the court and sets forth whatever information is deemed relevant (for example, experience and references).

Compensation is by voucher. At the conclusion of the representation the attorney completes a form indicating the total of in-court (compensated at the rate of $60 per hour) and out-of-court ($40 per hour) time.

There were recent changes in how individuals received appointments. At one time, appointments were made from the list at the first appearance in the district court, with the attorney then being notified by mail that he or she had been appointed to a case. The approach had two shortcomings. First, the attor-ney was not present at the first appearance, thus missing an early opportunity to speak with the client. The attorney then had to arrange to see the client in jail or try to locate the individual in the community. Second, some attorneys con-tended that appointments were not being equitably made from the list.

To address both issues, the district court now assigns attorneys to specific court days. The designated attorney will be appointed to all new indigent cases that come before the court for first appearance on that day. With seventy-eight people on the list, an attorney will have a "duty day" about once every two and a half months. This system equalizes the number of appointments, or at least eliminates biased use of the list. A disadvantage, however, is that it treats the attorneys as fungible commodities and can result in inappropriate appoint-ments when it is applied inflexibly by the court.

Monterey's Indigent Defense System[18]

Monterey's indigent defense services are provided primarily by the county pub-lic defender's office. Conflict cases are farmed out to a "consortium," which con-sists of six attorneys who contract with the county. Each consortium attorney handles a narrow range of cases and negotiates his own contract to provide those services. When neither the public defender's office nor a consortium attorney can be appointed, the court has a list of local attorneys on whom it can call.

The public defender's office has a staff of thirty-three individuals structured as follows: chief public defender, two assistant public defenders, eighteen deputy public defenders, seven secretaries, and five investigators. The office handles most of the indigent felony defendants. Felony cases are assigned to individual attorneys by the criminal division supervisor, taking work load and experience into account. Most of the new attorneys have worked in another public defender's office, usually in a metropolitan area. There is a low turnover rate, and those who have left have gone on to be judges or defenders in other jurisdictions or have gone into private practice. Training is primarily informal, by interoffice discussion, California Public Defender Association Briefs, bar courses, and communication with the bench.

The county contracts with six attorneys to provide indigent representation in conflict cases. Each attorney submits a monthly claim with a list of her or his active caseload to receive a monthly check from the county. The attorney must cover all expenses out of the contract (with the exception of investigative costs). The consortium attorneys tend to be experienced practitioners. All of them have been in practice for at least fifteen years. They include attorneys with prior experience in the public defender's office, including one of the former heads of the office.

When consortium attorneys are not able to take appointments, private attorneys are assigned. In 1987, there was no clear indication of what attorneys were eligible for these appointments, the process of how attorneys could be placed on the list was unspecified, and attorneys were not graded in a systematic way to handle different types of cases. More recently, the court has taken steps to formalize the assignment system by clarifying the criteria for appointment and what attorneys satisfy the criteria.

Globe's Indigent Defense System[19]

Gila County contracts with private lawyers for indigent services. From 1986 through 1989 three lawyers held contracts. A fourth attorney was added in 1990 to handle lesser felonies and juvenile dependency cases exclusively. Attorneys contract with the County Board of Supervisors, who fund indigent defense services. The system is not merely "low-bid," however, and the court plays a meaningful role in the process of awarding the contracts. Although the County Board of Supervisors issues a request for proposals, bids are returned to the judges of the court. Thereafter, applicants negotiate with the court before contracts are finalized. The system for assigning cases to each of the contract attorneys blends work load and geographic considerations. In theory, each contract attorney receives an equal number of new cases each year. One of the indigent defense attorneys practices almost exclusively in a remote community within the county (Payson-Pine), and the other attorneys occasionally practice there.

All of the attorneys have a private practice in addition to the Gila County contract. One attorney estimates that 60 percent of his work was indigent defense and 40 percent private practice. Another attorney supplements his Gila County practice with additional contract indigent defense work in an adjacent county, which compensates him on an hourly rather than flat-fee basis. All of the attorneys maintain an office in Gila County, except for the recently hired contract attorney, who handles the misdemeanors and less serious felony work.

The three attorneys who handle felony cases are veteran lawyers with more than fifteen years of experience in criminal practice, which includes forty to sixty felony cases each year. In Globe, the superiority of experience by indigent defense counsel over the deputy prosecuting attorneys is apparent and generally acknowledged. They go to trial infrequently, but they usually win when they do go.

Oxford's Indigent Defense System[20]

The state funds indigent defense in Maine, and Oxford County uses an assigned counsel system. Attorneys are appointed to a case by a judge from a list of available attorneys, with the assistance of the superior court clerk (in the instance of a direct indictment) and the chief deputy district court clerk (in the instance of a felony bind over). Attorneys who wish to be considered for assigned criminal cases inform the clerks of the respective courts who maintain the appointment lists. About twelve Oxford County lawyers accepted indigent criminal cases during the study period, with six of them receiving the majority of the appointments.

Although the state office manages the fiscal elements of the program, the local clerk of court processes the vouchers to get them approved by the judge and forwards them to the administrator in Portland. The state office reviews them and forwards them to Augusta for payment. Checks are written from the state capital in Augusta and mailed to the attorneys. Attorneys receive their checks four to ten weeks after submitting a voucher. The judges must approve vouchers submitted by counsel, and they may adjust the approved amount. The fee structure is set by the supreme court. No ceilings have been legislated for permissible attorney's fees, although the judge must approve the voucher. The judges have discretion to pay less than the full hourly rate.

Island's Indigent Defense System[21]

Island delivers indigent defense services through an assigned counsel system. In the 1970s an association of lawyers—Island County Defender's Association—was formed to certify lawyers for the service, to manage referrals and appointments, and to negotiate with the board of commissioners over fee schedules. The association maintained a governing board and employed a secretary to provide administrative services. The same secretary was hired later by the county commissioners as the full-time administrator of the indigent defense system. Through the association, the consortium of attorneys continued to speak to the county as a group, set standards for eligibility, and, in effect, controlled admission to the indigent defense practice. Thus, even though Island is classified as an assigned system, it has important elements characteristic of a public defender system.

The indigent defense administrator for the Island County Defender's Association runs a tight ship with lots of statistics, careful scrutiny of appointment documentation and the fees charged, review of defendant eligibility, and determination of partial ability to pay. She is responsible for quality control of services, fiscal control, and arrangement for promissory notes when clients have some ability to pay. There is an expectation that attorneys will meet with clients within forty-eight hours of admission to jail.

The assigned counsel system matches attorneys to case severity, with the more experienced attorneys getting the more serious cases. There are approximately twelve attorneys on the assigned counsel roster, all of whom have had several years of experience. Judges and other court personnel state that Island County's system appears to represent the values that should be present in a system of criminal defense—access to experienced attorneys who specialize in trial practice and criminal law and the opportunity for a "personal" relationship.

San Juan's Indigent Defense System

San Juan is an island community with no bridges to the mainland. Indigent defense service has been provided there since 1980 through a contract system. Before that time, defense was provided by an assigned counsel system, similar to Oxford County's. Most attorneys accepted appointments reluctantly, however. From 1979 to 1980, some local lawyers lobbied the county to revise the fee schedule upward; instead, a contract system was initiated by the county commissioners. Until recently, the contract was strictly on a low-bid criterion. The contract attorney assumed responsibility for all criminal, juvenile, and mental health cases, including all overhead. The court at the time was passive, under the theory that so long as there was a vehicle for appointment of counsel, the commissioners were free to fund the service in whatever manner they saw fit.

During the first year of the contract program, the contract attorney moved from the island to a mainland community, three hours distant by automobile and ferry. Thereafter, until 1990, a succession of three attorneys who did not live in the county held the contracts. One of these attorneys had previously been the deputy prosecutor responsible for criminal cases. Throughout this period there was general dissatisfaction with the contract service among the bar and criminal justice community, but no organized attempts to intervene with the commissioners were undertaken. Complaints generally had to do with the unavailability of the lawyer at critical times. Not only was the lawyer rarely available to clients immediately following arrest, but he also often would be late for, or entirely miss, scheduled court appearances. These proceedings would have to be rescheduled.

COMPARATIVE PERSPECTIVE

Indigent defense should be thought of in terms of a flexible system of interrelated elements rather than three mutually exclusive structures. There is no doubt that there are public defenders, assigned counsel, and contract attorneys and that the methods by which they receive appointments tend to be different. Looking at these systems in the nine courts, however, the following three lessons emerge.

First, there is no single organizational model of public defenders, assigned counsel, or contract attorneys. There are important variants within each of these three categories. Second, virtually all possible combinations of public defenders, assigned counsel, and contract attorneys are feasible. Courts have the opportunity to design the arrangements that meet their particular needs and circumstances. Third, indigent defense systems should not be assessed simply in terms of organizational structure and the assumed advantages of the preferred structure. Instead, the performance of a given structure should be measured in terms of how well the indigent defenders actually handle their cases. That topic is the subject of the next two sections.

TIMELINESS

The expeditious resolution of criminal cases is both a right guaranteed under the U.S. Constitution and a standard to which courts are held accountable. According to the Sixth Amendment, defendants are entitled to a speedy trial as well as the assistance of counsel. Consequently, indigent defenders have a fiduciary obligation to avoid unnecessary delays.

Timeliness is also a goal that the courts are expected to achieve. Both the American Bar Association (ABA) and the Conference of State Court Administrators (COSCA) have stipulated standards for courts. Specifically, the ABA states that all felony cases should take no longer than one year from the date of the arrest to be adjudicated. It is expected, moreover, that most cases should take considerably less than one year to reach final disposition. According to the ABA, 90 percent of all felony cases should be adjudicated within 120 days from the date of arrest and 98 percent should be adjudicated within 180 days from the date of arrest.

Length of Time from Arrest to Disposition

The indigent defenders consistently process the typical case in less time than privately retained attorneys, except in Island County. As shown in Table 3, the median number of days from the date of arrest to the date of adjudication for indigent defenders is less than it is for privately retained counsel in each of the eight other courts for all types of indigent defenders except for the small group of assigned counsel in Monterey. In Monterey, assigned counsel have a median

Table 3 Typical Length of Time That Indigent Defenders and Privately Retained Counsel Take to Resolve Cases (Median Number of Days from Date of Arrest to Adjudication,[a] Felony Dispositions)

	Detroit	Seattle[b]	Denver	Norfolk	Monterey	Globe	Oxford	Island	San Juan
Public defender	79	75	151	—	56	—	—	—	—
Contract attorney	—	—	—	—	78	125	—	—	79
Assigned counsel	62	—	162	114	115	—	134	156	—
Privately retained counsel	102	101	167	184	89	141	215	131	88
All cases	71	85	156	126	63	129	161	146	83

[a]Adjudication is the entry of a dismissal, guilty plea, deferred adjudication, or diversion, or verdict.

[b]In Seattle, the indigent defense attorneys represented are from three public defender firms (The Defender Association [TDA]; Associated Counsel for the Accused [ACA]; Society of Counsel Representing Accused Persons [SCRAP]). The typical case processing time for each firm [is] as follows: TDA, 89 days; ACA, 77 days; SCRAP, 59 days.

Table 4 Percent of Felony Cases Unresolved after 180 Days from the Date of Arrest for Indigent Defenders and Privately Retained Counsel (ABA Standards Stipulate That 2 Percent or Less of the Cases Should Be Unresolved)

	Detroit	Seattle[a]	Denver	Norfolk	Monterey	Globe	Oxford	Island	San Juan
Public defender	16.7%	19.0%	43.8%	—	8.3%	—	—	—	—
Contract attorney	—	—	—	—	3.9%	28.6%	—	—	0%
Assigned counsel	11.9%	—	45.5%	20.9%	20.0%	—	42.4%	44.6%	—
Privately retained attorneys	21.8%	26.4%	45.6%	51.1%	11.5%	27.2%	60.0%	47.2%	9.1%
All cases	14.4%	21.1%	44.2%	29.7%	8.0%	28.3%	49.1%	45.6%	3.4%

[a]In Seattle, the indigent defense attorneys represented are from three public defender agencies (The Defender Association [TDA]; Associated Counsel for the Accused [ACA]; Society of Counsel Representing Accused Persons [SCRAP]). The percentages of unresolved cases after 180 days for the three firms are as follows: TDA, 23.0%; ACA, 17.6%; SCRAP, 16.3%.

number of days (115) that is longer than the time associated with privately retained counsel (eighty-nine days). However, both the public defenders (fifty-six days) and the contract attorneys (seventy-eight days), which are the primary and secondary providers of indigent defense in Monterey, are more timely than privately retained counsel (eighty-nine days).

Meeting the ABA Standard

The same pattern of positive performance by indigent defenders emerges when the ABA's standard of resolving 98 percent of felony cases within 180 days of the arrest data is used. Only San Juan meets the standard; in the other eight courts more than 2 percent of the felony cases are still open at 180 days. However, as shown in Table 4, the percentages of cases remaining open after 180 days is consistently less for the indigent defenders in all the courts except Globe. In Globe, 28.6 percent of the cases represented by contract attorneys remain open after 180 days, and 27.2 percent of the cases represented by privately retained attorneys remain open after 180 days from the date of arrest. Additionally, in Monterey, relatively more of the cases with privately retained counsel meet the ABA standard than do the cases with assigned counsel. However, the two larger groups of indigent defenders in Monterey (public defender and contract attorneys) approximate the standard more closely than do the privately retained attorneys.

The quantitative results, which indicate that indigent defenders do well in terms of timeliness, have profound implications. One implication is that the expeditious adjudication of cases reduces the demand for additional court appearances and the length of time that defendants spend in jail awaiting disposition of their cases. The assembling of all the participants in the legal process for court proceedings and the pretrial detention of defendants are undeniably costly. Hence, indigent defenders contribute to cost savings by their timeliness.

Second, the closer approximation by indigent defenders to established time standards presents a picture that diverges from the popular image. A common view of indigent defenders is that they are engaging in dilatory tactics in one case in order to meet deadlines in other cases. Simply stated, they are viewed as unable to schedule their work, to satisfy time requirements, and to live within budgetary constraints. That point of view is not supported by the data from the nine courts under study. In terms of approximating time standards, indigent defenders perform better than privately retained attorneys. What other public institutions can make the claim that they perform as well as (or better than) the private sector?

Third, the achievement of timeliness frames the issue of effective representation in a new light. Instead of engaging in a philosophical debate over whether timeliness is inherently good or bad, one can ask the empirical question, Are the gains in efficiency made at the expense of the defendants? Are the rights or interests of defendants sacrificed in some way? The achievement of timeliness needs to be viewed side by side with information on the outcomes for defendants. The tasks of presenting and interpreting the necessary information are the subject of the next section.

PERFORMANCE AND INDIGENT DEFENSE

There are two basic approaches to assessing indigent defenders in the literature. The first approach has what may be called an input orientation. Indigent defenders are expected to represent their clients by being adequately prepared—meeting with clients, contacting witnesses, conducting research, reviewing presentence investigation reports, and so forth. Hence, a body of guidelines has been formulated that identifies how effective representation is to be conducted and the resources required to facilitate advocacy.[22]

The second approach has what may be called an output orientation.[23] Indigent defenders are expected to represent their clients by achieving favorable outcomes, such as acquittals and dismissals, charge reductions, noncustodial sentences, and the shortest possible periods of incarceration in prison. In this approach, the performance of indigent defenders is determined by comparing them with privately retained counsel. Do indigent defenders achieve the same percentage of favorable outcomes for their clients as privately retained counsel? This comparison sets a very high standard of evaluation for indigent defenders. There are several factors that have very little to do with the relative capabilities of attorneys that make it more difficult for indigent than nonindigent defendants to gain favorable outcomes. First, indigent defendants are more likely to be detained than defendants who can afford an attorney. Second, indigent defendants are more likely to have prior records that will be influential at sentencing. Third, indigent defendants are thought to be less assertive of their rights than defendants who can afford to pay for attorneys.[24]

Both of these approaches have their role to play in assessing indigent defense counsel. The first approach is appropriate for examining work that individual attorneys put into specific cases, but it provides no assessment of what the attorney accomplishes. Certainly, an attorney may meet with the client, interview witnesses, research the law, but do none of these activities effectively. Because the second approach draws conclusions concerning the performance of attorneys, it is the preferred orientation.

Conviction Rates

A fundamental concern to criminal defendants is gaining an acquittal or a dismissal. With a conviction comes the imposition of penalties. One basic goal of the defense attorney is to minimize the possibility of criminal penalties. In terms of measuring this goal, the standard is that the lower the conviction rate for a given set of attorneys, the more successful they are in gaining favorable outcomes for their clients.

The data indicate that indigent defenders perform as well as privately retained counsel in meeting this standard under a wide range of conditions. The conviction rates of defendants represented by public defenders, contract attorneys, assigned counsel, and privately retained counsel, when all nine courts are combined, are strikingly similar. Public defenders have a rate of 84.4 percent, contract attorneys have a rate of 83.6 percent, assigned counsel have a rate of 85.3 percent, and privately retained counsel have a rate of 83.4 percent.

There is no statistically significant difference (chi-square = 1.26, significance level = .77) among these rates.[25] Defendants are no worse off with one type of defense attorney than another, which means that defendants with privately retained counsel do no better, on average, than do indigent defendants with a publicly appointed attorney.

The similarity in the conviction rates among the different types of defense attorneys extends to cases that go to trial. Public defenders secured acquittal or dismissal in 23.2 percent of cases; contract attorneys, 28.6 percent; assigned counsel, 33.3 percent; and privately retained counsel, 25.6 percent. Thus indigent defenders are no less successful in gaining acquittals or dismissals for their clients than are privately retained counsel. There is no statistically significant relationship (chi-square = 2.74, significance level = .43) between the types of attorneys and the likelihood of conviction at trial.

These results raise an additional question. Are the conviction rates similar for different types of attorneys in both the large- and small-sized courts? This more refined question outstrips the available data to some extent. There are too few contract attorneys in either the large-sized or the small-sized courts to permit valid statistical testing. However, if all the indigent defenders are collapsed into one category, then this question can be addressed in terms of the conviction rates of publicly appointed attorneys versus privately retained counsel.

The data indicate that there is no linkage between the type of attorney and the likelihood of conviction either in the large-sized or in the small-sized courts. The conviction rates for publicly appointed and privately retained attorneys in the large courts (Detroit, Seattle, Denver, Norfolk, and Monterey) are 84.8 percent and 82 percent, respectively. In the small-sized courts (Oxford, Globe, Island, and San Juan), the parallel percentages are 84.1 and 86.3.[26] These are not statistically significant differences. Hence, within the limitations of the available data, the evidence indicates that indigent defenders do as well as privately retained counsel in terms of a fundamental criterion of performance. The likelihood of an indigent defendant being convicted is not influenced significantly by the fact that the defense attorney is publicly appointed.

Charge Reductions

From the perspective of the defendant and the defense attorney, any success is a victory. Given the fact that most defendants are convicted, one of the best outcomes that most defendants can realistically strive for is a reduction in the seriousness of charge. If the offense at conviction is a less serious offense than the offense with which the defendant was initially charged, this outcome is favorable to the defendant. The empirical question is, Do privately retained counsel have significantly different charge reduction rates from those of indigent defenders?

For the four types of defense attorneys, this question can be addressed only for the cases disposed of by guilty pleas, because the number of trials is limited for some categories of attorneys. The data reveal that there are significant differences in charge reduction rates among the categories of defense attorneys. The charge reduction rates for public defenders, contract attorneys, assigned counsel, and privately retained counsel are 25.7, 50.9, 26.4, and 31.9 percent, respectively. Contract attorneys do considerably better than the privately retained counsel, who do slightly better than the public defenders or the assigned counsel.[27] Hence, for cases involving guilty pleas, there are mixed results concerning the performance of indigent defenders. Some indigent defenders perform quite well whereas others perform less well than privately retained counsel.

If all indigent defenders are combined into one category, then the question of the linkage between type of attorney and charge reductions also can be examined for different-sized courts. From this perspective the size of the court produces opposite effects. In the large courts, privately retained attorneys gain more reductions (32 percent) than do publicly appointed counsel (26.3 percent). In the small-sized courts, privately retained counsel gain fewer reductions (28.7 percent) than do publicly appointed counsel (37.4 percent). Both sets of results are weak statistically, however.[28] In the large courts the correlation between the type of attorney and the likelihood of a charge reduction is very low (phi-square = .05). For the small-sized courts, the relationship is not statistically significant.[29] Hence, while the type of defense attorney may have some effect on charge reductions, the effect is negligible.

On the basis of these data, the performance of indigent defenders in gaining charge reductions is somewhat mixed. Contract attorneys do better than privately retained counsel, while public defenders and assigned counsel do less well. This connection, however, is weak statistically (Cramer's V = .15). Similarly, publicly appointed counsel gain more charge reductions in small-sized courts and fewer charge reductions in large-sized courts than do privately retained counsel. These connections, while demonstrating opposite effects, are weak. Thus, overall, indigent defenders perform about as well as privately retained counsel in obtaining charge reductions.

Incarceration Rates

The potential advantage that privately retained counsel have over indigent defenders should be the greatest in determining whether a convicted defendant is incarcerated in jail or prison, sentenced to probation, given community service, or fined. The prior record of the defendant is likely to play a major role in this decision. Unfortunately, the collection of data on the defendant's prior record was beyond the scope of this research. If it is true that indigent defendants are more likely to have prior records than nonindigent defendants, this missing information means that the examination of incarceration rates, without controlling for the effects of prior record, is tipped somewhat in favor of privately retained counsel. Yet, despite this potential advantage, privately retained counsel are only slightly more successful in keeping their clients out of jail or prison.

The incarceration rates are lower for cases represented by privately retained counsel. Assigned counsel and privately retained counsel have approximately the same incarceration rates (60.3 versus 57.1). Public defenders (78.2) and contract attorneys (74.6) are less successful in keeping their clients out of penal institutions. However, the association between the four types of defense attorneys and the corresponding incarceration rates is only moderate (Cramer's V = .20).[30] This correlation means that privately retained attorneys are more likely to gain favorable outcomes for their clients, but this advantage is limited. A majority of the convicted defendants represented by every type of defense attorney are incarcerated. The size of the majority is greater for indigent defense attorneys, but nearly six of every ten defendants represented by privately retained counsel are incarcerated.

How indigent defenders and privately retained counsel compare is seen more clearly when all indigent defenders are grouped together. Felony defendants with publicly appointed counsel are incarcerated 72.4 percent of the time, while those who privately retain their attorneys end up in prison or jail 58.2 percent of the time. The correlation between these two types of defense attorneys and the in/out decision is a very weak one (phi-square = .12).[31] The slightly better performance by privately retained counsel, moreover, appears to be due to the effect of public defenders on the population of all indigent defenders. The use of a public defender appears to influence the higher incarceration rate among publicly appointed attorneys. The question thus arises, If public defenders are excluded from the analysis, then what do the results look like? The absence of public defenders occurs naturally when the courts are separated according to size. Whereas public defenders work in four of the five large courts, they are not present in any of the four small courts. The results of this analysis show that privately retained attorneys perform better than publicly appointed attorneys in both the large courts and the small courts.

In the large courts, privately retained attorneys perform better (50.5 percent of clients incarcerated) than publicly appointed counsel (71.5 percent of clients incarcerated). The difference in incarceration rates is statistically significant, but it is limited, as indicated by a weak correlation coefficient (phi-square = .17).[32] The underlying reason why the connection is weak rests on the fact that indigent defenders represented 83 percent of defendants and obtained 74 percent of the sentences involving some penalty other than incarceration. Privately retained counsel represented 17 percent of the defendants and obtained 26 percent of the sentences involving nonincarceration. Given that indigent defenders cannot choose their clients, and privately retained counsel do have some control over whom they represent, these differences are much smaller than expected. Moreover, in the small-sized courts, the differences are in favor of publicly appointed counsel, although the incarceration rates are not statistically different. The incarceration rate is 77.4 percent for privately retained counsel and 75.2 percent for publicly appointed counsel, which is in the opposite direction of the advantage that privately retained counsel are expected to enjoy.[33]

Thus, privately retained counsel perform somewhat better than indigent defenders on the basic in/out dimension. However, the greater likelihood that privately retained counsel keep their clients out of jail or prison is limited both in magnitude and in the scope of the effects. In the small-sized courts, privately retained counsel and publicly appointed attorneys perform at the same level. Given the assumption that indigent defendants are much less likely to win favorable outcomes because of their prior records, limited ties to the community, and other social circumstances, the limited degree of success by privately retained counsel falls short of that expectation. The results suggest that indigent defenders are able to overcome the potential liabilities of their clients to a very great extent.

CONCLUSION

How frequently do indigent defenders gain favorable outcomes for their clients? Are they more successful than, less successful than, or equally as successful as privately retained counsel in gaining favorable outcomes? The evidence gained from an examination of felony dispositions in the nine courts is that indigent defenders generally are as successful as privately retained counsel. The conviction rates, the charge reduction rates, and the incarceration rates for their clients are similar to the outcomes associated with privately retained counsel. These results raise a couple of issues for future consideration.

First, the results are helpful in identifying what aspects of performance are translatable into management information systems and what aspects warrant further research and development. The measurement of case outcomes seems sufficiently feasible and the results seem sufficiently meaningful to merit inclusion into the monitoring of indigent defense systems. Consequently, judges, policy makers, and others concerned with the quality of indigent defense representation should take the necessary steps to gather information on how well indigent defenders do in gaining favorable outcomes for their clients.

However, the measures of performance in this article do not speak to the issue of lawyer-client relations, especially the time that indigent defenders give to individual defendants. How frequently do they meet with clients? What is the average amount of time spent with clients? Previous research has indicated that the amount of time that indigent defenders spend with their clients makes a difference in client satisfaction. The more time that is spent, the more defendants are satisfied with their attorneys.

Satisfaction should not be confused with productive work. Indigent defenders know how to husband resources and to gain the most favorable outcomes for their clients expeditiously. However, satisfaction is part of performance and deserves further examination. Future research needs to be conducted on this topic in order to establish more precisely what amount and what kind of time indigent defenders should be expected to devote to meeting with their clients, within the constraints of their caseloads.[34]

Second, the results suggest that judges, policy makers, attorneys, and others are not required to choose between timeliness and performance. Evidence from the nine courts in this study indicate that both goals are possible to achieve. The fact that these goals are not necessarily in conflict means that the task confronting the courts is to organize an indigent defense system responsible to community needs and circumstances that achieves both goals. That task, which is neither easy nor obvious, is possible. However, the lesson to be learned is that courts have the opportunity to design a system where both timeliness and performance are attained.

NOTES

1. Michael McConville and Chester L. Mirsky, "Criminal Defense of the Poor in New York City," 15 *New York University Review of Law and Social Change* 881 (1986–1987). An underlying theme to McConville and Mirsky's work is that indigent defenders are coopted by the courthouse community. This theme is a traditional one in the literature. See, for example, David Sudnow, "Normal Crimes: A Sociological Feature of the Penal Code in a Public Defender Office," 12 *Social Problems* 253 (1965); Abraham S. Blumberg, "The Practice of Law Is a Confidence Game: Organizational Co-optation of a Profession," 1 *Law and Society Review* 15 (1967); Dennis R. Eckart and Robert V. Stover, "Public Defenders and Routinized Criminal Defense Processes," 51 *Journal of Urban Law* 665 (May 1974); J. P. Levine, "The Impact of 'Gideon': The Performance of Public and Private Defense Lawyers," 8 *Polity* 215 (1975); Suzzane E. Mounts and Richard Wilson, "Systems for Providing Indigent Defense: An Introduction," 14 *New York University Review of Law and Social Change* 193 (1986).

2. See, for example, Lisa J. McIntyre, *The Public Defender: The Practice of Law in the Shadows of Repute* (Chicago: University of Chicago Press, 1987).

3. Some studies focus on very large communities. See, for example, Robert Hermann, Eric Single, and John Boston's study of New York, Los Angeles, and Washington, D.C., in *Counsel for the Poor: Criminal Defense in Urban America* (Lexington, Mass.: D. C. Heath, 1977). See also James Eisenstein and Herbert Jacob's study of Baltimore, Detroit, and Chicago in *Felony Justice: An Organizational Analysis of Criminal Courts* (Boston: Little, Brown, 1977). On the other hand, Peter Nardulli focuses exclusively on nine medium-sized

communities (DuPage, Peoria, and St. Clair counties in Illinois; Kalamazoo, Oakland, and Saginaw counties in Michigan; Dauphin, Erie, and Montgomery counties in Pennsylvania) in "Insider's Justice: Defense Attorneys and the Handling of Felony Cases," 77 *Journal of Criminal Law and Criminology* 379 (1986). Prior research with the broadest scope is a study of eight medium-sized and small-sized communities all located in Virginia by Larry J. Cohen, Patricia P. Semple, and Robert E. Crew, Jr., "Assigned Counsel versus Public Defender Systems in Virginia: A Comparison of Relative Benefits," in *The Defense Counsel*, edited by William F. McDonald (Newbury Park, Calif.: Sage Publications, 1983).

4. Some of the studies, in fact, do not compare indigent defenders with privately retained counsel. See, for example, McConville and Mirsky, "Criminal Defense of the Poor in New York City" (note 1). The lack of a comparison group poses severe methodological problems because evaluations require some form of comparison.

5. Hereafter the courts will be referred to by the names that they commonly are called in order to facilitate exposition. The names are Detroit, Seattle, Denver, Norfolk, Monterey, Oxford, Globe, Island, and San Juan.

6. Robert L. Spangenberg, Beverly Lee, Michael Batlaglia, Patricia Smith, and A. David Davis, *National Criminal Defense System Study: Final Report* (Washington, D.C.: U.S. Department of Justice, 1986).

7. Paul B. Wice, *Criminal Lawyers: An Endangered Species* (Newbury Park, Calif.: Sage Publications, 1978).

8. There are minor differences in the caseload composition of defense attorneys. All three basic categories of indigent

defenders tend to have the same distribution of felony cases. Most of their cases involve burglary and theft offenses, followed by, in descending order of frequency, crimes against the person, drug sale and possession, and other types of felonies. The only difference between their caseloads and those of privately retained counsel lies in the fact that privately retained counsel have more crimes against the person than burglary and theft cases. However, this difference is not sharp.

9. The population of Wayne County was 2,164,300 in 1986. The city of Detroit accounted for just over one-half of the total county population (1,086,220), making it the sixth-largest city in the United States. The total population living within the city, however, has been in decline since the 1950s. Approximately 39 percent of the Wayne County population is identified as nonwhite. Per capita income is $10,681, with just over 14 percent of the population living below the poverty level. Wayne County's crime rate was 9,864 serious crimes per 100,000 population.

10. In 1988, the Seattle primary metropolitan area had a population of 1,862,000, with the city of Seattle accounting for just under one-third of the total (502,000). Seattle, the twenty-fourth-largest city in the country, experienced a growth in population of 1.7 percent from 1980 to 1988; just over 12 percent of its population is identified as nonwhite. Of the nine communities under examination, Seattle had the second-highest per capita income ($13,192) and the lowest percentage of individuals living below the poverty line (7.7 percent).

11. Several years ago, the Seattle City Council, members of the bar, and some indigent defendants questioned whether there was insufficient minority representation on the board of directors and in management positions at TDA, ACA, and SCRAP. The response, in addition to increasing the awareness of affirmative action in the three agencies, was to create a fourth firm with management by minority-group members, Northwest Defenders Association (NDA). NDA, which did not represent felony cases in 1990–1991, is not investigated in this study.

12. The Defender Association, an outgrowth of Seattle's Model City Program, was created in 1967 with a staff of five. In 1969, 166 individuals were employed at TDA, seventy-one of whom were attorneys. It was the only agency that provided indigent defense services for all case types: felony, misdemeanor, juvenile offender, juvenile dependency, and municipal court cases.

13. In 1987, ACA employed eighty-three individuals, fifty-five of whom were professional staff. The types of cases handled by ACA are felony, misdemeanor, juvenile offender, and Seattle municipal court cases. The director of ACA values having a core of experienced attorneys (that is, four to six years), but he has reservations about "lifers." About 20 percent of the attorneys have five to seven years of experience, and most attorneys have about three years of experience.

14. In 1987, SCRAP employed 29.5 full-time equivalents, 18 of whom were professionals. Most attorneys are recent law school graduates. New attorneys start in juvenile offender or dependency and may work into felonies if they are interested. Most felony attorneys gain experience within the firm in other divisions, but there are some lateral hires of experienced felony lawyers. Felony attorneys are hired by an ad hoc, two-member hiring committee consisting of the felony supervisor and another felony lawyer. Tenure in the felony division was difficult to assess because the firm had been handling these cases for only about the last five years.

15. The defender firms have no funding in their own budgets for expert witnesses. Funds for experts are found in the superior court budget, and defenders obtain them through an order from the judge. The judge is able to sign off for up to $350. If a higher amount is requested, it goes to an audit committee for acceptance or rejection. Some of the attorneys who were interviewed were not aware of the procedure for obtaining an amount in excess of $350.

16. Denver is the largest city in the Rocky Mountain region. Its population of 505,000 in 1986 tended to be divided between a relatively affluent majority and a

very poor minority. A most striking feature of Denver is its crime rate of 10,557 serious crimes per 100,000 population.

17. Norfolk, Virginia, is a core city declining in population, with limited growth due to the out-migration of both middle-income residents and some poor residents (through the demolition of housing projects). Racial minorities constitute 38.4 percent of the population, and about 21 percent live below the poverty level. Norfolk had a violent crime rate in 1985 of 6,561 per 100,000.

18. The population of Monterey County was 340,000 in 1986. Approximately 15 percent of the county's population is Hispanic. In 1985, the per capita income was $10,420, with 11.4 percent of the population below the poverty level. Monterey County's crime rate was 5,419 serious crimes per 100,000 population.

19. Gila County is a large geographic area (4,752 square miles), approximately half the size of Rhode Island. It is located approximately 90 miles east of Phoenix in the state's copper mining region. It also includes a growing recreational and retirement community (Payson-Pine), although the Miami-Globe community is larger. Demographically, Gila County is a community of 37,000 persons, with 15 percent of the population identified as nonwhite (primarily Hispanic and American Indian, since the county is bordered on the east by two Indian reservations). The per capita income in 1985 was $7,399.

20. The population of Oxford County was 50,200 in 1986, approximately 4 percent of Maine's total population of 1,250,000. Oxford County is located in the southwestern mountain region of Maine. The basic industries in this area center around lumbering and paper production. The per capital income is $8,379, with just under 13 percent of the population living below the poverty level. Less than one-half of 1 percent of Oxford County is identified as nonwhite. The serious crime rate for Oxford was 1,781 index crimes per 100,000 population in 1985.

21. Island and San Juan counties are adjacent counties that consist only of islands. By Western United States standards they are very small in area (212 square miles for Island; 179 square miles for San Juan). Both counties are rural in character; however, a Naval Air Station in Island County gives Island a somewhat different flavor. Both counties have a low to virtually nonexistent minority population and high real estate values. The median value of homes in San Juan County is $87,300—the highest in the state and nearly one-third higher than the state median—and the median real estate value in Island County is nearly identical to the state median of $60,700. Crime rates are 2,278 and 2,843 per 100,000 population for Island and San Juan, respectively.

22. Roberta Rovner-Pieczenik, Alan Rapoport, and Martha Lane, *How Does Your Defender Office Rate? Self-Evaluation Manual for Public Defender Offices* (Washington, D.C.: Government Publications Office, 1977), especially pages 38–43 concerning measures of "attorney competence." American Bar Association Project on Standards for Criminal Justice, *Standards Relating to the Prosecution Function and the Defense Function* (Washington, D.C.: American Bar Association, 1971), especially pages 225–228 concerning the "duty to investigate." William Genego, "Future of Effective Assistance of Counsel: Performance Standards and Complete Representation," 22 *American Criminal Law Review* 181 (Fall 1984). National Study Commission on Defense Services, *Guidelines for Legal Defense System in the United States* (Washington, D.C.: National Legal Aid and Defender Association, 1976), especially pages 428–447 on "ensuring effectiveness."

23. See, for example, Hermann, Single, and Boston, *Counsel for the Poor* (note 3); Joyce Sterling, "Retained Counsel Versus the Public Defender," in William F. McDonald, ed., *The Defense Counsel* (Newbury Park, Calif.: Sage Publications, 1983), pp. 68–76; David Willison, "The Effects of Counsel on the Severity of Criminal Sentences: A Statistical Assessment," 9 *Justice System Journal* 87 (1984).

24. Some scholars suggest that it is utopian to expect that indigent defenders will perform as well as privately retained counsel. Willison, "The Effects of the

Severity of Criminal Sentences" (note 23), writes that indigent defenders will "fail to perform as successfully as privately retained counsel even if they are adequately funded and have workable caseloads so long as they continue to represent disadvantaged defendants facing serious criminal charges and possessing extensive criminal records" (88).

25. In this section, two basic statistical tests are applied to determine whether there is a connection between the different types of defense attorneys and performance and the strength of the connection. The first test is a test of significance. The test of significance indicates whether there is a systematic connection as opposed to a coincidental connection. The chi-square test is the particular test that is applied. This technique generates a number and a corresponding level of significance. The smaller the significance level, the less likely it is that the observed pattern could have happened by chance alone. In this article, the benchmark of .01 is used to determine when there are statistically significant differences (that is, results could have happened by chance alone only one time out of a hundred).

The second test is a test of association. If there is a systematic connection, how close is it? The test of association measures the strength of connection in terms of a correlation coefficient. The coefficient ranges in value from zero to one. Basically, the larger the value of the coefficient, the tighter the connection is between the different types of attorneys and various case outcomes. The phi-square and the Cramer's V correlations are the tests of association that are applied. Phi-square is appropriate for all two-by-two tables, and Cramer's V is appropriate for all the others. Finally, the rule of thumb is that coefficients below .20 are considered to be indications of weak connections between the types of attorneys and case outcomes, those from .21 to .40 are

considered to indicate moderate connections, and coefficients from .41 to 1.0 are considered to indicate strong connections.

26. Large courts: chi-square = 1.91, significance level = .17, phi-square = .03. Small courts: chi-square = .46, significance level = .49, chi-square = .46.

27. The relatively high level of success among contract attorneys may be due to the unusually high level of experience, especially among the contract attorneys in Monterey and Globe.

28. Chi-square = 48.12, significance level = .0001, Cramer's V = .15.

29. Large courts: chi-square = 4.43, significance level = .04, phi-square = .05. Small courts: chi-square = .46, significance level = .49, phi-square = .03.

30. Chi-square = 87.79, significance level = .0001, Cramer's V = .20.

31. Chi-square = 36.00, significance level = .0001, phi-square = .12.

32. Chi-square = 55.00, significance level = .0001, phi-square =.17.

33. Chi-square = .261, significance level = .01, phi-square = .03.

34. Jonathan D. Casper, "Did You Have a Lawyer When You Went to Court? No. I Had a Public Defender," *Yale Review of Law and Social Action* 4–9 (Spring 1971). More generally, researchers have found that the felony defendant's degree of satisfaction with the outcome of the case is shaped by the procedural fairness of the process. Procedural fairness includes measures of the defendant's views of the defense attorney's, prosecutor's, and judge's behavior (for example, Did your lawyer listen to you? Did the prosecutor pay careful attention to your case? Did the judge try hard to find out if you were guilty or innocent?). See also Jonathan D. Casper, Tom Tyler, and Bonnie Fisher, "Procedural Justice in Felony Cases," 22 *Law and Society Review* 483 (1988).

PART IV

Courts

The typical American courtroom is not in the public minds' eye what it is in actuality. Most lower criminal courts in city courtrooms have little of the quiet dignity one expects to see when decisions concerning individual freedom and justice are made. The scene is usually one of noise and confusion as attorneys, police, and prosecutors mill around conversing with one another and making bargains to keep the assembly line of the criminal justice process in operation. One might see a judge accepting guilty pleas and imposing sentences at a rapid pace, going through the litany of procedure in rote fashion. It is not surprising that visitors are shocked and that first offenders are confused by what they see.

The courts, like other parts of the justice system, function under conditions of mass production, congestion, and limited resources. Even in the courts, the interests of the organization and of the principal actors often take precedence over the claims of justice. The mass production of judicial decisions is accomplished because the front line bureaucrats in the system work on the basis of three assumptions. The first is that only people for whom there is a high probability of guilt will be brought before the courts; doubtful cases will be filtered out of the system by the police and the prosecution. Second, the vast majority of defendants will plead guilty. In most urban courts less than 10 percent of defendants plead not guilty. Third, those charged with minor offenses will be processed quickly. This usually means that all the defendants will be called together before the bench, the citation will be read by the clerk, individual pleas will be taken by the judge, and sentences quickly pronounced.

It is tempting to believe that adding more judges and constructing new facilities will relieve courtroom overload, but other factors contribute to the situation—for example, poor management, the rise or change in types of crime, and the presence of lawyers. What is criminalized by legislatures affects the amounts and types of cases seen in a courtroom. For example, the 1980s trend of criminalizing more low-level drug offenses increased the amount of drug cases handled by the courts—illustrating the assertion that courts are a mirror of the society that they serve. Some argue that the procedural requirements laid down by the U.S. Supreme Court have lengthened the processing time, yet observers point out that defendants are typically informed en masse of their rights by a droning bailiff. In addition, most defendants actually waive their right to a trial, and many do not even want the services of an attorney.

The problem of court congestion has become widely recognized during the past decades. Observers both inside and outside of government have deplored the fact that defendants in criminal cases often wait in jail for months before they come to trial, and increasingly more jurisdictions have passed speedy trial laws. More important than conditions in the criminal courts is the filtering effect, the administrative determination of guilt, and the exchange relationships that characterize the system. As long as the system is able to function in accordance with the needs of the players, the additional judges and courtrooms demanded by reformers will not bring about a shift to due process values.

TO BE A JUDGE

The judge is intended to be a neutral arbiter between the state and the accused. More than any other person in the system, the judge symbolizes and is expected to embody justice, thereby ensuring that the right to due process is respected and that the defendant is treated fairly. We recognize that the prosecutor and the defense attorney each represent a particular side in a criminal case. By contrast, the judge's black robe and gavel symbolize the impartiality we expect from our courts. The judge is supposed to act both in and outside the courthouse according to a well-defined role designed to prevent involvement in anything that could tarnish the judiciary's reputation. We expect judges to make careful, consistent decisions that uphold the ideals of equal justice for all citizens.

This image of judges devoting themselves to careful deliberations and thoughtful decisions does not, in fact, reflect the daily reality for most American judges. Lower court judges can face significant caseloads that require them to quickly exercise discretion in the disposition and punishment of minor offenses with little supervision from any higher court. Although judges are popularly portrayed as being forced to decide complex legal issues, in reality their courtroom tasks are routine. Because of the unending flow of cases, they operate with assembly-line precision; many judges, like many workers, soon tire of the repetition.

In most cities, criminal court judges occupy the lowest rank in the judicial hierarchy. Lawyers and citizens alike fail to accord them the same respect and prestige enjoyed by judges in civil and appellate courts. As with other professions, the status of criminal trial judges may be linked to the status of the people whom they serve. Criminal court judges deal with the lowliest and most despised segment of society—criminal defendants—and the work is often conducted in the busiest, noisiest, and least attractive courtrooms. The neverending flow of tragic stories, poor people, and substance abusers is a far cry from the solemn, wood-paneled, velvet-curtained marble temples that are more typical of higher courts. As a result, the possibility of moving to civil or appellate courts motivates many trial judges while they deal with the heavy caseloads and tough working conditions of the criminal court.

All judges are addressed as "Your Honor," and we must rise to our feet in deference whenever they enter or leave the courtroom. This respect and deference is not based on any certainty that each judge is highly qualified and fair. In some jurisdictions, judges are sometimes chosen for reasons that have little to do with either their legal qualifications or their judicial manner. Instead, they may be chosen because of their political connections, friendships with influential officials, or financial contributions to political parties. There is a strong reform movement to place men and women of quality on the bench. Reformers urge that judges be experienced experts in law. Many people believe that selection of judges on a nonpolitical basis will produce higher quality, more efficient, more independent, and consequently more impartial and fair members of the judiciary.

In opposition are those who argue that in a democracy the voters should elect the people charged with carrying out public policies, including judges. They contend that people chosen by their fellow citizens can better handle the steady stream of human problems confronting the judges of the nation.

THE COURTROOM: HOW IT FUNCTIONS

Although similar rules and processes are used in criminal cases throughout the nation, differences among courthouses are visible to anyone who has observed American courts. Some courts sentence offenders to longer terms than do others. In some jurisdictions, court delays and tough bail policies keep many of the accused in jail awaiting trial, while in other jurisdictions similar defendants gain pretrial release or have their cases resolved relatively quickly. Guilty pleas may make up 90 percent of dispositions in some communities but only 60 percent in others. How can we explain these differences among courts in various cities—differences which can exist even among different judges' courtrooms in the same city?

Social scientists have long recognized that the culture of a community—its shared beliefs and attitudes—has a great influence on how its members behave. Culture implies shared beliefs about proper behavior. Sets of shared beliefs can span entire nations or exist within types of smaller communities. Within any community, large or small, the shared beliefs of its culture can exert a powerful influence over people's decisions and behavior.

Researchers have identified a *local legal culture*—values and norms shared by members of a particular court community (judges, attorneys, clerks, bailiffs, and others)—regarding the handling of cases and court officials' expected behavior in the judicial process. The local legal culture influences court operations in three ways. First, shared values and expectations help participants distinguish between "our" court and other courts. Often a judge or prosecutor will proudly describe how "we" do the job differently and better than officials in the neighboring county or city. Second, norms—the shared values and expectations—tell members of a court community how they should treat one another. For example, mounting a strong adversarial defense may be viewed as not in keeping with the norms of one court, while it is the expected behavior in another. Third, norms describe how cases *should* be processed. The best example of this situation is the *going rate*, the shared local view about the appropriate sentence given the offense, the defendant's prior record, and other characteristics. The local legal culture also includes attitudes about issues such as the appropriateness of judicial participation in plea negotiations, when continuances—lawyers' requests for delays in court proceedings—should be granted, and which defendants are eligible for representation by a public defender.

The differences among local legal cultures help to explain why court decisions are dissimilar even though the formal rules of criminal procedure are basically the same. For example, we often think of judges applying their discretion in determining sentences for convicted offenders. While judges' discretion can be an important factor in sentencing, the concept of the "going rate" helps to show us that sentences are normally the product of shared understandings among the prosecutor, defense attorney, and judge involved in the plea bargaining or trial for a particular case. In one courthouse, shared understandings may impose probation on the first-time thief, but in other locales, different shared values among lawyers and judges may send such first offenders to jail or prison for the same offense.

Informal rules and practices arise within particular settings, and "the way things are done" differs from place to place. As one might expect, the local legal culture of San Francisco inevitably differs from that of Burlington, Vermont, or Baltimore—or for that matter, from neighboring Modesto, California. The customs and traditions of each jurisdiction vary because local practices are influenced by factors such as size, politics, and demographics. Among these, differences between urban and rural areas are a major factor.

SENTENCING

Sentencing is often difficult, since it is not merely a matter of applying clear-cut principles to individual cases. In one case, a judge may decide to sentence a forger to prison as an example to others despite his being no threat to community safety and probably not in need of rehabilitative treatment. In another case, the judge may impose a light sentence on a youthful offender who, although he has committed a serious crime, may be a good risk for rehabilitation if he can be moved quickly back into society.

Legislatures establish the penal codes that set forth the sentences that judges may impose, and there has been a significant increase in the use of sentencing guidelines, whereby the legislature proscribes or restricts the use or degree of discretion a judge has in sentencing. These laws generally give judges wide powers of discretion with regard to sentencing. They may combine various forms of punishment to tailor the sanction to the offender. The judge may stipulate, for example, that the prison terms for two charges are to run either concurrently (at the same time) or consecutively (one after the other) or that all or part of the period of imprisonment may be suspended. In other situations, the offender may be given a combination of a suspended prison term, probation, and a fine. Judges may also suspend a sentence as long as the offender stays out of trouble, makes restitution, or seeks medical treatment. The judge may also delay imposing any sentence but retain power to set penalties at a later date if the offender misbehaves.

Within the discretion allowed by the penal code, various elements in the sentencing process influence the decisions of judges. These may include the administrative context of the court, and the attitudes and values of the judges.

In the administrative context of the criminal courts, judges often do not have time to consider all the crucial elements of the offense and the special circumstances of the offender before imposing a sentence. Especially when the violation is minor, there is a tendency for judges to routinize decision making, announcing sentences to fit certain categories of crimes without paying much attention to the particular offender. Individuals convicted of minor offenses, and therefore possibly the most likely to be reformed, are frequently sentenced immediately after being found guilty or when they enter a guilty plea. If counsel requests a presentence report before imposition of sentence, the necessary delay may require that the defendant remain in jail—a price many are unwilling to pay.

That judges exhibit different sentencing tendencies is taken as a fact of life by the court community. These differences can be attributed to such factors as the conflicting goals of criminal justice, the differing backgrounds and social values of judges, and the influence of the local legal culture. Each of these factors influences a judge's exercise of discretion in sentencing offenders. In addition, a judge's perception of these factors can be dependent on his or her own attitudes toward the law, a particular crime, or a type of offender.

Who Gets the Harshest Punishment?

The prison population in most states contains a higher proportion of African Americans and Hispanic Americans than is found in the general population. In addition, poor people are more likely to be convicted of crimes than those with higher incomes. Is this situation a result of the prejudicial attitudes of judges, police officers, and prosecutors? Are poor people more liable to commit crimes that elicit a strong response from society? Are enforcement resources distributed so that certain groups are subject to closer scrutiny than other groups? Research on these and similar questions is inconclusive. Some studies have shown that members of racial minorities and the poor are treated more harshly by the system; other research has been unable to demonstrate a direct link between harshness of sentence and race or social class. These are a few of the questions that must be answered if we are to correct present inequities in the criminal justice system.

QUESTIONS FOR FURTHER EXPLORATION

1. What are the implications of the local legal culture and how do they explain both the behavior of actors in the system and how the system functions?

2. Explain the role that stigma or shame plays in influencing the behavior of a defendant. How does this influence your opinion about how the system works?

3. What are the collective beliefs about how judical decisions occur?

4. Discuss the importance and role of discretion on the judicial process. Do you support movements limiting discretion (mandatory sentencing)?

SUGGESTIONS FOR FURTHER READING

Eisenstein, James, Roy Flemming, and Peter Nardulli. *The Contours of Justice: Communities and Their Courts.* Pearson Education, Inc., 1988. A study of nine felony courts in three states. Emphasizes the impact of the local legal culture on court operations.

Eisenstein, James, and Herbert Jacob. *Felony Justice: An Organizational Analysis of Criminal Courts.* Boston: Little, Brown, 1977. Felony courts in three cities. Develops the concept of the courtroom workgroup and its impact on decision making.

Feeley, Malcolm M. *Court Reform on Trial.* New York: Basic Books, 1983. Study of court reform efforts such as diversion, speedy trial, bail reform, and sentencing reform. Notes the difficulties of bringing about change.

Gaylin, Willard. *The Killing of Bonnie Garland.* New York: Simon and Schuster, 1982. True story of the murder of a Yale student by her boyfriend and the reaction of the criminal justice system to the crime. Raises important questions about the goals of the criminal

sanction and the role of the victim in the process.

Rosenberg, Gerald. *The Hollow Hope.* Chicago: University of Chicago Press, 1991. Explores the efficacy of courts as policy makers, how decisions influence implementation, and the ability of the courts to enact social change.

Satter, Robert. *Doing Justice: A Trial Judge at Work.* New York: Simon and Schuster, 1990. A judge's view of the cases that he faces daily and the factors that influence his decisions.

Scheck, Barry, Peter Neufeld and Jim Dwyer. *Actual Innocence.* New York: Doubleday, 2000. Describes the harrowing stories of ten men wrongly convicted and the efforts of the Innocence Project to free them.

Zimgin, Franklin E., Gordon Hawkins, and Sam Kamin. *Punishment and Democracy: The Three Strikes and You're Out in California.* New York: Oxford University Press, 2001. Examines the origins, politics and impact of the three-strikes law in California.

14

✦

The Criminal Court Community in Erie County, Pennsylvania

James Eisenstein
Roy B. Flemming
Peter F. Nardulli

The traditional picture of the courtroom emphasizes adversarial attitudes, but a more realistic picture might emphasize the interaction among the major actors within the normative context of the work group and the local legal culture. As you read about the criminal court community in Erie County, Pennsylvania, think about the impact of the local legal culture and the interpersonal relationships among the principal actors on decision making. How might the court in Erie County differ from that in your home community?

SIZE, COMPOSITION,
AND COMMUNICATION
IN THE COURT COMMUNITY

E rie's criminal court community displayed several features that reflected the characteristics of the county it served. We begin our description of the court community by looking at these characteristics.

People tended to stay in Erie County. In 1980, 90 percent of its population had lived there at least since 1975, the highest proportion among our nine

Source: From *The Contours of Justice: Communities and Their Courts,* by James Eisenstein et al., pp. 74–103. Copyright © 1988 by James Eisenstein, Roy B. Flemming and Peter F. Nardulli.

counties.[1] Among the five "standard metropolitan statistical areas" (SMSAs) in our nine counties, the Erie SMSA showed the lowest rate of migration into the area (10 percent) from 1975 to 1980. The low influx of newcomers meant that people tended to know each other. Despite its population of 280,000, the county, and especially the city and its suburbs, exhibited the familiarity and extensive network of social ties usually associated with small towns. One person told us:

> Erie's an interesting community in that there are a lot of people in this community who are related to one another. I mean with strings, and cousins and distant cousins—that's the problem. A lot of the marriages— I can think of several older Republican families, and their families have married. There are a lot of small (100 to 200) industrial firms that have been run by older Erie families. It's in the school board; it's in the government; it's just everywhere.

These patterns facilitated the development of another feature of small towns, a highly effective and extensive community grapevine. An attorney who had lived in Pittsburgh commented that

> you could go over into another segment of Pittsburgh and nobody would know you. Here, someone once said, if you break a window at 10th and State, by the time you hit 6th and State, it's in the morning newspaper. There are grapevines all over the place.

Like many newspapers serving smaller towns, Erie's morning and evening papers combined a conservative editorial policy with "community booster-ism." Published by the same company, both papers' editorials called for harsher sentences, and the morning paper's managing editor was described as a "hard-line criminal justice man." Nevertheless, because the papers wanted to project an image of Erie as a nice community with few serious problems, they did not sensationalize crime, single out individuals for criticism, or engage in in-depth investigative reporting on the courts. A content analysis of the papers' coverage of crime found fewer and shorter articles about crime and the courts than in the other two Pennsylvania counties. Furthermore, the papers deliberately refrained from reporting an important feature of sentencing policy. One attorney told us that

> [E]verybody knows that prostitutes get six months or a year, and get out in ten days because the press doesn't follow it up. The press is there when the judge sentences them, but the press doesn't follow up, and the judge cuts them loose.

In fact, a prosecutor claimed that a reporter had written a story describing this practice, only to have it killed by his editors.

The newspapers' treatment of the courts probably also reflected the effects of social and business ties common in small communities. The head public defender's law firm and several of the judges had served as legal counsel to editors or publishers. Another attorney told us of his friendship with the editor:

"We do things in charitable organizations together. It's a small town . . . everybody knows everybody."

The criminal court community reflected many of the characteristics of the larger community just described. Lawyers referred to the Erie County bar as "small," even though more than 300 lawyers practiced there. As one stated, "It's an easy place to get to know everybody." Furthermore, a relatively small group of people formed the core of the criminal court community. Three of the five judges heard most of the cases. Nine attorneys staffed the district attorney's office and fourteen the public defender's. Together, these twenty-eight people handled half the cases. A group of about fifty private attorneys joined the prosecutors and judges to handle the other half of the caseload. But just five of them represented about 40 percent of defendants with private counsel. Thus a core group of thirty-three people disposed of about 70 percent of the caseload.

Familiarity extended to other participants as well. One attorney summarized the results of his analysis of about 700 of his case files: "The same names appeared over and over again. . . . You see family names. . . . You'll get the father, the older brother, the younger brother, the sister, the mother." Another lawyer said that the judges, being political creatures, also knew many of the defendants. A third told us, "Basically, you see the same [police] officers. . . . There are a lot of detectives but there are only a few that do any work."

The Erie court community's small size and the familiarity of its members with one another undoubtedly contributed to the effectiveness of its grapevine.[2] . . . A public defender confirmed our suspicion about its effectiveness when we asked if there were *any* secrets in the county: "I'll tell you. Probably not very many. Because if you get around and know the people, you'll find out."

The grapevine, the court community's small size, and the familiarity of its members together provided the conditions for developing strong social ties that went beyond the courthouse. The description of an experienced defense attorney's ties to people in the district attorney's office illustrates these relationships:

> [One] is a personal friend of mine. He's over at my house; I'm over at his. A lot of those guys are personal friends. I have a corporation with another prosecutor. That's the thing that's unique about this county. Most of the lawyers—there's a couple of cliques—where everybody knows everybody else. After trial we go out and have dinner. . . . That's just the way we are.

Of course, criticism and conflict usually gave way to moderation and cooperation under such circumstances. One attorney explained, "Sometimes you have to be very careful whom you criticize in this town just because you never know who you're talking to." Mutual accommodation and working things out provided the principal formula for dealing with each other. A prosecutor explained,

> Detectives get along pretty well with defense attorneys, too. There's not a great deal of animosity. . . . The police get along with the DAs; the DAs get along with the defense attorneys.

A significant feature of Erie's court community was the ability to talk things over. This same prosecutor said that he shared a goal with public defenders, that if their client needed a break, they should "come see me." The ability to "talk about it" extended to judges: "I don't really have a problem walking in and seeing them at just about any time subject to their schedule," observed a prosecutor. A former public defender explained why Erie was a nice county in which to practice:

> It's a little bit looser than a lot of counties in Pennsylvania where the judges don't even want to talk to the lawyers. We have easy access to our judges.

And a full-time prosecutor, when asked what one needed to know to understand Erie's court, replied:

> My experience here has been that it's—I don't want to say that it's a family operation necessarily—but it's a fairly close interpersonal sort of operation, with some notable exceptions, like the public defender's office . . . in terms of the relationships, most of them are based on individual relationships with each other. Like given lawyers in this office and given probation officers on the third floor, or even given lawyers and judges.

He continued his description later:

> The judges' secretaries make a big difference too. . . . It's all part of the wheels, the wheels of the system. The court administrator is the same as you. You have to know how to handle him . . . he's our age, he worked on our campaign right along with us, he's a hell of a nice guy.

Thus, cooperating, "going along," and adhering to established ways of treating others and doing things received powerful support in Erie.

If social relationships encouraged cooperation, they also provided the means for punishing those who refused. A prosecutor explained how he would get a postponement in a trial's starting date if key witnesses were unavailable when the 180-day deadline was about to expire:

> So I'm gonna have to lean on the defense counsel to get a waiver of the 180-day rule. The judge will do it for me if necessary. He'll just lean on the defense counsel. This is a small town.

And a nonlawyer familiar with the court's operations explained that attorneys who violated widely accepted informal rules of behavior "suffered in some way down the line" in their dealings with the judges. Thus, the high degree of familiarity and interdependency characteristic of Erie's criminal court community heightened communication among its members and facilitated adherence to implicit rules. Personal rivalries and conflicts were there too, especially among the heads of the principal offices, but not extensively enough to threaten the prevailing mood of cooperation and accommodation.

GEOGRAPHY OF ERIE'S CRIMINAL COURT COMMUNITY

Where people worked subtly shaped the structure and dynamics of Erie's criminal court community. Here we explore the effects of the layout of the courthouse.

Public officials liked the façade of the old courthouse (built in 1852) so much that they built a new wing duplicating it in 1929. Behind these two buildings, traditional in appearance with marble columns and staircases, sat the newest addition, built in the 1970s. Here were housed county officials on the first floor, four of the five judges and the district attorney's office on the second, the public defender, probation department, and coffee room on the third, and the jail on the fourth.

These arrangements facilitated communication. A few steps led judges from their chambers to their courtroom or their brethren's quarters. The district attorney's cramped quarters forced frequent encounters among its staff, a pattern reinforced by the practice of gathering to work, meet, and shoot the breeze in the centrally located conference room. Any judge's chambers could be reached in thirty seconds. . . . The courthouse coffee room [was] a center for socializing, gossiping, and nourishing the grapevine. The presence of other county offices on the first floor guaranteed that the grapevine would carry information about everybody's activities. It was also a convenient shorthand in discussing relations between the court (the "second floor") and its source of funds (the "first floor").

• • •

THE JUDGES

Unlike other enforcers of rules such as baseball umpires, judges find that their prestige, formal authority, and active participation place them at center stage in criminal courts. What kind of people are they? What attitudes, personality quirks, and decision patterns describe them? How do they get along with one another and with other members of the court community? These questions are a never-ending source of fascination and worry to other members of the court community. Though we can provide only brief answers, they will contribute much to understanding the criminal court community.

Five older, experienced "home-town boys" formed Erie's judiciary in 1980. One handled the juvenile docket; another devoted himself to probate. Only during trial terms did these two judges handle adult criminal cases, and then only by presiding over cases sent to them for trial. Our discussion consequently is focused on the three men who handled most of the criminal work load.

These three judges had served a total of thirty-five years. The youngest had already passed his sixtieth birthday and seventh year on the bench. The other two were sixty-four and sixty-seven, with thirteen and fifteen years' experience. Each indicated they were Republicans, though one of the other two was a Democrat, and the last an independent. Born and raised in Erie County, all three won election as district attorney between 1964 and 1970. Their election campaigns for DA and judge familiarized them with the county and its people. Commenting on his experience in campaigning for judge, one concluded that:

> I think it is an advantage because you tend to have a better feeling for people, and I think you've got a better feeling for problems, people's problems, practical problems. . . . I think it's easier to understand how people get into a situation that has led to some difficulty that ended up in court.

Their attitudes toward criminal law were distinctly conservative. In an article in *Pennsylvania Law Journal*, one publicly criticized the Warren Court's criminal law decisions, especially those such as *Miranda* dealing with confessions, as tipping the balance too far in favor of defendants; he went on to chastise the Pennsylvania Supreme Court for adhering too strictly to such decisions. In an interview with us, an Erie judge expressed views that reflected the tone of the entire court on such issues:

> The criminal law has become so much more detailed and complex, and in my opinion a little nauseous, and I'm losing interest. I really am opposed to a lot of criminal law decisions in Pennsylvania. . . . Frankly, I think they're basically absurd. . . .

All three scored low on our measure of the extent to which they believed in the due process guarantees for criminal defendants (the "due process" scale). When the attitudes of all five judges as a group were compared to those of judges in the other counties, only one other county's judges (Dauphin) scored lower. Questions measuring "belief in punishment" showed Erie judges ranked fourth.

Long service together and ideological compatibility facilitated good relations and a sense of comradery among the judges, one of them saying,

> Three of us have been district attorneys . . . all of us have been defense attorneys for a longer period of time, so we're pretty familiar with criminal law. I mean, I think we think alike without even talking. . . . I could tell you what the president judge thinks about criminal law without even talking to him.

Personal relations among four of the five judges appeared congenial, even close. Referring to the president judge, one commented that "He's over here every day talking to me and we're very close friends." The four normally gathered for morning coffee in the coffee room, engaged in social banter, shared opinions, and discussed common problems. The fifth judge, however, did not share in this fellowship. Younger, stern and aloof in personality, and strong in his views, his operating style differed sharply from that of his colleagues. We heard stories of his conflicts with the president judge, praise for his willingness to work hard, and descriptions of his distant manner. Prosecutors and defense attorneys ranked him as the least responsive to them and least involved in trying to encourage guilty pleas in order to avoid a trial.

The chief judge, called the president judge in Pennsylvania, exercised strong leadership, though his influence varied from one area to another. One judge described these differences:

> I assure you, when he expresses an opinion about my schedule I take that as something more than just an expression of opinion. But if he tells me that he disagrees with a sentence I may have imposed, or a particular finding that I made, I don't pay much attention to it.

The president judge sought to control sentencing in one area by prohibiting acceptance of "Accelerated Rehabilitative Disposition" (ARD) in retail theft cases.[3] He failed, however, to achieve complete adherence. We witnessed his close friend grant ARD in a retail theft; the other criminal judge expressed to us his willingness to do so if a good argument for it were made out to him.

His sway in matters of scheduling was great. A court official familiar with the judges' interactions concluded:

> As far as a unified judicial policy, as far as judges affixing their signature to a particular document or scheduling or something like that, the president judge dominates that. He's pretty much autonomous from the rest of the judges. . . . They can offer comments and suggestions. . . . But he has the ultimate say. All the other judges recognize that whatever the president judge wants, the president judge usually gets.

The president judge's descriptions of his duties conformed to this view. Asked if he facilitated joint decisions or bore the responsibility for running the court and exerting strong leadership, he replied:

> I think we have a little bit of both. I think like the saying, "The buck stops here." Somebody has to make the ultimate decision. That's the way it is. In other words, you receive all the input you can or should get or need. But eventually you're gonna have to make the decision.

He backed up his position with expressed willingness to meet direct challenges to his authority. What would you do, we asked, if a judge consistently violated the prohibition against granting ARD in retail theft cases. "I talk to him and try to understand," he replied. But what if the judge persisted? "You'd have to report to the judicial review board . . . if there is an established policy, I think the judge should adhere to it."

Thus, the chief judge in Erie acted much like the president of the United States—exercising strong executive leadership. But like the president, his ability to get his way by persuasion surpassed his ability to command and order. Even in matters of scheduling, his control sometimes failed. When the juvenile court judge refused to hear adult trials because of a backlog in his own docket, the president judge backed down.

This description fails to convey adequately the personalities of the judges or the substantial differences among them. One judge earned a reputation, a prosecutor mentioned, as

> notorious for settling the case . . . leaning on the case or requiring a plea . . . in the conference before the trial, in the recesses during the trial, all the way through.

Prosecutors and defense attorneys ranked him very high in his "involvement" in determining how cases would be disposed and low in his "responsiveness" to the problems of attorneys. Another judge presented the opposite profile: reluctant to be directive in settling a case and highly responsive to attorneys' requests and needs. Nearly everyone commented on his reluctance to make decisions.

If the Erie criminal court system benefited from its judges' experience, it also paid a price in interest and vigor. Some lawyers in the community believed that time had begun to pass the judges by. Our interviews picked up the loss of vigor. "I'm sort of winding down," one judge told us. "I'm getting closer to when I think I'll retire." Asked what he found satisfying and unsatisfying about his work, another replied:

> Well, I read a lot and I enjoy studying, and I did originally enjoy studying and writing opinions. I'll admit it's getting a little tedious now, but at first I did. And I liked trial work at first. I liked all those things. Now I'm getting to the point where I'm thinking about retirement, to be frank with you.

The relations of Erie's judges with other significant figures in the court-house presented a mixed picture. . . . The judges relied heavily on the probation department, routinely requiring a presentence report on convicted defendants from it before they imposed sentences. The chief probation officer enjoyed the judges' confidence, and had a crucial role in recommending which inmates in the overcrowded jail could be paroled to make room for a fresh recruit. But relations with the county executive and county council were strained. Products of Erie's old political system, the judges got on well with the old system's governing board, the three county commissioners. An individual who dealt with the new regime on behalf of the judges described the changes that came with the adoption of home rule in 1977:

> We're not dealing with three people any more. We're dealing with many more. . . . not only the county executive, but his director of finance, his personnel director, and his director of administration. . . . Not only that, but we have to deal with seven county councilmen, because everything has to go before them.

A judge lamented, "They don't understand the operations of the courts, and I think there is a sort of resentment there. They think the judges are high and mighty. . . ." The resentment was mutual. "They always try to cut us once they have satisfied the needs of the other people," observed a court administrator. A showdown over the judges' hiring of additional courtroom personnel and probation officers nearly occurred, and tension lingered. But the court's operations did not appear to be greatly threatened, and self-restraint avoided an all-out public battle. One judge, reminded that in Pennsylvania the court had the power to issue an order to the county for needed funds, remarked: "But you don't like to be dogmatic. You have to be a little bit politician to get along with people."

The "home-town," "old-style politician" character of the judges produced strong links between the judges and the larger community. They knew the county and its people well. Though they were somewhat isolated once on the bench, we got the impression that old ties and lines of communication did not disappear. A prosecutor intriguingly depicted the judges' informal contacts:

> **R:** There is an awful lot of hearsay about it. But my understanding of it is that it will break itself down generally into a contact from someone along the way. That's a contact in terms of "We'll take a look at this," or "Judge, what can you do about this?" or "Judge, what can you do about that?"
>
> **I:** Are these attorneys or political figures?
>
> **R:** Oh, anybody. Anybody. Political figures, people who you might not want to call political figures, people who worked in campaigns, that kind of thing.
>
> **I:** So the telephone lines are open?
>
> **R:** Yeah.
>
> **I:** And they pay attention to it?
>
> **R:** Oh sure. The chambers are open, and that's a very difficult thing to have to deal with.

However you interpret phrases like "the chambers are open" and "people who you might not want to call political figures," it is clear that major participants in the criminal process believed that the judges responded to outside influences on cases for reasons that went beyond facts and law.

PROSECUTOR'S OFFICE

Erie's prosecutors contrasted sharply with the judges in almost every characteristic. When the judges themselves were at equivalent stages in their careers, most members of the office had not been born. Five of its nine-member staff were thirty-one or younger, the oldest only forty-one, and the DA himself but thirty-two. As a group, these eight men and one woman had spent less than half their lives in Erie County; in fact, five indicated that they had moved to Erie for professional reasons. The judges counted three Republicans, one Democrat, and one independent; the prosecutors had two Republicans, six Democrats, and an independent. The DA, elected just a few months before our field research began, displayed a vigor, enthusiasm, and vision in his work that the judges did not. And if the judges stood as remnants of the old political order with strong ties to the community, the prosecutor came to office as an insurgent.

The story of the new DA's route to office illustrates how events and human values shape the life of a criminal court community. The highly regarded Democratic DA who hired him as a young assistant died suddenly in 1974. The judges appointed an experienced trial attorney in the office to replace him, and this individual, running as a Democrat, narrowly won a new term in 1975. Soon nearly everyone on the deceased DA's staff left, citing a litany of complaints about the new DA ("not giving a damn," "not bothering to delegate," "no organization," "no leadership"). The young assistant, who became a defense attorney after he quit, was increasingly dismayed at the deterioration of an office he felt had been a fine one. A combination of nostalgia and anger led him to challenge the incumbent's reelection in 1979.

Because both were Democrats, it meant a fight in the primary for the nomination. Anyone wise in the way of politics knows that challenging incumbents, especially in their own party's primary, usually results in failure. Established politicians counseled him to keep out; labor leaders refused to support him. Then the politically powerful mayor of Erie announced his support for a third candidate. But he stubbornly persisted, assembling a brain trust of politically experienced advisers, several of whom had also served with him in the deceased DA's office. They waged an aggressive campaign in the primary, criticizing the incumbent's loss of thirty-five cases for violating the speedy-trial rule, and hammering on the theme, "It's time to get tough." The incumbent suffered an astonishing defeat, receiving a paltry 10 percent of the vote. The results demonstrated how effective Erie's grapevine was in informing the community of the low regard in which he was allegedly held in the courthouse. Equally unusual was the insurgent's 20 percent margin of victory over the mayor's candidate.

The Republicans had a strong prospective candidate, the man who barely lost the DA's race in 1975. Personal problems, however, caused him to surprise everyone by declining to run, leaving the GOP with no candidate. The Democrats' insurgent candidate faced no opposition in the general election. Rebuffed by Democratic party and labor union leaders in the early stages of his campaign, bucked by the mayor of Erie, and not requiring anyone's assistance in the uncontested general election, he came to office with very few political obligations. Ironically, the new DA did face his potential GOP challenger, but in a different capacity. The Republican county executive fired the longtime incumbent Republican public defender and appointed him to the vacancy. The absence of organized, politically effective groups such as the American Civil Liberties Union, civil rights organizations, and even business groups capable of pressuring the office also contributed to the freedom enjoyed by the new DA. In fact, when asked what organizations or groups impinged on the office, office officials identified only the local rape crisis center.

Motivated by the desire to restore the office to what he believed to be its former competence and performance, and unencumbered by political debts, the new Erie district attorney came to office eager to make big changes. He began with a clear view of the potential his office offered, a view expressed when he was asked if the criminal court administrator could change the way in which cases were scheduled:

> He's not able to pull it off by himself. No. But the person who is, the guy who's got to be out on the point . . . is the district attorney—the combination lawyer, politician, administrator, social worker.

He started his initiatives before taking office, utilizing the general election campaign period to prepare an elaborate justification for increasing his budget. Initially rebuffed by the county executive, he finally prevailed by lobbying the county council to override the executive's veto of the increase. He consequently gained both an enhanced reputation for effectiveness and an additional $40,000.

The extra funds permitted basic restructuring of the office. Instead of five full-time assistants, he switched to three full-time and five half-time assistants. Only one attorney from the defeated incumbent's staff remained. His new full-time first assistant knew the criminal process well, because he had served as second assistant public defender. Two of the half-time assistants had also worked for the deceased DA, and a third had engaged in defense work for some time. The added half-timers gave the office some experienced "big guns" to handle the difficult cases and to help train the younger members of the staff who had never tried a case. The half-timers joined because of the new DA's leadership, not for the $12,000 salary. As one explained,

> I haven't been doing it for the money. It's a loss leader. It's a disaster. But it's fun. That's why you do it. That's why he has the staff that he has. It's an economic disaster, but you don't do everything for economic reasons in this world.

Several large changes in policy accompanied inauguration of the reinvigorated DA's office. And several of these flowed directly from the theme of the campaign. "It's time to get tough." The slogan reflected sentiment widely shared in the office, not merely campaign rhetoric. The office sought higher bail, especially in crimes of violence. "They oppose everything you do now," an experienced public defender complained. "You go in for a bond reduction and they oppose it, automatically." It became stingier in recommending lenient dispositions in less serious cases, including Accelerated Rehabilitative Disposition (ARD). The office's leadership felt the previous DA had agreed to plea bargains that reduced the seriousness of the charges "just for the sake of reduction." The new regime claimed it had stopped this practice, reducing charges only when the case was weak, a witness was missing, or the facts justified a lower charge. Finally, the office began writing what some referred to as "hate letters" to the probation department urging that its presentence reports to the judges recommend stiff sentences. Assistants also began appearing at sentencing to make their views known. A militant tenor about this practice arose from the interviews, as one assistant demonstrated:

That's another thing that's happening that didn't happen before. The judges, under the old regime, were not asking the district attorney to comment at the time of sentence. They are now. We have a right to comment.

Despite widespread agreement among the staff on the need to "get tough," Erie's prosecutors did not appear from the interviews to be vindictive, "grind defendants into the dust" individuals. One administrator volunteered that he retained his belief in due process, and admitted he would find it difficult to sentence some defendants. As a group, Erie's prosecutors held less strong "belief in punishment" views and less negative attitudes toward "due process" than their counterparts in the other two Pennsylvania counties. They ranked seventh among the nine counties in "belief in punishment" and third in "regard for due process."

The leadership style of Erie's new district attorney flowed naturally from the composition of the office. Seven of the eight staff attorneys owed their appointments to the DA. Several part-timers helped plan election strategy, shared memories of the old office, and considered themselves close friends of his. The staff strongly approved of the changes in policy instituted. Its members also socialized in the evening. Both attorneys and secretaries, for instance, attended performances by a band in which one of the lawyers played. A spirit of comradery and pride seemed to prevail. One assistant enthusiastically remarked, "He's assembled a hell of a staff. And that's fun. It's always fun to be associated with competent people. It's interesting." Despite the youth of the office, it had much experience in the criminal process and a high degree of self-assurance, as one administrator's boast showed: "We know all the angles, we know the ropes, we know the way the system works."

These factors encouraged an informal, loose management style. No written rules or manual of office policies existed. No formal procedures for checking staff performance, such as auditing monthly disposition statistics for each attorney, were employed. The DA and the first assistant spent much time in the conference room: the proximity of the courtrooms made it easy to drop in on the inexperienced assistants' performances; the grapevine filled in any gaps. The DA gained familiarity with the cases by reviewing all new matters as they came into the office.

The half-timers were former colleagues older than the DA, precluding a traditional "boss–employee" relationship. The degree of supervision thus varied depending on the assistant's experience. The half-timers felt free to exercise discretion consistent with the DA's views, as the comments of one suggest:

He knows me and I know him. If there is a question of policy, I would go and ask him. But generally, if a deal is to be made, I in my own discretion would make the deal, and I know he would accept it, just because I've been around. . . . I think we think alike, we act alike, and we have probably very similar attitudes on what law and order is and what justice is. . . . So consequently we really don't have any problems.

In fact, the DA did not always insist cases be handled as he would handle them, even when he became aware of such differences. An experienced assistant told us what happened when he discussed with his boss a plea bargain he had reached:

> He told me he disagreed with it. And I said, "Well, I think I have some pretty good reasons for doing it. . . ." He said, "Well, okay. I'm not going to overrule you. It's your decision."

Rookie assistants received closer scrutiny and direction, but typically through informal means. One, asked if his plea bargains were reviewed by the DA, explained:

> He does monitor that. Probably not on a formal basis as far as keeping a list. He very much stays in the conference room and just sort of sits here and sees what's going on, and asks, like, "Why did you do this?"

They often assisted veteran attorneys on difficult and important cases as part of their training. "Postmortems" in the conference room after trial were another way to give rookies feedback.

If internal office management and relations presented few problems and challenges, the same could not be said of external relations. The successful effort to obtain a budget increase was a significant though difficult victory in dealing with the county government. Like most members of criminal court communities everywhere, however, Erie's prosecutors felt county officials had little knowledge of or real interest in the operations of the criminal courts. The DA did not enjoy a close relationship with the Republican county executive, a political ally of the public defender. But he got on extremely well with the criminal court administrator, an employee of the judges who oversaw scheduling and other administrative matters pertaining to the criminal docket. In fact, everyone knew that the administrator participated actively in the DA's campaign. Good relations with the probation department also developed.

Interaction with several other organizations deserves brief mention. Relations with the news media seemed important to the office. One key office member, assessing the newspaper, strongly implied it favored the judges and the head public defender: "I've sensed that certain things will get printed and certain things won't get printed, and certain people get treated better in the media." The DA received better coverage from the broadcast media, appearing frequently on local television news programs. The office appreciated the cooperation the district justices showed, promptly forwarding copies of case documents after the preliminary hearing, but felt less happy about their refusal to toss out weak cases. Attitudes toward the police . . . varied from respect to disdain depending on the department.

Our description of the Erie DA's office would be incomplete without mentioning its desire to bring about a number of changes. It sought to enhance the office's investigative capabilities beyond the one county detective available, to institute a career criminal prosecution program, and to create a special unit to focus on consumer fraud, drug cases, and white-collar crime. The office's ambitious long-run agenda clashed with the bench's preferences. The judges engaged in almost no long-range planning. Major changes in the way things worked, indeed any changes, failed to excite them.

Our field research ended after the DA's first nine months, and so we could not assess his success in overcoming judicial apathy. His failure, however, to win the president judge's approval of a change in the structure of the criminal calendar demonstrated the need for judicial cooperation, and suggested the formidable obstacles to success that he faced.

PUBLIC DEFENDER'S OFFICE

If Erie's judges contrasted sharply with its prosecutors, the public defenders displayed many superficial similarities. The public defender himself had also assumed control recently. Though slightly larger, with thirteen attorneys (counting the head) handling adult criminal cases, the office's average age of thirty-three nearly matched that of the prosecutors. The staff also had three full-timers, including the first and second assistants, with the rest, including the head, part-timers. The new leader felt extensive changes needed to be made, and took steps to bring them about. He fired several people and encouraged others considered "deadwood" to retire. By June 1980, only two part-timers with the office when he took over in 1979 remained.

Despite these obvious similarities, however, major differences could be seen. All but three of the attorneys had lived in Erie County almost all their lives. Despite the head's status as a partisan Republican, the office had four Republicans, four Democrats, and five independents. Three women and two blacks worked there. The DA had one woman and no blacks. The PD's staff had much less experience in criminal law. The first assistant and the two holdover part-timers knew their way around criminal courts, though the first assistant won his knowledge in another state. But the other two full-timers were new both to the office and to criminal law, and five of the six other part-timers had served a year or less. The head PD owed his appointment to his political rather than legal activities. He practiced civil, not criminal, law, and had worked as a Washington lobbyist. Prominent in GOP politics, and narrowly defeated for DA in 1975, he played a central role in the county executive's campaign.

The office failed to achieve the esprit and social cohesion found in the prosecutor's office. The cramped third-floor offices provided space only for the full-timers. The others worked primarily from their private offices, appearing in the main office sporadically during trial terms. The PD called few staff meetings gathering everyone together. An assistant bothered by the lack of communication described several unsuccessful efforts to generate informal social get-togethers.

The head PD identified several long-range goals, including moving the main office out of the courthouse, establishing a student-intern program, and transforming the operation into a private corporation. Like the DA, he demonstrated considerable sophistication and political savvy in devising strategies to realize them. But he classified himself as a "short-run implementer" rather than a "long-range goal man."

Like nearly all supervisors we talked to in public defenders' offices, Erie's head PD believed his staff should be allowed wide autonomy in handling individual clients' cases.

> I am dealing with professionals and if they are good public defenders or good lawyers they have big egos. So that, to some extent, to get the best out of them, I have to take an equal or even a subordinate role in an individual case.

Some staff attorneys agreed that their discretion was not unduly limited. Asked what office policies influenced how he handled cases, one assistant public defender replied there were none. "And it's just like that person is a private client. I have complete latitude on the cases to do what I feel is in his best interest."

Several features of the office's relations outside the court community deserve mention. The head PD's relations with the county executive were very good, though no surprise given their close political ties. Like many aspects of life in other human communities, the effect of their ties on events, though powerful, was often quite subtle. For example, in January 1980, several assistant public defenders were, for various reasons, unavailable. Consistent with his desire to provide defendants with "continuous" representation by the same attorney, the head PD refused to reassign cases to other members of the office. The resulting disruption of the docket angered the rest of the court community, especially the judges. When we asked the public defender if his defiance of the judges might not lead to later trouble in the form of complaints from the judges to the county executive, he replied it would not be a problem due to the "independence" of the county executive from the president judge. Left unsaid was the fact that in such a dispute the public defender would win the county executive's support.

Like the prosecutor, the public defender received little pressure from the community. The private bar voiced few complaints about the office taking paying clients away from struggling attorneys, a situation the office attributed to its strict application of eligibility standards. The PD's law firm represented the newspapers, leading the prosecutors to claim that it received favorable coverage.

The office recognized the importance of district justices and probation officers, and sought to cultivate good relations with both. One policy the head PD pursued required cooperation by the district justices: disposition of minor charges at the preliminary-hearing stage. Erie's public defenders sounded a frequent refrain in discussing lower judges: "Some of the district judges are excellent; some are just dumb."

The lack of the same social cohesion and esprit found in the DA's office led to a less coherent "office view" among Erie's public defenders. The relative inexperience among its attorneys also made it difficult to summarize their attitudes neatly. We can, however, draw two useful conclusions. First, the office felt it did a very good job. An experienced assistant boasted:

> I think we give our clientele excellent service. I think we give the taxpayers a lot for their money. I think our services are really very effective, and are just as much—if not more—effective than private counsel.

The management orientation produced an emphasis on statistical measures of success. An office supervisor rattled off figures on performance in jury trials as proof of effectiveness:

> The public defender's staff had nine guilties, seven splits, nine not guilties, one hung, for twenty-six jury trials. The private bar had eleven guilties, five guilty of lesser offenses, seven not guilties. So we beat them in every category . . . we compare favorably with the private bar.

Several aspects of the head public defender's management style contrasted, though, with his expressed belief in autonomy. He believed strongly in "over-motioning," filing a whole series of pretrial motions as standard practice. Unlike the DA, he sought to implement and enforce this and other policies with formal written memos to the staff and a case file folder with places for the attorney to record every action taken. The data recorded there could then be used as a management tool. "I am not above evaluating lawyers and individual cases. That's one of the reasons I got this file-folder system," he informed us. He also differed from the DA in avoiding informal socializing with the staff: "It's fine when you're one or two years out of law school. But when you start fraternizing with people that you have to tell how to do things, it doesn't work." He used salary-increase allocations to reward some assistants, and gave no raises to others. Everyone knew he had fired several assistants. An individual who had served under the previous public defender summarized the changes as "a more formal and standardized basis now." Holdovers disliked his management style and some of the policies. One who quit complained: "Now it's kind of they're looking over your shoulder all the time. And when I've tried as many cases as I have, I don't need somebody looking over my shoulder."

Other stated policies contributed to the new regime's formal, strict tone. The office prohibited part-time assistants from representing paying criminal clients in their private practices, a common occurrence among part-time defenders in Montgomery County. It became stricter in applying criteria to determine eligibility of poor defendants for representation, and began keeping records of those turned down. It encouraged assistants to talk to defendants before preliminary hearings, tried to assign repeat clients to the attorney who handled the earlier case, and sought to provide a "continuous" or "vertical" defense (that is, have the same attorney represent the defendant from the initial stages to final disposition or sentencing). High turnover in the months just before our field research began, however, made such continuous assignment extremely difficult.

The head PD's management style thus contrasted with the DA's in his desire to establish and monitor compliance with formal policies, in his willingness to reward and punish assistants, in his rigidity, and in his lack of informality.

Did the PD succeed in running a tight ship and achieving conformity to his policies? The answer is complicated somewhat because assistants differed in their reaction to office policies. Acts that rankled old-timers as unnecessary interference were a perfectly acceptable and normal way of doing things for newcomers. A further complication arose from the head's spending relatively little time directly supervising the office. He remained uninvolved in day-to-day operations, and delegated much of the task of direct administration to the first assistant.

The first assistant employed a more informal and looser management style. He announced an open-door policy to assistants, especially the less experienced ones, and encouraged them to consult with him as equals in an atmosphere of low tension. He inserted memos in case files making suggestions to the trial attorney. "But," he told us, "I don't ever follow up to see if they do or not. It's none of my business." And he apparently failed to ensure that the head's wishes regarding "over-motioning" were met. One attorney said, "Each guy does as he sees fit—what he wants to do." The result was a public defender's office somewhat less tightly and formally run than the head sought, but also more formal and controlled than those in other counties.

Second, the office lacked a strong "defendant orientation" in the attitudes of its staff and its policies. Several assistants remarked that they could just as easily work for the prosecutor; one recent departee wanted to join the DA's staff. An assistant's answer to a question about his job's frustrations illustrated this attitude:

> Well, the frustration with being a public defender goes back to the fact that just basically our client is not what society is going to consider as an upstanding citizen by and large. . . . They don't really consider what they've done as wrong.

A recently departed assistant complained sentences were not harsh enough; another said he just got fed up with clients charged repeatedly with serious crimes lying each time about what happened. Public defenders in only one other county produced a higher mean on the "belief of punishment" measure, though they scored relatively high in "regard for due process." Finally, the office acquiesced in permitting defendants to accept a disposition entered in the records as "NPCOD," which stood for "Noll Pros (that is, dismissal by the prosecutor), Costs on Defendant." The office did not challenge the practice. And even though some defenders thought it was unfair for defendants to pay court costs when charges were dropped, they felt it was up to the defendant to accept or reject such a disposition.

ERIE'S PRIVATE DEFENSE BAR

In the first half of 1980, fifty different attorneys represented the 220 defendants who appeared on the arraignment docket in Erie's trial court. . . . Thirty-eight attorneys handled only one or two defendants. . . . Five men . . . handled the cases of ninety-one defendants, more than 40 percent of those privately represented. . . .

We found a few general characteristics of the defense bar. In the years just before our research began, several of the high-volume, established private defense attorneys began to cut back. Four of the five white male attorneys we spoke with had yet to reach their thirty-fifth birthdays. The gap in age between them and the fading group of old-timers interfered with the development of a cohesive defense bar, despite their familiarity with one another. One interviewee conveyed the tenor of relations among defense attorneys when he told us: "I'm not very active in the bar. I'm not crazy about most of them." . . . In 1980, only ten women practiced among the 300 lawyers in Erie; only the three assistant public defenders and an assistant prosecutor among them dealt with criminal matters. Except for several of the less active veteran specialists, the private defense bar enjoyed little status. Several had the reputation of benefiting their clients through, one prosecutor said, their "inexplicable access before certain judges" rather than through their legal ability. According to one judge, the top civil attorneys avoided criminal law.

Of course, the private defense bar had some communication and structure. As described earlier, a group of attorneys, including several currently handling criminal cases, joined in the effort to elect the new DA. They shared a common fate and interest. Several told us, for example, of widespread grumbling at the public defender's "slam" at the private bar when he hired an attorney from Pittsburgh to fill a vacancy.

· · ·

SOCIAL AND WORKING RELATIONSHIPS
IN ERIE'S COURT COMMUNITY

For the most part, encounters between the people who formed Erie's criminal court community on the surface displayed courtesy, cordiality, and cooperation. This pattern seemed especially prevalent in personal relations between rank and file members of the DA's and the PD's offices. Referring to assistant prosecutors, a PD said:

> The average "belief in punishment" for prosecutors was higher than for public defenders. Erie's judges, in keeping with their conservative views, expressed attitudes closer to those of the prosecutors than the public defenders. Public defenders' "regard for due process" was positive, and the difference exceeded that seen for belief in punishment.
>
> They're nice guys, you know. They're professionally enjoyable and you can get them aside over a cup of coffee and quite frankly tell them that they're just full of crap and they'll just laugh about it.

A former assistant defender expressed a similar view.

> If you don't normally give the DA's office a rough time—by rough I mean by being unavailable or not around—you say, "Listen, I've got a real important civil matter this morning. Can I start it this afternoon?" They're going to accommodate you.

The stereotyped image of the friendly way of life in small communities, the avoidance of conflict in favor of cooperation, and the unwillingness to offend, held true much of the time.

Under the surface in most small towns, college faculties, workers in fast-food restaurants, and most other places where people gather, we find another pattern, with personality clashes, disagreements, grudges, and lack of cooperation. Erie's criminal court was no exception. Relationships between a few prosecutors and public defenders were less friendly. But more significantly, relations between the principal personalities in the community displayed considerable tension, criticism, and dislike. It would be impossible (and tedious) to describe these conflicts in full detail, but we will briefly summarize the crucial characteristics of relations among the leading members of the criminal court community to convey this feature of Erie's court community.

The judges' cohesiveness, mutual friendship, long joint service, and strong leadership from the president judge produced a common outlook toward the DA and PD. They mentioned improvement in prosecutors' performances since the new DA took office, describing them as "better prepared," "more on the ball," "aggressive," "intelligent and scholarly." Nevertheless, all opposed his call for a change in the calendar, blaming the office for its failure to use the full two weeks of existing trial terms.

The judges expressed very different opinions about the public defender's office. "I'm not satisfied with the public defender," one judge revealed. "I think it's pathetic." He regarded its attorneys as "very inexperienced" and "incompetent." Resentment lingered over the office's failure to reassign the cases of PDs unable to work during the January trial term. The president judge demonstrated his lack of confidence by taking over himself the job of deciding which private attorneys would represent homicide defendants, a task formerly delegated to the PD. The PD wanted to reacquire this power, but the president judge refused.

Members of the prosecutor's office shared the judges' assessment of the public defender's office. Said one:

> It's really a sin what's happened up there in the last year. . . . They don't have a single experienced trial attorney on the staff. . . . He's picking real bad people. In consequence of doing that he's really destroying the reputation of the office that was good for a long time.

Another reported the common belief that the PD's appointment resulted from the return of a political debt.

> There may be some merit to it because he doesn't have any trial experience, doesn't have any criminal law experience, and doesn't have any administrative experience.

An experienced assistant summarized the office's view:

> As a generalization, by and large we don't particularly care for the public defender's office. We don't like the way they handle their office. We don't

think it's administered well and we just don't think too much of how they handle their clients.

Part of the explanation for this tension and dislike can be attributed to the relationship between the heads of the two offices. Though they professed mutual friendship, their assertions lacked credibility. In fact, one complained to us that the other had lied a lot to him. The opinions expressed by their staffs reflected the tension between them. A member of the PD's staff observed that the "political stuff" between them was both messy and petty, and that they were "at each other all the time." A counterpart in the DA's office expressed views that revealed their rivalry. "There is bad blood between [the DA] and [the PD]. The [PD] is a political creature." Relations between assistants in administrative positions in the two offices showed similar tension. Prosecutors voiced other criticisms, such as, "they wait too long, or wait till the last minute to do much of their work."

The PD's office mirrored the DA's views in its assessment. An administrator charged the DA's office with lack of respect, failure to do its homework, and poor performance in trials. The public defenders considered a supervisor in the DA's office to be a poor trial attorney and a rigid, unreasonable administrator. They felt the DA's office had "gone overboard" in getting tough, refusing to plea bargain when it should have, backing out on tentative agreements, and generally being "inflexible," "unyielding," and "unbending."

We alluded to the attitudes of the prosecutor's office toward the judges. They blamed the early end of trial terms not on themselves, but on the pressures exerted by the judges to settle cases in order to avoid trials. Seven of the prosecutors we interviewed indicated in one way or another that they regarded the bench as a whole, and the two judges close to retirement in particular, as lazy. Immediately after stating that the aloof judge was "the only worker on the court," a prosecutor interjected:

> while the other ones are—classic example—today: President judge is out to lunch at 11:15, back at 2:00, gone at 3:30, a month's vacation right during the middle of a court term.

They resented the president judge's refusal to alter the calendar. The one judge labeled "the only worker" received praise for his sentences. But the others' sentences appeared "very lenient" to the DA's office, especially the standard 11.5- to 23-month county jail sentences that frequently resulted in the defendant's release in a few days.

The public defenders said little about the judges. They neglected to complain about the harshness of sentences, an indirect expression of their apparent satisfaction. They shared the prosecutor's judgment that only one judge worked hard, that another was slow in making decisions, and that a third lacked much knowledge of criminal law. But administrators knew the judges did not think well of the office, telling us they got the idea the judges were displeased. This recognition, however, brought forth no efforts to modify the practices that aroused criticism.

AGE AND GENERATIONS
IN ERIE'S COURT COMMUNITY

Differences in the ages of judges, prosecutors, and public defenders in Erie and the prominence of "cohorts" were striking. . . . Data on the average age of judges (60.4 years) compared to those of prosecutors and public defenders (33.1 years and 32.9 years, respectively) confirms the size of Erie's generation gap. Only Kalamazoo's judges had a higher average age. Only Saginaw's judges had a higher average of years of service on the bench (12.8 versus Erie's 12.0). The ages of prosecutors and public defenders differed little from those in other counties. . . . Erie's prosecutors were a little older than the average for all nine counties, and its public defenders about a year younger.

Comparing the differences in age of the judge, prosecutor, and either the PD or private counsel who handled each defendant's case provides a clearer picture of Erie's generation gap. Judges averaged more than 30 years older than prosecutors and 28.6 years older than defense attorneys, a larger gap than in seven of the eight other counties. In fact, the gap in three counties was only about half as great, about 15 years.

STRUCTURE OF INFLUENCE

In Erie, the judges set the tone and rhythm of the criminal court. The president judge believed in exercising strong leadership, and he enjoyed the support and friendship of a cohesive group of three of the four other judges. The general policies of Erie's newspapers, and their relationship with the president judge in particular, insulated the judges from criticism. The county's long tradition of strong president judges reinforced his status. One important attorney in the community minced no words in describing his control: "This is a county, historically, that has had under-the-thumb kind of rule from the president judge, from the incumbent as well as his predecessors." One subtle indication of his stature appeared in a prosecutor's response to a question about how the county officials on the first floor reacted when the judges came down from the second to request their budget:

> Well, the judges don't come down for their budget. I think that's a classic illustration of how it works. The second floor doesn't go down to see the first floor. The first floor comes up.

It was clear that his power had entered its final stages as retirement loomed. But his ability to prevail on issues like the structure of the calendar remained. Though the prosecutor began making speeches calling for change, he acknowledged that if the president judge were to call him in and ask him to stop, he would have to comply.

The public defender exerted little influence within the court community. He lost the duty of assigning attorneys to homicide cases, had an inexperienced staff, and was regarded by judges, prosecutors, and the private bar as inexperienced in criminal work and highly political. Only his strong ties to the county executive provided him with significant support. The new district attorney enjoyed a good reputation among the private bar and the judges. Though he established an ambitious agenda for change, only the initiatives that could be implemented within his own office succeeded in the early months of his tenure. The impending retirement of two judges, his vigor, and his access to the broadcast media augured well for a rise in the DA's influence. At the time of our research, however, the president judge still dominated Erie's criminal court community. As one important community member said, "It's a one-horse county. It always has been."

SUMMARY

...The small size and extensive familiarity of the [Erie criminal] court community, which reflected characteristics of the county generally, contributed to the development of an effective grapevine, and to a tradition of informality and accommodation in interpersonal relations. The proximity of major participants in the courthouse facilitated informal interaction and exchange of information.

The principal characteristics of each of the three major sponsoring organizations—the judges, prosecutors, and public defenders—are described in some detail. For each, we look at the age and experience of its members, the content of policies and internal management styles, the degree of cohesion, the structure of attitudes, and the nature of relations with the newspapers, lower-court judges, and others. Comparing attitudes, we found both judges and prosecutors adhering more strongly to a belief in punishment than public defenders did; the judges were surprisingly negative in their regard for due process.

We found tension in relations between the public defender's office on the one hand, and judges and prosecutors on the other. The prosecutors criticized the judges for their lack of hard work, their leniency, and their unwillingness to change the calendar. Continuing a long tradition in Erie county, the judges, and the president judge in particular, exerted the most influence over the operations of the court community.

NOTES

1. *Editor's note:* The nine counties studied by the authors were Erie, Dauphin, and Montgomery counties, Pennsylvania; Kalamazoo, Oakland, and Saginaw counties, Michigan; and DuPage, Peoria, and St. Clair counties, Illinois.

2. *Editor's note:* The "grapevine" is the informal social and communication network found in organizations. It serves the function of providing court community members with information useful in the performance of their jobs. A public defender in Erie told the authors:

> I don't know how it is in other counties, but in this county the courthouse is just the fastest grapevine I've ever seen. If I

fire a secretary at 9 o'clock, the whole courthouse knows about it by 9:30.

3. Prosecutors could propose to the court that offenders without a serious prior criminal record arrested for a minor offense could be placed on ARD. Prosecution was deferred, and if the defendant fulfilled the conditions set forth, such as attending classes and avoiding subsequent arrest, the case was dropped and the defendant had no conviction added to his or her record.

15

The Process Is
the Punishment

Handling Cases in
a Lower Criminal Court

Malcolm M. Feeley

Many observers of the lower criminal courts are struck by the fact that the sentences seem to be so lenient. Malcolm Feeley's study of the Court of Common Pleas, New Haven, Connecticut, shows that the punishment given out by the judge is not the only cost imposed by the criminal justice system.

This article develops the argument that in the lower criminal courts the process itself is the primary punishment. I identify the costs involved in the pretrial process and examine the ways they affect the organization, as well as the way a defendant will proceed on his journey through the court. This examination should help explain why lower courts do not fit their popular image, and why cases are processed so quickly in the Court of Common Pleas, New Haven, Connecticut.

INTRODUCTION

The first set of factors I examine deals with the consequences of pretrial detention and the problems of securing pretrial release. The second explores the costs of securing an attorney. There are obvious financial outlays involved in retaining a private attorney, but there are also hidden costs associated with

Source: Malcolm M. Feeley, *The Process Is the Punishment* (New York: Russell Sage, 1971), pp. 199–243. Copyright © 1979 Russell Sage Foundation. References deleted. Reprinted by permission.

obtaining free counsel. A third set of factors deals with the problem of continuances. While delay often benefits the defendant, its importance for the defendant is often exaggerated, and it is crucial to distinguish defendant-induced delay from continuances which are arranged for the convenience of the court.

By themselves these costs may appear to be minor or even trivial in a process formally structured to focus on the crucial questions of adjudication and sentencing. However, in the aggregate, and in comparison with the actual consequences of adjudication and sentencing, they often loom large in the eyes of the criminally accused, and emerge as central concerns in getting through the criminal justice system.

These pretrial costs account for a number of puzzling phenomena: why so many people waive their right to free appointed counsel; why so many people do not show up for court at all; and why people choose the available adversarial options so infrequently. Furthermore, pretrial costs are part of the reason why pretrial diversion programs designed to *benefit* defendants and provide alternatives to standard adjudication do not receive a more enthusiastic response. The accused often perceive these programs as cumbersome processes which simply increase their contact with the system.

The relative importance of the pretrial process hinges on one important set of considerations. Students of the criminal courts often overlook what many criminologists and students of social class do not, that the fear of arrest and conviction does not loom as large in the eyes of many people brought into court as it does in the eyes of middle-class researchers. While I did not systematically interview a sample of defendants, I had informal and often extended discussions with dozens of defendants who were waiting for their cases to be called, and I watched still more discuss their cases with attorneys and prosecutors. While there were obvious and numerous exceptions, I was nevertheless struck by the frequent lack of concern about the stigma of conviction and by the more practical and far more immediate concerns about what the sentence would be and how quickly they could get out of court.

There are several reasons for this. First, many arrestees already have criminal records, so that whatever stigma does attach to a conviction is already eroded, if not destroyed.[1] Second, many arrestees, particularly young ones, are part of a subculture which spurns conventional values and for which arrest and conviction may even function as a celebratory ritual, reinforcing their own values and identity. In fact, they may even perceive it as part of the process of coming of age.[2] Third, lower-class people tend to be more *present*-oriented than middle-class people, and for obvious reasons.[3] Many defendants are faced with an immediate concern for returning to work or their children, and these concerns often take precedence over the desire to avoid the *remote* consequences that a (or another) conviction might bring. This *relative* lack of concern about conviction is reinforced by the type of employment opportunities available to lower-class defendants. If an employee is reliable, it may make little difference whether or not he pleads guilty to a minor charge emerging from a "Saturday night escapade." Indeed, an employer is not likely to find out about the incident unless his employee has to arrange to miss work in order to appear in court.

If the stigma of the criminal sanction is not viewed as a significant sanction, the concrete costs of the pretrial process take on great significance. When this occurs, the process itself becomes the punishment.

PRETRIAL RELEASE: AN OVERVIEW

A quick reading of relevant Connecticut statutes, case law, and administrative directives conveys the impression that the state has an unswerving commitment to prompt pretrial release. There is an elaborate multi-layered system for decision and review, there are a variety of pretrial release alternatives, and assurance of appearance at trial is the sole criterion for establishing release conditions.

The police are empowered to make the initial release decision and can either release a suspect at the site of the arrest or take him to the central booking facility. Once the suspect is booked, police retain the power to establish release conditions, and they may release suspects on a written promise to appear (PTA) or on bond, which they set. If they do not release the arrestee, at this point, the police are then required to notify a bail commissioner who in turn is supposed to "promptly conduct [an] interview and investigation as he deems necessary to reach an independent decision." If after this the accused is still not released, then the bail commissioner "shall set forth his reasons . . . in writing."[4] The accused has a third opportunity to seek release at arraignment and all subsequent appearances, at which time he can request the judge to consider a bond reduction or release on PTA.

This liberal release policy is reflected in practice as well. Table 1 indicates that 89 percent of those arrested were released prior to the disposition of their cases, and that 52 percent of them were released on nonfinancial conditions, by police field citation or PTA. Thirty-seven percent were released on bond, and only 11 percent were detained until disposition. Although the proportion of arrestees released pending trial is typically regarded as the most important measure of a jurisdiction's "liberality," it is far from a complete picture. Two additional questions must be answered. First, at what point in the process do people secure release? To identify as "released" only those who were free at the time their cases were disposed of is to overlook those who were held in detention for a while before eventually securing release. And if a person is released on bail, at what price was freedom purchased?

Length of Time in Pretrial Custody

Table 2 provides a breakdown of the length of time defendants in my sample were in custody before being released. Seventeen percent were released almost immediately on police citations. A much larger group—43 percent—was released within three hours after being taken to the "lockup," and a third group

Table 1 Release Detention Rates

Condition Immediately Prior to Disposition	N	%
Released on Citation	244	16%
Released on PTA	565	36
Released on Bond	567	37
(Subtotal released)	(1376)	(89%)
Detained	166	11
TOTAL	1542	100%

Table 2 Length of Time in Pretrial Detention

Length of Time	N	%
none	244	17%
0–3 hours	624	43
4–7 hours	82	6
8–12 hours	92	6
13–24 hours	308	21
2 days	31	2
3 days	10	1
4–7 days	12	1
8–20 days	18	1
over 20 days	17	1
	1438	99%*

*Rounding error.

was released within a period of thirteen to twenty-four hours after arrest. Many of the people in this group were released in court the morning after their arrest, at which time they were able to secure reductions in the amount of bond or contact a bondsman or family member to post bond; some pleaded guilty and were discharged from custody. However, 6 percent of the sample remained in pretrial custody for a period of two days or longer, and a small number were held three weeks or more.

• • •

Other arrestees secure delayed release because the lockup facility becomes overcrowded. On Saturday evenings police may "weed out" the lockup by granting PTA's to Friday evening's arrestees in order to make room for new arrivals. Women are housed in a separate facility in another location and are generally more likely to be released earlier on lower bond.

• • •

PRETRIAL RELEASE: PROCESS

The Role of the Police

Although most students of the pretrial process focus on judicial bail setting at arraignment, their observations may often miss the mark, since in many jurisdictions—including New Haven—the bulk of the pretrial release decisions is made by other people before the accused is ever presented in court. In New Haven it is not the judge or the bail commissioner who dominates the release process, but rather the police. They are responsible not only for arresting and charging suspects, but also for releasing them before a trial. A number of observers have commented that Connecticut in general, and New Haven in particular, has liberal policies on pretrial release. They attribute these to the multi-layered system of decision and review, and the existence of bail commissioners. But in fact one cannot attribute these practices directly to this elaborate system. In fact, they probably have more to do with the intuitive judgments of the initial decision makers, the police.

Unless a suspect is released on a field citation at the site of an arrest, the arresting officer takes him to the central booking facility. After the booking, the officer is required by departmental order to complete a detailed bail interview form which seeks information about the arrestee's ties to the community and other factors on which the release decision is to be based. The form also provides a space for reasons if the arrestee should not be released. Rarely is there anything that might be characterized as an "interview." Only occasionally is the bail interview form completed in detail, and whatever information it does record is likely to have been filled in *after* a release decision has already been made. While different officers have different practices, most of them require little more than the accused's name, address, and the charges being pressed before making a decision to release on PTA or a small bond.

If the charges are more serious, or if the arrestee has a prior record of arrests or failure to appear (and well over 50 percent do), then the officer may insist on a bond. In setting its amount, he often consults a "bail schedule." This document, prepared by the Judicial Department and adopted by a resolution of all Circuit Court judges in 1967, specifies a monetary amount for each type of charge, and provides for "discounts," depending upon the accused's ties to the community.

Although officers setting the conditions of release must complete a section of the bail interview form which calls for a statement of reasons if an arrestee is not released immediately, this section is rarely filled out. In my review of over 100 bail interview forms for people who were not immediately released, only a handful—15 or so—had this section completed. Only occasionally did they specify that the arrestee was a "poor risk" because he had no local address, or because he had a record of failures to appear. Most of the reasons related instead to the police officer's perception of the arrestee's condition, which was often characterized as "abusive," "threatening," or "wants to return to the incident," reasons which encouraged them to favor immediate situational justice or specific deterrence.

These officers are often in a dilemma. They are agents of the community, expected to enforce the law and make arrests. But then they must immediately turn around and release those very people whom they have just apprehended and arrested. It is not surprising that the tensions produced by these conflicting roles place a strain in the formal rules these people are charged with applying, and that they have taken advantage of the lax enforcement of the law to pursue their own conceptions of rough justice. Occasionally they use this detention power arbitrarily to administer their own system of punishment. Often they fear that an arrestee will return to a fight if he is released, so that they purposefully set bail beyond the arrestee's means in order to detain him until they think he has calmed down. The statutes on release make no provision for this latter concern, and the police can pursue it only by ignoring the literal letter of the law. But in bending the law in this "reasonable" direction, the door is opened for justifications to bend it for other, less benign reasons. Police may impose situational sanctions on arrestees whom they think deserve to "sit in jail for a time" because the courts will just "let them out."

$$\bullet\ \bullet\ \bullet$$

SECURING AN ATTORNEY

A person accused of a criminal offense must decide whether or not to obtain an attorney. This seemingly simple choice in fact involves a complex set of decisions: whether or not to get a lawyer; and who to get, a public defender or a private attorney; if a private attorney, then which one? The decision is confusing and costly in terms of both time and money.

Private Counsel

Unless an arrestee has had prior experience with a particular lawyer and has been satisfied, he is confused about what to do, whom to call, if anyone, how much it will cost him, and whether the amount is reasonable. He is overly suspicious and afraid of being taken advantage of. Some arrestees will call an attorney with whose name he or his friends are familiar. Others may turn to other inmates or their captors—the police—for advice, or perhaps to a bondsman. Still others, fearful of the expense, decide to do without representation.

If the arrestee telephones an attorney from the lockup, the attorney is likely to ask him a few questions about the charges, then ask to speak to the police officer in charge or contact a bail commissioner in an effort to get the bond lowered to an amount the arrestee can make. After this he may contact a bondsman. If the arrestee secures his release before arraignment, the case is scheduled for a week or two later, and in the interim the attorney will arrange an appointment with his caller. If the arrestee is not released, the attorney will try to meet his prospective client just before arraignment in order to argue for bail reduction and afterward hold a brief conference to discuss financial terms and the case.

It is important that an attorney assess his would-be client's ability to pay early on; once he has begun to represent a defendant, he is bound by the canon of ethics to continue his representation until disposition. While it is possible to withdraw later from the case, it can be awkward and embarrassing. Most attorneys can relate instances of being "taken" by clients, and the result is a rather hardnosed approach to fees, even among the more liberal "client-oriented" attorneys who are frequently young, not well-established, and in particular need of the income.

Fees and billing practices vary widely from attorney to attorney and from case to case. Most private attorneys expect an initial retainer based on their own assessment of the "worth of the case." As one private attorney observed:

> I want to get enough at the outset, so that if I don't get any more out of the case, I won't get burned. This amount varies. For instance, I told a guy it would cost a minimum of five hundred to take his case—it was a messy child-molesting thing—and perhaps more, but that I wanted five hundred dollars to begin with. He later called and said he could come up with three hundred, and I said I would take it. So now, even if he can't pay, I won't get burned too badly. . . . I suppose as I pick up business, I'll have to get tougher on this, but now I need the business and will take the chances. On a routine breach [of peace], or disorderly [conduct], I might very well take fifty dollars.

Although most attorneys bill clients based on the amount of time they spend—or say they spend—on a case (and all things being equal, they feel that the type of charge provides a rough indication of this), they also adjust this amount according to their assessment of their client's ability to pay. Some attorneys are critical of such billing practices, but those who use them claim that they allow the better-off to subsidize the less fortunate.

Some attorneys have experimented with a flat fee for a case, which in one small firm is $300 for a case in the lower court and $1,000 for a case in upper court. But this means that those people whose cases are disposed of quickly after only one or two court appearances pay an extremely high per hour or per appearance cost, while those whose cases require considerable research, investigation, court appearances, or a trial get a real bargain.

• • •

Public Defenders

In order to obtain a public defender a person must be poor. There are rather rigid guidelines for eligibility, but they are not strictly adhered to, and in fact most arrestees who apply for a PD routinely obtain one. There are several reasons for this. Perhaps most important is the prevailing belief among prosecutors, public defenders, and most judges that the formal guidelines are overly restrictive, and that by denying a person *free* counsel they are in effect denying him *any* counsel. As a consequence they may overlook an income ceiling or an obvious undervaluing of personal assets. Although some judges occasionally suggest it, few in fact seriously expect an applicant to sell his five-year-old automobile in order to raise an attorney's fee.

A second reason is the drive for administrative efficiency. The application form requires detailed information about the applicant's financial condition, and to verify all of it would require more effort than the PD is willing to extend in most cases. The PD's staff finds it far easier to take the partial information at face value and recommend assignment of a PD knowing that errors will be made. They justified this by arguing that it might permit a few more people to have a PD than deserve one, but at least it does not exclude those who do. In addition, PDs are reluctant to question or challenge ambiguous or inconsistent answers about income and assets, feeling that to do so would create an atmosphere of suspicion and hostility, and undercut their ability to gain the full confidence of their clients.

But it can still be difficult to obtain an attorney. In court, the prosecutor's first question to an unrepresented defendant is: "Do you want to get your own attorney, apply for a public defender, or get your case over with today?" The very way the question is phrased encourages people *not* to seek counsel, and suggests preferential treatment if they plead guilty immediately. If someone asks for a PD, then he is shunted off for an interview to determine his eligibility, and the interview itself can become a humiliating experience.

• • •

In light of the consistently lenient sentences and the casual way in which so many cases linger on, it is understandable why many defendants do not obtain attorneys—public or private—at all, and when they do, why so many of them desire little more than a quick and perfunctory meeting with their attorneys.

CONTINUANCES

Although defendants usually want to get their cases over with as quickly as possible, they are not always successful. The court has its own pace, which is often at odds with the defendant's self-interest. Defense attorneys and prosecutors usually turn (or return) their attentions to a case on the morning it is scheduled on the calendar, and if they are not able to resolve any differences before the calendar call, they will agree to a (or another) continuance. Problems which impede the resolution of a case can vary considerably, and a great many continuations stem from confusion and carelessness. A defense attorney may have overcommitted himself on that day, or in a more difficult case be unwilling to spend a few additional moments to track down a full-time prosecutor. Occasionally a defendant may appear in court only to find that his case is not on the calendar. Or the defense attorney may forget to show up. A court-ordered report such as a laboratory report on drugs may not have been completed, or a defendant's file may simply be lost. Whatever the reasons for delay, it may be two or three hours after the defendant has first taken his seat in the gallery before he is informed that his case will be continued. Rarely is this decision made in consultation with him or even with an appreciation of the problems it might involve for him. Unable to comprehend the details of court operations, most defendants are overwhelmed by the details of the processes. Rarely can they distinguish reasonable from unreasonable, careful from careless decisions, and they are left with generalized discontent and haunting suspicions.

But delay is not always the result of bumbling, and it is often a highly effective defense strategy. As one attorney observed:

> We can make life difficult for the prosecutors by filing a lot of motions. . . . So when I push a legalistic line I am not expecting to have a complicated legal discourse; rather it's part of my ammunition to secure my objectives. They know I'm serious and that I'll spend a lot of time to pursue it. I'll wear them down that way.

Motions may be filed one at a time, so that a case may be strung out over a long period. Strategic delay can also be secured by pleading not guilty and asking for a trial by jury. This request automatically provides a several-week (and at times a several-month) continuance, during which period the complainant may calm down or restitution can be arranged.

Because delay can be and often is an effective defense strategy, it can also be used successfully by a defense attorney to justify his own carelessness or actions performed for the sake of convenience. While public defenders may use it to cope with a pressing caseload, private attorneys may use it to boost their own fees or insure payment. In any case, all but the most knowledgeable of defendants will be unable to identify the *real* reasons for delay.

FAILURE TO APPEAR

The Causes of Nonappearance

For many arrestees the central question is not how to maneuver to reduce the chances of conviction, a harsh sentence, or the number of court appearances, but whether to show up in court at all. This consideration is not restricted to a small handful of "absconders" or would-be absconders; it concerns large numbers of arrestees. Roughly one-third of those in my sample missed one or more of their scheduled court appearances, and a substantial number (one person in five) never did return to court even after they received repeated letters of warning. While a number of these people had their cases terminated by a court action which called for a "bond forfeiture with no further action," about one in every eight or nine cases was never formally resolved by the court in any way, and are filed as outstanding, closed only if and when the accused is arrested on other unrelated charges. Most of those who fail to appear (FTA) are charged with minor misdemeanors, but the problem is by no means restricted to them. A third of the FTAs were charged with the most serious class of misdemeanors, and fully 20 percent of them were charged with felonies. Both in terms of absolute numbers and the seriousness of the charges, failures to appear present a serious and continuing problem for the court.

• • •

Like other efforts, mine to identify predictors of appearance/nonappearance focused on characteristics of *individual* defendants. Yet the discussion above suggests that the label FTA itself is problematic because it depends in part on whether a bondsman is present in court to secure a continuance and whether a prosecutor is willing to make accommodations for those who step out of the courtroom momentarily. Furthermore, by focusing on the *personal* characteristics of the defendant we overlook the importance of *organizational features* in the court which may encourage nonappearance. People without attorneys may *show up* in court with the same frequency as those with attorneys, but because their cases are not called until late in the day some of them give up and go home, either because they are bored and irritated or because they think a recess is an adjournment. My observations of the court lead me to believe that nonappearance is more likely to be accounted for in terms of how well defendants understand the operations of the court (for example, are they in the correct courtroom?), how much respect they have for the court, how seriously they take the proceedings, how aware they are of their scheduled court appearances, and what they believe the consequences will be if they fail to appear. In other words, the *interaction between the court organization and the accused* is likely to provide the best explanation for appearance or nonappearance.

PRETRIAL DIVERSION

One way for an accused person to reduce the chances of conviction and post-conviction penalty is to make an advance effort to "rehabilitate" himself. There are a variety of ways in which the accused can demonstrate this effort to the court. . . . One way is the Pretrial Diversion Program sponsored by the New Haven Pretrial Services Council. Representatives of this program approach new arrestees who meet its initial eligibility criteria, and offer them an opportunity to participate in its in-house group counseling program or to take advantage of its job placement services. If those who are accepted faithfully participate in these activities for a period of ninety days, then the program will recommend to the prosecutor that the charges be nolled.

Despite the seeming benefits which flow from this program, very few of the eligible arrestees take advantage of it. Estimates constructed from my sample indicated that over three-quarters of all arrestees met the program's *initial* eligibility requirements, but of the 800 eligibles for whom data were available, only 19, or 2.3 percent of them, actually participated in the diversion program. Officials of the diversion program attempt to account for these low numbers by pointing to the prosecutor's discretion to veto prospective participants who are otherwise eligible and interested. While these factors certainly limit the program's size, there is another much more important reason for its limited effectiveness: arrestees consider participation in the program itself a penalty that is much more severe than the one they think they will receive if they do *not* participate.

One evaluation of the program attempted to estimate what might have happened to the program's participants if they had not been "diverted."

Identifying a control group and tracing its path through the court, the researchers found that one-fifth to one-third of the "control group" obtained nolles or dismissals; most of them pleaded guilty and received a small fine of $10 to $20. *None* of them went to jail. In short, they concluded tentatively, those people who are eligible but decline to enter the diversion program are not likely to be treated harshly by the court.

In contrast, people who do participate in the program must agree to participate in regularly scheduled meetings for a three-month period with no definite assurances that their cases will be nolled afterward. It is not surprising, then, that so many people pass up the diversion program.

• • •

CONCLUSION: THE AGGREGATED EFFECTS
OF THE PRETRIAL PROCESS

The figures on pretrial costs presented in the preceding discussion are rough estimates and should not be interpreted as facts. Because they suggest comparisons between groups and costs which are themselves quite different, they must also be interpreted with caution. Still, these figures point to the inescapable conclusion that the costs of lower court—the tangible, direct, and immediate penalties extracted from those accused of minor criminal offenses—are not those factors which have received the greatest attention from legal scholars, social scientists, or indeed court officials. Liberal legal theory directs attention to formal outcomes, to the conditions giving rise to the application of the criminal sanction at adjudication and sentence. Much social science research has followed this lead, searching for the causes of sanctioning at these stages. But this emphasis produces a distorted vision of the process and the sanctions it dispenses. The real punishment for many people is the pretrial process itself; that is why criminally accused invoke so few of the adversarial options available to them.

This inverted system of justice dramatizes the dilemma of lower courts. Expanded procedures designed to improve the criminal process are not invoked because they might be counterproductive. Efforts to slow the process down and make it truly deliberative might lead to still harsher treatment of defendants and still more time loss for complainants and victims. Devices designed to control official discretion do not perform their expected functions (the failure to litigate bail is a clear case-in-point). And whereas rapid and perfunctory practices foster error and caprice, they do reduce pretrial costs and in the aggregate may render rough justice.

In light of the pretrial costs and the actual penalties meted out in the lower court, one is tempted to scoff at the formal theory which so ineffectively governs official behavior in the lower court and to dismiss it as unworkable and overly elegant—as proceduralism run amok—for the types of petty problems presented to the court. Would not simple summary justice with a minimum of procedures provide a more appropriate and workable set of standards? Perhaps the police court magistrate meting out immediate kadi-like justice without reliance on defense counsel—but also without the need for bail, repeated court appearances, and the like—might be more satisfactory. Or perhaps community-based courts might be more adept at ferreting out the underlying causes of conflict and providing ameliorating responses.

In a great many cases these alternatives might work more effectively; yet the impulse for formality, even with its manifest shortcomings, cannot be so quickly dismissed. While lower courts sentence very few people to terms in jail, in theory almost all of those appearing before them face a slim possibility of incarceration. While creating a record of petty criminal offenses may not significantly affect the future of most people who find themselves before the bench, it can have a long-lasting and unpredictable impact on some. Citizenship can be placed in jeopardy, careers destroyed, aspirations dampened, delinquent propensities reinforced. Such problems may be few in number, but they do occur. And it is impossible to tell in advance which cases may precipitate these more serious consequences, since the specific impact of a record may not make itself felt until much later in life.

As long as conviction for petty criminal offenses carries the possibility of a jail sentence or of jeopardizing one's future, the ideal of a formal, adversarial process will remain strong and attractive even to those who acknowledge that the process itself is the punishment for most people. However, there may be some alternatives which both facilitate the rapid handling of petty cases and protect the interests of the accused.

NOTES

1. Over half the arrestees in my sample had a record of prior arrests by the New Haven police, and a large proportion of them had records of conviction. These figures are probably drastically low, however, since local authorities do not systematically obtain records from other jurisdictions, either within or outside the state.

2. Discussions of arrest and conviction frequently assume that arrestees have a great fear of the stigma of a conviction and will go to great lengths to avoid being formally labeled as criminals. But my observations are consistent with the findings of many criminologists who have studied juvenile delinquency and concluded that the disproportionate rate of criminal conduct by young lower-class males stems from a subculture which promotes such activity as a social mechanism for becoming a male adult. Rather than being a brand of inferiority for many lower- and working-class youths, arrest and conviction often reinforce the values of their subculture and can even enhance their status among their peers. This has been noted time and again in the literature on juvenile courts, but altogether overlooked and ignored in "adult" courts. See Walter B. Miller, "Lower Class Culture as a Generating Milieu of Gang Delinquency," *Journal of Social Issues* 14 (1958): 5–19, and Albert K. Cohen, *Delinquent Boys: The Culture of the Gang* (New York: Free Press, 1955). Also see Edwin H. Sutherland and Donald Cressey, *Principles of Criminology,* 7th ed. (Philadelphia: J. B. Lippincott, 1966), pp. 183–199, and Richard Quinney, *The Social Reality of Crime* (Boston: Little, Brown, 1970), pp. 207–276.

3. See Edward Banfield, *The Unheavenly City* (Boston: Little, Brown, 1971), pp. 45–56; and Edward Banfield and James Q. Wilson, "Public Regardingness as a Value Premise in Voting Behavior," *American Political Science Review* 58 (1964): 876–887.

4. Connecticut General Statute 54–63 (C) (A).

16

❂

Maintaining the Myth
of Individualized Justice

Probation
Presentence Reports

John Rosecrance

The presentence investigation has been justified so that judges can individualize sentences to fit the particular circumstances of the offender as well as the offense. In many states probation officers are required to submit presentence reports prior to sentencing in all felony cases. But what is the function of these reports in a system where plea bargaining is so dominant? Is justice really individualized, or are sentence recommendations actually influenced by the administrative context of the system?

The Justice Department estimates that over 1 million probation presentence reports are submitted annually to criminal courts in the United States. The role of probation officers in the presentence process traditionally has been considered important. After examining criminal courts in the United States, a panel of investigators concluded: "Probation officers are attached to most modern felony courts: presentence reports containing their recommendations are commonly provided and these recommendations are usually followed" (Blumstein, Martin, and Holt 1983). Judges view presentence reports as an integral part of sentencing, calling them "the best guide to intelligent sentencing" (Murrah 1963: 67) and "one of the most important developments in criminal law during the twentieth century" (Hogarth 1971: 246).

Source: From John Rosecrance, "Maintaining the Myth of Individualized Justice: Probation Presentence Reports," *Justice Quarterly* 5 (June 1988), pp. 235–256. Footnotes and some references deleted. Reprinted by permission.

Researchers agree that a strong correlation exists between probation recommendations (contained in presentence reports) and judicial sentencing. In a seminal study of judicial decision making, Carter and Wilkins (1967) found 95 percent agreement between probation recommendations and sentence disposition when the officer recommended probation and 88 percent agreement when the officer opposed probation. Hagan (1975), after controlling for related variables, reported a direct correlation of .72 between probation recommendation and sentencing. Walsh (1985) found a similar correlation of .807.

Although there is no controversy about the correlation between probation recommendation and judicial outcome, scholars disagree as to the actual influence of probation officers in the sentencing process. That is, there is no consensus regarding the importance of the presentence investigator in influencing sentencing outcomes. On the one hand, Myers (1979: 538) contends that the "important role played by probation officer recommendation argues for greater theoretical and empirical attention to these officers." Walsh (1985: 303) concludes that "judges lean heavily on the professional advice of probation." On the other hand, Kingsnorth and Rizzo (1979) report that probation recommendations have been supplanted by plea bargaining and that the probation officer is "largely superfluous." Hagan, Hewitt, and Alwin (1979), after reporting a direct correlation between recommendation and sentence, contend that the "influence of the probation officer in the presentence process is subordinate to that of the prosecutor" and that probation involvement is "often ceremonial."

My research builds on the latter perspective and suggests that probation presentence reports do not influence judicial sentencing significantly but serve to maintain the myth that criminal courts dispense individualized justice. On the basis on an analysis of probation practices in California, I will demonstrate that the presentence report, long considered an instrument for the promotion of individualized sentencing by the court, actually de-emphasizes individual characteristics and affirms the primacy of instant offense and prior criminal record as sentencing determinants. The present study was concerned with probation in California; whether its findings can be applied to other jurisdictions is not known. California's probation system is the nation's largest, however, and the experiences of that system could prove instructive to other jurisdictions.

In many California counties (as in other jurisdictions throughout the United States) crowded court calendars, determinate sentencing guidelines, and increasingly conservative philosophies have made it difficult for judges to consider individual offenders' characteristics thoroughly. Thus judges, working in tandem with district attorneys, emphasize the legal variables of offense and criminal record at sentencing. Probation officers function as employees of the court; generally they respond to judicial cues and emphasize similar variables in their presentence investigations. The probation officers' relationship to the court is ancillary; their status in relation to judges and other attorneys is subordinate. This does not mean that probation officers are completely passive; individual styles and personal philosophies influence their reports. Idiosyncratic approaches, however, usually are reserved for a few special cases. The vast majority of "normal" (Sudnow 1965) cases are handled in a manner that follows relatively uniform patterns.

Hughes's (1958) work provides a useful perspective for understanding the relationship between probation officers' status and their presentence duties. According to Hughes, occupational duties within institutions often serve to maintain symbiotic status relationships as those in higher-status positions pass on lesser duties to subordinates. Other researchers (Blumberg 1967; Neubauer 1974; Rosecrance 1985) have demonstrated that although judges may give lip service to the significance of presentence investigations, they remain suspicious of the probation officers' lack of legal training and the hearsay nature of the reports. Walker (1985) maintains that in highly visible cases judges tend to disregard the probation reports entirely. Thus the judiciary, by delegating the collection of routine information to probation officers, reaffirms its authority and legitimacy. In this context, the responsibility for compiling presentence reports can be considered a "dirty-work" assignment that is devalued by the judiciary. Judges expect probation officers to submit noncontroversial reports that provide a facade of information, accompanied by bottom-line recommendations that do not deviate significantly from a consideration of offense and prior record. The research findings in this paper will show how probation officers work to achieve this goal.

In view of the large number of presentence reports submitted, it is surprising that so little information about the presentence investigation process is available. The factors used in arriving at a sentencing recommendation, the decision to include certain information, and the methods used in collecting data have not been described. The world of presentence investigators has not been explored by social science researchers. We lack research about the officers who prepare presentence reports, and hardly understand how they think and feel about those reports. The organizational dynamics and the status positions that influence presentence investigators have not been identified prominently. In this article I intend to place probation officers' actions within a framework that will increase the existing knowledge of the presentence process. My research is informed by fifteen years of experience as a probation officer, during which time I submitted hundreds of presentence reports.

Although numerous studies of probation practices have been conducted, an ethnographic perspective rarely has been included in this body of research, particularly in regard to research dealing with presentence investigations. Although questionnaire techniques, survey data, and decision-making experiments have provided some information about presentence reports, qualitative data, which often are available only through an insider's perspective, are notably lacking. The subtle strategies and informal practices used routinely in preparing presentence reports often are hidden from outside researchers.

The research findings emphasize the importance of *typing* in the compilation of public documents (presentence reports). In this paper "typing" refers to "the process by which one person (the agent) arrives at a private definition of another (the target)." A related activity, *designating*, occurs when "the typing agent reveals his attributions of the target to others." In the case of presentence investigations, private typings become designations when they are made part of an official court report. I will show that presentence recommendations are developed through a typing process in which individual offenders are subsumed into general dispositional categories. This process is influenced largely by probation officers' perceptions of factors that judicial figures consider appropriate; probation officers are aware that the ultimate purpose of their reports is to please the court. These perceptions are based on prior experience and are reinforced through judicial feedback.

METHODS

The major sources of data used in this study were drawn from interviews with probation officers. Prior experience facilitated my ability to interpret the data. Interviews were conducted in two three-week periods during 1984 and 1985 in two medium-sized California counties. Both jurisdictions were governed by state determinate sentencing policies; in each, the district attorney's office remained active during sentencing and generally offered specific recommendations. I did not conduct a random sample but tried instead to interview all those who compiled adult presentence reports. In the two counties in question, officers who compiled presentence reports did not supervise defendants.

Not all presentence writers agreed to talk with me; they cited busy schedules, lack of interest, or fear that I was a spy for the administration. Even so, I was able to interview thirty-seven presentence investigators, approximately 75 percent of the total number of such employees in the two counties. The officers interviewed included eight women and twenty-nine men with a median age of 38.5 years, whose probation experience ranged from one year to twenty-seven years. Their educational background generally included a bachelor's degree in a liberal arts subject (four had degrees in criminal justice, one in social work). Typically the officers regarded probation work as a "job" rather than a profession. With only a few exceptions, they did not read professional journals or attend probation association conventions.

The respondents generally were supportive of my research and frequently commented that probation work had never been described adequately. My status as a former probation officer enhanced the interview process greatly. Because I could identify with their experiences, officers were candid, and I was able to collect qualitative data that reflected accurately the participants' perspectives. During the interviews I attempted to discover how probation officers conducted their presentence investigations. I wanted to know when a sentencing recommendation was decided, to ascertain which variables influenced a sentencing recommendation decision, and to learn how probation officers defined their role in the sentencing process.

Although the interviews were informal, I asked each of the probation officers the following questions:

1. What steps do you take in compiling a presentence report?
2. What is the first thing you do upon receiving a referral?
3. What do you learn from interviews with the defendant?
4. Which part of the process (in your opinion) is the most important?
5. Who reads your reports?
6. Which part of the report do the judges feel is most important?
7. How do your reports influence the judge?
8. What feedback do you get from the judge, the district attorney, the defense attorney, the defendant, your supervisor?

In addition to interviewing probation officers, I questioned six probation supervisors and seven judges on their views about how presentence reports were conducted.

$$\cdots$$

FINDINGS

In the great majority of presentence investigations, the variables of present offense and prior criminal record determine the probation officer's final sentencing recommendations. The influence of these variables is so dominant that other considerations have minimal influence on probation recommendations. The chief rationale for this approach is "That's the way the judges want it." There are other styles of investigation; some officers attempt to consider factors in the defendant's social history, to reserve sentencing judgment until their investigation is complete, or to interject personal opinions. Elsewhere (Rosecrance 1987), I have developed a typology of presentence investigators that describes individual styles; these types include self-explanatory categories such as hard-liners, bleeding-heart liberals, and team players as well as moss-backs (those who are merely putting in their time) and mavericks (those who strive continually for independence).

All types of probation officers, however, seek to develop credibility with the court. Such reputation building is similar to that reported by McCleary (1978) in his study of parole officers. In order to develop rapport with the court, probation officers must submit reports that facilitate a smooth work flow. Probation officers assume that in the great majority of cases they can accomplish this goal by emphasizing offense and criminal record. Once the officers have established reputations as "producers," they have "earned" the right to some degree of discretion in their reporting. One investigation officer described this process succinctly: "When you've paid your dues, you're allowed some slack." Such discretion, however, is limited to a minority of cases, and in these "deviant" cases probation officers frequently allow social variables to influence their recommendation. In one report an experienced officer recommended probation for a convicted felon with a long prior record because the defendant's father agreed to pay for an intensive drug treatment program. In another case a probation officer decided that a first-time shoplifter had a "very bad attitude" and therefore recommended a stiff jail sentence rather than probation. Although these variations from normal procedure are interesting and important, they should not detract from our examination of an investigation process that is used in most cases.

On the basis of the research data, I found that the following patterns occur with sufficient regularity to be considered "typical." After considering offense and criminal record, probation officers place defendants into categories that represent the eventual court recommendation. This typing process occurs early in the course of presentence inquiry; the balance of the investigation is used to reaffirm the private typings that later will become official designations. In order to clarify the decision-making processes used by probation officers, I will delineate the three stages in a presentence investigation: (1) typing the defendant, (2) gathering further information, and (3) filing the report.

Typing the Defendant

A presentence investigation is initiated when the court orders the probation department to prepare a report of a criminal defendant. Usually the initial court referral contains such information as police reports, charges against the defendant, court proceedings, plea-bargaining agreements (if any), offenses in which the defendant has pleaded or has been found guilty, and the defendant's prior criminal record. Probation officers regard such information as relatively unambiguous and as part of the "official" record. The comment of a presentence investigator reflects the probation officer's perspective on the court referral:

> I consider the information in the court referral hard data. It tells me what I need to know about a case, without a lot of bullshit. I mean the guy has pled guilty to a certain offense—he can't get out of that. He has such and such a prior record—there's no changing that. So much of the stuff we put in these reports is subjective and open to interpretation. It's good to have some solid information.

Armed with information in the court referral, probation officers begin to type the defendants assigned for presentence investigation. Defendants are classified into general types based on possible sentence recommendations: a probation officer's statement indicates that this process begins early in a presentence investigation.

> Bottom line: it's the sentence recommendation that's important. That's what the judges and everybody wants to see. I start thinking about the recommendation as soon as I pick up the court referral. Why wait? The basic facts aren't going to change. Oh, I know some POs will tell you they weigh all the facts before coming up with a recommendation. But that's propaganda—we all start thinking recommendation right from the get-go.

At this stage in the investigation the factors known to probation officers are mainly legally relevant variables. The defendant's unique characteristics and special circumstances generally are unknown at this time. Although probation officers may know the offender's age, sex, and race, the relationship of these variables to the case is not yet apparent.

These initial typings are private definitions based on the officer's experience and knowledge of the court system. On occasion, officers discuss the case informally with their colleagues or supervisors when they are not sure of a particular typing. Until the report is complete, their typing remains a private designation. In most cases the probation officers type defendants by considering the known and relatively irrefutable variables of offense and prior record. Probation officers are convinced that judges and district attorneys are most concerned with that part of their reports. I heard the following comment (or versions thereof) on many occasions: "Judges read the offense section, glance at the prior record, and then flip to the back and see what we recommend." Officers indicated that during informal discussions with judges it was made clear that offense and prior record are the determinants of sentencing in most cases. In some instances judges consider extralegal variables, but the officers indicated that this occurs only in "unusual" cases with "special" circumstances. One such case involved a probation grant for a woman who killed her husband after she had been a victim of spouse battering.

Probation investigators are in regular contact with district attorneys and frequently discuss their investigations with them. In addition, district attorneys seem to have no compunction about calling the probation administration to complain about what they consider an inappropriate recommendation. Investigators agreed unanimously that district attorneys typically dismiss a defendant's social history as "immaterial" and want probation officers to stick to the legal facts.

Using offense and prior record as criteria, probation officers place defendants into dispositional (based on recommendation) types. In describing these types I have retained the terms used by probation officers themselves in the typing process. The following typology is community- (rather than researcher-) designated: (1) deal case, (2) diversion case, (3) joint case, (4) probation case with some jail time, (5) straight probation case. Within each of these dispositional types, probation officers designate the severity of punishment by labeling the case either lightweight or heavy-duty.

A designation of "lightweight" means that the defendant will be accorded some measure of leniency because the offense was minor, because the offender had no prior criminal record, or because the criminal activity (regardless of the penal code violation) was relatively innocuous. Heavy-duty cases receive more severe penalties because the offense, the offender, or the circumstances of the offense are deemed particularly serious. Diversion and straight-probation types generally are considered lightweight, while the majority of joint cases are considered heavy-duty. Cases involving personal violence invariably are designated as heavy-duty. Most misdemeanor cases in which the defendant has no prior criminal record or a relatively minor record are termed lightweight. If the defendant has an extensive criminal record, however, even misdemeanor cases can call for stiff penalties; therefore, such cases are considered heavy-duty.

Certain felony cases can be regarded as lightweight if there was no violence, if the victim's loss was minimal, or if the defendant had no prior convictions. On occasion, even an offense like armed robbery can be considered lightweight. The following example (taken from an actual report) is one such instance: a first-time offender with a simulated gun held up a Seven-Eleven store and then returned to the scene, gave back the money, and asked the store employees to call the police.

The typings are general recommendations; specifics such as terms and conditions of probation or diversion and length of incarceration are worked out later in the investigation. The following discussion will clarify some of the criteria for arriving at a typing.

Deal cases involve situations in which a plea bargain exists. In California, many plea bargains specify specific sentencing stipulations; probation officers rarely recommend dispositions contrary to those stipulated in plea-bargaining agreements. Although probation officers allegedly are free to recommend a sentence different from that contained in the plea bargain, they have learned that such an action is unrealistic (and often counterproductive to their own interests) because judges inevitably uphold the primacy of sentence agreements. The following observation represents the probation officers' view of plea-bargaining deals.

> It's stupid to try and bust a deal. What's the percentage? Who needs the hassle? The judge always honors the deal—after all, he was part of it. Everyone, including the defendant, has already agreed. It's all nice and neat, all wrapped up. We are supposed to rubber-stamp the package—and we do. Everyone is better off that way.

Diversion cases typically involve relatively minor offenses committed by those with no prior record and are considered "a snap" by probation officers. In most cases, those referred for diversion have been screened already by the district attorney's office; the probation investigator merely agrees that they are eligible and therefore should be granted diversionary relief (and eventual dismissal of charges). In rare instances when there has been an oversight and the defendant is ineligible (because of prior criminal convictions), the probation officer informs the court, and criminal proceedings are resumed. Either situation involves minimal decision making by probation officers about what disposition to recommend. Presentence investigators approach diversion cases in a perfunctory, almost mechanical manner.

The last three typings generally refer to cases in which the sentencing recommendations are ambiguous and some decision making is required of probation officers. These types represent the major consequences of criminal sentencing: incarceration and/or probation. Those categorized as joint (prison) cases are denied probation; instead the investigator recommends an appropriate prison sentence. In certain instances the nature of the offense (for example, rape, murder, or arson) renders defendants legally ineligible for probation. In other situations, the defendants' prior record (especially felony convictions) makes it impossible to grant probation. In many cases the length of prison sentences has been set by legal statute and can be increased or decreased only marginally (depending on the aggravating or mitigating circumstances of the case).

In California, the majority of defendants sentenced to prison receive a middle term (between minimum and maximum); the length of time varies with the offense. Those cases that fall outside the middle term usually do so for reasons related to the offense (for example, using a weapon) or to the criminal record (prior felony convictions, or, conversely, no prior criminal record). Those typed originally as joint cases are treated differently from other probation applicants: concerns with rehabilitation or with the defendant's life situation are no longer relevant, and proper punishment becomes the focal point of inquiry. This perspective was described as follows by a probation officer respondent: "Once I know so-and-so is a heavy-duty joint case I don't think in terms of rehabilitation or social planning. It becomes a matter of how long to salt the sucker away, and that's covered by the code."

For those who are typed as probation cases, the issue for the investigator becomes whether to recommend some time in jail as a condition of probation. This decision is made with reference to whether the case is lightweight or heavy-duty. Straight probation usually is reserved for those convicted of relatively innocuous offenses or for those without a prior criminal record (first-timers). Some probation officers admitted candidly that all things being equal, middle-class defendants are more likely than other social classes to receive straight probation. The split sentence (probation and jail time) has become popular and is a consideration in most misdemeanor and felony cases, especially when the defendant has a prior criminal record. In addition, there is a feeling that drug offenders should receive a jail sentence as part of probation to deter them from future drug use.

Once a probation officer has decided that "some jail time is in order," the ultimate recommendation includes that condition. Although the actual amount of time frequently is determined late in the case, the probation officer's opinion that a jail sentence should be imposed remains constant. The following comment typifies the sentiments of probation officers whom I have observed and also illustrates the imprecision of recommending a period of time in custody:

> It's not hard to figure out who needs some jail. The referral sheet can tell you that. What's hard to know is exactly how much time. Ninety days or six months—who knows what's fair? We put down some number but it is usually an arbitrary figure. No one has come up with a chart that correlates rehabilitation with jail time.

Compiling Further Information

Once an initial typing has been completed, the next investigative stage involves collecting further information about the defendant. During this stage most of the data to be collected consists of extralegal considerations. The defendant is interviewed and his or her social history is delineated. Probation officers frequently contact collateral sources such as school officials, victims, doctors, counselors, and relatives to learn more about the defendant's individual circumstances. This aspect of the presentence investigation involves considerable time and effort on the part of probation officers. Such information is gathered primarily to legitimate earlier probation officer typings or to satisfy judicial requirements; recommendations seldom are changed during this stage. A similar pattern was described by a presentence investigator:

> Interviewing these defendants and working up a social history takes time. In most cases it's really unnecessary since I've already decided what I am going to do. We all know that a recommendation is governed by the offense and prior record. All the rest is just stuffing to fill out the court report, to make the judge look like he's got all the facts.

Presentence interviews with defendants (a required part of the investigation) frequently are routine interactions that were described by a probation officer as "anticlimactic." These interviews invariably are conducted in settings familiar to probation officers, such as jail interviewing rooms or probation department offices. Because the participants lack trust in each other, discussions rarely are candid and open. Probation officers are afraid of being conned or manipulated because they assume that defendants "will say anything to save themselves." Defendants are trying to present themselves in a favorable light and are wary of divulging any information that might be used against them.

It is assumed implicitly in the interview process that probation officers act as interrogators and defendants as respondents. Because presentence investigators select the questions, they control the course of the interview and elicit the kind of responses that serve to substantiate their original defendant typings. A probationer described his presentence interview to me as follows:

> I knew what the PO wanted me to say. She had me pegged as a nice middle-class kid who had fallen in with a bad crowd. So that's how I came off. I was contrite, a real boy scout who had learned his lesson. What an acting job! I figured if I didn't act up I'd get probation.

A probation officer related how she conducted presentence interviews:

> I'm always in charge during the interviews. I know what questions to ask in order to fill out my report. The defendants respond just about the way I expect them to. They hardly ever surprise me.

On occasion, prospective probationers refuse to go along with structured presentence interviews. Some offenders either attempt to control the interview or are openly hostile to probation officers. Defendants who try to dominate interviews often can be dissuaded by reminders such as "I don't think you really appreciate the seriousness of your situation" or "I'm the one who asks the questions here." Some defendants, however, show blatant disrespect for the court process by flaunting a disregard for possible sanctions.

Most probation officers have interviewed some defendants who simply don't seem to care what happens to them. A defendant once informed an investigation officer: "I don't give a fuck what you motherfuckers try and do to me. I'm going to do what I fuckin' well please. Take your probation and stick it." Another defendant told her probation officer: "I'm going to shoot up every chance I get. I need my fix more than I need probation." Probation officers categorize belligerent defendants and those unwilling to "play the probation game" as dangerous or irrational. Frequently in these situations the investigator's initial typing is no longer valid, and probation either will be denied or will be structured stringently. Most interviews, however, proceed in a predictable manner as probation officers collect information that will be included in the section of the report termed "defendant's statement."

Although some defendants submit written comments, most of their statements actually are formulated by the probation officer. In a sociological sense, the defendant's statement can be considered an "account." While conducting presentence interviews, probation officers typically attempt to shape the defendant's account to fit their own preconceived typing. Many probation officers believe that the defendant's attitude toward the offense and toward the future prospects for leading a law-abiding life are the most important parts of the statement. In most presentence investigations the probation investigator identifies and interprets the defendant's subjective attitudes and then incorporates them into the report. Using this procedure, probation officers look for and can report attitudes that "logically fit" with their final sentencing recommendation.

Defendants who have been typed as prison cases typically are portrayed as holding socially unacceptable attitudes about their criminal actions and unrealistic or negative attitudes about future prospects for living an upright life. Conversely, those who have been typed as probation material are described as having acceptable attitudes, such as contriteness about the present offense and optimism about their ability to lead a crime-free life. The structuring of accounts about defendant attitudes was described by a presentence investigator in the following manner:

> When POs talk about the defendant's attitude we really mean how that attitude relates to the case. Naturally I'm not going to write about what a wonderful attitude the guy has—how sincere he seems—and then recommend sending him to the joint. That wouldn't make sense. The judges want consistency. If a guy has a shitty attitude but is going to get probation anyway, there's no percentage in playing up his probation problem.

In most cases the presentence interview is the only contact between the investigating officer and the defendant. The brevity of this contact and the lack of postreport interaction foster a legalistic perspective. Investigators are concerned mainly with "getting the case through court" rather than with special problems related to supervising probationers on a long-term basis. One-time-only interviews rarely allow probation officers to become emotionally involved with their cases; the personal and individual aspects of the defendant's personality generally are not manifested during a half-hour presentence interview. For many probation officers the emotional distance from offenders is one of the benefits of working in presentence units. Such an opinion was expressed by an investigation officer: "I really like the one-shot-only part of this job. I don't have time to get caught up with the clients. I can deal with facts and not worry about individual personalities."

The probation officer has wide discretion in the type of collateral information that is collected from sources other than the defendant or the official record. Although a defendant's social history must be sketched in the presentence report, the supplementation of that history is left to individual investigators. There are few established guidelines for the investigating officer to follow, except that the psychiatric or psychological reports should be submitted when there is compelling evidence that the offender is mentally disturbed. Informal guidelines, however, specify that in misdemeanor cases reports should be shorter and more concise than in felony cases. The officers indicated that reports for municipal court (all misdemeanor cases) should range from four to six pages in length, while superior court reports (felony cases) were expected to be six to nine pages long. In controversial cases (to which only the most experienced officers are assigned) presentence reports are expected to be longer and to include considerable social data. Reports in these cases have been as long as thirty pages.

Although probation officers learn what general types of information to include through experience and feedback from judges and supervisors, they are allowed considerable leeway in deciding exactly what to put in their reports (outside of the offense and prior-record sections). Because investigators decide what collateral sources are germane to the case, they tend to include information that will reflect favorably on their sentencing recommendation. In this context the observation of one probation officer is understandable: "I pick from the mass of possible sources just which ones to put in the report. Do you think I'm going to pick people who make my recommendation look weak? No way!"

Filing the Report

The final stage in the investigation includes dictating the report, having it approved by a probation supervisor, and appearing in court. All three of these activities serve to reinforce the importance of prior record and offense in sentencing recommendations. At the time of dictation, probation officers determine what to include in the report and how to phrase their remarks. For the first time in the investigation, they receive formal feedback from official sources. Presentence reports are read by three groups important to the probation officers: probation supervisors, district attorneys, and judges. Probation officers recognize that for varying reasons, all these groups emphasize the legally relevant variables of offense and prior criminal record when considering an appropriate sentencing recommendation. Such considerations reaffirm the probation officer's initial private typing.

A probation investigator described this process:

> After I've talked to the defendants I think maybe some of them deserve to get special consideration. But then I remember who's going to look at the reports. My supervisor, the DA, the judge; they don't care about all the

personal details. When all is said and done, what's really important to them is the offense and the defendant's prior record. I know that stuff from the start. It makes me wonder why we have to jack ourselves around to do long reports.

Probation officers assume that their credibility as presentence investigators will be enhanced if their sentencing recommendations meet with the approval of probation supervisors, district attorneys, and judges. On the other hand, officers whose recommendations are consistently "out of line" are subject to censure or transfer, or they find themselves engaged in "running battles" with court officials. During the last stage of the investigation probation officers must consider how to ensure that their reports will go through court without "undue personal hassle." Most investigation officers have learned that presentence recommendations based on a consideration of prior record and offense can achieve that goal.

Although occupational self-interest is an important component in deciding how to conduct a presentence investigation, other factors are also involved. Many probation officers agree with the idea of using legally relevant variables as determinants of recommendations. These officers embrace the retributive value of this concept and see it as an equitable method for framing their investigation. Other officers reported that probation officers' discretion had been "short-circuited" by determinate sentencing guidelines and that they were reduced to "merely going through the motions" in conducting their investigations. Still other officers view the use of legal variables to structure recommendations as an acceptable bureaucratic shortcut to compensate partially for large case assignments. One probation officer stated, "If the department wants us to keep pumping out presentence reports we can't consider social factors—we just don't have time." Although probation officers are influenced by various dynamics, there seems little doubt that in California, the social history that once was considered the "heart and soul" of presentence probation reports has been largely devalued.

SUMMARY AND CONCLUSIONS

In this study I provide a description and an analysis of the processes used by probation investigators in preparing presentence reports. The research findings based on interview data indicate that probation officers tend to de-emphasize individual defendants' characteristics and that their probation recommendations are not influenced directly by factors such as sex, age, race, socioeconomic status, or work record. Instead, probation officers emphasize the variables of instant offense and prior criminal record. The finding that offense and prior record are the main considerations of probation officers with regard to sentence recommendations agrees with a substantial body of research.

My particular contribution has been to supply the ethnographic observations and the data that explain this phenomenon. I have identified the process whereby offense and prior record come to occupy the central role in decision making by probation officers. This identification underscores the significance of private typings in determining official designations. An analysis of probation practices suggests that the function of the presentence investigation is more ceremonial than instrumental.

I show that early in the investigation probation officers, using offense and prior record as guidelines, classify defendants into types; when the typing process is complete, probation officers essentially have decided on the sentence recommendation that will be recorded later in their official designation. The subsequent course of investigations is determined largely by this initial private typing. Further data collection is influenced by a sentence recommendation that already has been firmly established. This finding answers affirmatively the research question posed by Carter (1967: 211):

> Do probation officers, after "deciding" on a recommendation early in the presentence investigation, seek further information which justifies the decision, rather than information which might lead to modification or rejection of that recommendation?

The type of information and observation contained in the final presentence report is generated to support the original recommendation decision. Probation officers do not regard defendant typings as tentative hypotheses to be disproved through inquiry but rather as firm conclusions to be justified in the body of the report.

Although the presentence interview has been considered an important part of the investigation, I demonstrate that it does not significantly alter probation officers' perceptions. In most cases probation officers dominate presentence interviews; interaction between the participants is guarded. The nature of interviews between defendants and probation officers is important in itself; further research is needed to identify the dynamics that prevail in these interactions.

Attitudes attributed to defendants often are structured by probation officers to reaffirm the recommendation already formulated. The defendant's social history, long considered an integral part of the presentence report, in reality has little bearing on sentencing considerations. In most cases the presentence is no longer a vehicle for social inquiry but rather a typing process that considers mainly the defendant's prior criminal record and the seriousness of the criminal offense. Private attorneys in growing numbers have become disenchanted with the quality of probation investigations and have commissioned presentence probation reports privately. At present, however, such a practice is generally available only for wealthy defendants.

The presentence process that I have described is used in the great majority of cases: it is the "normal" procedure. Even so, probation officers are not entirely passive actors in this process. On occasion they will give serious consideration to social variables in arriving at a sentencing recommendation. In special circumstances officers will allow individual defendants' characteristics to influence their report. In addition, probation officers who have developed credibility with the court are allowed some discretion in compiling presentence reports. This discretion is not unlimited, however; it is based on a prior record of producing reports that meet the court's approval, and is contingent on continuing to do so. A presentence writer said, "You can only afford to go to bar for defendants in a few select cases; if you try to do it too much, you get a reputation as being 'out of step.'"

This research raises the issue of probation officers' autonomy. Although I depict presentence investigators as having limited autonomy, other researchers contend that probation officers have considerable leeway in recommendation. This contradictory evidence can be explained in large part by the type of sentencing structure, the professionalism of probation workers, and the role of the district attorney at sentencing. Walsh's study (1985), for example, which views probation officers as important actors in the presentence process, was conducted in a jurisdiction with indeterminate sentencing, where the probation officers demonstrated a high degree of professionalism and the prosecutors "rarely made sentencing recommendations." A very different situation existed in the California counties that I studied: determinate sentencing was enforced, probation officers were not organized professionally, and the district attorneys routinely made specific court recommendations. It seems apparent that probation officers' autonomy must be considered with reference to judicial jurisdiction.

In view of the primacy of offense and prior record in sentencing considerations, the efficacy of current presentence investigation practices is doubtful. It seems ineffective and wasteful to continue to collect a mass of social data of uncertain relevance. Yet an analysis of courtroom culture suggests that the presentence investigation helps maintain judicial mythology as well as probation officer legitimacy. Although judges generally do not have the time or the inclination to consider individual variables thoroughly, the performance of a presentence investigation perpetuates the myth of individualized sentences. Including a presentence report in the court file gives the appearance of individualization without influencing sentencing practices significantly.

Even in a state like California, where determinate sentencing allegedly has replaced individualized justice, the judicial system feels obligated to maintain the appearance of individualization. After observing the court system in California for several years, I am convinced that a major reason for maintaining such a practice is to make it easier for criminal defendants to accept their sentences. The presentence report allows defendants to feel that their case at least has received a considered decision. One judge admitted candidly that the "real purpose" of the presentence investigation was to convince defendants that they were not getting "the fast shuffle." He observed further that if defendants were sentenced without such investigations, many would complain and would file "endless appeals" over what seems to them a hasty sentencing decision. Even though judges typically consider only offense and prior record in a sentencing decision, they want defendants to believe that their cases are being judged individually. The presentence investigation allows this assumption to be maintained. In addition, some judges use the probation officer's report as an excuse for a particular type of sentence. In some instances they deny responsibility for the sentence, implying that their "hands were tied" by the recommendation. Thus judges are taken "off the hook" for meting out an unpopular sentence. Further research is needed to substantiate the significance of these latent functions of the presentence investigation.

The presentence report is a major component in the legitimacy of the probation movement; several factors support the probation officers' stake in maintaining their role in these investigations. Historically, probation has been wedded to the concept of individualized treatment. In theory, the presentence report is suited ideally to reporting on defendants' individual circumstances. From a historical perspective this ideal has always been more symbolic than substantive, but if the legitimacy of the presentence report is questioned, so then is the entire purpose of probation.

Regardless of its usefulness (or lack of usefulness), it is doubtful that probation officials would consider the diminution or abolition of presentence reports. The number of probation workers assigned to presentence investigations is substantial, and their numbers represent an obvious source of bureaucratic power. Conducting presentence investigations allows probation officers to remain visible with the court and the public. The media often report on controversial probation cases, and presentence writers generally have more contact and more association with judges than do others in the probation department.

As ancillary court workers, probation officers are assigned the dirty work of collecting largely irrelevant data on offenders. Investigation officers have learned that emphasizing offense and prior record in their reports will enhance relationships with judges and district attorneys, as well as improving their occupational standing within probation departments. Thus the presentence investigation serves to maintain the court's claim of individualized concern while preserving the probation officer's role, although a subordinate role, in the court system.

The myth of individualization serves various functions, but it also raises serious questions. In an era of severe budget restrictions, should scarce resources be allocated to compiling predictable presentence reports of dubious value? If social variables are considered only in a few cases, should courts continue routinely to require presentence reports in all felony matters (as is the practice in California)? In summary, we should address the issue of whether the criminal justice system can afford the ceremony of a probation presentence investigation.

REFERENCES

Blumberg, Abraham (1967). *Criminal Justice.* Chicago: Quadrangle.

Blumstein, Alfred J., S. Martin, and N. Holt (1983). *Research on Sentencing: The Search for Reform.* Washington, D.C.: National Academy Press.

Carter, Robert M. (1967). "The Presentence Report and the Decision-Making Process." *Journal of Research in Crime and Delinquency* 4:203–11.

Carter, Robert M., and Leslie T. Wilkins (1967). "Some Factors in Sentencing Policy." *Journal of Criminal Law, Criminology, and Police Science* 58:503–14.

Hagan, John (1975). "The Social and Legal Construction of Criminal Justice: A Study of the Presentence Process." *Social Problems* 22:620–37.

Hagan, John, John Hewitt, and Duane Alwin (1979). "Ceremonial Justice:

Crime and Punishment in a Loosely Coupled System." *Social Forces* 58:506–25.

Hogarth, John (1971). *Sentencing As a Human Process.* Toronto: University of Toronto Press.

Hughes, Everett C. (1958). *Men and Their Work.* New York: Free Press.

Kingsnorth, Rodney, and Louis Rizzo (1979). "Decision-Making in the Criminal Courts: Continuities and Discontinuities." *Criminology* 17:3–14.

McCleary, Richard (1978). *Dangerous Men.* Beverly Hills, Calif.: Sage.

Murrah, A. (1963). "Prison or Probation?" In B. Kay and C. Vedder (eds.), *Probation and Parole.* Springfield, Ill.: Charles C Thomas, pp. 63–78.

Myers, Martha A. (1979). "Offended Parties and Official Reactions: Victims and the Sentencing of Criminal Defendants." *Sociological Quarterly* 20:529–46.

Neubauer, David (1974). *Criminal Justice in Middle America.* Morristown, N.J.: General Learning.

Rosecrance, John (1985). "The Probation Officers' Search for Credibility: Ball Park Recommendations." *Crime and Delinquency* 31:539–54.

——— (1987). "A Typology of Presentence Probation Investigators." *International Journal of Offender Therapy and Comparative Criminology* 31:163–77.

Sudnow, David (1965). "Normal Crimes: Sociological Features of the Penal Code." *Social Problems* 12:255–76.

Walker, Samuel (1985). *Sense and Nonsense about Crime.* Monterey, Calif.: Brooks/Cole.

Walsh, Anthony (1985). "The Role of the Probation Officer in the Sentencing Process." *Criminal Justice and Behavior* 12:289–303.

PART V

Corrections

Prison comes to mind most often when people think of corrections. This is understandable given the history of corrections, the folklore, films, and songs about prison life, and the fact that incarceration is the most visible aspect of the process. Many of us have seen the looming walls, barbed-wire fences, and searchlights of a prison. The prison is also brought to our attention by the media whenever there is inmate unrest or an escape. And it is the prison that legislators and politicians speak about when they debate changes in the penal code or appropriations for corrections.

Yet for students of criminal justice, it should be no surprise that less than one-third of offenders under supervision are in prisons and jails. Most offenders are punished in the community through probation, intermediate sanctions, and parole. Thus corrections refers to the great number of programs, services, facilities, and organizations responsible for the management of people accused or convicted of criminal offenses. Besides prisons and jails, corrections includes probation, halfway houses, education and work release, boot camps, parole supervision, counseling, and community service. Many of these alternatives to incarceration rely on advances in technology such as electronic anklets, video surveillance, or global positioning systems. These alternatives also rely on cheap and inexpensive invasive measures, such as regular urine and blood testing. Correctional programs operate in Salvation Army hostels, in forest camps, along roadsides, in medical clinics, and in urban storefronts.

Corrections is authorized by all levels of government, administered by both public and private organizations, and costs over $30 billion per year.

Corrections supervises almost six million adults and juveniles. Supervision is carried out by more than five hundred thousand administrators, psychologists, officers, counselors, social workers, and others. An astounding 2.7 percent of U.S. adults (1 of every 21 men and 1 out of every 100 women) is incarcerated, on probation, or on parole. This is particularly alarming when we realize that 1 of every 6 African-American adult males and 1 of 3 African-American young adult males (aged 18–34) are under some form of correctional supervision.

COMMUNITY CORRECTIONS

Since the early nineteenth century, supervision in the community has been recognized as an appropriate punishment for some offenders. Although probation had been developed in the 1840s and was widely used by the 1920s, incarceration remained the usual sentence for serious crimes until the 1960s. At that time, with a new emphasis on community corrections, judges sentenced increased numbers of offenders to sanctions carried out in the community. As a result, incarceration rates fell as probation was viewed as the "punishment of choice" for most first-time offenders.

However, as Americans became weary of crime in the 1980s, legislatures passed tough sentencing laws and stipulated that incarceration should be the new priority punishment. By 1990, criminal justice scholars recognized that many imprisoned offenders, if properly supervised, could be punished more cheaply in the community. At the same time, probation was clearly inappropriate for offenders whose crimes were serious and who could not be effectively supervised by officers with large caseloads. What was needed was a set of intermediate sanctions, less restrictive of freedom than prison but more restrictive than probation, such as intensive probation supervision, home confinement, monetary sanctions, and boot camps.

In coming years, community corrections can be expected to play a much greater role in the criminal justice system. The number of offenders supervised in the community is likely to increase as states try to deal with the high costs of incarceration. With incarceration rates at record highs, probation and intermediate sanctions appear to many criminal justice experts to be less expensive and just as effective as prison.

GOVERNING A SOCIETY OF CAPTIVES

The prison differs from almost every other institution or organization in modern society. Not only are its physical features different, but also it is a place where a group of persons devotes itself to managing a group of captives. Prisoners are required to live according to the rules of their keepers, and their movements are sharply restricted. Unlike managers of other government agencies, prison managers:

- Cannot select their clients
- Have little or no control over the release of their clients
- Must deal with clients who are there against their will
- Must rely on clients to do most of the work in the daily operation of the institution and to do so by coercion and without fair compensation for their work
- Must depend on the maintenance of satisfactory relationships between clients and staff

With these unique characteristics, how should a prison be run? What rules should guide administrators? As we can see from the factors just noted, wardens and other key personnel are asked to perform a difficult order, one that requires skilled and dedicated managers.

The correctional literature points to four factors that make the governing of prisons different from the administration of other public institutions, (1) the defects of total power, (2) the limited rewards and punishments that can be used by officials, (3) the exchange relations between correctional officers and inmates, and (4) the strength of inmate leadership.

The Defects of Total Power

Imagine a prison society comprised of hostile and uncooperative captives ruled by force, in which prisoners could be legally isolated from one another, physically abused until they cooperate, and put under continuous surveillance. Theoretically, such a society is possible. In reality, correctional officers have limited power, because many prisoners have little to lose by misbehaving and unarmed officers have only limited ability to force compliance with rules. Perhaps more important is the fact that forcing people to carry out complex tasks is basically inefficient. Prison efficiency is further diminished by the realities of the usual ratio of one officer to forty inmates and the potential danger of the situation.

Rewards and Punishments

Because there are few permissible situations for the use of physical coercion, corrections officials must gain compliance and maintain control through the use of limited rewards and punishments. For example, privileges such as good time allocations, choice job assignments, and favorable parole reports may be offered in exchange for obedience. The reward system is defective because most privileges are given to the inmate at the start of the sentence and are taken away only if rules are broken. Few additional rewards can be granted for progress or exceptional behavior, although a desired work assignment or transfer to the honor cell block will induce some prisoners to maintain good behavior. One problem is that the punishments for breaking the rules do not represent a great departure from the prisoner's usual status. Because they are already deprived of many freedoms and valued goods—heterosexual relations, money, choice of clothing, and so on—inmates have little else left to lose. The punishment of not being allowed to attend a recreational period may not carry much weight. Moreover there are legal limitations on what types of punishments can be imposed.

Gaining Cooperation: Exchange Relationships

One way that correctional officers obtain inmates' cooperation is through exchange relationships. Although the formal rules require a social distance between officers and inmates, physical closeness makes them aware that each is dependent on the other. The officers need the cooperation of the prisoners so that they will look good to their superiors, and the inmates depend on the guards to relax the rules or occasionally look the other way.

Correctional officers must be careful not to pay too high a price for the cooperation of their charges. Officers who establish subrosa relationships can be manipulated by prisoners into smuggling contraband or committing other illegal acts. Officers are under pressure to work effectively with prisoners and may be blackmailed into doing illegitimate favors in return for cooperation.

Inmate Leadership

Some officials also try to use inmate leaders to exercise control over convicts. Inmate leaders have been "tested" over time so that they are neither pushed around by other inmates nor distrusted as stool pigeons. Because staff can also rely on them, inmate leaders serve as the essential communications link between staff and inmates. By being able to acquire inside information and access to higher officials, inmate leaders command the respect of other prisoners and are granted special privileges by officials. In turn, they distribute these benefits to other prisoners, thus bolstering their own influence within the society. In practice, prison administrators of earlier eras were more successful at using inmate leaders to maintain order than are today's administrators. In most of today's institutions, prisoners are divided by race, ethnicity, age, and gang affiliation, so that no single leadership structure exists.

The Challenge of Governing Prisons

The factors of total power, rewards and punishments, cooptation, and inmate leadership exist in every prison and must be managed. How they are managed greatly influences the quality of prison life. Among many correctional administrators and officers is the belief that "the cons run the joint." Instead, successful wardens have made their prisons "work" by the application of management principles within the context of their own style of leadership. Prisons can be governed, violence can be minimized, and services can be provided if correctional executives and wardens exhibit leadership appropriate to the task. Governing prisons is an extraordinary challenge, but it can be and has been successfully accomplished.

QUESTIONS FOR FURTHER EXPLORATION

1. Rehabilitation has been subject to the criticism that it is unworkable and antithetical to criminal justice values. What might be concurring or opposing positions?

2. Argue a pro or con position for intermediate punishments. Do you believe they arise out of necessity, out of planning and evaluation,

or stem from our standards of justice?

3. How does research debunk the myth that prisons function as strictly authoritarian agencies?

4. Do the rules and norms of prison life dictate the inmate culture, or does the inmate culture shape the institution?

SUGGESTIONS FOR FURTHER READING

Clear, Todd R., and George F. Cole. *American Corrections,* 6th ed., Belmont, Calif.: Wadsworth, 2003. A comprehensive look at the corrections system.

DiIulio, John J., Jr. *Governing Prisons.* New York: Free Press, 1987. A critique of the sociological perspective on inmate society. DiIulio argues that governance by correctional officers is the key to the maintenance of good prisons and jails.

Earley, Pete. *The Hot House: Life inside Leavenworth Prison.* New York: Bantam Books, 1992. An eyewitness account of daily life in the United States Penitentiary in Leavenworth, Kansas, written by the first journalist given unlimited access to a maximum security institution of the Federal Bureau of Prisons.

Garland, David. *Punishment and Modern Society.* Chicago: University of Chicago Press, 1990. Argues against punishment purely as a function of crime control.

Johnson, Robert. *Deathwork: A Study of the Modern Execution Process,* 2nd ed. Belmont, Calif.: Wadsworth 1998. First-person account detailing the execution process, including the death watch team, warden, condemned prisoner, and official witness.

Morris, Norval, and Michael Tonry. *Between Prison and Probation: Intermediate Punishments in a Rational Sentencing System.* New York: Oxford University Press, 1990. Urges development of a range of

intermediate punishments that can be used to sanction offenders more severely than probation but less severely than incarceration.

Petersilia, Joan. *When Prisoners Come Home: Parole and Prisoner Reentry*, New York: Oxford University Press, 2003. An excellent overview of the crisis of exfelon reentry. Examines the impact of the incarceration and release of large numbers of inner-city men, who are mostly minorities, on the community.

Rothman, David J. *The Discovery of the Asylum: Social Order and Disorder in the New Republic.* Boston: Little, Brown, 1971. A history of the invention of the penitentiary. Rothman shows the links among the ideology of the 1830s, assumptions concerning corrections, and design of institutions.

Sheehan, Susan. *A Prison and a Prisoner.* Boston: Houghton Mifflin, 1978. A fascinating description of life in Green Haven Prison and the way one prisoner "makes it" through "swagging," "hustling," and "doing time." Contains an excellent discussion of the inmate economy.

Simon, Jonathon. *Poor Discipline: Parole and the Social Control of the Underclass.* Chicago: University of Chicago Press, 1993. Explores the use of parole to control poor and disadvantaged members of society.

17

❂

Between Prison
and Probation

Toward a Comprehensive
Punishment System

Norval Morris
Michael Tonry

With record-high incarceration rates and overwhelming probation caseloads, Morris and Tonry argue for the need for intermediate punishments. These sanctions can be used in the community to punish offenders who do not require the restrictions of prison as well as offenders who require more restrictions than those imposed by probation.

There [are now] more than 1,000,000 Americans aged 18 and over in prison and jail, and more than 2,500,000 on parole or probation. If one adds those on bail or released awaiting trial or appeal and those serving other punishments such as community service orders, the grand total under the control of the criminal justice system exceeds four million, nearly 2 percent of the nation's adult population.

The pressure of these numbers on insufficient and mostly old penal institutions and on sparsely staffed probation offices has sharpened interest in all punishments lying between the prison and the jail at one end and insufficiently supervised probation at the other—there is general agreement about the need to develop and expand "intermediate punishments" but the path to that end is far from clear.

There are two main lines of argument. First, it is submitted that there has been a failure in this country to develop and institutionalize a range of punishments lying between incarceration and probation. That argument can stand

Source: Norval Morris and Michael Tonry, *Between Prison and Probation*, (New York: Oxford University Press, 1990): pp. 9–33. Copyright © 1990 by Oxford University Press, Inc.

alone and would support an expansion of intermediate punishments without considering any questions of sentencing processes. The selection between those properly committed to prison and those sentenced to intermediate punishments cannot be based alone on the gravity of their crimes or the lengths of their criminal records, nor can the choice between probation and an intermediate punishment.

The second line of argument takes the matter further: for certain categories of offenders now in prison, some though not all could better be sentenced to intermediate punishments, and for certain categories of offenders now on probation, some though not all could be better subjected to more intensive controls in the community than probation now provides.

The first argument is obvious enough and does not deny the conventional wisdom; indeed, such is the extent of current experimentation with intermediate punishments that the ground is fertile and the time precisely right for their growth. The second argument will meet with more opposition since it seems to contradict the intuitive sense that like cases should be treated alike, that crimes of equal severity committed by criminals with equal criminal records should be punished identically. We regard this position as an erroneous application of principles of "just desert." A comprehensive and just sentencing system requires principled "interchangeability" of punishment of "like" cases, some going to prison, some receiving an intermediate punishment. Similarly, there must be principled interchangeability of punishment of like cases, with some being put on probation while others receive the more intensive control or qualitatively different experience of an intermediate punishment.

• • •

[The following is a bare statement of our recommendations:]

- Intermediate punishments should be applied to many criminals now in prison and jail and to many criminals now sentenced to probation or a suspended sentence.

- Intermediate punishments must be rigorously enforced; they should not, as is too often the present case, be ordered absent adequate enforcement resources.

- Breaches of conditions of intermediate punishments must be taken seriously by the supervising authority and, in appropriate cases, by the sentencing judge, if these punishments are to become credible sanctions.

- The fine should be greatly expanded, in amount and in frequency, both as a punishment standing alone and as part of a punishment package. Fines must be adjusted to the offender's financial capacity (to be achieved by a system of "day fines") and must be collected; this requires innovative assessment and enforcement arrangements, since at present fines are set too low, do not sufficiently match the means of the offender, and are too often not collected.

- The use of community service orders, standing alone or as part of a punishment package, should be greatly increased. Such punishments are applicable to the indigent and to the wealthy; they have much to contribute provided, as for other intermediate punishments, they are vigorously supervised and enforced.

- Intensive probation is a mechanism by which reality can be brought to all intermediate punishments. Allied to house arrest, treatment orders, residential conditions up to house arrest, buttressed by electronic monitoring where appropriate, and paid for by fees for service by the offender where that is realistic, intensive supervision has the capacity both to control offenders in the community and to facilitate their growth to crime-free lives.

- Current sentencing reforms, both proposals and developments, devote inadequate attention to intermediate punishments. Sentencing guidelines, legislative or voluntary, shaped by a sentencing commission or by a court system, must provide better guidance to the judiciary in the use of intermediate punishments if a comprehensive sentencing system is to be developed. In particular:
  1. there is a range of offense–offender relationships in which incarcerative and intermediate punishments are equally applicable;
  2. there is a range of offense–offender relationships in which intermediate punishments and lesser community-based controls are equally applicable;
  3. the sentencing judge requires adequate information about the offender and his financial and personal circumstances to decide on the applicability to each convicted offender of a fine, of a community service order, of a treatment or residential order, of intensive supervision, or of a split sentence involving incarceration and an intermediate punishment—or a mixture of several of these punishments;
  4. the judge should retain ultimate responsibility for the decision on the "back-up" sentence, that is, on what should be done if the conditions of an intermediate punishment are not adhered to.

- As intermediate punishments become part of a comprehensive sentencing system, their efficacy must be critically evaluated so that, in time, an effective treatment classification may emerge.

THE OVERUSE OF IMPRISONMENT
AND PROBATION

The figures again: 1,000,000 in prison and jail, over 2,500,000 on probation. How many of these would be better subjected to intermediate punishments cannot be precisely calculated but that the number is large can be confidently affirmed.

Who among the sentenced offenders now in prison or jail need not be there? One way to get at this question is to define the criteria that justify incarceration and then to ask how many in prison and jail do not meet those criteria.

Some years ago, one of us argued in *The Future of Imprisonment* that prison is an appropriate punishment only when one or more of the following three conditions is fulfilled:

- Any lesser punishment would depreciate the seriousness of the crime or crimes committed.
- Imprisonment is necessary for deterrence, general or special.
- Other less restrictive sanctions have been frequently or recently applied to this offender.

We hope it is not stubborn persistence in error that leads us to reaffirm allegiance to those propositions. They track ideas offered by the American Law Institute's *Model Penal Code* and by the American Bar Association's *Standards for Criminal Justice*. Both of these organizations and many other commentators on sentencing have expressed a preference for parsimony in incarceration with a presumption against that punishment unless it be necessary for one or more of these three purposes: to affirm the gravity of the crime, to deter the criminal and others who are like-minded, or because other sanctions have proved insufficient.

Judged by these criteria there are many in prison and jail who need not be there, who are at a shallow end of severity of crime and have criminal records that do not trigger any one of these selecting criteria. How many is a matter of guesswork. Prison wardens differ in their estimates, but it is common to hear talk of 10 to 15 percent. And there are other straws in the wind of this assessment.

In practice, there is another reason, and an increasingly popular reason, why convicted criminals are imprisoned. The sentencing judge may be skeptical that imprisoning a given criminal is necessary to reaffirm any behavioral standards, may doubt that it will have either a general or special deterrent effect, and may doubt that imprisonment will prove any more effective, whatever its purposes, than any other punishment. But this, at least the judge knows: an offender who is in prison will not be committing any crimes against other than the prison community. Incapacitation plays an increasing role in the sentencing decision and may in considerable part account for the present overcrowding of penal institutions.

Incapacitation is a function of risk-assessment. This becomes clear when "caps" are put on prison populations or on jail populations by court orders pursuant to Eighth Amendment suits. Those running the prisons or jails have frequently had to arrange, and have arranged, early release programs, freeing many who otherwise would be in prison or jail. Wisely they select for such release the lower-risk offenders, those who seem most likely to avoid crime, at least during the remainder of the period to which they had been sentenced. This, of course, is exactly what parole boards do, particularly when they are guided by parole prediction tables such as the "salient factor score" developed for the federal parole system. There are many now in prison who have a low likelihood of future criminality, particularly if that prediction is confined to crimes of personal violence.

In the broad sense, then, there are certainly prisoners who in terms of risk to society or other punitive purpose need not serve the prison terms now imposed. Within that group a number need never have been so sentenced had there existed a sufficient range of intermediate punishments to provide community protection from them.

Even more certainly, of the more than 2 million convicted offenders now sentenced to probation there are many who should be under closer supervision than ordinary probation provides and also many who by fines or by community service should make larger amends for their crimes than ordinary probation now provides. It would be misleading to suggest with any attempt at precision what that number might be, since it is in large part a function of what community-based treatment and control resources are available. But when one finds caseloads of 200 and more per probation officer in some of our cities, it is clear both that probation is often a merely token sanction providing scant community protection and that the number of probationers meriting middle-range intermediate punishment is large.

We have, in short, created a punishment system that is polarized and ill-adapted to the gradations of severity of crime and magnitude of future threat that are the grist of the mill of our criminal courts. Between overcrowded prisons and even more overcrowded probation, there is a near-vacuum of appropriate and enforced middle-range punishments. . . . Unless and until such intermediate punishments are developed and institutionalized, there can be no comprehensive punishment system suited to the realities of crime and criminals in this country.

THE UNDERUSE
OF INTERMEDIATE PUNISHMENTS

At last, there is an experiment with a day-fine system in this country, decades after it became entrenched in many European punishment systems. At last, federal fines have been raised to realistic levels, decades after the threats of white-collar crime and organized crime were understood. Some countries now treat the fine as their main punishment for quite serious crime; such a thought is brushed aside in the United States, a country otherwise dedicated to the power of the economic incentive. Why not, then, let the fine serve as a powerful penal disincentive rather than a mere adjunct to other punishments?

The reasons for the neglect of the fine as a weapon against other than minor crime are not clear. That the fine is an insufficiently used punishment is, however, clear beyond argument. It is seen as ineffective against the wealthy and inapplicable to the poor. Far too often, when a fine is imposed it is not collected, and this holds true in federal as well as state and local courts.

All that is now affirmed is that a system of fines graduated to the severity of the crime and the capacity of the criminal to pay, if imposed and collected, is an essential part of a comprehensive punishment system. The knowledge base exists to develop and implement such a system. Widespread experimentation has taken place in this country with various methods of assessing, imposing, and collecting fines and other countries have moved toward implementing such systems.

Unlike the other intermediate punishments we shall consider, the development of an effective system of fines could be achieved cheaply, without the development of any large-scale enforcement mechanisms. This is one area of the criminal justice system to which the private sector can make a significant contribution—and to its own profit. Private financial institutions are good at collecting debts; the courts are not.

All who have studied criminal punishments in this country, be they from the bleeding-hearted left or the lantern-jawed right, lament the state of the fine. There is less unanimity concerning the underuse of the other punishments in the middle range between prison and probation, but in our view the cases are equally strong.

The community service order is analogous to the fine, clearly applicable to the indigent, for whom a fine may be inappropriate, but also suited, either alone or as an adjunct to other punishments, to many who can and should pay fines. Later we tell the story of experimentation with this punishment in this country and abroad; for the time being all that is being suggested is that one important way in which the criminal can make amends to the community he has wronged—make a contribution to it given that he has inflicted injury on it—is by providing some form of community service that is needed and that otherwise would not be provided. In the destroyed inner-city areas there is much need for rehabilitation of otherwise unusable housing; there is unlimited work to be done to preserve our heritage of natural resources; our hospitals and all our community services stand in need of assistance—it seems obvious that there is ample opportunity here for some offenders, as part of their punishment or as their punishment, to give of their labor and skills to our benefit and possibly also to theirs.   *work release experience*

Intermediate punishments encompass a wide diversity of community-based treatments and controls of the convicted offender, ranging from house arrest, to halfway houses, to intensive probation with conditions of treatment or control vigorously enforced and, if appropriate, backed up by the emerging technology of electronic and telephonic monitoring. . . . The probation order has become the punishment of choice for a wide swath of crimes. Like prison, inadequately supplied with the resources to fulfill its mission, probation has been overwhelmed by numbers. But, this reality apart, it has come to be realized that many offenders require closer supervision than the usual probation order provides. Hence the development of these more intensive controls, combining elements of police supervision and casework assistance. . . . For some criminals, as a punishment standing alone, for others, as part of a larger punishment package, community-based punishments stand in urgent need of further development as a necessary and integral part of a comprehensive punishment system.

THE ENFORCEMENT
OF INTERMEDIATE PUNISHMENTS

As we surveyed experimentation with intermediate punishments, one pattern emerged which may go far to explain their small role in punishment policy and practice: an enthusiastic reformer, a judge as in the origins of the community service order, or an agency as in much experimentation with intensive supervision probation, seeks and finds funds to launch an experimental program of intermediate punishments. It "works well": the early enthusiasm of a new initiative leads the sentencing court and the community in which it is established to be satisfied with its observed results. It does not have a high failure rate; it is hard to know, however, whether the failure rate would have been higher or lower if some other punishment had been imposed on the same offenders. There is always the possibility that the new initiative skimmed the least threatening offenders from the pool of convicted offenders possibly suited to this new punishment; at any event, those who launch it and those who are subject to it feel [good] about it. It is written up in some popular literature and often featured on local or national television, usually with excessive claims of success. Then the task of building it into the larger punishment system in the city or state where it was established begins—and usually ends. The enthusiasm of the early reformers dissipates; they move on to other pastures. The other punishment agencies, prison and probation, are not excited by this new competition for their clientele, even though they recognize their overload. Bureaucratic inertia dominates. The "reform" is allowed quietly to die.

We draw two morals from this oft repeated experience. First, the designers and administrators of new initiatives must face and overcome daunting organizational, political, financial, and bureaucratic problems if new programs are to be institutionalized and their promised benefits achieved. Second, and more important for our purposes here, the development of a comprehensive punishment system requires the dedication of appreciable resources of men and women, money and materials, to the implementation and enforcement of a range of intermediate punishments if we are to move beyond experimentation.

• • •

It may be true that, in the long run, a punishment system making appropriate use of a range of punishments from probation through the middle range of punishments and on to imprisonment may be less expensive than one that relies excessively on prison; but that will be true, if at all, in the very long run. Community-based controls are labor intensive if they are to be effective. If the convicted offender is to be supervised effectively, with or without the assistance of electronic or similar monitoring, with or without, for example, regular drug testing, supervising officers cannot carry a large caseload. The "alternatives to imprisonment" movement sailed under false colors when it claimed immediate savings; prison budgets decline only when substantial numbers are taken out of the prison so that a prison or a wing of a prison may be closed—and that does not seem an immediate likelihood in most American jurisdictions.

And there is another aspect of reality that is not usually stressed by those who advocate this type of development of our punishment system: the intermediate punishment must be rigorously enforced, it must be "backed up" by enforcement mechanisms that take seriously indeed any breach of the conditions of the community-based sanction. This does not mean, for example, that the addict who once relapses in a treatment program must by that fact and without more be incarcerated; but it does mean that this relapse must be taken seriously and that there is a real possibility of the imposition of a prison term because of the relapse.

If a fine is imposed, adjusted to the criminal's financial circumstances and potential, and time given to pay if necessary, it is of the first importance that an effective and determined enforcement machinery be in place. It seems unnecessary to make such a point, but the record of failure to collect fines in the federal system, and similar experience in state and local fining practice, compel such a stressing of the obvious.

Here too the law must keep its promises. The promise of intermediate punishments demands for its fulfillment resources adequate to their support and sufficient for their determined enforcement.

SENTENCING TO
INTERMEDIATE PUNISHMENTS

Concerns for justice and fairness in sentencing will lead, in time, probably within 25 years, to the creation in most American states of comprehensive systems of structured sentencing discretion that encompass a continuum of punishments from probation to imprisonment, with many intermediate punishments ranged between. These systems may take the form of the sentencing guidelines now in place in Minnesota, Washington, and elsewhere, or they may take some other form, but they will all provide for interchangeability of punishments for like-situated offenders. They will establish ranges of interchangeable punishments, bounded by considerations of desert, that are presumed to be applicable to the cases governed by each range, subject to the right of the judge to impose some other sentence if he provides written reasons for so doing; the adequacy and appropriateness of those reasons will be subject to review by appellate courts that will consult a body of case law, a common law of sentencing, for guidance.

These predictions may seem millenarian, but they are the foreseeable extension of developments and practices that are already in place. Anyone who in 1970 predicted the radical changes in American sentencing practices that have taken place since that date would have seemed even more romantic than we do now. The developments that underlay the past two decades of evolution in American sentencing practices will continue to shape reform for decades to come in the directions that we have identified. . . .

In 1970 the indeterminate sentencing systems in the United States, federal and state, had continued virtually unchanged from at least 1930 and looked much the same everywhere. Premised at least in theory on commitment to the values of individualized sentencing and rehabilitative correctional programs, indeterminate sentencing systems gave officials wide-ranging discretion and freedom from external controls over their decisions. Criminal statutes and common law doctrines defined the elements of crimes. Statutes established maximum terms of probation and imprisonment, and maximum amounts of fines, that could be imposed. Occasionally, but rarely, the statutes established mandatory minimum prison terms for persons convicted of particular crimes. Prosecutors had complete control over charging and plea bargaining. Judges had little-fettered discretion to "individualize punishment" in deciding who received probation and who was sentenced to jail or prison, and, for those to be confined, to set minimum or maximum terms, and sometimes both. Parole boards, subject only to statutory provisions on parole eligibility, generally when a third of the maximum term had been served, decided who was released from prison prior to the expiration of their terms, when, and under what conditions.

None of these decisions—charging and plea bargaining, sentencing, paroling—was governed by legal or administrative decision rules and only rarely did these decisions raise issues cognizable in the appellate courts. Well-established doctrines based on notions of separation of powers and deference to administrative expertise led appellate courts to refuse to review prosecutorial and parole decisions on the substantive merits. Equivalent notions of comity between judges and deference to the better information of the trial judge caused appellate courts to accord extreme deference to the discretionary sentencing decisions of the trial judge.

When courts did consider appeals from parole and prosecutorial decisions, which was uncommon before 1970, the cases generally involved procedural issues. When appellate courts considered sentence appeals in the few states where such appeals were allowed, few sentences were overturned and they tended to be such gross departures from standard practice that the appeals courts felt comfortable concluding that they constituted an "abuse of discretion" or that they "offended the conscience."

In effect, prosecutors, judges, and parole boards were accountable for their decisions in individual cases only to their political constituencies and their consciences. Few would have guessed in 1970 that nearly every facet of indeterminate sentencing in theory and in practice would be decisively repudiated within a decade.

• • •

The theoretical attacks were most influentially advanced by Francis Allen in his 1964 book, *The Borderland of Criminal Justice*, and in 1974 by Norval Morris in *The Future of Imprisonment.* Their arguments had two major elements. First, from an ethical perspective, it is simply wrong to take or extend the state's criminal law powers over individuals for, ostensibly, their own good, especially in light of pessimistic findings on the correctional systems' abilities to rehabilitate offenders. Second, from a psychological perspective, it defies common experience to imagine that coerced participation in treatment programs will often facilitate personal growth and change. Generally, self-improvement is voluntary; coupling participation in treatment programs with a likelihood of earlier release motivated prisoners to participate, but often it did not motivate them to change.

Taken together, these critiques greatly undermined indeterminate sentencing and the practices and institutions that went with it. It is not easy to defend a major set of social institutions that are portrayed as based on unsound empirical, ethical, and psychological premises, as characterized by racial and class bias, by arbitrariness, by lawlessness, and by unfairness, and as conspicuously ineffective at achieving the larger social purposes of reducing crime and rehabilitating offenders—and few tried.

Hence American sentencing institutions and practices underwent more extensive and more radical changes between 1975 and 1985 than in any other decade in our history. Most of the changes attempted to structure or eliminate the discretionary decisions exercised by public officials. Although new initiatives affecting decision making by judges and prosecutors were not uncommon, it was the parole boards, the institutions that in theory based their decisions on rehabilitative predictions and assessments, that experienced the most drastic changes.

• • •

Many of the sentencing innovations since the midseventies have not achieved their proponents' aims. Mandatory sentencing laws, for example, had at best a modest short-term deterrent effect on the crimes they affect and usually produced very little change in sentencing practices. For serious crimes, the one- or two-year minimum sentence usually prescribed was generally less than would normally be imposed even without a mandatory sentencing law. For less serious offenses and offenders, lawyers and judges could usually devise a method for circumventing the mandatory sentence when its imposition seemed to them unduly harsh.

Voluntary guidelines for sentencing fared little better. Voluntary guidelines were voluntary in two senses; their development by judges was self-initiated and not in furtherance of a statutory directive, and whether and to what extent judges followed them was entirely in the hands of each individual judge. In most jurisdictions, voluntary guidelines seem to have had little effect on sentencing. Although courts in more than 40 states established voluntary guidelines between 1975 and 1980, in most places they were soon abandoned or soon became dead letters.

Statutory determinate sentencing laws did somewhat better and in some states, notably North Carolina and California, they seem to have reduced sentencing disparities and made sentencing somewhat more predictable. In other states, however, like Illinois and Indiana, the new laws offered no meaningful constraints on judicial discretion and proved to be no improvement on the indeterminate sentencing systems they replaced.

Parole guidelines in some jurisdictions, such as Minnesota and the federal system, accomplished much of what their creators had in mind. Consistently applied, they made release dates more predictable and served to even out disparities in the lengths of prison sentences meted out by judges. Their major shortcoming from a reform perspective was that they affect only those offenders who are sent to prison and accordingly have no effect whatever on the question of who is sentenced to prison or on what happens to those who are not imprisoned.

The sentencing reform initiative of the future is the combination of the sentencing commission and presumptive sentencing guidelines that Judge Frankel first proposed in 1972 as a solution to the lawlessness that he decried, that Minnesota first implemented in 1980, and that other jurisdictions have elaborated as the years have passed. Presumptive sentencing guidelines establish presumptions that govern judges' decisions whether to imprison an offender and, if so, for how long. The judge may conclude that special circumstances justify some other sentence or, in other words, that the presumption should be rejected. If so, the judge must explain his reasoning and its adequacy is subject to review by appeal of sentence to a higher court. Careful evaluations of the experience in Minnesota and later Washington showed that presumptive sentencing guidelines could reduce sentencing disparities, reduce differences in sentencing patterns associated with race, increase consistency in sentencing statewide, and make sentencing much more predictable, so that state sentencing policies could be related in a meaningful way to the availability of prison beds and other correctional resources.

Presumptive sentencing guidelines appear to be a way to address most of the major critiques of indeterminate sentencing. They reduce disparities and the potential for decisions based on invidious considerations of race and class. They provide decision rules to guide the sentencing choices judges make. Judges are made accountable because they must comply with the guidelines' presumptions or give reasons for doing something else. Sentence appeals become meaningful because appellate judges have some basis for assessing the correctness of the trial judge's decisions and the reasons that are invoked to justify them.

The wisdom of Judge Frankel's proposal, and the core of the sentencing commission idea, was its combination of the sentencing commission, sentencing guidelines, and appellate sentence review. All three elements were crucial. The creation of an administrative agency responsible for formulation of sentencing policy provided an institution much better situated than any legislature to accumulate specialized expertise to develop comprehensive sentencing policies and sufficiently removed from the glare of day-to-day legislative politics to approach these often controversial matters in a principled and thoughtful way. The resulting sentencing guidelines for the first time provided an instrument for the expression of finely tuned standards for exercise of the punitive powers of the state, and their presumptive character required that judges give reasons for their decisions to depart from the guidelines' presumptions. Those reasons, in turn, for the first time in this country provided the material for development of principled appellate review of sentences. . . .

A comprehensive sentencing system must provide guidance to judges in choosing among all available sentencing options, including probation, prison, and all the intermediate punishments that fall between them in severity and intrusiveness. . . . There is, however, one threshold that must be crossed before such a system becomes a viable possibility—the prison or probation, something or nothing, simplicities of too much present thought must be rejected.

• • •

Here we simply set out the components of a comprehensive sentencing system.

1. The principle of interchangeability of punishments must be recognized.

2. The "in/out" line must be erased to eliminate the false dichotomous prison-or-nothing simplicities.

3. In place of a two-part in-or-out sentencing grid, there should be at least four graded categories of punishment presumptions: "out," "out unless . . .," "in unless . . .," and "in."

4. Within the governing purposes *of* sentencing established by policymakers, the guidelines should permit the judge to look to the applicable purposes of punishment to be served *at* sentencing in choosing among the available interchangeable punishments.

5. The principle of interchangeability should be recognized for all crimes for which the presumptive prison sentence (for those cases where the applicable purposes at sentencing will best be served by incarceration) is two years or less.

6. The system should provide guidance for all sentencing decisions for all felonies and misdemeanors.

7. The choice among interchangeable punishments is for the judge to make, not the offender.

The preceding list does not address all of the issues our proposals raise. For example, it does not explain how the exchange rates between different punishments are to be determined or calculated, or how judges are to know what the governing purposes are *at* sentencing. We discuss such problems later. We believe, however, that they are simpler than at first appears and that their apparent difficulty results mainly from their novelty.

Our mission is to explain how in principle and in practice a comprehensive sentencing system, which incorporates a rich variety of intermediate punishments linked to one another and to probation and prison by a principle of interchangeability, can be established and implemented. Before we turn to that fuller explication and justification, a critical issue of justice as fairness must be mentioned and its implications noted.

Fitting intermediate punishments into a principled sentencing system has proved to be the Achilles heel of both sentencing reform proposals and practice. The central reason for this is (somewhat unexpectedly given the general human capacity to tolerate the sufferings of others with a degree of equanimity) a sense of unfairness when it is suggested that two equally undeserving criminals should be treated differently—since differently here means that one will be treated more leniently than the other.

The conceptual keystone of the argument is that a developed punishment theory requires recognition that precise equivalency of punishment between equally undeserving criminals in the distribution of punishments is in practice unattainable and is in theory undesirable. We argue that all that can be achieved is a rough equivalence of punishment that will allow room for the principled distribution of punishments on utilitarian grounds, unfettered by the miserable aim of making suffering equally painful. . . .

The first consequence is that it now becomes possible to move appreciable numbers who otherwise would be sentenced to prison into community-based intermediate punishments, having a roughly equivalent punitive bite but serving both the community and the criminal better than the prison term. It also becomes possible to move appreciable numbers who otherwise would be sentenced to token probationary supervision into intermediate punishments that exercise larger controls over them and provide us with larger social protection from their criminality. The advantages are obvious; it is a liberating idea—but it has its problems, theoretical and practical.

First, the theoretical problem. If appropriate guidance is to be given the sentencing judge under such a system of punishment, some "exchange rates" between punishments to achieve this rough equivalence must be stated in advance. There exist a few fledgling efforts to state these exchange rates; we believe that a principled system of punishment can be defined in which rough equivalence of punitive bite and identity of process in relation to stated purposes of punishment provide the necessary guidance to the judge and also give both the appearance and the reality of fairness to the community and to the convicted offender.

Among the practical problems that accompany such a purposive introduction of intermediate punishments into the body of a punishment system, none is more troublesome than its impact on existing class and race biases.

At present black adult males per hundred thousand are more than seven times as likely to be in prison as white adult males. The reasons for this are deeply rooted in history, social structure, and social attitudes; but it also seems clear that the criminal justice systems of this country—federal, state, and local—make some contribution to this sad result. Are we really proposing the introduction of a punishment system that by its expansion of intermediate punishments will make this racial skewing worse? At first blush it would appear so.

Take two addict-criminals convicted of selling relatively small amounts of cocaine on a number of separate occasions. Each has once before been convicted of illegal possession of marijuana. Each is aged 20. Criminal A is in college, the son of a loving and supportive middle-class family, living in a district where space is available in drug treatment programs. Criminal B has never met his putative father, lives in a high-rise apartment in a slum area with his mother and his two much younger siblings, welfare being their major financial support. The waiting list at the available drug treatment center is long, the waiting time three months.

You know the pigmentation of the two hypothetical but far from unreal criminals.

Are we really suggesting that Criminal B serve a jail or prison term with the hope that thereafter he can be fitted into a drug treatment program, while Criminal A should pay a substantial fine, be under intensive probationary supervision with a condition of regular attendance at a drug treatment program where he is tested regularly to ensure that he is drug-free, and be subjected possibly to house arrest in the evenings and weekends—electronically monitored if that be necessary? This will, of course, be the likely result. Is it unprincipled? We think not.

The criminal justice system lacks both resources and capacity to take on the task of rectification of social inequalities of race or class. It will do well if it does not exacerbate them. To insist that Criminal A go to jail or prison because resources are lacking to deal sensibly with Criminal B is to pay excessive tribute to an illusory ideal of equality. That is not the way equality of opportunity and equality of punitive pain is to be achieved; it is to be achieved by efforts to provide within the criminal justice system for Criminal B what exists for Criminal A, and to intercede by means other than the criminal justice system to eradicate the inequalities that generate the present discrimination.

The comprehensive punishment system we propose will, we believe, in the longer run reduce the impact of race and class on sentencing practice. The more clearly the exchange rates between punishments and the purposes each is to serve can be articulated in advance, the more possible it will be to reduce race and class biases in the selection of sanctions. Strong racial and class prejudices, conscious and less perceived, already drive sentencing practice; the substitution of purposive principles framed independently of race and class but necessarily having race and class correlates will make matters better, not worse.

18

✦

Racial Disproportions in US Prisons

Michael Tonry

Scholars around the world criticize that the United States is an outlier in punishing offenders, both with respect to the types of offenses and the severity of punishment. There remains continued debate about the disproportionate representation of minorities in the U.S. penal system. Tonry argues that the types of offenses or behaviors that American legislatures criminalize, and the American social policies that hace disenfranchised minorities, will continue a disproportionate representation for African Americans in U.S. prisons and jails.

Outside the United States, probably the best known characteristics of America's correctional system are that capital punishment continues in use and that American incarceration rates are four to 15 times higher than those in other developed countries. Within the United States, the most notable characteristics are the absolute numbers in confinement and that they are disproportionately black. Blacks in 1991 made up 12 percent of America's population but 48 percent of both prison and jail inmates.[1] Forty percent of the occupants of "death row" on 31 December 1991 were black. In public juvenile facilities in 1989, 48 percent were black. Americans of Hispanic origin, by contrast, America's second largest minority group, in 1991 constituted 9 percent of the general population, 13 percent of the prison population, 14 percent of the jail population, and 8 percent of the death row population.

Source: "Racial Disproportions in US Prisons" by Michael Tonry, *British Journal of Criminology*, vol. 34 (1994), pp. 97–155.

America's incarceration rates[2] are seen by many as evidence of draconian criminal justice policies. The overrepresentation of black offenders is seen by many as evidence of racial bias. Both critiques have merit; the latter rests, however, in part on a misconception that racial disproportion in prisons is markedly worse in the United States than elsewhere. This appears not to be the case.

Four findings stand out when incarceration rates are disaggregated by race in Australia, Canada, England and Wales, and the United States. First, the white American incarceration rate compared with those in other English-speaking countries, is not as much higher as is generally believed. Secondly, patterns of differential incarceration by race in England and Wales (white and black), Australia (non-Aboriginal and Aboriginal), and Canada (white and native) resemble American patterns. In all these countries, members of disadvantaged visible minority groups are seven to 16 times likelier than whites to be confined in correctional institutions.

Thirdly, when the different racial compositions of national prison populations are taken into account, apparent differences in national rates of incarceration diminish. Table 1, shown later in this essay, presents disaggregated incarceration rates for blacks, whites, and others for America and for England and Wales. It invites intriguing comparisons. If, for example, America's 1990 general population were, like England and Wales's in 1991, 94.1 percent white and 1.8 percent black, America's jails and prisons in 1990 would have housed 759.632 black and white inmates (the actual black and white total was 1,133,820). This assumes that incarceration rates by race would be the same as in 1990 (see Table 1). The national incarceration rate (assuming the 1990 rate of 241 per 100,000 for the residual 4.1 percent "other") would fall from 474 per 100.000 to 315.

When the opposite exercise is carried out, if England and Wales's black/white general population percentages were America's, the results would be more striking. In 1990, combining remand and sentenced prisoners, England and Wales incarcerated 77 whites per 100,000 whites and 547 blacks per 100,000 blacks. If the general population were 80 percent white, 12 percent black, there would be 30,732 white and 32,748 black prisoners and an overall incarceration rate (attributing the current 164 per 100,000 rate to the remaining 8 percent of prisoners) of 140 per 100,000. England and Wales would have more black than white prisoners and its national incarceration rate would be more than 50 percent higher (140 versus 89). This assumes that a six-fold increase in the black population would not be accompanied by heightened racial tensions that would exacerbate existing racial disproportions in confinement decisions and patterns (e.g., Hood 1992).

Fourth, racial disproportion in prisons within countries is distributed in ways not commonly recognized. In 1988, for example, black–white incarceration rate differentials in some southern American states were relatively low (4 to 1 in Mississippi, South Carolina, and Tennessee). In some states traditionally considered politically liberal and governmentally progressive, like Wisconsin (12 to 1), Iowa (16 to 1), Connecticut (17 to 1), and Minnesota (19 to 1), the differentials were much higher. Similar patterns exist in Australia where

Table 1 Black, White, and Other Incarceration Rates, 1990

		General Population	Prison Population	Jail Population	Prison + Jail Population	Rate per 100,000
United	White	199,686,000	369,485	206,713	576,198	289
States	Black	29,986,000	367,122	190,500	557,622	1,860
	Other	19,038,000	37,768	8,106	45,874	241
	Total	248,710,000	774,375	405,319	1,179,694	474
England	White	46,946,751	36,300	—	—	77
and	Black	898,025	4,910	—	—	547
Wales	Other	2,045,501	3,350	—	—	164
	Total	49,890,277	44,520	—	—	89

Note: UK numbers do not equal column total in original source.
SOURCES: Jankowski 1992, tables 2.1, 2.3, 5.6; Home Office 1991, table 7; Bureau of the Census 1992, table 16.

Aboriginal–non-Aboriginal differentials ranged from 3.4 to 1 in Tasmania to 19.7 to 1 in Western Australia in January 1993.

This essay examines racial differences in incarceration, mostly in the United States but with occasional mention of other English-speaking countries. To anticipate the conclusion, a large part (but by no means all) of the long-term incarceration rate differential by race in the United States results from racial differences in participation in the kinds of crime, like homicide, robbery, and aggravated assault, that typically result in prison sentences; a recent short-term worsening of racial incarceration differences results from foreseeable discriminatory effects of conscious policy decisions of the Reagan and Bush administrations in launching and conducting the federal "War on Drugs." More generally, rough comparability in majority and minority group incarceration patterns in Australia, Canada, England and Wales and the United States exposes the failure of social policies aimed at assuring full participation by members of minority groups in the rewards and satisfactions of life in industrialized democratic countries.

One caveat concerning data reliability needs mention. Analyses such as this one that depend on unadjusted general population census data share the limits of the data. In the United States, for example, the decennial population survey conducted by the US Bureau of the Census undercounts members of minority groups. With a complete general population census, the black population count would be higher, which would make black denominators in incarceration rates larger and the resulting black rates lower. Similarly, after blacks, whites, Native-Americans, and Asians are counted, the 1990 census reports nearly 10,000,000 respondents as "others," which distorts denominators, and rates, in unknown ways. Likewise, the prison and jail censuses report residual "other, not known, or not reported" categories which necessarily lend imprecision to these data. In this essay, I rely on official black and white counts and generally do not adjust for estimates of the racial composition of "other" groups, except in Figure 1 showing long-term trends where Hispanics are included within black and white counts.

Here is how this essay is organized. Part 1 (Long-term Trends) describes long-term patterns of racial differences in incarceration rates in the United States. Part 2 (Cross-national Comparisons) examines American and other countries' comparative reliance on incarceration. Part 3 (Sub-national Comparisons) shows American state-by-state comparisons. Part 4 (Explanation of Minority Over-representation) examines the underlying causes of both long-term patterns and recent worsening of racial differentials in incarceration rates. Part 5 (Redressing Racial Imbalance) suggests lessons for criminal justice and social welfare policies that derive from those differences.

LONG-TERM TRENDS

That members of ethnic and racial minority groups are disproportionately involved in common law crimes and disproportionately ensnared in the American criminal justice system by itself, is neither unprecedented nor especially worrisome. These patterns typically characterize low-income immigrant groups and typically abate as subsequent generations are assimilated into American economic and social life.

America's first national crime commission, the US National Commission on Law Observance and Enforcement (1931), concentrated on two subjects— prohibition and "crime among the foreign-born." The commission's final report examined patterns of criminality among the foreign-born in general and Mexican immigrants in particular. The fundamental findings were that crime was less common among the foreign-born than among either non-immigrants or the immigrants' children and grandchildren. The relatively low involvement by immigrants in crime should come as no surprise. Most chose the uncertainties and dislocations of immigration and were determined to work hard and succeed. For many, material conditions of life in America as immigrants compared favourably with conditions in the natal homeland.

The problem of immigrant crime was preponderantly among the second and third generations to whom English was a native tongue, to whom worse conditions in the old country were mere words, and on whom relative deprivation could have a corrosive effect. Victims too often of ethnic stereotyping and discrimination, enjoying fewer legitimate opportunities than did assimilated middle-class and working-class youth, second and third generation immigrants were especially susceptible to the allure of juvenile gangs and especially likely to exploit illicit opportunities when legitimate opportunities were few, unattractive, or blocked (Glazer and Moynihan 1963).

Mass immigration declined after the 1930s. From 1900 to 1930, the United States received nearly 19 million people, thereafter falling to 1.5 million from 1930 to 1950 and 2.5 million during the 1950s (Bureau of the Census 1992, table 5). By the 1950s, the phrase "crime and the foreign-born" had an archaic if not xenophobic ring, and had disappeared as a major symbol of crime problems.

In retrospect, "crime and the foreign-born" as a prominent public policy problem in the 1920s and 1930s was a foreseeable, and foreseeably temporary, product of the transition of newly arrived immigrants into what was once called a "melting pot." Similar patterns appeared among southern black farm labourers and tenant farmers, made technologically obsolete by the mechaniza- tion of agriculture, who migrated to northern cities in the 1950s and 1960s. Employment rates were higher, and welfare dependency was lower among southern-born black migrants in the 1960s and 1970s than among northern- born blacks (despite the higher average education among the northern-born) (Wilson 1987: 55–6; Katz 1989: 203). Participation in crime by adult migrants was less extensive than was that of their children. Recent reports of developing Asian youth gangs look like a variation on a familiar story, as the children of Asian immigrants of the 1970s and 1980s face the problems confronted by children of eastern and southern European immigrants early in the twentieth century.

Unfortunately, the migration-is-comparable-to-immigration hypothesis is at best a partial explanation of modern patterns of crimes and punishments of American blacks. If the immigration analogy were apt, crime among Northern American blacks should be little more salient today, 45 years after the begin- ning and 25 years after the end of the major South-to-North migration, than was crime among Southern and Eastern Europeans in the 1950s.

The American pattern of social and economic progress by blacks is much more complicated. Something akin to Disreali's two nations is appearing within the American black community. A large portion of the black population is becoming much more fully assimilated into American economic and social life; black/white gaps in education, household income, residence patterns, and various public health measures are closing. By some measures—e.g., personal and household incomes of college-educated younger blacks, especially females—some groups of blacks are doing as well or better than their white peers (Jaynes and Williams 1989; Hacker 1992; Jencks 1992).

However a minority of blacks, disproportionately located in "Rust belt" and "Snow belt" cities, are not making progress and by many measures—wel- fare dependence, labour force participation, illegitimacy, single-parent house- holds, crime victimization, criminality—are doing worse. It is from this group, sometimes (and sometimes controversially) called the black urban underclass, that black offenders and prisoners grossly disproportionately come.

For the urban black underclass, at least, the immigration hypothesis does not appear to explain social conditions or criminality. Explanations abound and range from conservative "culture of poverty" and "welfare dependence" (Murray 1984) arguments to centrist social and structural accounts that emphasize the flight of unskilled jobs and the black middle class from the inner city and general economic conditions (Wilson 1987) to liberal "legacy of racism" (Lemann 1991 and radical "contemporary racial discrimination" expla- nations. Whatever the ultimate reasons, and those mentioned here are but a few among many that have been offered, American blacks' involvement in crime and their presence in jails and prisons remain high.

Figure 1 shows demographic trends in selected American correctional populations. Because of variation in statistical and reporting systems, data for different populations cover different periods. Recent changes and inconsistencies in reporting of data on Hispanics complicate some trend reports. Until 1980, Hispanics generally were included in black and white counts, sometimes with separate supplementary counts of Hispanics alone. More recently, some reports count non-hispanic whites, non-hispanic blacks, Hispanics, and others (sometimes reporting data on Asians and Native Americans). When possible, I have included Hispanics within racial groupings.

Figure 1a shows admissions to state and federal prisons by race from 1960 to 1989, the most recent date for which national admissions data on race have been published. White percentages declined and black percentages increased continuously. Between 1986 and 1989, the racial mix reversed, from 53 percent white, 46 percent black to 53 percent black, 46.5 percent white. The black proportion has probably continued to grow (as is shown for selected states in part 4 (Explanation of Minority Over-representation)).

Figure 1b shows the racial composition of state and federal prison populations on census dates for selected years from 1960 to 1980 and successively from 1985 to 1990. The continuous trend is one of decreasing white and increasing black percentages. By 1990, American prisons housed as many blacks as whites. Reported black numbers in recent years are an understatement because many Hispanics, some of whom are black, are reported as "race unknown" by some states, including Florida and Texas, which have sizeable Hispanic populations.

Figure 1c shows the composition on census dates of jail populations for selected years from 1960 to 1978 and for successive years from 1983 to 1991. The trend again is one of continuing white decrease and black increase in population composition, reaching near parity in 1991 when 50 percent were white and 48 percent black.

The patterns shown in Figure 1 for adult offenders also characterize juveniles. The proportion of whites in custody in public juvenile facilities fell from 70 percent in the 1950s to 60 percent in the late 1970s. By 1980, 42 percent of confined juveniles were black, 40 percent were white, and 15 percent were Hispanic (if adult patterns hold, roughly two-thirds are white and one-third are black). Between 1987 and 1989, the number of confined white juveniles fell by 5 percent, while the number of confined black juveniles grew by 14 percent (Calahan 1986, tables 5–30, 5–31; Allen-Hagen 1991; Krisberg and DeComo 1992).

Most people are instinctively uneasy about black rates of incarceration that appear to be three to four times higher than white rates. The uneasiness is warranted but the disproportion is far greater than three or four to one. The initial tendency to compare American blacks' proportion of the general population, 12 percent, to their presence in the prison and jail populations, 48 percent, is understandable, but wrong, and it greatly underestimates the

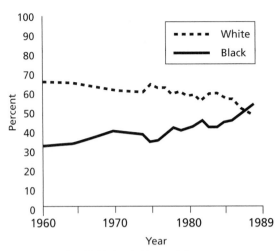

Hispanics are included in black and white populations

FIGURE 1a Admissions to Federal and State Prisons by Race, 1960–89 (Langan 1991; Gilliard 1992; Perkins 1992; Perkins and Gilliard 1992)

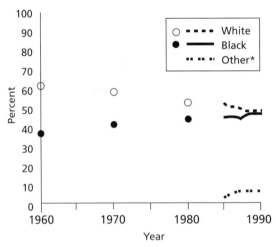

*Hispanics in many states, Asians, Native Americans

FIGURE 1b Prisoners in State and Federal Prisons on Census Date, by Race, 1960–90 (for 1960, 1970, 1980: Calahan 1986, table 3.31; for 1985–90: Bureau of Justice Statistics 1987, 1989a, 1989b, 1991a, 1991b)

scale of the problem. The better comparison is between racially disaggregated incarceration rates measured as the number of confined persons of a racial group per 100,000 population of that group. By that measure, black incarceration rates are six to seven times higher than white incarceration rates. Table 1

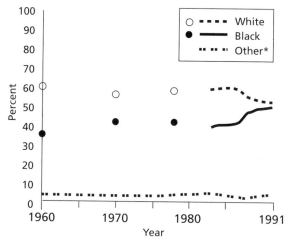

* White and black figures for 1988 and 1991 are estimated: white non-Hispanic, black non-Hispanic, and Hispanic reported: Hispanic racial breakdown assumed to be the same as in 1990 for which racial data were reported.

FIGURE 1c Jail Inmates at Mid-year, by Race, 1960–91 (for 1960–83: Calahan 1986, table 4.15, 4.21; for 1984–91: Bureau of Justice Statistics 1984, 1985, 1991c, 1992)

shows racially disaggregated jail and prison incarceration rates for the United States and for England and Wales for 1990.

Hereafter, in this article, racially disaggregated incarceration rates, and their ratios. as illustrated in Table 2, are regularly used as indicators of racial patterns in the criminal justice system.

CROSS-NATIONAL COMPARISONS

Racial disproportions in the United States among jail, prison, and juvenile inmates, awful as they are, are not radically different from those in Australia, Canada, and England and Wales.

The conventional cross-national comparisons of incarceration rates, limited and methodologically flawed as they are, show gross American incarceration rates to be much higher than those for other countries. Table 3, for example, shows one recent estimate of incarceration rates in 22 countries in the late 1980s.

Cross-national comparisons are best seen as crude order-of-magnitude indicators and not as anything more precise. Different countries handle and report pre-trial detainees and short- and long-term prisoners in different ways. In Canada, for example, sentences of two years or longer are served under the authority of the national prison system; sentences under two years are adminis-tered by the provinces. In the United States, pre-trial detainees and convicted

Table 2 Ratios of Racial Incarceration Rates 1990

	Black	White	Ratio
England and Wales	547	77	7.10
United States	1,860	289	6.44

offenders are distributed among federal, state, and local authorities. The US Bureau of Prisons handles all federal confinement, including pre-trial. In most states, the state prison system houses offenders sentenced to terms of one year or longer and county institutions house pretrial detainees and under one year sentenced offenders. There are, however, exceptions. Some states, like Connecticut and Delaware, have unified state departments of corrections that house detainees and all convicted offenders. In other states, local jails house offenders serving longer sentences; Pennsylvania's county facilities, in which terms up to five years can be served locally, are the extreme case.

The organization of corrections in the United States presents problems for counting offenders. If, for example, a count of all confined convicted offenders is wanted, data must be obtained from the Federal Bureau of Prisons, 50 state departments of corrections, the District of Columbia, and upwards of 3,312 county jails.

The most accessible source of population data is a series entitled "Prisoners in America," which is compiled and reported semi-annually and reports all confined offenders under the jurisdiction of the Federal Bureau of Prisons and the departments of corrections of the 50 states and the District of Columbia. Counts are provided for total populations on a census date (including detainees and short-term prisoners in unified systems) and prisoners serving sentences of one year or longer. Jail populations are less reliably known. There have been a number of special censuses (in 1972, 1978, 1983, and 1989) and since the early 1980s, an annual "Jail Inmates" report, based partly on estimates, has been published.

The only feasible way to calculate national incarceration rates is to combine the census-date population data reported for a given year in "Prisoners in America and Jail Inmates." So calculated, both aggregate and racially disaggregated incarceration rates climbed steadily between 1972 and 1991.

It appears that patterns of differential incarceration by race in Australia, Canada, England and Wales, and the United States are much more similar than differences in their gross incarceration rates suggest. As noted earlier, the ratio of black to white incarceration rates in England and Wales in 1990 was 7.10:1, slightly higher than America's 6.44:1. Differential incarceration of Aboriginal people in Australia makes these patterns appear modest. The Royal Commission into Aboriginal Deaths in Custody (1990) found that "for Australia as a whole, adult Aboriginal people are 15.1 times more likely than adult non-Aboriginal people to be in prison, but they are only 8.3 times more likely to be serving non-custodial correctional orders." Biles 1993*b* shows that,

Table 3 Incarceration Rates for 22 Countries, 1989

Country	Rate per 100,000
United States	426
South Africa	333
Soviet Union	268
Hungary	196
Malaysia	126
Northern Ireland	120
Hong Kong	118
Poland	106
New Zealand	100
United Kingdom	97
Turkey	96
Portugal	83
France	81
Austria	77
Spain	76
Switzerland	73
Australia	72
Denmark	68
Italy	60
Japan	45
Netherlands	40
Philippines	22

SOURCE: Mauer 1990.

among persons 17 years and older, Aboriginals were 18.2 times likelier than non-Aboriginals to have been incarcerated on 30 June 1991. Comparisons with Canada are especially difficult because most Canadian jurisdictions, including Ontario, have prohibited the collection and dissemination of racially disaggregated statistics, except concerning the native population. Data obtained privately, excluding Quebec, from the Canadian Centre for Justice Statistics, a division of Statistics Canada, indicate that in 1986–7 natives were admitted to correctional institutions at a rate of 2,662 per 100,000 native population, compared with 315 non-native admissions per 100,000 non-native population (Birkenmayer 1992). Although these are admissions rather than population data as for the other countries, the admission ratio of 8.45:1 native to non-native is not unlike the population ratios of the other countries.

There seems to be general agreement that violent crime rates are higher in the United States than in other developed countries and that property crime rates are among, but not invariably, the highest. World Health Organization and Interpol comparisons of officially recorded crimes show American crime rates that are much higher than other countries' (Kalish 1988). Cross-national comparisons of official crime records are, however, subject to even more measurement problems than are incarceration comparisons. Just as national governments increasingly look to victimization surveys for an independent measure of crime that is less subject than police records to variability in reporting and recording, efforts have been made to obtain cross-national victimization data. The most ambitious effort to date concluded that victim-reported crime in the United States was higher than in most developed countries but that, for some offences, American rates were lower than elsewhere, and that the differences between American and other countries' rates were much lower than is revealed by official-rate comparisons (Van Dijk, Mayhew, and Killias 1990; Van Dijk and Mayhew 1993).

When America's higher crime rates are taken into account, three findings stand out. First, relative to crime rates, America's incarceration rates are closer to other countries' rates than might otherwise be expected. Secondly, relative to white incarceration rates, or absolutely, America's black incarceration rate is shockingly high. Thirdly, relative to white incarceration rates, Australia, Canada, and England and Wales handle their most prominent visible minority groups no less differentially harshly than does the United States.

The overriding problem turns out not to be a unique American problem of overreliance on incarceration but a general problem in English-speaking white-dominant countries that minority citizens are locked up grossly out of proportion to their numbers in the population.

SUB-NATIONAL COMPARISONS

Another way to look at comparative incarceration rates is to stop the analytical lens down to focus on sub-national incarceration rates. England and Wales make up one unitary legal system, unlike the federal systems of Australia, Canada, and the United States. I lack provincial data for Canada, but state-level incarceration data are available for the United States and Australia.

Table 4 shows racially disaggregated incarceration rates and racial ratios for males in 1988 for 49 states and the District of Columbia. These data encompass state prisons only and do not count persons confined in county jails or in federal facilities. Thus, these data are not comparable to the inclusive England data. None the less, England and Wales's white incarceration. rate of 77 per 100,000, its black rate of 547, and its racial ratio of 7.10 are not greatly different from what those of a number of American states would be if adjustments were made for non-comparability of the data. A few American states have lower white male incarceration rates than in England and Wales some have lower black male incarceration rates, and many have lower racial ratios.

Table 5 shows Australian national and state incarceration numbers, rates per 100,000 population, and ratios for Aboriginals and non-Aboriginals in January 1993. The national ratio of rates was 12.8, nearly double the black/white ratio in the United States.

Table 4 Ratio of Black-to-White Incarceration by State, 1988

State	INCARCERATION RATES White per 100,000	Black per 100,000	Black/White Ratio
Hawaii	190	530	2.79
Maine	104	311	3.00
North Dakota	63	199	3.14
Alaska	349	1,296	3.72
Tennessee	108	402	3.72
South Carolina	217	829	3.82
Mississippi	135	562	4.16
Idaho	157	712	4.52
Alabama	164	757	4.62
New Mexico	213	983	4.62
Georgia	148	686	4.64
New York	165	781	4.74
North Carolina	136	665	4.88
New Hampshire	90	472	5.22
Arizona	329	1,725	5.25
Montana	136	714	5.26
West Virginia	72	382	5.33
Indiana	155	830	5.34
Arkansas	139	745	5.37
Louisiana	159	903	5.68
Kentucky	146	829	5.69
California	218	1,266	5.81
National	155	965	6.24
Virginia	116	738	6.38
Colorado	148	994	6.69
Nevada	279	1,954	7.01
Oklahoma	200	1,406	7.02
Florida	147	1,045	7.11
Missouri	145	1,033	7.14
Delaware	235	1,722	7.34
Maryland	114	873	7.67
Texas	109	874	8.05
Ohio	140	1,137	8.13
South Dakota	115	952	8.28
Michigan	145	1,224	8.46
Kansas	156	1,382	8.83
Oregon	180	1,657	9.22
Washington	86	856	9.97
Illinois	74	739	9.96
New Jersey	95	946	9.98
Massachusetts	72	775	10.82
Nebraska	98	1,099	11.24
Wisconsin	84	966	11.52
Pennsylvania	72	940	12.97
Wyoming	174	2,302	13.23
Rhode Island	132	1,752	13.24
Dist. of Columbia	150	2,143	14.31
Utah	105	1,503	14.35
Iowa	85	1,395	16.33
Connecticut	83	1,383	16.58
Minnesota	42	797	19.01

SOURCES: Proband 1991; Bureau of the Census 1992; Flanagan and Maguire 1990.

Table 5 Aboriginal and Non-Aboriginal Incarcerated Populations, January 1993

	Non-Aboriginal Prisoners	Rates 100,000	Aboriginal Prisoners	Rates 100,000	Ratio of Rates
New South Wales*	5,388	86.2	614	868.5	10.1
Victoria	2,123	47.4	121	728.9	15.4
Queensland	1,685	56.1	422	629.9	11.2
Western Australia	1,201	71.7	566	1,415.0	19.7
South Australia	938	63.9	169	1,056.3	16.5
Tasmania	251	54.9	16	183.9	3.4
NorthernTerritory	124	101.1	308	804.2	8.0
Australia	11,710	67.1	2,216	861.3	12.8

SOURCE: Biles 1993a from Australian Institute of Criminology data.

These data, which because of their inclusiveness are more comparable than American data to those from England and Wales show that England and Wales incarcerate proportionately more whites than most Australian states and proportionately fewer blacks than is the case with Aboriginals in Australia.

England and Wales's middling location in these measures relative to the United States and Australia suggests that disproportionate black incarceration is a much greater problem in England than is commonly acknowledged, an oversight made possible only by the small number of blacks in England's general population.

EXPLANATIONS OF MINORITY OVER-REPRESENTATION

Among numerous questions presented by the preceding data on incarceration of members of minority groups, three stand out. What causes the broad long-term patterns of overincarceration of blacks? Why do some not conspicuously punitive jurisdictions—Minnesota, Wisconsin, Victoria—have racial incarceration ratios that are especially unfavourable to blacks? Why has racial disproportionality in American prisons worsened in recent years? Although these same questions appear to apply equally to Australia, Canada, England and Wales, and the United States, my comments here concern the United States; appropriately adapted they may also apply to other countries.

Long-Term Racial Disproportion

Much, not all, black over-representation in American prisons over the past 20 years appears to be associated with disproportionate participation by blacks in the kinds of crimes—"imprisonable crimes" like homicide, robbery, aggravated assault, rape—that commonly result in prison sentences. Alfred Blumstein some years ago (1982) analysed black and white incarceration patterns in relation to arrest patterns (and, from victim surveys, victims' identifications of assailants' races, when known) and concluded that 80 percent of the disproportion appeared to result from blacks' participation in imprisonable crimes. The remaining 20 percent, he speculated, included some mixture of racially discriminatory discretionary decisions and other, arguably legitimate, sentencing considerations like prior criminal record. Hood (1992) in his study of Crown Courts in the English Midland; similarly concluded that 80 percent of black-white incarceration differences "can be accounted for by the greater number of black offenders who appeared for sentence . . . and by the nature and circumstances of the crimes they were convicted of" (p. 205).

Blumstein's conclusion that involvement in crime, not racial bias, explains much of the black disproportion among prisoners in the early 1980s is consistent with most recent reviews of empirical research on discrimination in sentencing (Wilbanks 1987). Most analyses of the past 15 years using multivariate techniques do not reveal racial bias as a major predictor of sentencing outcomes.

Most likely, however, if Blumstein's study were redone today, his imprisonable crimes analyses would be less powerful (e.g., Hawkins 1986). As noted below, drug offenders make up a steadily increasing proportion of prisoners, and they are even more disproportionately black than are other felony offenders.[3] Although I see no reason to believe that court processing is more racially biased than in recent years, both the national policy decision to launch a War on Drugs and local police decisions to focus on street trafficking foreseeably increased black arrests, prosecutions, convictions, and incarcerations.

The absence of research evidence of invidious discrimination is not evidence of its absence. Bias no doubt remains common—sometimes as a matter of conscious ill-will, more commonly as a result of unconscious stereotyping and attribution by middle-class and white officials of special dangerousness to underclass minority offenders. Moreover, all but the most sophisticated studies can be confounded by cross-cutting biases that result in harsher treatment of some black offenders and less harsh treatment of offenders (generally black) whose victims are black. Another complication is that many of the arguably legitimate bases for distinguishing among offenders, such as the nature of a criminal record, systematically adversely affect blacks (whose average first arrest is at a younger age than the average first arrest for whites and who, controlling for age and offence, are likely to have accrued more prior arrests and convictions, which may themselves result from earlier conscious and unconscious discrimination against blacks). None the less, at day's end, there is relatively little empirical basis for concluding that all or a large portion of the long-term disproportion in prison numbers results from invidious racial discrimination in processing of cases once arrests have been made.

Variations in Racial Ratios

That Minnesota and Wisconsin, generally considered among America's most socially and politically progressive states, and leaders in setting enlightened sentencing and corrections policies, have the most racially disproportionate incarceration rates in the country may strike many as surprising. They achieved that dishonour not only in the data reported here but in earlier analyses using 1979 (Hawkins 1985) and 1982 (Blumstein 1988) data.

At least three considerations partly explain the seeming anomaly. First, in jurisdictions in which blacks constitute a small percentage of the population, like Minnesota and Wisconsin (and England), the minority population is typically concentrated in urban areas. Crime rates are higher in urban than in suburban and rural areas; that a preponderantly urban black population experiences higher rates of criminality and incarceration than do groups that are more widely dispersed geographically is to be expected. In states like Georgia, Mississippi, and South Carolina, blacks live throughout the state and thus come from low, moderate, and high crime areas.

Secondly, black Americans are likelier than whites to be unemployed, ill educated, and to have been raised in single-parent households and impoverished circumstances (Jaynes and Williams 1989). All of these things are associated with increased participation in crime and, not unnaturally, are also associated with heightened arrest and incarceration probabilities (Blumstein *el al.* 1986).

Thirdly, in states like Minnesota, Iowa, and Wisconsin that have relatively low incarceration rates, prison spaces are principally used for persons convicted of violent and otherwise especially serious crimes. If the black populations of such states are small in number, concentrated in urban areas, and socially disadvantaged, they are disproportionately likely to be involved in serious crimes. By contrast, in states like Georgia, Alabama, California, and Texas, in which imprisonment rates are high, reflecting incarceration of many persons convicted of less serious crimes, larger proportions of white offenders are imprisoned and racial disproportions are less.

No doubt racial discrimination, especially in unconscious forms related to stereotyping and attribution of threatening characteristics to minority offenders, also plays a role in the extreme racial incarceration ratios in states like Minnesota. None the less, much of the variation appears explicable in terms of crimes committed and previous criminal records.

The Short-Term Worsening of Racial Ratios

Racial disproportion has worsened markedly in recent years, as is shown both by Figure 1 and by a series of recent analyses showing that one in four black American males aged 20 to 29 is in jail or prison, on probation or parole (Mauer 1990) and that in the District of Columbia (Miller 1992*a*) and Baltimore (Miller 1992*b*), 42 and 56 percent, respectively, of black males aged 18 to 35 were under the control of the criminal justice system.

The recent worsening is the result of deliberate policy choices of federal and state officials to "toughen" sentencing, in an era of falling and stable crime rates, and to launch a "War on Drugs" during a period when all general population surveys showed declining levels of drug use, beginning in the early 1980s (e.g., National Institute on Drug Abuse 1991).

At every level of the criminal justice system, empirical analyses demonstrate that increasing black disproportion has resulted from the War on Drugs—in

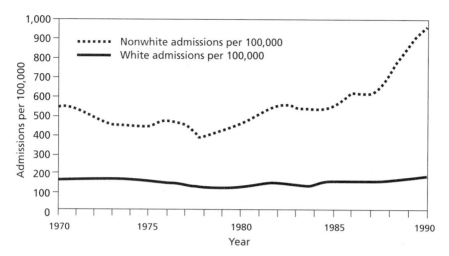

FIGURE 2 Prison Admissions per 100,000 General Population, North Carolina, by Race, 1970–90 (Clarke 1992)

juvenile institutions (Snyder 1990), in jails (Flanagan and Maguire 1992, table 6.49). and in state (Flanagan and Maguire 1992, table 6.81; Perkins 1992, tables 1–5) and federal (US Sentencing Commission 1991) prisons. The experience in several state prison systems is illustrative.

Figure 2 shows black and white admissions per 100,000 same-race population to North Carolina prisons from 1970 to 1990. White rates held steady during the entire period. Black rates doubled between 1980 and 1990 from a higher starting point, increasing most rapidly after 1987. According to Stevens Clarke, the foremost scholar of North Carolina sentencing and corrections trends, the War on Drugs has increasingly targeted blacks: "in 1984 about twice as many whites (10,269) as blacks (5,021) were arrested for drug offenses ... By 1989, annual drug arrests of blacks had grown by 183 percent, reaching 14,192; drug arrests of whites increased only by 36 percent (to 14,007)" (Clarke 1992: 12).

Figure 3 shows increases in prison commitments in Pennsylvania for 1980–90 for drug and other offences by race and sex. Drug commitments of black males increased by 1,613 percent during the decade; white males by 477 percent. The pattern for females was similar, though the differences were less dramatic. In 1990, 11 percent of Pennsylvanians were black; 58 percent of state prisoners were black (Clark 1992).

Figure 4 shows white and non-white drug commitments to Virginia prisons from 1983 to 1989. Sixty two percent of drug offenders committed in 1983 were white, 38 percent were non-white. By 1989, those percentages had more than reversed; 65 percent of drug commitments were non-white, 35 percent were white. Drug commitments have continued to rise since 1989; current data would show worse racial disproportion.

Phrased most charitably to the officials who launched and conducted America's latest War on Drugs, worsening of racial incarceration patterns was a

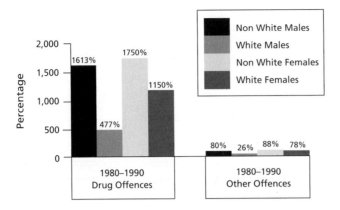

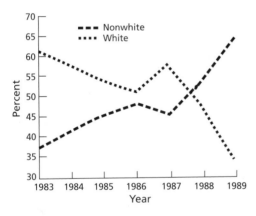

FIGURE 3 Percentage Growth in Prison Commitments in Pennsylvania, by Race, Sex, and Offence, 1980–90 (Clark 1992)

FIGURE 4 New Drug Commitments in Virginia, by Race, 1983–9 (Austin and McVey 1989)

foreseen but not intended consequence. Less charitably, the recent blackening of America's prison population is the product of malign neglect.

REDRESSING RACIAL IMBALANCE

Problems of race and punishment in America are both more severe than is generally recognized and yet, controlling for crime rates, not all that much worse than in other English-speaking countries. Although increasing numbers of American blacks are moving into the middle-class, for a sizeable minority the traditional pattern of assimilation of in-migrants is not working. In any case, the immigration analogy patently does not hold for black residents of southern states. In the black urban underclass, rates of unemployment, illegitimacy, single-parent households, delinquency, and other correlates of social disorganization are far higher than in other population groups.

These patterns pose formidable—if obvious—policy problems. Concern for victims rights to live their lives free from fear, assaults, and property loss obliges the state to respond to predatory crime and criminals. Because much crime is intra-racial, concern for minority victims necessarily occasions criminal justice system intervention in the lives of minority offenders. In so far as predatory crime is concentrated in the inner cities and predatory criminals disproportionately come from groups that lack opportunities, resources, and social supports, blacks are likely to continue to be disproportionately present among arrestees and defendants.

None the less, there are things that could be done to diminish racial disproportion. First, although the criminal law cannot acknowledge extreme social adversity as an affirmative defence, at all stages from prosecution to sentencing and parole, adversity can be recognized as an informal mitigating circumstance to justify diversion from prosecution and avoidance of prison in all possible cases and to justify provision of drug and alcohol treatment, remedial education, vocational training and placement. and supportive social services to minority and other disadvantaged offenders.

Secondly, designers of law enforcement policies should take account of foreseeable racial effects of alternative policy choices. Although American constitutional law sometimes distinguishes between actions taken with the purpose of discriminating against blacks, and actions taken for other purposes but with knowledge that they will systematically disadvantage blacks, policymakers should generally treat purpose and knowledge as moral equivalents (as they are in criminal law *mens rea* doctrines). The decision heavily to favour law enforcement over prevention and treatment strategies in the American War on Drugs, for example, was pre-ordained to affect young black males especially severely and for that reason alone (there are others) the "War" should never have been launched.

Thirdly, policy makers generally should begin to look to delinquency and criminality as diagnostic markers of group social distress. Among recent immigrant groups, those in which offending is conspicuously more common than in other contemporaneous immigrant groups should be targeted for social services and supports. South-east Asian tribal immigrants in the United States like the Meo and the Hmong, for example, were less well-situated than the Vietnamese, many of whom were educated urban dwellers, to succeed in America's capitalist economy. If second and third generation Meo and Hmong people demonstrate unusually high levels of criminality (it is too soon to tell), that will be powerful evidence that, as a group, they are having particular difficulty adjusting to life in a new country and, accordingly, that the state should allocate resources to help them overcome barriers to assimilation.

American blacks are the paradigm case of an identifiable subgroup that needs special aid in entry into full participation in American life. Fewer than 30 years have passed since discrimination against blacks in many settings ceased to

be legal and full legal rights have only slowly, and as yet imperfectly, been institutionalized in day-to-day life. All American blacks suffer from the legacy of
slavery and legal racism and many, especially southern agricultural migrants and
their children and residents of inner city underclass areas, have suffered from
inadequacies in education, employment opportunities, and health care.
American social policy since the 1970s has not provided adequate educational
programmes, housing, and income support to disadvantaged blacks, and their
disproportionate participation in crime is in part the result. The War on Drugs
has worsened the prospects for disadvantaged blacks by giving a majority of
young urban black males criminal records, thereby diminishing prospects for
jobs, marriage, and law-abiding material success. Conversely, the deteriorating
life chances of underclass black males have made them less promising prospects
as life partners of black women and are contributing to declining marriage
rates and accelerating illegitimacy and single-parent households among black
women.

Americans have a remarkable ability to endure suffering by others. Racially
disaggregated incarceration patterns show that black Americans are suffering
severely. Whether the recent presidential election will produce a more caring
government and a more compassionate climate, prepared to deal seriously with
the problems of disadvantaged American blacks, remains to be seen. If not, the
intolerable racial disproportion in America's prisons and jails is likely long to
continue.

NOTES

1. With some exceptions, prisons hold convicted offenders serving terms or one year
or longer; jails hold pretrial detainees and
convicted offenders serving terms up to
one year.

2. "Incarceration rate," as used in this essay,
refers to the numbers confined on a census
date, or the average daily confined population, per 100,000 residents.

3. More recently Blumstein (1993) analysed
1991 data and concluded that 75 percent of
the variance could be explained on the
basis of arrests (the decline resulted from
black over-representation among the
greatly increased numbers of those arrested
for drug offences).

REFERENCES

Allen-Hagen, B. (1991), *Public Juvenile Facil-
ities, Children in Custody 1989.*
Washington. DC: US Department of
Justice, Office of Juvenile Justice and
Delinquency Prevention.

Austin, J., and McVey, A. D. (1989), *The
Impact of the War on Drugs.*
San Francisco: National Council on
Crime and Delinquency.

Biles, D. (1993a), Personal correspondence
with the author, 23 March (1993b),
"Imprisonment in Australia," *Overcrowded Times*, 4(3): 4–6.

Birkenmayer, A. (1992), Communication
from the Chief, Corrections Program.
Canadian Centre for Justice Statistics,
Statistics Canada.

Blumstein A. (1982), "On the Racial Disproportionality of United States' Prison Populations," *Journal of Criminal Law and Criminology,* 73: 1259–81.

——— (1988), "Prison Populations: A System Out of Control?" in M. Tonry and N. Morris, eds, *Crime and Justice*, vol. 10. Chicago: University of Chicago Press.

——— (1993), "Racial Disproportion of U.S. Prison Populations Revisited," *University of Colorado Law Review,* 64: 743–60.

Blumstein, A., Cohen, J., Roth, J., and Visher, C., eds. (1986), *Criminal Careers and "Career Criminals."* Washington, DC: National Academy Press.

Bureau of Justice Statistics (1984), *The 1983 Jail Census.* Washington, DC: US Department of Justice.

——— (1985), *Jail Inmates, 1983.* Washington, DC: US Department of Justice.

——— (1987), *Correctional Populations in the United States, 1985.* Washington, DC: US Department of Justice.

——— (1989*a*), *Correctional Populations in the United States, 1987.* Washington, DC: US Department of Justice.

——— (1989*b*), *Correctional Populations in the United States, 1986.* Washington, DC: US Department of Justice.

——— (1991*a*), *Correctional Populations in the United States, 1989.* Washington, DC: US Department of Justice.

——— (1991*b*), *Correctional Populations in the United States, 1988.* Washington, DC: US Department of Justice.

——— (1991*c*), *Census of Local Jails, 1988.* Washington, DC: US Department of Justice.

Bureau of Justice Statistics (1992), *Jail Inmates, 1991.* Washington, DC: US Department of Justice.

——— (1992), *Statistical Abstract of the United States—1992.* Washington, DC: US Government Printing Office.

Calahan, M. W. (1986), *Historical Corrections Statistics in the United States, 1850–1984.* Washington, DC: US Department of Justice, Bureau of Justice Statistics.

Clark, S. (1992), "Pennsylvania Corrections in Context," *Overcrowded Times,* 3(4): 4–5.

Clarke, S. H. (1992), "North Carolina Prisons Growing," *Overcrowded Time,* 3 (4): 1. 11–13.

Flanagan, T. J., and Maguire, K., eds (1990), *Sourcebook of Criminal Justice Statistics, 1989.* Washington, DC: US Government Printing Office.

——— (1992), *Sourcebook of Criminal Justice Statistics, 1991.* Washington, DC: US Government Printing Office.

Gilliard, D. K. (1992), *National Corrections Reporting Program, 1987.* Washington, DC: US Department of Justice, Bureau of Justice Statistics.

Glazer N., and Moynihan, D. (1963), *Beyond the Melting Pot.* Cambridge, MA: MIT Press.

Hacker, A. (1992), *Two Nations: Black and White, Separate, Hostile, Unequal.* New York: Scribner.

Hawkins, D. F. (1985), "Trends in Black–White Imprisonment: Changing Conceptions of Race or Changing Conceptions of Social Control?," *Crime and Social Justice,* 24: 187–209.

——— (1986), Race, Crime Type, and Imprisonment, *Justice Quarterly* 3: 251–69.

Home Office (1991), *The Prison Population in 1990.* London: Home Office, Statistical Department.

Hood, R. (1992), *Race and Sentencing.* Oxford: Oxford University Press.

Jankowski, L. W. (1992), *Correctional Populations in the United States, 1990.* Washington, DC: US Department of Justice, Bureau of Justice Statistics.

Jaynes, D. G., and Williams R. M., Jr., eds (1989), *A Common Destiny: Blacks and American Society.* Report of the Committee on the Status of Black Americans, National Academy of Sciences. Washington, DC: National Academy Press.

Jencks, C. (1992), *Rethinking Social Policy.* Cambridge, MA: Harvard University Press.

Kalish, C. (1988), *International Crime Rates.* Washington, DC: US Department of Justice, Bureau of Justice Statistics.

Katz, M. (1989), *The Undeserving Poor.* New York: Pantheon.

Krisberg, B., and Decomo, R. (1992), *National Juvenile Custody Trends 1978–89.* Washington, DC: US Department of Justice, Office of Juvenile Justice and Delinquency Prevention.

Langan, P. A. (1991), *Race of Persons Admitted to State and Federal Institutions, 1926–86.* Washington, DC: US Department of Justice, Bureau of Justice Statistics.

Lemann, N. (1991), *The Promised Land—The Great Black Migration and How It Changed America.* New York: Alfred Knopf.

Mauer, M. (1990), "Young Black Men and the Criminal Justice System," Washington, DC: The Sentencing Project.

Miller, J. G (1992*a*), "42% of Black DC Males, 18 to 35. Under Criminal Justice System Control, *Overcrowded Times,* 3.3 :1, 11.

———— (1992*b*). "56 Percent of Young Black Males in Baltimore Under Justice System Control," *Overcrowded Times.* 3(6): 1, 10, 16.

Murray, C. (1984), *Losing Ground—American Social Policy, 1950–1980.* New York: Basic.

National Institute on Drug Abuse (1991), *National Household Survey on Drug Abuse: Population Estimates 1990.* Washington, DC: US Government Printing Office.

Perkins, C. (1992), *National Corrections Reporting Program, 1989.* Washington, DC: US Department of Justice, Bureau of Justice Statistics.

Perkins, C., and Gilliard, D. K. (1992), *National Corrections Reporting Program,* 1988. Washington, DC: US Department of Justice, Bureau of Justice Statistics.

Proband, S. C. (1991), "Black, White Incarceration Rates," *Overcrowded Times.* 2(3): 6–7.

Royal Commission into Aboriginal Deaths in Custody (1990), *Report.* Canberra.

Snyder, H. N. (1990), *Growth in Minority Detentions Attributed to Drug Law Violators.* Washington, DC: US Department of Justice, Office of Juvenile Justice and Delinquency Prevention.

US National Commission on Law Observance and Enforcement (1931), *Report on Crime and the Foreign Born.* Washington, DC: US Government Printing Office.

US Sentencing Commission (1991), *The Federal Sentencing Guidelines: A Report on the Operation of the Guidelines System and Short-term Impacts on Disparity in Sentencing, Use of Incarceration, and Prosecutorial Discretion and Plea Bargaining.* Washington, DC: US Sentencing Commission.

Van Dijk, J., and Mayhew, P. (1993), *Criminal Victimisation in the Industrialised World: Key Findings of the 1989 and 1992 International Crime Surveys.* The Hague: Ministry of Justice.

Van Dijk, J., and Mayhew, P., and Killias, M. (1990), *Experiences of Crime Across the World: Key Findings from the 1989 International Crime Survey.* Boston: Kluwer.

Wilbanks, W. (1987), *The Myth of a Racist Criminal Justice System.* Monterey, CA: Brooks/Cole.

Wilson, W. J. (1987), *The Truly Disadvantaged: The Inner City, the Underclass, and Public Policy.* Chicago: University of Chicago Press.

19

The Society of Captives

The Defects of Total Power

Gresham M. Sykes

In theory, prisons are organized in an authoritarian manner. In such a "society of captives," one might assume that guards have only to give orders and inmates will follow them. Because the guards have a monopoly on the legal means of enforcing rules, many people believe that there should be no question about how the prison is run. In reality, however, the relationship between the guards and the prisoners is based on a more fragile foundation. As this article shows, there are limitations on the ability of correctional officers to use total power.

" **F**or the needs of mass administration today," said Max Weber, "bureaucratic administration is completely indispensable. The choice is between bureaucracy and dilettantism in the field of administration."[1] To the officials of the New Jersey State Prison the choice is clear, as it is clear to the custodians of all maximum security prisons in the United States today. They are organized into a bureaucratic administrative staff—characterized by limited and specific rules, well-defined areas of competence and responsibility, impersonal standards of performance and promotion,

Source: Selection from Gresham M. Sykes, *The Society of Captives: A Study of a Maximum Security Prison* (copyright © 1958 by Princeton University Press: Princeton Paperback, 1971), pp. 40–first 2 paragraphs p. 53. Reprinted by permission of Princeton University Press. Portions of this article concerning the corruption of the guards' authority are to be found in Gresham M. Sykes, *Crime and Society* (New York: Random House, 1956).

and so on—which is similar in many respects to that of any modern, large-scale enterprise; and it is this staff which must see to the effective execution of the prison's routine procedures.

Of the approximately 300 employees of the New Jersey State Prison, more than two-thirds are directly concerned with the supervision and control of the inmate population. These form the so-called custodian force which is broken into three eight-hour shifts, each shift being arranged in a typical pyramid of authority. The day shift, however—on duty from 6:20 A.M. to 2:20 P.M.—is by far the largest. As in many organizations, the rhythm of life in the prison quickens with daybreak and trails off in the afternoon, and the period of greatest activity requires the largest number of administrative personnel.

In the bottom ranks are the wing guards, the tower guards, the guards assigned to the shops, and those with a miscellany of duties such as the guardianship of the receiving gate or the garage. Immediately above these men are a number of sergeants and lieutenants, and these in turn are responsible to the warden and his assistants.

The most striking fact about this bureaucracy of custodians is its unparalleled position of power—in formal terms, at least—vis-à-vis the body of men which it rules and from which it is supposed to extract compliance. The officials, after all, possess a monopoly on the legitimate means of coercion (or, as one prisoner has phrased it succinctly, "They have the guns and we don't"); and the officials can call on the armed might of the police and the National Guard in case of an overwhelming emergency. The twenty-four-hour surveillance of the custodians represents the ultimate watchfulness, and presumably noncompliance on the part of the inmates need not go long unchecked. The rulers of this society of captives nominally hold in their hands the sole right of granting rewards and inflicting punishments and it would seem that no prisoner could afford to ignore their demands for conformity. Centers of opposition in the inmate population—in the form of men recognized as leaders by fellow prisoners—can be neutralized through the use of solitary confinement or exile to other state institutions. The custodians have the right not only to issue and administer the orders and regulations which are to guide the life of the prisoner, but also the right to detail, try, and punish any individual accused of disobedience—a merging of legislative, executive, and judicial functions which has long been regarded as the earmark of complete domination. The officials of the prison, in short, appear to be the possessors of almost infinite power within their realm; and, at least on the surface, the bureaucratic staff should experience no great difficulty in converting their rules and regulations—their blueprint for behavior—into a reality.

It is true, of course, that the power position of the custodial bureaucracy is not truly infinite. The objectives which the officials pursue are not completely of their own choosing and the means which they can use to achieve their objectives are far from limitless. The custodians are not total despots, able to exercise power at whim, and thus they lack the essential mark of infinite power, the unchallenged right of being capricious in their rule. It is this last which distinguishes terror from government, infinite power from almost infinite power, and the distinction is an important one. Neither by right nor by intention are the officials of the New Jersey State Prison free from a system of norms and laws which curb their actions. But within these limitations the bureaucracy of the prison is organized around a grant of power which is without an equal in American society; and if the rulers of any social system could secure compliance with their rules and regulations—however sullen or unwilling—it might be expected that the officials of the maximum security prison would be able to do so.

When we examine the New Jersey State Prison, however, we find that this expectation is not borne out in actuality. Indeed, the glaring conclusion is that despite the guns and the surveillance, the searches and the precautions of the custodians, the actual behavior of the inmate population differs markedly from that which is called for by official commands and decrees. Violence, fraud, theft, aberrant sexual behavior—all are commonplace occurrences in the daily round of institutional existence in spite of the fact that the maximum security prison is conceived of by society as the ultimate weapon for the control of the criminal and his deviant actions. Far from being omnipotent rulers who have crushed all signs of rebellion against their regime, the custodians are engaged in a continuous struggle to maintain order—and it is a struggle in which the custodians frequently fail. Offenses committed by one inmate against another occur often, as do offenses committed by inmates against the officials and their rules. And the number of undetected offenses is, by universal agreement of both officials and inmates, far larger than the number of offenses which are discovered.

Some hint of the custodial bureaucracy's skirmishes with the population of prisoners is provided by the records of the disciplinary court which has the task of adjudicating charges brought by guards against their captives for offenses taking place within the walls. The following is a typical listing for a one-week period:

Charge	Disposition
1. Insolence and swearing while being interrogated	1. Continue in segregation
2. Threatening an inmate	2. Drop from job
3. Attempting to smuggle roll of tape into institution	3. 1 day in segregation with restricted diet
4. Possession of contraband	4. 30 days loss of privileges
5. Possession of pair of dice	5. 2 days in segregation with restricted diet
6. Insolence	6. Reprimand
7. Out of place	7. Drop from job. Refer to classification committee for reclassification
8. Possession of homemade knife, metal, and emery paper	8. 5 days in segregation with restricted diet

9. Suspicion of gambling or receiving bets	9. Drop from job and change Wing assignment
10. Out of place	10. 15 days loss of privileges
11. Possession of contraband	11. Reprimand
12. Creating disturbance in Wing	12. Continue in segregation
13. Swearing at an officer	13. Reprimand
14. Out of place	14. 15 days loss of privileges
15. Out of place	15. 15 days loss of privileges

Even more revealing, however, than this brief and somewhat enigmatic record are the so-called charge slips in which the guard is supposed to write out the derelictions of the prisoner in some detail. In the New Jersey State Prison, charge slips form an administrative residue of past conflicts between captors and captives and the following accounts are a fair sample:

> This inmate threatened an officer's life. When I informed this inmate he was to stay in to see the Chief Deputy on his charge he told me if he did not go to the yard I would get a shiv in my back.
>
> Signed: Officer A _____

> Inmate X cursing an officer. In mess hall inmate refused to put excess bread back on tray. Then he threw the tray on the floor. In the Center, inmate cursed both Officer Y and myself.   Signed: Officer B _____

> This inmate has been condemning everyone about him for going to work. The Center gave orders for him to go to work this A.M. which he refused to do. While searching his cell I found drawings of picks and locks.   Signed: Officer C _____

> Fighting. As this inmate came to 1 Wing entrance to go to yard this A.M. he struck inmate G in the face.   Signed: Officer D _____

> Having fermented beverage in his cell. Found while inmate was in yard.   Signed: Officer E _____

> Attempting to instigate wing disturbance. When I asked him why he discarded [sic] my order to quiet down he said he was going to talk any time he wanted to and _____ me and do whatever I wanted in regards to it.   Signed: Officer F _____

> Possession of home-made shiv sharpened to razor edge on his person and possession of 2 more shivs in cell. When inmate was sent to 4 Wing officer H found 3" steel blade in pocket. I ordered Officer M to search his cell and he found 2 more shivs in process of being sharpened.
>
> Signed: Officer G _____

> Insolence. Inmate objected to my looking at papers he was carrying in pockets while going to the yard. He snatched them violently from my hand and gave me some very abusive talk. This man told me to _____ myself, and raised his hands as if to strike me. I grabbed him by the shirt and took him to the Center.   Signed: Officer H _____

Assault with knife on Inmate K. During Idle Men's mess at approximately 11:10 A.M. this man assaulted Inmate K with a home-made knife. Inmate K was receiving his rations at the counter when Inmate B rushed up to him and plunged a knife in his chest, arm, and back. I grappled with him and with the assistance of Officers S and V, we disarmed the inmate and took him to the Center. Inmate K was immediately taken to the hospital.   Signed: Officer I _____

Sodomy. Found inmate W in cell with no clothing on and inmate Z on top of him with no clothing. Inmate W told me he was going to lie like a _____ _____ _____ to get out of it.
                                             Signed: Officer J _____

Attempted escape on night of 4/15/53. This inmate along with inmates L and T succeeded in getting on roof of 6 Wing and having home-made bombs in their possession.   Signed: Officer K _____

Fighting and possession of home-made shiv. Struck first blow to Inmate P. He struck blow with a roll of black rubber rolled up in his fist. He then produced a knife made out of wire tied to a toothbrush.
                                             Signed: Officer L _____

Refusing medication prescribed by Doctor W. Said "What do you think I am, a damn fool, taking that _____ for a headache, give it to the doctor."   Signed: Officer M _____

Inmate loitering on tier. There is a clique of several men who lock on top tier, who ignore rule of returning directly to their cells and attempt to hang out on the tier in a group.   Signed: Officer N _____

It is hardly surprising that when the guards at the New Jersey State Prison were asked what topics should be of first importance in a proposed in-service training program, 98 percent picked "what to do in event of trouble." The critical issue for the moment, however, is that the dominant position of the custodial staff is more fiction than reality, if we think of domination as something more than the outward forms and symbols of power. If power is viewed as the probability that orders and regulations will be obeyed by a given group of individuals, as Max Weber has suggested, the New Jersey State Prison is perhaps more notable for the doubtfulness of obedience than its certainty. The weekly records of the disciplinary court and charge slips provide an admittedly poor index of offenses or acts of noncompliance committed within the walls, for these form only a small, visible segment of an iceberg whose greatest bulk lies beneath the surface of official recognition. The public is periodically made aware of the officials' battle to enforce their regime within the prison, commonly in the form of allegations in the newspapers concerning homosexuality, illegal use of drugs, assaults, and so on. But the ebb and flow of public attention given to these matters does not match the constancy of these problems for the prison officials who are all too well aware that "incidents"—the very thing they try to minimize—are not isolated or rare events but are instead a commonplace. The number of "incidents" in the New Jersey State

Prison is probably no greater than that to be found in most maximum security institutions in the United States and may, indeed, be smaller, although it is difficult to make comparisons. In any event, it seems clear that the custodians are bound to their captives in a relationship of conflict rather than compelled acquiescence, despite the custodians' theoretical supremacy, and we now need to see why this should be so.

In our examination of the forces which undermine the power position of the New Jersey State Prison's custodial bureaucracy, the most important fact is, perhaps, that the power of the custodians is not based on authority.

Now power based on authority is actually a complex social relationship in which an individual or a group of individuals is recognized as possessing a right to issue commands or regulations and those who receive these commands or regulations feel compelled to obey by a sense of duty. In its pure form, then, or as an ideal type, power based on authority has two essential elements: a rightful or legitimate effort to exercise control on the one hand and an inner, moral compulsion to obey, by those who are to be controlled, on the other. In reality, of course, the recognition of the legitimacy of efforts to exercise control may be qualified or partial and the sense of duty, as a motive for compliance, may be mixed with motives of fear or self-interest. But it is possible for theoretical purposes to think of power based on authority in its pure form and to use this as a baseline in describing the empirical case.

It is the second element of authority—the sense of duty as a motive for compliance—which supplies the secret strength of most social organizations. Orders and rules can be issued with the expectation that they will be obeyed without the necessity of demonstrating in each case that compliance will advance the subordinate's interests. Obedience or conformity springs from an internalized morality which transcends the personal feelings of the individual; the fact that an order or a rule is an order or a rule becomes the basis for modifying one's behavior, rather than a rational calculation of the advantages which might be gained.

In the prison, however, it is precisely this sense of duty which is lacking in the general inmate population. The regime of the custodians is expressed as a mass of commands and regulations passing down a hierarchy of power. In general, these efforts at control are regarded as legitimate by individuals in the hierarchy, and individuals tend to respond because they feel they "should," down to the level of the guard in the cell block, the industrial shop, or the recreation yard. But now these commands and regulations must jump a gap which separates the captors from the captives. And it is at this point that a sense of duty tends to disappear, and with it goes that easily won obedience which many organizations take for granted in the naïveté of their unrecognized strength. In the prison, power must be based on something other than internalized morality, and the custodians find themselves confronting men who must be forced, bribed, or cajoled into compliance. This is not to say that inmates feel that the efforts of prison officials to exercise control are wrongful or illegitimate; in general, prisoners do not feel that the prison officials have usurped positions of power which are not rightfully theirs, nor do prisoners feel that the orders and regulations which descend upon them from above represent an illegal extension of their rulers' grant of government. Rather, the noteworthy fact about the social system of the New Jersey State Prison is that the bond between recognition of the legitimacy of control and the sense of duty has been torn apart. In these terms the social system of the prison is very similar to a *Gebietsverband*, a territorial group living under a regime imposed by a ruling few. Like a province which has been conquered by force of arms, the community of prisoners has come to accept the validity of the regime constructed by their rulers but the subjugation is not complete. Whether he sees himself as caught by his own stupidity, the workings of chance, his inability to "fix" the case, or the superior skill of the police, the criminal in prison seldom denies the legitimacy of confinement.[2] At the same time, the recognition of the legitimacy of society's surrogates and their body of rules is not accompanied by an internalized obligation to obey and the prisoner thus accepts the fact of his captivity at one level and rejects it at another. If for no other reason, then, the custodial institution is valuable for a theory of human behavior because it makes us realize that men need not be motivated to conform to a regime which they define as rightful. It is in this apparent contradiction that we can see the first flaw in the custodial bureaucracy's assumed supremacy.

Since the officials of prison possess a monopoly on the means of coercion, as we have pointed out earlier, it might be thought that the inmate population could simply be forced into conformity and that the lack of an inner moral compulsion to obey on the part of the inmates could be ignored. Yet the combination of a bureaucratic staff—that most modern, rational form of mobilizing effort to exercise control—and the use of physical violence—that most ancient device to channel man's conduct—must strike us as an anomaly and with good reason. The use of force is actually grossly inefficient as a means for securing obedience, particularly when those who are to be controlled are called on to perform a task of any complexity. A blow with a club may check an immediate revolt, it is true, but it cannot assure effective performance on a punch-press. A "come along," a straitjacket, or a pair of handcuffs may serve to curb one rebellious prisoner in a crisis, but they will be of little aid in moving more than 1,200 inmates through the mess hall in a routine and orderly fashion. Furthermore, the custodians are well aware that violence once unleashed is not easily brought to heel and it is this awareness that lies behind the standing order that no guard should ever strike an inmate with his hand—he should always use a nightstick. This rule is not an open invitation to brutality but an attempt to set a high threshold on the use of force in order to eliminate the casual cuffing which might explode into extensive and violent retaliation. Similarly, guards are under orders to throw their nightsticks over the wall if they are on duty in the recreation yard when a riot develops. A guard without weapons, it is argued, is safer than a guard who tries to hold on to his symbol of office, for a mass of rebellious inmates may find a single nightstick a goad rather than a restraint and the guard may find himself beaten to death with his own means of compelling order.

In short, the ability of the officials to physically coerce their captives into the paths of compliance is something of an illusion as far as the day-to-day activities of the prison are concerned and may be of doubtful value in moments of crisis. Intrinsically inefficient as a method of making men carry out a complex task, diminished in effectiveness by the realities of the guard-inmate ratio,[3] and always accompanied by the danger of touching off further violence, the use of physical force by the custodians has many limitations as a basis on which to found the routine operation of the prison. Coercive tactics may have some utility in checking blatant disobedience—if only a few men disobey. But if the great mass of criminals in prison are to be brought into the habit of conformity, it must be on other grounds. Unable to count on a sense of duty to motivate their captives to obey and unable to depend on the direct and immediate use of violence to ensure a step-by-step submission to the rules, the custodians must fall back on a system of rewards and punishments.

Now if men are to be controlled by the use of rewards and punishments—by promises and threats—at least one point is patent: The rewards and punishments dangled in front of the individual must indeed be rewards and punishments from the point of view of the individual who is to be controlled. It is precisely on this point, however, that the custodians' system of rewards and punishments founders. In our discussion of the problems encountered in securing conscientious performance at work, we suggested that both the penalties and the incentives available to the officials were inadequate. This is also largely true, at a more general level, with regard to rewards and punishments for securing compliance with the wishes of the custodians in all areas of prison life.

In the first place, the punishments which the officials can inflict—for theft, assaults, escape attempts, gambling, insolence, homosexuality, and all the other deviations from the pattern of behavior called for by the regime of the custodians—do not represent a profound difference from the prisoners' usual status. It may be that when men are chronically deprived of liberty, material goods and services, recreational opportunities, and so on, the few pleasures that are granted take on a new importance and the threat of their withdrawal is a more powerful motive for conformity than those of us in the free community can realize. To be locked up in the solitary-confinement wing, that prison within a prison; to move from the monotonous, often badly prepared meals in the mess hall to a diet of bread and water; to be dropped from a dull, unsatisfying job and forced to remain in idleness—all, perhaps, may mean the difference between an existence which can be borne, painful though it may be, and one which cannot. But the officials of the New Jersey State Prison are dangerously close to the point where the stock of legitimate punishments has been exhausted and it would appear that for many prisoners the few punishments which are left have lost their potency. To this we must couple the important fact that such punishments as the custodians can inflict may lead to an increased prestige for the punished inmate in the eyes of his fellow prisoners. He may become a hero, a martyr, a man who has confronted his captors and dared them to do their worst. In the dialectics of the inmate population, punishments and rewards have, then, been reversed and the control measures of the officials may support disobedience rather than decrease it.

In the second place, the system of rewards and punishments in the prison is defective because the reward side of the picture has been largely stripped away. Mail and visiting privileges, recreational privileges, the supply of personal possessions—all are given to the inmate at the time of his arrival in one fixed sum. Even the so-called good time—the portion of the prisoner's sentence deducted for good behavior—is automatically subtracted from the prisoner's sentence when he begins his period of imprisonment. Thus the officials have placed themselves in the peculiar position of granting the prisoner all available benefits or rewards at the time of his entrance into the system. The prisoner, then, finds himself unable to win any significant gains by means of compliance, for there are no gains left to be won.

From the viewpoint of the officials, of course, the privileges of the prison social system are regarded as rewards, as something to be achieved. That is to say, the custodians hold that recreation, access to the inmate store, good time, or visits from individuals in the free community are conditional upon conformity or good behavior. But the evidence suggests that from the viewpoint of the inmates the variety of benefits granted by the custodians is not defined as something to be earned but as an inalienable right—as the just due of the inmate which should not turn on the question of obedience or disobedience within the walls. After all, the inmate population claims these benefits have belonged to the prisoner from the time when he first came to the institution.

In short, the New Jersey State Prison makes an initial grant of all its rewards and then threatens to withdraw them if the prisoner does not conform. It does not start the prisoner from scratch and promise to grant its available rewards one by one as the prisoner proves himself through continued submission to the institutional regulations. As a result a subtle alchemy is set in motion whereby the inmates cease to see the rewards of the system as rewards, that is, as benefits contingent upon performance; instead, rewards are apt to be defined as obligations. Whatever justification might be offered for such a policy, it would appear to have a number of drawbacks as a method of motivating prisoners to fall into the posture of obedience. In effect, rewards and punishments of the officials have been collapsed into one and the prisoner moves in a world where there is no hope of progress but only the possibility of further punishments. Since the prisoner is already suffering from most of the punishments permitted by society, the threat of imposing those few remaining is all too likely to be a gesture of futility.

Unable to depend on that inner moral compulsion or sense of duty which eases the problem of control in most social organizations, acutely aware that brute force is inadequate, and lacking an effective system of legitimate rewards and

punishments which might induce prisoners to conform to institutional regulations on the grounds of self-interest, the custodians of the New Jersey State
Prison are considerably weakened in their attempts to impose their regime on
their captive population. The result, in fact, is, as we have already indicated, a
good deal of deviant behavior or noncompliance in a social system where the
rulers at first glance seem to possess almost infinite power.

Yet systems of power may be defective for reasons other than the fact that
those who are ruled do not feel the need to obey the orders and regulations
descending on them from above. Systems of power may also fail because those
who are supposed to rule are unwilling to do so. The unissued order, the deliberately ignored disobedience, the duty left unperformed—these are cracks in
the monolith just as surely as are acts of defiance in the subject population. The
"corruption" of the rulers may be far less dramatic than the insurrection of the
ruled, for power unexercised is seldom as visible as power which is challenged,
but the system of power still falters.

Now the official in the lowest ranks of the custodial bureaucracy—the guard
in the cell block, the industrial shop, or the recreation yard—is the pivotal figure
on which the custodial bureaucracy turns. It is he who must supervise and control the inmate population in concrete and detailed terms. It is he who must see
to the translation of the custodial regime from blueprint to reality and engage in
the specific battles for conformity. Counting prisoners, periodically reporting to
the center of communications, signing passes, checking groups of inmates as they
come and go, searching for contraband or signs of attempts to escape—these
make up the minutiae of his eight-hour shift. In addition, he is supposed to be
alert for violations of the prison rules which fall outside his routine sphere of
surveillance. Not only must he detect and report deviant behavior after it occurs;
he must curb deviant behavior before it arises as well, as when he is called on to
prevent a minor quarrel among prisoners from flaring into a more dangerous situation. And he must make sure that the inmates in his charge perform their
assigned tasks with a reasonable degree of efficiency.

The expected role of the guard, then, is a complicated compound of
policeman and foreman, of cadi [judge], counselor, and boss all rolled into one.
But as the guard goes about his duties, piling one day on top of another (and
the guard too, in a certain sense, is serving time in confinement), we find that
the system of power in the prison is defective not only because the means of
motivating the inmates to conform are largely lacking but also because the
guard is frequently reluctant to enforce the full range of the institution's regulations. The guard frequently fails to report infractions of the rules which have
occurred before his eyes. The guard often transmits forbidden information to
inmates, such as plans for searching particular cells in a surprise raid for contraband. The guard often neglects elementary security requirements and on
numerous occasions he will be found joining his prisoners in outspoken criticisms of the warden and his assistants. In short, the guard frequently shows evidence of having been "corrupted" by the captive criminals over whom he
stands in theoretical dominance. This failure within the ranks of the rulers is

seldom to be attributed to outright bribery-bribery, indeed, is usually unnecessary, for far more effective influences are at work to bridge the gap supposedly
separating captors and captives.

In the first place, the guard is in close and intimate association with his
prisoners throughout the course of the working day. He can remain aloof only
with great difficulty, for he possesses few of those devices which normally serve
to maintain social distance between the rulers and the ruled. He cannot withdraw physically in symbolic affirmation of his superior position; he has no
intermediaries to bear the brunt of resentment springing from orders which
are disliked; and he cannot fall back on a dignity adhering to his office—he is a
hack or a *screw* in the eyes of those he controls and an unwelcome display of
officiousness evokes that great destroyer of unquestioned power, the ribald
humor of the dispossessed.

There are many pressures in American culture to "be nice," to be a "good
Joe," and the guard in the maximum security prison is not immune. The guard
is constantly exposed to a sort of moral blackmail in which the first sign of
condemnations, estrangement, or rigid adherence to the rules is countered by
the inmates with the threat of ridicule or hostility. And in this complex interplay, the guard does not always start from a position of determined opposition
to "being friendly." He holds an intermediate post in a bureaucratic structure
between top prison officials—his captains, lieutenants, and sergeants—and the
prisoners in his charge. Like many such figures, the guard is caught in a conflict
of loyalties. He often has reason to resent the actions of his superior officers—
the reprimands, the lack of ready appreciation, the incomprehensible order—
and in the inmates he finds willing sympathizers. They, too, claim to suffer from
the unreasonable irritants of power. Furthermore, the guard in many cases is
marked by a basic ambivalence toward the criminals under his supervision and
control. It is true that the inmates of the prison have been condemned by society through the agency of the courts, but some of these prisoners must be
viewed as a success in terms of a worldly system of values which accords high
prestige to wealth and influence even though they may have been won by
devious means; and the poorly paid guard may be gratified to associate with a
famous racketeer. Moreover, this ambivalence in the guard's attitudes toward
the criminals nominally under his thumb may be based on something more
than a sub-rosa respect for the notorious. There may also be a discrepancy
between the judgments of society and the guard's own opinions as far as the
"criminality" of the prisoner is concerned. It is difficult to define the man convicted of deserting his wife, gambling, or embezzlement as a desperate criminal
to be suppressed at all costs, and the crimes of even the most serious offenders
lose their significance with the passage of time. In the eyes of the custodian, the
inmate tends to become a man in prison rather than a criminal in prison, and
the relationship between captor and captive is subtly transformed in the
process.

In the second place, the guard's position as a strict enforcer of the rules is
undermined by the fact that he finds it almost impossible to avoid the claims of

reciprocity. To a large extent the guard is dependent on inmates for the satisfactory performance of his duties; and like many individuals in positions of power, the guard is evaluated in terms of the conduct of the men he controls. A troublesome, noisy, dirty cell block reflects on the guard's ability to "handle" prisoners and this ability forms an important component of the merit rating which is used as the basis for pay raises and promotions. As we have pointed out above, a guard cannot rely on the direct application of force to achieve compliance nor can he easily depend on threats of punishment. And if the guard does insist on constantly using the last few negative sanctions available to the institution—if the guard turns in charge slip after charge slip for every violation of the rules which he encounters—he becomes burdensome to the top officials of the prison bureaucratic staff who realize only too well that their apparent dominance rests on some degree of cooperation. A system of power which can enforce its rules only by bringing its formal machinery of accusation, trial, and punishment into play at every turn will soon be lost in a haze of pettifogging detail.

The guard, then, is under pressure to achieve a smoothly running tour of duty not with the stick but with the carrot, but here again his legitimate stock is limited. Facing demands from above that he achieve compliance and stalemated from below, he finds that one of the most meaningful rewards he can offer is to ignore certain offenses or make sure that he never places himself in a position where he will discover them. Thus the guard—backed by all the power of the state, close to armed men who will run to his aid, and aware that any prisoner who disobeys him can be punished if he presses charges against him—often discovers that his best path of action is to make "deals" or "trades" with the captives in his power. In effect, the guard buys compliance or obedience in certain areas at the cost of tolerating disobedience elsewhere.

Aside from winning compliance "where it counts" in the course of the normal day, the guard has another favor to be secured from the inmates which makes him willing to forgo strict enforcement of all prison regulations. Many custodial institutions have experienced a riot in which the tables are turned momentarily and the captives hold sway over their quondam captors; and the rebellions of 1952 loom large in the memories of the officials of the New Jersey State Prison. The guard knows that he may some day be a hostage and that his life may turn on a settling of old accounts. A fund of goodwill becomes a valuable form of insurance and this fund is almost sure to be lacking if he has continually played the part of a martinet. In the folklore of the prison, there are enough tales about strict guards who have had the misfortune of being captured and savagely beaten during a riot to raise doubts about the wisdom of demanding complete conformity.

In the third place, the theoretical dominance of the guard is undermined in actuality by the innocuous encroachment of the prisoner on the guard's duties. Making out reports, checking cells at the periodic count, locking and unlocking doors—in short, all the minor chores which the guard is called on to perform—may gradually be transferred into the hands of inmates whom the guard has come to trust. The cell block runner, formally assigned the tasks of delivering mail, housekeeping duties, and so on, is of particular importance in this respect. Inmates in this position function in a manner analogous to that of the company clerk in the armed forces and like such figures they may wield power and influence far beyond the nominal definition of their role. For reasons of indifference, laziness, or naïveté, the guard may find that much of the power which he is supposed to exercise has slipped from his grasp.

Now power, like a person's virtue, once lost is hard to regain. The measures to rectify an established pattern of abdication need to be much more severe than those required to stop the first steps in the transfer of control from the guard to his prisoner. A guard assigned to a cell block in which a large portion of power has been shifted in the past from the officials to the inmates is faced with the weight of precedent; it requires a good deal of moral courage on his part to withstand the aggressive tactics of prisoners who fiercely defend the patterns of corruption established by custom. And if the guard himself has allowed his control to be subverted, he may find that any attempts to undo his error are checked by a threat from the inmate to send a *snitch-kite*—an anonymous note—to the guard's superior officers explaining his past derelictions in detail. This simple form of blackmail may be quite sufficient to maintain the relationships established by friendship, reciprocity, or encroachment.

It is apparent, then, that the power of the custodians is defective, not simply in the sense that the ruled are rebellious, but also in the sense that the rulers are reluctant. We must attach a new meaning to Lord Acton's aphorism that power tends to corrupt and absolute power corrupts absolutely. The custodians of the New Jersey State Prison, far from being converted into brutal tyrants, are under strong pressure to compromise with their captives, for it is a paradox that they can ensure their dominance only by allowing it to be corrupted. Only by tolerating violations of "minor" rules and regulations can the guard secure compliance in the "major" areas of the custodial regime. Ill-equipped to maintain the social distance which in theory separates the world of the officials and the world of the inmates, their suspicions eroded by long familiarity, the custodians are led into a *modus vivendi* with their captives which bears little resemblance to the stereotypical picture of guards and their prisoners.

The fact that the officials of the prison experience serious difficulties in imposing their regime on the society of prisoners is sometimes attributed to inadequacies of the custodial staff's personnel. These inadequacies, it is claimed, are in turn due to the fact that more than 50 percent of the guards are temporary employees who have not passed a Civil Service examination. In 1952, for example, a month and a half before the disturbances which dramatically underlined some of the problems of the officials, the deputy commissioner of the Department of Institutions and Agencies made the following points in a report concerning the temporary officers of the New Jersey State Prison's custodian force:

1. Because they are not interested in the prison service as a career, the temporary officers tend to have a high turnover as they are quick to resign to accept more remunerative employment.

2. Because they are inexperienced, they are not able to foresee or forestall
    disciplinary infractions, the on-coming symptoms of which the more
    experienced officer would detect and take appropriate preventive
    measures against.

3. Because they are not trained as the regular officers, they do not have the
    self-confidence that comes with the physical training and defensive
    measures which are part of the regular officers' pre-service training and,
    therefore, it is not uncommon for them to be somewhat timid and
    inclined to permit the prisoner to take advantage of them.

4. Because many of them are beyond the age limit or cannot meet the
    physical requirements for regular employment as established by Civil
    Service, they cannot look forward to a permanent career and are therefore
    less interested in the welfare of the institution than their brother officers.

5. Finally, because of the short period of employment, they do not recognize
    the individual prisoners who are most likely to incite trouble or commit
    serious infractions, and they are at a disadvantage in dealing with the large
    groups which congregate in the cellblocks, the mess hall, the auditorium,
    and the yard.

The fact that the job of the guard is often depressing, dangerous, and possesses relatively low prestige adds further difficulties. There is also little doubt
that the high turnover rate carries numerous evils in its train, as the comments of the deputy commissioner have indicated. Yet even if higher salaries
could counterbalance the many dissatisfying features of the guard's job—to a
point where the custodial force consisted of men with long service rather
than a group of transients—there remains a question of whether or not the
problems of administration in the New Jersey State Prison would be eased to
a significant extent. This, of course, is heresy from the viewpoint of those who
trace the failure of social organizations to the personal failings of the individuals who man social organizational structure. Perhaps, indeed, there is some
comfort in the idea that if the budget of the prison were larger, if higher
salaries could be paid to entice "better" personnel within the walls, if guards
could be persuaded to remain for longer periods, then the many difficulties of
the prison bureaucracy would disappear. From this point of view, the problems of the custodial institution are rooted in the niggardliness of the free
community and the consequent inadequacies of the institution's personnel
rather than flaws in the social system of the prison itself. But to suppose that
higher salaries are an answer to the plight of the custodian is to suppose, first,
that there are men who by reason of their particular skills and personal characteristics are better qualified to serve as guards if they could be recruited; and
second, that experience and training within the institution itself will better
prepare the guard for his role, if greater financial rewards could convince him
to make a career of his prison employment. Both of these suppositions, however, are open to some doubt. There are few jobs in the free community

which are comparable to that of the guard in the maximum security prison and which, presumably, could equip the guard-to-be with the needed skills. If the job requirements of the guard's position are not technical skills, but turn on matters of character such as courage, honesty, and so on, there is no assurance that men with these traits will flock to the prison if the salary of the guard is increased. And while higher salaries may decrease the turnover rate— thus making an in-service training program feasible and providing a custodial force with greater experience—it is not certain if such a change can lead to marked improvement. A brief period of schooling can familiarize the new guard with the routines of the institution, but to prepare the guard for the realities of his assigned role with lectures and discussions is quite another matter. And it seems entirely possible that prolonged experience in the prison may enmesh the guard deeper and deeper in patterns of compromise and misplaced trust rather than sharpening his drive toward a rigorous enforcement of institutional regulations.

We are not arguing, of course, that the quality of the personnel in the prison is irrelevant to the successful performance of the bureaucracy's task, nor are we arguing that it would be impossible to improve the quality of the personnel by increasing salaries. We are arguing, however, that the problems of the custodians far transcend the size of the guard's paycheck or the length of his employment and that better personnel is at best a palliative rather than a final cure. It is true, of course, that it is difficult to unravel the characteristics of a social organization from the characteristics of the individuals who are its members, but there seems to be little reason to believe that a different crop of guards in the New Jersey State Prison would exhibit an outstanding increase in efficiency in trying to impose the regime of the custodians on the population of prisoners. *The lack of a sense of duty among those who are held captive, the obvious fallacies of coercion, the pathetic collection of rewards and punishments to induce compliance, the strong pressures toward the corruption of the guard in the form of friendship, reciprocity, and the transfer of duties into the hands of trusted inmates—all are structural defects in the prison's system of power rather than individual inadequacies.*

The question of whether these defects are inevitable in the custodial institution—or in any system of total power—must be deferred. For the moment it is enough to point out that in the New Jersey State Prison the custodians are unable or unwilling to prevent their captives from committing numerous violations of the rules which make up the theoretical blueprint for behavior and this failure is not a temporary, personal aberration but a built-in feature of the prison social system. It is only by understanding this fact that we can understand the world of the prisoners, since so many significant aspects of inmate behavior—such as coercion of fellow prisoners, fraud, gambling, homosexuality, sharing stolen supplies, and so on—are in clear contravention to institutional regulations. It is the nature of this world which must now claim our attention.

NOTES

1. Max Weber, *The Theory of Social and Economic Organization,* ed. Talcott Parsons (New York: Oxford University Press, 1947), p. 337.

2. This statement requires two qualifications. First, a number of inmates steadfastly maintain that they are innocent of the crime with which they are charged. It is the illegitimacy of their particular case, however, rather than the illegitimacy of confinement in general, which moves them to protest. Second, some of the more sophisticated prisoners argue that the conditions of imprisonment are wrong, although perhaps not illegitimate or illegal, on the grounds that reformation should be the major aim of imprisonment and the officials are not working hard enough in this direction.

3. Since each shift is reduced in size by vacations, regular days off, sickness, and so on, even the day shift—the largest of the three—can usually muster no more than ninety guards to confront the population of more than 1,200 prisoners. The fact that they are so heavily outnumbered is not lost on the officials.

20

Mature Coping

The Challenge of Adjustment in Contemporary Prisons

Robert Johnson

Each prisoner must answer the question, "How am I going to do my time?" Some decide to withdraw and isolate. Others decide to become full participants in the convict social system. The choice, influenced by prisoners' values and experiences, helps determine strategies for survival and success. Johnson argues that adjustment to prison requires "mature coping," dealing with life's problems as a responsive and responsible human being.

Prisons today are meant to be less painful than their predecessors. We do not intentionally impose physical, mental, or emotional suffering on inmates. The pains experienced in contemporary prisons, for all intents and purposes, originate in psychological stresses. And though these stresses can be quite substantial, today's prisons offer more opportunities for constructive adaptation than did earlier prisons. Still, although contemporary prisons may be comparatively civilized and potentially civilizing, adjustment to prison is always a challenge. We must understand this challenge in the larger context of the offender's adjustment to life, and work to facilitate mature adjustment both in and out of prison.

The pains of life in contemporary prisons are real. There is no point in denying them. Nor does it make sense to see pain merely as an obstacle to correctional work, for it is an obstacle that can never be circumvented. Pain is an enduring feature of the correctional enterprise. We must accept this hard real-

Source: Reprinted from Robert Johnson, *Hard Time*, 3rd ed. (Belmont, CA: Wadsworth, 2002), pp. 82–125 with permission of the publisher. Some footnotes omitted.

ity and quite explicitly attempt to promote growth through adversity. This is a genuine correctional agenda. For people who cope maturely with prison, I will argue, are people who have grown as human beings and been rehabilitated in the process.

Imprisonment is a disheartening and threatening experience for most men and women. Typically, prisoners find their careers disrupted, their relationships suspended, their hopes and dreams gone sour. Few inmates have experienced comparable stress in the free world, or have developed coping strategies or perspectives that shield them from prison problems. Although prisoners differ from each other, and may feel the pressures of confinement somewhat differently, they concur on the extraordinarily stressful nature of life in maximum security penal institutions. Moreover, for many inmates—male, as well as female—the stresses of imprisonment are aggravated because they cope with prison in immature and ultimately destructive ways. All too often, this is compounded by the immature actions of the staff. Tough, rebellious inmates and callous, insensitive guards may well be the public models of deportment commonly seen on prison yards ... but they are not models for mature problem solving. The hard stoicism of the prisoner who can "take it" without flinching and "dish it out" without remorse is particularly destructive in today's overcrowded prisons, where close and often abrasive contact calls for tact, diplomacy, and the ability to transcend stereotypical roles and relationships. Chronic tension and violence are testimonials to failures of adjustment under these conditions.

Of course, living in prison has never been easy, and it never will be. This holds true whether prisons are crowded or sparsely populated and whether prisoners are veterans or novices. And simply to survive is not enough. Prisoners must cope maturely with the demands of prison life; if they do not, the prison experience will simply add to their catalog of failure and defeat. Mature coping, in fact, does more than prevent one's prison life from becoming yet another series of personal setbacks. Mature coping is at the core of what we mean by correction or rehabilitation and, thus, creates the possibility of a more constructive life after release from prison.

Let me now examine the three major attributes of mature coping, show that much of what passes for adjustment among persistent felons falls short of this goal, and explain why men and women who respond maturely to prison stress are likely to become reformed citizens. . . .

MATURE COPING

Mature coping means, in essence, dealing with life's problems like a responsive and responsible human being, one who seeks autonomy without violating the rights of others, security without resort to deception or violence, and relatedness to others as the finest and fullest expression of human identity. It is of course true that most inmates have not been fully or even largely habilitated—equipped or trained—to behave in these ways; thus, to speak of their need for *re*habilitation is, in a sense, to put the cart before the horse. But like all people, prisoners have some natural inclinations toward autonomy, security, and relatedness to others, and the experience of prison can build on those inclinations. The result, in my view, can be said to comprise their personal rehabilitation or correction.

Dealing with Problems and Achieving Autonomy

Mature coping means, first, dealing with problems: meeting problems head-on, using all resources legitimately at one's disposal. This aspect of mature coping involves "assertiveness," a sense of "personal efficacy," and an "internal locus of control" with respect to one's immediate environment.

In effect, mature coping is doing the best you can with what is rightfully yours. But persistent and serious criminals, who regularly become prison inmates, don't settle for what is rightfully theirs. They have been described, aptly, as "hasty hedonists" and "jungle cats" who live by a preemptive version of the Golden Rule: "do unto others as they would do unto you . . only do it first."[1] The flamboyant posturing often characteristic of this lifestyle is captured in the following statement by a man who is currently serving time for a murder he committed while making a drug deal to support himself "in the life":

> Straight people don't understand. I mean, they think dudes is after the
> things straight people got. It ain't that at all. People in the life ain't looking
> for no home and grass in the yard. . . . We the show people. The glamour
> people. Come on the set with the finest car, the finest women, the finest
> vines. Hear people talking about you. Hear the bar get quiet when you
> walk in the door. Throw down a yard and tell everybody drink up. See.
> It's rep. It's glamour. That's what it's about. What else a dude gon do in this
> . . . world. You make something out of nothing.[2]

People like this can be masters at making something out of nothing. They are possessed of "delinquent egos" that help them to "make hay in the few moments sun is shining" on their slum street corners and associated hot spots, and they are ready to do so at the expense of others. Persistent offenders (especially persistent violent offenders) often have an inflated—though precarious—sense of their personal worth, which makes ordinary people mere fodder for their criminal exploits.

This impulsive and often predatory hedonism is adaptive in the short run. Jungle cats may survive and even prosper in prisons and ghettos, settings where persons with "middle class egos"—that "sell immediacy short" and are "other directed"—would be "pounced upon and consumed."

But many, perhaps even most, chronic felons are by no means masters of the criminal arts or even adept hedonists. Crime for them is not a lifestyle to which they aspired as a result of planning and choice. It is a way of life they selected by default. Many are bumbling, ineffectual people of limited intelligence. Some-—no one knows how many—appear to be saddled with a host of biomedical deficits that, often in conjunction with low IQ, limit their ability to cope with life in conventional ways. These offenders are inept at virtually everything they do, including crime. . . .

Most offenders, whether due to personal or social deficits, or both, are not "able to analyze situations rationally or to make choices that facilitate their desires."[3] For most offenders, then, "coping difficulties are a central cause of the maintenance and repetition of criminal acts, if not their origin.'[4] The problems they confront in life are fairly typical, centering on interpersonal and financial difficulties, but their coping efforts are unsystematic, unsustained, and, at best, ineffectual. Too often, their coping efforts *aggravate* the very problems they are intended to solve, making matters worse rather than better.

These offenders are better characterized as troubled and troublesome people rather than devil-may-care rogues. They lead lives of pain and inflict pain on others in response to their own inadequacy. For male convicts, relations with women can be destructive and controlling in the extreme. As one convict observed, absolutely without remorse or shame, women are ready candidates for abuse. "I cracked her a good one," he related in an interview with Earley,

> because she had it coming. Now, I don't believe in beating up women, but if my old lady is talking to some man, she's gonna get knocked to the floor every time because I know old ladies are good for three things: giving pussy, cooking, and taking care of kids, and if I see her talking to other man, I know she ain't cooking, I know she ain't taking care of his kids, so she and him must be talking about pussy.[5]

There is joy in crime for men such as this, including the crime of wif-beating, but that joy tends to be short-lived. Their lives are deeply unsatisfying.

For men and women who have self-esteem problems, limited cognitive and interpersonal skills, and few conventional opportunities for success, crime can be quite attractive. As Halleck has observed, "If favorable opportunities for altering the internal or external environment are not available, criminal action looms as a seductive antidote to an unbearable feeling of helplessness."[6] Robbie Wideman expressed this helplessness quite eloquently, if a bit melodramatically when he observed, "We see what's going down. We supposed to die. Take our little welfare checks and be quiet and die."[7] In contrast to the menial occupation and anonymous existence of the unskilled laborer, a life that looks like death to the average felon, crime offers a "moment of autonomy," high excitement, and a chance for camaraderie with peers. . . .[8] There is also an element of hope for the future, born of the sense that one is attacking one's problems directly by taking what one cannot properly lay claim to. Fittingly, criminals see themselves as rebels serving the cause of their own self-aggrandizement.

Some criminals commit crimes sporadically and without any discernible pattern. Others adopt crime as way of life. For this latter group, known as chronic or lifestyle criminals, "Crime can be understood as a lifestyle characterized by a global sense of irresponsibility, self-indulgent interests, an intrusive approach to interpersonal relationships, and chronic violation of societal rules, laws, and mores."[9] Lifestyle criminals exempt themselves from the constraints of law-abiding lives; neither laws nor conventional jobs are suitable for them. Only crime, "with its accompanying irresponsibility and self-indulgence," meets their needs.[10] Prison doesn't deter them because they know they can survive prison.[11] Conventional adjustments, on the other hand, have little going for them. They offer both the meager rewards of a middle-class life, which is seen as "exceedingly boring and something to avoid at all cost."[12] They are also discouraged by the threat of failure at conventional living; for them, fear of failure can be great, as they have been repeatedly bruised by failures in living throughout their lives. A conventional life is thus seen as a high-cost, low-reward proposition. Naturally, these chronic offenders do what comes easily, what they enjoy, and what they do best: crime.

The difficulty is that crime offers only illusory benefits. Appearances to the contrary, crime is bad business practice and a miserable way to make a living. The plain fact is that "street crime . . . doesn't pay. It's quite irrational by sound business standards. . . . [T]he criminal stands a 78% chance of winding up in jail before attaining even [the] minimal goal" of a poverty-level income.[13] It is, of course, hard to come by reliable estimates of earnings from crime, at least in part because criminals routinely overestimate their take from crime. Even so, there is absolutely no evidence for the common belief that many street criminals get rich as a result of their criminal exploits. As a general rule, earnings from crime are at best modest and "below the earnings these criminals could make at work."[14] The proficient predators—the cream of the criminal crop, notably more sophisticated drug dealers, organized car thieves and some high-priced prostitutes—may do somewhat better in material terms, but even they pay a high price for what amounts to short-term pleasures and conquests.

Chronic felons often complicate already badly managed lives by denying rather than facing and resolving their problems. They may successfully resist efforts by loved ones to discipline and control them, displaying "a maddening disregard for the inevitable consequences" of their destructive actions.[15] They are deeply immersed in the street life, a life in which one lives from moment to moment, anesthetized by drugs and insulated from concerns about the future. "[T]he average pattern" among felons while in the free world, for example, has been described as

> one of casual unplanned days, with greater dependence on friends than family or work, and little focus or goals. . . . [T]his way of spending time was also accompanied by a constant high level of alcohol and drug use. Many subjects must have gone through their days in a haze, and it is not surprising that there was little planning and few efforts at changing anything.[16]

The various elements of this lifestyle "all act to channel the effects of inadequate coping ability into violent and antisocial actions."[17] They make it easy to deny one's own problems as well as the damage done to others by one's self-serving forays.

Denial is a coping strategy that, when used to excess, always backfires. Problems denied simply do not disappear. Chronic offenders know this—or should know this—but they ignore its implications for their lives and go about business as usual. They act as if they are invulnerable. "In much the same way as a young child contemplates his invulnerability while donning a

Superman costume, the lifestyle criminal is unrealistic in how he appraises himself, his attributes, and his chances of avoiding the consequences of his antisocial actions.[18] The very nature of antisocial actions may be distorted in the minds of felons. Criminals regularly minimize the seriousness of their crimes and the degree to which they are culpable for their crimes. They may, for example, convince themselves that their crimes, even crimes of violence, are mere games:

> Ain't nobody gon get killed. You just into cowboy and Indin shit like in the movies. You the gangsters but you the good guys too. No problem. . . . That's the way we was. Stone gangsters. Robbing people. Waving guns in people's face. Serious shit. But it was like playing too. A game. A big game and we was just big kids having fun. Guns wasn't real. Bullets wasn't real. Wasn't planning on hurting nobody. Pow. Pow. You know. Fall over. I got you. No, you didn't. You missed. Pow. Pow. I got you. You lying. I got you first. Cowboy and Indin shit like the old days. . . .[19]

Chronic offenders tend to let situations deteriorate until they become unmanageable, often ignoring repeated warnings that their criminal exploits are leading to disaster or that relationships or jobs are in trouble. When failure inevitably materializes—when, for example, criminal games result in apprehension and confinement—they react with bitter fatalism, as if the cards were always stacked against them. Alternatively, impulses reign; the chronic offenders strike out blindly at the immediate cause of frustration (such as the boss who fires them or the police officer who arrests them) and do not analyze the deeper sources of their problems. Tragically, crime victims often bear the brunt of their impotent anger.

Chronic felons combine poor self-control with limited insight into the dynamics of their adjustment. They are, in Walters' observations, "lazy" in thought and behavior and, moreover, "overly accepting" of their own half-baked ideas about life and adjustment.[20] Remember that Jean Harris saw her fellow female inmates as "children with adult desires and criminal experiences."[21] This view has been expressed by noted reformers, including Katherine Davis, an early warden of Bedford Hills, who observed: "They are not like bad girls. They are bad girls. They are strong individualists. So are children. Social consciousness is asleep in the criminal as it is in the child. In both it must be awakened, and after it is awakened, trained."[22] Unsurprisingly, these children in adult bodies act as pawns of what they take to be an arbitrary fate, juxtaposing passivity and impulsivity where informed and modulated action are called for. This immature behavior is promoted, even extolled, in prison culture where the whim of the moment often rules. Ironically, what is touted on the prison yard as strength or toughness amounts to nothing more than a posture of psychological denial that is leavened, to personal taste, with short-run hedonism and resentment of authority. Behind bars, such a stance may have a romantic side. . . . It pits innocent and aggrieved cons against gratuitously emasculating hacks. But adopting an identity of this sort virtually ensures failure at conventional living in the free world.

Security without Deception or Violence

The second characteristic of mature coping is addressing problems without resort to deception or violence, except when necessary for self-defense. Deception and violence are primitive behaviors. Except when engaged in to prevent immediate physical harm—itself a primitive self-defense situation—deception and violence represent gross and reprehensible violations of the integrity of other human beings. Regrettably, deception and violence flourish in dangerous and unstable environments, where there is a chronic absence of trust in oneself and others, and preemptive strikes—hurting someone first and asking questions later—masquerade under the mantle of practical wisdom. Thus, in prisons and on slum streets, deception and violence are a regular feature of daily life and adjustment and, indeed, are seen as normal, even desirable behaviors.

Deception in one's dealings with others is, of course, a possibility in any social circumstance. It is apparently the case that the prospect of deception, which greatly complicates human social interaction, has been an important force in the evolution of the human psyche. The psyche must be attuned not only to peoples' words and deeds but also to the thoughts behind those words and deeds: to the thoughts people have about how others think as interactions unfold. To be sure, deception is a possibility in any interaction; and, in some cases, unlike violence, deception can be harmless—as when one passes along false compliments meant to put someone at ease. But, as a general rule, deception of others is a destructive force because it impedes cooperation and undermines solidarity. It is therefore of crucial significance that deception is a *central* feature of prison culture. Indeed, Empey reminds us, "deception is the name of the game" in prison; "[a]mong officials as well as among inmates, it will be the most skillfull manipulator who most often gets what he wants"[23]—or what she wants. In women's prisons, manipulation is a preeminent consideration as well, particularly in the dealings of women inmates with male staff. "The danger here," noted Owen, "is getting manipulated. The men who try to game you will give up. Women will continue over a much longer time; they are more patient, will work on you a little bit at a time."[24]

To be sure, manipulation is also "the name of the game" on slum streets and in other areas marked by poverty and crime. In these settings, as in prisons, cooperation is comparatively rare and hence, honesty has limited adaptive value in public social encounters. (Here, as in prisons, people are expected, at the very least, to be cagey. Telling the truth as a matter of course implies gross naïveté and may be the equivalent of revealing one's hand in a game of poker before the game is over.) Violence, moreover, is met with explicit approbation in these same milieus is considered a hallmark, if not *the* hallmark, of toughness and respect. "All my life," said one female inmate, "I wanted to look hard, to look mean," echoing sentiments common in men's prisons as well.[25] Tough cons, male or female, revel in their power and are admired—or at least feared—in the prison world.

The operating premise on slum streets as well as prison yards would appear to be that lying to and physically harming others are but behavioral cousins on a continuum of adaptive abuse. Whether on slum streets or in prison, the world is populated by victimizers who exploit others and a host of prospective victims variously known as "punks, chumps, pigeons, or fags." Even one's friends are presumed to be less than fully trustworthy and thus are potential candidates for exploitation. Since others are devalued, they become fair game. The authorities (police or guards) are seen as impotent and irrelevant; people are on their own, forced to make their own way. In what amounts to a social jungle, it is the weak versus the strong, with no holds barred. Bonds of trust built on words have little value. Small wonder so many people arm themselves in these environments. For them, a knife (in prison) or a gun (on the streets) is "like an American Express card . . . you don't leave home without it."[26]

This cynical and ultimately adolescent view of life—where there are no shades of grey, no tempered emotions, no feelings of concern or sadness for the "stupid bastard" butchered in the cell next door or the "punk motherfucker" ripped off with impunity—is common on slum streets. It is at the very heart of prison culture, however, in which anger and fear are the dominant emotions. . . .

Caring for Self and Others: Self-Actualization through Human Relationships

The third characteristic of mature coping is making an effort to empathize with and assist others in need, to act as though we are indeed members of a human community who can work together to create a more secure and gratifying existence. The point is that one can achieve autonomy and security—that is, control of one's life—through relatedness to others. "Deep individual connections to others and the experience of benevolent persons and institutions result in feelings of safety and trust."[27] With trust in ourselves and in the world, "both individuals and groups can acquire confidence in their ability to gain security and fulfill essential motives through connection and cooperation."[28]

In the free world, poor social bonds are expressed in a routine distrust of others, especially strangers. But even the worst slum has room for civility and relationships. There is, in other words, a "social order" that has its roots in the expectation of minimal standards of conscience and community. That social order is less robust these days, given the inroads made by guns and violence in low-income areas, including in inner-city schools, but it remains the case that the "decent" people still outnumber the "street" people and hold out to each other and their children the prospect of a civil life in slum communities.

In prison, by contrast, men and women are explicitly and almost unanimously encouraged to be uncivil and amoral, that is, "'to do their own time' and ignore the suffering and inhumanity that surround them."[29] (For women, the admonition "to do your own time" is expressed as "mind your own business") To be sure, there are a few permissible exceptions. One may have relationships with one's "main man" or fellow convicts or gang members; one may take care of one's prison lover or family, though these and other such arrangements seem at least in part to reflect calculated efforts to assure one's personal protection and perhaps further one's criminal objectives. Certainly these relationships are typically impermanent. "Niantic love comes and goes," one inmate told Rierden, referring to the instability of "homosexual dyads" or love relationships in that women's prison. "Most women just like to play house."[30] Presumably, others "play" at being family—though the relationships are no doubt important while they last. Be this as it may, the prison's version of decorum typically calls for restraint in matters of affection and concern for others in the prison world, whatever one's true feelings might be. (This is readily apparent in most men's prisons, as well as in women's prisons when one focuses on the convict world. There, toughness is prized and the "culture demand sharp survival skills and a quick eye for the ever-shifting hierarchy" of power. There are, as a result, few real friendships in prison. There are even fewer Good Samaritans (who surely would deserve "an army of friends") and fewer still who will own up to this rather egregious lapse from manliness or toughness. In the words of one prisoner, "You've got to keep in mind that [another person's problem] doesn't concern you . . . You want to help the guy, but prison is no place to be a Good Samaritan if you want to come out in one piece."[31]

The prison community is quite different from any free world community. Relations there are distinctly calculating and transient. "In prison," notes Seymour,

> there are no primary ties, few alliances that extend beyond the immediate situation, and few norms that transcend the bounds of one's immediate relationships. Adjusting means the ability to survive and cope with each other's company. Membership in groups is temporary and artificial, and where groups may be friendly, there are few friends. Mutual aid is given, but with an emphasis on reciprocity, not altruism. Cultural dissension is part of a perceived war of prisoners against each other, and sitting out the war is a major goal.[32]

To "make it" as an inmate, one must live in the present, ever suspicious and alert to the depredations and betrayals of others, drawing what little sustenance one can from the meager and often exploitive emotional ties available in the prison community. Our prisons are moral cesspools, then, as much because of the callous disregard for others they promote as for the overt abuse that takes place there. Naturally, to the extent prisoners are permitted (by officials) and encouraged (by their peers) to treat others in need with indifference and even contempt, the greater will be their willingness to victimize others when it suits their interests.

PRISON ADJUSTMENT AND PERSONAL REFORM: RECONCILING PUBLIC AND PRIVATE CULTURES

Mature coping contradicts standard cultural prescriptions about appropriate prisoner deportment. The public culture of the prison has norms that dictate behavior "on the yard" and in other public areas of the prison such as mess halls, gyms, and the larger program and work sites. This culture emphasizes an almost automatic use of hostility and manipulation in one's relations with fellow inmates and especially with the staff and makes friendly and caring behavior— again, especially with respect to the staff, look servile and silly.

Thus, it is not surprising that prisoners often value roles that are, from the point of view of the larger society, distinctly antisocial. Goodstein's research, for example, reveals that most male inmates (43.5 percent of the maximum security prisoners in her sample) would like to think of themselves as tough and rebellious in their dealings with staff, as "right guys" who take no guff from the "wrong guys," their keepers. Another 34.7 percent claim to value deception in their relations with staff, which they view as a legitimate, even mandatory, tactic in winning ealy release from confinement. A few prisoners (5.4 percent) take pride in being institutionalized; they punctuate leisure time with work at easy high-status prison jobs, all the while studiously avoiding programs and other activities that might have rehabilitative value upon their release from prison. Only 16.3 percent expressly attempt to maintain a "generally positive attitude toward [their] environment."[33] This type of inmate "accepts the authority of the prison's official social system but maintains his commitment to life outside the institution."[34] While many inmates privately value this adjustment, the only men who publicly admit to these beliefs are the much-maligned "square johns" no self-respecting convict would be caught dead with on the yard.

Square johns, whether male or female, are a minority of a typical prison, though this adaptation appears to be more common in women's prisons than in men's prisons. As Owen has noted,

> A significant minority of women at CCWF . . . maintain an identity that is not embedded in the prison culture. Members of this minority, made up of short-termers, middle-class women with little investment in a criminal identity, and those who have moved away from participation in the prison culture, may have little connection to "familying" and emotional relationships with other women.[35]

Square johns, male or female, tend to endorse or aspire to conventional values. They also tend to have stable family ties, which gives them something to fall back on during difficult periods of confinement and something to look forward to at the end of their prison terms. Their generally solid social skills and good behavior make them excellent candidates for higher-level prison jobs, particularly in women's prisons, and their commitment to getting back out to their families gives them an added reason to avoid trouble in the prison community. Put differently, they have a stake in the world of the prison officials rather than in the world of the convicts. From the perspective of the larger free community, these offenders are advantaged. Yet the very fact of confinement is a considerable stigma in the middle-class circles they hail from or wish to enter. And to make it in prison, where they tend to be pariahs, they must scrupulously avoid the convict world. They typically adjust in the manner of lifers— taking one day at a time, carefully apprising the risks and benefits of their actions, and trying above all to avoid trouble, which would jeopardize the prison life they have built for themselves.

Some inmates adjust better than others, but there are few success stories in prison, few real winners. The predatory convicts who dominate the prison yard are stereotypes of adolescent immaturity. They have been described (by means of psychological tests) as "individuals who adhere to procriminal attitudes, who are self-centered, exploitive of others, easily led [by peers), and anxious to please [peers]; they recidivate at high rates, particularly when the prison experience has boosted their self-esteem, (by proving how tough they are) and when their exploitive behavior features violence—when they have become, in other words, hardened criminals. Their recidivism is sometimes obscured by the fact that they may appear to make the transition back to civilian life fairly well. Like Goffman's prisoners who follow an "intransigent line," they attempt to deny the reality of prison and behave behind bars as though they are not really subject to the rules and restrictions of the prison.[36] For example, they break institutional rules with regularity and are openly hostile to the authorities and the prison the authorities represent. When they leave prison, they can pick up civilian life fairly readily since they live in a way that is, psychologically speaking, a continuation of their prison adjustment.

Before long, however, their proclivity to victimize others as a routine feature of daily life gets them in trouble with the law. Free citizens, known derisively as *square johns*, do not play prison games. On release, hard-core convicts find that ploys that work in the prison fail miserably in the free world. In the words of one such predatory convict interviewed by Earley:

> I can walk into any prison in this country, any prison, and know
> immediately what's happening. I can deal with this crazy prison
> environment, with the so-called worst of the worst convicts in Marion
> and the so-called prison predators and all that baloney," he explained. "But
> in the outside world, I'm always getting tripped up. Every time I mess
> with a Square John, I end up getting fucked because you people have no
> concept of jailhouse respect and absolutely no honor. . . . You see," he
> continued, "in here, I know how to play all the games and play them well,
> but out on the streets, the deck always seems to be stacked against me.[37]

Such encounters may imperil the precarious and often inflated sense of self that many convicts develop from their criminal exploits, adding urgency to the needs to dominate and control the ebb and flow of prison life. . . .

Some convicts mellow over time and become "institutionalized," or, in Goffman's terms, "colonized." They serve many prison sentences, and eventually come to make the prison their "home away from home." . . .

Fleisher found a number of Lompoc inmates who had adopted an institutionalized adjustment. For these men, captivity is the norm, freedom the anomaly. They prefer prison to the free world because they have found, through hard experience, that freedom "means freedom to be out of work, freedom to be out of money, freedom to be without clean clothes, freedom to be without an apartment, and freedom to resume an alcohol or drug dependency, or both."[38] Prison, in contrast, means relative security. A similar picture emerges for female convicts. For many such women, as Owen observes, "prison is a better and safer place than their disrupted and disruptive lives on the streets."[39] One's needs are taken care of, and one's reputation as a tough character is assured by a history of prison survival. Institutionalized prisoners can assume menacing postures and may flaunt their indifference to the pains of imprisonment, but they are, in the final analysis, pathetic figures whose self-doubt and personal inadequacy consign them to a life of prison. This pathos may be more apparent with women who "don't have nothing to go home to." As one such woman observed,

> I don't know my younger boy at all. I don't know what he looks like. I have never lived with my seven-year-old. I have seen him only once. *Convicts have always been my family* [emphasis added]. My heart's desire is to have someone close to me who is blood, rather than just convicts as family.[40]

Like their more combative comrades, institutionalized male and female convicts win their battle with the prison but lose the larger war of survival in the free world. Since institutionalized prisoners are veterans of the prison, they "know the ropes" and can "play the angles"; after years of hard experience, they have enough sense to "keep their noses clean." They lead a manipulative and calculating existence and usually have what is, by prison standards, a materially comfortable life behind bars. They are "model prisoners," not in the sense that they exemplify the staff's version of the ideal prisoner—they do not—but because being a prisoner is what they do best. Where the predatory convicts simmer with hostility and yearn for freedom, these prisoners have become so acclimated to the prison routine that they become dependent upon it for a sense of security and self-esteem. This dependency is a double-edged sword, however, because it entails a loss of personal control that in turn promotes "higher levels of stress" than experienced by inmates who adapt to prison on their own terms. The central legacy of institutional dependency is the reduced ability to cope in situations where one must rely on one's own initiative. Accordingly, institutionalized prisoners find it very difficult to make the transition to the free world, which has become alien, a place that swallows up fellow prisoners rather than offers an opportunity for a new life. "When somebody leaves here," said one female inmate, "those of us stuck here know that unless they come back, they're most likely out of our life for good. It's a great big black hole out there, and you just learn to accept that."[41] Because institutionalized offenders cannot rely on the dictates of authorities, on an explicit code of conduct, and on preordained schedules, they recidivate almost immediately.

In terms of the norms and mores that make up the public culture of the prison, the undisputed losers of prison games are known as "inmates," a term that in this context is meant to set the run-of-the-mill prisoners—the "masses"—apart from the more savvy convicts. Yet most inmates get by; they are neither victims (of the convicts) nor victimizers (like the convicts). Some of the more sophisticated ones become institutionalized, usually by carving out a narrow but safe round of life in conformity with the officials' view of prison decorum. . . . But from the larger population of inmates are drawn such low-status types as "punks," "dings," "scapegoats," and offenders who are—or who become—flagrantly mentally ill. These inmates are often devastated psychologically by the prison experience. . . . These men and women are impaired for the purposes of adjustment in the free world and prone to escalating traumas in the prison.

Kupers provides a composite picture of a mentally disordered inmate: "He or she suffered massive and repeated traumas early in life, had a great difficulty coping with the stress of harsh prison conditions, and then acted out and was sent to a punitive segregation unit where the isolation and idleness aggravated the mental disorder."[42] These offenders are difficult to understand and manage. As a result, they get into trouble repeatedly and then are placed in high-security and supermax prisons, which overcome their limited coping skills. As one such inmate at Pelican Bay, a supermax prison, told Kupers:

> Sometimes I feel overwhelmed. I get trepidations, nervous, agitated, I go off the deep end. I don't really hear voices, just get to feeling like I can't breathe, the cell is getting smaller. Panic! It feels closed in, my heart pounds, these symptoms build up over days. . . It's the SHU [Special Housing Unit] that's making me this nervous. There's nothing like this at other prisons. Here I feel like I'm in a kennel, closed off from life itself. I feel like I live in a coffin, like a tomb."[43]

Such comments reveal extreme stress but were not uncommon. Indeed, these sentiments were shared by most of the mentally ill offenders interviewed by Kupers. "A majority of the inmates I have interviewed in super-maximum control units talk about their inability to concentrate, their heightened anxiety, their intermittent disorientation and confusion, their experience of unreality, and their tendency to strike out at the nearest person when they reach their 'breaking point."[44] These mentally ill inmates, sometimes released directly from supermax prisons into the free world, recidivate at rates considerably above more typical offenders.

Poor coping is disturbingly common in prison. Yet mature behavior and, hence, the prospect of successful adjustment upon release can be found in prison on a more regular basis than might first be supposed. One reason is that "the actions available to inmates are constrained, and many of the ineffective, diversionary, or destructive actions they might take on the outside are precluded."[45] In prison, one cannot normally turn to hard drugs or heavy drinking to escape one's problems; nor can one beat one's spouse or children to let off steam. It is also much harder to deny problems:

> While an inmate can still . . . deal with [a problem] ineffectively, it is difficult to avoid dealing with it in some fashion, because the institutional world is so confined and restricted. An inmate's problems are inevitably part of his daily life, and they must be encountered regularly.[46]

Confinement also promotes an increase in introspection and critical examination of one's actions. As one Canadian prisoner aptly observed, with perhaps a hint of irony, "I'm glad to be here because I had the opportunity to think a lot. You are alone and you learn about yourself. When I'm outside, I haven't the time for that. I'm too busy."[47] It can thus be the case that "the constraints of imprisonment can paradoxically make it easier for inmates to cope relatively more effectively with problems," at least with respect to the daily adjustment difficulties that surface behind bars.[48]

The adjustment of lifers (life-sentence prisoners) often reflects the legacy of improved coping created by the constraints of prison. Ethnographic accounts of prison adjustment among lifers, emphasize that they tend to see prison as a home—an involuntary one, to be sure—but still a domestic world in which they have an investment; they care about such things as the level of cleanliness, the quality of the food, the variety of activities, and even relations with their keepers. In contrast, these concerned citizens of the prison community see their short-sentence counterparts as rude visitors or disruptive tourists who have nothing to lose. Lifers, who feel they have everything to lose since prison is all they have, strive to make the most of the resources available in prison. As a result, they obey the rules and generally stay out of trouble, secure good jobs, participate in programs, involve themselves in organized clubs and recreation, and generally fill their days with structured activities—all so that they might live fully in the present and give as little thought as possible to the world they left behind.

A recent longitudinal study by Zamble reinforces these observations and traces the emergence of improved coping among a sample of twenty-five male Canadian long-termers over a seven-year study period. Zamble documents that these long-termers did not suffer "generalized emotional damage" as was speculated by some early penologists and critics of the prison.[49] Confirming early ethnographic studies, Zamble found that these long-termers tended to fill their days with "structured activities and regular routines, such as those of preferred institutional employment."[50] They were correspondingly "less interested in the unstructured or aimless activities that typify institutional socialization."[51]

Those "unstructured or aimless activities" avoided by long-termers are often at the heart of the prison's public culture. It is this life in the prison yard that often pushed prisoners into destructive activities and, ultimately, contributed to high rates of recidivism. Lifers saw clearly that trouble would reduce the quality of their prison lives:

> Unlike the very weak contingencies between behavior and consequences that the system presents to most prisoners, long-term inmates learn that misbehavior results in tangible diminution of the quality of their lives. Even if the contingencies are only inconsistently enforced, over a period of years the consequences of maladaptive behaviors are sure to be triggered.[52]

Lifers shared the perception that "short-termers were irresponsible and rowdy, and that mixing with them was likely to lead to trouble."[53] Short-termers had little to lose, and the link between their behavior and deprivations while in prison was weak. Lifers had much to lose, and over time this became quite clear to them. In general, they learned that they had to be more careful and controlled about prison living.

Zamble's long-termers, unlike short-termers, exploited constraints available in the prison community so that they could lead structured, controlled, and ultimately autonomous lives. For example, they explicitly and consciously chose the cell over the yard as the main arena for their daily life in prison. They did this because they could control the routine in the cell. Life in the sheltered confines of the cell was more autonomous than life elsewhere in the prison.

Life in the cell and away from the yard offered a sensible withdrawal from the myriad emotional and interpersonal problems, and resulting problems with authorities, that present themselves in the public world of prison. The prisoners developed a few relationships with others facing long terms, for support and protection, but they consciously held themselves back from involvement in the regular prison social life, which featured "confusion and uncertainties" and, in general, trouble.

Consistently, Zamble's lifers showed improvements in coping competence as their sentences unfolded. Their behavior became more controlled and more reflective. They were more likely to seek social support and to deal with problems rather than avoid them:

> The changes in coping modes are generally in the direction toward more
> normal and mature ways. . . . Thus, in general, there seems to have been
> some improvement in subjects' coping abilities over time in prison. . . .
> [T]hey were working more at controlling their behavior in problem
> situations, seeking solace and advice from others more than before, and
> were less likely to avoid dealing with problems. Although the statistical
> evidence is weak, more of them may also have been monitoring, analyzing,
> and planning their responses. As a result their efforts seemed more effective
> in dealing with problems, with lower risk of exacerbation.[54]

Better coping produced a host of benefits. There was, for example, an increase in prosocial attitudes and a decrease in disciplinary problems over time. Prisoners suffered less distress, as revealed in "a decrease over time in stress-related medical symptomology," including a decrease in anxiety and depression, as well as "some improvement in measures of general health." Daily emotions tied to situational pressures within the prison remained constant since the pressures themselves were unchanged. Hence, emotional states like anger, boredom, or loneliness were unaffected by improved coping skills. Nor did the prisoners see themselves as happy or beset with fewer problems. They coped better, then, and suffered fewer impairments, but prison life remained difficult.

One reason prisoners cope better over time is that the stresses of prison life, though high at the outset, tend to level out as time passes. Prison life then becomes fairly predictable. Continuity of prison conditions is largely assured because prison offers a life marked by routines; prison thus offers many opportunities for acclimatization and adjustment. As a result, almost all prisoners, though especially long-termers, cope better over time with the problems and pressures of imprisonment. That is, they become acclimated to the prison environment. These inmates learn to live with predictable constraints. Accordingly, they lead "compromise existences in which they achieve compromise goals, operating within available constraints" that are fixed by recurrent features of prison life.

Some of the constraints on behavior imposed by prison can be circumvented, and this, in turn, can undermine constructive efforts at coping. The public prison culture might be seen as a means doing just that, under the guise of ameliorating the pains of imprisonment. The "right guy," for example, can readily obtain contraband, sometimes including hard drugs. Moreover, as the putative model of prison deportment, the right guy would seem by definition to be free of the need for critical introspection. Certainly the right guy lives on the yard, in the middle of the prison fray, not sequestered in his cell. He scorns programs as the refuge of the weak or effeminate. Nevertheless, most inmates are not right guys and, judging by what they do as distinct from what they say, they do not aspire to that role. (As we have seen, most female inmates do not adopt convict roles, either.) Instead, they disavow the mainline prison culture and the destructive behavior it promotes. These inmates may or may not subscribe, on a verbal level, to the convict code; they may or may not claim that "doing time" and "sticking together against the screws" are the wellsprings of prison life. What is important is that they show, through their actions, that they wish to avoid contact with the so-called prison community. For men and women, desire to avoid the mainline prison culture appears in some instances to be a source of deterrence and presumably can be converted to a motive for personal reform.

Disaffection from the public prison culture is not unexpected. The values so saliently reflected in this culture landed these men and women in prison, a setting that has been known to give many a hasty hedonist a moment's pause. Moreover, most inmates see the dominant or public prison culture as causing more problems than it solves in the here-and-now world of the prison, a direct and immediate relationship between behavior and consequences that even the hastiest and least reflective of hedonists can appreciate. As a result, most prisoners, and not only lifers, want to shelter themselves from this culture, not immerse themselves in its adolescent games. This often means passing for a convict in one's public dealings with prisoners and staff (which one judiciously attempts to minimize) but evolving a markedly different lifestyle in one's private prison life.

The actual "day-to-day concerns" of the typical prisoner, whether male or female, "do not revolve around status, power, or honor in the prison world"[55] As Toch's research has made abundantly clear, most male prisoners attempt to carve out a private prison world composed of niches or sanctuaries, offering sheltered settings and benign activities that insulate them from the mainline prison. Owen has made this same point quite effectively in her study of women in prison. "Women manage their prison sentences by carving out a life that provides for some measure of privacy and safety, a range of activity, a satisfying program, a living situation that is fairly comfortable, and a degree of material comforts."[56] Lifers, both male and female, seem especially likely to secure niches. Too, prisoners characterized by an internal locus of control and corresponding sense of self-efficacy seem to "hold the advantage in obtaining, and maintaining, niches."[57] The larger point, however, is that the adjustment efforts of virtually all prisoners reveal a range of ecological options that support life "off the yard," in the relative privacy of the cell or, more exotically, in the physical and social settings that form the backwaters and byways of penal institutions.

The maximum-security prison, in other words, is not a monolith. . . . Today's prisons, moreover, provide substantial ecological diversity in the form of "varying degrees of privacy from irritants such as noise or crowding, safety from insult or attack, structure and consistency of procedures, support services that facilitate self-improvement, feedback or emotional support, activity to fill time, and freedom from circumscription of one's autonomy.[58] This observation, drawn from research in men's prisons, applies equally to penal institutions for women, which offer striking ecological diversity across living units. "Each of the cottages has its own particular culture," Rierden is told by an experienced officer at Niantic, a women's prison. Some settings, Rierden learns, "are as different as night from day."[59] Prisoners, male or female, who use the environmental diversity of prisons to create niches live not as role types or stereotypes parading about the prison yard but as individuals within small and manageable worlds, often, as with Zamble's lifers, built around their private cell activities. . . . Moreover, these prisoners, male as well as female, treat their peers and officers, some of whom have helped them in their adjustment efforts, as specific individuals who in some instances deserve a measure of respect and even affection, not as anonymous "cons" or "hacks" who are, by definition, candidates for abuse.

Those prisoners who live outside the mainstream of prison culture have created for themselves a mosaic of prison worlds and adjustments in which stress is reduced and in which mature coping is possible. One option is to use niches as sanctuaries from stress and nothing more; in effect, to take prison life one day at a time and go about business as usual. This is probably the most common mode of prison adjustment, especially among those serving short sentences, but it has obvious drawbacks. "If inmates anesthetize themselves against the pains of imprisonment—or of life—by narrowing their vision, they are truly taking a short-sighted approach. In helping to deal with the present they are cutting themselves off from most of the possibilities of future improvement."[60] A better strategy is to use niches as arenas for constructive social learning, that is, as places where one feels secure enough to respond maturely to stress instead of avoiding it. It is reasonable to suppose that prisoners who adapt in this fashion, like those studied by Zamble, may be more likely to handle general life stresses in mature ways when they leave prison. They may be able, in other words, to honor the minimal obligations of citizenship, which amount to navigating life's difficulties without preying upon or otherwise exploiting others. A central correctional task, then. . . . is to arrange prison environments that promote mature coping as an exercise in citizenship and as a desirable alternative to the immature response fostered by the public inmate culture.

GENERAL DYNAMICS OF ADJUSTMENT

At first blush, it sounds painfully naive to postulate a direct and positive link between prison adjustment and subsequent adjustment in the free world. To use the language of formal psychology the "behavior contingencies" of prisons and the free world are markedly different. What one learns in prison should have little direct relevance to free-world situations "where one must structure one's own life, conditions are more varied, choices are required, and the range of possible behaviors is greatly enlarged." . . .[61]

However, there is and always has been a general similarity between the adjustment problems posed in prison and those in the outside world; for there is an important sense in which prison life and life in general are related. Prison problems are essentially exaggerated—though sometimes greatly exaggerated—versions of problems experienced in normal life. As a former inmate once observed, "The pain of imprisonment is offset by the discovery that you are strong enough to take it."[62] And, because essentially "the same system of pain and reward" operates both in prison and "in the outside world, you realize that you can succeed there, too."[63]

Imprisonment is painful because it deprives one of liberty, goods and services, heterosexual contacts, autonomy, and security. It also puts an enormous strain on personal relationships with loved ones outside the walls (including children, a special concern of inmate mothers) and suspends or even ruins any notion of a conventional occupational career. Yet all of us suffer these pains to some degree. None of us is as free as we would like, has all the goods and services we would like, is completely satisfied by our sexual outlets, or is as autonomous or secure as we would like. None of us is free from strain in our personal and family lives or in our jobs or careers. It is also true that all of us must cope with time:

> [T]ime transcends the conventional social order. Prisoners can be snatched from that order but not from time. Time imprisons us all. When the prisoner returns to society after serving his time, in an important sense he's never been away.[64]

Certainly the correspondence between general life problems and prison problems is especially salient for the lower-class men and women who make up the vast bulk of our prison populations. Indeed, we know that many of these people come from urban slums that are, in some respects at least, as harsh and depriving as the prisons they wind up in! "Doing time" in one ghetto or another is a familiar if uncongenial experience in their lives.

Thus, it can plausibly be argued that inmates who learn to cope maturely with the stresses posed by confinement are learning to cope maturely with the stresses of life. Moreover, while immature coping typically complicates problems (even the most proficient predator must contemplate the army of enemies he is cultivating), mature coping enables one to solve problems or at least make them more manageable. These successes in coping are apt to build self-confidence and encourage more ambitious behavior, such as taking on new challenges, learning new skills, and generally engaging the world rather than running from opportunities or exploding when pressure mounts. At this juncture, prisoners are no longer embroiled full-time in a dog-eat-dog fight for survival or trapped in a cycle of personal failure and defeat. They are thus more likely to sample traditional correctional programs in an effort to remedy personal deficiencies. More generally, they are ready to tackle the hard job of rebuilding their lives.

Central to this thesis is the notion that healthy self-esteem mediates coping behavior in any environment and must be enhanced if mature behavior is to occur. (Healthy self-esteem features a positive sense of one's worth that is realistic and stable, as distinct from the exaggerated, groundless, and unstable self-regard that characterizes egotists.) The psychological sequence underlying this adaptive process has been identified by Toch and can be paraphrased as follows:

1. Mature problem-solving efforts are likely to succeed and this builds healthy self-esteem and encourages more mature behavior.

2. A history of successful mature coping efforts produces a confident, resilient person who can learn from occasional failures rather than be demoralized or even traumatized by them; in short, success breeds success and makes failure manageable.

3. Immature behavior generally produces failure, which, in turn, lowers self-esteem and further inhibits effective problem solving.

4. A history of failure produces chronically low self-esteem, with the result that the person spends more time nursing hurt feelings and less time attending to the environment; stated differently, failure breeds failure and, eventually, crippling self-doubt.

Given this sequence, we cannot "engage in stress amelioration without being involved in rehabilitating people (inmates) or in developing them (staff)."[65] We find, in Zamble's words, "a self-reinforcing cycle of improvement" that sparks continuing efforts at "monitoring and controlling" dysfunctional behavior.[66]

The easy logical flow of this psychological sequence should not lead us to believe that building healthy self-esteem is, in practice, a simple business. Bandura reminds us that people sometimes go to great lengths to defend their self-images and to discount the implications of successful experiences at new ways of living.[67] Persistent offenders often resist change because they take pride in their criminal exploits, including the considerable feat of prison survival. For them, life has been a matter of repeated and painful experiences of failure at conventional living; their only successes, modest as they may be in objective terms, have been at criminal activities. A self image as a serious criminal—as a lone warrior set apart from an unjust world, as many male convicts like to see themselves—may well be inflated and unstable but it helps to reduce the pains of rejection by the larger society and is something an offender will cling to until a viable alternative is found. Nevertheless, a history of successes at conventional activities, though it may be slow in coming, is necessary for healthy self-esteem and improved coping competence to develop.

Stress management and personal reform, then, are linked in direct if sometimes complicated ways. This connection forms the core of the correctional agenda; for stress, more than any other aspect of the prison experience, defines the quality of life and adjustment behind bars. As Toch and I have noted,

Stress is an important feature of prison life, and indeed may be the central feature of prison life as it is experienced by the prisoners themselves. Stress can contaminate programs, undermine adjustment efforts, and leave a residue of bitterness and resentment among inmates. It can make the prison a destructive and debilitating institution; to ignore stress is to relegate prisons to the business of warehousing spoiled (and spoiling) human resources. Stress must be controlled if prisons are to become environments in which the work of corrections, in any sense of the word, can take place.[68]

Ultimately, the prison itself must deal competently, meaning *maturely*, with stress. Porporino and Zamble are surely correct when they maintain that

> there is a general consensus that imprisonment should not be damaging. Prisons should not change individuals for the worse. Social objectives [of imprisonment] are not met to the extent that imprisonment serves to exacerbate psychological vulnerabilities and emotional difficulties, reinforce pro-criminal attitudes and aggressive behavior patterns, or curtail the development of coping skills needed to function in the outside world.[69]

Stated positively, prisons must be "resilient environments, settings orchestrated by line and managerial staff to meet the adjustment needs of prisoners."[70] The premise is that "even environments of stress such as prisons can become settings for survival and milieus for personal growth." Even maximum-security prisons, in other words, can promote mature adjustment, and they must do just that if they are to play a viable role in the correctional process.

NOTES

1. Nettler (1984:209); Schwendinger and Schwendinger (1967:98).
2. Wideman (1984:131).
3. Zamble (1990:138).
4. Zamble and Porporino (1990:56).
5. Earley (1992:416–417).
6. Halleck (1967:72).
7. Wideman (1984:132).
8. Halleck (1967:77).
9. Walters (1990:71).
10. Walters (1990:106).
11. Walters (1990:107).
12. Walters (1990:109).
13. Mueller (1985:18).
14. Freeman (1994:190).
15. Wideman (1984:66).
16. Zamble, Porporino, and Kalotay (1984:58).
17. Zamble, Porporino, and Kalotay (1984:128).
18. Walters (1990:88).
19. Wideman (1984:145).
20. Walters (1990:88–89).
21. Harris (1988:94).
22. Quoted in Harris (1988:291).
23. Empey (1982:25).
24. Owen (1998:170).
25. Owen (1998:58).
26. Montgomery (1994:A4).
27. Staub (1989:265).
28. Staub (1989:265).
29. Johnson and Toch (1988:20).
30. Rierden (1997:26).
31. For men, see Lerner (1984:17). For women, see Rierden (1997:32).
32. Seymour (1977:195–196).
33. Goodstein (1979:253).
34. Goodstein (1979:253).
35. Owen (1998:148).
36. Goffman (1961).
37. Earley (1992:249–250).

38. Fleisher (1989:22–23).

39. Owen (1998:40).

40. Owen (1998:55).

41. Rierden (1997:117).

42. Kupers (1999:39).

43. Kupers (1999:55).

44. Kupers (199:56–57).

45. Zamble, Porporino, and Kalotay (1984:69–70).

46. Zamble, Porporino, and Kalotay (1984:70).

47. Quoted in Besozzi (1993:37).

48. Zamble, Porporino, and Kalotay (1984:69–70).

49. Zamble (1992a:410); see also, Flanagan (1988).

50. Zamble (1992b:13–14).

51. Zamble (1992b:13–14).

52. Zamble (1992a:423).

53. Zamble (1992b:29).

54. Zamble (1992b:20).

55. Seymour (1988:268). See also Owen (1998).

56. Owen (1998:117).

57. Goodstein and Wright (1989:245).

58. Johnson and Toch (1988:18).

59. Rierden (1997:9).

60. Zamble, Porporino, and Kalotay (1984:80).

61. Zamble, Porporino, and Kalotay (1984:136).

62. Gates (1991:68).

63. Gates (1991:68).

64. Wideman (1984:36).

65. Toch (1988:37–38).

66. Zamble (1990:34).

67. Bandura (1977:200–202).

68. Johnson and Toch (1988:20).

69. Porporino and Zamble (1984:403).

70. Toch (1975:326).

REFERENCES

Bandura, A. "Self-efficacy: Toward a unified theory of behavioral change. *Psychological Review 84* (March 1977): 191–215.

Besozzi, C. "Recidivism: How inmates see it." *Forum on Corrections Research* 5(3) 1993:35–38.

Earley P. *The Hot House: Life Inside Leavenworth.* New York: Bantam Books, 1992.

Empey, L. "Implications: A game with no winners." In A.J. Manocchio and J. Dunn. *The Game: Two Views of a Prison.* Beverly Hills: Sage, 1982: 241–52.

Flanagan, T. J. "Lifers and long-termers: Doing big time." In R. Johnson and H. Toch (eds.). *The Pains of Imprisonment.* Prospect Heights, IL: Waveland Press, 1988:115–45.

Fleischer, M. S. *Warehousing Violence.* Beverly Hills: Sage, 1989.

Freeman, R. B. "The labor market." In J. Q. Wilson and J. Petersilia (eds.). *Crime.* San Francisco: ICS Press, 1994: 171–91.

Gates, M. "The excavation." American University: Unpublished manuscript, 1991.

Coffman, E. *Asylums.* New York: Anchor Books, 1961.

Goodstein, L. "Inmate adjustment to prison and the transition to community life." *Journal of Research in Crime and Delinquency* 16(2) 1979:246–72.

Goodstein, L., D. L. Mackenzie, and R. L. Shotland. "Personal control and inmate adjustment to prison." *Criminology* 22(3) 1984:343–69.

Goodstein, L., and K. N. Wright. "Inmate adjustment to prison." In L. Goodstein and D. L. MacKenzie (eds.). *The American Prison: Issues in Research and Policy.* New York: Plenum Press, 1989:229–51.

Halleck, S. *Psychiatry and the Dilemma of Crime.* New York: Harper & Row, 1967.

Hallinan, J. T. *Going Up The River: Travels in a Prison Nation.* New York: Random House, 2001.

Hannerz, U. *Soulside*. New York: Columbia University Press, 1969.

Harris, J. *They Always Call Us Ladies: Stories from Prison*. New York: Kensington Publishing, 1988.

Johnson, R., and H. Toch. "Introduction." In R. Johnson and H. Toch (eds.). *The Pains of Imprisonment*. Prospect Heights, IL: Waveland Press, 1988:13–21.

Kupers, T. A. *Prison Madness: The Mental Health Crisis Behind Bars and What We Must Do About It*. San Francisco, CA: Jossey-Bass Publishers, 1999.

Lerner, S. "Rule of the cruel." *The New Republic,* October 15, 1984:17–21.

Montgomery, L. "'Urban survival' rules at issue in trial." *The Washington Post*, October 26, 1994:A4.

Mueller. J. "Crime is caused by the young and restless." *Wall Street Journal,* March 6, 1985:18.

Nettler G. *Explaining Crime*. New York: McGraw-Hill, 1984.

Osgood, D. W, E. Gruber, M. A. Archer, and T. M. Newcomb. "Autonomy for Inmates: counterculture or cooptation?" *Criminal Justice and Behavior* 12 (1) 1985:71–89.

Owen, B. *"In the Mix": Struggle and Survival in a Women's Prison*. Albany: State University of New York Press, 1998.

Porporino, F, and E. Zamble. "Coping with imprisonment." *Canadian Journal of Criminology* 26(4) 1984:403–21.

Rierden, A. *The Farm: A Lift Inside a Women's Prison*. Amherst, MA: University of Massachusetts Press, 1997.

Schwendinger, H., and J. Schwendinger. "Delinquent stereotypes of probable victims." In M. W Klein (ed.). *Juvenile Gangs in Context: Theory, Research, and Action*. Englewood Cliffs, NJ: Prentice-Hall, 1967.

Seymour, J. "Niches in prison." In H. Toch. *Living in Prison: The Ecology of Survival*. New York: Free Press, 1977:179–205.

Staub, E. *The Roots of Evil: The Origins of Genocide and Other Group Violence*. New York: Cambridge University Press, 1989.

Toch, H. *Men in Crisis: Human Breakdowns in Prison*. Chicago: Aldine, 1975.

Toch, H. "Studying and reducing stress." In R. Johnson and H. Toch (eds.). *The Pains of Imprisonment*. Prospect Heights, IL: Waveland Press, 1988:25–44.

Walters, G. D. *The Criminal Lifestyle: Patterns of Serious Criminal Conduct*. Beverly Hills: Sage, 1990.

Wideman, J. E. *Brothers and Keepers*. New York: Holt, Rinehart & Winston, 1984.

Zamble, E. "Behavioral and psychological considerations in the success of prison reform." In J. W. Murphy and J. E. Dison (eds.). *Are Prisons Any Better?: Twenty Years of Prison Reform*. Newbury Park, CA: Sage, 1990: 129–45.

Zamble, E. "Behavior and adaptation in long-term prison inmates: Descriptive longitudinal results." *Criminal Justice and Behavior* 19(4) 1992a:409-25.

Zamble, E. "Personal communication relative to coping patterns among long-term prison inmates." (1992b).

21

❂

Well-Governed Prisons
Are Possible

John J. DiIulio, Jr.

Political scientist John DiIulio challenges the view of Sykes and other sociologists that prisons should be analyzed from the perspective of the inmate society. He argues that because of the dominance of the view that "the cons run the joint," the importance of good management has been neglected.

Although a disputatious lot, public management scholars tend to agree strongly (if implicitly) on one thing: public management matters. They share a belief ("faith" might be a better word) that how public organizations are managed has a significant bearing on how, and how well, those organizations perform. They assume that how public executives, managers, and line workers behave affects significantly what and how much their organizations produce in the way of public safety, health, education, environmental protection, national security, and so on. This assumption undergirds every public administration text and many books and articles on the organization of the White House, Congress, and the lesser bodies that form each institution.

Source: "Well-Governed Prisons Are Possible," by John J. DiIulio, Jr.
Author's Note: Portions of this article have been adapted from my previously published works, including "Recovering the Public Management Variable: Lessons from Schools, Prisons, and Armies," *Public Administration Review* (March/April 1989): 127–133; *No Escape: The Future of American Corrections* (New York: Basic Books, 1991), Chap. 1; and "Understanding Prisons: The New Old Penology," *Law and Social Inquiry* 16 (Winter 1991): 65–86.

For example, many studies now suggest that student performance on standardized tests and other measures of educational attainment is largely a function of school management, which is defined in terms of such hard-to-measure factors as how teachers structure their classes, how principals lead their teachers, and how superintendents coordinate their principals. In popular and scholarly discourse, these works are often lumped together and called the "effective-schools" literature.[1] This literature deepens one's faith in the efficacy of the public management variable. Broadly stated, if society's goal is to make students literate and social, then it matters greatly how the schools are managed. The studies indicate that simply paying teachers more, "tinkering" with testing devices, or "fiddling" with pupil-to-teacher ratios does not work.

WELL-GOVERNED PRISONS

No literature is available on prisons that parallels the "effective-schools" literature. Most of the research on prisons has been done by sociologists and focuses heavily on the social order of the cell blocks.[2] The "ineffective-prisons" literature might be the most fitting label for the past five decades of research on prisons.

Most works on prisons by sociologists and penologists embody grave doubts about the efficacy of prison management. Indeed, most of this literature suggests that prison managers can do virtually nothing to improve conditions behind bars: if prisons develop a distinctive social system along racial and ethnic lines, reinforced by an informal but powerful distribution of authority, then policy makers can do little more than take notice, while prison managers must compromise their formal authority. To the extent that any of these studies relate prison management practices to the quality of life behind bars, the results are maddening: prisons that are managed in a tight, authoritarian fashion are plagued by disorder and inadequate programs; prisons that are managed in a loose "participative" fashion are equally troubled; and "mixed" cell block management regimes do no better.

But general faith in the efficacy of public management, the existence of numerous (though admittedly laughable) "prison administrator" textbooks and former wardens'"how-to" memoirs, and a few quite recent empirical studies of prison management conspire to challenge this perplexing view of these "barbed-wire bureaucracies."

My *Governing Prisons: A Comparative Study of Correctional Management* reports on three years of exploratory research on prison management in the Texas, Michigan, and California departments of corrections.[3] In sum, that book analyzed intersystem, intrasystem, and historical variations in the quality of life, which were measured in terms of three criteria: order (rates of individual and collective violence and other forms of misconduct), amenity (availability of clean cells, decent food, and so on), and service (availability of work opportunities, educational programs, and so forth).

Using the simplest sort of approach and having weighed the possibility of problems in the data, I found no evidence that levels of order, amenity, and service varied directly with any of these factors: a "better class" of inmates; greater per capita spending; lower levels of crowding; lower inmate-to-staff ratios; greater officer training; more modern plant and equipment; more elaborate systems to sensitize official decision makers to the views (especially the grievances) of inmates; more elaborate systems to improve inmate–staff and inmate–inmate race relations (including the existence of a more racially "representative" officer force); and a more routine use of repressive measures, including official and quasi-official beatings of "troublemakers" by officers or by designated inmate "trustees."

All roads, it seemed, led to the conclusion that the quality of prison life depended mainly on the quality of prison management. This conclusion was teased from a close analysis of the history, politics, penological credo, and administration of each system and was bolstered by two natural experiments in the data. To simplify greatly, prison organizations that were led strongly by a stable team of like-minded executives, structured in a paramilitary, security-driven bureaucratic fashion, and coordinated proactively in conjunction with the demands of relevant outside actors (including key legislators, community activists, judges, and overseers) had higher levels of order, amenity, and service than prison organizations that were managed in other ways, *even when* the former institutions were more crowded, spent less per capita, had higher inmate–staff ratios, and so on. The research supported this conclusion: *"The only findings of this study that, to me at least, seem indisputable, is that . . . prison management matters."*[4]

Other recent studies are part of what might be termed the emerging "well-governed prisons" literature. Bert Useem, analyzing major prison riots in the United States between 1971 and 1986, provides ample evidence that the riots were due mainly to a breakdown in security procedures—the daily routine of numbering, counting, frisking, locking, contraband control, and cell searches that is the heart of administration in most prisons.[5] The main determinants of prison riots are obvious and proximate factors relating to the quality of prison management. Crowding, underfunding, court intervention, festering inmate–staff or inmate–inmate racial animosities, and other widely cited causes of prison disorders may make riots more likely, but only failed security management makes them "inevitable."[6] In short, how prisons are managed may increase or decrease the probability of an inmate living out his term in a safe, lawful environment.

Similarly, my *Principled Agents: The Cultural Bases of Behavior in a Federal Government Bureaucracy* shows how efficacious prison management can be.[7] The Federal Bureau of Prisons is recognized far and wide as one of the nation's most successful correctional agencies. Almost without exception, its prisons have been safe and humane; they have improved every decade since the agency came into being. There are two popular but false explanations for the bureau's success relative to state prison systems. The first explanation is that the bureau has always gotten "a better class of criminals." Historically, however, the bureau has never held only white-collar offenders: in mid-1988, for example,

46 percent of its prisoners had a history of violence; and each year the states transfer many of their "too-hard-to-handle" inmates to "the Feds." The second explanation is that the bureau's annual per-inmate expenditures far exceed the states'; in fact, historically the agency has spent almost exactly at the national median. Furthermore, like many state systems, the bureau has had overcrowding, poorly designed cell houses, staff shortages, and other problems that adversely affect the quality of prison life. But the bureau has met these challenges better, and with greater consistency, than any other correctional agency in the land.

The reason: bureau management. In sum, unlike most state prison systems, the bureau has had stable and talented executive leadership (only four directors in its first fifty-seven years of existence); a progressive inmate classification system; an elaborate system of audits, transfers, and other internal "checks and balances"; a positive, closely knit organizational culture; and many other positive features. State and local agencies that have copied bureau management practices have improved. For example, recent analysis of intrasystem differences in the New York City system documents the comparative strengths of "unit management," a form of correctional administration pioneered by the bureau in which security staff and noncustodial personnel are given responsibility for a wing of an institution and trained to work cohesively.[8] In these and other recent studies, prison management emerges as the crucial variable in determining the quality of life behind bars.

GENERAL PRINCIPLES OF GOOD CORRECTIONAL LEADERSHIP

Successful correctional leaders differ in many ways, from their own penological credos to their personal styles. However, in certain crucial aspects, they and the organization they lead are the same.

One important trait shared by successful correctional leaders is devotion to building or maintaining an organizational culture. James Q. Wilson has defined *organizational culture* as "a persistent, patterned way of thinking about the central tasks of and human relationships within an organization. Culture is to organization what personality is to an individual. Like human culture generally, it is passed on from one generation to the next."[9] As Wilson has observed, unlike students of business administration, students of public administration have not puzzled much over "creating the right organizational culture," and little is known about how government executives "define tasks and motivate workers to perform those tasks."[10]

While the literature of public administration includes nothing of note about the relationship between correctional leadership and organizational culture, certain interlocking patterns are clear. In *No Escape: The Future of American Corrections,* I identified six general principles of good leadership drawn from my observations of correctional managers in both state and national agencies.[11] Let us examine these principles closely.

1. *The successful leaders focus, and inspire their subordinates to focus, on results rather than process, on performance rather than procedures, on ends rather than means.* Managers are rewarded (or not) according to whether the cell blocks are clean, the inmates safe, the classes orderly, the industry productive, the staff turnover rate low, the escape rate zero, and so on. A warden who fails to deliver these goods cannot excuse himself by reciting budget woes, crowding problems, red tape, too many "heavies," or anything else.

   Some of the successful correctional leaders have concentrated more or less exclusively on results, but all of them have stressed results in accordance with their sense of the organization's mission and primary objectives. But in each case, a clear mission statement existed and the institutions were organized and managed around it.

2. *Organizational culture is custodial at core.* Doctors, nurses, secretaries, counselors, accountants, and other nonuniformed institutional staff are trained to think as correctional officers first, and the primary responsibility of every employee is to protect the inmates and to keep them from escaping. Leaders have made institutional safety and security their top priority and have worked hard to see to it that the organization's formal and informal (peer group) incentive structure mirrored this emphasis.

   In the Federal Bureau of Prisons, for example, all staff members have undergone the same basic training. They have been required to take target practice and are expected to join shoulders with uniformed officers in the event of a major disturbance. The spectacle of middle-aged secretaries in skirts toting guns on the perimeter of a prison amazed (and distressed) some on-site observers of the 1987 hostage incident at the bureau's Atlanta Penitentiary—but it was an example of the kind of management that has made the bureau a close-knit family organization with high esprit de corps and little of the workaday tension between treatment and custodial personnel that has harmed other corrections agencies. Similarly, a Michigan prisons research analyst was amused when he telephoned his counterpart in the Texas Department of Corrections and was told that the fellow was out hunting down escapees. Such practices accounted for the once-healthy staff morale and good relations among Texas prison workers at all levels.

   As Wilson points out, public organizations that have strong management and a concomitantly strong sense of mission sometimes suffer from resistance to needed administrative changes, slowness in adapting to new political circumstances, and other problems.[12] The net effect, however, is almost always positive, and correctional organizations that have been led in ways that promote a strong custodial culture have everywhere been more safe and humane than those that have not.

3. *Leaders of successful institutions follow the MBWA principle: management by walking around.* "Walking" George Beto, director of the Texas Department of Corrections from 1962 to 1972, takes the prize for this approach to management, but his successful peers come in as close seconds.

   New Jersey's William Fauver, for example, began his practice of "feet-on" leadership when he was the warden of Trenton State Prison. As he later recalled: "When I first came to Trenton, a warden walking around without a bodyguard was unheard of. I felt it was necessary—a symbolic thing that says you're in charge." He has continued this practice as commissioner, making regular visits (not "tours" or "inspections") to each of his facilities.

   The same has been true for other successful leaders. None are strangers to the cell blocks; each knows the facilities almost as well as he knows his own home, and he is always on the scene (often in the center of things) when major trouble erupts. MBWA keeps correctional managers from becoming hostages to (often distorted or incomplete) reports from the field and helps them escape the iron bars of paperwork. Moreover, it gives the staff greater personal respect for their chief and also enhances his reputation among the inmates.

   In prison and jail settings, one's personal reputation is crucial: inmates who lie about their criminal exploits or "punk out" when challenged physically by their peers are not respected; and officers who are easily intimidated, break their word, or do not act in a "firm but fair" manner are not taken seriously. Everyone "looks through" the uniform to the person inside it. Of senior officers who have weak personal reputations, one often hears comments such as "He's just a paper captain," or "His bars aren't for real," or (from inmates), "He's Major No-Balls."

   Correctional leaders who have not practiced MBWA have not made a reputation; instead, staff and inmates have made one for them. In most cases, the reputation they fastened to the director was not flattering ("removed," "chickenshit," "out of touch," "head up his ass," and so on). Leaders who have practiced MBWA have not always done so successfully, but most have.

4. *Successful leaders make significant alliances with key politicians, judges, journalists, reformers, and other outsiders with the ability to affect the organization's fiscal health, statutory authority, and public image.* Among the strategies employed by successful correctional leaders are throwing parties for key outsiders (in some cases at the executive's personal expense), responding quickly and cordially to legislative inquiries for information, lecturing in public, attending conferences, freely granting interviews, publishing articles and essays, and developing good personal relationships with top officials in other law-enforcement agencies—or, when that failed, creating interagency procedures to "force" and routinize cooperation.

   Above all else, important outsiders are invited into the facilities to see for themselves what conditions are like and how things operate. Often, events are staged; for example, an inmate college graduation ceremony. Just as often, however, the outsiders (including judges) are invited to take a long, hard look at what is going on. Sometimes they like what they see; other times they do not. In some instances, the resultant political fallout, press coverage, and public attention is favorable; in other cases, it causes fresh headaches for the director and his staff.

But successful correctional leaders follow a policy of openness and alliance building, and in the long run they are better than leaders who do not. Leaders who try to keep the outsiders out, or who simply ignore them, are more likely to wind up fired, burned out, or forced to resign, even when their institutions do not fare as badly as those of other systems where leaders are more open.

Successful leaders take it as axiomatic that the general public can neither know nor care enough about correctional staff (or the unpopular people they supervise) to furnish anything like sturdy political support for their institutions. Instead, they have made such broad appeals only one component, and by no means the largest one, of the strategy for handling outside "coaches, customers, and critics."[13] They consciously manage their agency's external relations with as much zeal as they have managed their cell blocks.

5. *Successful leaders rarely innovate, but their innovations are far-reaching and the reasons for them are made known in advance to both inmates and staff.* Changes are made slowly, allowing staff and inmates plenty of time to learn the new ways and "get on board." For the most part, the innovations address a current or potential problem that most of those who live and work in the facilities already acknowledge as serious. As often as not, the innovations represent a fundamentally new way of achieving an old mission, rather than being a new mission itself. And in most cases, the old practices are abolished without any implication that they (and hence those who followed and believed in them) failed or were misguided: rather, they are presented as necessary or unavoidable responses to changed circumstances and "sold" to inmates and staff accordingly.

Correctional line staff are notoriously sensitive to what their leaders "do for the inmates" versus "what they do for us." Signs of appreciation, tangible and symbolic, for the public service that line staff perform tend to be few and to come from within the organization. As one warden stated, at times it is almost as though there were a sibling rivalry between inmates and line officers. Thus, to give inmates a new athletic facility without making a commensurate gesture toward line staff, or to enhance inmates' eligibility for college and vocational courses without improving (or at least attempting to improve) the educational benefits of staff, can erode staff loyalty to "the brass," harm labor–management relations in other areas, and cost a director much of whatever personal and professional capital with line workers he may have accumulated over the years. Thus, many "innovations" in correctional settings are in actuality attempts to correct this sort of real or perceived imbalance.

6. *Successful leaders are in office long enough to understand and, as necessary, to modify the organization's internal operations and external relations.* Most

correctional leaders who are successful serve for at least six consecutive years in one position; some, for over a decade. With respect to length of service, there have been four kinds of correctional leaders, which I classify (with shameless alliteration) as flies, fatalists, foot soldiers, and founders.

Over the past two decades, corrections officers have served an average of only three years before quitting, getting fired, or moving on to another agency; several have stayed in office less than a year. These flies of summer have either come and gone unnoticed or have attempted to reform the agency in one fell swoop. The former flies are inconsequential; the latter buzzed loudly and were a nuisance until they were swatted down by reality.

The fatalists served similarly brief terms that began and ended with their complaining about the futility of incarceration and the hopelessness of institutional reform. Often, they had little or no previous experience managing correctional institutions. In some cases, they were talented and energetic people who convinced key decision makers that their institutions were beyond repair; several brought about deinstitutionalization schemes of one sort or another. Whatever the results of these schemes (usually the results have been poor to mixed), the fatalists did nothing to achieve institutional reform but did succeed in abolishing some institutions.

Compared to the flies and most of the fatalists, the foot soldiers served long terms. Whether they inherited their job from a fly, a fatalist, or a founder, they worked in the trenches to make whatever incremental improvements they could, usually in a pragmatic spirit unleavened by a commitment to any particular penological theory. When what they inherited was good, they tried to preserve as much of it as they could and to consolidate new administrative measures around old routines. W. J. Estelle in Texas, Steve Bablitch in Wisconsin, and Orville Pung in Minnesota would rank among the foot soldiers.

The founders were those who created an agency or reorganized it in major and positive ways. Generally, like directors James V. Bennett and Norman A. Carlson of the Federal Bureau of Prisons, and New Jersey's William Fauver and William Lecke, they served long terms.

Not every leader who served a long term has done good things organizationally. And some leaders are hard to classify meaningfully. But the record suggests that foot soldiers and founders are a boon to the quality of institutional life; indeed, if I were forced to choose between one mediocre leader for ten years and a succession of four talented ones over the same period, I would probably entrust the institutions to the former.

SUMMARY

Throughout the nineteenth century and the early part of the twentieth, studies of prisons focused more on the administrators than on the inmates. Prison governance was the central and abiding focus of these studies. To permit prisoners to associate freely was to abandon them to criminal mischief and corruption and to raise the likelihood of criminal disorders behind bars.

Beginning in the 1940s with the publication of research by sociologists, there was a shift in focus from sympathy for the work of prison administrators to sympathy for prison inmates. Whereas the "old penology" maintained that prisons must be governed strictly by duly appointed officials, the "new penology" maintained that prisons must be governed by the prisoners themselves.

In the 1960s the prison population became increasingly black and Hispanic. In a spate of studies, a second generation of new penologists documented the rise of a younger, more aggressive, more politicized breed of convict chieftains. These new inmate leaders were far less willing and able to get other inmates to go along with even the most basic wishes of the administration. Prison populations became fractionalized along racial and ethnic lines. The pliable con-boss was succeeded by the inflexible prison gang leader. The society of captives, it seemed, was about to run out of control.

The old penology, of course, had a cure for this virus of inmate dominance: namely, rigorous internal controls, rule enforcement, and the atomization of the "prison community." And in the few corrections agencies where old penologists remained at the helm, that is precisely the medicine they administered.

To old penologists, prison administrators were admirable public servants, inmate associations behind the walls were to be restricted and minimized, and any form of inmate self-government was considered a nightmare. To new penologists, prison administrators were damnable ogres, prisoners were responsible souls, and complete inmate self-government was a pleasant dream. By the mid-1980s, the new penologists' dream had come true in many places, but with precisely the ill consequences that the old penologists would have predicted.

Publication in 1987 of *Governing Prisons* gave rise to what has been called the "new old penology," a shift of attention from the society of captives to the government of keepers.[14] In that book I presented empirical evidence and arguments that tight administrative control was often more conducive to decent prison conditions (and possibly rehabilitation) than loose administrative control; highlighted the moral and practical sophistry of inmate self-government schemes; and otherwise restored some, though by no means all, of the claims of the old penology. This approach to understanding prisons pushes administrators back to the bar of attention, is inclined to treat them at least as sympathetically as it treats their charges, and attempts to translate empirically grounded research on prisoner behavior into ideas about how to manage toward more safe and humane conditions behind bars.

The "new old penology" posits as central that, other things being equal, correctional leaders who follow the precepts discussed above produce more in the way of safe and humane conditions behind bars than leaders who do not. It is time to stop treating correctional management as an impossible job. And it is long past time to stop offering lame sociological excuses for real failures of administration. What Sykes called the "society of captives" can be governed well or ill.

NOTES

1. Edward B. Fiske, "New Look at Effective Schools," *New York Times,* April 15, 1984, Section 12.

2. Major works in this large literature include Donald Clemmer, *The Prison Community* (New York: Holt, Rinehart & Winston, 1940); Gresham M. Sykes, *The Society of Captives: A Study of a Maximum Security Prison* (Princeton: Princeton University Press, 1958); Donald R. Cressey (ed.), *The Prison: Studies in Institutional Organization and Change* (New York: Holt, Rinehart & Winston, 1961); John Irwin, *The Felon* (Englewood Cliffs, N.J.: Prentice-Hall, 1970); John Irwin, *Prisons in Turmoil* (Boston: Little, Brown, 1980).

3. John J. DiIulio, Jr., *Governing Prisons: A Comparative Study of Correctional Management* (New York: Free Press, 1987).

4. Ibid., p. 256.

5. Bert Useem, *States of Siege: U.S. Prison Riots, 1971–1986* (New York: Oxford University Press, 1988).

6. Contrary to much of the "ineffective-prisons" literature, Useem's carefully documented work provides no support for the theory that security-driven management and prison violence vary inversely. The idea that the more prison authorities do to control inmates, the more inmates will run out of control is intriguing, counterintuitive, and wholly without empirical evidence to support it. For a discussion of this theory, see DiIulio, *Governing Prisons,* pp. 22–23, and Useem, *supra.*

7. John J. DiIulio, Jr., *Principled Agents: The Cultural Bases of Behavior in a Federal Government Bureaucracy,* Journal of Public Administration Research and Theory (July 1994): 4.

8. John J. DiIulio, Jr., *Interim Report on Corrections in New York City* (New York: New York City Board of Corrections, September 10, 1987); and Richard J. Koehler, Memo to First Deputy Mayor Stanley Brezenoff, New York City Department of Corrections, April 19, 1988.

9. James Q. Wilson, *Bureaucracy: What Government Agencies Do and Why They Do It* (New York: Basic Books, 1989), p. 91.

10. Ibid.

11. John J. DiIulio, Jr., *No Escape: The Future of American Corrections* (New York: Basic Books, 1991), Chap. 1.

12. Wilson, *Bureaucracy.*

13. This alliterative phrase is from Richard A. McGee, *Prisons and Politics* (Lexington, Mass.: Lexington Books, 1981). McGee directed the California penal system for several decades.

14. The term was coined by Bert Useem in "Correctional Management: How to Govern Our 'Cities,'" *Corrections Today* (February 1990): 88.

22

❂

What Works?
Questions and Answers
about Prison Reform

Robert Martinson

rehabilitation

Publication of this article in 1974 framed the debate about rehabilitation as a correctional goal. This recidivism-based research was much cited by practitioners and policy makers alike, as the reason for shifting to determinate sentences and for limiting discretionary release on parole. While Martinson fought to correct what he felt was a misinterpretation of this influential work, it is credited with reducing the role of treatment programs.

• • •

One of the problems in the constant debate over "prison reform" is that we have been able to draw very little on any systematic empirical knowledge about the success or failure that we have met when we *have* tried to rehabilitate offenders, with various treatments and in various institutional and non-institutional settings. The field of penology has produced a voluminous research literature on this subject, but until recently there has been no comprehensive review of this literature and no attempt to bring its findings to bear, in a useful way, on the general question of "What works?" My purpose in this essay is to sketch an answer to that question.

Source: Robert Martinson, "What Works? Questions and Answers about Prison Reform," *The Public Interest,* No. 35 (1974), pp. 22–54. Footnotes and references have been deleted.

THE TRAVAILS OF A STUDY

. . .

What we set out to do in this study was fairly simple, though it turned into a massive task. First we undertook a six-month search of the literature for any available reports published in the English language on attempts at rehabilitation that had been made in our corrections systems and those of other countries from 1945 through 1967. We then picked from that literature all those studies whose findings were interpretable—that is, whose design and execution met the conventional standards of social science research. Our criteria were rigorous but hardly esoteric: A study had to be an evaluation of a treatment method, it had to employ an independent measure of the improvement secured by that method, and it had to use some control group, some untreated individuals with whom the treated ones could be compared. We excluded studies only for methodological reasons: They presented insufficient data, they were only preliminary, they presented only a summary of findings, their results were confounded by extraneous factors, they used unreliable measures, one could not understand their descriptions of the treatment in question, they drew spurious conclusions from their data, their samples were undescribed or too small or provided no true comparability between treated and untreated groups, or they had used inappropriate statistical tests and did not provide enough information for the reader to recompute the data. Using these standards, we drew from the total number of studies 231 acceptable ones, which we not only analyzed ourselves but summarized in detail so that a reader of our analysis would be able to compare it with his independent conclusions.

These treatment studies use various measures of offender improvement: recidivism rates (that is, the rates at which offenders return to crime), adjustment to prison life, vocational success, educational achievement, personality and attitude change, and general adjustment to the outside community. We included all of these in our study, but in these pages I will deal only with the effects of rehabilitative treatment on recidivism, the phenomenon which reflects most directly how well our present treatment programs are performing the task of rehabilitation. The use of even this one measure brings with it enough methodological complications to make a clear reporting of the findings most difficult. The groups that are studied, for instance, are exceedingly disparate, so that it is hard to tell whether what "works" for one kind of offender also works for others. In addition, there has been little attempt to replicate studies; therefore one cannot be certain how stable and reliable the various findings are. Just as important, when the various studies use the term "recidivism rate," they may in fact be talking about somewhat different measures of offender behavior—i.e., "failure" measures such as arrest rates or parole violation rates, or "success" measures such as favorable discharge from parole or probation. And not all of these measures correlate very highly with one another. These difficulties will become apparent again and again in the course of this discussion.

With these caveats, it is possible to give a rather bald summary of our findings: *With few and isolated exceptions, the rehabilitative efforts that have been reported so far have had no appreciable effect on recidivism.* Studies that have been done since our survey was completed do not present any major grounds for altering that original conclusion. What follows is an attempt to answer the questions and challenges that might be posed to such an unqualified statement.

EDUCATION AND VOCATIONAL TRAINING

1. *Isn't it true that a correctional facility running a truly rehabilitative program—one that prepares inmates for life on the outside through education and vocational training—will turn out more successful individuals than will a prison which merely leaves its inmates to rot?*

If this is true, the fact remains that there is very little empirical evidence to support it. Skill development and educational programs are in fact quite common in correctional facilities, and one might begin by examining their effects on young males, those who might be thought most amenable to such efforts. A study by New York State (1964) found that for young males as a whole, the degree of success achieved in the regular prison academic education program, as measured by changes in grade achievement levels, made no significant difference in recidivism rates. The only exception was the relative improvement, compared with the sample as a whole, that greater progress made in the top seven per cent of the participating population—those who had high I.Q.'s, had made good records in previous schooling, and who also made good records of academic progress in the institution. And a study by Glaser (1964) found that while it was true that, when one controlled for sentence length, more attendance in regular prison academic programs slightly decreased the subsequent chances of parole violation, this improvement was not large enough to outweigh the associated disadvantage for the "long-attenders." Those who attended prison school the longest also turned out to be those who were in prison the longest. Presumably, those getting the most education were also the worst parole risks in the first place.

IMP POINT!

. . .

In sum, many of these studies of young males are extremely hard to interpret because of flaws in research design. But it can safely be said that they provide us with no clear evidence that education or skill development programs have been successful.

TRAINING ADULT INMATES

When one turns to adult male inmates, as opposed to young ones, the results are even more discouraging. There have been six studies of this type; three of them report that their programs, which ranged from academic to prison work experience, produced no significant differences in recidivism rates, and one—by Glaser (1964)—is almost impossible to interpret because of the risk differentials of the prisoners participating in the various programs.

Two studies—by Schur (1948) and by Saden (1962)—do report a positive difference from skill development programs. In one of them, the Saden study, it is questionable whether the experimental and control groups were truly comparable. But what is more interesting is that both these "positive" studies dealt with inmates incarcerated prior to or during World War II. Perhaps the rise in our educational standards as a whole since then has lessened the differences that prison education or training can make. The only other interesting possibility emerges from a study by Gearhart (1967). His study was one of those that reported vocational education to be non-significant in affecting recidivism rates. He did note, however, that when a trainee succeeded in finding a job related to his area of training, he had a slightly higher chance of becoming a successful parolee. It is possible, then, that skill development programs fail because what they teach bears so little relationship to an offender's subsequent life outside the prison.

One other study of adults, this one with fairly clear implications, has been performed with women rather than men. An experimental group of institutionalized women in Milwaukee was given an extremely comprehensive special education program, accompanied by group counseling. Their training was both academic and practical; it included reading, writing, spelling, business filing, child care, and grooming. Kettering (1965) found that the program made no difference in the women's rates of recidivism.

Two things should be noted about these studies. One is the difficulty of interpreting them as a whole. The disparity in the programs that were tried, in the populations that were affected, and in the institutional settings that surrounded these projects makes it hard to be sure that one is observing the same category of treatment in each case. But the second point is that despite this difficulty, one can be reasonably sure that, so far, educational and vocational programs have not worked. We don't know why they have failed. We don't know whether the programs themselves are flawed, or whether they are incapable of overcoming the effects of prison life in general. The difficulty may be that they lack applicability to the world the inmate will face outside of prison. Or perhaps the type of educational and skill improvement they produce simply doesn't have very much to do with an individual's propensity to commit crime. What we do know is that, to date, education and skill development have not reduced recidivism by rehabilitating criminals.

THE EFFECTS
OF INDIVIDUAL COUNSELING

2. But when we speak of a rehabilitative prison, aren't we referring to more than education and skill development alone? Isn't what's needed some way of counseling inmates, or helping them with the deeper problems that have caused their maladjustment?

This, too, is a reasonable hypothesis; but when one examines the programs of this type that have been tried, it's hard to find any more grounds for enthusiasm than we found with skill development and education. One method that's been tried—though so far, there have been acceptable reports only of its application to young offenders—has been individual psychotherapy. For young males, we found seven such reported studies. One study, by Guttman (1963) at the Nelles School, found such treatment to be ineffective in reducing recidivism rates; another, by Rudoff (1960), found it unrelated to *institutional* violation rates, which were themselves related to parole success. It must be pointed out that Rudoff used only this indirect measure of association, and the study therefore cannot rule out the possibility of a treatment effect. A third, also by Guttman (1963) but at another institution, found that such treatment was actually related to a slightly *higher* parole violation rate; and a study by Adams (1959b and 1961b) also found a lack of improvement in parole revocation and first suspension rates.

• • •

There have been two studies of the effects of individual psychotherapy on young incarcerated *female* offenders, and both of them (Adams, 1959; Adams, 1961) report no significant effects from the therapy. But one of the Adams studies (1959) does contain a suggestive, although not clearly interpretable, finding: If this individual therapy was administered by a psychiatrist or a psychologist, the resulting parole suspension rate was almost two-and-a-half times *higher* than if it was administered by a social worker without this specialized training.

There has also been a much smaller number of studies of two other types of individual therapy: counseling, which is directed towards a prisoner's gaining new insight into his own problems, and casework, which aims at helping a prisoner cope with his more pragmatic immediate needs. These types of therapy both rely heavily on the empathetic relationship that is to be developed between the professional and the client. It was noted above that the Adams study (1961b) of therapy administered to girls, referred to in the discussion of individual psychotherapy, found that social workers seemed better at the job than psychologists or psychiatrists. This difference seems to suggest a favorable outlook for these alternative forms of individual therapy. But other studies of such therapy have produced ambiguous results. Bernsten (1961) reported a Danish experiment that showed that socio-psychological counseling combined with comprehensive welfare measures—job and residence placement, clothing, union and health insurance membership, and financial aid—produced an improvement among some short-term male offenders, though not those in either the highest-risk or the lowest-risk categories. On the other hand, Hood, in Britain (1966), reported generally non-significant results with a program of counseling for young males. (Interestingly enough, this experiment *did* point to a mechanism capable of changing recidivism rates. When boys were released from institutional care and entered the army directly, "poor risk" boys among both experimentals *and* controls did better than expected. "Good risks" did worse.)

So these foreign data are sparse and not in agreement; the American data are just as sparse. The only American study which provides a direct measure of the effects of individual counseling—a study of California's Intensive Treatment Program (California, 1958), which was "psychodynamically" oriented—found no improvement in recidivism rates.

· · ·

GROUP COUNSELING

Group counseling has indeed been tried in correctional institutions, both with and without specifically psychotherapeutic orientation. There has been one study of "pragmatic," problem-oriented counseling on *young* institutionalized males, by Seckel (1965). This type of counseling had no significant effect. For adult males, there have been three such studies of the "pragmatic" and "insight" methods. Two (Kassebaum, 1971; Harrison, 1964) report no long-lasting significant effects. (One of these two did report a real but short-term effect that wore off as the program became institutionalized and as offenders were at liberty longer.) The third study of adults, by Shelley (1961), dealt with a "pragmatic" casework program, directed towards the educational and vocational needs of institutionalized young adult males in a Michigan prison camp. The treatment lasted for six months and at the end of that time Shelley found an improvement in attitudes; the possession of "good" attitudes was independently found by Shelley to correlate with parole success. Unfortunately, though, Shelley was not able to measure the *direct* impact of the counseling on recidivism rates. His two separate correlations are suggestive, but they fall short of being able to tell us that it really is the counseling that has a direct effect on recidivism.

With regard to more professional group *psychotherapy*, the reports are also conflicting. We have two studies of group psychotherapy on young males. One, by Parsons (1966), says that this treatment did in fact reduce recidivism. The improved recidivism rate stems from the improved performance only of those who were clinically judged to have been "successfully" treated; still, the overall result of the treatment was to improve recidivism rates for the experimental group as a whole. On the other hand, a study by Craft (1964) of young males designated "psychopaths," comparing "self-government" group psychotherapy with "authoritarian" individual counseling, found that the "group therapy" boys afterwards committed *twice* as many new offenses as the individually treated ones. Perhaps some forms of group psychotherapy work for some types of offenders but not others; a reader must draw his own conclusions, on the basis of sparse evidence.

With regard to young females, the results are just as equivocal. Adams, in his study of females (1959a), found that there was no improvement to be gained from treating girls by group rather than individual methods. A study by Taylor of borstal (reformatory) girls in New Zealand (1967) found a similar lack of any great improvement for group therapy as opposed to individual therapy or even to no therapy at all. But the Taylor study does offer one real, positive finding: When the "group therapy" girls *did* commit new offenses, these offenses were less serious than the ones for which they had originally been incarcerated.

• • •

As with the question of skill development, it is hard to summarize these results. The programs administered were various; the groups to which they were administered varied not only by sex but by age as well; there were also variations in the length of time for which the programs were carried on, the frequency of contact during that time, and the period for which the subjects were followed up. Still, one must say that the burden of the evidence is not encouraging. These programs seem to work best when they are new, when their subjects are amenable to treatment in the first place, and when the counselors are not only trained people but "good" people as well. Such findings, which would not be much of a surprise to a student of organization or personality, are hardly encouraging for a policy planner, who must adopt measures that are generally applicable, that are capable of being successfully institutionalized, and that must rely for personnel on something other than the exceptional individual.

TRANSFORMING

THE INSTITUTIONAL ENVIRONMENT

3. *But maybe the reason these counseling programs don't seem to work is not that they are ineffective per se, but that the institutional environment outside the program is unwholesome enough to undo any good work that the counseling does. Isn't a truly successful rehabilitative institution the one where the inmate's whole environment is directed towards true correction rather than towards custody or punishment?*

This argument has not only been made, it has been embodied in several institutional programs that go by the name of "milieu therapy." They are designed to make every element of the inmate's environment a part of his treatment, to reduce the distinctions between the custodial staff and the treatment staff, to create a supportive, non-authoritarian, and non-regimented atmosphere, and to enlist peer influence in the formation of constructive values. These programs are especially hard to summarize because of their variety; they differ, for example, in how "supportive" or "permissive" they are designed to be, in the extent to which they are combined with other treatment methods such as individual therapy, group counseling, or skill development, and in how completely the program is able to control all the relevant aspects of the institutional environment.

One might well begin with two studies that have been done of institutionalized adults, in regular prisons, who have been subjected to such treatment; this is the category whose results are the most clearly discouraging. One study of such a program, by Robison (1967), found that the therapy did seem to reduce recidivism after one year. After two years, however, this effect disappeared, and the treated convicts did no better than the untreated. Another study, by Kassebaum, Ward, and Wilner (1971), dealt with a program which had been able to effect an exceptionally extensive and experimentally rigorous transformation of the institutional environment. This sophisticated study had a follow-up period of 36 months, and it found that the program had no significant effect on parole failure or success rates.

The results of the studies of youth are more equivocal. As for young females, one study by Adams (1966) of such a program found that it had no significant effect on recidivism; another study, by Goldberg and Adams (1964), found that such a program *did* have a positive effect. This effect declined when the program began to deal with girls who were judged beforehand to be worse risks.

As for young males, the studies may conveniently be divided into those dealing with juveniles (under 16) and those dealing with youths. There have been five studies of milieu therapy administered to juveniles. Two of them—by Laulicht (1962) and by Jesness (1965)—report clearly that the program in question either had no significant effect or had a short-term effect that wore off with passing time. Jesness does report that when his experimental juveniles did commit new offenses, the offenses were less serious than those committed by controls. A third study of juveniles, by McCord (1953) at the Wiltwych School, reports mixed results. Using two measures of performance, a "success" rate and a "failure" rate, McCord found that his experimental group achieved both less failure *and* less success than the controls did. There have been two positive reports on milieu therapy programs for male juveniles; both of them have come out of the Highfields program, the milieu therapy experiment which has become the most famous and widely quoted example of "success" via this method. A group of boys was confined for a relatively short time to the unrestrictive, supportive environment of Highfields; and at a follow-up of six months, Freeman (1956) found that the group did indeed show a lower recidivism rate (as measured by parole revocation) than a similar group spending a longer time in the regular reformatory. McCorkle (1958) also reported positive findings from Highfields. But in fact, the McCorkle data show, this improvement was not so clear: The Highfields boys had lower recidivism rates at 12 and 36 months in the follow-up period, but not at 24 and 60 months. The length of follow-up, these data remind us, may have large implications for a study's conclusions. But more important were other flaws in the Highfields experiment: The populations were not fully comparable (they differed according to risk level and time of admission); different organizations—the probation agency for the Highfields boys, the parole agency for the others—were making the revocation decisions for each group; more of the Highfields boys were discharged early from supervision, and thus removed from any risk of revocation. In short, not even from the celebrated Highfields case may we take clear assurance that milieu therapy works.

In the case of male youths, as opposed to male juveniles, the findings are just as equivocal, and hardly more encouraging. One such study by Empey (1966) in a residential context did not produce significant results. A study by Seckel (1967) described California's Fremont Program, in which institutionalized youths participated in a combination of therapy, work projects, field trips, and community meetings. Seckel found that the youths subjected to this treatment committed *more* violations of law than did their non-treated counterparts.

• • •

So the youth in these milieu therapy programs at least do no worse than their counterparts in regular institutions and the special programs may cost less. One may therefore be encouraged—not on grounds of rehabilitation but on grounds of cost-effectiveness.

WHAT ABOUT MEDICAL TREATMENT?

4. *Isn't there anything you can do in an institutional setting that will reduce recidivism, for instance, through strictly medical treatment?*

A number of studies deal with the results of efforts to change the behavior of offenders through drugs and surgery. As for surgery, the one experimental study of a plastic surgery program—by Mandell (1967)—had negative results. For non-addicts who received plastic surgery, Mandall purported to find improvement in performance on parole; but when one reanalyzes his data, it appears that surgery alone did not in fact make a significant difference.

One type of surgery does seem to be highly successful in reducing recidivism. A twenty-year Danish study of sex offenders, by Stuerup (1960), found that while those who had been treated with hormones and therapy continued to commit both sex crimes (29.6 per cent of them did so) and non-sex crimes (21.0 per cent), those who had been castrated had rates of only 3.5 per cent (not, interestingly enough, a rate of zero; where there's a will, apparently there's a way) and 9.2 per cent. One hopes that the policy implications of this study will be found to be distinctly limited.

As for drugs, the major report on such a program—involving tranquilization—was made by Adams (1961b). The tranquilizers were administered to male and female institutionalized youths. With boys, there was only a slight improvement in their subsequent behavior; this improvement disappeared within a year. With girls, the tranquilization produced worse results than when the girls were given no treatment at all.

THE EFFECTS OF SENTENCING

5. *Well, at least it may be possible to manipulate certain gross features of the existing, conventional prison system—such as length of sentence and degree of security—in order to affect these recidivism rates. Isn't this the case?*

At this point, it's still impossible to say that this is the case. As for the degree of security in an institution, Glaser's (1964) work reported that, for both youth and adults, a less restrictive "custody grading" in American federal prisons was related to success on parole; but this is hardly surprising, since those assigned to more restrictive custody are likely to be worse risks in the first place. More to the point, an American study by Fox (1950) discovered that for "older youths" who were deemed to be good risks for the future, a minimum security institution produced better results than a maximum security one. On the other hand, the data we have on youths under 16—from a study by McClintock (1961), done in Great Britain—indicate that so-called Borstals, in which boys are totally confined, are more effective than a less restrictive regime of partial physical custody. In short, we know very little about the recidivism effects of various degrees of security in existing institutions; and our problems in finding out will be compounded by the probability that these effects will vary widely according to the particular *type* of offender that we're dealing with.

The same problems of mixed results and lack of comparable populations have plagued attempts to study the effects of sentence length. A number of studies—by Narloch (1959), by Bernsten (1965), and by the State of California (1956)—suggest that those who are released earlier from institutions than their scheduled parole date, or those who serve short sentences of under three months rather than longer sentences of eight months or more, either do better on parole or at least do no worse. The implication here is quite clear and important: Even if early releases and short sentences produce no improvement in recidivism rates, one could at least maintain the same rates while lowering the cost of maintaining the offender and lessening his own burden of imprisonment. Of course, this implication carries with it its concomitant danger: the danger that though shorter sentences cause no worsening of the recidivism rate, they may increase the total amount of crime in the community by increasing the absolute number of potential recidivists at large.

• • •

More important, the effect of sentence length seems to vary widely according to type of offender. In a British study (1963), for instance, Hammond found that for a group of "hard-core recidivists," shortening the sentence caused no improvement in the recidivism rate. In Denmark, Bernsten (1965) discovered a similar phenomenon: That the beneficial effect of three-month sentences as against eight-month ones disappeared in the case of these "hard-core recidivists." Garrity found another such distinction in his 1956 study. He divided his offenders into three categories: "pro-social," "anti-social," and "manipulative." "Pro-social" offenders he found to have low recidivism rates regardless of the length of their sentence; "anti-social" offenders did better with short sentences; the "manipulative" did better with long ones. Two studies from Britain made yet another division of the offender population, and found yet other variations. One (Great Britain, 1964) found that previous offenders—but not first offenders—did better with *longer* sentences, while the other (Cambridge, 1951) found the *reverse* to be true with juveniles.

To add to the problem of interpretation, these studies deal not only with different types and categorizations of offenders but with different types of institutions as well. No more than in the case of institution type can we say that length of sentence has a clear relationship to recidivism.

DECARCERATING THE CONVICT

6. *All of this seems to suggest that there's not much we know how to do to rehabilitate an offender when he's in an institution. Doesn't this lead to the clear possibility that the way to rehabilitate offenders is to deal with them* outside *an institutional setting?*

This is indeed an important possibility, and it is suggested by other pieces of information as well. For instance, Miner (1967) reported on a milieu therapy program in Massachusetts called Outward Bound. It took youths 15½ and over; it was oriented toward the development of skills in the out-of-doors and conducted in a wilderness atmosphere very different from that of most existing institutions. The culmination of the 26-day program was a final 24 hours in which each youth had to survive alone in the wilderness. And Miner found that the program did indeed work in reducing recidivism rates.

But by and large, when one takes the programs that have been administered in institutions and applies them in a non-institutional setting, the results do not grow to encouraging proportions. With casework and individual counseling in the community, for instance, there have been three studies; they dealt with counseling methods from psycho-social and vocational counseling to "operant conditioning," in which an offender was rewarded first simply for coming to counseling sessions and then, gradually, for performing other types of approved acts. Two of them report that the community-counseled offenders did no better than their institutional controls, while the third notes that although community counseling produced fewer arrests per person, it did not ultimately reduce the offender's chance of returning to a reformatory.

• • •

PSYCHOTHERAPY
IN COMMUNITY SETTINGS

There is some indication that individual psychotherapy may "work" in a community setting. Massimo (1963) reported on one such program, using what might be termed a "pragmatic" psychotherapeutic approach, including "insight" therapy and a focus on vocational problems. The program was marked by its small size and by its use of therapists who were personally enthusiastic about the project; Massimo found that there was indeed a decline in the recidivism rate. Adamson (1956), on the other hand, found no significant difference produced by another program of individual therapy (though he did note that arrest rates among the experimental boys declined with what he called "intensity of treatment"). And Schwitzgebel (1963, 1964), studying other, different kinds of therapy programs, found that the programs *did* produce improvements in the attitudes of his boys—but, unfortunately, not in their rates of recidivism.

And with *group* therapy administered in the community, we find yet another set of equivocal results. The results from studies of pragmatic group counseling are only mildly optimistic. Adams (1965) did report that a form of group therapy, "guided group interaction," when administered to juvenile gangs, did somewhat reduce the percentage that were to be found in custody six years later. On the other hand, in a study of juveniles, Adams (1964) found that while such a program did reduce the number of contacts that an experimental youth had with police, it made no ultimate difference in the detention rate. And the attitudes of the counseled youth showed no improvement. Finally, when O'Brien (1961) examined a community-based program of group psychotherapy, he found not only that the program produced no improvement in the recidivism rate, but that the experimental boys actually did worse than their controls on a series of psychological tests.

PROBATION OR PAROLE VERSUS PRISON

But by far the most extensive and important work that has been done on the effect of community-based treatments had been done in the areas of probation and parole. This work sets out to answer the question of whether it makes any difference how you supervise and treat an offender once he has been released from prison or has come under state surveillance in lieu of prison. This is the work that has provided the main basis to date for the claim that we do indeed have the means at our disposal for rehabilitating the offender or at least decarcerating him safely.

One group of these studies has compared the use of probation with other dispositions for offenders; these provide some slight evidence that, at least under some circumstances, probation may make an offender's future chances better than if he had been sent to prison. Or, at least, probation may not worsen those chances. A British study, by Wilkins (1958), reported that when probation was granted more frequently, recidivism rates among probationers did not increase significantly. And another such study by the state of Michigan in 1963 reported that an expansion in the use of probation actually improved recidivism rates—though there are serious problems of comparability in the groups and systems that were studied.

• • •

Quite a large group of studies deals not with probation as compared to other dispositions, but instead with the type of treatment that an offender receives once he is *on* probation or parole. These are the studies that have provided the most encouraging reports on rehabilitative treatment and that have also raised the most serious questions about the nature of the research that has been going on in the corrections field.

Five of these studies have dealt with youthful probationers from 13 to 18 who were assigned to probation officers with small caseloads or provided with other ways of receiving more intensive supervision (Adams, 1966—two reports; Fiestman, 1966; Kawaguchi, 1967; Pilnick, 1967). These studies report that, by and large, intensive supervision does work—that the specially treated youngsters do better according to some measure of recidivism. Yet these studies left some important questions unanswered. For instance, was this improved performance a function merely of the number of contacts a youngster had with his probation officer? Did it also depend on the length of time in treatment? Or was it the quality of supervision that was making the difference, rather than the quantity?

INTENSIVE SUPERVISION:
THE WARREN STUDIES

The widely reported Warren studies (1966a, 1966b, 1967) in California constitute an extremely ambitious attempt to answer these questions. In this project, a control group of youths, drawn from a pool of candidates ready for first admission to a California Youth Authority institution, was assigned to regular detention, usually for eight to nine months, and then released to regular supervision. The experimental group received considerably more elaborate treatment. They were released directly to probation status and assigned to 12-man caseloads. To decide what special treatment was appropriate within these caseloads, the youths were divided according to their "interpersonal maturity level classification," by use of a scale developed by Grant and Grant. And each level dictated its own special type of therapy.

• • •

"Success" in this experiment was defined as favorable discharge by the Youth Authority; "failure" was unfavorable discharge, revocation, or recommitment by a court. Warren reported an encouraging finding: Among all but one of the "subtypes," the experimentals had a significantly lower failure rate than the controls. The experiment did have certain problems: The experimentals might have been performing better because of the enthusiasm of the staff and the attention lavished on them; none of the controls had been *directly* released to their regular supervision programs instead of being detained first; and it was impossible to separate the effects of the experimentals' small caseloads from their specially designed treatments, since no experimental youths had been assigned to a small caseload with "inappropriate" treatment, or with no treatment at all. Still, none of these problems were serious enough to vitiate the encouraging prospect that this finding presented for successful treatment of probationers.

This encouraging finding was, however, accompanied by a rather more disturbing clue. As has been mentioned before, the experimental subjects, when measured, had a lower *failure* rate than the controls. But the experimentals also had a lower *success* rate. That is, fewer of the experimentals as compared with the controls had been judged to have successfully completed their program of supervision and to be suitable for favorable release. When my colleagues and I undertook a rather laborious reanalysis of the Warren data, it became clear why this discrepancy had appeared. It turned out that fewer experimentals were "successful" because the experimentals were actually committing more offenses than their controls. The reason that the experimentals' relatively large number of offenses was not being reflected in their failure rates was simply that the experimentals' probation officers were using a more lenient revocation policy. In other words, the controls had a higher failure rate because the controls were being revoked for less serious offenses.

So it seems that what Warren was reporting in her "failure" rates was not merely the treatment effect of her small caseloads and special programs. Instead, what Warren was finding was not so much a change in the behavior of the experimental youths as a change in the behavior of the experimental *probation officers*, who knew the "special" status of their charges and who had evidently decided to revoke probation status at a lower than normal rate. The experimentals continued to commit offenses; what was different was that when they committed these offenses, they were permitted to remain on probation.

The experimenters claimed that this low revocation policy, and the greater number of offenses committed by the special treatment youth, were *not* an indication that these youth were behaving specially badly and that policy makers were simply letting them get away with it. Instead, it was claimed, the higher reported offense rate was primarily an artifact of the more intense surveillance that the experimental youth received. But the data show that this is not a sufficient explanation of the low failure rate among experimental youth; the difference in "tolerance" of offenses between experimental officials and control officials was much greater than the difference in the rates at which these two systems detected youths committing new offenses. Needless to say, this reinterpretation of the data presents a much bleaker picture of the possibilities of intensive supervision with special treatment.

"TREATMENT EFFECTS" VERSUS
"POLICY EFFECTS"

This same problem of experimenter bias may also be present in the predecessors of the Warren study, the ones which had also found positive results from intensive supervision on probation; indeed, this disturbing question can be raised about many of the previously discussed reports of positive "treatment effects."

This possibility of a "policy effect" rather than a "treatment effect" applies, for instance, to the previously discussed studies of the effects of intensive supervision on juvenile and youthful probationers. These were the studies, it will be recalled, which found lower recidivism rates for the intensively supervised.

• • •

One must conclude that the "benefits" of intensive supervision for youthful offenders may stem not so much from a "treatment" effect as from a "policy" effect—that such supervision, so far as we now know, results not in rehabilitation but in a decision to look the other way when an offense is committed. But there is one major modification to be added to this conclusion. Johnson performed a further measurement (1962b) in his parole experiment: He rated all the supervising agents according to the "adequacy" of the supervision they gave. And he found that an "adequate" agent, whether he was working in a small *or* a large caseload, produced a relative improvement in his charges. The converse was not true: An *in*adequate agent was more likely to produce youthful "failures" when he was given a *small* caseload to supervise. One can't much help a "good" agent, it seems, by reducing his caseload size; such reduction can only do further harm to those youths who fall into the hands of "bad" agents.

So with youthful offenders, Johnson found, intensive supervision does not seem to provide the rehabilitative benefits claimed for it; the only such benefits may flow not from intensive supervision itself but from contact with one of the "good people" who are frequently in such short supply.

having a "good" parole officer makes the difference.

INTENSIVE SUPERVISION OF ADULTS

The results are similarly ambiguous when one applies this intensive supervision to adult offenders. There have been several studies of the effects of intensive supervision on adult parolees. Some of these are hard to interpret because of problems of comparability between experimental and control groups (general risk ratings, for instance, or distribution of narcotics offenders, or policy changes that took place between various phases of the experiments), but two of them (California, 1966; Stanton, 1964) do not seem to give evidence of the benefits of intensive supervision. By far the most extensive work, though, on the effects of intensive supervision of adult parolees has been a series of studies of California's Special Intensive Parole Unit (SIPU), a 10-year-long experiment designed to test the treatment possibilities of various special parole programs. Three of the four "phases" of this experiment produced "negative results." The first phase tested the effect of a reduced caseload size; no lasting effect was found. The second phase slightly increased the size of the small caseloads and provided for a longer time in treatment; again there was no evidence of a treatment effect. In the fourth phase, caseload sizes and time in treatment were again varied, and treatments were simultaneously varied in a sophisticated way according to personality characteristics of the parolees; once again, significant results did not appear.

The only phase of this experiment for which positive results were reported was Phase Three. Here, it was indeed found that a smaller caseload improved one's chances of parole success. There is, however, an important caveat that attaches to this finding: When my colleagues and I divided the whole population of subjects into two groups—those receiving supervision in the North of the state and those in the South—we found that the "improvement" of the experimentals' success rates was taking place primarily in the North. The North differed from the South in one important aspect: Its agents practiced a policy of returning both "experimental" and "control" violators to prison at relatively high rates. And it was the North that produced the higher success rate among its experimentals. So this improvement in experimentals' performance was taking place only when accompanied by a "realistic threat" of severe sanctions.

. . .

THE EFFECTS OF COMMUNITY TREATMENT

In sum, even in the case of treatment programs administered outside penal institutions, we simply cannot say that this treatment in itself has an appreciable effect on offender behavior. On the other hand, there is one encouraging set of findings that emerges from these studies. For from many of them there flows the strong suggestion that even if we can't "treat" offenders so as to make them do better, a great many of the programs designed to rehabilitate them at least did not make them do *worse*. And if these programs did not show the advantages of actually rehabilitating, some of them did have the advantage of being less onerous to the offender himself without seeming to pose increased danger to the community. And some of these programs—especially those involving less restrictive custody, minimal supervision, and early release—simply cost fewer dollars to administer. The information on the dollar costs of these programs is just beginning to be developed but the implication is clear: *that if we can't do more for (and to) offenders, at least we can safely do less.*

There is, however, one important caveat even to this note of optimism: In order to calculate the true costs of these programs, one must in each case include not only their administrative cost but also the cost of maintaining in the community an offender population increased in size. This population might well not be committing new offenses at any greater rate; but the offender population might, under some of these plans, be larger in absolute *numbers*. So the total number of offenses committed might rise, and our chances of victimization might therefore rise too. We need to be able to make a judgment about the size and probable duration of this effect; as of now, we simply do not know.

DOES NOTHING WORK?

7. Do all of these studies lead us irrevocably to the conclusion that nothing works, that we haven't the faintest clue about how to rehabilitate offenders and reduce recidivism? And if so, what shall we do?

We tried to exclude from our survey those studies which were so poorly done that they simply could not be interpreted. But despite our efforts, a pattern has run through much of this discussion—of studies which "found" effects without making any truly rigorous attempt to exclude competing hypotheses, of extraneous factors permitted to intrude upon the measurements, of recidivism measures which are not all measuring the same thing, of "follow-up" periods which vary enormously and rarely extend beyond the period of legal supervision, of experiments never replicated, of "system effects" not taken into account, of categories drawn up without any theory to guide the enterprise. It is just possible that some of our treatment programs *are* working to some extent, but that our research is so bad that it is incapable of telling.

Having entered this very serious caveat, I am bound to say that these data, involving over two hundred studies and hundreds of thousands of individuals as they do, are the best available and give us very little reason to hope that we have in fact found a sure way of reducing recidivism through rehabilitation. This is not to say that we found no instances of success or partial success; it is only to say that these instances have been isolated, producing no clear pattern to indicate the efficacy of any particular method of treatment. And neither is this to say that factors *outside* the realm of rehabilitation may not be working to reduce recidivism—factors such as the tendency for recidivism to be lower in offenders over the age of 30; it is only to say that such factors seem to have little connection with any of the treatment methods now at our disposal.

From this probability, one may draw any of several conclusions. It may be simply that our programs aren't yet good enough—that the education we provide to inmates is still poor education, that the therapy we administer is not administered skillfully enough, that our intensive supervision and counseling do not yet provide enough personal support for the offenders who are subjected to them. If one wishes to believe this, then what our correctional system needs is simply a more full-hearted commitment to the strategy of treatment.

It may be, on the other hand, that there is a more radical flaw in our present strategies—that education at its best, or that psychotherapy at its best, cannot overcome, or even appreciably reduce, the powerful tendency for offenders to continue in criminal behavior. Our present treatment programs are based on a theory of crime as a "disease"—that is to say, as something foreign and abnormal in the individual which can presumably be cured. This theory may well be flawed, in that it overlooks—indeed, denies—both the normality of crime in society and the personal normality of a very large proportion of offenders, criminals who are merely responding to the facts and conditions of our society.

This opposing theory of "crime as a social phenomenon" directs our attention away from a "rehabilitative" strategy, away from the notion that we may best insure public safety through a series of "treatments" to be imposed forcibly on convicted offenders. These treatments have on occasion become, and have the potential for becoming, so draconian as to offend the moral order of a democratic society; and the theory of crime as a social phenomenon suggests that such treatments may not be only offensive but ineffective as well. This theory points, instead, to decarceration for low-risk offenders—and, presumably, to keeping high-risk offenders in prisons which are nothing more (and aim to be nothing more) than custodial institutions.

But this approach has its own problems. To begin with, there is the moral dimension of crime and punishment. Many low-risk offenders have committed serious crimes (murder, sometimes) and even if one is reasonably sure they will never commit another crime, it violates our sense of justice that they should experience no significant retribution for their actions. A middle-class banker who kills his adulterous wife in a moment of passion is a "low-risk" criminal; a juvenile delinquent in the ghetto who commits armed robbery has, statistically, a much higher probability of committing another crime. Are we going to put the first on probation and sentence the latter to a long term in prison?

Besides, one cannot ignore the fact that the punishment of offenders is the major means we have for *deterring* incipient offenders. We know almost nothing about the "deterrent effect," largely because "treatment" theories have so dominated our research, and "deterrence" theories have been relegated to the status of a historical curiosity. Since we have almost no idea of the deterrent functions that our present system performs or that future strategies might be made to perform, it is possible that there is indeed something that works—that to some extent is working right now in front of our noses, and that might be made to work better—something that deters rather than cures, something that does not so much reform convicted offenders as prevent criminal behavior in the first place. But whether that is the case and, if it is, what strategies will be found to make our deterrence system work better than it does now, are questions we will not be able to answer with data until a new family of studies has been brought into existence. As we begin to learn the facts, we will be in a better position than we are now to judge to what degree the prison has become an anachronism and can be replaced by more effective means of social control.

- Idea of justice for criminals.
- disparity between seriousness of offense and the actual risk.

23

❁

Reentry Reconsidered

A New Look
at an Old Question

Jeremy Travis
Joan Petersilia

Prison policy influences the social fabric of the community, and has a strong interrelationship with social policy and other areas of public law. This discussion illustrates the legislative role in sentencing, and the failure to understand the ways in which the political system impacts the daily wheels of justice. Increased or mandated sentencing fails to consider the issue of how to integrate offenders back into mainstream society.

L ast year, about 585,000 individuals—nearly 1,600 a day—left state and federal prisons to return home. On one level, this is not particularly noteworthy. Ever since prisons were built, prisoners have faced the challenge of moving from confinement in correctional institutions to liberty on the street. Yet, as we argue in this article, from a number of policy perspectives, the age-old issue of prisoner reintegration has taken on critical importance as we enter the new century. Furthermore, we believe that a renewed research and policy

Note: Several of the papers contained in this special issue were originally commissioned for the "Reentry Roundtable," a conference held in October 2000 and funded by the Open Society Institute. The authors are grateful to the Open Society Institute for their financial support of the Roundtable, and to Amy Solomon and Jake Rosenfeld of the Urban Institute for their substantive and editorial assistance on this special issue.

Source: Jeremy Travis and Joan Petersilia, *Crime and Delinquency* (New York: Sage, 2001), pp. 291–313.

focus on the phenomenon of prisoner reentry can breathe life into old debates about the purposes of punishment, the relationship between offenders and society, and the consequences of the arrest, incarceration, and return of offenders.

We first view the reentry phenomenon through a jurisprudential lens. We argue that a reentry perspective sheds light on three natural experiments in justice policy: namely, the fourfold increase in per capita rates of incarceration, the disintegration of a unified sentencing philosophy, and the weakening of parole as a coherent approach to prisoner reintegration. We then discuss recent changes in the profile of returning prisoners. Third, we examine linkages between the reentry phenomenon and five related social policy domains. Finally, we explore some implications of this reentry perspective for the development of new policies.

SENTENCING POLICY
THROUGH A REENTRY LENS

Over the past generation, sentencing policy in the United States has been characterized by three interrelated developments, one well known, two less so: the growth in imprisonment rates, the fragmentation of sentencing philosophy, and the weakening of parole. Taken together, they have had profound consequences on the reintegration of released prisoners.

The Growth of Imprisonment

The per capita rate of imprisonment in America hovered at about 110 per 100,000 from 1925 to 1973, with little variation (Blumstein & Beck, 1999). Starting in 1973, however, the rate of imprisonment has grown steadily, so that our rate is now 476 per 100,000, over four times the 1973 level (Beck, 2000a). State prisons now house 1.2 million people (Beck, 2000a). There are an additional 596,485 people in local jails, a threefold increase since 1980 (Bureau of Justice Statistics, 2000a).

There has been a nearly parallel growth in the size of the population under parole supervision. In 1980, there were 220,000 people on parole, serving the remainder of their prison sentences under community supervision. By 1999, that number had grown to 713,000, a more than a threefold increase. Similarly, the probation population increased between 1980 and 1999, from 1.2 million to 3.8 million (Bureau of Justice Statistics, 2000a).

As a natural, predictable consequence of the nation's experiment with increased levels of imprisonment, more people leave prison to return home, typically under some form of criminal justice supervision. As Figure 1 shows, the number of people released from state and federal prisons has increased from 154,000 in 1980 to about 585,000 in 2000. Because the average length of prison stay has also increased over time, there has been a slight lag between intake levels and release levels in the prison systems. But by 1998 there were similar numbers admitted (615,000) as released (547,000) (Beck, 2000b; Bureau of Justice Statistics, 2000b). Furthermore, now that the nation's prison

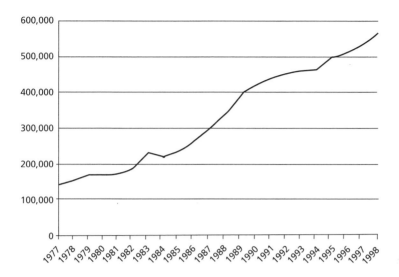

FIGURE 1 Sentenced prisoners released from State and Federal Jurisdictions, 1977–1998

Source: BJS, National Prisoner Statistics data series (NPS-1)

population is moving toward equilibrium, and even declining in some states, we can expect that the reentry cohorts may soon peak as well.

In summary, the burden on the formal and informal processes that should work together to support successful reintegration of prisoners has increased enormously. On one level, if the capacity to manage reintegration had kept pace with the flow of released prisoners—as the capacity to incarcerate has basically kept pace with the increase in detained prisoners—then, perhaps, the reentry phenomenon today would be no different than in times past. To borrow the language of the assembly line, the throughput would simply be at a higher level of production. But, as will be shown … the exponential increase in release cohorts has placed exponentially greater strains on the communities where prisoner removal and return are concentrated. And the philosophical and operational capacity to manage the higher production of released prisoners has not kept pace.

The Fragmentation of Sentencing Philosophy

A second, lesser-known development in our sentencing philosophy has been what Michael Tonry (1999, p. 1) called the "fragmentation of American sentencing policy." A generation ago, we had a unifying national sentencing philosophy, what Tonry called "a distinctly American approach to sentencing and corrections, usually referred to as indeterminate sentencing, and it had changed little in the preceding 50 years" (p. 1). Under this approach, all states provided judges with broad ranges of possible sentences, authorized the release of prisoners by parole boards, supervised prisoners after release, and explicitly embraced rehabilitation of offenders as the goal of corrections (Tonry, 1999).

That philosophy came under attack from the left and right ends of the political spectrum. Liberals critiqued indeterminate sentencing by judges and discretionary release decisions by parole boards as presenting opportunities for distortions of justice. Widely disparate sentences for similar offenses and similar offenders were critiqued as violating fundamental principles of fairness. The unreviewable nature of the decisions was seen as presenting opportunities for disparate racial outcomes. And the lingering uncertainty regarding the culmination of a prison term, dependent on the seemingly arbitrary decision of a parole board, was critiqued as adding unnecessary stress to the period of imprisonment (Frankel, 1973).

The criticism from the right was equally fierce. The imposition of indeterminate sentences, with low minimum and high maximum prison terms, was criticized as a fraud on the public. A resurgent belief in "just desserts," the idea that criminal behavior warrants a punishment proportionate to the offense, resonated with a new public belief that the criminal justice system was too lenient (Hirsch, 1976; Wilson, 1975). A review of the literature on the effectiveness of rehabilitation, captured in the famous phrase "nothing works," weakened the intellectual underpinning of the stated purpose of sentencing and correction (Martinson, 1974). Finally, the use of early release as a mechanism to manage burgeoning prison populations strained public confidence in the integrity of the governmental process for managing the severity of punishment (Wright, 1998).

Under attack from left and right, the philosophy of indeterminate sentencing, once embraced by all 50 states and enshrined in the Model Penal Code, lost its intellectual hold on U.S. sentencing policy. Beginning with the abolition of parole in Maine in 1975, "nearly every state has in some way repudiated indeterminate sentencing" and replaced it with a variety of state experiments (Tonry, 1996, p. 4; Tonry, 1999). As of 1998, 17 states had created sentencing commissions, quasi-independent administrative bodies that have designed sentencing grids that significantly constrain judicial sentencing discretion (Rottman et al., 2000). Legislation creating mandatory minimum sentences has been enacted in all 50 states (Austin et al., 1995). Three-strikes laws have lengthened prison terms for persistent offenders in 24 states (Austin et al., 1999). Forty states have enacted truth-in-sentencing laws requiring that violent offenders serve at least 50% of their sentences in prison; of these 40 states, 27 and the District of Columbia require violent offenders to serve at least 85% of their sentences in prison (Ditton & Wilson, 1999).

These developments in U.S. sentencing philosophy can be analyzed from a number of different perspectives. One could analyze their effects on the level of incarceration, the profile of the prison population, plea bargaining practices, or prosecutorial discretion, to name a few. A reentry perspective focuses attention on the impact of these developments on the process of release and reintegration—on the timing of the release decision, the procedures for making the release decision, the preparation of the prisoner for release, the preparation of the prisoner's family and community for his release, supervision after release, and the linkages between in-prison and post-release activities.

For example, as a result of these changes in sentencing philosophy, fewer prisoners are being released because of a parole board decision (see Table 1). In

1990, 39% were released to supervision by parole board action, and 29% by mandatory release; by 1998, those figures had been reversed, and 26% were released by parole board decision, and 40% by mandatory release (Beck, 2000b). With widespread adoption of truth-in-sentencing statutes, these trends can be expected to continue, so that release by parole board will become a vestige of a bygone era, retained in some states but in others, reserved for an aging prison cohort sentenced under the old regime.

The policy and research questions posed by this development have implications for corrections management. Does the absence of a discretionary release process remove an incentive for good behavior? If so, can the loss of that incentive be replaced with another, equally effective incentive? Does the automatic nature of release diminish the prisoner's incentive to find a stable residence or employment on the outside, the factors that traditionally influenced release decisions? Does a mandatory release policy increase or decrease a correctional agency's coordination between life in prison and planning for life outside of prison? Does mandatory release remove the ability of a parole board to revisit the risk posed by the offender, once his prison behavior has been observed? The psychological literature on coping and adaptation in prison concludes that long-term imprisonment may cause depression, anxiety, and mental breakdown (Liebling, 1999). If more inmates are "maxing out," the parole board has no ability to correct for risk-related variables that may have presented themselves during imprisonment. And, if parole boards have little authority to extend inmate sentences, what role does that leave for victims? Recent research shows that more than 70% of parole boards now invite victims to attend the parole hearing (Petersilia, 1999). As parole boards release fewer prisoners in the future, these victims' rights become less meaningful (Herman & Wasserman, 2001).

The absence of a dominant sentencing philosophy has also left the current sentencing regime—actually, a national crazy quilt made up of piecemeal sentencing reforms—without a public rationale that would explain the relationship between imprisonment and release. Under the old regime, it was straightforward: when a prison sentence was imposed (under a variety of justifications), the amount of time served would depend on a later determination of release readiness. Release decisions and postrelease supervision were part and parcel of the sentencing framework. Under a just-desserts model, for example, the purpose of a period of postrelease supervision is unclear. Under a mandatory minimum sentence, why should an offender serve any more time in the community? If prisons started to look more like jails, with fixed-date releases, what is the rationale for any supervision after release? Why not just show the prisoners the door when they have served their time?

The Weakening of Parole

The increase in incarceration and fragmentation of our sentencing philosophy have created strains on the raison d'etre and management of parole agencies. Reflecting the notion of a continuous flow from prison to community, with a focus on the endpoint of rehabilitation and reintegration, the word parole actually has two operational meanings: it refers both to the agency making a

Table 1　Inmate Releases Decisions, 1990–1998

	RELEASED TO SUPERVISION				
Year	Parole Board	Mandatory Release	Other Conditional	Expiration of Sentence	Other
1990	39.4	28.8	15.5	12.7	3.6
1995	32.3	39.0	10.1	14.5	4.0
1996	30.4	38.0	10.2	16.7	4.7
1997	28.2	39.7	10.4	16.8	4.9
1998	26.0	40.4	11.2	18.7	3.7

SOURCE: Beck, 2000a.

release decision (the parole board) and the agency supervising the offender in the community (typically the "division of parole").

A focus on returning prisoners does not begin with a discussion of parole populations, however, because some prisoners are released without supervision. Returning to Table 1, we see that in 1998, 18.7% of the released prisoners were released because their sentence had expired, and another 3.7% were released without supervision, meaning that 22.4% of the 1998 release cohort of 547,000—or about 123,000—left prison with no legal supervision. This form of release is increasing steadily as determinate sentencing reforms take hold— in 1990, only 16.3% of the released cohort were released without supervision, meaning that about 69,000 left prison unconditionally that year (Beck, 2000b).

There are two views of this development. On the one hand ... parole supervision has not been proven effective at reducing new arrests, and has been shown to increase technical violations (Petersilia & Turner, 1993). Intensive supervision program clients are subject to much closer surveillance than others under supervision, and more of their violations may come to official attention, resulting in more returns to jail or prison. If noncompliance with technical conditions signaled that offenders were "going bad," then returning them to incarceration might prevent future crime. However, research on the issue has shown no support for the argument that violating offenders on technical conditions suppressed new criminal arrests (Petersilia & Turner, 1993). So, simply increasing parole supervision does not lead to fewer crimes. Therefore, why force more offenders into an ineffective system of supervision? Perhaps, as James Austin (2001) argued, certain offenders who pose low risks should simply be released.

On the other hand, if the transition from prison life to community life is difficult, and if some form of supervision can make that transition more effective, then the loss of a legal connection would appear counterproductive. This view becomes particularly compelling when one considers the stories of prisoners who serve the last years of their sentence in maximum security, then are released to the street without supervision because they reached the end of their sentence. And from a purely a public safety standpoint, the status of parole allows law enforcement greater search and seizure powers, and a quick way to remove offenders from the street if they commit a new crime. In this view, both society and ex-offenders stand to benefit from legal supervision.

The increase in prison populations has had the predictable impact on parole caseloads without proportionate increases in resources. As discussed earlier, in 1999 there were 713,000 individuals on parole (or other form of conditional release), more than triple the number on parole in 1980 (Bureau of Justice Statistics, 2000a). Spending has not kept pace with this growth in supervision caseloads. In the 1970s, parole officers handled caseloads averaging 45 offenders; today, most officers are responsible for about 70 parolees (Rottman et al., 2000). At the same time, per capita spending per parolee has decreased from more than $11,000 per year in 1985 to about $9,500 in 1998 (J. P. Lynch & Sabol, 2001).

The nature of parole supervision has shifted over the past two decades as well. The parole field has uneasily accommodated two potentially conflicting objectives, one more akin to social work, one more akin to law enforcement. The introduction of new surveillance technologies, particularly urine testing and electronic monitoring, has provided enhanced capacity to detect parole violations and, thereby, to increase the rate of revocations of liberty (Kleiman, 1999). Signaling a shift in emphasis, recent surveys of parole officers show that more of them prioritize the law enforcement function of parole, rather than its service or rehabilitation functions (M. Lynch, 1998).

For these and other reasons, the rate of parole violations has increased significantly over recent years. In 1985, 70% of parolees successfully completed their parole term; by 1997, that number had dropped to 44%. Conversely, the percentage of those who fail on parole has increased from less than a third of all parolees in 1985 to 54% in 1997 (Petersilia, 1999). Almost 9% of all parolees nationally are counted as absconding-meaning their whereabouts are unknown to parole agents (Bonczar & Glaze, 1999).

This rise in rates of parole failures, coupled with an increasing base of parole populations, has had profound impacts on the nation's prison population. In 1980, parole violators constituted 18% of prison admissions; they now constitute 37% of prisoners coming in the front door. In 1998, this meant that 207,000 of the 565,000 people admitted to prison were parole violators, individuals who had either been returned to prison on a technical violation or for committing a new offense (Beck, 2000a). The combination of this increase with the leveling off of new prison commitments from new convictions means that parole revocations are now a significant factor in the rising prison populations.

Just as the collapse of a unifying sentencing philosophy has resulted in enormous state variation in punishment regimes, it has also resulted in wide differences in parole practices. For example, in California, 65% of the individuals admitted to that state's prisons in 1997 were parole violators; in Florida, parole violators accounted for 12% of new admissions; in Pennsylvania, 33% (Petersilia, 1999). Nationally, parole violators serve on average another 5 months in prison (Austin et al., 2000).

Taken together, these three developments paint a picture of a system that has lost its way. More people are going to prison under differing sentencing philosophies and returning home through a system of reintegration that has diminished capacity to perform that function and now serves more to return reentry failures to prison's front door. One need not engage in illusions about the capacity of this population to obey the law to conclude that the constructs of philosophy, law, policy, and practice are out of alignment. A return to the preexisting arrangement is unlikely; nor is it necessarily desirable in all respects. But, in our view, any sentencing regime should retain a focus on the reintegration goal. No matter what punishment philosophy sends prisoners to prison, no matter how their release is determined, with few exceptions they all come back. It is hard to find a coherent reentry philosophy in the current state of affairs.

THE PROFILE OF REENTERING PRISONERS

The profile of returning prisoners is changing in ways that pose new challenges to successful reentry. The basic demographics have not changed much over the past 20 years. The parole population is mostly male, although the number of incarcerated females has risen steadily over the past decade. Their median age is 34; the median education level is 11th grade. More than half (55%) of the returning offenders in 1998 were White, while 44% were African-American. Twenty-one percent of offenders on parole in 1998 were Hispanics, who may be of any race (Bonczar & Glaze, 1999).

One characteristic that has changed is the crime for which the offenders were convicted. Reflecting the arrest activities of the "war on drugs," the percentage of released offenders who had been convicted of drug offenses increased significantly during the past 20 years. More than one third (35%) of prisoners released to parole in 1997 had been incarcerated for a drug offense, up from 28% in 1990 and 12% in 1985. Over the same time period, the percent of parolees who had been convicted of violent offenses declined. In 1997, about a quarter of offenders coming into parole had convictions for violent offenses, down from a third (35%) in 1985 (Beck, 2000b).

The profile of returning prisoners is changing in other respects. Due to shifting sentencing policies, including mandatory minimums and truth-in-sentencing laws, the average length of stay in prison is increasing. Those released to parole in 1997 served an average of 27 months in prison—5 months longer than those released in 1990 (Beck, 2000b). This longer time in prison translates into a longer period of detachment from family and other social networks, posing new challenges to the process of reintegration.

More sobering is the decrease in the preparation of these prisoners for their release. As shown in Figure 2, in 1997 approximately a third of the inmates about to be released participated in vocational (27%) or educational (35%) programs—down from 31% and 43%, respectively, in 1991. The level of participation in prerelease planning did not decline, but only 12% of prisoners about to be released participate in prerelease planning at all. Of the entire prison population, an estimated 7% report participation in prison industries, whereas 24% are altogether idle (Austin et al., 2000).

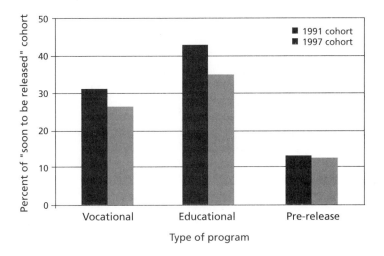

FIGURE 2 Offenders to Be Released in the Next 12 Months: Percent
Participating in Prison Programs, 1991 and 1997 (based on preliminary
analysis of data for forthcoming Urban Institute Crime Policy Report).

The inescapable conclusion is that we have paid a price for prison expansion, namely a decline in preparation for the return to community. There is less treatment, fewer skills, less exposure to the world of work, and less focused attention on planning for a smooth transition to the outside world.

Another important perspective is that the growing numbers of returning offenders are increasingly concentrated in neighborhoods already facing enormous disadvantage. A majority of prisoners are released into counties that contain the central cities of metropolitan areas. In 1996, an estimated two thirds of the 489,000 state prison releases were released into these counties. Fewer than 50% of 220,000 prisoners were released into these counties in 1984 (J. P. Lynch & Sabol, 2001). Presumably, the releases are more highly concentrated within the central cities of these core counties than they are in the nearby suburbs. And the central cities typically are less wealthy than neighboring areas, and they face other challenges such as loss of labor market share to suburban regions (J. P. Lynch & Sabol, 2001).

Research also suggests high concentrations of prisoners in a relatively small number of neighborhoods within the central cities of the core counties. For example, J. P. Lynch and Sabol (2001) have conducted analyses using data on Ohio state prisoners from Cuyahoga County, which includes the city of Cleveland. More than two thirds of the county's prisoners and most of the block groups with high rates of incarceration come from Cleveland. Concentrations are such that three tenths of 1% of the block groups in the county account for approximately 20% of the county's prisoners. In such "high-rate" block groups, somewhere between 8% and 15% of the young Black males are incarcerated on a given day.

High rates of removal and return of offenders may further destabilize disadvantaged neighborhoods. Recent research by Todd Clear and Dina Rose indicates that high incarceration and return rates may disrupt a community's social network, affecting family formation, reducing informal control of children and income to families, and lessening ties among residents. Clear, Rose, and Ryder (2001) also argue that when removal and return rates hit a certain tipping point, they may actually result in higher crime rates, as the neighborhood becomes increasingly unstable and less coercive means of social control are undermined.

However, the question of whether incarceration policies of the past 15 years have had a beneficial or detrimental effect on the social capital of communities is far from settled (J. P. Lynch & Sabol, 2000b). Alternative theories suggest that this tipping point may differ across communities and that, in some cases—particularly in very high-poverty, high-crime areas—incarceration may be an effective tool for controlling crime. Research shows that residents in these communities want a greater police presence and more attention to the chronic crime problems surrounding them. We do not yet know the relative benefits of removal and returns in various types of communities—there are clearly incapacitation benefits to crime control in many communities, but those may erode without a focus on reentry and reintegration.

In sum, the prisoners moving through the high-volume, poorly-designed assembly line that has, in many respects, lost a focus on reintegration, are less well prepared individually for their return to community, and are returning to communities that are not well prepared to accept them.

SOCIAL POLICY DIMENSIONS OF REENTRY

A focus on reentry highlights connections between criminal justice policy and other social policy domains that are provocative and suggest new directions for research and policy. In this section, we set aside issues of criminal justice policy—e.g., the purposes of punishment—and examine, instead, the overlapping considerations with other policy domains.

Health Policy

The population moving through correctional facilities in the United States presents serious health problems; the question is how to coordinate criminal justice and health policies in ways that improve health outcomes and, secondarily, justice outcomes. Interestingly, a period of incarceration often has positive consequences for the health status of a prisoner—in part because adequate health care is constitutionally required, but also because the food and living environment are more conducive to better health outcomes than many situations in the community. Yet the consequences for a prisoner's mental health may be adverse, and for substance abusers the effects of incarceration depend heavily on the management of the risk of relapse.

The overlap between the public health population and the criminal justice population is striking. For example, as Hammett (2001) shows, nearly one quarter of all people living with HIV or AIDS, one third living with Hepatitis C, and one third with tuberculosis in the United States in 1997 were released from a correctional facility (prison or jail) that year. These data suggest that correctional facilities could provide efficient access to large numbers of people posing serious public health risks, but embracing this challenge would require reconfiguration of the health and justice professions. For criminal justice policymakers, attention would need to be paid to diagnostic screening and treatment capabilities in all prisons and jails. From a reentry perspective, the two professions would need careful collaboration to ensure a smooth transition of care from prison or jail to community health care. Whether this capacity exists, and whether criminal justice supervision could increase the likelihood of healthy outcomes, are open questions.

Some 80% of the state prison population report a history of drug and/or alcohol use, including 74% of the "soon-to-be-released" prisoners (Beck, 2000b; Mumola, 1999). However, in-prison treatment is not readily available to those who need it. Despite a significant infusion of federal monies to fund treatment in state prisons, only 10% of state inmates reported participating in professional substance abuse treatment since admission, down from 25% in 1991 (Bureau of Justice Statistics, 1999). (When one includes participation in drug abuse programs, such as self-help groups and educational programs, the participation rates increase to 24% of the 1997 prison population, down from 30% in 1991 [Bureau of Justice Statistics, 1999].) Of the soon-to-be-released group who were using drugs in the month prior to incarceration, only 18% had participated in treatment since prison admission. And only 22% of the alcohol abusers had participated (Beck, 2000b).

The concern about the connections between criminal justice policy and drug treatment policy is brought into sharp focus by two distinct research findings. First, there is a significant body of evaluation literature demonstrating that in-prison drug treatment in the period leading up to release can, if combined with treatment in the postrelease period, significantly reduce both drug use and recidivism (Harrison, 2001). So, careful planning of treatment programs, along with supervision during reentry, will enhance health and safety. The second research finding comes from research on the brain. This research concludes "addiction is a brain disease" (Leshner, 1998, p. 2). Consequently, the return of a former addict to his old neighborhood places him at high risk of relapse, in part because the old haunts act as a trigger to his brain mechanisms and heighten the cravings. So, the criminal justice policy of requiring a parolee to return to his community may merely be placing a recovering addict at the crossroads of greatest risk.

Inmates with mental illness are also increasingly being imprisoned—and ultimately, being released. In 1998, the Bureau of Justice Statistics estimated that 16% of jail or prison inmates reported either a mental condition or an overnight stay in a mental hospital (Ditton, 1999). There are relatively few public mental health services available, and studies show that even when they are available, mentally ill individuals fail to access available treatment because they fear institutionalization, deny that they are mentally ill, or distrust the mental health system (Lurigio, 2001). Untreated mentally ill individuals may engage in criminal behaviors that eventually lead to arrest and conviction.

Family and Child Welfare Policy

One of the undeniable aspects of imprisonment is that relationships with family are strained. Not surprisingly, then, the increase in incarceration has significant consequences for family and child welfare policy. Most prisoners are parents—about one half of the men and two thirds of the women. According to the Bureau of Justice Statistics, in 1999 more than 1.5 million minor children in the United States had a parent who was incarcerated, an increase of more than a half million since 1991. About 7% of all African-American children currently have a parent in prison (Mumola, 2000).

Incarceration has consequences for child rearing. When fathers are imprisoned, about 90% of their children remain in the custody of their mothers. When mothers are incarcerated, however, fewer than a third of their children stay with their fathers, placing new demands on the extended family, peer networks, and child welfare systems (Hagan & Dinovitzer, 1999).

The high rates of incarceration in poor neighborhoods create a high level of ongoing disruption in family relationships. Sometimes, the removal of a family member is a good outcome—someone who has been violent in the home, draining resources to support a drug habit, or otherwise posing negative consequences for the family's well-being. But the removal of large numbers of mostly male young adults also drains the community of a key ingredient of social capital—community men. These complex relationships, combined with the great distance between many prisons and prisoners' communities, require creative management on the part of the families and the private and governmental support systems that could minimize the harm to children and families.

The reentry perspective focuses policy attention on the moment of release. How is the family prepared for this moment? How is the prisoner prepared? If there is a history of dysfunction, whose responsibility is it to minimize the harm? Particularly in the instance of domestic violence or child abuse, what is the role of the state and the police in managing the reentry safely?

Workforce Participation

The current strong economy presents unusual opportunities for linkages between ex-offenders and the world of work. Approximately two thirds of prisoners had a job just prior to their incarceration (J. P. Lynch & Sabol, 2000a). However, released offenders have very low employment rates, suggesting that incarceration may reduce the employability and future earnings of young men (Western, Kling, & Weiman, 2001). The stigma of incarceration makes ex-inmates unattractive for entry-level or union jobs; civil disabilities limit ex-felons access to skilled trades or the public sector; and incarceration undermines the social networks that are often necessary to obtain legitimate employment. Moreover,

Nagin and Waldfogel (1998) found that the effect of imprisonment on employment and future earnings is particularly pronounced for inmates over age 30, suggesting that as the prison and parole population ages, employment prospects become bleaker.

Civic Participation

In many ways, prisoners leave prison with only part of their debt to society paid. Much more is owed, and it may never be paid off. For example, one of the traditional consequences of a felony conviction has been the loss of voting rights. The laws of 46 states and the District of Columbia contain such stipulations. Fourteen states permanently deny convicted felons the right to vote. Eighteen states suspend the right to vote until the offender has completed the sentence and paid all fines. As a result, some 4 million Americans, 1.4 million of whom are African American (equaling 13% of the Black male adult population), are disenfranchised in this way (Fellner & Mauer, 1998).

In a spate of laws beginning in the late 1980s, a number of states now require that sex offenders be registered with the police upon release from prison, and/or that the community be notified in some way that a sex offender is living in the neighborhood. Today, every state requires convicted sex offenders to register with law enforcement on release (so-called Megan's laws).

These kinds of disqualifications and burdens (for a review, see Petersilia, 1999) constitute a very real component of the punishment—taken together, they reflect a philosophy akin to internal exile under which ex-offenders are cut off from civic participation, banned from certain employment opportunities, and required to display their status as ex-offender when required.

Racial Disparities

No discussion of imprisonment would be complete without a focus on the impact of incarceration on different racial groups. Bonczar and Beck (1997) calculated that in 1991, an African-American male had a 29% chance of being incarcerated at least once in his lifetime, 6 times higher than that for White males. In fact, the Bureau of Justice Statistics estimated that 9% of Black males in their late 20s and 3% of Hispanic males in their late 20s were in prison at the end of 1999 (Beck, 2000a). Looked at differently, more than one third of Black male high school dropouts were in prison or jail in the late 1990s; a higher percentage of this group were imprisoned than employed (Western & Pettit, 2000).

The consequences of imprisonment on minority communities—and our democracy—are profound. Just the impact on voting rights and civic participation generally is very disturbing. Denying large segments of the minority population the right to vote will likely alienate them further and spawn beliefs about the state that are contentious (Clear, Rose, & Ryder, 2001). Greater alienation and disillusionment with the political process also erodes residents' feelings of commitment and makes them less willing to participate in local activities. This is important because our most effective crime fighting tools require community collaboration and active engagement (Sherman et al., 1997). An increase in alienation between the community and the agencies of justice will make it more difficult for those agencies to turn back to communities and ask for assistance in neighborhood-based approaches (Petersilia, 2000).

It strikes us that this abbreviated summary of some of the data presented at the Reentry Roundtable that we co-hosted in October 2000 (most of which are found in the articles in this volume) argue strongly for strategic engagement between these varied policy sectors and criminal justice policy using the moment of reentry as the focal planning point. For example, the high degree of public health concerns presented by the criminal justice population is a compelling case for coordination of health care in the prison and in the community. Similarly, the creation of seamless treatment systems for returning prisoners with histories of substance abuse would keep a significant number of offenders from returning to prison. The linkage between prison-based work and community-based work also seems manageable, particularly in a low-unemployment economy. Furthermore, we applaud the work underway in a number of states to reconsider the reach of the current voter disqualification laws. Finally, we hope that the new community focus on reentry, with geocoded data, and analysis of the impact of imprisonment and reentry on poor, minority communities can provide a new dimension to the ongoing debate about the impact of criminal justice on our pursuit of racial justice.

IMPLICATIONS OF THE REENTRY PERSPECTIVE

We find the reentry perspective helpful in shining light into the dusty corners of some old debates about criminal justice policy. We have three particular corners in mind: the logic of parole, the mission of corrections, and the allocation of public and private responsibilities for the reintegration of offenders. Our overarching conclusion resembles the rallying cry of welfare reformers—we think we should abolish the system of parole as we know it, and replace it with a new system focused squarely on the goal of reintegration.

The Logic of Parole

Parole has both operational and jurisprudential meanings for criminal justice policy. At an operational level, it refers both to a method of making release decisions and a form of community supervision. As this article has demonstrated, we have concluded that both operational meanings of the word have lost political ground in recent years. We think a reentry analysis makes a compelling case for a reconsideration of the jurisprudential logic of parole as well. The central tenet of our parole system is the idea that a prisoner is expected to serve a portion of his sentence in the community, and he risks return to prison—often for the remainder of his sentence—if he fails to meet certain conditions.

We would substitute a new, two-part jurisprudential logic, namely that (a) completion of a prison sentence represents payment of a debt to society, and (b) every substantial period of incarceration should be followed by a period of managed reentry. In other words, we think it is important to decouple the rationale for the imposition of a sentence to imprison for a period of time from the rationale for community supervision for a period of time. The former should be justified in terms of deterrence, retribution, rehabilitation or incapacitation, the traditional underpinnings of a criminal sentence; the latter should be justified in terms of reintegration. In this view, if a criminal sentence requires imprisonment, the sentence would be served when the prison phase is completed. After completion of the prison sentence, the reentry phase would begin. For released prisoners who pose little risk and can accomplish reintegration easily, the reentry phase could be quite short, perhaps as short as a month. For those who pose greater risks and face greater difficulty reestablishing themselves, the reentry phase would be longer, but upper bounds would be established proportionate to both the risk and the original offense.

Supervision during this period would be the responsibility of a new, community-based entity ... The expectations placed on the returning prisoner would be related to successful reintegration—for example, getting a job, staying sober, attending mental health counseling, or making restitution to the victim. Failure to meet expectations during this period of managed reentry would not result in return to prison, as in traditional parole jurisprudence, because the sentence has been served with the completion of the prison term. Rather, as with drug courts, failure could result in graduated sanctions, up to a short deprivation of liberty, if those sanctions are demonstrably effective at changing behavior. In this system, if the released prisoner commits a new crime, it would be treated as a new crime to be prosecuted in a traditional manner, not as a violation of a condition of release as often happens now.

There are important and interesting experiments in this new approach to the task of reintegration. The Wisconsin Sentencing Commission articulated this risk-based philosophy in its final report and Wisconsin has launched pilot projects to test these ideas (Smith & Dickey, 1999). Washington state has embraced a risk-based approach to postprison supervision (Lehman, in press). The new concept of a reentry court reflects these principles as well (Travis, 2000). As originally proposed, reentry courts would have the authority to impose sanctions for failure to meet conditions associated with a reintegration plan, but not on the theory that the original sentence remains in effect. These courts would also provide a public forum that would underscore the importance of the work of reintegration for the offender and the community alike. We recognize that some sentencing reforms, such as the federal system's, have implemented a new status of "supervised release" to replace parole, but we prefer a new conceptualization of the connection between the reintegration mandate and our sentencing jurisprudence, not a reinstatement of parole under a different name.

For our proposal to take full shape, two revisions to a state's sentencing framework would be required. First, the duration of the criminal sentence would be defined as coinciding with completion of the prison term. The truth-in-sentencing philosophy reflects this idea somewhat, but with an emphasis on creating a fixed prison term. In our proposal, by contrast, we would still allow for early completion of a prison term (and thereby early completion of the criminal sentence) upon a showing of good conduct in prison in order to create incentives for conforming behavior in prison life. Second, a new legal status of reentry supervision would be created, with upper time limits, and incentives for early completion. During this period following prison release, the power of the state to revoke liberty would be statutorily limited to a system of graduated, parsimonious sanctions related to failures to meet reentry conditions. We believe these statutory clarifications would reflect a public recognition of the need to reintegrate returning prisoners into our society.

The Mission of Corrections

We think that the departments of corrections should also embrace the new mission of reintegrating returning prisoners. To do this, corrections agencies would be expected (and funded) to create a seamless set of systems that span the boundaries of prison and community. For example, corrections agencies would create linkages between in-prison jobs training and community-based employment and job training and between in-prison health care and community-based health care. They would be expected to link mental health services on both sides of the wall, or to work with community-based domestic violence services when a prisoner with a history of spousal abuse is released. They would be expected to give a prisoner the tools to succeed—for example, identification, driver's license, access to social security or other benefits, or housing, upon release. Where necessary, the department of corrections would be authorized to purchase services to ensure a smooth transfer of responsibility, for example, the first few months' rent if no private housing is available, or transitional mental health counseling to help cushion the shock of return, if community-based care is not available.

Just as welfare reform forced welfare agencies to shift from a dependency model to a model of transition to independence, so too a reentry perspective should force corrections agencies to take practical steps to move prisoners toward independence. In the case of welfare reform, this shift meant that welfare agencies invested in child care, job training, and employee assistance programs—whatever it took to move the client from welfare to work. Similarly, we would expect corrections agencies to make strategic investments in transitional services to move prisoners toward independence. The necessary step here is that corrections agencies must embrace reintegration as a goal, and we note with interest that the Ohio Department of Rehabilitation and Corrections, under the leadership of Reginald Wilkinson, has officially adopted this new mandate (Wilkinson, in press).

Allocation of Responsibilities for Reintegration

Who is responsible for successful reintegration? Clearly, the released prisoner has an important role to play, a role that we think is enhanced if made visible and explicit, as in a reentry court. We have also argued that a corrections agency has a role to play, creating a seamless linkage between in-prison programs and community programs to increase the chances of successful reintegration. Yet, our reentry analysis suggests that many of the key activities are distinctly local. For example, this discussion implies that the health, child welfare, job placement, drug treatment, and other service entities need to be mobilized to support prisoner reintegration. Most of these are city- or county-level functions and therefore require the leadership of the mayor or other executive. In our traditional configuration of responsibilities, we have oddly placed responsibility for "reentry management" in a state agency, typically a parole division or a corrections agency. Yet, we have also created community supervision functions in probation or pretrial release agencies, which are often county or city based. These artificial distinctions are barriers to reentry management.

We think it's important to move these activities as close to the community as possible. This is where the problems and assets can be found—the risks to relapse can be identified here; the positive power of social networks can be found here. Ultimately, reentry management should be community-based, with a focus on marshalling community resources to assist in successful reintegration. The legal status of the individual—whether on parole, probation, or pretrial release, whether adult or juvenile—matters somewhat, but we could envision a community supervision system that embraced all types of individuals, in all types of legal relationships with the criminal justice system. We are impressed by the idea of a community justice development organization, now being developed by the Center for Alternative Sentencing and Employment Services (CASES) in New York City. This idea borrows from the successes of community development corporations over the past 20 years that have managed the creation of housing, employment opportunities, and economic growth as intermediaries between federal, state, and local governments responsible for those functions and community institutions that are sometimes better at carrying them out. The researchers and planners at CASES have analyzed the probation and parole caseloads of certain neighborhoods and have asked a simple question: Why can't supervision of those individuals be organized along neighborhood lines, with much of the supervisory responsibility devolved to a community-based entity?

The creation of a community-based intermediary working on criminal justice issues could conceivably win the trust of the community and coalesce community capacity such as churches, small businesses, service providers, schools, and civic institutions to support the work of reintegration of returning prisoners. This new entity could broker the relationship between those institutions and the formal agencies of the justice system. The state system could then devolve the supervision functions of reentry management to the community justice development corporation and retain responsibility for the imposition of sanctions to a reentry court or other backstop system. The function of the government employees now called parole officers would be redefined in this new paradigm. Some of those functions would be performed by community justice corporation employees; other functions more related to enforcement of conditions of reentry would be performed under the auspices of the reentry court or other governmental entity. As with drug courts, it would be important that "carrots and sticks" be used in concert to produce the desired behavioral outcomes.

In sum, we find this reentry perspective suggests new ways of thinking about the underpinnings of our concept of parole, a new mandate for corrections, and a new mission at the local level to coalesce public and private capabilities to increase positive outcomes of the reentry process. This realignment of philosophy and operational capacity is not just about crime policy; it is ultimately about community well-being. And maybe good crime policy results will follow.

REFERENCES

Austin, J. (2001). Prisoner reentry: Current trends, practices, and issues. *Crime & Delinquency*, 47, 314–334.

Austin, J., Bruce, M. A., Carroll, L., McCall, P. L., & Richards, S.C. (2000, November). *The use of incarceration in the United States.* Paper prepared for the annual meeting of the American Society of Criminology, San Francisco.

Austin, J., Clark, J., Hardyman, P., & Henry, D. A. (1999). Impact of "three strikes and you're out." *Punishment & Society,* 1, 131–162.

Austin, J., Jones, C., Kramer, J., & Renninger, P. (1995). *National Assessment of Structured Sentencing, Final Report.* (Bureau of Justice Statistics Publication No. NJS 167557). Washington, DC: U.S. Department of Justice, Bureau of Justice Assistance.

Beck, A. (2000a). *Prisoners in 1999.* Bureau of Justice Statistics Bulletin. (Bureau of Justice Statistics Publication No. NCJ 183476). Washington DC: U.S. Department of Justice, Bureau of Justice Statistics.

Beck, A. (2000b, April 13). *State and Federal Prisoners Returning to the Community: Findings from the Bureau of Justice Statistics.* Paper presented at the First Reentry Courts Initiative Cluster Meeting, Washington DC. For more information, see http://www.ojp .usdoj.gov/bjs/pub/pdf/sfprc.pdf

Blumstein, A., & Beck, A. (1999). Population growth in U.S. prisons, 1980–1996. In M. Tonry and J. Petersilia (Eds.), *Prisons.* Chicago: University of Chicago Press.

Bonczar, T.P., & Beck, A. (1997). *Lifetime Likelihood of Going to State or Federal Prison.* In Bureau of Justice Statistics, Special Report. (Bureau of Justice Statistics Publication No. NCJ 160092). Washington, DC: U.S. Department of Justice, Bureau of Justice Statistics.

Bonczar, T.P., & Glaze, L.E. (1999). *Probation and Parole in the United States, 1998.* In Bureau of Justice Statistics bulletin. (Bureau of Justice Statistics Publication No. NCJ 178234.) Washington, DC: U.S. Department of Justice, Bureau of Justice Statistics.

Bureau of Justice Statistics. (1999). *Correctional Populations in the United States, 1997.* Washington, DC: U.S. Department of Justice, Bureau of Justice Statistics.

Bureau of Justice Statistics. (2000a, June 23). *Correctional population trends.* Washington, DC: U.S. Department of Justice, Bureau of Justice Statistics. Retrieved February 22, 2001, from the World Wide Web: http://www.ojp.usdoj.gov/bjs/keytabs.htm

Bureau of Justice. (2000b, August 2). *Sentenced prisoners admitted to State or Federal jurisdiction.* Washington, DC: U.S. Department of Justice, Bureau of Justice Statistics. Retrieved February 22, 2001, from the World Wide Web: http://www.ojp.usdoj.gov/bjs/dtdata.htm#justice

Bureau of Justice. (2000c, June 9). *Total sentenced prisoners released from state or federal jurisdiction.* Available: http://www.ojp.usdof.gov/bjs/dtdata.htm#justice

Clear, T., Rose, D.R., & Ryder, J.A. (2001). Incarceration and the community: The problem of removing and returning offenders. *Crime & Delinquency, 47,* 335–367.

Ditton, P. M. (1999). *Mental Health and Treatment of Inmates and Probationers.* In Bureau of Justice Statistics, Special Report. (Bureau of Justice Statistics Publication No. NCJ 174463). Washington, DC: U.S. Department of Justice, Bureau of Justice Statistics.

Ditton, P. M., & Wilson, D.J. (1999). *Truth and Sentencing in State Prisons.* In Bureau of Justice Statistics, Special Report. (Bureau of Justice Statistics Publication No. NCJ 170032). Washington, DC: U.S. Department of Justice, Bureau of Justice Statistics.

Fellner, J. & Mauer, M. (1998). *Losing the Vote: The Impact of Felony Disenfranchisement Laws in the United States* (Criminal Justice Briefing Sheet No. 1046). Washington, DC: The Sentencing Project. Available: http://www.sentencingproject.org/pubs/pubs.html#9080

Frankel, M. (1973). *Criminal Sentences: Law Without Order.* New York: Hill and Wang.

Hagan, J. & Dinovitzer, R. (1999). Collateral consequences of imprisonment for children, communities, and prisoners. In M. Tonry and J. Petersilia

(Eds.), *Prisons.* Chicago: University of Chicago Press.

Hammett, T. M. Health-related issues in prisoner reentry. *Crime & Delinquency, 47,* 390–409.

Harrison, L. D. (2001). The revolving prison door for drug-involved offenders: Challenges and opportunities. *Crime & Delinquency, 47,* 462–484.

Herman, S., & Wasserman, C. (2001). A role for victims in offender reentry. *Crime & Delinquency, 47,* 428–445.

Hirsch, A. von. (1976). *Doing Justice: The Choice of Punishments.* (Rep. of the Committee for the Study of Incarceration). New York: Hill and Wang.

Kleiman, M. (1999). *Getting Deterrence Right: Applying Tipping Models and Behavioral Economics to the Problems of Crime Control. Perspectives on Crime and Justice: 1998–1999 Lecture Series,* 3. (Bureau of Justice Statistics Publication No. NCJ 178244). Washington, DC: National Institute of Justice.

Lehman, J. D. (in press). Re-inventing community corrections in Washington state. *Corrections Management Quarterly,* 5(3).

Leshner, A. I. (1998). "Addiction is a brain disease—and it matters." *National Institute of Justice Journal,* No. 237, 2–6.

Liebling, A. (1999). Prison suicide and prisoner coping. In M. Tonry and J. Petersilia (Eds.), *Prisons.* Chicago: University of Chicago Press.

Lurigio, A. Effective services for parolees with mental illnesses. *Crime & Delinquency, 47,* 446–461.

Lynch, J. P., & Sabol, W. J. (2000a. December 5). *Analysis of Bureau of Justice Statistics Data: Survey of Inmates of State Correctional Facilities, 1991 and 1997.* Urban Institute First Tuesdays presentation, Washington DC.

Lynch, J. P., & Sabol, W. J. (2000b). Prison use and social control. In *Policies, Processes and Decisions of the Criminal Justice System.* Washington, DC: U.S. Department of Justice.

Lynch, J. P,. & Sabol, W. J. (2001). Prisoner reentry in perspective (Urban Institute Crime Policy Report). In *Crime policy report*. Washington, DC: Urban Institute Press.

Lynch, M. (1998). Waste managers? New penology, crime fighting, and the parole agent identity. *Law and Society Review, 32*, 839–869.

Martinson, R. (1974). What works? Questions and answers about prison reform. *Public Interest*, 35, 22–45.

Mumola, C. J. (1999). *Substance abuse and treatment, state and federal prisoners, 1997*. In Bureau of Justice Statistics, special report (Bureau of Justice Statistics Publication No. NCJ 172871). Washington, DC: U.S. Department of Justice, Bureau of Justice Statistics.

Mumola, C. J. (2000). *Incarcerated Parents and Their Children*. In Bureau of Justice Statistics, special report (Bureau of Justice Statistics Publication No. NCJ 182335). Washington, DC: U.S. Department of Justice, Bureau of Justice Statistics.

Nagin, D., & Waldfogel, J. (1998). The effects of conviction on income through the life cycle. *International Review of Law and Economics*, 18, 25–40.

Petersilia, J. (1999). Parole and prisoner reentry in the United States. In M. Tonry and J. Petersilia (Eds.), *Prisons*. Chicago: University of Chicago Press.

Petersilia, J. (2000). When prisoners return to the community: Political, economic, and social consequences. In *Sentencing & Corrections, Issues for the 21st Century*, 9. (Bureau of Justice Statistics Publication No. NCJ 184253). Washington, DC: National Institute of Justice.

Petersilia, J., & Turner, S. (1993). Intensive probation and parole. In M. Tonry and J. Petersilia (Eds.), *Crime and Justice: A review of research* (Vol. 17). Chicago: University of Chicago Press.

Rottman, D. B., Flango, C.R, Cantrell, M.T., Hansen, R., & LaFountain, N. (2000). *State Court Organization 1998*. (Bureau of Justice Statistics Publication No. NCJ 178932). Washington, DC: U.S. Department of Justice, Bureau of Justice Statistics.

Sherman, L., Gottfredson, D., MacKenzie, D., Eck, J., Reuter, P., & Bushway, S. (1997). *Preventing Crime: What Works, What Doesn't, What's Promising*. College Park: University of Maryland Press.

Smith, M. E., & Dickey, W. J. (1999). Reforming' sentencing and corrections for just punishment and public safety. In *Sentencing & Corrections, Issues for the 21st Century*, 4. (Bureau of Justice Statistics Publication No. NCJ 175724). Washington, DC: National Institute of Justice.

Tonry, M. (1996). *Sentencing Matters*. New York: Oxford University Press.

Tonry, M. (1999). The fragmentation of sentencing and corrections in America. In *Sentencing & Corrections, Issues for the 21st Century*, 1. (Bureau of Justice Statistics Publication No. NCJ 175721). Washington, DC: National Institute of Justice.

Travis, J. (2000). But they all come back: Rethinking prisoner reentry. In *Sentencing & Corrections, Issues for the 21st Century*, 7. (Bureau of Justice Statistics Publication No. NCJ 181413). Washington, DC: National Institute of Justice.

Western, B., Kling, J. R., & Weiman, D. F. The labor market consequences of incarceration. *Crime & Delinquency*, 47, 410–427.

Western, B., & Pettit, R. (2000) Incarceration and racial inequality in men's employment. *Industrial and Labor Relations Review*, 54, 3–16.

Wilkinson, R.A. (2001). Offender reentry: A storm overdue. *Corrections Management Quarterly*, 5(3).

Wilson, J.Q. (1975). *Thinking About Crime*. New York: Vintage Books.

Wright, R.F. (1998). *Managing Prison Growth in North Carolina through Structured Sentencing*. National Institute of Justice, Program Focus. (Bureau of Justice Statistics Publication No. NCJ 168944). Washington, DC: National Institute of Justice.

PART VI

Policy Perspectives

This nation was founded on a premise of freedom from governmental interference, and that citizens are innocent until, or if, the state can prove otherwise. We have never been unconcerned about crime, or the process of the state response to it. However, the advent of television, the growth in national media, sunshine laws, changes in our cultural norms, and a growth in poverty and a seeming underclass, has elevated crime to a seat at the daily dinner table of policy and political debate. Crime and the administration of justice have been increasingly prominent on the public policy agenda since the mid-1960s. During this period, Congress has created and abolished the Law Enforcement Assistance Administration (LEAA), two presidential commissions have made extensive suggestions for reform, and billions of dollars have been spent in attempts to reduce crime and improve the justice system. Initially, an air of certainty about the causes of crime and the way to reform criminals characterized official and scholarly statements on the problem. Like the bulk of policy research, rationality and scientific reasoning drove research agendas in criminal justice. But only during the past few years have the true dimensions of crime and the potential for dealing with it been viewed with a new realism, in part because humans confound true scientific approaches and limit possibilities for authentic experimentation. As James Q. Wilson, a leading exponent of this realistic stance, stated, our efforts to understand and curb the rise in crime have been frustrated by "our optimistic and unrealistic assumptions about human nature." This view is a far cry from the previously prevalent belief that crime, like poverty, could be ended if only there were enough money to apply the techniques of the social and behavioral sciences to the "root causes"—poor housing, unemployment, and racial prejudice.

The close of the twentieth century saw hopes rise and fall, as research has provided a glimmer of hope for those who believe that the social sciences have the analytical tools to understand crime and to contribute to formation of public policies to deal with it. This research appears to be more systematic, to be based on empirical findings, and to challenge much of the "conventional wisdom" about crime, criminal behavior, and the administration of justice. There is a new appreciation of the complex dimensions of criminal behavior and of the fact that the law-enforcement function is only one role of the police. The courts are increasingly viewed as organizations composed of small groups, and it is recognized that rehabilitative techniques have had a low success rate—although it can be argued that efforts have never been extensive enough to accurately evaluate their efficacy. In addition, the dominant approach has been that criminal justice is a system.

Research should be one essential variable included in formulating public policies. If government decisions were not influenced by politics, one might be able to show how the findings of social scientists could be directly applied to solving a public problem. Ideally, policies should reflect state-of-the-art research, the best of our expert wisdom.

Yet public decisions arise from a complicated confluence of public and legislative recognition of a problem, well-defined and measured solutions in the policy realm, and negotiation in the political arena. A political tug-of-war among interest groups is very apparent in certain policy areas like gun control, where both sides are well organized, have bolstered legal claims allowing them to fight their cause in multiple branches of government, and have substantial public support. Yet other areas, such as drug legalization, have varying levels of support from interest groups, which often provide a source of funds which can help fund candidates, buy advertising and raise issue awareness. Some policy proposals and solutions sit on a proverbial shelf, until a notorious crime or declaration of innocence breathes new life into the cause, as has been seen off and on for decades with the death penalty, as well as different forms of mandatory and "three strikes" sentencing. Ideally, the tools of policy and empiricism serve to neutralize these forces.

There is a natural regulation of which criminal justice issues gain attention, cycling with the balance of power between congressional and executive branches. Political platforms and parties prioritize their issues, such as the Democrats' emphasis on Violence Against Women Act (VAWA) and Community Oriented Policing (COPS), or the Republicans' emphasis on Three Strikes You're Out laws and an increase in expenditures for security. Who is in power, specific events and crises, and current cultural norms can significantly affect the national mood. In turn, legislatures may respond to what they believe the public perceives the problem to be, and not the evidence that is generated by data. Thus, solutions discussed by experts usually have little relation to the operational plans that emerge from the policy process.

We know that Americans feel strongly about crime, and feel it is deserving of governmental attention. With equal certainty, we know that Americans remain strong in their feelings about the preservation of individual liberty and self-governance. Although Americans are fearful of crime, and want action to address it, what remains unclear is precisely what action the polis would condone. Increases in press coverage of focusing events such as the tragedy at the World Trade Center, and local stories like Columbine and Lacey Peterson help prioritize crime as a top public concern, but political communication research tells us that the media can only tell us what to think about, not what to think. Thus, Americans' real policy preferences toward crime control remain unclear. Debate over criminal justice policies may be discussed in the press, in legislative assemblies, and in private conversations. Should the police be allowed unfettered discretion in the name of preserving public safety for air travel in the wake of 9/11? Should sentences emphasize incapacitation or rehabilitation? Should we disarm our citizens or respect their liberty to decide whether to have guns in their homes? Should the War on Drugs be continued?

Discussions of these and similar questions get to basic questions about crime and justice policies in a democracy. During the three decades we've seen a shift in public opinion and policy direction. Until the mid-1970s, the recommendations of the 1967 report of the President's Commission on Law Enforcement and Administration of Justice seemed to hold sway at both the federal and state levels of government. The commission declared that crime was caused essentially by disorganization in American society; that agencies engaged in enforcement, adjudication, and corrections lacked sufficient resources; and that rehabilitation had been insufficiently emphasized in the treatment of offenders. The writers of the report recommend eliminating social conditions that bring about crime, doing away with social and racial injustices in order to achieve the ideals of the American ethic, and reintegrating those who commit crime into their communities.

The middle of the 1970s saw a shift in criminal justice policies that mirrored the ascendance of conservative political leaders. Since that time, the conservative critique of the liberal policies of the 1960s has been constant. The critique gained credence during the 1970s in part because research cast doubt on many previous policies. Debate about "what works" sparked a reconsideration of the role of rehabilitative programs. Committees of the National Academy of Sciences recommended that greater weight be given to policies of incarceration and deterrence. Questions were raised about the dangers posed by the practice of allowing bail to repeat offenders, the prosecution of career criminals, lengths of incarcerative sentences, and the broader efforts to reduce crime through social reform.

The election of Ronald Reagan in 1980 consolidated the shift in crime control policies. Actions taken during the Reagan, Bush, and Clinton administrations, and copied in most states, placed greater emphasis upon increasing resources for police and prosecutors, raising sentence lengths, increasing the use of incarceration, tightening the insanity defense, and abolishing parole release. These policies are expected to continue during the current administration.

Now that we have experienced almost twenty years of harsher crime control policies, have they made a difference? Some will point to the leveling off of the crime rate since the mid-1970s and argue that the tougher policies have worked. Opponents point to the doubling of the incarcerative population during the past decade as proof that these policies have failed. Is another shift in crime and justice policies in the offing? Will the costs of the War on Drugs and increased use of prison cause taxpayers to raise questions about the future of these policies? Will concerned citizens again call for policies that emphasize justice over crime control? As our memories fade from our nation's great tragedy of 9/11, will we be left scarred and more tolerant of law enforcement's presence, or will the roots of liberty ultimately grow deeper?

QUESTIONS FOR FURTHER EXPLORATION

1. Should legislators be responsible to public opinion and pass the laws about issues that citizens are concerned about, or should legislators be guided by studies, research, and practice?

2. How might interest groups influence the criminal justice system? Provide more than one example.

3. Should lawmakers and criminal justice system actors consider the role and influence of race on the adversarial process?

4. Do drugs cause crime, or do drugs create an environment for crime to exist? Defend your position.

5. Are public health officials, lawyers, legislators, or criminal justice system actors best suited to address the problem of guns and drugs?

6. How are drugs classified? Explain how drug effects are divided for the purpose of analysis.

SUGGESTIONS FOR FURTHER READING

Gest, Ted. 2001. *Crime and Politics: Big Government's Erratic Campaign for Law and Order.* New York: Oxford University Press. An experienced journalist provides the analytical descriptions of the political interests and events that shaped federal crime policy on such issues as gun control and narcotics laws.

Horney, Julie, and Cassia Spohn. "Rape Law Reform and Instrumental Change in Six Urban Jurisdictions," 25 *Law and Society Review* 117 (1991). Characterizes rape reform law as symbolic, and recommends monitoring implementation and enforcement of these laws.

Rossi, Peter H., and Richard A. Berk. *Just Punishments: Federal Guidelines and Public Views Compared.* New York: Aldine de Gruyter, 1997. Examines agreement between public perceptions of crime seriousness, and policies for sentencing of convicted offenders set forth by the United States Sentencing Commission.

Sampson, Robert, and John Laub. *Crime in the Making: Pathways and Turning Points Through Life.* Cambridge, Mass.: Harvard University Press, 1993.

Walker, Samuel, Cassia Spohn, and Miriam DeLone. 2003. *The Color of Justice: Race Ethnicity and Crime in America*, 3rd ed. Belmont, CA: Wadsworth. An excellent overview of the links between crime, race, and ethnicity.

24

✦

Black Man's Burden

Race and the Death Penalty in America

Charles J. Ogletree, Jr.

The influence of race in the criminal justice system is well documented. Professor Ogletree examines the history of race and the death penalty. He raises important questions for both abolitionists and retentionists.

Nearly 120 years ago, Frederick Douglass, the former slave and great African American leader, described the American criminal justice system as follows: "Justice is often painted with bandaged eyes. She is described in forensic eloquence, as utterly blind to wealth or poverty, high or low, white or black, but a mask of iron, however thick, could never blind American justice, when a black man happens to be on trial."[1] Sadly, little has changed in the century and a half since Douglass had cause to condemn the state of the justice system in America. Nowhere is this more true than in the application of the "ultimate punishment"—the punishment of death.

After September 11th, America's attitudes about crime and punishment shifted dramatically. Americans, without regard to race, class, or religion, were all shocked by the tragic circumstances of the terrorist attack, and have not been reluctant to seek vengeance. The response in the African American community has been particularly surprising, given the history of racial discrimination in America. As I discuss the intersection of race and criminal justice,

Source: Charles J. Ogletree, Jr. Black Man's Burden: Race and the Death Penalty in America, 81 *Oregon Law Review* 15 (2002). Some footnotes deleted.

specifically in the context of capital punishment, it is critical to reveal some facts that are frequently ignored in this country today. African Americans are, by and large, conservative. They are among our nation's most patriotic citizens. They are prepared to sacrifice their own liberty by supporting governmental efforts to protect their security. Even though discriminatory treatment by law enforcement against African Americans is well documented, a recent survey indicates that an overwhelming majority of African Americans support the racial profiling of Muslims and Arab-Americans as a result of September 11th.[2]

Like the entire criminal justice system, the administration of the death penalty in America places a disproportionate burden on African Americans. The focus of my comments will be on race and capital punishment. Beyond my concerns about race, the death penalty faces challenges from a number of other quarters as well. Among the most recent developments:

- On June 20, 2002, the Supreme Court decided Atkins v. Virginia,[3] holding that it is unconstitutional to execute the mentally retarded. Writing for the court, Justice Stevens followed previous decisions articulating how the Eighth Amendment's prohibition on cruel and unusual punishment is to be applied. The Court noted that prohibited forms of punishment are not fixed, but rather vary according to "evolving standards of decency that mark the progress of a maturing society." When the Supreme Court upheld executions of the mentally retarded thirteen years ago in Penry v. Lynaugh,[4] Justice Sandra Day O'Connor's reasoning for the majority was based on a determination that there was no national consensus against the practice—that is, executing the mentally retarded did not violate Americans' notions of decency at the time. Since that case was decided in 1989, the number of death penalty states barring executions of the retarded has grown from two to eighteen, such that eighteen of thirty-eight death penalty states—and thirty of fifty states total—bar executions of the mentally retarded. In Atkins, Justice O'Connor was again in the majority, but this time holding that "evolving standards of decency now prohibit executing the mentally retarded.[5]

- Further evidence of the shift in attitude came in late February 2002, when the Georgia Parole Board commuted the death sentence of a mentally ill defendant to life in prison. We will watch carefully Supreme Court cases in the near future since we can see that even staunch supporters of capital punishment, like Justice O'Connor, are noticing the public mood shifting away from the death penalty.

- In addition, the Supreme Court issued a stay of execution on February 15, 2002, to Thomas Miller-El, an African American death row inmate in Texas who claims that prosecutors deliberately kept African Americans off the jury during his murder trial. Miller-El's case could provide some much-needed clarity to the Supreme Court's jurisprudence on racial discrimination in jury selection, and, as I will discuss shortly, could also provide one step toward reducing the disparities in sentencing rates of people of color sitting on death row.

- The Supreme Court also recently found unconstitutional state death penalty laws that allow the judge, rather than the jury, to decide whether the death penalty will be imposed. This case, Ring v. Arizona,[6] implicates capital punishment laws in nine states, calling into question up to 800 death sentences.

- More recently, a federal district court judge in New York struck down the Federal Death Penalty Act as unconstitutional because it "deprived innocent people of a significant opportunity to prove their innocence . . . [and] creates an undue risk of executing innocent people."[7] On September 24, 2002, a federal district judge in Vermont overturned a death sentence based on a finding that the Federal Death Penalty Act determines for imposition of the death penalty in a manner inconsistent with Sixth Amendment and Due Process rights. The court also noted that "[c]apital punishment is under siege."[8]

- And finally, Professor James Liebman of Columbia Law School released the second part of his comprehensive study of error rates in capital sentencing in early 2002. The initial findings from two years ago showed an error rate in capital sentencing of 68%—that is, more than two out of every three death sentences were overturned due to "serious error." [9] Further study has shown that the states that use the death penalty most often have error rates that exceed the national average, and that the occurrence of capital sentencing error is higher in states that have a higher proportion of African Americans in the population.[10]

In addition to issues regarding who should be eligible for execution, who makes that decision, and how to guarantee accuracy and avoid error, there is a fundamental issue regarding the role that race has played in the death penalty in America. I will discuss a number of racial elements of the application of capital punishment, and I will specifically mention the impact of the death penalty on black defendants, black victims, and black communities. In the context of race, I will note the connection between the current system of capital punishment and the historical use of extra-judicial lynchings against blacks during the Jim Crow era. Based on this analysis I will then raise some questions regarding the best strategies for abolitionists who want to address the racially disparate impact of the death penalty.

I. THE LEGACY OF LYNCHING

In a sense, to take a historical view, the racially disproportionate application of the death penalty can be seen as being in historical continuity with the long and sordid history of lynching in this country. It is also notable in this regard that the states of what is often called the "Death Belt"—the southern states that together account for over 90% of all executions carried out since 1976—overlap considerably with the southern states that had the highest incidence of extra-legal violence and killings during the Jim Crow era. This similarity appears to be more than mere coincidence or correlation—and indeed, a cursory evaluation of some of the factors that explain the high incidence of lynching shows that many of those factors are present in the impulse to impose capital punishment today.

Before evaluating the factors that motivated lynchings in America, it is instructive to begin with a case study.[11] While the facts of the case described in the Supreme Court's decision of United States v. Shipp[12] seem astonishing in many respects, they were altogether common in many places in this country at the time.

In a cemetery in Chattanooga, Tennessee, lies an unremarkable headstone for Ed Johnson, a black man born in 1882 who died at the hands of a white lynch mob on March 19, 1906. The inscription reads: "God bless you all. I am an innocent man . . . Farewell until we meet again in the sweet by and by."

Ed Johnson was a young, uneducated African American who grew up in Chattanooga. He had no job, no home, and no immediate family. In the early 1900s, he was wrongly accused of raping a white woman. During his trial, he was taunted by the public, the press, and even by a member of the jury. The trial judge and the Tennessee trial courts ignored both these procedural injustices and his actual innocence. An all-white jury convicted him of rape, and there was vocal demand for him to be lynched. The lives of two black lawyers and a white Supreme Court justice intersected in an effort to save Ed Johnson from an unfair conviction and an illegal lynching.

Noah Parden and his law partner, Styles Hutchins, feared that the local sheriff, Joseph Shipp, would allow an unruly, white lynch mob to kill Ed Johnson before Johnson's conviction and sentence could be reviewed. Parden and Hutchins took the unprecedented step of traveling to Washington, D.C., to ask the Supreme Court to hear Mr. Johnson's appeal.

In what may be the first argument ever made by African American lawyers before a Justice of the United States Supreme Court, Parden and Hutchins met with Justice John Marshall Harlan and urged him to intervene to prevent Johnson's lynching in Tennessee. Many recall Justice Harlan's powerful and lonely dissent in Plessy v. Ferguson,[13] in which he argued:

> [I]n view of the Constitution, in the eye of the law, there is in this country no superior, dominant, ruling class of citizens. There is no caste here. Our Constitution is colorblind, and neither knows nor tolerates classes among citizens. In respect of civil rights, all citizens are equal before the law. The humblest is the peer of the most powerful. The law regards man as man, and takes no account of his surroundings or of his color when his civil rights as guaranteed by the supreme law of the land are involved. [14]

Parden and Hutchins were fortunate that Justice Harlan accepted their arguments that the Supreme Court should intervene to ensure an opportunity for appellate review of a fatally defective conviction. Justice Harlan issued a stay of execution, prohibiting the state of Tennessee from executing Johnson. Despite this impressive victory, Sheriff Shipp and the white lynch mob ignored the Supreme Court's directive. As the Supreme Court subsequently determined, Sheriff Shipp facilitated the mob's efforts to remove Mr. Johnson from jail and to lynch him. In fact, Mr. Johnson was lynched, shot and his body mutilated. In an unprecedented step, the U.S. Department of Justice filed contempt of court charges in the Supreme Court against Sheriff Shipp and several associates. They were convicted, but in further irony to Ed Johnson's death, received sentences of less than three months.

Unfortunately, the tragic circumstances did not end with Ed Johnson's lynching. The two African American lawyers, Parden and Hutchins, became frequent targets of death threats, were ostracized by African Americans in their own community for stirring up racial tensions, and virtually lost their law practice.

Even Parden's minister publicly opposed the effort to appeal Johnson's conviction to the Supreme Court, telling the Chattanooga News that "[t]he best [element] of the colored people do not approve of reopening the case and the colored lawyers who are advocating it are making a serious mistake, not only for themselves but for the community in which they live."

The Johnson case is but one example of many lynchings that took place in the South—the Tuskegee Institute estimates that nearly 5,000 lynchings took place between 1882 and 1968. While lynchings no longer occur at the same frequency as during the Jim Crow era, the practice certainly did not stop in the 1960s—to give one prominent example, just four years ago [2000] in Texas, an African American was chained by two white assailants to the back of a pickup truck, and was dragged through the streets until he was decapitated.

A number of factors appear to have motivated the practice of lynching. At a fundamental level, lynching was an expression of racism and racial discrimination—it reflected an effort to assert the superiority of whites over blacks. A number of sociologists, including Gunnar Myrdal, have suggested that lynching was a tool used to maintain racial caste distinctions and to keep blacks in a position of subjugation.[15] As such, it served not only to eliminate individual blacks who had violated social norms, but also functioned as a powerful incentive for blacks to "learn their place." Even a summary glance at the statistics presented in more recent examinations of racial disparities in capital sentencing, to be discussed shortly, demonstrates that racial discrimination is still a powerful force in the decisions the legal system makes about who gets to live and who will die.

In addition, a number of historians have commented on the recreational element of extralegal killings. As one historian wrote: "In rural [areas] . . . lynchings, manhunts and kidnappings certainly offered a degree of 'excitement' to otherwise culturally deprived southerners. The noted social critic H.L. Mencken said as much when he argued that the gala events surrounding lynchings were pathological substitutes for more normal community activities."[16] . . .

Lynchings served a number of other purposes as well. The impulse may have been an expression of anti-state sentiments, or more specifically, a concern that state judicial processes were not to be trusted to reach the correct outcome. In this regard, lynchings may have reflected concern with the possibility of acquittals, or a concern for the delay between the moment of judgment and the moment when the sentence would be carried out.

In addition, lynching can be seen as a manifestation of a peculiar culture of violence in America's southern states. A number of historians have discussed the southern "code of honor," which justified extreme violence when that code was breached, and thus promoted and countenanced lynching and mob violence.

Given the many similarities between the illegal but often officially sanctioned practice of lynching, and the current imposition of the death penalty, it seems at times that the only difference between lynching and capital punishment is the gloss of legality and procedural regularity that the latter enjoys. In this regard, application of the death penalty may be fairer than the vigilante justice that characterized the Jim Crow era, but not by much.

In fact, a number of scholars and activists have referred to America's history of lynching and Jim Crow as the appropriate point of reference for an understanding of the dynamics of our current legal system. Reverend Jackson used the title "Legal Lynching" for his book on the death penalty;[17] and Professor Emma Coleman Jordan has hypothesized that "lynching [is] a contemporary civic metaphor for the black experience within the American legal system." [18]

II. RACE AND THE DEATH PENALTY

This history of lynching and the reasons for its prevalence will be useful to bear in mind as we consider the ways in which race still predominates in the American criminal justice system.

A. Racial Discrimination in Jury Selection

An examination of recent findings just in the area of racial jury composition illustrates this point. Race has historically played a role in the ability of black defendants to invoke their right under the U.S. Constitution to a fair and impartial jury of their peers, and the racial composition of the jury is of particular importance in capital cases. These rights are dramatically undermined by the use of peremptory jury challenges as a pretext for discriminating against people of color.

Some background into the relevant history and caselaw is necessary at this point. In the 1986 decision Batson v. Kentucky,[19] the Supreme Court held that prosecutorial use of peremptory challenges to exclude potential jurors on the basis of race violated the Equal Protection Clause. In a concurring opinion. Justice Thurgood Marshall (who had other problems with the decision, to be discussed in a moment) celebrated the decision as a "historic step toward eliminating the shameful practice of racial discrimination in the selection of juries."[20]

Before Batson, prosecutors routinely struck black jurors based purely on racism, or gross racial prejudice and generalizations. The history of criminal prosecution in Dallas County, Texas, is illustrative of this point. The prosecutor's office in Dallas County prepared a jury selection instruction book that included the following instruction: "Do not take Jews, Negroes, Dagos,

Mexicans or a member of any minority race on a jury no matter how rich or well educated."[21] Even once the instruction manual was revised to remove the explicitly racist terms, prosecutors were still advised to eliminate "any member of a minority group" from a petit jury. [22]

While such blatant and outrageous instructions now seem to be a relic of the past, existing statistical evidence reveals the continuing disproportionate use of peremptory challenges to remove blacks from the venire. As one commentator has explained, the discriminatory use of peremptory challenges is the single most significant means by which racial prejudice and bias are injected into the jury selection system."[23]

Batson has been viewed as a major accomplishment in the effort to eliminate this form of jury discrimination. The Court in Batson reaffirmed the principle, established in Strauder v. West Virginia,[24] that a state denies a black defendant equal protection by putting him on trial before a jury from which members of his race have been purposefully excluded. Moreover, Batson reaffirmed the principle, announced in Swain v. Alabama,[25] that a state's purposeful denial of jury participation on the basis of race also violates the excluded juror's Fourteenth Amendment right to equal protection.

The Batson decision, however, left to the trial courts the important issue of determining whether a defendant had established a prima facie case of discrimination, and whether the prosecution had rebutted that prima facie showing. The Supreme Court has since provided lower courts with little direction regarding how those determinations are to be made, and has declined to give lower courts more information on how to determine when a prosecutor's race-neutral justifications for challenges are acceptable.

State and lower federal courts have shown widely different views regarding the existence of a prima facie case under Batson. At the trial level, many courts frequently accept explanations that are no more than after-the-fact rationalizations for challenges which appear to have been made on subconsciously racial grounds. For example, although the Alabama Supreme Court has insisted that "[n]o merely whimsical or fanciful reason will suffice as an adequate explanation,"[26] trial courts have not always scrutinized prosecutorial explanations closely. In Wallace v. Alabama,[27] the prosecutor explained that he challenged:

- A young black female because she was a homemaker and lacked knowledge of what life was like out on the street;
- Another young black female because she was a student who did not indicate that she was working, and therefore "would not have had the necessary experience to be able to draw on and make a judgment in this case";
- An older black female who was retired, and might be more sympathetic because she "appeared to be a grandmotherly type";
- A young black male who had a beard, which the prosecutor explained meant he was likely to "go against the grain";
- A middle-aged black man because he was unemployed and therefore might be irresponsible; and

- A middle-aged black female because she appeared to be in the same age group as the defendants' parents or mothers.

Amazingly, the trial court found the prosecutor's thin, allegedly "race-neutral" explanations sufficient to rebut the prima facie case of discrimination, and the appeals court affirmed.

In Missouri v. Alexander,[28] a prosecutor explained that he challenged a black juror because the juror was unemployed, did not understand one of the questions asked during voir dire, and lived in a high crime neighborhood. Unemployment, lower education, and crime are found more frequently in minority communities, yet the court seemed unconcerned that minorities might be excluded disproportionately because of these reasons.

B. Disproportionate Imposition of Capital Punishment

Death penalty opponents have been pursuing claims of racial discrimination in the application of the death penalty for a long time. A number of major death penalty cases were actually brought as racial discrimination claims, even though the Supreme Court chose to decide the cases on other grounds. One example is Coker v. Georgia,[29] in which the Supreme Court invalidated laws that imposed the death penalty for the crime of rape.

Coker had argued in his brief to the Supreme Court that capital sentencing was tainted by an impermissible degree of racial bias. Coker presented evidence that over a twenty-year period in the South, black men accused of raping white women were more than eighteen times as likely to be sentenced to death as white men accused of the same crime. But the Supreme Court decided the case solely on the grounds that the death penalty was disproportionate to the crime of rape, and was thus in violation of the Eighth Amendment's prohibition on cruel and unusual punishment. The Court completely sidestepped the racial issue—remarkably, there is not a single mention of race, or of Coker's racial argument, in the Court's reported opinion.

●●●

The Supreme Court's silence on the racial disparities in Coker is instructive—the Court was doing its best to avoid discussing the overwhelming evidence of racial disparity, and it succeeded. But less than ten years after Coker, the Court confronted the issue of racial discrimination in capital sentencing head-on, in the landmark case of McCleskey v. Kemp.[30]

Professor David Baldus' seminal study on racial disparities in the imposition of the death penalty[31] served as the centerpiece of the McCleskey case, in which Warren McCleskey's lawyers argued that the racially discriminatory application of Georgia's death penalty statute violated the Equal Protection Clause of the Fourteenth Amendment. The study revealed racial disparities in the imposition of the death penalty in the state of Georgia, and identified the race of both the defendant and the victim as determinative factors in whether a defendant would be sentenced to death. Specifically, the study noted:

[D]efendants charged with killing white victims were 4.3 times as likely to receive a death sentence as defendants charged with killing blacks. According to this model, black defendants were 1.1 times as likely to receive a death sentence as other defendants. Thus, the Baldus study indicates that black defendants . . . who kill white victims have the greatest likelihood of receiving the death penalty.[32]

Professor Baldus also noted a remarkable disparity in the rate at which the death penalty was sought—"prosecutors sought the death penalty in 70% of the cases involving black defendants and white victims; 32% of the cases involving white defendants and white victims; 15% of the cases involving black defendants and black victims; and 19% of the cases involving white defendants and black victims."[33]

Writing for the 5-to-4 majority in McCleskey, Justice Lewis Powell conceded that the Baldus study was "valid statistically,[34] but concluded that it only demonstrated a risk that race factored into some capital sentencing determinations. The Court determined that the risk of racial discrimination in capital sentencing determinations was negligible:

The likelihood of racial prejudice allegedly shown by the study does not constitute the constitutional measure of an unacceptable risk of racial prejudice. The inherent lack of predictability of jury decisions does not justify their condemnation. . . . At most, the Baldus study indicates a discrepancy that appears to correlate with race, but this discrepancy does not constitute a major systemic defect. Any mode for determining guilt or punishment has its weaknesses and the potential for misuse. Despite such imperfections, constitutional guarantees are met when the mode for determining guilt or punishment has been surrounded with safeguards to make it as fair as possible. [35]

While premising its holding on the determination that racial disparity in the administration of the death penalty did not constitute a "constitutionally significant risk of racial bias," Justice Powell articulated another reason for his holding, which seemed to indicate a fear that treating McCleskey's claim as legitimate would open up a Pandora's Box and reveal the pervasive role of race in criminal processes:

McCleskey's claim, taken to its logical conclusion, throws into serious question the principles that underlie our entire criminal justice system. The Eighth Amendment is not limited in application to capital punishment, but applies to all penalties. Thus, we accepted McCleskey's claim that racial bias has impermissibly tainted the capital sentencing decision, we could soon be faced with similar claims as to other types of penalty. . . . [T]here is no limiting principle to the type of challenge brought by McCleskey. The Constitution does not require that a State eliminate any demonstrable disparity that correlates with a potentially irrelevant factor in order to operate a criminal justice system that includes capital punishment.[36]

Thus, despite overwhelming evidence of discrimination, the response of the courts has been to deny relief on the grounds that patterns of racial disparities are insufficient to prove racial bias in individual cases. Justice William Brennan criticized this approach, remarking:

> It is tempting to pretend that minorities on death row share a fate in no way connected to our own, that our treatment of them sounds no echoes beyond the chambers in which they die. Such an illusion is ultimately corrosive, for the reverberations of injustice are not so easily confined.[37]

While the Court offered a number of rationalizations to deny Warren McCleskey relief, Justice Brennan's strongly worded dissent left no doubt as to the significance of race in the application of the death penalty. As Justice Brennan explained:

> At some point in this case, Warren McCleskey doubtless asked his lawyer whether a jury was likely to sentence him to die. A candid reply to this question would have been disturbing. First, counsel would have to tell McCleskey that few of the details of the crime or of McCleskey's past criminal conduct were more important than the fact that his victim was white. Furthermore, counsel would feel bound to tell McCleskey that defendants charged with killing white victims in Georgia are 4.3 times as likely to be sentenced to death as defendants charged with killing blacks. In addition, frankness would compel the disclosure that it was more likely than not that the race of McCleskey's victim would determine whether he received a death sentence: 6 of every 11 defendants convicted of killing a white person would not have received the death penalty if their victims had been black. . . . Finally, the assessment would not be complete without the information that cases involving black defendants and white victims are more likely to result in a death sentence than cases featuring any other racial combination of defendant and victim. The story could be told in a variety of ways, but McCleskey could not fail to grasp its essential narrative line: there was a significant chance that race would play a prominent role in determining if he lived or died.[38]

Regrettably, Justice Powell did respond to Justice Brennan's challenge, but only after he left the Court. When interviewed by his biographer and asked whether there were any decisions he would change, he stated that he would have voted differently on McCleskey.[39]

What Justice Brennan characterized as the "reverberations of injustice" are still being felt today. A number of recent studies show that racially disproportionate death penalty sentencing is as pervasive as ever, and continues to plague the capital punishment system.

C. Recent Empirical Findings

Two recent studies by Professor Baldus report a number of key findings. First, as I discussed earlier, Batson has not been particularly successful in eliminating racially-motivated peremptory challenges in capital trials.[40] Second, and perhaps more importantly, there is a distinct correlation between the likelihood that a jury will return a capital sentence and the number of blacks on the jury—the more black jurors there are, the less likely the jury is to return a death sentence.[41] This correlation grows even stronger when the capital defendant is black.

A recent study from Professor William Bowers, resulting from his work with the Capital Jury Project, confirms the finding that the more black members there are on a jury, the less likely the jury is to return a death sentence.[42] Again, the pattern is even more noticeable when the defendant is black. Professor Bowers interviewed capital jurors to identify what might explain this striking result, and his findings confirm the assertion that capital sentencing is unacceptably susceptible to racial factors. Jurors listed three main considerations that weighed into a decision whether to apply the death penalty: lingering doubts about the defendant's guilt, the extent of the defendant's remorsefulness, and the defendant's future dangerousness. In each consideration, black jurors viewed black defendants more favorably than did white jurors. When evaluations of the defendant's character are so starkly different along racial lines, and when the result of the evaluation means the difference between lethal injection or life in prison, we can see that battles over who sits on the jury really are battles for life or death.

D. Burdens Resulting from Racially Disproportionate Capital Sentencing

In light of the continued racial imbalance in the application of the death penalty, the burden that the Supreme Court's decision in McCleskey places on blacks continues to operate at a number of levels. At the first, most obvious level, the racially disproportionate sentencing of blacks puts black defendants in the position of having their actions judged and punished more harshly than similarly situated white defendants.

At a second level, however, the racial imbalance in how death sentences are handed out shows a disregard for black victims. Disproportionate application of the death penalty in cases where the victim is white compared to cases where the victim is black reflect a disturbing racial calculus: White lives are considered to be more valuable than black lives, because the killing of a white is treated as a more serious crime—a crime worthy of a more severe punishment—than the killing of a black.

And at a third level, following from this devaluation of black life, we can see that the judicial failure to acknowledge racially disproportionate capital sentencing shows a systemic disregard for black communities. By treating the lives of black victims as being less valuable than the lives of white victims, the Court's death penalty jurisprudence deprives black communities of equal access to and treatment by the justice system. Professor Randall Kennedy has pointed out a seeming paradox in claims of this kind—he notes that because most killers of blacks are other blacks, correcting the systemic bias that assigns more lenient punishment to killers of blacks would ultimately result in more blacks being sent to death row. Kennedy argues that "the [black] community as a whole is disadvantaged by the relative leniency extended to killers of blacks, but black . . . criminals who murder Negroes benefit from the undervaluation of black victims. Remedying that bias . . . might move some black criminals closer to the gas chamber." [43]

The fallacy of this assertion, with all due respect to my colleague, Professor Kennedy, is that he assumes the way to rectify this imbalance is to move in the direction of executing more people—that is, he claims that the way to address the undervaluation of black life is to sentence black killers of other blacks to death at the same (higher) rate at which black killers of whites are sentenced to death. However, we could approach the problem instead by ceasing to over-value white life so much—that is, we could decrease the rate at which we execute black killers of whites such that it matches the rate at which we execute black killers of blacks. Rather than executing more people, we could execute fewer.

More importantly, the undervaluation of black life is not just evident in our capital sentencing rates, but is seen in the grossly racially disproportionate way in which our entire system of criminal justice operates. These racial differences occur at every stage of criminal processing, from arrest, prosecution, and jury selection to trial conduct, sentencing, and parole.

Justice Powell's majority opinion in McCleskey recognized this reality, when he noted, as I quoted earlier, that "McCleskey's claim, taken to its logical conclusion, throws into serious question the principles that underlie our entire criminal justice system."[44] Justice Powell recognized that if statistical evidence of racially disparate impact sufficed to call the procedural regularity of the death penalty into question, every stage of the criminal justice system would be vulnerable to the same charge. Unfathomably, rather than taking that as a reason to reject the death penalty imposed in McCleskey's case, Justice Powell claimed that the Court should punt on the issue, leaving it instead to the legislature to deal with if it so chose. As Justice Brennan suggested in his dissenting opinion, this astounding rationale "[t]aken on its face . . . seems to suggest a fear of too much justice."[45] This is exactly the claim I am making with respect to the disregard for black defendants, black victims, and black communities that we see in the way the death penalty is administered—capital punishment is but one particularly egregious example of the system-wide failure to offer to blacks the same amount of justice.

CONCLUSION: STRATEGIC QUESTIONS
FOR DEATH PENALTY OPPONENTS

This discussion of the current state of the system of capital punishment in America leads to an obvious question: Now what? What strategies can we pursue to move toward the possible objectives identified in the title of this conference—Abolition, Moratorium, or Reform? And as an abolitionist, I must ask as well: How do we choose which of these objectives to pursue most vigorously?

Professors Carol Steiker and Jordan Steiker have argued that the history of constitutional regulation of the death penalty since the Gregg v. Georgia[46] decision in 1976 has focused almost entirely on making incremental refinements to procedural aspects of the capital sentencing process.[47] If we think of opposition to the death penalty as having been effective mostly along the lines of incremental procedural fixes, it does not take much of a stretch to see that the current system of capital punishment is really in continuity with the American history of extra-legal violence and lynching—it is just more procedurally protected and has the minor additional virtue of being legal.

This point raises important issues of strategy for those who oppose the death penalty. As an abolitionist, I feel that we must constantly be asking what the likely outcome will be from any arguments we raise against the death penalty. Most arguments of unconstitutionality could be addressed in ways that actually strengthen, or further entrench, the system of capital punishment in this country. As one commentator recently noted: "[B]y focusing on flaws in the operation of the death penalty, opponents run the risk of surrendering the moral argument. They might also find themselves inadvertently helping to repair a system they would rather see eliminated," ending up with a "modernized, sanitized death penalty." [48]

For example, the issue of innocence and DNA testing has been much in the news lately. [On January 13, 2000], Illinois Governor George Ryan imposed an indefinite moratorium on executions in his state, following the exoneration of thirteen prisoners who had been incorrectly sent to death row. And the recent book by Barry Scheck, Peter Neufeld, and Jim Dwyer—*Actual Innocence*—conducted an extensive analysis of the risks of executing innocent defendants and suggested that there is some evidence that we have already executed defendants who were wrongly convicted.[49] The risk of executing the innocent can be a powerful argument for the abolition of the death penalty, but it can also be used by retentionists to strengthen their position as well. Say that the resources are made available to deploy DNA testing in every capital case, and the identity of the defendant is positively identified each time—concern about innocence would no longer be a valid objection to the death penalty. As one author argued recently:

> DNA evidence will in fact lead to greater support for the death penalty in the long run. . . . While many people in this country currently may be concerned by the potential for mistakes in determining the guilt of a defendant, once they are convinced that there is little likelihood of mistake, the majority will continue to support the death penalty.[50]

As another example, a number of recent legal challenges to the system of capital punishment in America have focused on the "death row phenomenon"—the claim that extensive incarceration under the conditions on death row causes such psychological trauma as to constitute cruel and unusual punishment in violation of the Eighth Amendment. A number of abolitionists have argued that the procedural requirements of the administration of the death penalty in America result in so many levels of direct and collateral review that all condemned prisoners face the possibility of an indeterminate and inordinately long stay on death row. Indeed, a number of foreign and international tribunals have accepted this claim. Again, however, there is a retentionist argument lurking here—if there is a problem with excessive delay in the execution of a death sentence, we should just pass more laws like the Antiterrorism and Effective Death Penalty Act of 1996 (AEDPA), to restrict the opportunities for collateral review of a death sentence.

It is even possible that a moratorium, such as that in place in Illinois, and as proposed nationwide by the American Bar Association, could serve as a means for marshaling support for the continued use of capital punishment rather than its abolition. A recent survey of public opinion on death penalty matters reveals that about the same percentage of Americans favor a moratorium as favor the death penalty, and notes that these results are not necessarily inconsistent.[51]

All of these examples raise the question whether any of the successes that the abolition movement has achieved, especially since the death penalty was reinstated after Gregg, have brought us any closer to getting rid of capital punishment for good; or whether at each juncture we have only pointed out the most glaring errors so that retentionists could fix them and then say—see, it's okay for us to have the death penalty, we've fixed the irregularities in the system. This is not an unimportant concern; after all, most of the procedural protections now provided for in the administration of capital punishment came out of constitutional challenges to the death penalty.

One way that the strategy of incremental, procedural change might succeed is to force what might be called the "Blackmun Revelation." As Justice Harry Blackmun wrote in his dissenting opinion in Callins v. Collins,[52] just months before stepping down from the Supreme Court:

> From this day forward, I no longer shall tinker with the machinery of death. For more than 20 years I have endeavored—indeed, I have struggled—along with a majority of this Court, to develop procedural and substantive rules that would lend more than the mere appearance of fairness to the death penalty endeavor. Rather than continue to coddle the Court's delusion that the desired level of fairness has been achieved and the need for regulation eviscerated, I feel morally and intellectually obligated simply to concede that the death penalty experiment has failed.[53]

The Blackmun Revelation is thus that none of these incremental changes ever ultimately remedy the problem, so at some point we must conclude that perhaps the problem cannot be remedied.

This is the same revelation that Justice Powell reached, as I mentioned earlier, although regrettably he was off the Court by this time. As Justice Powell's biographer has claimed, his statement that he would change his vote in McCleskey was based not on fundamental moral opposition to the death penalty, but rather on a concern that it could never be fairly and non-arbitrarily administered.

As Justice Blackmun further stated in Callins:

> Twenty years have passed since this Court declared that the death penalty must be imposed fairly, and with reasonable consistency, or not at all, see Furman v. Georgia, and, despite the effort of the States and courts to

devise legal formulas and procedural rules to meet this daunting challenge, the death penalty remains fraught with arbitrariness, discrimination, caprice, and mistake. This is not to say that the problems with the death penalty today are identical to those that were present 20 years ago. Rather, the problems that were pursued down one hole with procedural rules and verbal formulas have come to the surface somewhere else, just as virulent and pernicious as they were in their original form. [54]

Are we just chasing these problems down one hole, only to have them reappear, just as virulent and pernicious, from another? How can we shape our advocacy and activism to put the death penalty away for good?

The struggle for racial equality is inextricably tied to the struggle for fairness in the criminal justice system. And in both of these struggles, there is a long road ahead. Six months before he died, Justice Marshall spoke from Independence Hall in Philadelphia, where he received the Liberty Bell Award on July 4, 1992. He described the unfinished journey to racial equality as follows:

> I wish I could say that racism and prejudice were only distant memories . . . and that liberty and equality were just around the bend. I wish I could say that America has come to appreciate diversity and to see and accept similarity.
>
> But as I look around, I see not a nation of unity but of division—Afro and white, indigenous and immigrant, rich and poor, educated and illiterate.
>
> But there is a price to be paid for division and isolation. . . .
>
> We cannot play ostrich. Democracy cannot flourish amid fear. Liberty cannot bloom amid hate. Justice cannot take root amid rage. . . . We must go against the prevailing wind. We must dissent from the indifference. We must dissent from the apathy. We must dissent from the fear, the hatred and the mistrust. We must dissent from a government that has left its young without jobs, education, or hope. We must dissent from the poverty of vision and the absence of moral leadership. We must dissent because America can do better, because America has no choice but to do better. . . .
>
> Take a chance, won't you? Knock down the fences that divide. Tear apart the walls that imprison. Reach out; freedom lies just on the other side.[55]

NOTES

1. Frederick Douglass, The United States Cannot Remain Half-Slave and Half-Free, Speech on the Occasion of the Twenty-First Anniversary of Emancipation in the District of Columbia, delivered in the Congregational Church, Washington, D.C. (April 16, 1883), in *The Life and Writings of Frederick Douglass, Reconstruction and After* 357 (Philip S. Foner, ed., 1975).

2. See Mark Z. Barabak, America Attacked; *Times* Poll; U.S. Keen to Avenge Attacks, *L.A. Times*, Sept. 16, 2001, A1 (noting that 68% of non-white poll respondents supported racial profiling of "people who fit the theoretical description of a terrorist").

3. 122 S. Ct. 2242 (2002).

4. 492 U.S. 302 (1989).

5. Atkins, 122 S. Ct. at 2252.

6. 122 S. Ct. 2428 (2002).

7. United States v. Quinones, 205 F. Supp. 2d 256, 257 (S.D.N.Y. 2002).

8. See United States v. Fell, 2002 WL 31113946 (D.Vt. 2002).

9. James S. Liebman et al., A Broken System: Error Rates in Capital Cases, 1973–1995 i, 4–5 (2000), available at http://justice.policy.net/proactive /newsroom/release.vtml?id=18200.

10. See James S. Liebman, et al., *A Broken System, Part II: Why There Is So Much Error in Capital Cases, and What Can Be Done About It* ii–iii (2002), available at http:// justice.policy.net/proactive/newsroom /release.vtml? id-26641.

11. The case of Ed Johnson's lynching is described in detail in Mark Curriden & Leroy Phillips, Jr., *Contempt of Court: The Turn-of-the-Century Lynching that Launched 100 Years of Federalism* (New York: Faber and Faber, 1999).

12. 214 U.S. 386 (1909).

13. 163 U.S. 537 (1896).

14. Id. at 559 (Harlan, J., dissenting), quoted in Curriden & Phillips, supra note 21, at 11.

15. See Gunnar Myrdal, *An American Dilemma: The Negro Problem and Modern Democracy, Transaction* 36, 563 (1944).

16. Walter T. Howard, *Lynchings: Extralegal Violence in Florida During the 1930s* 139 (Selinsgrove, PA: Susquehanna University Press, 1995).

17. Jesse Jackson, *Legal Lynching: Racism, Injustice, and the Death Penalty* 26 (1996) (quoting the past of Walla Walla prison in Washington).

18. Emma Coleman Jordan, *Crossing the River of Blood Between Us*: Lynching, Violence, Beauty, and the Paradox of Feminist History, 3. *J. Gender Race & Just.* 545, 547 (2000).

19. 476 U.S. 79 (1986).

20. Id. at 102 (Marshall, J., concurring).

21. Id. at 104 n.3.

22. Id. at 104.

23. Theodore McMillian & Christopher J. Petrini, Batson v. Kentucky: A Promise

Unfulfilled, 58 UMKC L. Rev. 361,363 (1990).

24. 100 U.S. 303 (1879).

25. 380 U.S. 202 (1965).

26. Jackson v. Alabama, 516 So. 2d 768, 772 (Ala. 1986).

27. 530 So. 2d 849 (Ala. Crim. App. 1987).

28. 755 S.W.2d 397 (Mo. Ct. App. 1988).

29. 433 U.S. 584 (1977).

30. 481 U.S. 279 (1987).

31. See David C. Baldus et al., Comparative Review of Death Sentences: An Empirical Study of the Georgia Experience, 74 *J. Crim. L. & Criminology* 661 (1983).

32. McCleskey, 481 U.S. at 287.

33. Id.

34. Id. at 292 n.7.

35. Id. at 282 (quoting case syllabus).

36. Id. at 314–19 (citations omitted).

37. McCleskey, 481 U.S. at 344 (Brennan, J., dissenting).

38. Id. at 321–322 (citations omitted).

39. See John C. Jeffries, Jr., Justice Lewis F. Powell, Jr. 451(1994). In addition, Justice Powell noted that he now thought capital punishment should be abolished entirely. Id.

40. See David C. Baldus et al., The Use of Peremptory Challenges in Capital Murder Trials: A Legal and Empirical Analysis, 3 *U. Pa. J. Const. L.* 3 (2001); David C. Baldus et al., Racial Discrimination and the Death Penalty in the Post-Furman Era: An Empirical and Legal Overview, with Recent Findings from Philadelphia, 83 *Cornell L. Rev.* 1638 (1998).

41. See Baldus et al., *Use of Peremptory Challenges*, supra note 78, at 85 fig. 6.

42. See William J. Bowers et al., Death Sentencing in Black and White: An Empirical Analysis of the Role of Jurors' Race and Jury Racial Composition, 3 *U. Pa. J. Const. L.* 171 (2001).

43. See Randall L. Kennedy, McCleskey v. Kemp: Race, Capital Punishment, and the Supreme Court, 101 *Harv. L. Rev.* 1388, 1393 (1988).

44. McCleskey, 481 U.S. at 314–15.

45. Id. at 339 (Brennan, J., dissenting).

46. 428 U.S. 153 (1976).

47. See Carol S. Steiker & Jordan M. Steiker, Sober Second Thoughts: Reflections on Two Decades of Constitutional Regulation of Capital Punishment, 109 *Harv. L. Rev.* 355 (1995).

48. Thomas Healy, Death Penalty Support Drops as Debate Shifts; Foes Turning Focus from Moral Issues to Flaws in the System, *Baltimore Sun,* July 25, 2001, at 1A.

49. See Jim Dwyer, Peter Neufeld & Barry Scheck, Actual Innocence (2000).

50. John B. Wefing, Wishful Thinking by Ronald J. Tabak: Why DNA Evidence Will Not Lead to the Abolition of the Death Penalty, 33 *Conn. L. Rev.* 861, 861–62 (2001).

51. See Richard Morin and Claudia Deane, Support for Death Penalty Eases; McVeigh's Execution Approved, While Principle Splits Public, *Wash. Post,* May 3, 2001, at A9.

52. 510 U.S. 1141 (1994).

53. Id. at 1145 (Blackmun, J., dissenting from denial of certiorari).

54. Id. at 1144–45.

55. Carl T. Rowan, *Dream Makers, Dream Breakers: The World of Justice Thurgood Marshall* 453–54 (quoting Justice Marshall) (1993).

25

❊

Unintended Consequences of Politically Popular Sentencing Policy

The Homicide Promoting Effects of "Three Strikes" in U.S. Cities (1980–1999)

Tomislav Kovandzic
John J. Sloan
Lynne Vieraitis

Three strikes laws are a popular sentencing requirement passed by legislatures, often in response to public outrage over individual case examples of horrible crimes committed by a person with a criminal history. The expectation is that these laws will prevent future crimes committed by repeat offenders. Yet as a wide array of political science literature has demonstrated, sometimes legislation does not have its desired effect. Kovandzic et al demonstrate that three strikes legislation is having an undesirable outcome.

Source: From Tomislav Kovandzic, John J. Sloan, and Lynne Vieraitis, Unintended Consequences of Politically Popular Sentencing Policy: The Homicide Promoting Effects of "Three Strikes" in U.S. Cities (1980–1999), *Criminology and Public Policy,* vol. 1, no. 3 (2002), pp. 399–424, with some editing.

Facing public pressure to address high violent crime rates in the late 1980s and early 1990s, policy makers responded by strengthening existing laws targeting repeat offenders. Between 1993 and 1996, twenty five states and the federal government enacted "three-strikes" laws mandating longer prison terms for offenders with prior convictions who were subsequently convicted of serious crimes like murder, rape, aggravated robbery, aggravated assault, and kidnapping (Austin and Irwin, 2001).

The rationale for these laws is grounded in the "expected utility" principle of classic and neoclassic theory, which states that criminals calculate the potential benefits and costs of their actions and are less likely to commit crime when expected costs outweigh rewards. Enhanced terms of incarceration mandated by these laws are thus assumed to raise the expected costs (or lower the expected benefit) for offenders subject to them with the result that crime levels would decrease.

The problem is that three-strikes laws, like other initiatives aimed at controlling crime, may result in significant unintended consequences. Criminologists and other experts on sentencing have identified possible negative side effects of three-strikes laws, including: the high costs of incarcerating aging inmates (Shichor and Sechrest, 1996; Walker, 2001); the costs of building and operating additional prisons; difficulties controlling inmates serving life sentences; and the impact on courts as more defendants facing a "third strike" charge demand jury trials. Previous research on the application of repeat-offender laws has also highlighted the racial disparity that results because of the increased incarceration of minorities (Crawford, Chiricos, and Kleck, 1998) and the laws' failure to reduce crime rates through deterrence or incapacitation (Kovandzic, 2001; Macallair and Males, 1999; Marvell and Moody, 2001). Perhaps most alarming, however, is the recent finding by Marvell and Moody (2001) that homicide rates actually *increase* following passage of three-strikes laws.

According to Marvell and Moody (2001), criminals facing lengthy prison terms upon conviction for a third strike may take steps to reduce the chances of being caught, prosecuted, and convicted by changing their *modus operandi*. They may, for example decide to kill victims, witnesses, or police officers to reduce the chance of apprehension.[1] As Marvell and Moody (2001:91) suggested, "Everything else being the same, when the penalties for a crime and for an exacerbated version of that crime are similar, the criminal can be expected to commit the exacerbated version if that reduces the chances of apprehension and conviction." In effect, an offender with "two strikes" faces sentence for a "third strike" that would equal the sentence he/she would face upon being convicted of homicide. Circumstances such as these, according to Marvell and Moody (2001:92), result in little marginal deterrence for offenders, creating little dissuasion from committing the homicide if doing so would lessen the chances of resistance by victims, arrest by the police, or conviction at trial.[2]

Accepting the above logic and assuming the circumstances described are indeed rare, their impact on homicide rates can still be relatively large (Marvell and Moody, 2001:92–93). As they demonstrated, assuming that the above circumstances are present in only 1 of every 1,000 violent crimes, because the ratio of homicide to all other violent crimes is approximately .006, additional homicides created by the law would increase the total number of homicides in a three-strikes state by approximately 17 percent.

To test their hypothesis that three-strikes laws increase homicide, Marvell and Moody (2001) evaluated three-strikes laws in 24 states for the period 1970–1998. Using regression analysis, they found that three-strikes laws increased homicide rates by 10 to 12 percent over the short term (or roughly 1,400 additional homicides in all 24 three-strikes states) and by 23 to 29 percent over the long term (roughly 3,300 additional homicides per year). The impact occurred in almost all 24 states with three-strikes laws. Results for rape, robbery, assault, burglary, larceny, and auto-theft were generally nonsignificant and were often in the unexpected positive direction. Because there is virtually no evidence that the laws have any crime reduction impacts through deterrence or incapacitation that might compensate for the additional homicides, the authors called for the repeal of three-strikes laws.

The finding that laws designed to decrease crime actually increased homicide, arguably the most serious of all crime, underscores the need for additional research on the potential lethal impact of three-strikes laws. Given the enormity of Marvell and Moody's (2001) findings and their implications for criminal justice policy, it was decided to reexamine the relationship between rates of homicide and the adoption of three-strikes laws.

As a general rule, we follow the procedures used by Marvell and Moody, except that we use cities (as opposed to states) as our unit of analysis and we extend the study period to 2000, which provides us with two additional years of post-intervention data. We believe cities are the preferred unit of analysis for revisiting the three-strikes and homicide question because they exhibit greater within-city variation in homicide rates over time (and factors affecting homicide rates) that can be obscured when larger units of analysis such as states or metropolitan areas are used. It is precisely this within-city variation in homicide rates that we are trying to explain with the adoption of three-strikes laws. In addition, cities minimize the likelihood of within-unit variation, which can be a source of aggregation bias when larger, more heterogeneous units such as states or metropolitan areas are used. The greater such bias, the more problematic any inferences about individual-level behavior—such as inferring that prospective three-strike defendants might kill victims and witnesses to reduce the chance of identification while using state or metropolitan area data. The following discussion summarizes the procedures, results, and policy implications of our research.

METHODS

To test whether the passage of three-strikes laws cause an increase in homicides, a multiple time series design was employed, with panel data from 1980 to 1999 for all 188 U.S. cities that had a population of 100,000 or more in 1990, and for which relevant data were available. Of the 188 cities, 110 resided in states that passed three-strikes laws between 1993 and 1996. The multiple time series design is considered one of the best quasi-experimental research designs for assessing the impact of changes in criminal justice policy when a more thorough experimental control is not possible or practical. (Berk, et al., 1979; Campbell and Stanley, 1963, pp. 55–57).[3] The main advantage of the design is that it allows us to treat the adoption of three-strike laws as a sort of "natural experiment," with the 110 cities residing within three-strike states as "treatment cities" and the 78 no-change cities as "controls."[4] Specifically, changes in homicide rates in the treatment cities from the pre-three strike law period to the post-three strike law period are compared to changes in homicide rates observed in the control cities. If three-strike laws increase homicide then the adoption cities should experience, on average, an increase in homicide greater than that experienced in the nonadoption cities in or around the time the laws were adopted. To further strengthen the basis for causal inference, the estimated impacts of three-strikes laws on homicides were compared to the impacts on other types of crimes. This additional analysis controls for missing variables that could be confounded with the passage of three-strikes laws. Another causal variable would be confounded with the law only if it influenced homicide and other crimes differently, and if it changed markedly following the passage of three-strike laws.

Each three-strikes law was represented using a binary dummy variable scored 1 starting the full first year after the law went into effect, and 0 otherwise. In the year a law went into effect, the dummy variable is the portion of the year remaining after the effective date. For cities in states without three-strikes laws the dummy variable is coded zero for all years. Inferences about the effect of three-strikes laws on homicide rates are based on the sign and statistical significance of the three-strikes dummy variable. A positive and significant estimate suggests that homicide rates have grown faster (or declined at slower rate) in three-strike cities as compared to cities without the laws, while a negative and significant coefficient points to the contrary. The laws and their effective dates were obtained from Marvell and Moody (2001), and were verified by checking relevant secondary sources.[5]

The main dependent variable is the homicide rate per 100,000 population. These data were obtained from the FBI *Uniform Crime Reports* (1981–2001), which only reports homicide counts for a city if the responsible law enforcement agency submits 12 complete monthly reports.[6]

Control Variables

The analysis includes seven specific control variables that prior macro-level crime research and theory suggests are important correlates of homicide. The decision as to which control variables to include was based on a review of previous macro-level studies linking homicide rates to the structural characteristics of ecological units like cities (see Kovandzic, et al.). The specific control variables included in the homicide models were: percent African Americans, percent of the population ages 18 to 24, percent of female headed households, percent of the population living below the poverty line, per-capita income, percent of the population living alone, and state-level prison population. Most of these variables account for causal processes emphasized by strain/deprivation, social disorganization, and opportunity/routine activities theories.[7]

Analytic Methods

Similar to Marvell and Moody (2001), reliance was placed on a statistical technique known as regression analysis that allows us to determine whether a relationship exists between the adoption of three-strike laws and homicide rates after other effects have already been taken into consideration. The regressions are also "weighted by the city population" because of the very high level of instability in homicide rates over time in smaller cities. By weighting the regressions by city population less emphasis is placed on the smaller cities and more on the larger, which experience much more stable homicide rates over time.

Another problem must be addressed in the regression analysis is what happens if three-strikes laws are adopted at the same time as an upward national trend in homicide rates? The solution to this problem is to add a separate dummy variable for each year in the homicide regression. For example, one variable equals 1 for all observations during 1980 and zero for all other times. In essence, the year dummies control for the average change in homicide rates from one year to the next that are due to nationwide forces. As a result, if the homicide rate increases nationally from 1995 to 1996, the year-dummy variables will measure the average increase in homicide rates between those two years and allow us to determine if there was an additional increase, even after controlling for this national increase, in cities that resided in states adopting three-strikes laws. Similarly, a separate dummy variable for each city was included in the homicide regression, and they control for unobserved factors that remained approximately stable during the study period that caused homicide rates to differ from city to city. Examples of these factors might include economic deprivation, criminal gun ownership, and law enforcement strategies. Including the city dummy variables avoids the possibility the findings may show that three-strike laws appear to increase homicide simply because the cities with these laws happened to have high homicide rates to begin with. Rather, the findings will allow us to test whether, on average, the homicide rate increases in cities *after* the adoption of three-strikes laws.

The results provide exceptionally strong support for Marvell and Moody's (2001) claim that homicide rates grew faster (or declined at a slower rate) in three-strikes cities as compared to non-adoption cities. The findings imply that passage of a three-strikes law increased homicides, on average, by 13 to 14 percent over the short-term, and 16 to 24 percent over the long-term. This translates to approximately 8 additional homicides in each three-strikes city in the first year (or 880 homicides in all 110 three-strike cities) and roughly 1,300 homicides per year in the 110 three-strikes cities in the last year. These results are virtually identical to those obtained by Marvell and Moody (2001), who found a 10 to 12 percent in homicides the first year the laws were in effect (about 1,400 homicides per year in all the three-strike states) and a 23 to 29 percent increase in homicides in the last year of the analysis (about 3,300 homicides per year across the three-strikes states).

Are the Results for Homicide
Due to Rival Causal Factors?

As Marvell and Moody (2001) noted, because the theoretical arguments for why three-strikes laws might increase homicide rates do not apply to other crimes, the finding that homicide rates are positively associated with the adoption of three-strikes laws would not be very compelling if other crimes also increased following their implementation. Such a finding would suggest that some other, unmeasured, variable(s) that changed during the 1993 to 1995 time frame (e.g., drug market and/or gang activity) was responsible for the observed homicide increases in three-strike cities, something that could also have affected violent and property crime rates more generally. On the other hand, if homicide was the only crime that increased following passage of the laws, one can virtually rule out the possibility that factors confounded by the passage of three-strikes laws could have accounted for increases in homicide. To examine this possibility, the date was reanalyzed with total reported crime (not including homicide) and violent crime (not including homicide) as the dependent variables. The results of these analyses showed little evidence that the apparent positive association between the passage of three-strike laws and homicide rates is due to the effects of omitted factors not included in our regression analysis.

In another set of analyses, total crime and violent crime as independent variables was added into the regression analysis. The rationale for doing so was that if violent crime was growing faster in three-strikes cities compared to non-three strikes cities, it could have accounted for most, if not all, of the impact. Adding total crime and violent crime to the analyses, however, yielded results similar to the analyses without these variables. Thus, there is no evidence that overall growth in violent crime in three-strikes cities was responsible for the observed increases in homicide rates in these cities.[8]

Addressing Potential Simultaneity Bias

Another potential threat to the results presented above is simultaneity bias. Simultaneity is possible because policy makers might have responded to growing crime problems by passing three-strikes laws, i.e., states with higher homicide rates may have been more prone to pass three-strikes laws. It can be safely assumed, however, that homicide rates probably did not have an immediate impact on the passage of three-strikes laws because it takes considerable time for crime statistics to be compiled and for states to enact crime legislation. Also, it is unlikely that state governments would enact legislation based solely on crime rates in the current year, while not considering crime in earlier years. No evidence was found that increases in homicide rates prompted state legislatures to enact three-strikes laws.

Individual City Results

Like most criminal justice policy evaluations of legal interventions, there is an implicit, albeit unlikely, assumption that the impact of the intervention under study is identical across all ecological units. Recent research by, among others, Black and Nagin (1998), McDowall, Loftin, and Wiersema (1992), and Pesaran and Smith (1995) suggests, however, that the assumption in regression analysis of a constant impact of legal interventions across ecological units is probably unrealistic. At present, by aggregating the three-strikes law dummy variables into a single variable, it was assumed that all cities located in states with three-strikes laws would exhibit similar changes in homicide rates. As Marvell and Moody (2001) noted, however, this assumption is probably unrealistic given variation in (1) the publicity surrounding the passage of the laws, (2) differences in the severity of the laws, (3) the amount of discretion prosecutors and judges have in applying the laws, and (4) other contemporaneous changes in criminal law and operations. All of these factors are likely to vary across and within cities in three-strikes states and are probably important in influencing criminals' awareness of the laws, the perceived extent of their use, and the eventual actions of criminals at crime scenes. In such a situation, there will be a distribution of effects for three-strikes laws instead of one common impact. On the other hand, one might expect a few cities to witness increases in homicide following the passage of three-strikes laws as a matter of chance alone, and it is impossible to tell which these are. To explore this issue, we followed Marvell and Moody's (2001) recommendation of creating separate law variables for each city, which are scored 1 for the law in the particular city and 0 elsewhere.

When the three-strikes laws are represented by separate dummy variables, the results vary widely, but the overall impression is the same: three-strikes laws increased homicide rates. As noted above, it is possible that variation in the severity of the laws and their enforcement might be responsible for these results. Similar to Marvell and Moody (2001:101–102), we categorized California and Georgia as having especially "severe" laws (based on statutory wording) and Connecticut, Florida, Indiana, Kansas, Louisiana, Maryland, North Carolina, and Utah as having laws that are probably less severe than most. Regarding enforcement of the laws, we used the results of the survey conducted by the Campaign for an Effective Crime Policy, which noted greater application of the laws in California, Nevada, Florida, Georgia, and Washington (Dickey and Hollenhorst, 1998).[9] Like Marvell and Moody (2001), we found that the most severe laws appeared to have the smallest impact on homicide rates, suggesting that increased murders committed in these cities may have been offset by some deterrence effects. For example, results indicate that while the coefficients on the three-strikes variables were disproportionately positive, only 4 of the 82 individual law variables for cities in California are significant and positive, while none are significant and positive for the 8 individual cities in Georgia. On the other hand, 9 of the 22 significant and positive individual city law variables were in states with laws that could be considered weaker than most. Likewise, the coefficients for the individual city law variables do not give the impression that homicide rates increased more in areas where the laws were applied most often. A possible exception is Nevada, where 2 of the 4 individual city law variables (both for Las Vegas) were significant and positive. Beyond that, however, there is little evidence that increased application of the laws produced greater increases in homicide.

There are numerous reasons why the laws might not have similar or even stronger impacts for three-strike cities located in states where the laws are strictly enforced, but we cannot determine which of them explain the results. First, the lack of any apparent positive impact of three-strikes laws in these cities could be due to counterbalancing effects of the increases in homicides being offset by the laws deterrent and incapacitative effects. Another possible explanation for the lack of stricter third-strike laws increasing homicide is criminal migration. If criminals leave states where the laws are strictly enforced to commit crimes in states where the laws are rarely applied or do not exist, increases in homicide might roughly cancel out the decreases in homicide due to criminals relocating. Finally, since it is highly unlikely prospective three-strike offenders would have accurate information about how often three-strike sentences are imposed in their particular location, one could argue that variation in sentencing practices across cities is largely irrelevant for purposes of assessing the effects of three-strikes laws on crime. Nonetheless, there is little doubt that the impact of the laws in cities where the laws were applied most frequently was positive.

CONCLUSION AND IMPLICATIONS

This study revisited the claim by Marvell and Moody (2001) that homicide rates might increase following the passage of three-strikes laws. Using city-level panel data for 1980 to 1999 and numerous control variables, it was found that in cities with three-strikes laws, homicide rates increased on average 13 to 14 percent over the short-term and 16 to 24 percent over the long term, compared to cities without the laws.

The present findings lend further support to existing theoretical and empirical research demonstrating the disutility and potentially lethal danger of three-strikes laws. Despite their public support and political popularity, policy-makers should seriously consider repealing three-strikes laws. They are simply not the panacea for the nation's violent crime may actually exacerbate the most serious crime—homicide.

Three-strikes laws are based on the principle of incapacitation—violent recidivist criminals would be unable to commit further crimes while incarcerated. But it was also hypothesized that these laws would also deter others from continuing or contemplating crime. Inherent in this hypothesis is the assumption that offenders are rational, weighing the costs and benefits of criminal behavior prior to engaging in it. That is, offenders must reason that the potential benefits of crime outweigh its costs. If true, a "rational" offender with a criminal history that includes two felony convictions could calculate that the best way to minimize the risk of apprehension and subsequent conviction as a three-strikes offender would be to eliminate victims or police officers—those who could increase the likelihood of the offender being caught and prosecuted. This would be a rational (i.e., calculated) response in that it minimizes an important cost—apprehension.

The public's fear of crime and its frustration with repeat offenders was largely induced by the amplification of violent crime in the national media, in particular, the saturation of attention afforded to a few select, albeit horrendous, cases (e.g., Polly Klaas). Public outcry over these cases galvanized policymakers to "get tough" and "do something" to "fix" the crime problem. In response, legislators passed three-strikes laws.

Although policymakers anticipated the laws would "fix the problem" by deterring active criminals and incapacitating repeat offenders (thus preventing them from preying upon citizens), the climate of fear and hysteria in which the statutes were passed actually increased the likelihood of failure and/or unintended negative consequences. In a climate of fear or "moral panic," people are more willing to believe that something must be done and done quickly without looking carefully at the full set of possible consequences of the proposed solutions (see: Kleck, 1999).

Based on the theoretical and empirical research on three strikes legislation and with the recognition that policymaking is inherently a political process, we offer the following suggestions to policymakers and criminal justice researchers. First, legislators should be aware of "claimsmakers" and media distortion of social problems and resist passing "quick fix" solutions in a climate of public fear. Second, policymakers should take more care to weigh, not just the potential benefits of a proposed crime control solution but the potential costs as well, and researchers should become more active in providing assistance in this process. Third, researchers should resist the tendency to separate policy criticism, positive or negative, from criminological science by continuing to conduct empirical studies of major crime control policies to assess their impact and more importantly, analyze and discuss the implications of their findings. Considering the impact of crime control policies on not only offenders, but the public in general, researchers have an obligation to inform policymakers of the potential benefits as well as the costs of these policies. Future research can assist in this process.

Two studies have now found that three-strikes laws increase homicide rates. Future research, however, is clearly warranted and might take several approaches. One avenue for future research would involve conducting surveys of active offenders in three strikes states to determine whether offenders are aware of three strikes enhancements and if so, to what lengths they would go to avoid detection and prosecution. One such a study was done in California, but was limited to interviews with active juvenile offenders (Schafter, 1999). Further research of this nature would, through interviews with active offenders, reveal either the possible crime-promoting or the deterrent effects of these laws. Additional research could also examine, using official data combined with surveys of judges and prosecutors, the extent to which these laws are actually implemented. This would allow researchers to examine variation in the implementation of the laws, as well as the impact on crime rates of variability in their application. Finally, future research could expand the scope of the present study by including serious crimes of violence (e.g., robbery, aggravated assault) and serious property crimes (e.g., burglary) as the dependent variable. Such a study would address the extent to which three-strikes laws impact other serious crimes.

As Dye (1978:3) observed, "[p]ublic policy is whatever government chooses to do or not to do," and when government "chooses to do something," the outcome of that choice can affect citizens both directly and indirectly through intended and unintended consequences. Of course, not all unintended consequences are negative. The problem becomes the extent the impacts of a policy may actually "backfire" and make the target of the problem worse.

Criminal justice policies have consequences for both individuals and society as a whole, some of which are unintended and some of which are not necessarily positive. As the present study demonstrated, these unintended consequences can be lethal. While this is only the second published study that examined the possible homicide promoting effects of three-strikes laws, it contributes to a growing body of literature on how these laws failed to reduce crime and other unintended negative side. In light of previous theoretical and empirical research on the "costs" of three-strikes laws, we join others advocating their repeal. It is possible that policymakers and the public are willing to "pay" some of these "costs," however, it is questionable as to whether they are willing to "pay" in human lives.

NOTES

1. Recent evidence lends supports to the claim that offenders may respond to three-strikes laws with increased lethality. For example, in a survey of 500 juveniles housed in a residential lock-up facility outside Los Angeles, Schafer (1999) found that 54 percent of the juveniles indicated they "would kill or would probably kill" witnesses or police officers to avoid a life sentence that would accompany a third strike under California law. This figure increased to 65 percent among self-identified gang members. In addition, Moody [and colleagues] (2000) found that three-strikes laws increased the number of police officers killed in the line of duty by 25 percent. This translates to one additional police officer murdered every two and a half years in the average three-strikes state.

2. As Marvell and Moody (2001) note, this reasoning assumes the likelihood of arrest for the current offense is equal to the likelihood of arrest for homicide. However, clearance rates for homicide are substantially higher than are clearance rates for other forms of serious violence, and far greater than clearance rates for property crimes. Therefore, the criminal's self-interest would preclude the commission of a homicide during another offense.

3. The multiple time series design has been utilized in many recent evaluations of criminal justice interventions including, juvenile curfew laws (McDowall, et al., 2000), firearm sentence enhancement laws (Marvell and Moody, 1995), concealed-carry handgun laws (e.g., Ayres and Donahue, 2003; Lott and Mustard, 1997; Lott, 2000), Brady law (Ludwig and Cook, 2000), and earlier studies examining the effects of three-strike laws (Kovandzic, et al., 2002; Marvell and Moody, 2001; Shepherd, 2002).

4. Additional advantages of the MTS design include (1) the ability to enter proxy variables for omitted variables that cause homicide rates to vary across years and cities (the proxy variables, which number nearly 400 here, are discussed further below), (2) it provides a larger sample size (n= 3,320 or more) allowing us to enter numerous control variables in the homicide models to control for factors that might be correlated with other explanatory variables, and therefore lead to spurious associations among these variables, and (3) it provides for greater statistical power (due to the large sample size), and thus makes it possible to detect more modest effects of three-strikes laws on homicide rates.

5. Three-strike laws in Montana, Vermont, and South Carolina were not examined here because they did not have a city with a population greater than 100,000 in 1990.

6. Homicide data were missing for 53 observations and were scored as missing data. Despite having a population greater than 100,000 in 1990, a decision was made to drop the following cities because of severe reporting problems during the study period: Moreno Valley, CA, Rancho Cucamonga, CA, Santa Clarita, CA, Overland Park, KS, Kansas City, KS, Cedar Rapids, IA, and Lowell, MA.

7. Year 2000 data were obtained from the U.S. Census Bureau website (http://www.census.gov) using American Fact Finder.

Income data for 1980 to 1999 were obtained from the U.S. Bureau of Economic Analysis website (http://www.bea.doc.gov). Income data are county-level estimates and we used these values as imperfect substitutes for city-level income. Personal income data was converted from a current dollar estimate to a constant-dollar 1967 basis by dividing personal income by the consumer price index (CPI). The prison population variable is the number of inmates sentenced to state institutions for more than a year (year-end estimates), available annually at the state-level. We used these values as proxies for city-level imprisonment. State-level prison population data were obtained from the Bureau of Justice Statistics website (http://www.ojp.usdoj.gov/bjs/).

8. We also tried adding a binary dummy variable for the 33 states subject to the Brady law, which became effective on February 28, 1994, and mandated background checks for prospective handgun purchasers. The addition of the Brady law dummy had very little impact on the results reported above.

9. As Marvell and Moody (2001) note, the survey is not complete and does not take into account the possibility that prosecutors may be using the laws as leverage during the plea bargaining process in order to get defendants (probably in weak cases) to accept more severe sentences that they would otherwise not accept.

REFERENCES

Austin, James (1996). The effect of "three strikes and you're out" on corrections. In David Shichor and Dale K. Sechrest (eds.), *Three Strikes and You're Out: Vengeance as Public Policy.* Thousand Oaks, CA: Sage.

Austin, James and John Irwin (2001). *It's About Time: America's Imprisonment Binge.* Belmont, CA: Wadsworth.

Baltagi, B.H., and J.M. Griffin (1997). Pooled Estimators vs. Their Heterogeneous Counterparts in the Context of Dynamic Demand for Gasoline. *Journal of Econometrics* 77:303–327.

Becker, Gary .S. (1968). Crime and punishment: An economic approach. *Journal of Political Economy* 76:169–217.

Belsley, David A., Edward Kuh, and Roy E. Welsh (1980). *Regression Diagnostics.* New York: John Wiley & Sons.

Black, D.A. and D.S. Nagin. (1998). Do right-to-carry laws deter violent crime? *Journal of Legal Studies* 27:209–219.

Campbell, Donald T. and Julian Stanley (1963). *Experimental and Quasi-Experimental Designs for Research.* Boston, MA: Houghton Mifflin.

Clear, Todd R. (2002). Reply to Gene Czajkoski. *The Criminologist* 27(2):5.

Cohen, Stanley (1972). *Folk Devils and Moral Panics.* London: MacGibbon and Kee.

Crawford, Charles, Ted Chiricos, and Gary Kleck (1998). Race, racial threat, and sentencing of habitual offenders. *Criminology* 36:481–511.

Cushman, Robert C. (1996). Effect on a local criminal justice system. In David Shichor and Dale K. Sechrest (eds.), *Three Strikes and You're Out: Vengeance as Public Policy.* Thousand Oaks, CA: Sage.

DiIulio, John J. (1994). Instant replay. *American Prospect* 18:12–18.

Dye, Thomas R. (1978). *Understanding Public Policy.* Third Edition. Englewood Cliffs, NJ: Prentice-Hall.

Economic and Demographic Research (1992). *An Empirical Examination of the Application of Florida's Habitual Offender Statute.* Tallahassee, FL: Joint Legislative Management Committee of the Florida Legislature.

Ehrlich, Issac (1973). Participation in illegitimate activities: A theoretical and empirical investigation. *Journal of Political Economy* 81:521–565.

Federal Bureau of Investigation (1979–2000). *Crime in the United States: The Uniform Crime Reports.* Washington, DC: U.S. Government Printing Office.

Fishman, Mark (1976). Crime waves as ideology. *Social Problems* 25:531–543.

Flanagan, Timothy J., James W. Marquart, and Kenneth G. Adams (eds.) (1998). *Incarcerating Criminals: Prisons and Jails in Social and Organizational Context.* New York: Oxford.

Gilsinan, James F. (1990). *Criminology and Public Policy: An Introduction.* Englewood Cliffs, NJ: Prentice-Hall.

Granger, Clive W.J. (1969). Investigating Causal Relations by Econometric Models and Cross-Spectral Methods. *Econometrica* 37:424–438.

Greene, William H. (1993). *Econometric Analysis.* New York: Macmillan.

Greenwood, Peter C., Peter Rydell, Allan F. Abrahamse, Jonathan P. Caulkins, James Chiesa, Karyn E. Model, and Stephen P. Klein (1996). Estimated benefits and costs of California's new mandatory-sentencing law. In David Shichor and Dale K. Sechrest (eds.), *Three Strikes and You're Out: Vengeance as Public Policy.* Thousand Oaks, CA: Sage.

Hamilton, James D. (1994). *Time Series Analysis.* Princeton, NJ: Princeton University Press.

Hendry, David F. (1995). *Dynamic Econometrics.* New York: Oxford University Press.

Kappler, Victor E., Mark Blumberg, and Gary W. Potter (1996). *The Mythology of Crime and Justice* (2e). Prospect Heights, IL: Waveland.

Kleck, Gary (1999). There are no lessons to be learned from Littleton. *Criminal Justice Ethics* 18(1):2–6.

Kovandzic, Tomislav V. (2001). The impact of Florida's habitual offender law on crime. *Criminology* 39:179–203.

Kovandzic, Tomislav V., Lynne M. Vieraitis, and Mark R. Yeisley (1998). The structural covariates of urban homicide: Reassessing the impact of income inequality and poverty in the post-Reagan era. *Criminology* 36:569–599.

Land, Kenneth C., Patricia L. McCall, and Lawrence E. Cohen (1990). Structural covariates of homicide rates: Are there any invariances across time and social space? *American Journal of Sociology* 95:922–963.

Levin, Andrew and Chien-Fu Lin (1992). Unit root tests in panel data: Asymptotic and finite-sample properties. Discussion paper No. 92–93. Department of Economics, University of California, San Diego, CA.

Levitt, Steven D. (1996). The effect of prison population size on crime rates: Evidence from prison overcrowding litigation. *Quarterly Journal of Economics* 111:319–351.

Lott, John R. and David B. Mustard (1997). Crime, deterrence, and right-to-carry concealed handguns. *Journal of Legal Studies* 26:1–68.

Ludwig, Jens and Philip Cook J. (2000). Homicide and suicide rates associated with implementation of the Brady Handgun Violence Prevention Act. *Journal of American Medical Association* 284:585–591.

Macallair, Dan and Males, Mike (1999). *Striking Out: The Failure of California's "Three Strikes and You're Out" Law.* San Francisco, CA: The Justice Policy Institute.

Marvell, Thomas B. and Carlisle E. Moody (1994). Prison population growth and crime reduction. *Journal of Quantitative Criminology* 10:109–140.

Marvell, Thomas B. and Carlisle E. Moody (1995). The impact of enhanced prison terms for felonies committed with guns. *Criminology* 33:247–281

Marvell, Thomas B. and Carlisle E. Moody (2001). The lethal effects of three strikes laws. *The Journal of Legal Studies* 30:89–106.

McCorkle, Richard C. and Terance D. Miethe (2002). *Panic: The Social Construction of the Street Gang Problem.* Upper Saddle, NJ: Prentice Hall.

McDowall, David, Colin Loftin, and Brian Wiersema (1992). A comparative study of the preventive effects of mandatory sentencing laws for gun crimes. *Journal of Criminal Law and Criminology* 83:378–394.

McDowall, David, Colin Loftin, and Brian Wiersema (2000). The impact of youth curfew laws on juvenile crime rates. *Crime and Delinquency* 46:76–91.

Merton, Robert K. (1936). The unintended consequences of purposive social action. *American Sociological Review* 1:894–904.

Moody, Carlisle E., Thomas B. Marvell, and Robert J. Kaminski (2000). Unintended consequences: Three strikes laws and the killing of police officers. Unpublished manuscript.

Nagin, Daniel (1978). General deterrence: a review of the empirical evidence. In Alfred Blumstein, Jacqueline Cohen, and Daniel Nagin (eds.), *Deterrence and Incapacitation: Estimating the Effects of Criminal Sanctions on Crime Rates.* Washington, DC: National Academy Press.

Patch, Peter C. (1998). The three strikes law and control of crime in California. *ACJS Today* 17(3):1–4.

Pesaran, M. Hasem and Ron Smith (1995). Estimating long-run relationships from dynamic heterogeneous panels. *Journal of Econometrics* 68:79–113.

Pindyck, Robert S. and Daniel L. Rubinfeld (1991). *Econometric Models and Economic Forecasts.* New York: McGraw Hill. SAS Institute.

SAS Institute (1993). *SAS/ETS User's Guide,* Version 6, Second Edition. Cary, NC: SAS Institute.

Schafer, John R. (1999). The deterrent effects of three-strikes law. *FBI Law Enforcement Bulletin* 68:6–10.

Shepherd, Joanna M. (2002). Fear of the First Strike: the Full Deterrent Effect of California's Two- and Three-Strikes Legislation. *Journal of Legal Studies,* 31:159–201.

Shichor, David and Dale K. Sechrest (1996). Three strikes as public policy: Future implications. In David Shichor and Dale K. Sechrest (eds.), *Three Strikes and You're Out: Vengeance as Public Policy.* Thousand Oaks, CA: Sage.

Skolnick, Jerome (1995). How not to deal with crime: The 1994 American Society of Criminology Presidential Address. *Criminology* 33:1–15.

Stigler, George J. (1970). The optimum enforcement of laws. *Journal of Political Economy* 78:526–536.

Stolzenberg, Lisa and Stewart J. D'Alessio (1997). Three strikes and you're out: The impact of California's new mandatory sentencing law and serious crime rates. *Crime and Delinquency* 43:457–469.

Surette, Ray (1998). *Media, Crime, and Criminal Justice: Images and Realities.* Belmont, CA: Wadsworth.

United States Bureau of the Census (1983). *County and City Data Book: 1983.* Washington, DC: U.S. Government Printing Office.

United States Bureau of the Census (1994). *County and City Data Book: 1994.* Washington, DC: U.S. Government Printing Office.

Walker, Samuel (2001). *Sense and Nonsense about Crime and Drugs: A Policy Guide.* Belmont, CA: Wadsworth.

Wu, Yangru (1996). Are real exchange rates nonstationary? Evidence from a panel data set. *Journal of Money, Credit, and Banking* 28:54–63.

Zimring, Franklin E. (2001). The new politics of criminal justice: Of "'three strikes,' truth-in-sentencing, and Megan's laws." In National Institute of Justice (ed.), *Perspectives on Crime and Justice: 1999–2000 Lecture Series.* Washington, DC: National Institute of Justice.

26

The Great American Gun Debate

What Research Has to Say

Gary Kleck

The gun control movement gained national momentum and credibility when former Reagan White House Press Secretary Jim Brady and his wife Sarah joined forces with many Democrats and policy groups in sponsoring the Handgun Violence Protection Act (commonly known as the Brady Bill). No policy area has more active public participation than gun control, from the legions of members in the National Rifle Association, to the effective grassroots efforts of the gun control movement. Yet public opinion and politics are not reflective of the state of the research. Gary Kleck argues that gun control has become highly politicized with little attention paid to credible evidence, and that public rhetoric does not reflect the reality of the data.

O n April 21, 1999, two young men armed with guns and explosives entered their high school in Littleton, Colorado, murdered 13 people, wounded 31 others, and then committed suicide. The mass killing set off a media frenzy and renewed calls for stricter gun laws. Yet no wave of new restrictions on guns followed Littleton, prompting pro–gun control commentators to wonder why more Americans did not push for tougher controls and prompting anti–gun control critics to respond that guns were not the problem. Spokespersons for gun control advocacy groups such as Handgun Control Inc. (later the Brady Campaign) asserted that tighter controls over gun shows would have prevented the tragedy, while representatives of the National Rifle Association contended that gun show controls were irrelevant, noting that one

Source: Written specifically for this book.

of the killers was, at the time of the shootings, old enough to buy rifles and shotguns from any gun store in Colorado. In short, the usual people said the usual things that constitute the Great American Gun Debate. Virtually ignored in the public debate and media coverage however, was the enormous body of scholarly knowledge that had accumulated in the preceding decades, and that would have shed some light on the heated debate. This chapter summarizes that body of knowledge.

THE TRADITION OF GUN OWNERSHIP
IN THE UNITED STATES

In contrast to most other nations, gun ownership has always been widespread in the United States. An average of about 46 percent of U.S. households reported owning guns in surveys in recent decades, and it is widely believed that the true share could easily be 5–10 percentage points higher. Furthermore, gun ownership may well have been even higher in the past, when the nation was more rural, and hunting and other shooting sports were more widely pursued (Kleck 1997, Chapter 3). Lindgren and Heather (2002) estimated, based on probate records from 1774, that 52 percent of male "wealthholders" (persons who had any property that needed to be allocated to heirs after their death) in the thirteen colonies owned guns at the time of their death, a figure considerably higher than the percent of elderly males who reported personally owning guns in the 1990s.

By international standards, the share of U.S. households with guns is extraordinarily high. The nearest known competitor is Switzerland, where about a third of households have guns, mainly due to military service requirements (Killias 1990). There were probably over 260 million guns in private hands in the United States at the end of 1999, about 36 percent of them handguns. The size of the U.S. gun stock—especially the handgun stock—increased enormously from the 1960s through the 1990s, though the share of U.S. households with guns showed little change. One obvious policy implication of this huge existing stock is that an enormous supply of guns would remain available, to criminals and noncriminals alike, even if all further manufacture and importation of guns ceased immediately (Kleck 1997, Chapter 3). In contrast, only a few hundred thousand guns are used to commit violent crimes each year. Thus, the available supply greatly exceeds criminal demand.

Perhaps what is most striking about the patterns of gun ownership in the United States is the fact that ownership is generally highest in those groups where violence is lowest. Although both gun ownership and violence are more frequent among males and Southerners, gun ownership is also higher among whites than blacks, higher among middle-aged people than young people, higher among married people than unmarried people, higher among richer people than poor people, and higher in rural areas and small towns than urban areas. These patterns are all the reverse of the distribution of violent criminal behavior (Kleck 1997, Chapter 3).

Most owners of guns in general, and long guns in particular, own them primarily for recreational reasons unrelated to crime. About half of handgun owners, however, as well as some long gun owners, own guns mainly for protection against crime. Most American gun ownership is culturally patterned, linked with a rural hunting subculture. The culture is transmitted across generations, with gun owners being socialized from childhood by their parents into gun ownership and use. Thus, much gun ownership results from membership in subcultural groupings and the acceptance of norms and values favorable to gun ownership and use.

Discussing the conflicts among Americans over gun control, Bruce-Briggs (1976) contrasted "two alternative views of what America is and ought to be" (p. 61) Sociologists would identify these views as elements of two distinct subcultures:

> On the one side are those who take bourgeois Europe as a model of a civilized society: a society just, equitable, and democratic; but well ordered, with the lines of responsibility and authority clearly drawn, and with decisions made rationally and correctly by intelligent men for the entire nation. On the other side are persons whose model is that of the independent frontiersman who takes care of himself and his family with no interference from the state. They are "conservative" in the sense that they cling to America's unique pre-modern tradition—a nonfeudal society with a sort of medieval liberty writ large for everyman. (p. 61)

In the gun-hunting subculture of rural and small town America, a boy's introduction to guns and hunting is an important rite of passage to manhood. Stinchcombe and his associates (1980) portrayed much gun ownership as resulting from membership in a rural hunting culture originating in the early settlement of the American frontier. They argued that the culture is found today primarily in rural areas and small towns, and among ethnic and religious groups whose ancestors came to the United States early in its preindustrial history. Persons with a family tradition of hunting and an exposure to regional values and norms encouraging hunting—especially in the South and West—are more likely to own guns. Recreational gun owners are likely to have parents who owned guns, to have obtained their first gun at an early age, and to have been trained in gun use, suggesting socialization into a sporting gun culture (Lizotte and Bordua 1980).

In contrast, among persons who own guns for protection, there is no evidence of socialization into a gun-owning subculture. Protective gun owners commonly obtain their first guns as adults, without training in gun use, and without any family background in gun ownership. Defensive handgun owners are more likely to be disconnected from any gun subcultural roots; their gun ownership is less likely to be accompanied by association with other gun owners in connection with gun-related activities, or by training in the safe handling of guns. Defensive ownership is more likely to be an individualistic response to life circumstances perceived as dangerous (Lizotte and Bordua 1980).

The evidence supports a simple explanation of the unusually high level of gun ownership in America. Most of the guns in America are rifles and shot-guns, and most of these are owned for hunting and for other shooting sports common among hunters. Unlike European nations with a feudal past, the United States has had both widespread ownership of farmland and millions of acres of public lands available for hunting. Rather than being limited to a small land-owning aristocracy, hunting has been accessible to most ordinary Americans. Having the income and leisure to take advantage of these resources, millions of Americans have hunted for recreation, long after it ceased to be essential to survival for any but an impoverished few. High gun ownership lev-els have not resulted from a lack of strict gun control laws; instead widespread gun ownership predated any push for controls over firearms, and later discour-aged the enactment of restrictive gun laws.

Beginning in the mid–1960s, concerns about crime began to drive up handgun acquisition. Crime rates rose rapidly in the period 1964–1974, then leveled off; crime rates showed short-term fluctuations through 1992, then steadily declined through 2000. Although some Americans responded to rising crime rates by calling for stricter gun controls, others responded by acquiring guns, mostly handguns, for self-protection. As a result, the stock of guns owned, especially handguns, increased rapidly in the 1970s and 1980s, and more slowly in later decades.

THE USE OF GUNS IN VIOLENCE

It is well known that guns are used in many violent crimes in the United States. There were as many as 430,000 violent crimes committed in the United States in 2000 by offenders armed with guns, though not all of the perpetrators actually used the guns during criminal incidents. About 23 percent of robberies and five percent of assaults were committed by gun-armed offenders in 2000 (U.S. Bureau of Justice Statistics 2002). Two-thirds of homicides that year (about 10,180) were committed with guns (U.S. Federal Bureau of Investigation 2001, pp. 19, 67).

It is not so widely known that large numbers of crime victims in America also use guns in self-defense, usually against criminals without guns. Based on sixteen national telephone surveys of probability samples of the adult U.S. pop-ulation, the best available evidence indicates that victims use guns in self-protection considerably more often than offenders commit crimes using guns. For example, victims used guns defensively about two to two and a half million times in 1993 (Kleck and Gertz 1995).

Defensive gun use is effective in preventing injury to the victim and prop-erty loss. Research based on interviews with large nationally representative samples of crime victims consistently indicates that those who use guns during crime incidents are less likely to be injured or lose property than those who either adopt other resistance strategies or do not resist at all. These effects are usually produced without shooting the gun or wounding a criminal—only 24 percent of gun defenders even fired the gun (including warning shots), only 16 percent tried to shoot the perpetrator, and at most 8 percent wounded the offender (evidence summarized in Kleck 1997, Chapter 5).

There is also evidence indicating that some criminals may be deterred from making some criminal attempts in the first place by the prospect of victim gun use against them. Criminals interviewed in prison indicate that they have refrained from committing crimes because they believed a potential victim might have a gun, and crime rates have dropped substantially after highly publicized instances of prospective victims arming themselves or receiving training in gun use, or victims using guns against criminals. Evidence also supports the hypothesis that U.S. burglars are careful to avoid residences where the victims are home because they fear being shot. Although 43 percent of British residential burglaries are committed while victims are home, only 9 percent of residential burglaries in the United States are committed under such circumstances (research summarized in Kleck 1997, Chapter 5). In sum, many criminals use guns to commit violence and other crimes, while many victims also use guns to avoid injury and property loss. Thus, there are both harms from gun use by criminals and benefits from gun ownership and use by victims.

The research on gun use by victims is very consistent—it reduces the likelihood of harm. The best established effect of gun use by aggressors, on the other hand, is a "lethality effect"—if an aggressor attacks and wounds a victim with a gunshot, the victim is more likely (probably about three to four times more likely) to die than if wounded with a knife, the weapon most likely to be used by a lethally minded attacker if a gun were not available (Kleck 1997, Chapter 7).

On the other hand, it is not so widely known that when criminal aggressors possess guns in a crime incident, they are substantially less likely to attack and injure their victims in the first place. At least nineteen studies have found that offenders possessing guns are less likely to injure their victims than offenders with other weapons or no weapons. The explanation appears to be that possession of a lethal weapon enables aggressors to intimidate victims without actually attacking them, in crimes where the offender's goal is not to kill the victim. Since a killing cannot occur if a wound is not inflicted, this is a fatality-reducing effect of aggressor gun possession. Thus, even gun possession by aggressors has some inadvertently violence-reducing effects, along with the violence-increasing "lethality effect." Nevertheless, the net effect of offender gun possession is that it increases the likelihood that a violent crime will result in the death of the victim.

Because gun possession among largely noncriminal prospective victims has beneficial effects, and gun possession among criminals has a mixture of both harmful and inadvertently beneficial effects, it is not self-evident what the net effect of overall gun ownership levels on violence rates is likely to be. U.S. research on crime rates in macrolevel units like cities and states has produced distinctly mixed results on this issue. Most of the research is seriously flawed. In particular, most studies fail to properly model the possibility of a two-way relationship between violence rates and gun ownership rates, making it impossible to interpret the meaning of a positive association between the two (i.e., higher violence rates are found where there are higher gun levels). Although more guns may lead to more crime, higher crime rates might also motivate more people to acquire guns for self-protection. The more sophisticated studies, which address this possible reciprocal causation, mostly have found that higher crime rates cause higher gun ownership levels, but that general gun ownership levels have no net effect on rates of violence and crime, including homicide. This finding does not preclude the possibility that gun ownership among criminals and other high-risk subsets of the population increases violence rates, but it does suggest that any such effects are counterbalanced by violence-reducing effects of guns in the hands of crime victims and prospective victims.

GUN CONTROL IN AMERICA

The United States is unusual in having a Constitution that limits what the national government may do to restrict gun ownership. The meaning of the Second Amendment to the U.S. Constitution is heavily debated but the consensus of scholars is that, although the provision does recognize an individual's right to keep and bear arms, including guns, current Supreme Court doctrine also holds that the Constitution does not restrict what state and local governments may do to restrict gun ownership. Thus, because most criminal law is made at the state level, and would be so regardless of the interpretation of the Second Amendment, the Amendment actually has little current effect on the strictness of gun controls in the United States.

More significant politically, the vast majority of Americans believe that they have a right to own guns, and oppose gun controls that would interfere with that right. The enormous body of evidence on American public opinion and gun control can easily be summarized: most Americans are willing to support a wide array of moderate regulatory controls aimed at keeping guns away from criminals, juveniles, and other high-risk groups, but oppose prohibitionist controls. That is, most Americans oppose gun bans or other controls that would preclude them from legally acquiring or owning guns. As a result, there is a huge number, and bewildering variety, of gun control laws in the United States, but almost none of them ban guns outright or seriously limit noncriminal citizens' access to guns. Three large cities (Washington, DC, Chicago, and New York) effectively ban the private possession of handguns among their residents, but no laws at either the federal or state levels ban ownership of all guns or even just handguns.

Federal Law

Under the federal system of government in the United States, criminal laws are made at the national, state, and local levels. The vast majority of criminal laws, including gun control laws, are made at the state level. Federal gun laws are both less numerous than state laws and less restrictive than the laws prevailing in most states. Complicating things still further, local governments in some states are allowed to make some gun law, and the strictest controls of all in the United States are those enacted by municipal governments (U.S. Bureau of Justice Statistics 1996; Brady Campaign to Prevent Gun Violence 2003; National Rifle Association 2003).

Under federal law, all persons in the regular business of selling guns must have a federal firearms dealer's license. Anyone purchasing a gun of any kind from a licensed dealer must pass a background check for a criminal conviction and other disqualifying attributes. It is unlawful for a convicted felon to purchase a gun or for a dealer to sell a gun to a felon. It is unlawful for any convicted felon to possess a gun of any kind, regardless of how it was obtained. It is unlawful in the United States for a juvenile to possess a handgun, and unlawful to sell guns to juveniles.

Although all licensed dealers must record the identity of each gun buyer and the particulars of the gun transferred, there is no national registry of guns or gun owners, since records of active dealers are not centralized in federal government hands. There is also no federally mandated permit required for purchasing guns, nor any license required to own guns, though such controls are common at the state level. Thus, it is deliberate national policy that there be no national registry of guns or gun owners that could be used to facilitate the mass confiscation of guns. Perhaps most significant of all, gun transfers between private persons, i.e., nonlicensees, are not subject to any background check under federal law.

State Law

Each of the fifty states has a different array of gun laws. Some states have controls stricter than the average level prevailing among democracies outside the United States (United Nations 1997, pp. 11–17), while others have only very limited controls. No state bans the private possession of guns, including handguns, though a few large cities ban handgun possession. Six states ban the purchase or possession of certain models of semiautomatic firearms loosely labeled "assault weapons," guns that fire just one shot at a time but look like, or were adapted from, military guns that could fire like machine guns. Almost all of the states forbid possession or purchase of handguns by convicted felons and juveniles, and most also ban other higher risk categories of persons, such as mentally ill persons and illicit drug users, from firearm purchase or possession.

Twelve states require a permit to purchase a handgun, and five of these also require a permit to buy a long gun. Although twenty-five states require that records of gun sales be reported to state or local authorities, only nine have state-mandated handgun registration systems, and only two states register long guns. Although registration was once justified as a way to identify the perpetrators of individual crimes, the current rationale is that a record system that can trace the history of crime guns can help identify gun trafficking operations.

Thirteen states require a minimum waiting period of anywhere from one to fourteen days before buyers may take delivery of handguns they have purchased; five of these states also mandate waiting periods for long guns. The rationale for waiting periods has also changed. When it was thought that significant numbers of murderers acquired guns in the heat of passion to kill their victims, it was argued that the waiting period served as a "cooling-off" period during which the murderous impulse could fade. When it was found that virtually no killers acquired guns at the last minute from the licensed dealers likely to observe the waiting period, gun control advocates highlighted the advantages of being able to conduct more thorough background checks than just the "instant" computer check mandated by federal law.

There are also diverse laws governing the concealed carrying of firearms in public places. In thirty-four states, covering over half the nation's population, adult residents without a criminal record may get a permit allowing concealed carrying of guns in public places if they pass a background check and complete a course teaching both firearm safety and the law pertaining to self-defense and firearms. In seven other (mostly urban) states, concealed carrying by civilians is completely forbidden, while in the remaining states, permits are technically available at the discretion of authorities but in practice are rarely granted, making these states effectively identical to those banning carrying.

GUN CONTROL LAWS
AND THE SUPPLY OF GUNS TO CRIMINALS

Much U.S. gun law is concerned with regulating the sale and purchase of guns to keep guns away from criminals. These regulations mostly cover transactions involving licensed gun dealers (U.S. Bureau of Alcohol, Tobacco and Firearms 1980). The limitation of this regulatory focus is that many guns are acquired through private, largely unregulated, channels. Even among members of the general, mostly noncriminal, population, about one-third of guns were acquired by their present owners from private parties (DMI 1979, p. 71; Cook and Ludwig 1997, p. 25). Although nominally regulated in some jurisdictions, these transactions are largely invisible to legal authorities under existing law, and are even more common routes to gun possession among criminals. The best work on the ways that criminals get guns was done by Wright and Rossi (1986), who surveyed over 1,800 imprisoned felons in ten states about their guns. Among 943 felon handgun owners, 44 percent had acquired their most recently acquired handgun through a purchase, usually from a source other than a dealer; 32 percent had stolen the gun; 9 percent rented or borrowed it; and 8 percent each obtained it in trade or as a gift. Only 16 percent of the total had obtained their handgun by a purchase from a conventional retail dealer (p. 185).

On the other hand, black market dealers were also unimportant as sources of guns—only 2.9 percent of the felons mentioned a "black market source," and only 4.7 percent got the gun from a "fence" (dealer in stolen goods). Although many criminals, such as residential burglars, occasionally sell guns they have stolen, large-scale illicit gun trafficking organizations are rare, and are responsible for only a tiny share of the guns acquired by American criminals. Thus, although many criminals get their guns from unlicensed sources, they rarely get them from black market dealers regularly engaged in the business of selling illegal guns. Most of the felons' guns were obtained outside of licensed, easily regulated channels, yet not from persons in the business of illegal gun selling.

The federal agency charged with enforcing the federal gun laws, the Bureau of Alcohol, Tobacco and Firearms and Explosives (ATF), devotes a significant share of its resources to suppressing illicit gun trafficking activity. The ATF has been the primary source of information used to support the claim that organized gun trafficking is a significant source of criminal guns, yet their own data indicate that each year they catch fewer than 15 traffickers who dealt in more than 250 guns, and that the average number of guns trafficked per trafficking case was just 33 in fiscal year 1997 (ATF 1998, p. 17; 2000, p. 24). The "illicit gun dealers" that come to law enforcement attention turn out to be numerous, but each "dealer" handles so few guns that arresting them could have little or no impact on the availability of guns to criminals. Criminals do occasionally sell guns for profit, but this is mostly a low-volume activity done as a by-product of other criminal activities, such as burglary, drug-dealing, or trafficking in stolen property. The gun "traffickers" caught by the ATF in fiscal year 1997 accounted for only 51,540 known guns (ATF 1998, p. 17), many of which were not sold to criminals, since gun traffickers almost never sell exclusively to prohibited persons (Vizzard 2000, p. 31). Even if half of these guns ended up in criminal hands, they would claim only about one percent of the estimated two million plus guns acquired annually by criminals (Kleck 1999). Furthermore, it is not known if any of the handful of criminals who get guns as a result of trafficking activity would not simply turn to other sources if trafficked guns were not available. Consequently, organized gun trafficking appears to be of little significance in supplying guns to criminals.

As a result of the enormous numbers of guns owned by Americans, there are at least 600,000 guns stolen in a typical year in the United States, so that at any one time there are millions of stolen guns circulating among criminals. The volume of gun theft is so large that, even if one could completely eliminate all voluntary transfers of guns to criminals, including either lawful or unlawful transfers, involving either licensed dealers or private citizens, and even if police could confiscate all firearms from all criminals each year, a single year's worth of gun theft alone would be more than sufficient to rearm all gun criminals and supply the entire set of guns needed to commit the current number of gun crimes (about 430,000 in 2000) (Kleck 1997, pp. 90–4; U.S. Bureau of Justice Statistics 2002). As a result, large-scale gun trafficking (as distinct from burglars occasionally selling guns they have stolen) is largely superfluous to supplying criminals with guns in most areas. The only likely exceptions are a few cities, such as New York and Boston, with unusually low levels of gun ownership in the general population and thus an unusually small stock of guns available to be stolen.

These estimates imply serious limits on the results that can be realistically expected from controls applied only to voluntary (nontheft) transfers such as gun sales. One cannot substantially reduce the flow of water through a sieve by blocking just a few of the holes, especially if one cannot block the largest holes.

Since burglary and other forms of theft are already illegal and severely punished, the gun theft figures imply that, to have any further impact, gun controls must decrease possession and use of firearms by the small high-risk subset of owners most likely to use guns for criminal purposes, above and beyond efforts to prevent them from acquiring guns in the first place.

For example, conceal carry license laws are intended to reduce unlicensed possession of guns in public places, without necessarily preventing anyone from acquiring a gun or keeping it in their home. Likewise, bans on possession of guns by convicted criminals could deter some criminals from possessing guns anywhere, without directly blocking their initial acquisition. Similarly, laws enhancing penalties for committing violent crimes if committed with firearms could conceivably reduce the *use* of guns in crimes, without preventing any criminals from acquiring guns in the first place.

THE IMPACT OF GUN LAWS ON VIOLENCE

The enormous number and variety of gun controls, and the huge variation in strictness of controls across different states and cities, makes the United States a natural laboratory for evaluating the impact of gun control laws. In nations where a single set of laws prevail everywhere, the only practical way of assessing any given control's impact on violence rates is to make crude comparisons of national violence rates before and after introduction of the new measure. Unfortunately, there is very little longitudinal data available on other factors that influence violence rates, making it impossible to control for any significant number of other determinants of violence rates. Thus, there is almost no ability to separate the effects, if any, of a new law from the effects of changes in other factors. As a result, longitudinal evaluations of legal impact are virtually worthless (Britt, Kleck, and Bordua 1996). On the other hand, because far more data are available describing multiple areas at a given point in time such as a Census year, crosssectional studies of many different legal jurisdictions, with explicit controls for confounding factors, give considerably more power for separating the impact of a given gun law from the effects of other factors.

One review of the results and weaknesses of 39 U.S. studies of the impact of gun control laws on crime rates indicated that most of the studies found no impact of gun laws on violence rates. Of the 16 studies providing at least mixed support for a gun law impact, 12 were unacceptable univariate time series case studies, usually of a single law in a single nonrandomly selected area, and three of these were evaluations of the same law (Kleck 1997, pp. 35–359, 378–379).

The most sophisticated and comprehensive evaluation of gun law impact was done by Kleck and Patterson (1993). It is unique in generating comparative evidence on the impact of such a large number of different kinds of gun control. These authors assessed the impact of nineteen major types of gun control on rates of homicide, robbery, aggravated assault, rape, suicide, and fatal gun accidents. They separately examined gun and nongun violence (e.g., gun homicide vs. nongun homicide), as well as the impact of gun laws on gun ownership levels. They controlled for dozens of possible confounding factors and gun ownership levels, assessed both state and city controls, and used multiple sources of information on gun laws.

Some gun controls were probably designed to reduce violence by reducing gun ownership levels, but none of the nineteen common types of gun laws showed consistent evidence of reducing gun ownership. Only two of the regulations, requiring a license to possess guns, and prohibiting possession by mentally ill persons, showed even mixed support for an impact. Of course, for many gun regulations, such as carry controls or add-on penalties, these findings are not surprising, since the laws were not intended to reduce gun ownership.

Other gun controls may operate to restrict ownership only among "high-risk" groups such as criminals or alcoholics. However, the results also indicated that most U.S. state and local controls fail to reduce gun use in acts of violence, undercutting the idea that gun ownership was reduced even in the limited subsets of the population that commit violent crimes. One reasonable explanation for this failure would be the huge size of the U.S. gun stock. With over 260 million guns in private hands, it is hard to deny guns to anyone who truly wants one.

As to the impact of gun laws on violence rates, the findings generally indicated that gun controls common in the United States appear to exert no significant negative effect on total violence rates. Of 102 tests of the direct effects of 19 different major types of gun law on 6 different categories of crime and violence, only three tests unambiguously supported the gun law efficacy hypothesis, while fifteen others provided ambiguous support.

Favorite policies of the American public and gun control advocacy groups, such as waiting periods and gun registration, clearly do not reduce violence rates to any measurable degree. Neither the Kleck-Patterson research, nor any other research, has ever indicated that these controls reduce any form of violence. On the other hand, the gun control strategy most favored by the gun owner groups, mandatory add-on penalties for committing crimes with a gun, is also ineffective.

Why do so many varieties of gun control laws appear to have no impact on many of the types of violence that frequently involve guns? First, gun laws intended to have their effects by reducing gun ownership levels, either in the general population or, more usually, within various high-risk subsets, may fail simply because they do not achieve their proximate goal of reducing gun ownership. Second, given that the best research indicates that general gun ownership levels do not have a net positive effect on crime and violence, even if gun laws did reduce general gun ownership, this reduction on the number of guns would have no net negative impact on total violence rates. On the other hand, laws that reduced gun availability among criminals in particular, without disarming noncriminal victims, might reduce violence. Unfortunately, no research has managed to distinguish gun availability among criminals from that among noncriminals.

Many U.S. gun laws regulate only handguns, or regulate handguns more stringently than long guns such as rifles or shotguns, which are far more numerous. This permits the substitution of the less regulated long guns for the more heavily regulated handguns. This common feature of U.S. gun laws can have the undesirable effect of encouraging some prospective criminals to substitute the more lethal long guns. The implication for the homicide rate is that the harmful effects of long gun substitution by some criminals could either cancel out or even outweigh the beneficial effects of denying handguns to other criminals, and produce a net increase in homicide. This is why regulating only handguns can be a risky course (Kleck 1997, Chapter 4).

It has been argued that local or state controls fail because guns from jurisdictions with weaker controls "leak" into those with stricter controls. This argument misleads with regard to any kind of possession ban, since the illegality and risks of possessing firearms in a restrictive jurisdiction are unaffected by the presence or absence of controls in surrounding areas—only controls over acquisition of guns are affected by interjurisdictional leakage. With respect to controls over acquisition, advocates have argued that federal measures are therefore called for (e.g., Newton and Zimring 1969). Research on the relatively weak federal regulations existing prior to the Brady Act generally found these controls to be ineffective (Zimring 1975; Magaddino and Medoff 1984), and an early (perhaps premature) evaluation of the 1994 Brady Act points to the same conclusion (Ludwig and Cook 2000).

Most case studies of changes in gun law investigate increases in gun control restrictiveness. However, there is as much to be learned about the efficacy of gun controls from decreases in strictness as there is from increases. Between 1986 and 1998, 22 states amended their gun laws to make it easier for noncriminal adult residents to get permits allowing them to carry concealed firearms in public places. Critics of these laws feared that the increase in legally authorized gun carriers would result in increased acts of violence involving permit holders. These fears were not realized. For example, statewide data on permit revocations in Florida indicated that only about eight persons a year had their carry permits revoked due to a gun crime conviction; 194,356 people held permits on September 30, 1995 (Kleck 1997, pp. 367–372).

The first sophisticated study of the impact of these laws conducted by John Lott and David Mustard (1996), who analyzed crime trends in all 3,000 counties in the nation for which requisite data were available and studied every shall issue carry law passed between 1977 and 1992. Their results indicated that violence rates, including gun homicide rates, declined after these laws went into effect, and declined more in the states that liberalized carry laws than in those that did not. Many attempts to replicate these findings, however, failed to do so; instead they generally found nonsignificant negative associations between crime rates and passage of the laws (Kovandzic and Marrell 2003).

Lott and Mustard believed that the laws caused substantial reductions in violence rates by deterring prospective criminals afraid of encountering an armed victim. This would be surprising in light of the modesty of the intervention. The 1.3 percent of the population in places like Florida who obtained permits would represent at best only a slight increase in the share of potential crime victims who carry guns in public places, given that about 10 percent of Americans at least occasionally carried guns in public places for self-protection even before these laws were passed (Kleck 1997, p. 212). Moreover, if those who got permits were merely legitimating what they were already doing before the new laws, it would mean there was no increase at all in carrying or in actual risks to criminals. Thus, changes in carry laws may not have increased criminals' perceptions of risk from armed victims. Nevertheless, contrary to what critics expected, crime did not increase when it became easier for noncriminals to get carry permits.

Some have sought to assess gun law impact through crossnational comparisons of violence rates. Typically, pairs of nations are compared, but are arbitrarily selected so as to prove whatever point the analyst wishes; or many nations are compared and any observed differences in violence are arbitrarily attributed to differences in gun control strictness. The most common paired comparison is made between the United States and Great Britain. The latter does indeed have both stricter gun laws and less homicide than the United States, and the residents of Great Britain rarely kill one another with guns. However, there is little reason to believe that gun controls play any role in the lower British total homicide rates. Conclusions to the contrary typically rely on static comparisons of the two nations in fairly recent years. These comparisons overlook one crucial fact: Great Britain had far less violence than the United States long before the former had strict gun laws. Causation cannot run backward in time, so controls implemented after 1920 could not have produced the low homicide rates already prevailing in Great Britain prior to 1920.

Before 1920, gun control was at least as lenient in Great Britain as in the United States—there were few significant controls on any common gun type. The Library of Congress referred to the pre–1903 period in Great Britain as "the era of unrestricted [gun] ownership" (p. 75), while noting for the 1903–1920 period that although a license was required to obtain a gun, "licenses were available on demand" (U.S. Library of Congress 1981, pp. 75–76). Since 1920, British controls have been made progressively stricter, first in response to the Russian revolution and political unrest at home, and only later as a means of crime-control (U.S. Liberary of Congress (p. 76; Kopel 1992, pp. 70–74).

In 1919, the homicide rate for England and Wales was 0.8 per 100,000 (Archer and Gartner 1984). It has been estimated that the homicide rate for the entire United States was 9.5 in 1919 (Kleck 1991, p. 393), 11.9 times as large as the British rate. By 1983–1986, the homicide rate for England and Wales was 0.67, and the rate in the United States was 7.59 (Killias 1990, p. 171), 11.3 times as high as the English rate. Thus, after more than sixty years of increasingly stringent gun regulation, Great Britain's homicide rates relative to the United States had actually gotten worse.

SELECTED RECENT TRENDS AND
POSSIBLE FUTURE DEVELOPMENTS

The most significant federal gun legislation passed since 1968 is the Brady Handgun Violence Prevention Act, or the Brady Act, which become effective on February 28, 1994. It provided for a waiting period of five working days between purchase and delivery of a handgun, during which a background check on the prospective buyer had to be performed. The law applied only to purchases from federally licensed dealers, initially covered only handguns, and operated only in the 26 states that did not already have similar background checks in effect under state laws (U.S. Congressional Research Service 1994). The background checks were thereby extended to about 39 percent of the U.S. population not already covered by state checks. The waiting period requirement, emphasized heavily by the press during debate over the measure, was only a temporary provision, in effect only until November 29, 1998, after which a national "instant record check" system was in place, capable of performing computerized checks of criminal history files that could be accomplished in a few minutes at the point of purchase. At that time, the waiting period was dropped, with the background checks extended to cover rifles and shotguns as well as handguns. The law prohibited law enforcement agencies from retaining records of the gun purchases or conveying information about them to anyone other than those carrying out the checks (U.S.C. 922(s)(6)(B)), thereby preventing the establishment of a national registry of gun owners.

The principle shortcoming of the law is that it does not cover nondealer transactions, which probably account for the majority of transfers of guns to criminals (Wright and Rossi 1986, p. 183; U.S. Bureau of Justice Statistics 2001, p. 6). Nevertheless, many attempts by criminals to buy guns from dealers were denied as a result of the law. It is, however, impossible to tell from denials how many criminals were actually prevented from getting handguns, since it is unknown how many of those blocked from buying firearms in gun stores simply acquired them instead from unlicensed sellers, from licensed dealers by using phony identification documents to avoid identification as a disqualified person, or through use of "straw purchasers" (who had no disqualifying attributes) to make the purchase on their behalf. None of this, however, contradicts the assertion that the law may reduce violence, since there may well be some persons who will commit serious acts of violence in the future but who would not be sufficiently motivated and able to make use of these evasion strategies. Since the Brady law only blocked future gun acquisitions, without taking guns away from anyone who already had them, its effects, if any, will become evident only gradually in the future. For what it is worth, an early evaluation of the first few years of the law's operation found no impact on homicide or suicide rates (Ludwig and Cook 2000).

As previously discussed, at the state level, one of the most important and highly publicized developments in the past fifteen years was the widespread passage of "right to carry" or "shall issue" laws promoted by gun owner organizations, especially the National Rifle Association (NRA). These laws made it easier for noncriminals to get permits to carry concealed weapons in public. Arguably of even greater significance, but largely unheralded, was the passing of "state preemption" laws, which now exist in 36 of the 50 states. These laws forbid local governments from passing their own gun controls—the state government "preempts" the field of gun control for itself. The significance of these measures is that, although most political struggles over gun control involved just a single kind of control in a single jurisdiction, these laws forbade the passing of almost any kind of gun control in future, while also eliminating many local controls implemented in the past for thousands of jurisdictions. This was even more significant given that the strictest gun laws in the United States have generally been passed at the local level. Indeed, local governments have been the only ones willing to pass bans on handgun possession.

Perhaps in response to defeats in legislatures, gun control advocacy organizations in recent years have shifted much of their efforts to the courts, helping others to bring civil lawsuits against gun manufacturers. If widely successful, the lawsuits could either bankrupt gun makers and produce a de facto ban on the further manufacture of firearms, or make guns prohibitively expensive and thereby bring about a de facto ban on gun buying, without benefit of new legislation. Some of the lawsuits are brought by individual persons, and others by municipal governments, many of them with the assistance of the Brady Campaign through its Legal Action Project. The suits are based on novel legal theories that manufacturers were negligent for: (1) producing and selling guns lacking certain safety devices (e.g., "personalized gun" technologies, not yet available in proven form, that prevent anyone but the authorized user from firing the gun), (2) allegedly marketing guns to prohibited buyers such as criminals or juveniles, (3) marketing guns based on allegedly false claims that guns can be useful for self-defense, or (4) simply manufacturing too many guns, in excess of the demand among noncriminals.

Municipal governments have also brought suits based on a public nuisance theory that gun manufacturers should be held liable to city governments for the costs of gun violence—the costs of police and courts, medical care of the wounded, and so forth. So far, although lawsuits against gun manufacturers have occasionally been won on more orthodox legal grounds, such as defects (as conventionally understood) in design or manufacture, none of these new theories has yet been accepted by any court.

The strictness and character of gun law in the United States reflects the broad themes of public opinion. Most Americans oppose bans on ownership of major categories of guns, but support a wide variety of moderate regulatory measures aimed at keeping guns away from criminals. Some moderate controls proposed, however, have not been voted into law, despite majority support. This has been due to the efforts of gun owner organizations, the most prominent of which is the NRA. Their success in recent decades has largely come about because support for moderate control measures is widespread but weak; while opposition, concentrated among gun owners, is narrower but more intense. As a result, opponents of stricter controls have been more effectively mobilized by the gun owner organizations to take politically significant actions such as contacting their elected representatives, casting their votes based largely on a candidate's stand on gun issues, and making contributions to pro-gun candidates and organizations (Kleck 1997, Chapter 10; Vizzard 2000).

In this political context, much of recent gun control legislation has been weak and unlikely to influence rates of crime or violence. For legislators faced with many voters who would be mildly disappointed if they voted "no" on new gun controls, and a smaller number who would be intensely hostile if they voted "yes," the politically prudent compromise has been to pass weak "feel good" measures that are unlikely to have any measurable impact on crime or seriously anger gun owners. The most likely future trend is more of the same—symbolic, minor changes in gun laws touted as major advances by supporters and decried as disasters by opponents.

Another possible future trend, however, is increased federalization of the criminal law in the gun control area, paralleling trends in other areas of law. Traditionally, Congress has had little to do with the criminal laws prevailing in America, most of which have been enacted at the state level. Congress was supposed to address issues that were inherently national in character, such as national defense and commerce with other nations, and crime was regarded as a state and local matter. As crime became a political issue beginning in the 1960s, and "tough on crime" stances became popular political positions in the 1970s and 1980s, many Congressmen saw potential political rewards in adopting similar positions.

Federal criminal laws passed in the 1980s and 1990s often duplicated state laws, merely adding federal penalties on top of existing state penalties, and outside of the area of drug control were of little substance regarding crime control. A federal ban on gun possession among juveniles (already forbidden by almost all states) was a prime example of such a duplicative measure in the area of gun control.

After the September 11, 2001 terrorist attacks, gun control advocacy groups worked to link gun control with terrorism. No new federal controls, however, resulted from these efforts. They may have failed because major acts of terrorism in the United States have typically involved explosives rather than firearms. In any case, Republican control of the presidency and both houses of Congress after the 2002 elections made any new federal restrictions on guns unlikely in the near term.

REFERENCES

Archer, Dane, and Rosemary Gartner (1984), *Violence and crime in cross-national perspective.* New Haven, CT: Yale University Press.

Brady Campaign to Prevent Gun Violence. (2003). http://www.bradycampaign.org /legislation/state/index.asp.

Britt, Chester, III, Gary Kleck, and David J. Bordua (1996), "A reassessment of the D.C. gun law: some cautionary notes on the use of interrupted time series designs for policy impact assessment." *Law & Society Review* 30:361–380.

Bruce-Briggs, Barry (1976), "The great American gun war." *The Public Interest* 45:37–62.

Cook, Philip J., and Jens Ludwig (1997), *Guns in America*. Summary Report. Washington, DC: Police Foundation.

DMI (Decision-Making-Information) (1979), *Attitudes of the American electorate toward gun control*. Santa Ana, CA: Author.

Killias, Martin (1990), "Gun ownership and violent crime: the Swiss experience in international perspective." *Security Journal* 1:169–174.

Kleck, Gary (1991), *Point blank: Guns and violence in America*. New York: Aldine de Gruyter.

——— (1997), *Targeting guns: Firearms and their control*. New York: Aldine de Gruyter.

——— (1999), "BATF gun trace data and the role of organized gun trafficking in supplying guns to criminals." *St. Louis University Public Law Review* 18(1):23–45.

Kleck, Gary, and Marc Gertz (1995), "Armed resistance to crime: the prevalence and nature of self-defense with a gun." *Journal of Criminal Law and Criminology* 86:150–187.

Kleck, Gary, and E. Britt Patterson (1993), "The impact of gun control and gun ownership levels on violence rates." *Journal of Quantitative Criminology* 9:249–288.

Kopel, David (1992), *The Samurai, the mountie, and the cowboy*. Buffalo, New York: Prometheus.

Kovandzic, Tomislav V., Thomas B. Marrell (2003), "Right-to-carry concealed handguns and violent crime." *Criminology and Public Policy* 2(3): 263–396.

Lindgren, James, and Justin Lee Heather (2002), "Counting guns in early America." *William and Mary Law Review* 43(5):1777–1842.

Lizotte, Alan J., and David J. Bordua (1980), "Firearms ownership for sport and protection: two divergent models." *American Sociological Review* 45:229–244.

Lott, John, and David B. M. Mustard (1997), "Crime, deterrence and right-to-carry concealed handguns." *Journal of Legal Studies* 26:1–68.

Ludwig, Jens, and Philip J. Cook (2000), "Homicide and suicide rates associated with implementation of the Brady Handgun Violence Prevention Act." *Journal of the American Medical Association* 284(5):585–591.

Magaddino, Joseph P., and Marshall H. Medoff (1984), "An empirical analysis of federal and state firearm control laws." Pp. 225–258 in *Firearms and violence: Issues of public policy*, edited by Don B. Kates, Jr. Cambridge, MA: Ballinger.

National Rifle Association Institute for Legislative Action (2003), Information available at NRA Web site at http://www.nra.org.

Newton, George D., and Franklin Zimring (1969), *Firearms and Violence in American Life*. A Staff Report to the National Commission on the Causes and Prevention of Violence. Washington, DC: U.S. Government Printing Office.

Stinchcombe, Arthur, Rebecca Adams, Carol A. Heimer, Kim Lane, Scheppele, Tom W. Smith, D. Garth Taylor (1980), *Crime and punishment—Changing attitudes in America*. San Francisco: Jossey-Bass.

United Nations (1997), *Draft—United Nations International Study on Firearm Regulation*. Vienna: Crime Prevention and Criminal Justice Division, United Nations Office at Vienna.

U.S. Bureau of Alcohol, Tobacco and Firearms (1980), *State laws and published ordinances, firearms—1980*. Washington, DC: Department of the Treasury.

——— (1998), *ATF Annual Report, 1997*. Washington, D.C.: Department of the Treasury.

——— (2000), *Following the gun*. Washington, DC: Department of the Treasury.

U.S. Bureau of Justice Statistics (1996), *Survey of state procedures related to firearm sales*. Washington, DC: Department of Justice.

——— (2001), *Firearm use by offenders*. Washington, DC: U.S. Government Printing Office.

───── (2002), *Criminal victimization in the United States, 2000.* Department of Justice. http://www.ojpus.doj.gov/bjc/abstract/cvusst.htm.

U.S. Congressional Research Service (1994), "Brady Handgun Violence Prevention Act." CRS Report for Congress number 94–14 GOV, January 6, 1994. Washington, DC: Library of Congress.

U.S. Federal Bureau of Investigation (2001), *Crime in the United States, 2000: Uniform crime reports.* Washington, DC: U.S. Government Printing Office.

U.S. Library of Congress (1981), *Gun control laws in foreign countries.* Law library.

Washington, DC: U.S. Government Printing Office.

Vizzard, William J. (2000), *Shots in the dark: The policy, politics, and symbolism of gun control.* Lanham, MD: Rowman & Littlefield.

Wright, James D., and Peter H. Rossi (1986), *Armed and considered dangerous: A survey of felons and their firearms.* New York: Aldine de Gruyter.

Zimring, Franklin E. (1975), "Firearms and federal law: The Gun Control Act of 1968." *Journal of Legal Studies* 4:133–198.

27

Between Politics
and Reason

Drugs and Crime

Erich Goode

In the 1980s, there were significant public conversations exploring the link between crime and drugs, and citizens witnessed extensive public outreach efforts, as well as popularized rhetoric like "Just Say No." Yet there are conservatives and liberals alike who unite in support of drug legalization. These unlikely bedfellows agree that the economic incentives from the illicit drug trade are what increase the likelihood of drug crime, not the actual use of drugs. Goode examines the lack of a causal link between drugs and crime, and explains the positions of warring public, policy, and political factions.

Drugs and crime are intimately related in the public mind. When a gangland execution is reported in the media, most of us immediately begin thinking about a possible drug connection. Drugs are behind the extraordinarily high murder rate in the nation's largest cities, we feel. Innocent bystanders are gunned down on the street—and behind every such slaying, drugs are seen as being responsible. Decent, honest, law-abiding citizens are held hostage to drug dealers, afraid to leave their apartments at night. Robbery, burglary, auto theft, simple larceny—these and other property crimes are committed on a massive scale to pay for millions of drug habits. Assault, rape, reckless endangerment, child abuse, automobile fatalities: Much of it is committed when the offender is under the influence.

Source: Erich Goode, "Drugs and Crime," *Between Politics and Reason: The Drug Legalization Debate*, (New York: St. Martin's Press, 1997)

The connection between drugs and crime is real, of course, although somewhat exaggerated in the public's mind, and in the media as well. All researchers recognize that determining the causal link between drug use and criminal acts is not an easy matter. If the police discover a body in a known crack house, was the killing drug-related? Not necessarily. The deceased may have died of natural causes, or as a result of actions completely unrelated to drugs. To some degree, the designation "drug related" is a construct, not an objective reality (Brownstein, 1993). Even the fact that drugs and crime are frequently found together or *correlated* does not demonstrate their *causal* connection. Still, all observers agree that the drugs–crime connection is strong. Drug users do have a significantly higher than average crime rate. In fact, the recreational users of *all* drugs-alcohol and tobacco included—have a substantially higher crime rate than do drug abstainers. (Let's return to this theme momentarily.) What's behind this connection? What causes it? And what can we do about it? Quite obviously, the criminalizers and the legalizers have precisely the opposite solution. The criminalizers think that severe penalties will take the criminals off the street, discourage potential offenders from breaking the law, and lower the crime rate. The legalizers think that removing criminal penalties from the currently illegal drugs would sever the drugs–crime connection by removing the motives for property crime (because drugs would be cheap) and violent crime as well (because there would be no illegal empire to protect). How would it work? And would it be successful?

One building block of the legalization position is that it is law enforcement itself that is largely responsible for the high rate of crime in our society. If the currently illegal drugs were to be legalized, they say, the crime rate would decline sharply and drastically. Legalization would "take the crime out of drugs," its advocates argue. This will take place in at least four distinctly different ways.

First, since, under legalization, drug possession would no longer be a crime, not arresting addicts and users—and, in all likelihood, petty, street-level user-dealers as well—would free up the criminal justice system to the tune of hundreds of thousands of arrests per year, and keep hundreds of thousands out of the nation's prisons, and put them into treatment programs.

Second, since drugs would be sold legally and at low cost, addicts and drug abusers would no longer be forced to commit crimes in order to obtain their substances of choice. Their current crime rate is a function of the illegality of cocaine and heroin; transform that legal status, and the crime rate of hard-drug users will plummet, again, freeing up our criminal justice system so that it can focus largely on the violent criminal.

Third, legalization would result in the deflation of the profits earned by dealers which, in turn, would result in the virtual elimination of gang "turf" wars and other violent disputes that erupt around the drug trade. As much as half the urban street violence can be traced to the drug trade; eliminate drug profits, violence will decline, and many lives will be saved.

And fourth, legalization would virtually wipe out organized crime, at least that sector of it that earns its livelihood by selling the currently illegal drugs. A major source of the underworld's profits will be eliminated overnight; organized crime will shrink correspondingly.

Do these arguments in favor of legalization make sense? Will legalization reduce or "take a bite out" of crime? Are these points empirically sound? What evidence do we have to address these points? Conceptually, at least, we have to make a distinction between crimes committed by users in the course of their everyday lives and those committed by dealers in the course of their illicit business. In addition, we have to keep the distinction between crimes of violence and property crimes fresh in our mind. These two distinctions will become relevant as our discussion unfolds.

DRUG CRIMES

If drug possession and sale are legalized, by definition all the current drug crimes would no longer be against the law. In this sense, legalization would produce a direct and immediate drop in the crime rate as a result of taking the drug laws off the books. Or would it? This depends entirely on the specific legalization program under consideration. The details of the plan under consideration are far from a trivial matter. Details represent a series of conditions which determine or influence what the targeted population is likely to do, and that is different for different conditions.

Many legalization plans propose controls for the currently illegal drugs similar to those now in place for alcohol. Alcohol is a legal substance; anyone above a certain age may purchase it. Let's be clear about this: In the United States, there are far more arrests related directly to the use, possession, and sale of alcohol, a *legal* substance, than is true for all the illegal drugs. In 1994, according to the Federal Bureau of Narcotics, arrests for drug abuse violations numbered 1.3 million. But there were just under 1.4 million arrests for driving under the influence, over half a million for violations of the liquor laws, and nearly three-quarters of a million for drunkenness. (This does not count the arrests for violations that are code words for alcohol-related offenses, such as disorderly conduct and vagrancy.) Of course, this statement must be met with a strong qualifier: Though there are many alcohol-related *arrests*, and consequently, a sizable segment of jail or temporary holding facilities is devoted to them, there are very few arrests that result in *prison incarceration*. In contrast, over 60 percent of federal and 26 percent of state prisoners (and a third of newly incarcerated state offenders) are incarcerated for drug offenses (Butterfield, 1995). Alcohol offenses tie up a huge proportion of police and jail resources, but practically none in prisons. In any case, if the laws and their enforcement against the now-illicit drugs were similar to those now operating for alcohol, it is clear that this would *not* eliminate drug crimes or arrests on drug charges. It is not inconceivable that, under legalization, the current drug arrest figures may actually *rise* as a result of two developments: One, as I argued, under legalization, more people will use drugs; and two, the police will use charges like public intoxication and driving while under the influence as a new means of controlling drug abuse. In any case, an alcohol-type legal control system *will not* eliminate drug arrests—and it may actually increase them.

The marijuana decriminalization or "harm reduction" program that now prevails in the Netherlands is often cited by legalizers as a model drug plan the United States might adopt. Yet, it has not resulted in the disappearance of drug crimes. Recall that in the Netherlands, the possession and sale of small quantities of marijuana, while technically against the law, are tolerated in practice; the possession and sale of large quantities of marijuana remain a crime—both in the law and in its enforcement. Moreover, the possession and sale of the hard drugs by users, addicts, and petty street dealers, again, while illegal, results in very few arrests. Yet, as we've seen, in the Netherlands, roughly a third of the prison population is made up of drug offenders; most were arrested for the sale of substantial quantities of the hard drugs. This is comparable to the United States, where, again, just over a quarter of the state prison population is made up of drug violators (Butterfield, 1995). Clearly, then, *certain* legalization or decriminalization programs will not eliminate drug crimes.

Picture a far more modest legalization scheme: some form of drug maintenance or a prescription plan. In the United States at present, as we've seen, roughly 100,000 narcotic addicts are enrolled in methadone maintenance programs. Under these programs, narcotic addicts are not granted complete, free, or unrestricted access to any psychoactive substance they wish to take. Instead, they are administered maintenance doses of methadone, a slow-acting narcotic. These doses are administered orally rather than injected, so that they do not produce a high or intoxication. However, only a minority of the nation's narcotic addicts are enrolled in these programs (100,000 out of between half a million to a million), partly because funding for them is limited and partly because most narcotic addicts do not want to be maintained—they want to get high. *Most* enrollees violate the terms of the program by taking illegal drugs; most drop out of the program against the advice of the staff, presumably to return to a life of addiction; most continue to commit criminal behavior, even when they are enrolled in the program. However, roughly a third to 40 percent, as I pointed out earlier, are helped in some major way, as a result of a significant decline in their use of heroin and other drugs, as well as a reduction in their crime rate. If drug legalization is to look anything like the current methadone maintenance program for narcotic addicts, then what we should expect is a significant drop in the overall rate of illegal drug use for enrollees as a whole (to perhaps one-half or one-third of their previous level). However, roughly a third of all enrollees will continue to take illegal drugs frequently, and will drop out of the program; a third will take them less frequently, and will bounce in and out of the program; and a third will remain semi-abstemious as a result of the program (Hubbard, et al., 1989). Again, while this is an improvement, it does not result in an *elimination* of drug crimes among addicts. If legalization is to look like our present methadone maintenance program, we should expect similar results. In fact, perhaps we should expect *poorer* results, since, now, methadone programs only enroll the addicts who are *most* committed to giving up illegal drug use. If these programs were to be expanded, they will inevitably enroll a far higher percentage of less-committed addicts and, hence, a higher volume of drug violations.

Considering methadone maintenance programs forces us to face an obvious dilemma in "fine tuning" the dispensing of drugs in any legalization system.

On the one hand, if the restrictions are as strict as they are for our current methadone maintenance program, many users, abusers, and addicts will not be willing to enroll because it does not give them the drug they want, or the drug in sufficient doses, or administered the way they want. Most users want to get high, they do not wish simply to be maintained and, hence, refuse to enroll in a maintenance program. As a consequence, a restrictive program, such as the methadone programs we now have, will result in *many* drug violations among users, including enrollees.

On the other hand, under a viable legalization program, what are our criteria for eligibility to be? Should anyone above a certain age be allowed to obtain any quantity of any drug, no matter how large, at any level of potency? What would the price of newly legal drugs be pegged at? The price of the currently illegal drugs is hugely inflated above what they cost to manufacture under free-market conditions—by a factor of 20 to 50 times. Should drugs be priced at what the market will bear? If this means selling crack at 50 cents a dose, within the budget of any sixth-grader—so be it? If not, will an illicit market step in and supply what the market wants, but cannot obtain legally?

The fact is, under almost any conceivable form of legalization, that is one with some restrictions, an illicit market will "continue to thrive alongside the legal one" (Kraar, 1990, p. 71). The lower legal prices are (and the more accessible drugs are), the smaller this illicit market will be; the higher legal prices are (and the less accessible drugs are), the larger it will grow. If there is an "iron law of prohibition" it is this: *An illicit market in a hugely desired product will shrink only to the extent that the demand for that product is satisfied; to the extent that it is not, the illicit market will grow correspondingly.* The claim that legalization will dry up an illicit drug market seems extraordinarily naive, given that it fails to stipulate the single most crucial factor: the price and availability of the newly legalized substances. Is it really possible that any informed observer imagines that free and ready availability of drugs will not significantly increase their use and abuse and, hence, multiply the damage they cause?

Hence, the dilemma can be stated quite simply: The more restrictive the program, the larger the volume of illicit use, and therefore the more frequent the drug crimes; the less restrictive the program, the smaller the volume of illicit use—but, almost certainly, the greater the legal use (Moore, 1990a, p. 16). Programs with *many* restrictions will have little licit but much illicit use, whereas programs with *few* restrictions will have much licit but little illicit use. Programs which claim to wipe out drug distribution crimes will do so only at the expense of distributing psychoactive substances to anyone who wants them, and will encourage use; to the extent that there are restrictions, an illicit market will arise to meet that demand. The same economic market principle operates for less-than-full legalization programs as for our current punitive policy. The only legalization plan that would result in eliminating drug-related crimes or arrests for sale and possession is a complete free-market or laissez-faire program (Szasz, 1992), which calls for virtually no restrictions on drugs whatsoever. This plan has no likelihood whatsoever of implementation in the foreseeable future. As I said earlier, it is difficult to imagine any legislator or serious policy analyst urging a program that calls for controls on powerful and dangerous psychoactive drugs that are no more stringent than those that apply to the possession and sale of tomatoes.

THE DRUG USE–PROPERTY CRIME
CONNECTION: THREE MODELS

Currently, drugs and crime are connected in very specific ways; their connection bears directly on the issue of whether or not property crime would decline under legalization. At least three "models" spell out the different *ways* they could be connected: the "enslavement" or "medical" model, the "criminal" model, and the "intensification" model.

The *enslavement* (or "medical") model is the one that has been adopted by the legalizers. It goes as follows. Addicts and abusers become "enslaved," unable to control their use of the drug; they spend so much money on it that they are unable to support their habit by working at a regular, legitimate job. Consequently, they *must* engage in crime; they have no choice in the matter. The enslavement model argues that addiction came first and crime followed as a consequence; addicts turn to crime *because* of their addiction. In the absence of addiction, those persons who are now enslaved to a drug would not commit moneymaking crimes, at least not to the same degree. Under legalization, in contrast heroin and cocaine would cost just a dollar or so per dose, and a huge slice of crime would be wiped out virtually overnight (Inciardi, 1992, pp. 150, 153, 159, 248, 263). The enslavement model makes two assumptions: first, that addicts and abusers are motivated to use their drugs of choice primarily because they want to avoid painful, body-wracking withdrawal symptoms and, second, that they will be satisfied with maintenance and will not seek intoxication or a high.

The *criminal* model argues that it is not *addicts who turn to crime* but *criminals who turn to drugs*. Long before they become dependent on heroin and cocaine, those who eventually do so were *already* engaging in a variety of criminal activities. Persons who eventually become drug addicts and abusers were delinquents and criminals *first*; only later do they turn to drug use. The *type of person* who engages in criminal behavior—moneymaking crimes included—is the same type of person who experiments with and becomes dependent on drugs. Addiction has nothing to do with their criminal behavior; they are not enslaved to a drug so much as *participants on a criminal lifestyle*. Their drug use is a *reflection* or an *indicator* of that lifestyle; it is a later phase of a deviant *tendency* or *career*. Take away the drugs and they would still commit a great deal of crime; make drugs inexpensive, and they would still commit a great deal of crime; make drugs legal, again, and they would still commit a great deal of crime. Such persons belong in prison, this argument holds; legalization isn't going to reform their criminal tendencies (Inciardi, 1992, pp. 151, 160–163).

The *intensification* model represents something of a blend or compromise between the enslavement and the criminal models (Inciardi, 1992, pp. 158, 163, 248). It argues that, yes, criminal careers are *already* well established long before someone abuses, becomes dependent on, or even uses illegal drugs. Take away the drugs and, indeed, these same persons would *still* commit crimes vastly in excess of the rate of the general population. Legalization will *not* eliminate their criminal activities; indeed, most drug-dependent persons are deeply entrenched in a criminal lifestyle—dependency or no dependency, drugs or no drugs. Drug abuse and criminal activity are simply *part and parcel* of the way some people live. Drugs and crime are not causally connected so much as manifestations of the same deviant tendencies. *On the other hand*, the heavy use of cocaine and heroin certainly *intensifies* the likelihood that addicts and abusers will commit crimes, especially moneymaking crimes. Researchers have followed samples of heroin addicts over a period of years. The number of days on which these addicts committed crimes was extremely *high* during periods of nonaddiction (that is, during abstention or when enrolled in a methadone maintenance program)—but *strikingly lower* than the number of days during which they remained addicted (Anglin and Speckart, 1988; Nurco, et al., 1988). The conclusions are inescapable: Drug abuse does not *create* or *cause* criminal behavior, but it does *intensify* or *drive* it. Legalization would not *wipe out* moneymaking crime among addicts and abusers, but it may very well *reduce* it (Inciardi, 1992, pp. 158, 163, 248).

Would some form of drug legalization reduce the incidence of moneymaking crimes among drug addicts and abusers to practically zero? Almost certainly not. Most are involved in crime as a way of life; very few have a legitimate job; very few have enough education to make them marketable. Most commit crimes just to stay alive. In the world of chronic street-drug abuse, criminal activity is routine, deeply entrenched. It is simply how a certain segment of the abuser population earns money to obtain what it wants. Legalization is not going to change this very much. On the other hand, would legalization *reduce* the likelihood that heroin addicts and cocaine abusers would commit moneymaking crimes? In all likelihood, yes. Now, as we've seen, the total amount of crime committed by addicts who are enrolled in treatment programs declines to between one-half and one-third of its former level (Hubbard, et al., 1989). Remember, however, that methadone maintenance clients represent a fairly small, self-selected sample of addicts who are motivated to succeed; if all addicts were able to walk into such a program whenever they felt the impulse to rehabilitate themselves, would their crime rate be as affected as is the case now, with a more restrictive program? If legalization were to increase the number of addicts and abusers significantly and strikingly, the total crime rate may very well increase along with it. And under legalization, would users, who would then spend less money on drugs, begin spending the same amount on other goods and services and, as a consequence, commit the same amount of crime? This is a distinct possibility.

DRUGS AND VIOLENCE: THREE MODELS

As we saw, crimes of violence must be at least conceptually separated from property crime. Their dynamics are not necessarily the same; in fact, their motives are quite different. (At the same time, most of the same persons who commit crimes of violence also commit property crime.) The legalization model, at any rate, rests on a sharp distinction between them. As with the connection between drug use and moneymaking crimes, we encounter three models of the drugs-violence nexus, or why violence is more common among drug abusers than the rest of our citizenry: the *psychopharmacological* model, the *economic-compulsive* model, and the *systemic* model (Goldstein, 1985; Goldstein, et al., 1989). They do not correspond exactly to the three models for money-making crimes I just spelled out, although the economic-compulsive model is similar to the enslavement model above, and the systemic model corresponds more or less to the criminal model. It is important to note that these three models are *not* mutually exclusive; that is, one is not right, while the other two are wrong. In fact, one could be right in explaining the dynamics of a particular criminal event, while, for another specific crime, another model best explains its unfolding. All may be right in explaining the drug use-violence link for different specific crimes; on the other hand, it is possible that one of them best explains a great deal *more* drug-caused acts of violence than the other two.

The *psychopharmacological* model says that drugs cause violence because of their *direct* effects. As a result of taking a specific drug, this model argues, users become irritable, excitable, impatient, and irrational and, hence, are much more likely to engage in criminal behavior. Judging by their direct or pharmacological effects, it might seem reasonable that narcotics would depress or reduce violent behavior because of their soothing, calming, soporific effect; marijuana as well is more likely to lower the user's violent tendencies and hence, reduce the incidence of violent behavior as well. In contrast, again, simply going on their direct pharmacological effects, cocaine and amphetamine would seem to increase the criminal behavior of users as a result of these drugs' tendency to stimulate overall activity, alertness, edginess, suspicion, paranoia, and behavioral fixations. It should also be said that heroin and the narcotics could generate an excitable, impatient, irritable state *during withdrawal* (Inciardi, 1992, p. 161).

The *economic-compulsive* model argues that what causes the higher rate of violence among addicts and abusers is not so much the direct or pharmacological effects of drugs but the fact that users are dependent on drugs and, thus, engage in a great deal of violent crime that is a *by-product* of that dependency. In supporting a costly drug habit, addicts and abusers have to commit such crimes as theft, prostitution, and robbery; in committing them, they come into abrasive and sometimes violent confrontation with victims, bystanders, and the police. Moneymaking crimes *become* violent crimes inadvertently, by accident, without design, simply because victims and others fight back or because drug abusers often lack good judgment about using the most effective means of carrying out the deed. They are not "really" violent criminals, this reasoning goes, they're just involved in moneymaking activities that unwittingly *force* them to become violent upon occasion. Their violence is an extension of their "enslavement" to drugs.

The *systemic* model argues that drug abusers are more likely to be violent than the rest of us because drug abuse is densely woven into a lifestyle that is, by its very nature, violent. This is especially the case when we consider drug selling in addition to the use and abuse of illegal drugs. One cannot be a drug dealer, especially in the inner city, without facing the possibility of violence; it is a world that is *saturated* with violence. In a study of over 400 homicides in New York City, Goldstein [and colleagues] (1989) found that over half were "drug related." Four out of 10 of *all* these homicides, and eight out of 10 the drug-related homicides, specifically involved cocaine. The connection in nine out of 10 of the cases of cocaine-related homicides was *systemic* in nature. It was *the social context of the drug trade* that generated the vast majority of these killings; these homicides were results of territorial disputes, robbery of a drug dealer, assaults to collect a debt, punishment of a drug worker, disputes over a drug theft, and disputes involving a dealer's selling bad drugs.

In other words, the world of selling cocaine, especially in certain contexts, is an ugly, brutal, violent, *inherently disputatious* world. Arguments are frequent. Predators roam the street looking for opportunities to rip dealers off or muscle in on their territory. Dealers dilute the merchandise for a fatter profit. Users attempt to acquire merchandise without paying for it. Huge sums of cash are exchanged; valuable merchandise—illegal drugs—is moving from one location to another, from hand to hand, apartment to apartment, vehicle to vehicle. The temptation to cheat, steal, and shortchange is always great. Violence is a means of social control in such a world; it is an ever-present reality.

But we can take this a step further: It is not only the world of drug dealing in which violence is common (although this is especially the case); so is the street world of drug abuse generally. A later study by the same research team (Goldstein, et al., 1991) obtained detailed, day-by-day accounts of the criminal activities and drug use of nearly 300 street cocaine users for eight weeks, or 56 days. The sample was divided into nonusers (former cocaine users—that is, they were nonusers for the period of this study), "small" users (who spent less than $34 per day on cocaine during the study), and "big" users (who spent more than $34 per day on cocaine). The researchers sampled men and women equally. This study provides a somewhat different slant on the reality of the connection between drug, especially cocaine, abuse and violence than the study cited earlier.

About half the sample were involved with at least one seriously violent episode during the eight weeks of the study (55 percent for the men, 59 percent for the women). However, the violence in which men were involved was mainly as a *perpetrator*, while the violence most of the women were involved in was as a *victim*. Moreover, as volume of cocaine use increased, the men were increasingly likely to be involved in violence as a perpetrator, while for the women, as cocaine use increased, the likelihood of being a victim of violence increased (pp. 356, 357). For men, violence as perpetrator was related to involvement in robbery; for women, violence as victim was related to domestic disputes with lovers, boyfriends, and husbands, as well as to disputes with friends and acquaintances. In this study, alcohol played a prominent role in violent episodes, and an extraordinarily high proportion of the violent events reported by the sample stemmed from the psychopharmacological dimension, and far less from the systemic or economic-compulsive dimensions (p. 361). And in most of these events, alcohol—not cocaine—was the drug most intimately connected to violence. Interestingly, of all the categories in the sample, the "big" male cocaine users were the *most* likely to be involved in violence, but their violence was *least* likely to be related to cocaine use or distribution (p. 364).

The conclusions we can draw from this study seem clear. Heavy, chronic street abusers of illegal drugs are involved in a great deal of violence. Heavy (or "big") male cocaine users are often victimizers; they frequently engage in a variety of crimes, both economic and violent. The specific motive of paying for and supporting a drug habit is almost beside the point. Rather, most engage in crime more or less as a way of life. Even crimes with an economic motive, such as robbery, often turn violent. Many of their acts of violence are alcohol-related. Women, too, are frequently implicated in acts of violence, but more often as a victim than as a perpetrator. It is almost inevitable that women who are involved in the illegal street drug scene will be victimized; in fact, the more they use cocaine, the greater that likelihood is. Drug use either places them in vulnerable situations or is a measure or indicator of their involvement in the violence-saturated street drug scene. It is extremely unlikely that legalization will transform the violent nature of the world of heavy, chronic drug abuse very much. That violence is a part of the way that frequent, heavy drug users live their lives; it is *systemic* to their subculture. In assuming that the ordinary, routine, day-to-day, garden-variety violence will decline substantially if the currently illegal drugs were to be legalized, the legalizers do not make a terribly compelling argument.

THE DRUGS–CRIME
CONNECTION GENERALLY

The connection between drug use and criminal behavior is strong, intimate, and, in all probability, ineradicable. But is it causal in nature? If so, what is the *nature* of the causal relationship between them? As we've seen, the causal connection is extremely complex. Certainly illegality and, hence, the cost of illegal drugs influence the crime *rate*, that is the exact *magnitude* of crime. But illegality and cost do not determine *criminality*. Recall that, among cocaine abusers, the drug that was most intimately connected with violence was alcohol, not cocaine, and that the more that they used cocaine, the less that cocaine played a role in their violence (Goldstein, et al., 1991).

The role of the unexpected is made stunningly clear when we examine the correlation between *legal* drug use and criminal behavior. The relationship between alcohol and tobacco use and the commission of crime is strong and

significant. Practically every study that has ever been conducted on this relationship has found that drinkers and smokers are *more likely* to engage in criminal behavior of all kinds—both property crime and crimes of violence—than
is true of substance abstainers. Moreover, the more that one drinks, at any rate,
the greater this likelihood is (Akers, 1984; O'Donnell, et al., 1976, pp. 82, 83).
Again, what's the causal connection? And if this is true of crime's connection
with *legal*—and fairly inexpensive—drugs, what does this say about the impact
that legalization will have on the criminality of users of the currently *illegal*
drugs? Then, too, if systemic violence is characteristic of heavy users of illegal
drugs (cocaine and heroin, at any rate), what accounts for the higher crime rate
of drinkers and smokers? After all, most consumers of alcohol and tobacco are
presumably not members of a criminal subculture; where does their higher rate
of criminality come from?

Let's be clear about this: *Most* drinkers and smokers are law-abiding; most
do not engage in crime—serious crime at any rate—and most are not "criminals." When criminologists assert a connection between drug use and crime,
they are talking about a correlation, a *statistical*, not an absolute, relationship. *In
comparison with* alcohol and tobacco abstainers, drinkers and smokers have a
higher rate of criminal offenses. Of course, there are many drinkers and smokers in the population, so this does add up to a lot of crimes, but *very few* of them
commit the crimes that are likely to lead to arrest and incarceration. Still, when
we're talking about differences, they are significant. And they do shed light on
what is likely to happen if the currently illegal drugs were to become legalized.
So, what accounts for the relationship? What's the explanation?

The explanation, according to some criminologists, is quite simple. Crime
does not cause drug use, and drug use does not cause crime; attempting to
determine a causal relationship between them is "a waste of time and money"
(Gottfredson and Hirschi, 1990, p. 234). It is not even necessary to refer to a
criminal subculture, they say. (Although it may be a factor in the equation.)
What's important is that "*crime and drug use are the same thing*—that is, manifestations of low self-control" (pp. 233–234; the italics are mine). Essentially, this
argument goes, the *type of person* who uses psychoactive substances (alcohol and
tobacco included) is also the type of person who commits criminal offenses.
Both drugs and crime "provide immediate, easy, and certain short-term pleasure" (p. 41). Both entail engaging in an activity that satisfies a hedonistic desire
for something that involves a measure of danger, risk, or harm, either to oneself
or to another. And who is willing to take such risk, to expose oneself to such
danger, to harm oneself or another? An actor who lacks self-control. After all,
the pleasure is immediate, but the pain takes place over the long run. Hence, it
is an inability to control one's desire for risky pleasures that is the key here, and
that may be found both in substance abuse and in criminal activity.

Again, this is not to say that all or most substance users engage in (nondrug)
crime. Or that all or most criminals are substance users or abusers. (Although
the second statement probably is true.) What it is to say is that drug users and
criminals are essentially the same people, at least those who use drugs and commit crime at a certain level of frequency and seriousness; these two denizens are

cut from the same cloth. The kind of person who engages in one activity is likely to engage in the other; they are, in fact, motivated by the same impulse.

This fundamental fact has important implications for what is likely to happen if the currently illegal drugs were to be legalized. The fact is, the routine, garden-variety criminal behavior of the vast majority of heavy substance abusers is likely to be fundamentally *unchanged* under a program of drug legalization. Currently, the day-to-day lives of drug abusers is saturated with crime and violence; under legalization, by what magical formula is this going to be transformed overnight? If drugs were distributed inexpensively, would our current abusers commit the same level of crime to obtain more nondrug commodities? Hard-core drug abusers are typically uneducated (most are not even high school graduates), unskilled, and essentially unemployable. How will legalization change this? How will abusers obtain the basics, such as food and shelter, to live after drugs are legalized? It is not clear that legalization can transform a way of life very much. Sure, among current abusers, moneymaking crimes may decline, but this is likely to be purchased at the cost of drawing a greater number of users into the drug scene, and increasing their involvement in the drug subculture. Being able to obtain drugs legally will not change the fact that most drug abusers, now and in the future, are low impulse control, high-crime perpetrators. It is difficult to imagine what will turn them into law-abiding citizens, although some feasible programs could, conceivably, lower their crime rate a bit.

VIOLENCE, DEALING, AND ORGANIZED CRIME

Would legalization eliminate or substantially reduce the volume of violence that stems from drug dealing? It depends on the exact program in question. Extremely liberal programs relying on the ready availability of drugs on demand may very well eliminate the need for an illicit drug market, and thus have the projected impact. But as with users generally, without a source of income and essentially unemployable in legitimate jobs, how will the dealers of today earn their livelihood? Will crime, including violence, become their only source of income? What will replace what they now have? And will legalization wipe out or weaken organized crime? (Keep in mind that "organized crime" is a good deal *less* organized—that is, far more decentralized—than most people think.) The repeal of Prohibition didn't wipe out organized crime in the 1930s; in fact, Prohibition capitalized the later enterprises, some of them legal, that organized crime turned its attention and talents to. What would these ambitious, daring entrepreneurs have in store for us if a major source of their income were to be eliminated overnight? Would they become more ruthless in taking over legal enterprises? Would they turn their attention to more or less legal financial speculation? Would their new enterprises entail more, or less, danger to the public than the sale of drugs does now? Or, would the old organized criminals now be selling legal drugs? Would they then be in much the same position that purveyors of alcohol and tobacco are now? After having "gotten rich from illegal drugs," would dealers then "launder their images and play key roles in the now-legal distribution system" (Jacobs, 1990, p. 29)? Would their new, legal source of income magnify their power and influence? It's anyone's guess. But one thing is certain: A legal change is not going to force them out of business. They'll do *something*, but whether this will involve more—or less—mischief for the rest of us has to remain in the realm of speculation.

Of course, the other side of the equation is that, to the extent that legalization programs are more restrictive, an illicit market will be correspondingly larger. As we've seen, illicit drug dealing can be shrunk down *only* to the extent that the current demand for these drugs can be met. To the extent that restrictions block access to them, an illicit market will flourish correspondingly. And, of course, as I've argued, increases in use are an extremely likely consequence of less-restricted access. An illicit market can be diminished, and whatever benefits there are in a reduction in the crime rate along with it, only at the expense of an increase in availability and therefore use. As with use specifically, this represents one of the central dilemmas in the issue of legalization.

SUMMARY

If a knowledgeable observer were to summarize the probable impact of legalization on criminal behavior, it would go something like this.

Legalization is likely to reduce economic crimes among current heroin and cocaine abusers to a certain extent, although probably not dramatically. But drug abusers commit a great deal of crime in their day-to-day lives, and most of that volume is not going to be affected very much. Moreover, we do not know what the impact of increased use is likely to have on the crime rate of current nonusers. And what are current dealers, high and low, going to do once their livelihood is taken away? To imagine that they will turn into law-abiding citizens overnight is fanciful. An experienced gambler is not likely to wager much money on the bet that legalization will have a dramatic impact on the crime rate.

REFERENCES

Akers, Ronald L. (1984), "Delinquent Behavior, Drugs and Alcohol: What Is the Relationship," *Today's Delinquent*, 3(1): 19–47.

Anglin, M. Douglas, and George Speckart (1988), "Narcotics Use and Crime: A Multisample, Multimethod Analysis." *Criminology*, 26 (May): 197–233.

Brownstein, Henry J. (1993), "What Does 'Drug-Related' Mean? Reflections on the Problem of Objectification." *The Criminologist*, vol. 18 (March/April): 1, 5–7.

Butterfield. Fox (1995), "More in U.S. Are in Prisons, Report Says." *The New York Times*, August 10, p. A14.

Goldstein, Paul J. (1985), "The Drugs/Violence Nexus: A Tripartite Conceptual Framework." *Journal of Drug Issues*, 15 (Fall): 493–506.

Goldstein, Paul J., Henry H. Brownstein, Patrick J. Ryan, and Patricia A. Bellucci (1989), "Crack and Homicide in New York City, 1988: A Conceptually Based Event Analysis," *Contemporary Drug Problems*, 16 (Winter): 651–687.

Gottfredson, Michael R., and Travis Hirschi (1990), *A General Theory of Crime.* Stanford, Calif.: Stanford University Press.

Grasmick, Harold G., Robert J. Bursik, Jr., and Bruce J. Arneklev (1993), "Reductions in Drunk Driving as a Response to Increased Threats of Shame Embarrassment, and Legal Sanctions." *Criminology*, 31 (February): 41–67.

Hubbard, Robert L., et al. (1989), *Drug Abuse Treatment: A National Study of Effectiveness.* Chapel Hill: University of North Carolina Press.

Inciardi, James A. (1992), *The War on Drugs II.* Mountain View, Calif.: Mayfield.

Jacobs, James B. (1990), "Imagining Drug Legalization." *The Public Interest*, no. 101 (Fall): 28–42.

Kraar, Louis (1990), "How to Win the War on Drugs," *Fortune*, March 12, pp. 70–71, 74–75, 78–79.

Moore, Mark H. (1990a), "Drugs: Getting a Fix on the Problem and the Solution." *Yale Law and Policy Review*, 8 (1): 8–35.

Moore, Mark H. (1990b), "Supply Reduction and Drug Law Enforcement." In Michael Tonry and James Q. Wilson (eds.), *Drugs and Crime.* Chicago: University of Chicago Press, pp. 109–157.

Nurco, Dand N., Thomas E. Hanlon, Timothy W. Kinlock, and Karen R. Duszynski (1988), "Differential Criminal Patterns of Narcotic Addicts Over an Addiction Career," *Criminology* 26 (August): 407–423.

O'Donnell, John A., et al. (1976), *Young Men and Drugs—A Nationwide Survey.* Rockville, Md.: National Institute on Drug Abuse.

Szasz, Thomas (1992), *Our Right to Drugs: The Case for a Free Market.* New York: Praeger.

28

✪

Putting Justice Back into Criminal Justice

Notes for a Liberal Criminal Justice Policy

Samuel Walker
George F. Cole

Almost forty years ago the President's Commission on Law Enforcement and Administration of Justice recommended crime policies that attacked the causes of crime, that rehabilitated offenders, and that upheld civil rights. Many of these ideas have been criticized by conservatives as not effectively dealing with crime control. Samuel Walker and George Cole argue that the policies of the past four decades have not reduced crime and that liberal policies are more likely to achieve justice.

INTRODUCTION

The principal thrust of criminal justice policy for the last forty years has been the effort to enhance crime control: to arrest, prosecute, convict, and punish more offenders—or at least those who are guilty of serious crimes. There has been an increase in the number of actions that are criminalized; the War on Drugs serves as a prime example. That effort, which should be seen as a vast social experiment, has failed. We do not control crime any more effectively now than we did before, and have strained our correctional system

Source: "Putting Justice Back into Criminal Justice: Notes for a Liberal Criminal Justice Policy," by Samuel Walker and George F. Cole, 2003.

well beyond its capacity. The time has come for a new direction in criminal justice policy. It is time to focus less on the tool of the law and reintroduce justice back into criminal justice.

The conservative domination of criminal justice policy is the result of several forces. Persistently high crime rates have produced deep public frustration about crime and about efficacy of the criminal justice system, and the perceived leniency of judges. Fear of crime, moreover, is inextricably bound up with issues of race—as evidenced by the Willie Horton issue in the 1988 presidential election. The 1990s gave us the debate over disparate punishments for powder versus crack cocaine, and in the twenty-first century we are still grappling with racial profiling and police brutality, as evidenced by the beating of Abner Louima (1997), the killing of Amadou Diallo (1999), and the Cincinnati riots in 2001. Evidence of the conservative mood on crime policy is everywhere. The philosophy of rehabilitation has been abandoned in favor of a new interest in punishment, retribution, incapacitation, and deterrence. But beyond punishing a broader range of crimes for a longer time, we are also turning to forms of punishment that are particularly liberty invasive—detaining people past their sentence if they are still designated as dangerous, or requiring compulsory medication for sex offenders if they are "potentially" violent. There has been particular interest in identifying and punishing the so-called career criminal or high-rate offender.[1] In its zeal to combat drugs, Congress and state legislatures have imposed long mandatory minimum sentences for drug offenders. The number of people incarcerated has skyrocketed 300 percent.[2] And, since the death penalty was reinstituted in 1977, more than eight hundred and twenty five individuals have been executed and by 2003 more than thirty-seven hundred were on death rows.[3]

The Supreme Court has followed the popular mood as expressed in national elections. On crime policy issues the Court has a razor-thin conservative majority. Unlike the Warren court in the 1960s, the Court today is willing to side with the asserted claims of law-enforcement officials. It has sanctioned drunk driving checkpoints, a public safety exception to the *Miranda* warning, and a good faith exception to the exclusionary rule, has dramatically limited the use of habeas corpus as an avenue of relief for convicted offenders, has allowed the use of pretextual traffic stops by police officers, and has held schools liable for student-on-student harassment.

This, at any rate, is the conventional wisdom about national crime policy over the past forty years. Upon closer inspection, however, the matter is a lot more complex. Change in the criminal justice system has not been completely dominated by a conservative agenda. There have been a number of very important changes that reflect the traditional liberal values of due process and equal protection. A surprising number of reforms have in fact achieved their stated goals.[4] These successes form the building blocks for a new direction in national criminal justice policy.

TWO DEADLY MYTHS ABOUT
CRIMINAL JUSTICE POLICY

Creating a liberal criminal justice policy has to begin by demolishing two prevalent myths about national crime policy.

The first is that liberal reforms don't work. While many reforms reflecting liberal social values did prove to be failures, others have succeeded and represent significant improvements in criminal justice policy. The second myth is that conservative "get-tough" crime-fighting policies do work. There is no evidence to support this belief. We can view the past forty years as a vast social experiment in which conservative crime policies have been tried and found wanting.

THE FOUNDATIONS OF A LIBERAL
CRIMINAL JUSTICE POLICY

A liberal criminal justice policy begins with a renewed commitment to the traditional liberal values of fairness and equality. These values are embodied in the constitutional principles of due process, equal protection of the law, and protection against cruel and unusual punishment. In many, but not always all, cases, liberal values are consistent with civil libertarian principles. The criminal justice system has two basic goals: to control crime and ensure justice. The time has come to put a renewed emphasis on justice for people who are the victims of discrimination at the hands of the system.

A renewed commitment to a national policy based on liberal values does not mean that every proposal cloaked in the garb of justice and fairness is a good idea. Good intentions alone do not make for good crime policy. Some of the well-intentioned reforms of the 1960s did fail. And we now see that the noble goals inherent in determinate sentencing have resulted in net-widening, particularly for those already disenfranchised. Nor does a commitment to liberal values mean that criminal behavior is excused. Wrongdoing should be punished. There is nothing inconsistent between liberal values and punishing those people found guilty of a serious crime. Liberal values, however, do require that use of the most serious penalties be carefully limited and tailored to the crime involved.

The second key element in a liberal criminal justice policy is a sober appreciation of the limits of the criminal justice system. We should not ask it to do things it cannot do. Criminal justice officials need to learn how to "just say no." When the public and elected officials ask it to do things that are beyond its power, responsible officials have a professional and social obligation to explain why they cannot. Already, for example, some police chiefs have been willing to publicly say that more arrests will not solve the nation's drug problem. The evidence on the limits of some of the more popular crime control programs is explored in detail later in this essay.[5]

The third element of a liberal approach to crime would be to direct public attention to the social problems that underly criminal behavior. This point flows inexorably from a recognition of the limits of the criminal process. The problems the criminal justice system is asked to handle (murder, robbery) are the end product of larger forces, which in turn are influenced by social policies related to employment, housing, race relations, transportation, social welfare, and so on.

The limits of the criminal justice system are best symbolized by the police officer called for the third time to a domestic disturbance. The people involved have a lot of problems: unemployment, alcohol abuse, psychological problems, and so on. The officer cannot solve those problems. At best, he or she can do a professional job of resolving the immediate dispute. Policies based on liberal values should attempt to enhance that professionalism. But the ultimate solution to this particular domestic incident lies elsewhere, outside the justice system.

The Myth of Liberal Failure

The conservative mood that began in the mid-1970s and reached its peak with the election of Ronald Reagan as president in 1980 was based in part on a reaction against liberal social programs of the 1960s. According to the conventional wisdom, those policies failed. With respect to criminal justice policy, that indictment is partly true. But it is also true that we know many liberal reforms in criminal justice were tempered in the compromises that are characteristic of the legislative process. Our large-scale omnibus crime bills of the 1990s illustrate how difficult it is to maintain the integrity or spirit of the research idea or philosophy. The task of policy analysis at the moment is to sort out the failures and the successes.

The proper point of reference for this analysis is the 1967 report of the president's crime commission, *The Challenge of Crime in a Free Society*.[6] The commission's recommendations had two broad thrusts. The first was that more money needed to be spent on criminal justice. The administration of justice would be substantially improved by hiring more police, raising their salaries, subsidizing their education, expanding their training, developing more sophisticated communications technology, expanding pretrial services for arrestees, creating more community-based treatment programs for convicted offenders, funding research, and so on. This approach was consistent with liberal social policy generally: investing in programs to deal with social problems (for example, the so-called War on Poverty). Furthermore, the commission recommended that the federal government undertake, for the first time, comprehensive assistance to state and local criminal justice agencies.

In many respects, this goal was achieved. Spending on criminal justice did increase substantially. The federal government did initiate a comprehensive program of financial assistance. Whether or not all this spending improved the administration of justice, however, is another question altogether. Much of the increase in spending has been a result of inflation and rising crime rates. It is not clear that the spending has improved either the crime control effectiveness of the system or the quality of justice.

The second general element of the crime commission's recommendations was a general belief in rehabilitation. This consisted of several different parts. The first was the optimistic belief that criminal offenders would be rehabilitated (or corrected, or treated, or resocialized) into productive law-abiding lives. The second element was the belief that this could be more effectively achieved in a community-based setting. There was a strong anti-institutional current in the commission's recommendations. Diversion was better than prosecution; probation was better than imprisonment; parole was better than long imprisonment.

It is the commitment to rehabilitation that has been the target of the strongest reaction over the past twenty years. The concept of rehabilitation fell into disrepute and is, today, the object of much derision. The reaction against rehabilitation was summed up by Robert Martinson's survey of correctional treatment programs. Asking the basic question, "What works?" he found that few programs could persuasively demonstrate their effectiveness.[7] Although he did find that some programs were more effective than alternatives, the public translated his findings into the conclusion that "nothing works."

The idea that nothing works has, on occasion, been inflated into a general indictment of criminal justice reform, particularly reforms reflecting liberal values. Some analysts argue that well-intentioned reforms backfire and aggravate the problem they set out to correct.[8] Other analysts argue that reforms are simply negated by the informal resistance of criminal justice officials.[9]

The most extreme versions of the nothing-works argument arise from the literature on correctional programs. Martinson's report seemed to indict all rehabilitation programs. One widely cited example of failure is the so-called "net-widening" phenomenon. Some evaluations indicated that programs designed to divert offenders from the criminal justice system actually brought more people under some form of official control.

With respect to the issue of rehabilitation, the critics have a good point. Few correctional treatment programs have persuasively demonstrated that a convicted offender is less likely to recidivate because he or she received a particular kind of "treatment" as opposed to a conventional form of punishment or treatment. Thus, the prisoner who participated in group therapy sessions is no less likely to recidivate than the offender who did his time in prison and was released at the same time; intensive parole supervision is no more successful than normal supervision. The list could be extended.

The Hidden Successes of Criminal Justice Reform

Not all of the crime commission's recommendations failed, however. A number of them have had considerable vitality and are responsible for significant improvements in the administration of justice. Nearly all are consistent with liberal values. The most important of these goals are (1) the control of discretion, (2) the reduction of official misconduct, and (3) equal employment opportunity. In addition, there is a new goal, (4) community renewal, which is an indirect result of the crime commission's work.

Controlling Discretion

Perhaps the most important recommendation made by the crime commission was one that did not receive much attention at the time: the control of discretion by criminal justice officials. In fact, it is largely hidden in the commission's report, buried among innumerable other recommendations. It was most explicit with respect to the police, where the commission recommended that "police departments should develop and enunciate policies that give police personnel specific guidance for the common situations requiring exercise of police discretion."[10] It also recommended that departments develop "a comprehensive regulation" on officer use of firearms.[11] With respect to plea bargaining, the commission recommended the "establishment of explicit policies for the dismissal or informal disposition" of cases,[12] along with a written record for guilty pleas (pp. 337–338). Correctional agencies, meanwhile, were advised to adopt "explicit standards and administrative procedures" for decisions affecting prisoners.[13]

The commission's recommendations were part of a broader recognition of the phenomenon of discretion. The pioneering field research by the American Bar Foundation has identified discretion as one of the key elements of a new paradigm of the administration of justice. This paradigm was embodied in the now-famous flowchart of the criminal justice system. It not only provided a graphic representation of the "system" but also focused attention on the many decision points in the system.

In the intervening years, the control of discretion has become one of the central issues in criminal justice policy. Every decision point in the system has been subject to new controls. The police department SOP (Standard Operating Procedure) manual has become a large document and the principal instrument of contemporary police management. Bail decisions have been subject to controls by several different types of bail reform. Prosecutors' decisions to charge and to accept guilty pleas have been subject to both legislative and administrative controls. Sentencing, through mandatory provisions and sentencing guidelines have been instituted to limit discretion. Prisoners' rights litigation produced an intricate network of controls over correctional decisions, particularly disciplinary actions against inmates.

There are several notable examples of positive gains resulting from new controls over discretion. Restrictive deadly force policies have reduced the number of citizens shot and killed by the police. This has been accomplished without endangering police officers or contributing to an increase in the crime rate. Even more important, Lawrence W. Sherman's and Ellen G. Cohn's data indicates that the limits on shootings have reduced the racial disparity in persons shot and killed, from about 6:1 to 3:1.[14] Given the urgent nature of the race issue in American society, this reduction in police shootings is extremely important.

There are also new police department policies attempting to control officer discretion with respect to domestic violence and high-speed pursuits. It is still too early, however, to say whether these policies have had a significant effect on routine police practices.

Other attempts at discretion control have also produced some modest gains. The bail reform movement of the 1960s, which sought to guide bail-setting decision of judges, did reduce the number of pretrial detainees in many cities, thereby reducing discrimination against defendants because of their economic status. Some analysts, however, suggest that this reduction might have occurred even without the benefit of "reform." There is also some evidence that administrative controls over plea negotiations, in the form of written standards about dismissals and charge reductions, have resulted in greater consistency in case disposition.

The results of attempting to control judicial sentencing discretion through sentencing guidelines are even more dramatic. The greatest success appears to have occurred in Minnesota, where formal guidelines have significantly limited the use of imprisonment and have reduced, although not eliminated, racial and economic disparities in sentencing.[15] Minnesota has the second lowest imprisonment rate in the entire country (Maine is slightly lower). Moreover, it maintained a very low rate through the 1980s and 1990s while other states were drastically increasing their prison populations. As will be discussed below, limiting the use of imprisonment yields additional benefits in terms of maintaining humane conditions within prisons.

These successes represent building blocks for a more comprehensive effort to control discretion. One of the principal items on the agenda of a liberal criminal justice policy should be to continue the effort to control discretion for the purpose of reducing and eliminating racial and economic injustice. Formal controls over discretionary decision making should be extended to those decision points that remain free of controls. The most important of all is the arrest decision. Apart from the new policies on domestic violence, the decision of the police officer to take a suspect into custody is unregulated. A second extremely important area involves the complex relationship between the various decisions that constitute plea bargaining and sentencing.

Reducing Official Misconduct

A second major goal should be the elimination or reduction of official misconduct. The control of discretion is one means of achieving this goal, although there are several other means as well.

In the 1960s the most important attacks on official misconduct came through Supreme Court decisions. The exclusionary rule *(Mapp v. Ohio)* was essentially an attempt to eliminate illegal searches and seizures. The *Miranda* warning was an attempt to eliminate or reduce coercive interrogations. The *Gault* decision imposed some minimal standards of due process in juvenile court proceedings. The many prisoners' rights decisions have reduced some of the more barbaric practices in prisons.

One of the most important corollary effects of these Supreme Court decisions was a transformation of the working environment of policing. A study of narcotics detectives in Chicago found that court decisions had forced significant improvements in training and supervision. At the same time, a new generation of officers had come to accept the principles underlying court decisions protecting individual rights. Many stated that formal, externally imposed limits on police powers were a necessary means of controlling police conduct.[16]

Another important area of police misconduct involves the unjustified use of physical force and abusive language directed at citizens. The crime commission recommended that police departments create a formal process for handling citizen complaints. As a part of that, it also recommended that every department have a separate internal-affairs unit. To a large extent these recommendations have been fulfilled. Formal complaint procedures are now standard items in virtually all big-city departments. Despite this progress, the problem of police misconduct continues—as the killing of Amadou Diallo by New York City officers, the indictment of forty-three officers in Cleveland for cocaine dealing, and corruption of Los Angeles officers assigned to the Ramparts area clearly indicate. However, the number of fatal shootings is down since the 1970s, and grotesque incidents of physical brutality are rare rather than common events. Most observers believe that with the exception of certain departments, police behavior has in fact improved in most cities and counties over the past thirty years.[17]

Public attention has now focused on the effectiveness of police disciplinary procedures. The belief that they are inadequate has led to the creation of some form of civilian oversight procedures in about 80 percent of the police departments in the fifty largest cities.[18]

One of the most important consequences of the 1991 beating of Rodney King in Los Angeles has been the new focus on the phenomenon of the "problem-prone" officer. Investigations in Los Angeles, Kansas City, Boston, Houston, and elsewhere have consistently found that a small percentage of officers are involved in a disproportionate number of citizen complaints.[19]

The U.S. Civil Rights Commission identified this problem in 1981 and recommended that police departments create "early-warning systems" to identify these officers and take appropriate remedial steps.[20] Apparently, no department followed this recommendation. In the wake of the Rodney King incident, however, several police departments have begun to address the problem. A liberal criminal justice program would emphasize the reduction of police misconduct through the development of "early-warning" procedures in all police departments.

A major part of a liberal criminal justice program would be to continue the movement to instill respect for legal principles in criminal justice agencies and to encourage the growth of self-regulation. One form of self-regulation is accreditation. Litigation against police misconduct led to the creation of the Commission on Accreditation for Law Enforcement Agencies, which by 1998 accredited more than 460 agencies. Administrative rule making—controls over deadly force, handling of domestic violence, and high-speed pursuits—may be the most promising avenue for controlling police behavior in the immediate future.

Another significant area of official misconduct involves the abuse of prison inmates: physical brutality, prolonged sentences to solitary confinement, absence of due process in disciplinary procedures, and the violation of other individual rights such as access to reading material, visits, mail, and so forth. The crime commission called for "explicit standards and administrative procedures" regarding decisions affecting prisoners, but it did not give the matter a great deal of attention.[21] The commission's report was published before the modern prisoners' rights movement began. Since then, litigation based on constitutional principles has created a vast body of prisoners' rights, including physical facilities, services and programs, and the rights and privileges of inmates.

This litigation has had a far-reaching impact on American prisons. Many of the grossest abuses have been eliminated. Formal disciplinary procedures have been established. Also, litigation stimulated the correctional accreditation movement, which has resulted in the development of minimum standards for institutions. As is the case with the police, these developments represent a step in the direction of self-regulation and a transformation of the working environment of institutions. This is an important and overdue development that a liberal criminal justice program would continue to foster.

Many of the gains of the prisoners' rights movement began to be eroded in the 1980s, however. The dramatic increase in prison populations resulted in severe overcrowding, which, in turn, aggravated tensions among inmates, overloaded prison programs, and made routine supervision and discipline far more difficult.

The key to maintaining humane conditions in prisons—and in the process reducing both misconduct by officials and violence by inmates—is to limit the use of imprisonment. The state of Minnesota has shown that this can be done. The use of sentencing guidelines to control judicial discretion is a viable technique for limiting imprisonment. By limiting prison populations, states will be able to maintain humane conditions inside prisons within the constraints of limited state budgets.

Providing Equal Employment Opportunity

The crime commission also recommended the hiring of more racial minorities and women in policing. The commission produced devastating data on the underrepresentation of African-Americans (then referred to as Negroes) in big-city police departments. In 1967 they represented 38 percent of the population of Atlanta but only 9.3 percent of the police force; 23 percent of the population of Oakland but only 2.3 percent of the police; 29 percent of the population of Detroit but only 3.9 percent of the police force.[22] Significantly, the employment of Hispanic Americans was not even mentioned.

In the intervening years, there has been considerable progress in minority employment. A study of the nation's 62 local police departments serving a population of 250,000 or more found that from 1990 to 2000 the percentage of African American officers rose to 20 percent of the force, Hispanic rose to 14 percent, and Asian/Pacific Islanders/Native Americans to 3.2 percent. The fact that minority officers constitute 38 percent of these departments represents a dramatic change in staff composition. In some departments the percentage of minority officers on the force equals the percentage of minorities in the community.[23]

Increased racial-minority employment has furthered several important goals. Most important, it represents a commitment to the principle of equality. In the process it has created real employment opportunities for thousands of people of color. It also has some positive impact on police–community relations. A more diverse police force does not appear to be an all-white occupying army. Diversity also alters the police subculture such that, today, national organizations representing African-American officers offer a different point of view on such issues as civilian review and police brutality. Together with the growing number of female officers, minority officers have shattered the once-homogeneous police subculture.

At the same time, however, increased minority employment has not fulfilled all the objectives of reformers. The impact on police–community relations is indirect at best. Studies of police behavior have found no significant differences between white and black officers. Thus, minority employment does not automatically translate into improved police work.

With respect to women in policing, there has been a revolution in social policy since the mid-1960s. At that time, women represented an estimated 1 percent of all sworn officers and were relegated to second-class status in police work: excluded from patrol work and restricted to juvenile, clerical, or other peripheral tasks. In some departments they were barred from promotion to the highest ranks as a matter of official policy. The *Task Force Report* (but not the main report) delicately raised the question of recruiting more women officers and assigning them to patrol duty.[24]

Following the crime commission's recommendation, the Police Foundation conducted an experiment on women on patrol in 1973. This was followed by similar experiments. Evaluations of these experiments reached consistent conclusions: despite minor differences, women officers performed just as well as male officers in routine patrol duty. The formal barriers to female recruitment quickly fell, in large part because of federal civil rights laws. The presence of women in policing increased to about 10 percent of all sworn officers by 1997. Informal barriers to employment, however, have remained.[25]

As has been the case with racial-minority employment, the addition of female officers has enhanced the principle of equality, provided real job opportunities for many women, and diversified the police subculture. At the same time, the addition of female officers has not fulfilled all reform expectations. The performance of female officers is essentially the same as male officers; thus, they are not fundamentally better able to mediate disputes. This notion rested on an inverse sexist stereotype of women as more verbal and nurturing than men.

There has also been progress in terms of the employment of women in other parts of the criminal justice system. The enrollment of women in law schools has increased substantially, and more women are securing jobs as prosecutors and defense attorneys, as well as election and appointment as judges. Women are also being employed as correctional officers in male institutions.

The increase in racial-minority and female employment in criminal justice represents a good beginning. But it is only a beginning. In every occupation category, both groups remain underrepresented. The studies of employment in policing all conclude that affirmative action plans have been critical to increased racial-minority and female employment. In 2003 the Supreme Court approved affirmative action for colleges and universities and the decision may be applied to criminal justice employment practices. A liberal criminal justice program would reaffirm the commitment to equal employment opportunity in all aspects of the criminal justice system.

Stimulating Community Renewal

Another important goal of a liberal criminal justice program is community renewal. Specifically, this refers to programs that criminal justice agencies might undertake to help communities resist the downward spiral of deterioration. This goal rests on the recognition that the criminal justice system cannot, by itself, control crime. It is a last-resort mechanism that comes into play only when all other instruments of social control have failed.

Some of the most creative thinking in policing over the past two decades argues that the police might play a vital role in community renewal. This idea has been given the label "community policing." The essence of community policing is that the police should de-emphasize traditional crime fighting in favor of attention to long-range problem solving and attention to small signs of disorder in the community.

Community policing is an indirect result of the crime commission's work. First, the commission's *Task Force Report: The Police* was the first full statement of the idea that the police have a diverse and complex role, with only a small part of their work being devoted to crime fighting.[26] This point was reinforced by the field studies of policing sponsored by the commission.[27] Subsequent studies found that increased patrol presence did not reduce crime[28] and that faster response time did not result in more arrests. All of this research demolished the "crime fighter" image of the police role.

Drawing upon this accumulated research, first Herman Goldstein and then James Q. Wilson and George Kelling sketched out new models of policing. Wilson and Kelling argued that the capacity of the police to control crimes was very limited and that, instead, they should concentrate on the less serious problems of disorder (which they identified by the metaphor of "broken windows").[29] This was designed to accomplish two things. First, it would enhance feelings of community safety. Second, it would help to arrest the process of community deterioration at an early stage and, thus, help prevent neighborhoods from sinking into serious crime. Wilson and Kelling's "Broken Windows" article was enormously influential and, more than anything else, launched the community policing movement.

Herman Goldstein, meanwhile, had already developed the concept of "problem-oriented policing."[30] He argued that the police should disaggregate the different aspects of their role and develop strategies to address particular ones. Problem-oriented policing is really a planning process. It does not tell the police what to do; it tells them only how to approach their mission in a different fashion. Community policing, at least as defined by Wilson and Kelling, did have a specific content. By de-emphasizing crime fighting, however, both approaches involved a very different conception of the police role.

In *Fixing Broken Windows*, a book written in response to the Wilson and Kelling article, George L. Kelling and Catherine Coles call for strategies to restore order and reduce crime in public spaces.[31] They point to many American cities where the police are paying greater attention to "quality-of-life crimes"—by arresting subway fare-beaters, rousting loiterers and panhandlers from parks, and aggressively dealing with those obstructing sidewalks, harassing, and soliciting. By handling these "little crimes," they argue that the police not only reduce disorder and fear but their actions help to stem deterioration of the community.

By the 1990s, community policing and problem-oriented policing had, together, become a national movement. Many, if not most, police departments claimed to be engaged in one or the other. Community policing received a major boost with the 1994 Violent Crime Control Act, which provided $8 billion to hire 100,000 additional police officers. The program is administered by the Office of Community Oriented Police Services (COPS), which requires that departments develop a community policing plan in order to receive the federal funds for additional officers.[32]

The jury is still out on community policing. There is the danger that it will be destroyed by its own early success. It has quickly become a fad, in some cases nothing more than a rhetorical phrase with no content. As was the case with team policing thirty years ago, many departments are jumping on the bandwagon with no planning. In some instances, community policing has become a trendy label for putting more police on the streets in response to community fears about crime. Even under the best of circumstances—assuming careful planning, training, and supervision—there are serious limits to what community policing could accomplish in the way of community renewal. The key word here is *renewal*. Taking Wilson and Kelling at their word, the police might be able to help communities resist the downward spiral of deterioration. That, however, assumes the existence of a viable community. Yet in the most crime-ridden neighborhoods today, no such community exists. One of the main characteristics of economically devastated neighborhoods is the absence of the institutions and informal networks that make up a "community." Indeed, one could argue that drug gangs thrive because they fill that void, providing identity, protection, work, and income. In this respect, community policing has been oversold.

Nonetheless, community policing represents a bold concept of the police role. It recognizes that the police cannot, by themselves, control crime, but that they might be able to help communities renew themselves and resist the forces that lead to high levels of crime.

The blunt fact is that the police cannot create a community where one does not exist. No amount of creative community policing can hope to overcome the devastating effect of massive unemployment and declining job opportunities—the conditions that affect today's inner cities. The real solution to the crime problem lies outside the realm of criminal justice policy: in the realm of economic policy and job creation. This conclusion is not based on liberal sentimentality about the "roots" of crime; it reflects a sober assessment of what the criminal justice system can and cannot do.

THE FAILURE OF TOUGH CRIME CONTROL

For the past forty years, national criminal justice policy has been dominated by a conservative "get tough with crime" approach. This represents a far longer period than the heyday of 1960s liberalism. We can now look back and evaluate it as we would any other social experiment.

Contrary to public opinion and the claims of politicians, rates for many crimes have dropped since the early 1980s. The National Crime Victimization Surveys have shown that the greatest declines are in property crimes, but crimes of violence have also dropped, especially since 1993.[33] These declines, however, can be attributed largely to demographic changes, particularly the aging of the baby boom generation, fewer users of crack cocaine, and the positive economic climate of the 1990s. There is little evidence that the "tough on crime policies" have had much impact on the crime problem.[34]

What is evident is that the conservative experiment has been costly. Operating the criminal justice system costs taxpayers more than $100 billion a year. A major portion of these resources could be diverted to the underlying causes of criminal behavior—poor housing, unemployment, and racial injustice. Another price of the tough crime control policies has been an erosion of civil rights and liberties—especially for racial and ethnic minorities. Tough incarceration policies have devastated poor communities. With large numbers of young males in prison, families live in poverty, and children grow up without guidance from their fathers and older brothers.

It is now the conventional wisdom, even among conservatives, that traditional police crime control efforts will not reduce crime. Adding more patrol officers, increasing response time, and adding more detectives will not produce either fewer crimes or more arrests. The evidence is also overwhelming on the long-standing controversy over the exclusionary rule. Studies have convincingly found that the rule affects a tiny percentage of criminal cases at best.

With respect to bail, the federal government and many states have adopted some form of preventive detention that is designed to allow judges to deny bail to allegedly dangerous offenders. The Supreme Court upheld the federal law in 1987. The impact of preventive detention on crime has been negligible. Prior studies indicated that serious crime by persons on pretrial release was confined to a small percentage of defendants and that it was impossible to identify exactly which ones they were. Evaluations of the federal preventive detention law have found little change in the total percentage of defendants being held before trial. Judges have always practiced a covert form of preventive detention. The new procedures have yielded no gain.[35]

With respect to the disposition of criminal cases, studies have persuasively demonstrated that plea bargaining is not a loophole by which dangerous people beat the system. Persons who have committed a serious crime against a stranger, who have a prior criminal record, and against whom there is solid evidence are charged with the top offense, convicted of that offense, and sentenced to prison. "Career criminal" prosecution programs have produced no net gain in the imprisonment of dangerous criminals because those people were being treated fairly harshly under normal conditions.[36]

With respect to sentencing, there has been an enormous increase in imprisonment. The prison population more than tripled between 1980 and 2000. With more than two million behind bars, the size of the United States prison population is now the world's largest. This growth has largely resulted from changes to sentencing statutes that emphasize retribution and incapacitation through policies or mandatory minimums, "three strikes," "truth in sentencing," and restrictions on parole release. Community corrections, initially conceptualized as an alternative to incarceration, are now being used to extend sentences. Split sentences are not replacing lengthy sentences, they are being used in addition to them.

Trends with respect to drug offenses dramatize the failure of the conservative experiment even further. In every state and the federal system, the most dramatic change has been the increase in the number of incarcerated drug offenders. Yet there is no evidence that this has curbed the drug problem through either incapacitation or deterrence. In fact, the problem of drug gangs and gang-related violence worsened in the early 1990s—after more than fifteen years of increasing use of imprisonment. The much-publicized idea of selective incapacitation had no effect on policy, in large part because normal prosecution and sentencing were already highly selective.

Nor has the revival of the death penalty had any discernible effect on crime. The sudden upsurge in murders in the early 1990s, almost all of them related to inner-city drug gang activity, occurred after a yearly average of more than twenty people were executed in the mid-1980s. Only at the end of the century were a few politicians, such as Governor George Ryan of Illinois, willing to raise questions about the possibility that innocent people have been executed.

In short, the conservative criminal justice program of "getting tough" with crime has failed in all of its manifestations.

CONCLUSION

A sound criminal justice policy begins with a sober respect for the limits of what can be accomplished through the criminal justice system.

The first principle is that criminal justice agencies—police, courts, prisons—cannot make significant changes in the level of criminal behavior. This is where much of the liberal thinking of the 1960s went wrong. It assumed that the right kind of programs—diversion of minor offenders, community-based treatment programs, and the like—would affect the lives of offenders: resocializing them into law-abiding lives. There is no reason to believe that today. By the same token, it should be noted that many of the popular conservative crime control programs of the past thirty years assume an ability to change people's behavior. To cite one example: the concept of deterrence assumes that by raising the cost of crime, potential offenders will choose not to offend. Altering criminal justice programs, in short, has little effect on criminal behavior.

The crime commission also assumed that pouring more money into the justice system—for more personnel, better equipment, better training, more research—would enhance the crime control capacity of the system. There is no support for that assumption either.

This is not to say that many of the crime commission's proposals were entirely wrong. More money, resources, and research may not reduce crime but it can help to improve the *quality* of justice. And that is an important goal. By the same token, community-based programs for convicted offenders may not rehabilitate them, but they may well be cheaper and more humane forms of punishment. By 2002 and 2003, financial stresses have forced a member of states to consider ways to reduce their prison populations and the attendant costs.

If our capacity to affect the behavior of criminals and potential criminals is very limited, we can control the behavior of criminal justice officials. The evidence indicates that we can control their discretion, we can reduce misconduct, and we can eliminate employment discrimination. These goals, which reflect the liberal values of fairness and equality, are the proper goals of a national criminal justice policy.

NOTES

1. Alfred Blumstein et al., *Criminal Careers and "Career Criminals"* (Washington, D.C.: National Academy Press, 1986).

2. U.S. Department of Justice, Bureau of Justice Statistics, *Bulletin* (April, 2003).

3. NAACP Legal Defense and Educational Fund, *Death Row USA* (Winter, 2003).

4. A full discussion of these developments is in Samuel Walker, *Taming the System: The Control of Discretion in Criminal Justice, 1950–1990* (New York: Oxford University Press, 1993).

5. The limits of the "get-tough" approach are examined in Samuel Walker, *Sense and Nonsense about Crime and Drugs: A Policy Guide*, 5th ed. (Belmont, Calif.: Wadsworth, 2001).

6. U.S. President's Commission on Law Enforcement and Administration of Justice, *The Challenge of Crime in a Free Society* (Washington, D.C.: Government Printing Office, 1967).

7. Robert Martinson, "What Works? Questions and Answers about Prison Reform," *Public Interest* 35 (Spring, 1974): 22–54.

8. Eugene Doleschal, "The Dangers of Criminal Justice Reform," *Criminal Justice Abstracts* 14 (March, 1982): 133–152.

9. Malcolm Feeley, *Court Reform on Trial* (New York: Basic Books, 1983).

10. President's Commission, *The Challenge of Crime*, p. 104.

11. Ibid., p. 119.

12. Ibid., p. 134.

13. Ibid., pp. 181–182.

14. Lawrence W. Sherman and Ellen G. Cohn, *Citizens Killed by Big City Police, 1970–1984* (Washington, D.C.: Crime Control Institute, 1986).

15. Terance D. Miethe and Charles A. Moore, "Socioeconomic Disparities under Determinate Sentencing Systems: A Comparison of Preguideline and Postguideline Practices in Minnesota," *Criminology* 23 (May, 1985): 337–363. Minnesota Sentencing Guidelines Commission, *Guidelines and Commentary*, rev. ed. (St. Paul: August, 1981).

16. "The Exclusionary Rule and Deterrence: An Empirical Study of Chicago Narcotics Officers," *University of Chicago Law Review* 54 (1987): 1016–1069.

17. Samuel Walker, *Police Accountability: The Role of Citizen Oversight* (Belmont, Calif.: Wadsworth, 2001), p. 45.

18. Ibid., p. 40.

19. Ibid., p. 110.

20. Samuel Walker, *The Police in America*, 3d ed. (New York: McGraw-Hill, 1999), p. 285.

21. President's Commission, *The Challenge of Crime*, pp. 181–182.

22. President's Commission, *Task Force Report: The Police* (Washington, D.C.: Government Printing Office, 1967), p. 168.

23. Brian A. Reaves and Andrew L. Goldberg, *Local Police Departments, 1997*. (Washington, D.C.: Bureau of Justice Statistics, U.S. Government Printing Office, 2000).

24. President's Commission, *Task Force Report: The Police*, (Washington, D.C.: Government Printing Office, 1967), p. 168.

25. U.S. Department of Justice, Bureau of Justice Statistics, *Fiscal Year 1996: At a Glance* (Washington, D.C.: Government Printing Office, 1996), p. 25.

26. President's Commission, *Task Force Report: The Police*.

27. Albert Reiss, *The Police and the Public* (New Haven, Conn.: Yale University Press, 1971).

28. George Kelling et al., *The Kansas City Preventive Patrol Experiment* (Washington, D.C.: The Police Foundation, 1974).

29. James Q. Wilson and George L. Kelling, "Broken Windows: The Police and Neighborhood Safety," *Atlantic Monthly* 249 (March, 1982): 29–38.

30. Herman Goldstein, "Improving Policing: A Problem-Oriented Approach," *Crime and Delinquency* 25 (1979): 236–258; Herman Goldstein, *Problem-Oriented Policing* (New York: McGraw-Hill, 1990).

31. George L. Kelling and Catherine M. Coles, *Fixing Broken Windows: Restoring and Reducing Crime in our Communities* (New York: Free Press, 1996).

32. U.S. Office of Community Oriented Policing Services, *COPS Office Report* (Washington, D.C.: Government Printing Office, 1997).

33. U.S. Department of Justice, Bureau of Justice Statistics, *National Crime Victimization Survey* (August, 2000).

34. *The Crime Drop in America*, ed. Alfred Blumstein and Joel Wallman (New York: Cambridge University Press, 2000).

35. Lynn Zimmer, "Proactive Policing against Street-Level Drug Trafficking," *American Journal of Police IX* (1990, No. 1), 43–74.

36. Eleanor Chelimsky and Judith H. Dahmann, *National Evaluation of the Career Criminal Program: Final Report* (McLean, Va.: Mitre Corp., 1979).

Index